2nd Edition

THE HUMAN QUEST FOR MEANING

Personality and Clinical Psychology

Irving B. Weiner

University of South Florida

Series Editor

This series of books is intended to provide information about personality processes and their implications for the science and practice of clinical psychology. To this end, the books in the series integrate conceptual formulations, research findings, and practical recommendations concerning a broad range of topics, including theoretical perspectives on the nature of personality; biological and psychosocial influences on personality development; continuity and change in dimensions of personality across the lifespan; personality characteristics likely to foster adjustment difficulties; classification of abnormal personality patterns associated with psychopathological conditions; assessment procedures for evaluating individual differences in personality and identifying types of psychopathology; and methods of ameliorating adjustment problems, treating psychological disturbances, and promoting positive mental health.

"The human heart is a meaning-making organ. Living meaningfully with intention is a fulcrum that can counter the gravity of any predicament. In *The Human Quest for Meaning* a host of old pros provide the theory, research, and methods of meaning-centered practice."

–Jeffrey K. Zeig, PhD, The Milton H. Erickson Foundation, Arizona

"This new edition of *The Human Quest for Meaning: Theories, Research, and Applications* presents much of the best thinking and research on the human quest for meaning done in clinical, experimental, and social psychology today. Paul T. P. Wong has done a commendable job in selecting and bringing together leading researchers and their ideas. This book is destined to become a classic textbook in positive psychology, counseling, and the existential philosophy of psychology."

–Alexander Batthyany, PhD, lecturer of philosophy of psychology and cognitive science, University of Vienna; director, Viktor Frankl Institute, Vienna; author, *Empirical Research on Logotherapy and Meaning-Oriented Psychotherapy* and *Mind and Materialism*; principal editor, *Collected Works of Viktor Frankl* (14 volumes)

"This is a book of enormous scope and diversity. Reflective of Paul Wong's philosophical legacy, this work combines some of the best literature on meaning research with some of the wisest and most personally meaningful applications of that literature. I strongly recommend this volume."

–Kirk J. Schneider, PhD, author (with Orah Krug), *Existential-Humanistic Therapy* and *Existential-Integrative Psychotherapy*; editor, *Journal of Humanistic Psychology*; vice president, Existential-Humanistic Institute, California

"Meaning matters! That's the persuasive message of this evidence-based review of the roots and fruits of meaning. Anyone interested in the human quest for meaning need look no further than this synopsis of state-of-the-art scholarship."

–David Myers, PhD, professor of psychology, Hope College, Michigan; author, *The Pursuit of Happiness*

"Anyone interested in the concept of meaning, whether student or senior faculty, researcher or clinician, will find this volume difficult to put down. Each chapter broadens and deepens our understanding of this fascinating topic. As a whole, the volume should be treasured as a compendium of contemporary thought about meaning."

–Susan Folkman, PhD, professor of medicine emeritus, University of California, San Francisco (UCSF)

"Paul Wong is the expert on the psychology of meaning, and this edited volume shows why. Within these chapters he has assembled a comprehensive, authoritative, and cutting-edge review of the topic. This book is not to be placed on the shelf and forgotten. It is an essential resource for both researchers and practitioners who want a deeper understanding of why meaning matters."

–Robert A. Emmons, PhD, professor of psychology, University of California, Davis; editor-in-chief, *The Journal of Positive Psychology*

"With absolute conviction, this is the most comprehensive, scholarly statement to date on the nature of meaning and purpose in life. There is no better example of the deep dialogue between science, philosophy, and practice than this classic work. Anybody who is interested in this topic should have a copy on their bookshelf."

–Todd B. Kashdan, PhD, professor of psychology, George Mason University, Virginia; author, *Curious? Discover the Missing Ingredient to a Fulfilling Life* and *Designing Positive Psychology*

"Like the previous edition, this book represents a landmark contribution to the study of meaning. This stimulating volume is essential reading for researchers and practitioners interested in the topic of meaning. It will set the intellectual agenda in this field for years to come."

–Camille B. Wortman, PhD, professor of psychology, Stony Brook University, New York; coauthor, *Traumatic Bereavement* and *Treatment for Survivors of Sudden Death*

2nd Edition

THE HUMAN QUEST FOR MEANING

Theories, Research, and Applications

Edited by

PAUL T. P. WONG

Routledge
Taylor & Francis Group
New York London

Routledge
Taylor & Francis Group
711 Third Avenue
New York, NY 10017

Routledge
Taylor & Francis Group
27 Church Road
Hove, East Sussex BN3 2FA

Routledge is an imprint of Taylor & Francis Group, an Informa business

Printed in the United States of America on acid-free paper
Version Date: 20110812

International Standard Book Number: 978-0-415-87677-3 (Hardback)

Library of Congress Cataloging-in-Publication Data

The human quest for meaning : theories, research, and applications / edited by
Paul T.P. Wong. -- 2nd ed.
p. cm. -- (Personality and clinical psychology series)
Includes bibliographical references and index.
ISBN 978-0-415-87677-3 (hardback : alk. paper)
1. Meaning (Psychology) I. Wong, Paul T. P. II. Title. III. Series.

BF463.M4H86 2011
153--dc23 2011028347

Visit the Taylor & Francis Web site at
http://www.taylorandfrancis.com

and the Routledge Web site at
http://www.routledgementalhealth.com

Contents

Foreword

Making Meaning

Like you, I am searching for meaning. More precisely, I am working on constructing a meaningful life. With that goal in mind, I read this book with great interest, looking for guidance borne out of theory and science. I found more than I expected as the chapters nudged me toward deep reflection about my life and what matters most. Here I share some of my discoveries and encourage you to see this book for what it is—an intervention that could inspire you to make meaning.

Thinking about meaning conjures up memories of conversations with important people in my life. The first I will recount was a conversation, or series of discussions, between my mentor and me. While hanging out in his office, C. R. "Rick" Snyder and I chatted about our meaningful lives and the science that might explain them. Of course, we believed that hope had lots to do with meaning, and indeed, some of his research supported this notion. He and David Feldman were curious about hope's links to various conceptualizations of meaning. Through their simple psychometric study, they found very high correlations between hope and meaning measures that were rooted in three different theories and measured with different tools. These findings, and my conversations with Rick, suggested to me that hope might be necessary but not sufficient for meaning.

Hope is necessary but not sufficient for meaning. Is that true? Well, I could launch a 10-year program of study to test this theory. With other plans for the next decade, I decided to approach this unscientifically. I talked to the person that contributes most to my life's meaning, and I observed the most hopeful person I know to determine how hope and meaning coexisted in daily life.

Alli, my wife of 18 years, is my role model of a flourishing person. She is very happy and makes meaning for herself and others daily. How does she do it? That is what I asked her. "I think about where I need to go. I think about it everyday," she said. At the same time that she focuses on where she is going, she works hard each day to enjoy herself. Her simultaneous hot pursuit of the future and cool enjoyment of the present, and the experiences of my psychotherapy clients who found hope while suffering, affirm that the passionate pursuit of goals that matter to you and others is integral to a meaningful life.

So hope may be necessary for meaning, but is it sufficient for meaning? Are high-hope people meaning-making machines by nature? I thought I would try to answer this question by spending time with my super-hopeful 6-year-old son Parrish. He repeatedly demonstrated that he is an expert at nexting, futurecasting, persisting, and celebrating when he reaches his goals. With hope in abundance, he is able to make the most of daily life. Despite this, I am not sure how much meaning he has in his life, and he certainly doesn't think abstractly enough to complete a meaning-in-life questionnaire. Said differently, I am not certain that he is yet psychologically capable of constructing meaning. He passionately pursues goals of having fun and learning about the world around him, so maybe he is primed for meaning making. However, his hope may not be sufficient for meaning. Is he cognitively and emotionally ready to make meaning? (That question would take another ten years of research to answer, but instead I will spend that decade watching Parrish build up to purpose and meaning.) Development issues certainly have an effect on meaning making. Thus, hope's effects on meaning making have to be considered across the lifespan. So, in the lack of compelling evidence to determine whether hope is sufficient for meaning, I will hedge and say that it may or may not be. This conclusion is not satisfying but meaningful all the same.

The chapters in this volume sparked these personal reflections, and the reflections have helped me make more meaning. I hope the book has the same effect on you.

SHANE J. LOPEZ

Lawrence, Kansas

Editor

Paul T. P. Wong received his PhD from the University of Toronto. He has held professorial positions at various universities, including Trent University, the University of Toronto, and Trinity Western University. He is a registered clinical psychologist in Ontario. His meaning-centered counseling and therapy has gained increasing recognition. He is the president of the International Network on Personal Meaning and editor of the *International Journal of Existential Psychology and Psychotherapy*, which will be renamed the *International Journal of Personal Meaning* in 2012. He has published extensively on the subjects of the meaning of life and the meaning of death. Recently, he was the guest editor of the special issue on death acceptance in *Death Studies* and the "Positive Psychology" section in *Canadian Psychology*.

Contributors

Arthur Aron, PhD, is professor of psychology at the State University of New York at Stony Brook. His research centers on the self-expansion model of motivation and cognition in personal relationships, including the neural underpinnings and real-world applications of the model. He currently serves on the editorial boards of the *Journal of Personality and Social Psychology*, *Personal Relationships*, and the *Journal of Social and Personal Relationships.* In addition to authoring journal articles and chapters, he has written several books, including a statistics textbook now in its sixth edition. He is a fellow of the American Psychological Association, the Association for Psychological Science, the Society of Personality and Social Psychology, and the Society for the Psychological Study of Social Issues. He has received major grants from the National Science Foundation, the Fetzer Institute, the Templeton Foundation, and the Social Science and Humanities Research Council of Canada. In 2006, he received the Distinguished Research Career Award for the International Association for Relationship Research.

Elaine N. Aron, PhD, codeveloped the self-expansion model with Arthur Aron and, using the model, continues to collaborate with him on research on love and relationships. In recent years, however, her main research work has focused on two other themes. One is the temperament or personality trait of sensory-processing sensitivity. She has published numerous studies on the highly sensitive person, including surveys, laboratory experiments, and neuroimaging studies, theoretical and review papers, professional books (the recently released *Psychotherapy and the Highly Sensitive Person*) and several books for the general public on the topic, including the best-selling *The Highly Sensitive Person.* She also writes a widely-read quarterly newsletter for the public on the topic. Her newest line of research focuses on the interaction of basic hierarchical and relational social motives ("ranking and linking") and their relationship to self-esteem. In addition to engaging in her scientific work on the topic, she has recently published *The Undervalued Self* for the general public. She conducts her research at the State University of New York at Stony Brook, where she shares a lab with Arthur Aron. She is also a licensed clinical psychologist who maintains a small psychotherapy practice and teaches public and professional workshops.

Lisa G. Aspinwall, PhD, is associate professor of psychology at the University of Utah. Her research program examines self-regulatory processes and future-oriented thinking as people seek to anticipate, prevent, understand, and manage important negative outcomes, especially in the domain of health. She has studied such questions in a wide range of topic areas, including psychosocial adjustment to cancer, and most recently, genetic testing for familial cancer.

Roy F. Baumeister, PhD, is the Francis Eppes Eminent Scholar and professor of psychology at Florida State University, where he also serves as head of the social psychology graduate program. He received his PhD in social psychology in 1978 from Princeton University, and his research and teaching have also taken him to the University of California, Berkeley; Case Western Reserve University; the University of Texas at Austin; the Max-Planck-Institute for Psychological Research in Munich (Germany); the University of Virginia; and the Center for Advanced Study in the Behavioral Sciences (at Stanford). He studies a broad range of topics including self-control, the need to belong, sexuality, aggression, social rejection, power, self-esteem, consciousness, free will, gender, and culture.

Denise R. Beike, PhD, is a professor of psychology and director of experimental training at the University of Arkansas, Fayetteville. Her primary areas of research are autobiographical memory, the self, and emotions, particularly regret. She has authored or coauthored 23 journal articles and book chapters and coedited the book, *The Self and Memory.*

James E. Birren is emeritus professor of gerontology and psychology, and founding dean of the Andrus Gerontology Center of the University of Southern California. His career includes serving as chief of the Section on Aging of the National Institute of Mental Health from 1950 to 1964, and head of the Division on Aging of the National Institute of Child Health and Human Development. He is a past president of the Gerontological Society of America; the American Society on Aging; the California Council on Gerontology and Geriatrics; and the Division of Adult Development and Aging of the American Psychological Association. His awards include the Brookdale Award for Gerontological Research; Brookdale Distinguished Scholar; and honorary doctorates from the University of Gothenberg, Sweden, Northwestern University, and St. Thomas University, Canada. He has published extensively on aging. He has been the series editor of the *Handbooks of Aging* and *The Encyclopedia of Gerontology* and written numerous books and articles on aging.

Lawrence G. Calhoun is professor of psychology at the University of North Carolina at Charlotte and a licensed clinical psychologist. Although his parents were North American, he was born and raised in Brazil. He is coauthor or coeditor of 8 books and of more than 100 articles published in professional journals. He teaches undergraduate and graduate students, and is a recipient of the Bank of America Award for Teaching Excellence and of the University of North Carolina Board of Governors Award for Excellence in Teaching. For many years his scholarly work has been focused on the responses of persons encountering major life crises, particularly the phenomenon of posttraumatic growth.

Charles S. Carver, PhD, is distinguished professor of psychology at the University of Miami, where he has spent his entire professional career. He received his doctoral degree from the University of Texas at Austin in personality psychology. His work spans the areas of personality psychology, social psychology, health psychology, and, more recently, experimental psychopathology. His research has been supported at various times by the National Science Foundation, the American Cancer Society, and the National Cancer Institute. He has been honored by Divisions 8 and 38 of the American Psychological Association for his career contributions to the areas of health and social psychology. He served for six years as editor of the *Journal of Personality and Social Psychology*'s section on Personality Processes and Individual Differences and is currently an associate editor of *Psychological Review.* He is author of nine books and over 310 articles and chapters.

Travis S. Crone, PhD, is an assistant professor of psychology at the University of Houston–Downtown. His primary areas of research interest are nonconscious goal structures, autobiographical memory, and meaning making.

Edward L. Deci, PhD, is the Helen F. and Fred H. Gowen Professor in the Social Sciences at the University of Rochester. For 40 years Deci has been engaged in a program of research on human motivation, much of it with Richard M. Ryan, that has led to and been organized by self-determination theory. He has published ten books, including *Intrinsic Motivation* (1975) and *Intrinsic Motivation and Self-Determination in Human Behavior* (coauthored with R. M. Ryan, 1985). A grantee of NIH, NSF, and IES, and a fellow of the American Psychological Association and the Association for Psychological Science, he has lectured at more than 90 universities around the world.

Daniel T. Gingras holds a Bachelor of Arts (Honours), majoring in psychology. His undergraduate thesis focused on how sources of perceived meaning in life relate to the quality of life in chronic pain sufferers. His current interests include Aristotelian philosophy, medieval Christian philosophy and theology, and ethics in modern society. He currently resides in Cambridge, Ontario, with his wife Rachel and is pursuing a career in sales for industrial software applications and educational materials.

Joshua A. Hicks, PhD, is an assistant professor of psychology at Texas A&M University. His research focuses on the dynamic interplay of individual differences and situational factors in predicting important outcomes such as meaning in life, the link between substance use and behavior, judgment and decision making processes, and personality development.

Laura A. King, PhD, is the Frederick A. Middlebush Professor of Psychological Sciences at the University of Missouri, Columbia. A personality psychologist, she has focused her research on well-being, motivation, narrative approaches, folk theories of the Good Life, and individual differences in the intuitive information processing. She has published over 80 articles and chapters and is currently editor of the *Journal of Personality and Social Psychology: Personality Processes and Individual Differences.*

Eric Klinger, PhD, is professor emeritus of psychology at the University of Minnesota, Morris and (adjunct) Minneapolis. His research activities focus on motivational processes, especially as these and emotional processes influence attention, recall, and thought content. He has contributed to basic theory of motivation and its extension to substance use, treatment of alcoholism, and depression. A fellow of the American Association for the Advancement of Science and of the American Psychological Association, a charter fellow of the American Psychological Society, and a holder of the Henry A. Murray Award of the Society for Personality and Social Psychology, Eric Klinger is the author of more than 125 publications, including authoring or editing six books.

Neal Krause, PhD, is the Marshall H. Becker Collegiate Professor in the Department of Health Education and Health Behavior at the School of Public Health, University of Michigan. His research interests focus on the ways in which older people cope with stressful life events. He is especially interested in the role that social support and religion play in this regard. He conducted the first nationwide longitudinal survey to focus exclusively on religion and health among older Whites and older African Americans. He recently completed the first nationwide survey on religion and health among older Mexican Americans.

Maurits G. T. Kwee, PhD, Em. Hon. Prof., clinical psychologist, is a faculty member of the Taos Institute (United States) and Tilburg University (Netherlands) PhD program. A psychotherapist for more than three decades and cofounder of the Trans-Cultural Society for Clinical Meditation, Japan, Dr. Kwee is presently president of the Institute for Relational Buddhism, Netherlands. Among his publications are a dozen books and more than 100 articles in professional journals. His latest book is *New Horizons in Buddhist Psychology: Relational Buddhism for Collaborative Practitioners* (2010). He conducts master classes, seminars, and workshops on relational Buddhism and Buddhist psychotherapy.

Samantha L. Leaf earned her PhD at the University of Utah. She is currently is a senior research associate at ISA Associates, Inc., in Alexandria, Virginia. Her research interests include cancer prevention and screening, adjustment to cancer diagnosis, and psychosocial and behavioral aspects of genetic testing. She is currently involved in the development and testing of web-based interventions designed to reduce disease risk and increase preventive health behaviors in a variety of health domains, including cancer, HIV/AIDS, and cardiovascular disease.

Sancy A. Leachman, MD, PhD, is a dermatologist with a specialized clinical and research focus on genetic skin disorders and hereditary melanoma. She directs the Melanoma and Cutaneous Oncology Program as well as the Familial Melanoma Research Program at Huntsman Cancer Institute at the University of Utah in Salt Lake City. Her research interests include the basic mechanisms leading to melanoma predisposition in hereditary melanoma, the development of chemoprevention agents for use in the hereditary melanoma population, and the role of genetic testing in improving compliance with melanoma prevention recommendations.

Salvatore R. Maddi, PhD, received his PhD in clinical psychology from Harvard in 1960 and went on to be a professor at the University of Chicago from 1959 to 1986, and the University of California, Irvine from 1986 to the present. His research and theoretical interests concern personality hardiness as a factor in performance effectiveness and health, especially in stressful circumstances, and this work has facilitated his ongoing consulting and psychotherapeutic services. During his career, he has received many distinctions and awards here and abroad and is sought after as a speaker, consultant, and expert witness.

Dan P. McAdams, PhD, is professor of psychology and professor of human development and social policy at Northwestern University. A personality and life-span developmental psychologist, he focuses his research on themes of generativity, redemption, and commitment in human lives, with a special emphasis on the kinds of narratives that midlife adults construct to make meaning out of their lives. He is the author most recently of *The Redemptive Self: Stories Americans Live By*.

Marvin J. McDonald is director of the MA program in counselling psychology at Trinity Western University. His recent research and publications are built upon collaborations with colleagues and students in the investigation of trauma therapy, secondary traumatic stress, bicultural identity, spiritual questing, and family health. He is currently cultivating projects that draw upon French phenomenology to enrich empirical inquiry into human thriving and flourishing. The work of Immanuel Levinas and Jean-Luc Marion, in particular, provide resources for deepening and intensifying relationally-grounded tactics for investigation.

Joav Merrick, MD, MMedSci, DMSc, is professor of pediatrics and child health and human development affiliated with Kentucky Children's Hospital, University of Kentucky, Lexington, and the Division of Pediatrics, Hadassah Hebrew University Medical Centers, Mt. Scopus Campus, Jerusalem. Dr. Merrick is also the medical director of Health Services, Division for Intellectual and Developmental Disabilities, Ministry of Social Affairs and Social Services, Jerusalem, and the founder and director of the National Institute of Child Health and Human Development in Israel. He is the author of numerous publications in the field of pediatrics, child health and human development, rehabilitation, intellectual disability, disability, health, welfare, abuse, advocacy, quality of life, and prevention. Dr. Merrick received the Peter Sabroe Child Award for outstanding work on behalf of Danish children in 1985 and the International LEGO-Prize ("The Children's Nobel Prize") for an extraordinary contribution towards improvement in child welfare and well-being in 1987.

Gregory E. Miller, PhD, is codirector of the Psychobiological Determinants of Health Laboratory. After receiving a PhD in clinical psychology at the University of California, Los Angeles, he completed a clinical internship at the Western Psychiatric Institute and Clinic, followed by a postdoctoral fellowship in health psychology at Carnegie Mellon University. Dr. Miller joined the faculty of Washington University in Saint Louis in July 2000, and after three years there, accepted his current position at the University of British Columbia, where he is professor of psychology. Dr. Miller has received a number of honors for his research including the Young Investigator Award from the Society of Behavioral Medicine, the Early Career Award from the American Psychosomatic Society, and the Distinguished Scientific Award for Early Career Contributions from the American Psychological Association. He is an associate editor at two journals, *Psychological Bulletin* and *Psychosomatic Medicine.*

Crystal L. Park, PhD, is professor of clinical psychology at the University of Connecticut, Storrs, and affiliate of the University of Connecticut Center for Health, Intervention and Prevention. Her research focuses on multiple aspects of coping with stressful events, including the roles of religious beliefs and religious coping, the phenomenon of stress-related growth, and the making of meaning in the context of traumatic events and life-threatening illnesses, particularly cancer and congestive heart failure. She is coauthor of *Empathic Counseling: Meaning, Context, Ethics, and Skill* and coeditor of *The*

Handbook of the Psychology of Religion and Spirituality and the recently published *Medical Illness and Positive Life Change: Can Crisis Lead to Personal Transformation?*

Nansook Park, PhD, is associate professor of psychology at the University of Michigan and a nationally certified school psychologist (NCSP) with a research and practice background in clinical and school psychology. She studies character strengths and virtues among children and youth and takes a cross-cultural and life-span developmental approach to her work. She is also interested in character education and strength-based practice. Her studies of children and youth well-being have been recognized by several national and international honors. She is a member of the Annenberg/Sunnylands Commission on Positive Youth Development and the International Positive Psychology Association Board of Directors, an associate editor of *Applied Psychology: Health and Well-Being*, and a consulting editor of the *Journal of Positive Psychology.*

Christopher Peterson, PhD, is professor of psychology and organizational studies at the University of Michigan. He also holds an appointment as Arthur F. Thurnau Professor in recognition of his excellence in undergraduate teaching. In 2003, he was named by the Institute for Scientific Information as among the world's 100 most widely-cited psychologists over the past 20 years and has authored more than 300 scholarly publications. In 2010, he received the Golden Apple Award at the University of Michigan, honoring him as the university's outstanding teacher. His work focuses on character strengths and virtues, and his most recent books are *Character Strengths and Virtues* (2004) and *A Primer in Positive Psychology* (2006).

Gary T. Reker, PhD, is professor emeritus in the Department of Psychology at Trent University, Peterborough, Ontario, Canada. As a life-span developmental psychologist, he has focused his writing and research interests on positive psychology and the aging process, particularly on the topics of personal meaning in life, personal optimism, subjective well-being, death attitudes, creative coping, spirituality, resilience, and successful aging. A related area of interest is the development of measuring instruments, including the Perceived Well-Being Scale, the Future Orientation Test, the Life Attitude Profile–Revised, the Sources of Meaning Profile–Revised, the Death Attitude Profile–Revised, the Locus of Evaluation Scale, the Coping Schemas Inventory, the Peterborough Existential Regret Scale, the Spiritual Transcendence Scale, the Multidimensional Resilience Inventory, the Multidimensional Existential Regret Inventory, and the Successful Aging Scale. He coedited *Existential Meaning: Optimizing Human Development Across the Life Span* and is the author of many published articles in peer-reviewed journals and book chapters. He is actively involved in the Gerontological Society of America and the International Institute for Reminiscence and Life Review.

Richard M. Ryan, PhD, is a professor of psychology, psychiatry, and education at the University of Rochester. He is a widely published researcher and theorist in the areas of human motivation, development, and psychological well-being, having published over 300 articles and books. He is a fellow of several professional organizations, including the American Psychological Association and the American Educational Research Association. He is a licensed clinical psychologist with a practice in psychotherapy and consultation to schools and organizations and has served as director of clinical training at Rochester. Ryan is also an award-winning teacher and educational researcher and is currently editor-in-chief of the psychological journal *Motivation & Emotion.*

Carol D. Ryff, PhD, is director of the Institute on Aging and Marie Jahoda Professor of Psychology at the University of Wisconsin–Madison. She studies psychological well-being, including how it varies by age, gender, socioeconomic status, ethnic and minority status, and cultural context as well as by the challenges and transitions individuals confront as they age. Whether well-being is protective of good physical health is another interest pursued through linkages to biomarkers (neuroendocrine, immune, and cardiovascular) and neural circuitry. A guiding theme in her work is human resilience—that is, how some individuals are able to maintain, or regain, well-being in the face of significant life challenge. She has generated over 120 publications and currently directs the MIDUS (Midlife in the United States) longitudinal study, based on a national sample of Americans. Funded by the National Institute on Aging, MIDUS II is a major forum for studying health as an integrated biopsychosocial process. She also directs MIDJA (Midlife in Japan), a parallel to MIDUS, for which she received an NIH Merit Award.

Michael F. Scheier is professor and head of psychology at Carnegie Mellon University. His research falls at the intersection of personality, social, and health psychology. His current research focuses on the effects of dispositional optimism on psychological and physical well-being, and on the health benefits of goal adjustment when confronting adversity. He is a fellow in Divisions 8 and 38 of the American Psychological Association (APA), and in the Society of Behavioral Medicine. He has received awards for Outstanding Contributions to Health Psychology and the Donald T. Campbell Award for distinguished lifetime contributions to social psychology (offered by APA Divisions 38 and 8, respectively). He has served Division 38 (Health Psychology) in the past as chair of the Nominations and Election Committee, as associate editor of *Health Psychology*, and as president.

Daniel T. L. Shek, PhD, FHKPS, BBS, JP, is chair professor of applied social sciences in the Department of Applied Social Sciences at The Hong Kong Polytechnic University, advisory professor of East China Normal University, and honorary professor of Kiang Wu Nursing College of Macau. He is chief editor of the *Journal of Youth Studies*, consulting editor of the *Journal of Clinical Psychology*, and international consultant of the *American Journal of Family Therapy*. He is chair of the Action Committee Against Narcotics of the Government of Hong Kong Special Administrative Region. He has published 46 books, 76 book chapters, and more than 300 articles in international refereed journals.

Dov Shmotkin, PhD, is affiliated with the department of psychology at Tel Aviv University. He serves as a senior researcher in the Herczeg Institute on Aging at Tel Aviv University. He is engaged in theory and research on the pursuit of happiness in the face of adversity. This work expands his studies on subjective well-being across the life span as well as on the long-term traumatic effects among Holocaust survivors. He also conducts research on aging processes. His studies in this area examine biographical experiences (e.g., trauma) and personal time perspective in relation to physical and mental health in later life.

Amit Shrira, PhD, is a postdoctoral researcher in the Israel Gerontological Data Center at the Paul Baerwald school of social work and social welfare, the Hebrew University of Jerusalem, and a teaching associate in the department of psychology at Tel Aviv University. His main research interests include long-term traumatic effects in old age, especially the Holocaust trauma and its intergenerational transmission. He also investigates the respective roles of meaning in life and subjective well-being in regulating long-term traumatic effects.

Jeanne M. Slattery, PhD, is professor of psychology at Clarion University, Clarion, Pennsylvania. Her writing primarily focuses on the roles of meaning and spirituality in psychotherapy. She is coauthor of *Empathic Counseling: Meaning, Context, Ethics, and Skill* and author of *Counseling Diverse Clients: Bringing Context Into Therapy*. She also maintains a small private practice.

Kristin L. Sommer is an associate professor of psychology at Baruch College, City University of New York. She also holds appointments on the doctoral faculties in industrial/organizational psychology and social/personality psychology at the Graduate Center. Dr. Sommer's primary research interests lie with the effects of peer and coworker rejection on individual performance motivation and social behaviors. She also conducts research on self-regulation, social influence, and motivated decision-making processes in small groups. Dr. Sommer teaches undergraduate and doctoral courses in research methods and social psychology as well as a course on research design in work organizations as part of Baruch College's Executive Master's Program in Management of Human Resource and Global Leadership in Taipei and Singapore.

Michael F. Steger, PhD, is an associate professor at Colorado State University, where he is the director of the Laboratory for the Study of Meaning and Quality of Life. He is also affiliated with North-West University in South Africa. His research focuses on meaning in life, well-being, health-promotion and health-risk, along with topics in psychopathology. He recently coedited *Designing Positive Psychology*, and another coedited book, *Meaning and Purpose in the Workplace*, is scheduled to be published in 2013.

Tyler F. Stillman, PhD, received a Bachelor of Science in psychology from the University of Utah, and later received his PhD in social psychology from Florida State University under the supervision of Roy F. Baumeister. Currently, Dr. Stillman lives in Cedar City, Utah, with his wife Debra and their three children. He is assistant professor of marketing and management in the School of Business at Southern Utah University. His research interests vary widely and include evolutionary psychology, meaning in life, conspicuous consumption, and financial risk. Dr. Stillman does not enjoy camping, kayaking, hunting, or hiking. He would rather be indoors and in a climate-controlled environment—preferably in a comfortable chair.

Cheryl M. Svensson, PhD, has been involved in the field of aging since the 1970s. She graduated from the first Masters in Gerontology program at the University of Southern California in 1977 and completed her PhD in psychology from the University of Lund, Sweden. She is both an educator and researcher focusing on the components of well-being and old age. Cheryl works closely with James Birren to develop and expand the Birren Autobiographical Studies program. She has taught guided autobiography classes at universities, libraries, and senior centers and is now teaching others to become guided autobiography instructors in live, interactive, online classes.

Richard G. Tedeschi is professor of psychology at the University of North Carolina at Charlotte, and serves as graduate coordinator for the Clinical-Community Psychology program. He is a licensed psychologist specializing in bereavement and trauma, and has led support groups for bereaved parents for more than 20 years. Dr. Tedeschi is a fellow of the American Psychological Association, Division of Trauma Psychology, a subject matter expert for the U.S. Army's Comprehensive Soldier Fitness Program, and president of the North Carolina Psychological Association. With his colleague Lawrence Calhoun, he has published books on posttraumatic growth, an area of research that they have developed that examines personal transformations in the aftermath of trauma. These books include *Trauma and Transformation* (1995), *Posttraumatic Growth* (1998), *Facilitating Posttraumatic Growth* (1999), *Helping Bereaved Parents: A Clinician's Guide* (2004), and the *Handbook of Posttraumatic Growth* (2006).

Adrian Tomer, PhD, is professor in the department of psychology at Shippensburg University of Pennsylvania. Since completing his doctoral training at the University of Florida in 1989, he has conducted research, published, and organized international symposia on the topics of death and dying and meaning, as well as on other gerontological and methodological issues. He developed (with Grafton Eliason) a comprehensive model of death anxiety. Dr. Tomer has published three books and numerous articles and/or chapters. These include *Existential and Spiritual Issues in Death Attitudes* (edited with Grafton Eliason and Paul Wong and published by Lawrence Erlbaum, 2007), *Death Attitudes and the Older Adult* (Taylor & Francis, 2000) and (with Bruce Pugesek and Alexander von Eye) *Structural Equation Modeling: Applications in Ecological and Evolutionary Biology* (Cambridge University Press, 2003). He is currently engaged in theoretical and empirical investigation of the comprehensive model of death with the goal of generalizing the model to death acceptance. Recently, Paul T. P Wong and Adrian Tomer served as guest editors of a special issue of *Death Studies* dedicated to death acceptance.

Søren Ventegodt, MD, MMedSci, EU-MSc-CAM, is the director of the Nordic School of Holistic Medicine and the Quality of Life Research Center in Copenhagen, Denmark, as well as director of and lecturer at Inter-University College, International Campus, Denmark, working in collaboration with Inter-University Consortium for Integrative Health Promotion, Inter-University College in Graz, Austria, and the Austrian Ministry of Education, Science and Culture. He is also responsible for the Clinical Research Clinic for Holistic Medicine and Sexology in Copenhagen and is a popular speaker throughout Scandinavia. He has published numerous scientific or popular articles and a number of books on holistic medicine, quality of life, and quality of working life. Recently, he has written textbooks on holistic psychiatry and holistic sexology. His most important scientific contributions are the comprehensive SEQOL questionnaire, the very short QOL5 questionnaire, the integrated QOL theory, the holistic process theory, the life mission theory, and the ongoing Danish Quality of Life Research Survey, 1991–1994, in connection with follow-up studies of the Copenhagen Perinatal Birth Cohort, 1959–1961, initiated at the University Hospital of Copenhagen by the late professor of pediatrics Bengt Zachau-Christiansen.

Netta Weinstein, PhD, is an assistant professor at the University of Essex. She has published both empirical and review articles concerned with the impact of human motivation on well-being and has received a number of awards recognizing this work, including the Alfred Baldwin Award for Excellence in Research and a Fellowship and Presenter's First Prize at the Gallup Positive Psychology summit. Her findings have been reviewed in such popular media as *Scientific American* and *CNBC*. In addition to conducting her research, she has taught courses focusing on the dynamics and outcomes of human motivation.

Lilian C. J. Wong, BSc, MA, PhD, received her MA in educational psychology from the University of Texas at Austin, and PhD in counselling psychology from the University of British Columbia. She was associate professor in the graduate program in counselling psychology at Trinity Western University, and associate professor of psychology at Tyndale University College. Previously she was psycho-educational consultant and school psychologist for several school boards in Ontario and British Columbia. She has been recognized internationally for her research on multicultural competencies in clinical supervision. She is cochair for the Supervision and Training Section of The Society of Counseling Psychology (Division 17) of the American Psychological Association. She serves on the steering committee of the Ontario Coalition of Mental Health Professionals, and also sits on the boards of directors for the International Network on Personal Meaning, Canadian Association for Child and Play Therapy, and Canadian Humanistic and Transpersonal Association. She is vice president of the Meaning-Centered Counselling Institute. She is coeditor of the *Handbook in Multicultural Perspectives on Stress and Coping* (2006), *The Positive Psychology of Meaning and Spirituality* (2007), and *Addiction, Meaning, and Spirituality* (2011).

Carsten Wrosch, PhD, addresses the importance of self-regulation processes for preventing distress and improving psychological well-being among individuals who experience difficult life circumstances. In addition, his work examines how such benefits derived from effective self-regulation can further contribute to adaptive patterns of biological functioning and good physical health. His research areas include adjustment to unattainable goals, the experience of life regrets, and managing age-related problems across the adult life span.

Acknowledgments

It has taken far more time than anticipated to complete this edited volume—primarily because of my health issues. I am grateful to all the contributing authors for their patience and understanding. I also want to express my heartfelt thanks to my research assistants—Scott Bulloch, Daniel Gingras, and Jennifer Chu—for their contributions to various aspects of this project. Needless to say, I really appreciate my wife Dr. Lilian Wong's unfailing support, without which I might not be able to complete this project amid many competing demands. Finally, I owe a debt of gratitude to Marta Moldvai, senior editorial assistant at Routledge, who has a special way of gently nudging me forward without giving me undue pressure.

So many readers of the first edition have told me that they valued it as their Bible for meaning research and applications and have inquired when the second edition will be published. To all my faithful readers, I dedicate this volume.

PAUL T. P. WONG

Introduction

A Roadmap for Meaning Research and Applications

"What is the meaning of life?" is probably the most persistent and important question ever asked. The human propensity for grappling with existential questions has long been evident in the chronicles of philosophy, religion, and literature. The broad appeal of trade publications like Viktor Frankl's *Man's Search for Meaning* and Rick Warren's *Purpose Driven Life* also attests to the widespread public interest in meaning and purpose. Jerome Bruner (1990) has made a compelling case to make meaning the central construct of psychology. In spite of the long history of the human concern for meaning, psychological research on this topic is quite recent.

Wong and Fry (1998) represent the first major publication on empirical research on meaning of life and its vital role in well-being, resilience, and psychotherapy. Back then, I predicted that meaning will take its rightful place at the center stage of psychology, along with self-efficacy and optimism. This prediction has come true, largely as a result the exponential growth of positive psychology, which identifies what makes life worth living as one of the cornerstones of this new movement (Seligman & Csikszentmihalyi, 2000).

This second edition has 21 new chapters, reflecting the rapidly expanding field of research on the role of meaning in flourishing. Some chapters have been so extensively revised that they can be treated as new chapters. Apart from providing a considerable amount of new material, this revised edition also shows better integration between chapters. This introductory chapter provides an overview of the significant advances in meaning-oriented research and applications.

What Is the Meaning of Meaning of Life?

People routinely talk about their needs for meaningful relationships or meaningful work; but when confronted with the question of meaningful living, they may become uneasy and defensive. Their first reaction is often "What do you mean by the meaning of life?" Even in academic circles, students often ask, "What is the meaning of meaning?" In order to address this common concern, I want to proceed by clarifying the different types and components of meaning.

Situational Meaning Versus Existential Meaning

It is helpful to distinguish between specific meaning and global meaning (Park & Folkman, 1997), or situational meaning and ultimate meaning

(Frankl, 1946/1985). This fundamental distinction can also be framed as situational meaning versus existential meaning (Reker & Chamberlain, 2000; Chapter 20, this volume). Existential meaning actually involves at least seven related questions (Wong, 2010): Who am I? What should I do with my life to make it worthwhile? What can I do to find happiness and life satisfaction? How can I make the right choices in an age of moral ambiguity and conflicting values? Where do I belong and where do I call home? What is the point of living in the face of suffering and death? What happens after death? These questions are concerned with one's philosophy of life and worldviews to make sense of life. All chapters in the volume touch on different combinations of these fundamental questions simply because it would be difficult to fully understand the meaning of life without addressing existential concerns.

Structure and Functions of Meaning

Another approach to understanding the meaning of life is to focus on the structure and functions of meaning. My PURE model (see Chapters 1 and 28, this volume) operationally defines meaning as consisting of four essential components: purpose, understanding, responsible action, and enjoyment or evaluation. Life would not be meaningful in the absence of any of these ingredients. Functionally, these components entail the four major psychological processes for the good life: motivational (purpose), cognitive (understanding), social and moral (responsibility), and affective (enjoyment or evaluation). This model provides a comprehensive framework for individuals to reflect and determine whether they have indeed found something worth living and dying for. All the contributors to this volume address some or all of these four basic components of meaning.

Subjective Versus Objective Meaning

The study of meaning has always been plagued by the subjective versus objective controversy. Meaning is subjective because individuals have to determine for themselves what kind of life is meaningful to them. Their decisions can be entirely based on how they make sense of themselves and the world. A purely subjective stance would lead to the logical conclusion that one can live a meaningful life by being a tyrant, serial killer, or pedophile. Therefore, there is the need for an objective frame of reference regarding the meaning of life, independent of personal biases. An objective principle of meaning is a truth claim that can be verified by empirical research. Psychologists engage in meaning research because they believe that it is possible to discover general principles of meaningful living.

Meaning in life needs to include both subjective and objective perspectives. Frankl (1946/1985) emphasizes that meaning can be discovered by individuals according to their subjective, phenomenological experience. But he also stresses that the discovery of meaning needs to be based on the principles of authenticity and time-honored universal values. Generally, one's meaning of life is more likely to be beneficial when there is congruence between subjective and objective meaning.

When research findings do not resonate with real-life experiences, we need to question the validity of the research. Furthermore, when we apply research findings without taking into account individual differences and cultural contexts, it may result in misapplication. Better integration between research and application can be achieved if researchers keep in mind the importance of both objective evidence and subjective experience as suggested by William James (1912) and Thomas Nagel (1989). All the chapters in the section on applications have found a way to incorporate both subjective and objective perspectives.

Content Versus Processes of Meaning

Content refers to experiences, activities, goals, and emotional states that imbue life with meaning, whereas processes refer to the psychological mechanisms or adaptive efforts in the quest for meaning. Steger, Frazier, Oishi, and Kaler (2006) make an important distinction between the presence of meaning and the search for meaning. However, mere presence of meaning does not indicate what makes life worth living. My implicit theory research (Wong, 1998a) has identified eight sources of meaning: happiness, achievement, intimacy, relationship, self-transcendence, self-acceptance, and fairness. This finding has been replicated in Asian cultures (Kim, Lee, & Wong, 2005; Lin & Wong, 2006; Takano & Wong, 2004). McDonald, Wong, and Gingras (Chapter 17, this volume) introduce a brief version of the Personal Meaning Profile (PMP) for the convenience for researchers and clinicians.

With respect to searching for meaning, the process is neither simple nor straightforward. For example, there are at least six different stages in the process of the search for meaning that have very different meanings and implications for well-being: (a) the inertia stage, in which individuals have not yet embarked on the quest for meaning; (b) the exploratory stage, in which individuals are struggling to find meaning but have not yet discovered one; (c) the discovery stage, in which individuals have already experienced some success in finding meaning in the major domains of life; (d) the completion stage, in which individuals cease their quests for meaning because they have found satisfactory answers to all their existential concerns; (e) the emergency stage, in which something horrible happens and shatters the assumptive world of individuals, triggering a quest for meaning; and (f) the stagnant stage, in which individuals get stuck in their search because they ask the wrong questions or come to conclusions that do not provide any closure or satisfaction.

In view of the complexities of the quest for meaning, a low score on Steger et al.'s (2006) Searching for Meaning Subscale can mean different things. That is why the subscale has been either negatively correlated to well-being (Chapters

13 and 23, this volume) or unrelated to well-being (Steger et al., 2006). Such inconsistency in findings can be resolved only by additional research on what type of meaning seeking is beneficial and what type is not, as Wong and Watt (1991) have done to resolve a similar controversy surrounding life review. The meaning of searching for meaning can be further clarified by studying when people do engage in which types of meaning search (Wong & Weiner, 1981).

Levels of Meaning

Given the complexity of the world we live in as well as the complexity of meaning as a construct, Peterson (1999, 2007) has proposed three levels of analysis. At the first level, meaning emerges because it helps us to understand what happens to us in everyday living and to decide how to respond in an adaptive way. This level has to do with self-regulation, self-maintenance, and self-propagation; meaning is broadly based on instincts, drives, motivation, emotions, and psychosocial processes involved in goal planning and goal striving. At the second level, meaning emerges because of encounters with something unexpected, negative, or threatening. For example, when our plans are blocked or when our cherished beliefs are threatened, we experience frustration, anxiety, fear, guilt, or anger. Meaning is adaptive in our attempts to overcome obstacles, uncertainties, and conflicts by exploring alternative solutions in order to keep hope alive. At the third level, meaning arises for two reasons. First, the realization that all our beliefs and endeavors are no longer valid puts us in a state of confusion and anxiety, thus creating a need for myth making, religion, and spirituality in order to restore meaning. Second, when all our basic needs are fully satisfied, boredom or atrophy may set in, thus setting the stage for exploration, curiosity, fantasy, or metanarratives in order to restore meaning.

Maslow's (1943) hierarchy of needs represents another way to conceptualize the different levels of meaning, beginning with meeting biological needs and moving toward self-actualization, which includes spirituality and transpersonal experiences. Several chapters in this volume (Chapters 1, 2, and 11) implicitly make reference to different levels of meaning.

What Is the Meaning of Life? Theoretical Perspectives

Meaning of life, especially the ultimate meaning of life, is too deep and complex to be fully understood by human beings. Solomon, one of the wisest persons who ever lived, conceded to this difficulty a long time ago in the book of Ecclesiastes. This daunting task has not prevented people from attempting to understand the mysteries of the human condition through different theoretical lenses.

The Positive Psychology Perspective

The positive psychology perspective seems most intuitive and self-evident. It is very appealing to believe that life is good and that we live in a wonderful world because we have the freedom and ability to pursue our dreams. Who doesn't want to enjoy life? Who doesn't want to do what one does best and what one loves most? Solomon came to the same conclusion during the early stages of his meaning quest: "A man can do nothing better than to eat and drink and find satisfaction in his work. This too I see is from the hand of God" (Ecclesiastes 2:24, New International Version).

According to positive psychology, positive affect and personal strengths are what make life worth living. King and Hicks (Chapter 6, this volume) have provided convincing evidence that positive affect plays a causal role in the experience of meaning even in the absence of realistic evidence that life is meaningful. They are correct in suggesting that the cultivation of positive feelings even in mundane activities can contribute to our overall sense of meaning in life. It is true that when people are in good moods, they are more inclined to see life as meaningful. But there are limitations to positive affect because moods are fleeting, and hedonic happiness invariably returns to a set point. The biggest challenge is to maintain positive affect when one is overwhelmed by pain and sadness. In noxious and disastrous situations, such as the 9/11 attacks and the 3/11 tsunami, only meaning can give us some sense of hope (Frankl, 1946/1985; Wong, 2009).

Peterson and Park (Chapter 13, this volume) studied the relationship between character strengths, well-being, and meaning in older people. They employed two meaning measurements. One is based on the Meaning of Life Orientation subscale (Peterson, Park, & Seligman, 2006). The other is the Meaning in Life Questionnaire developed by Steger et al. (2006). What is noteworthy is that the top four character strengths most significantly related to meaning orientation and presence of meaning are religiousness, gratitude, hope, and zest for life. The high correlation between religiousness and meaning confirms previous research on the inherent connection between meaning and spirituality (Pargament, 1997; Wong, 1998b). This finding suggests that religiosity or philosophy of life about the big picture is an essential aspect of meaning in life.

Peterson and Park (Chapter 13, this volume) conclude, "Positive psychologists stress that their interest extends beyond 'happiness' yet routinely use life satisfaction or happiness measures as the chief outcome of interest (e.g., Seligman, Steen, Park, & Peterson, 2005). Perhaps measures of meaning should be employed as well" (p. 292, this volume). I would go even further: Why not study the effect of acquiring a meaning mindset on a wide range of well-being and strengths measures (Wong, in press-b)?

The Self-Determination Perspective

Self-determination is clearly involved in choosing a preferred life goal as well as in making the necessary adjustments to achieve it. Several chapters in this volume employ this theoretical perspective (Chapters 1, 14, and 24).

Weinstein, Ryan, and Deci (Chapter 4, this volume) provide the most comprehensive and compelling account of meaning in life in terms of self-determination theory (SDT): "As described by SDT then, the meaning-making process is intrinsic to our natures and responsible for helping individuals create what Dittmann-Kohli (1991) called a coherent life course.... As individuals internalize and integrate new experiences, values, and behaviors they experience greater internal harmony, purpose, and wholeness (Ryan & Deci, 2001)." The ability to integrate both humanistic-existential theories and the social-personality processes makes SDT a very powerful theory in providing the mechanisms for meaningful and authentic living.

Weinstein et al. present the self-determination perspective, which incorporates intrinsic motivation and self-knowledge as main determinants. "In short, to find true meaning, individuals must get to know who they truly are—that is, know what is valuable and important to them—and act in accord with that knowledge." They conclude that meeting the intrinsic needs for relatedness, autonomy, and competence also contributes to a sense of life meaning and fulfillment, whereas extrinsic values, goals, and purposes typically do not yield basic need satisfactions. Their SDT perspective focuses on intrinsic motivation and integrates different aspects of personality and experiences of life as a unified whole. Of interest to note that like my dual-systems model, SDT also suggests that meaning can be facilitated by mindfulness.

Integrative Perspectives

A complete theory of meaning of life needs to integrate both positive and negative experiences. Aside from the inevitable physical decline evident in aging, illness, and death, life is unpredictable and hard for most people. Even when things are going well and one's cup is overflowing with blessings, a single misfortune can destroy one's world of happiness—just witness the recent catastrophes in Japan. When bad things happen, meaning is needed in order to make sense of suffering and make it more bearable. This is the main message in Shmotkin and Shrira's chapter in this volume (Chapter 7). They focus on the distinction between subjective well-being and meaning in life and consider how the two concepts serve different purposes and functions in the hostile-world scenario. Subjective well-being allows people to manage the hostile-world scenario, whereas meaning-making systems allow the hostile-world scenario to be interpretable. Both subjective well-being and meaning in life are major assets in dealing with trauma.

Shmotkin and Shrira embrace both hedonic (subjective well-being) and eudaimonic (meaning-in-life) approaches, arguing that each offers important insight for how one deals with a hostile world. Specifically, in dealing with the adverse contingencies of life, subjective well-being facilitates regulatory processes that make the adverse situation manageable, whereas meaning in life facilitates reconstructive processes that make suffering interpretable.

Steger's (Chapter 8, this volume) theoretical perspective focuses on cognition and purpose. Steger provides a comprehensive cognitive definition of meaning that includes existential elements:

> Meaning is the web of connections, understandings, and interpretations that help us comprehend our experience and formulate plans directing our energies to the achievement of our desired future. Meaning provides us with the sense that our lives matter, that they make sense, and that they are more than the sum of our seconds, days, and years. Comprehending our experience in this way builds the cognitive component of meaning in life. The cognitive component of meaning in life thus refers to the understandings that we develop of who we are, what the world is like, and how we fit in with and relate to the grand scheme of things.

The purpose aspect of meaning, according to Steger, also has an existential quality. Life goals are most meaningful when they flow from a person's sense of the self and place in the world. Citing Frankl (1946/1985), Steger advocates that individuals need to develop a clear vision of what they are trying to accomplish: "I argue that the goals people develop are most beneficial when they arise naturally from the unique ways they comprehend life."

Sommer, Baumeister, and Stillman (Chapter 14, this volume) define meaning in life in terms of four basic needs (purpose, efficacy, value, and self-worth). When people are not able to fulfill these four needs because of misfortunes, they resort to meaning reconstruction in order to maintain a sense of meaning. More important, the authors point out, "Negative events are thus not evaluated in isolation but interpreted according to one's life scheme or storylike representation of the self." Thus, one needs a philosophy of life and a narrative construction of the self in order to make sense of negative events.

They also point out that purposeful pursuit of meaningful goals—not just any goals—leads to greater psychological well-being. What is meaningful has to be derived from one's intrinsic motivation and sense of self in the larger scheme of things. This point is also emphasized by Wrosch, Scheier, Miller, and Carver (Chapter 24, this volume) and McAdams (Chapter 5, this volume).

Sommer et al. (Chapter 14, this volume) conclude that "successfully dealing with the process of aging also corresponds with spiritual and religious practice." According to their research, people find meaning and purpose when they "absorb and participate in large systems of meaning, such as religion (or democracy, conservation movements, etc)." This is consistent with my contention that we need to develop a meaning mindset as the best way to face negative events and aging.

Klinger (Chapter 2, this volume) employs the evolutionary perspective. According to this view, both animal life and human life "consist of a virtually continual succession of goal pursuits" in order to meet life's necessities. As a result, sustained and persistent goal striving "constitutes an imperative of purpose." He emphasizes that "the human brain cannot sustain purposeless living." Goal striving and positive affect independently contribute to the sense that life is meaningful. The absence of adequate goals or the blocking of major life goals may lead to feelings of meaninglessness, depression, and addiction.

Ryff's chapter in this volume (Chapter 11) is a good example of the integrative approach because her theory of meaning and well-being incorporates humanistic and existential theories, psychosocial adaptive processes, and neurophysiological substrates. The definition of existential well-being or eudaimonic well-being emphasizes meaning, purpose, personal growth, and mastery. I have always considered the six dimensions of psychological well-being (autonomy, environmental mastery, personal growth, positive relations with others, purpose in life, and self-acceptance) as the gold standard of well-being because it is more comprehensive than subjective well-being. It is most interesting that her components of psychological well-being correspond to the components of personal meaning (Wong, 1998a).

Steger (Chapter 8, this volume) is correct in pointing out that "one problem with this body of research is that it has often accumulated in the absence of a unifying theoretical framework." Wong's complex dual-systems model (see Chapter 1, this volume) is an attempt to provide a comprehensive framework that incorporates the large amount of research data related to the various dimensions of meaning. The dual-systems model also incorporates various theoretical perspectives in a coherent manner.

The Personality Perspective

Maddi's theory of hardiness (see Chapter 3, this volume) is rooted in the existential theory that emphasizes people's quest for meaning in order to overcome existential anxiety about uncertainties and meaninglessness. A disposition toward hardiness consists of three components: challenge, control, and commitment. Together, these three components enable people to cope with stress and maintain a sense of meaning in the face of adversity.

Maddi focuses on adaptive cognitive-behavioral responses to ontological threats in order to create a positive future. Meaning is created through creative problem solving, symbolization, imagination, and social support, thereby restoring a sense of meaning and well-being. The existential courage and decision to confront and experience uncertainty and threat are important for the experience of meaning. His approach further supports my contention that one cannot fully understand the meaning of life without considering the existential philosophical dimension.

According to McAdams (Chapter 5, this volume), there are three levels of personality: (a) dispositional traits, (b) characteristic adaptations, and (c) integrative life stories, evolving in a complex social and cultural context. Meaning making happens at all three levels of personality. Certain dispositional profiles, such as high levels of extraversion, conscientiousness, openness to experience, and low levels of neuroticism, tend to be associated with an overall feeling that life has meaning and purpose.

McAdams's main focus, however, is on the narrative approach to discovering the existential meaning of the human condition. Narrative construction allows for the examination and transformation of negative events into positives to make life meaningful. More important, it provides a framework that integrates the different fragments of one's life to produce a coherent narrative identity.

Wong (Chapter 1, this volume; see also in press-a, in press-b) has recently proposed that a meaning mindset may also serve as a powerful personality trait. Such individuals as Socrates, Mahatma Gandhi, and Martin Luther King, Jr., dedicated their lives to pursue an ideal, a mission, even when such pursuits put their lives at risk. This meaning-mindset hypothesis is especially relevant for developing a positive psychology for the suffering masses, among them cancer patients and trauma victims. Frankl (1946/1985) managed to retain a strong sense of meaning in life and helped others to do so in Nazi concentration camps. Emmons (1999) makes the case that "growth is possible to the degree to which a person creates or finds meaning in suffering, pain, and adversity" (p. 144).

Narrative Perspective

Apart from McAdams (Chapter 5, this volume), several other contributors, among them Sommer, Baumeister, and Stillman (Chapter 14, this volume) and Slattery and Park (Chapter 22, this volume), also favor a narrative approach. Reker, Birren, and Svensson (Chapter 18, this volume) discuss the importance of restoring meaning through autobiographical methods. They report on individuals' ability to transform old meanings into new ones that enable them to achieve a broader and deeper understanding of themselves and of life. "One's horizon expands along with the ability to see the bigger picture. One's worldview undergoes reconstruction and expansion with a renewed sense of connectedness with self, with others, and with all living things." Their chapter lends more credence to the deep-and-wide hypothesis of positive transformation.

Beike and Crone (Chapter 15, this volume) provide further support that a coherent life story helps make sense of life and "provides both temporal and causal explanations for events." In addition, they point out that the story needs to be morally grounded as understood by the social context in which the story is situated. "These well-defined narratives place the self contextually in space and time and integrate the person's life experience and self-concept, thereby providing a sense of a self with purpose (McAdams, 2006)."

The Relational Perspective

Aron and Aron's chapter in this volume (Chapter 9) is important because it emphasizes that other people matter. Their relational theory is about the expansion of the self to the extent of self-transcendence through relationships. Their chapter on love covers a wide variety of topics related to the centrality of relationships in meaningful living. Their self-expansion model encompasses two fundamental principles: (a) the motivational principle to expand one's potential efficacy and (b) the inclusion-of-other-in-the-self principle to expand the self through relationships with others. "It is important to see from another perspective why caring for others is central to meaning."

Aron and Aron conclude that "caring for others is central to meaning." They provide an evolutionary account of the need for caring for something beyond our personal self: "Social units, whether families or businesses, small towns or whole countries (that is whether genetically related or not), tend to survive better if they emphasize cooperation, altruism, sharing, and the general sense that the group is more important than the individual."

An auxiliary of this general principle is that one can be "part of something very large and almost eternal," which takes us to the mystical realm of religion and self-transcendence. In other words, spirituality, religion, myth making, and God are essential for meaningful living simply because they represent our need to serve and belong to something beyond ourselves.

Chapter 12, by Kwee, represents a very different theoretical approach to meaning of life. According to Buddhist psychology, what matters most is not what one can get from the world or whether one's needs are met but what takes place on the inside. This quantum shift of mindset calls for a spiritual awakening or enlightenment, which enables the person to see life differently. It is through this radical inner transformation that one sees life as being meaningful. Mindful meditation is a means to cultivate wisdom and compassion, which characterize the Buddhist vision of meaningful living. "Thus," according to Kwee, "from a Buddhist point of view meaning is derived from the compassion and empathic care for joyful relationships."

Resilience and the Threats to Meaning

In an ideal world, one needs to be concerned only with what is good and right. But in an imperfect world inhabited by imperfect people, we all have to cope with people problems, our own limitations, and predicaments inherent in the human condition. Existential psychologists have long recognized such inherent threats to meaning of life as alienation, death anxiety, freedom, and meaninglessness (Yalom, 1980). Major life disruptions and traumas, especially sexual abuse and domestic violence, can also lead to the shattering of one's assumptive world (Janoff-Bulman, 1992) and create a meaning crisis. Tomer (Chapter 10, this volume) and Wong (Chapter 28, this volume) emphasize the importance of acceptance as an effective way to deal with death anxiety. In terms of the mechanisms, resilience also involves disengagement, reengagement, and goal adjustment, which create meaning in negative situations (Chapters 2, 15, and 27, this volume).

Wong (Chapters 1 and 28, this volume) explains that meaning-centered resilience strategy calls for practicing the ABCDE, which stands for acceptance, belief, commitment, discovery, and evaluation. Each of these components is essential for adaptive success. The challenge for meaning researchers and practitioners is to transform negatives into positives, knowing the fact that the bad is stronger than the good (Baumeister & Vohs, 2004). Wong's dual-systems model (Chapter 1, this volume) is one of the several theoretical accounts of such a transformation. Wong postulates that (a) positive outcomes depend on self-regulation of the interactions between approach and avoidance systems within a specific context and (b) optimal functioning depends on achieving an optimal balance between approach and avoidance systems. The dual-system also includes components of culture, personality traits, and mindful awareness.

Tedeschi and Calhoun (Chapter 25, this volume) emphasize that negative events can spur people on the road to growth and personal transformation. "So, in our growth toward meaningful, wise living, traumas can serve the purpose of the crystallization of discontent that Baumeister (1991) describes as provoking changes in meaning." The key to posttraumatic growth (PTG) is the ability to reconstruct the assumptive world about the self and one's life. This meaning-making ability allows one to create a new narrative that facilitates one's positive change and growth. The discovery of new ways of perceiving life and negative events can lead to better adjustment. According to Tedeschi and Calhoun, their "evolving model of PTG (Calhoun & Tedeschi, 2006) emphasizes cognitive-emotional processes that require people who have suffered trauma to navigate a difficult path to rebuilding a shattered assumptive world." This is consistent with Wong's deep-and-wide hypothesis about the positive potentials of negative life events.

Sickness

Sickness, especially life-threatening illnesses, can trigger death anxiety and the quest for meaning. In her chapter on the role of meaning in coping with cancer, Park (Chapter 23, this volume) describes a study that shows that meaning making results in higher levels of self-esteem, optimism, and self-efficacy. Park's description of meaning systems resembles what I call a meaning mindset (Chapter 1, this volume): "Together, global beliefs and goals, and the resultant sense of life meaning, form individuals' meaning systems. Meaning systems comprise the lens through which individuals interpret, evaluate, and respond to their experiences."

Park also points out, however, that meaning seeking and meaning making may also result in distress. For example, rumination or developing a very negative view of life can lead to depression. This notion is similar to Peterson and Park's (Chapter 13, this volume) finding of a negative correlation between search for meaning and character strengths. Such negative effects may reflect bumps on the road in meaning seeking.

Aspinwall, Leaf, and Leachman (Chapter 21, this volume) demonstrate the importance of meaning attribution and personal responsibility in coping with cancer. For example, believing that God expects people to take responsibility for their own health leads to more health-promoting and disease-avoiding behaviors, whereas believing that cancer is God's will increases the belief that cancer is inevitably fatal. Their study provides empirical support for the idea that even when we have no control over the bad things that happen to us, we can still have control over our attitude and beliefs (Frankl, 1946/1985). In short, to believe in our personal responsibility for achieving a positive outcome can increase health-promoting behavior.

Aspinwall et al. conclude that finding meaning from adverse situations contributes to both mental and physical well-being. More specifically, religious and spiritual beliefs and practices are thought to serve as a central component of an individual's general orienting system, which helps the individual understand, appraise, and derive meaning from stressful life events and ultimately helps that individual decide how to react. Their conclusion provides further support to the two general principles that (a) self-transcendence is a key ingredient of a meaningful life and (b) finding meaning is a key ingredient of resilience.

Wrosch et al. (Chapter 24, this volume) emphasize the importance of disengagement and reengagement in self-regulation when the original goals become unattainable and one's sense of meaning is threatened. Subjective well-being depends not only on the pursuit of a meaningful goal but also on the ability to reinvest one's energy in an alternative goal when the original goal is repeatedly blocked. Trying a different pathway and switching to an alternative life goal both represent the deep-and-wide coping strategy.

Aging

The inevitability of aging and death poses a unique challenge to the task of meaningful living. This inevitability is no longer just a matter of overcoming situational stress because it has to do with the global stress of human existence. Once again we are confronted with an existential crisis that can be resolved only through meaning making and transcendence.

Krause (Chapter 19, this volume) points out that research suggests "meaning making is a lifelong process that is important at every point in the life course." He concludes that people who have a deep sense of meaning in life enjoy better mental and physical health than do individuals who have not been able to find meaning in life. Krause defines meaning in terms of values, purpose, goals, and the ability to reconcile the past. He adds an existential layer to the definition of meaning: "Although clearly linked to values, a sense of purpose is conceptually distinct. It has to do with believing that one's actions have a set place in the larger order of social life and that one's behavior fits appropriately into a larger, more important social whole." In other words, purpose implies that one's cherished values and goals are chosen according to one's worldviews and life orientation.

A goal not only inspires what Frankl calls "will to meaning" but also evokes commitment to a plan of actions. "A goal or plan instills the belief that no matter how bleak things may seem at the moment, there is still a way to get through these difficulties; and, further, that if these goals or plans are executed faithfully, hard times will eventually subside." His findings are clearly supportive of the efficacy of Wong's ABCDE coping strategy. He also recognizes the need for social support; family members and close friends can help restore a sense of meaning in life in older adults by reminders that it is still possible to pursue cherished values with commitment and dedication.

Reker and Wong (Chapter 20, this volume) present a research program on healthy aging. They compared successful and unsuccessful agers in institutions and the community on a variety of well-being measures. Their chapter highlights the pivotal role of meaning in psychosocial adjustment to aging. They found that both meaning and spirituality are associated with successful aging.

Dying

Becker (1973) emphasizes the terror of death because of the human capacity to foresee one's demise. Research supporting terror management theory (Pyszczynski, Greenberg, & Solomon, 2002) demonstrates how the unconscious motive to defend against this terror can lead to violence and aggression. Similarly, Peterson (1999) observes that a strong commitment to religious beliefs and meaning systems, when threatened, can lead to evil and violence. Tomer (Chapter 10, this volume) and Wong (Chapter 28, this volume) emphasize the importance of acceptance as an effective way to deal with death anxiety. Tomer's chapter is an excellent resource on how people ascribe different meanings or values to death and how meaning influences different death attitudes as measured by Wong, Reker, and Gesser (1994). More specifically, Tomer concludes that viewing death as meaningful was related to less fear of the unknown, whereas viewing death as purposeless was related to greater fear of the unknown.

Meaning-Centered Interventions

Wong (Chapter 28, this volume) summarizes the main contributions of logotherapy and presents the latest developments of integrative meaning-centered therapy. He stresses that meaning therapy serves the dual function of healing what is broken and bringing out what is good and right about individuals. After describing the defining characteristics of the meaning approach, he introduces PURE and ABCDE as the two major meaning-based intervention strategies to facilitate healing and personal growth.

Beike and Crone (Chapter 15, this volume) highlight the temporal dimension of meaning in memory reconstruction. Negative or traumatic memories are persistent primarily because of the strength of their negative emotional content, and they are more resistant to modification or reconstruction than are positive memories. Healing of painful memories depends on allowing emotions to fade and gaining a sense of closure. Upon recollecting such "closed memories," people report discovering more insight and meaning from their memories. "An initially crushing blow can be seen as a meaningful turning point toward happiness if one can shed the emotion that narrows the variety of meanings that can be applied."

Effective meaning-oriented interventions depend on understanding the cultural context. According to Slattery and Park (Chapter 22, this volume), a woman who has undergone trauma, for example, "needs to create a narrative that helps her develop coherent and consistent global and appraised meanings that are understandable and consistent within her culture and context. Until she is able to create satisfying context-consistent resolutions between global and appraised meanings, she is likely to remain symptomatic (Gray et al., 2007)."

Slattery and Park emphasize the distinction between global meaning and appraised situational meaning as a motivation or an incentive for change. Examples are provided of how changes in global meaning, appraised meaning, or behavior can facilitate positive change. This intervention makes use of the negative emotion of tension and unease to motivate positive change. They point out that for problems that cannot be directly "repaired" or solved through behavioral change, as in sexual assault, illness, or death, meaning-making efforts are often most effective in facilitating positive change.

Ventegodt and Merrick (Chapter 26, this volume) point out that a holistic approach to meaning of life needs to balance between sexuality and sense of coherence. "Sexuality is often a quality ascribed to the body, and sense of coherence is often a quality ascribed to the spiritual dimension of human beings; by seeing these qualities as being heart-qualities, love and sexuality are transformed to something more whole and holy."

In a holistic approach to therapy, which integrates the physical with the psychological and spiritual, meaning has emerged as an important element. During clinical interviews regarding the quality of life of the client, the authors emphasize the importance of recovering a sense of meaning in life and reestablishing one's life mission to facilitate healing. Emphasis is also on the actual experience of being engaged in meaningful pursuits and using all one's resources and physical, mental, and spiritual potentials. This holistic consciousness-oriented approach "will help people become valuable not only to themselves but also to each other."

The chapter by Shek (Chapter 16, this volume) represents a cross-cultural perspective of meaning. From his cross-sectional and longitudinal studies on Chinese students across socioeconomical statuses, he shows that purpose is not only positively correlated with psychological well-being and school adjustment but also negatively correlated with antisocial behavior and substance abuse. These findings emphasize the importance of meaning and purpose in contributing to youth resilience in a Chinese population. He points out that adolescents with stronger endorsement of positive Chinese beliefs about adversity are more resilient. Another important aspect of his chapter is his conclusion that family functioning is related to adolescent meaning in life. Thus, for meaning and resilience in the Chinese adolescent population, perceived family functioning is important.

Wong and Wong (Chapter 27, this volume) emphasize the role of meaning in resilience. They define resilience in terms of bouncing back and bouncing up beyond the baseline, citing the notion that what does not kill you can make you stronger. They provide additional evidence on the deep-and-wide hypothesis in effective coping with adversity. Reinforcing Shek's findings, Wong and Wong reiterate the need to take into account cultural context and family systems in meaning-oriented interventions.

Conclusions

I hope that this brief guided tour has not only given readers a sweeping view of the lay of the land but also revealed a bold new vision for the future of meaning-oriented research and applications. The human quest for meaning is probably the best kept secret to the greatest human adventure—namely, that it has always been here, springing from the deepest yearnings of the human heart, confronting the mysteries, uncertainties, and fears of human existence, and pursuing dreams and ideals that know no boundaries. The never-ending quest for meaning and significance has taken human race to the sublime heights of truth, goodness, and beauty, as well as to the hideous lows of atrocities, aggression, and oppression against fellow human beings (Frankl, 1946/1985; Peterson, 1999; Pyszczynski et al., 2002). The future of humanity hinges on understanding and harnessing the unlimited potentials of meaning seeking and meaning making.

Meaning research is a complex business. This volume shows that we need rigorous theoretical analysis, sophisticated research methods, and deep philosophical insight in order to understand the uniquely human capacity for meaning seeking and meaning making. No one theory or research paradigm can discover the whole truth about meaningful living. Not even scientific research can do justice to this ancient, universal, grand story of human adventure, which reaches the deep recesses of unconsciousness and the mystical realms of spirituality. In meaning research, psychologists can benefit from the great wisdoms and insights from philosophy, religion, and literature about the human striving to live fully, vitally, and authentically. Most of the chapters in this volume reflect the benefits of cross-fertilization between science and humanities.

There is already extensive literature on the vital role of meaning in integrating various aspects of human needs and functions in the service of survival and flourishing (Wong & Fry, 1998). In this revised edition, all chapters offer some new findings or insights about the adaptive benefits of meaning. Having a clear sense of meaning and purpose can not only pull us out of depression, misery, and anxiety but also give us the motivation, optimism, and strength we need to flourish. Steger's chapter (Chapter 8, this volume) contains the most detailed information about the benefits of meaning. Klinger (Chapter 2, this volume) concludes that "goal pursuits influence most of an individual's cognitive processing, emotional responses, and therefore consciousness as well as choices and overt actions. Goal striving appears also to form one of the main determinants of persons' sense that their lives are meaningful." Thus, the meaning advantage is that it is capable of both increasing well-being and decreasing psychopathology. The dominant message from this volume is that meaning is the foundation of positive psychology because it is the key component of positive affect, well-being, physical health, resilience, relationship, achievement, spirituality, successful aging, and dying well.

This book will serve as a rich resource not only for researchers and clinicians but for all those seeking to make life better. I invite readers to make good use of this book in their own personal quest for meaning. I also challenge researchers and practitioners to discover the potential of a meaning mindset in transforming society and culture to create a social ecology conducive to human flourishing.

References

Baumeister, R. F. (1991). *Meanings of life*. New York, NY: Guilford Press.

Baumeister, R. F., & Vohs, K. D. (Eds.). (2004). *Handbook of self-regulation: Research, theory, and application*. New York, NY: Guilford Press.

Becker, E. (1973). *The denial of death*. New York, NY: Free Press.

Bruner, J. (1990). *Acts of meaning*. Cambridge, MA: Harvard University Press.

Emmons, R. A. (1999). *The psychology of ultimate concerns*. New York, NY: Guilford Press.

Frankl, V. E. (1985). *Man's search for meaning* (Rev. and updated). New York, NY: Washington Square Press/Pocket Books. (Originally published 1946)

Gray, M. J., Maguen, S., & Litz, B. T. (2007). Schema constructs and cognitive models of posttraumatic stress disorder. In L. P. Riso, P. L. du Toit, D. J. Stein, & J. E. Young (Eds.), *Cognitive schemas and core beliefs in psychological problems: A scientist-practitioner guide* (pp. 59–92). Washington, DC: American Psychological Association.

James, W. (1912). *Essays in radical empiricism* (Essay 2, para. 1). New York, NY: Longman, Green.

Janoff-Bulman, R. (1992). *Shattered assumptions: Towards a new psychology of trauma.* New York, NY: Free Press.

Kim, M., Lee, H. S., & Wong, P. T. (2005, August). *Meaning of life according to Koreans: The Korean Personal Meaning Profile.* Poster presented at the annual convention of the American Psychological Association, Washington, DC.

Lin, A., & Wong, P. T. (2006, August). *The meaning of life: According to a Chinese sample.* Paper presented at the annual convention of the American Psychological Association, New Orleans, Louisiana.

Maslow, A. H. (1943). A theory of human motivation. *Psychological Review, 50,* 370–396.

Nagel, T. (1989). *The view from nowhere.* New York, NY: Oxford University Press.

Pargament, K. I. (1997). *The psychology of religion and coping: Theory, research, practice.* New York, NY: Guilford Press.

Park, C. L., & Folkman, S. (1997). Meaning in the context of stress and coping. *General Review of Psychology, 1,* 115–144.

Peterson, C., Park, N., & Seligman, M. E. (2006). Greater strengths of character and recovery from illness. *Journal of Positive Psychology, 1,* 17–26.

Peterson, J. B. (1999). *Maps of meaning: The architecture of belief.* New York, NY: Routledge.

Peterson, J. B. (2007). The meaning of meaning. In P. T. P. Wong, L. C. J. Wong, M. J. McDonald, & D. W. Klaassen (Eds.), *Proceedings of Meaning Conferences: The positive psychology of meaning and spirituality* (pp. 11–32). Abbotsford, BC: INPM Press.

Pyszczynski, T., Greenberg, J., & Solomon, S. (2002). *In the wake of 9/11: The psychology of terror.* Washington, DC: American Psychological Association.

Reker, G. T., & Chamberlain, K. (Eds.). (2000). *Exploring existential meaning: Optimizing human development across the life span.* Thousand Oaks, CA: Sage.

Seligman, M. E., & Csikszentmihalyi, M. (2000). Positive psychology: An introduction. *American Psychologist, 55,* 5–14.

Seligman, M. E. P., Steen, T., Park, N., & Peterson, C. (2005). Positive psychology progress: Empirical validation of interventions. *American Psychologist, 60,* 410–425.

Steger, M. F., Frazier, P., Oishi, S., & Kaler, M. (2006). The Meaning in Life Questionnaire: Assessing the presence of and search for meaning in life. *Journal of Counseling Psychology, 53,* 80–93.

Takano, Y., & Wong, P. T. (2004, July/August). *Meaning of life according to a Japanese sample.* Paper presented at the annual convention of the America Psychological Association, Honolulu, Hawaii.

Wong, P. T. P. (1998a). Implicit theories of meaningful life and the development of the Personal Meaning Profile (PMP). In P. T. P. Wong & P. S. Fry (Eds.), *The human quest for meaning: A handbook of psychological research and clinical applications* (pp. 111–140). Mahwah, NJ: Erlbaum.

Wong, P. T. P. (1998b). Spirituality, meaning, and successful aging. In P. T. P Wong & P. S. Fry (Eds.), *The human quest for meaning: A handbook of psychological research and clinical applications* (pp. 359–394). Mahwah, NJ: Erlbaum.

Wong, P. T. P. (2009). Viktor Frankl: Prophet of hope for the 21st century. In A. Batthyany & J. Levinson (Eds.), *Anthology of Viktor Frankl's logotherapy.* Phoenix, AZ: Zeig, Tucker & Theisen.

Wong, P. T. P. (2010). What is existential positive psychology? *Internationl Journal of Existential Psychology and Psychotherapy, 3,* 1–10.

Wong, P. T. P. (in press-a). Positive psychology 2.0: Towards a balanced interactive model of the good life. *Canadian Psychology.*

Wong, P. T. P. (in press-b). Reclaiming positive psychology: A meaning-centered approach to sustainable growth and radical empiricism. *Journal of Humanistic Psychology.*

Wong, P. T. P., & Fry, P. S. (Eds.). (1998). *The human quest for meaning: A handbook of psychological research and clinical applications.* Mahwah, NJ: Erlbaum.

Wong, P. T. P., Reker, G. T., & Gesser, G. (1994). Death Attitude Profile–Revised: A multidimensional measure of attitudes toward death. In R. A. Neimeyer (Ed.), *Death anxiety handbook: Research, instrumentation, and application* (pp. 121–148). Washington, DC: Taylor & Francis.

Wong, P. T. P., & Watt, L. (1991). What types of reminiscence are associated with successful aging? *Psychology and Aging, 6*, 272–279.

Wong, P. T. P., & Weiner, B. (1981). When people ask "why" questions and the heuristic of attributional search. *Journal of Personality and Social Psychology, 40*, 650–663.

Yalom, I. D. (1980). *Existential psychotherapy.* New York, NY: Basic Books.

I
Theories

1
Toward a Dual-Systems Model of What Makes Life Worth Living

PAUL T. P. WONG

Trent University

What makes life worth living? This is probably the most important question ever asked in psychology because it is vitally related to human survival and flourishing. It is also a highly complex question with no simple answers to the extent that it touches all aspects of humanity—biological, psychological, social, and spiritual. Thus, only a holistic approach can provide a comprehensive picture of meaningful living. To further complicate matters, every person has his or her own ideas on what constitutes the good life. Many people believe that money is the answer; that is why money remains the most powerful motivator in a consumer society. Others, especially those in academia, believe that reputation matters most. For those people living in abject poverty, heaven is being free from hunger. Given such individual differences in values and beliefs, is it even possible to provide general answers based on psychological research?

Viktor Frankl (1946/1985) found a way to reconcile general principles with individual differences. On the one hand, he emphasized that it was up to each individual to define and discover meaning in life; on other hand, he devoted most of his professional life trying to uncover the principles that could facilitate individuals' quests for meaning. His main finding is that "the will to meaning" is the key to living a worthy and fulfilling life regardless of personal preferences and circumstances (Frankl, 1946/1985; Chapter 28, this volume). The present chapter represents an extension of Frankl's work in a more precise and empirically testable model.

Numerous psychological models have been proposed to account for meaning in life. For example, the existential perspective tends to focus on learning to live with the dark side of the human condition, such as suffering, meaninglessness, loneliness, and death, and creating meaning through one's courageous choices and creative actions (Sartre, 1990; Yalom, 1980). In contrast, positive psychology emphasizes positive experiences and emotions as the pillars of a worthwhile life (Seligman, 2002; Seligman & Csikszentmihalyi,

2000). The dual-systems model provides a bridge between these two intellectual traditions and integrates various streams of research relevant to the question of the meaning of life.

The dual-systems model attempts to address three important issues vital to developing a comprehensive psychological account of a meaningful life: (a) what people really want and how to achieve their life goals, (b) what people fear and how to overcome their anxieties, and (c) how people makes sense of the predicaments and paradoxes of life. The first two issues are instrumental in nature, having to do with adaptive mechanisms, whereas the last issue is philosophical and spiritual in nature, having to do with how one makes sense of the self and one's place in the world. Answers to the first two issues depend on one's philosophy of life.

What Do People Really Want?

It is a truism that for life to be worth living, people need to enjoy living and feel satisfied that their needs and wants are met. Maslow's (1943) hierarchy model posits that people need to meet all five levels of needs in order to be self-actualized. Peterson and Seligman (2004) propose that people want to live a life of pleasure, engagement, and meaning in order to live a really happy life. Baumeister (1991) emphasizes that meaning in life depends on purpose, efficacy, value, and self-worth. Based on implicit theory research, I directly asked people what they really wanted in order to live an ideal meaningful life if money were no longer an issue (Wong, 1998b). Based on numerous studies, I have found that the worthy life consisted of the following components: happiness, achievement, relationship, intimacy, religion, altruism, self-acceptance, and fair treatment. All the foregoing models implicitly assume that (a) we know that the various psychological needs are markers of the good life and (b) we know how to meet these needs.

Unfortunately, we do not live in an ideal world with perfect justice, equal opportunities, and unlimited resources for all individuals to get what they want in life. Fate often intervenes, such as earthquakes and accidents, which totally disrupt one's life. Another relevant issue is that we are not perfect. Most people do make mistakes and often derail their own best efforts because of some such character defects as greed and blind ambition. At the end of their earthly journey, some people may discover that they have not really lived even though they were successful in realizing all their dreams and wishes. Finally, there is a philosophical dimension. People need to reflect on the big picture and learn to come to terms with such existential givens as sickness, aging, and death, which pose a constant threat to their dreams of a good life. They also need to examine their own lives to make sure they do not spend a lifetime chasing after the wind.

What Do People Want to Avoid?

We do not need empirical proof that all people naturally avoid pain, suffering, and death. Similarly, we want to be free from deprivation, discrimination, oppression, and forms of ill-treatment. We also shun rejection, opposition, defeat, failure, and all the obstacles that prevent us from realizing our dreams. We want to stay away from difficult people who upset us and make our lives miserable. Finally, we all struggle with our own limitations—areas of weaknesses and deficiencies.

In addition to the foregoing litany of woes, we also need to be concerned with the existential anxieties inherent in the human condition (Yalom, 1980). No one really enjoys suffering, but meaning in life depends on discovering the meaning of suffering (Frankl, 1946/1985). Furthermore, our ability to achieve the good life depends on our efficacy in coping with stresses, misfortunes, and negative emotions. The dual-systems model not only recognizes the inevitable unpleasant realities of life but also specifies the mechanisms of translating negativity into positive outcomes.

How Do People Make Sense of Life?

People may not be able to articulate their philosophy of life, but they all possess one; for we all have assumptions, beliefs, values, and worldviews that help us make sense of our lives. The huge literature on attribution research suggests that people are both lay scientists and philosophers (e.g., Weiner, 1975; Wong, 1991; Wong & Weiner, 1981).

Our philosophy about what constitutes the good life can determine how we make choices and how we live. Those people who believe that the good life is to eat, drink, and be merry will spend their lives on the hedonic treadmill. Those who believe that the purpose of life is to serve God will devote their lives to fulfilling God's calling.

Every philosophy of life leads to the development of a certain mindset—a frame of reference or prism—through which we make value judgments. For example, hedonism will contribute to a happiness-mindset that values positive experiences and emotions as most important for subjective well-being. Some of the widely used instruments of life satisfaction reflect the happiness-mindset. For example, the well-known Subjective Well-Being Scale (SWBS) by Diener, Emmons, Larsen, and Griffin (1985) include such items as "My conditions of life are excellent" and "So far I have gotten the important things I want in life."

In contrast, a eudaimonic philosophy (Aristotle, trans. 2004) is conducive to a meaning mindset that considers virtue as the key to flourishing. The joy of living comes from doing good. As a case in point, Jim Elliot died young as a missionary because he chose the path of self-sacrifice to serve God and others: "He is no fool who gives what he cannot keep to gain what he cannot lose" (Elliot, 1989, p. 15). Mahatma Gandhi, who gave his life in the struggle for freedom for his country, wrote, "Joy lies in the fight, in the attempt, in the suffering involved, not in the victory itself" (Attenborough, 2008, p. 3). A sense of life satisfaction can come from the defiant human spirit of fighting with courage and dignity. In *Myth of Sisyphus*, Albert Camus (1942/1991) concludes that "the struggle itself toward the heights is enough to fill a man's heart. One must imagine Sisyphus happy" (p. 123). This type of life satisfaction can best be measured by a psychological instrument that focuses on eudaimonic well-being (Huta, 2009; Waterman, 2008).

Why do I focus on the meaning mindset? For most people, life is full of hardships and struggles. A life of endless happiness without pain can only be achieved by reducing human beings to robots or brains connected to machines capable of delivering constant stimulation to the brain's pleasure center. Even when individuals are successful beyond their wildest dreams, their lives are not exempt from physical pain and psychological suffering. Moreover, a single-minded pursuit of personal happiness and success is not sustainable—eventually, it will lead to despair, disillusion, and other psychological problems (Schumaker, 2007). Thus, Schumaker advocates the creation of a society that will "attach greater value to the achievement of a meaningful life" (2007, p. 284).

The meaning mindset focuses on the person (Maslow, 1962; Rogers, 1995) as meaning-seeking and meaning-making creatures. It also capitalizes on the human capacity for reflection and awakening (Wong, 2007). The ability to reflect on and articulate one's worldview can facilitate positive changes. The meaning mindset also involves understanding the structure, functions, and processes of meaning (Wong, in press-a, in press-b). Without a personally defined meaning and purpose, individuals would experience life as being on a ship without a rudder. An enduring passion for living comes only from commitment to a higher purpose. In short, a meaning mindset will facilitate the dual process of striving for authentic happiness and overcoming adversities.

The Basic Postulates of the Dual-Systems Model

The basic tenets of logotherapy (Chapter 28, this volume) are applicable to the dual-systems model. The following postulates are specific to the dynamic interaction between positives and negatives (see Figure 1.1).

1. In reality, positives and negatives often coexist. It is rare, if not impossible, to have purely positive or negative conditions (Chapters 5, 7, 8, 11, 12, 14, 21, and 22, this volume).
2. Similar to the concept of yin and yang, every positive or negative element contains a seed of its opposite. For example, one can be happy about a promotion but worried about the extra stresses involved. By the same token, one can feel sad about losing a job but feel happy that one can go back to school for retraining. Thus, a purely either–or dichotomy is inadequate in capturing the complexities of human experiences.
3. The approach and avoidance systems coexist and operate in an interdependent fashion. The approach system represents appetitive

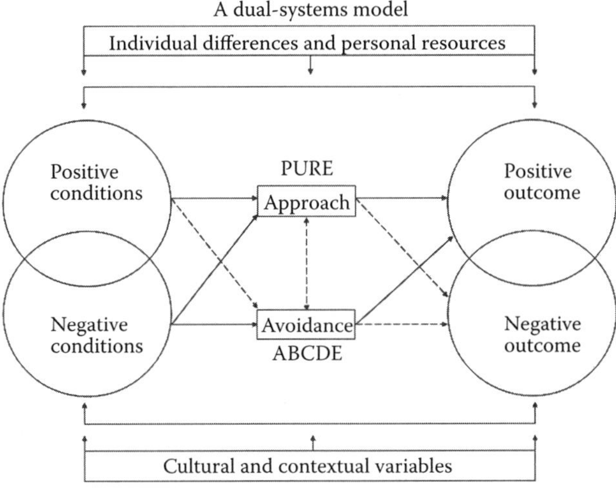

Figure 1.1 Schematic of the key components and links in the dual-systems model.

behaviors, positive affects, goal strivings, and intrinsic motivations. The avoidance system represents defensive mechanisms against noxious conditions, threats, and negative emotions. Both systems need to interact with each other in order to optimize positive outcomes (Chapters 2, 7, and 11, this volume). In other words, neither system can function effectively all by itself over the long haul. For example, an appetitive system will eventually implode unless it is checked by the warning of risks and discomforts associated with overconsumption. The approach and avoidance systems each involve different emotional-behavioral processes and neurophysiological substrates. When the two systems work together in a balanced and cooperative manner, the likelihood of survival and flourishing is greater than when the focus remains exclusively on either approach or avoidance.

4. Different systems predominate in different situations. In countries that enjoy peace and prosperity, the approach system predominates in everyday-life situations. However, in areas devastated by war or natural disaster, the avoidance system predominates. Yet no matter which system predominates, individuals are always better off when they make good use of the two complementary systems. For example, even in desperate times of coping with excruciating pain and impending death, the joy of listening to beautiful music can make life worth living.
5. When a person is not actively engaged in approach or avoidance, the default or neutral stage is regulated by the awareness regulation system. The Pavlovian orienting response (Pavlov, 1927/2003) is a good example of this effortless attention system. Mindful awareness is also

important because it is primarily concerned with being fully attuned to the here and now; as a result, it makes us open to new discoveries of the small wonders and miracles of being alive.

6. Meaning plays a pivotal role in the dual-systems model. Meaning is involved in life protection as well as life expansion, thereby contributing to enhancing well-being and health and buffering against negatives (Chapters 7, 8, and 20, this volume).
7. Self-regulation systems are shaped by individual differences, personal resources, and cultural or contextual variables (Chapters 2, 7, 11, 20, 21, and 22, this volume).

A Description of the Dual-Systems Model

Individual Differences

How we make sense of the environment and respond to various situations reflect individual differences. The Big Five personality factors (McCrae & Costa, 1987) are relevant; for example, openness is related to mindful awareness, and conscientiousness is related to responsible actions. One's mindset is relevant to making value judgments. The story one lives by can also make a difference (Chapters 5, 14, and 18, this volume). Finally, individual differences in psychological resources may affect efficacy in coping with the demands of life (Wong, 1993).

Culture and Cultural Context

Both personality and adaptation efforts are shaped by cultural contexts (Chapter 16, this volume; Wong & Wong, 2005). Cultural influence is especially strong in shaping our perception, thinking, and meaning construction (Bruner, 1990; Shweder, 1991). In fact, the complete process from antecedent conditions to outcomes can be influenced by culture. What is positive and negative are shaped by cultural norms. It is not possible to understand the good life apart from various contextual factors. Recently, Sheldon (2009) also proposed a multilevel model of human flourishing involving biological and cognitive levels of the persons within supportive social contexts and cultures. Similarly, DelleFave (2009) emphasized that optimal experiences vary according to cultural contexts and meaning making.

Antecedent Conditions

Positive and negative conditions tend to overlap. The overlapping area indicates ambiguous or neutral conditions in which there is no urgent need for either approach or avoidance. There are no purely positive or negative conditions, however; for even at the extreme positive or negative end, elements of the opposite may still exist. In fact, the model posits that some negativity is not only inevitable but also beneficial for our well-being over the long haul.

For instance, it never hurts to remind ourselves of the fragility and finitude of life and be aware of the risks of overconfidence and greed.

Outcomes

Positive outcomes result from successful adaptations. They include states of satisfaction, success, personal growth, and meaning fulfillment. Positive outcomes are accompanied by such positive emotions as happiness, satisfaction, and relief. Positive outcomes have the capacity of reinforcing behaviors that precede them.

Negative outcomes represent ineffective or unsuccessful adaptations. They include states of deprivation and frustration. They are accompanied by such aversive and negative emotions as anger and anxiety.

Positive and negative outcomes overlap because there is often a downside for every gain, and an upside for every loss. The dual-system also posits that a balanced attitude is better than being carried away by the ecstasy of success or dragged down to the abyss by defeat.

The Approach System

The approach system predominates when conditions are positive. More specifically, the positive-approach system seeks to do what is pleasant, engaging, meaningful, and what contributes to growth and life expansion. It includes all the appetitive aspects of life, among them consummatory behaviors, incentive motivation, pursuit of happiness and success, and all positive motivations. The positive system not only provides the energies and goals for a purpose-driven life but also generates positive emotions that make one feel life is worth living. Positive experiences and emotions come from both intrinsic and extrinsic motivations. Intrinsic motivation includes the striving for competence, creativity, justice, doing good, and experiencing the "flow." Extrinsic motivations include positive feelings of goal attainment and the rewards that come from success. The dual-systems model emphasizes the value of pursuing a higher purpose as the main pathway to meaningful living. Limiting one's goals to fulfilling one's physical desires or misguided selfish ambitions may lead to transitory happiness and may even result in regression and unhappiness (Chapters 4, 7, 9, 14, 15, 21, and 22, this volume).

The avoidance system intersects with the approach system at three junctures. First, even before embarking on the pursuit of a life goal, individuals always face elements of apprehension and fear of failure that may trigger an avoidance tendency. Second, individuals might encounter a setback or opposition in the process of striving toward a goal. Third, once a goal is achieved, the outcome might not be 100% positive. Success may create a backlash, invite a storm of criticisms, or lead individuals to a sense of disillusion and disappointment. Such interactions with negativity can be employed to increase wisdom and resilience for meaningful living.

The positive system can facilitate the avoidance system in at least four ways. First, maintaining a hopeful and positive attitude can reduce the threat of negative conditions. Second, a strong-approach response in spite of anxieties can reduce the avoidance tendency. Third, positive outcomes of success can lead to a reappraisal of the negative condition as less threatening. Finally, discovering the benefits and positive meanings of setbacks can reduce the adverse effects of negative outcomes.

The PURE Model

PURE represents the four ingredients that define meaning: Purpose, Understanding, Responsible Action, and Enjoyment or Evaluation. (see Chapter 28, this volume, for a more detailed explanation). PURE adds a meaning perspective to approach-oriented activities. This extra layer of meaning enables us to become aware of what we are striving for and thus avoid blindly pursuing things that will destroy us in the end. A clear sense of purpose and significance can also increase the motivation for goal striving (Wong, 1998a).

Purpose: The Motivational Component Purpose is the most important component in the meaning structure because it serves several functions as the engine, the fuel, and the steering wheel. Purpose includes goals, directions, incentive objects, values, aspirations, and objectives and is concerned with such questions as these: What does life demand of me? What should I do with my life? What really matters in life? A purpose-driven life is an engaged life committed to pursuing a preferred future. Purpose determines one's life direction and destiny. A meaning mindset increases the likelihood that one's life purpose is consistent with one's life calling and highest values.

Klinger (Chap. 2, p. 31, this volume) emphasizes that

> the human brain cannot sustain purposeless living. It was not designed for that. Its systems are designed for purposive action. When that is blocked, they deteriorate, and the emotional feedback from idling those systems signals extreme discomfort and motivates the search for renewed purpose, renewed meaning. This accounts for Viktor Frankl's (1946/1963; 1969) observation of a *will to meaning.*

Understanding: The Cognitive Component Understanding encompasses cognitive activities, a sense of coherence, making sense of situations, understanding one's own identity and other people, and effectively communicating and building relationships. It is concerned with such questions as these: What has happened? What does it mean? How do I make sense of the world? What am I doing here? Who am I? A life with understanding is a life with clarity and coherence. Weinstein, Ryan, and Deci (Chap. 4, p. 92, this volume) emphasize self-knowledge: "In short, to find true meaning, individuals must get to know who they truly are—that is, know what is valuable and important to them—and act in accord with that knowledge." According to Steger (Chapter 8, this volume), the cognitive component of meaning in life refers to the understandings of who we are, what the world is like, and how we fit in. People often depend on narratives to make sense of life; Sommer, Baumeister, and Stillman (Chap. 14, p. 299, this volume) suggest that their findings "reveal that the construction of narratives provides individuals with an opportunity to restructure events in memory in ways that reflect positively on the self and add a sense of coherence and stability."

Responsible Action: The Behavioral Component Responsible action includes appropriate reactions and actions, doing what is morally right, finding the right solutions, making amends. It is concerned with such questions as these: What is my responsibility in this situation? What is the right thing to do? What options do I have? What choices should I make? A worthy life is based on the responsible exercise of human freedom and personal agency. Frankl (1946/1985) emphasizes the need to be aware of the demand of each situation. A meaning mindset will predispose individuals to do what is right and behave responsibly in the face of pressures and temptations.

Evaluation: The Emotional or Evaluative Component Evaluation includes assessing the degree of satisfaction or dissatisfaction in a given situation or in life as a whole. It is concerned with such questions as these: Have I achieved what I set out to do? Am I happy with how I have lived my life? If this is love, why am I still unhappy? A meaningful life is based on reflection and self-evaluation. A strong sense of dissatisfaction will likely trigger the quest for meaning and activate the PURE model one more time. A meaningful life is a happy and fulfilling life, even when the process of searching for meaning may be unpleasant and costly. Happiness is an inherent component of meaning because satisfaction flows naturally from what is meaningful and virtuous. If we have truly implemented the previous three steps of P, U, and R, then the inevitable consequence is to enjoy a sense of purpose, significance, and happiness.

Well-being not only reflects healthy functioning and happiness (Ryan & Huta, 2009) but also serves as an evaluative function in the self-determination process (Ryan, Huta, & Deci, 2008). According to King and Hicks (Chap. 6, pp. 135–136, this volume), "Experiences that bring us joy are likely to be those experiences that make our lives meaningful."

The Avoidance System

The avoidance regulation system encompasses the tendency to avoid pain and overcome adversities. It involves the primitive fight-or-flight or freeze coping responses, unconscious defense mechanisms, as well as intentional coping endeavors. The system also includes warning signals that protect individuals from potential threats and things that are wrong in their lives. Paradoxically, existential anxieties are important to spur us on to living vitally and authentically. Accepting the growth potentials of negative conditions can strengthen the approach system (Chapters 7, 10, 15, 24, and 27, this volume).

Some individuals prefer to bury their heads in the sand in avoidance and denial. They may also resort to drugs or other addictions and distractions to shield themselves from the painful realities of life (Chapter 26, this volume). They may try to devote all their time and energy to pursuing instant happiness with quick fixes, but such efforts are doomed to failure because the reality of existential and situational problems eventually catches up to them and blows up in their faces. The approach system can help strengthen these individuals through the following pathways:

1. The motivation to overcome a solvable negative condition can add to the positive motivation of approach, resulting in stronger motivation. For example, the motivation to avoid failure can augment the desire to achieve success.
2. Problem-solving behaviors can increase the likelihood of achieving positive outcomes.
3. The process of struggling to overcome a very stressful situation will increase resilience and build character strengths (Chapters 5, 10, 11, 24, and 27, this volume).
4. When a problem is totally unsolvable and beyond one's control, then one seeks to transform and transcend the situation through the ABCDE strategy (to be explained later). This process typically involves some kind of self-transformation and strengthening of one's belief and value systems. The ability to transcend unsolvable life problems and existential givens will increase one's capacity to cope with life demands (Chapters 5, 7, 8, 10, 18, 21, 24, and 26, this volume).

The human story is one of tenacious and heroic struggles; otherwise, the human race would not have survived for so long. It has been said that necessity is the mother of invention, or frustration is the father of creativity. It has also been said that what does not kill you makes you stronger—a statement originally made by Friedrich Nietzsche and popularized by Viktor Frankl. Thus, negative experiences and negative affects can be energizing and life expanding.

ABCDE: The Transformative Process

The ABCDE intervention strategy is the main tool in dealing with negative life experiences in situations of unavoidable suffering. Totally different from the ABCDE sequence involved in the rational-emotive therapy process (Ellis,

1962, 1987), this present ABCDE is similar to acceptance and commitment therapy in its emphasis on commitment to adaptive action rather than correcting one's thinking. Simply put, ABCDE stands for Acceptance, Belief and affirmation, Commitment to specific goals or actions, Discovering the meaning and significance of self and situations, and Evaluation of the outcome and enjoying the positive results. These components generate corresponding principles:

1. *Accept* and confront the reality—the *reality principle.*
2. *Believe* that life is worth living—*the faith principle.*
3. *Commit* to goals and actions—*the action principle.*
4. *Discover* the meaning and significance of self and situations—*the Aha! principle.*
5. *Evaluate* the foregoing—*the self-regulation principle.*

ABCDE is essential for insolvable problems, but it is also helpful in coping with problems that are within one's control. For example, the wisdom of accepting one's limitations and deficiencies can provide relief from unnecessary anxieties and enable one to choose a career that capitalizes on one's strengths.

Meaning-Based Self-Regulation Systems

Both PURE and ABCDE are meaning-based self-regulation systems. People make sense of their situations and then decide on their reactions. Furthermore, they evaluate their progress in their efforts to achieve positive goals or overcome negative conditions. Self-regulatory feedback enables individuals to adjust their strategies and reset their goals. Disillusion and depression will set in when individuals persist in pursuing a career goal for which they do not have the necessary talents. Positive systems may also come to a crushing halt when disaster strikes, such as being diagnosed with terminal cancer. In such cases, negative systems are needed to make the necessary changes in order to adapt to the new reality.

Individuals who are exposed only to positive outcomes and positive conditions tend to be locked in an upward spiral until they implode. Such individuals tend to lose their sense of reality and do not know when to stop. They are also ill prepared for obstacles because they have not had the opportunity to develop sufficient inner strength to cope with adversities. The downward spiral refers to the vicious cycle of avoidance leading to more avoidance. Repeated exposure to negative events may make people overvigilant and fearful. These predictions are based on the dual-systems model as schematized in Figure 1.2.

Hypotheses Based on the Dual-Systems Model

The dual-systems model affirms that one can still squeeze out meaning and satisfaction from negative situations, which people instinctively avoid, but

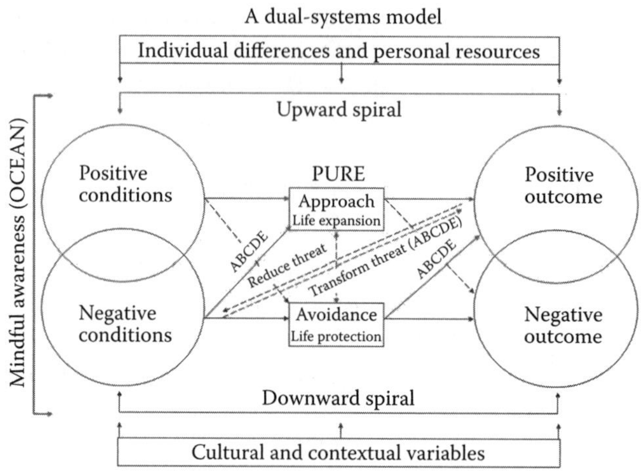

Figure 1.2 Interactions and meaning-based regulations within the dual-systems model.

also guards against the excesses and pitfalls in the sole pursuit of success and happiness. According to this model, decision making is a dialectic process of managing paradoxes and dilemmas. For example, when one's energy is taken up with denying and avoiding death, one may miss out on the opportunities and challenges of living a vital and fulfilling life. The paradox is that one can live fully only by accepting death. A balanced vibrant life will result from the process of managing optimal negative–positive interactions in each situation. What is optimal depends not only on situational demands but also on the criterion measure. For example, if one is interested in enhancing subjective well-being, then a high level of positivity is preferred (Fredrickson, 2009). However, if one is interested in developing resilience, then a high level of negativity may be necessary (Frankl, 1946/1985; Wong, 2009b).

The following hypotheses can provide a rich and comprehensive account of what makes life worth living. These hypotheses also have the heuristic value of generating new ideas for research and application.

Mindful Awareness Hypothesis

The mindful awareness system is primarily concerned with the self-regulation of attention and emotional reactions while we are not actively engaged in approach or avoidance activities (Chapter 12, this volume). By focusing on what is happening while it is happening, we become more attuned to the immediate environment. Mindful awareness clears your mind so that you can hear and see more clearly (Chapter 4, this volume). Mindful awareness is like a master regulation system that monitors what is going on in all waking hours. It explores and appraises situations with equanimity.

Mindful awareness consists of the following components: openness, compassion, empathy, acceptance, and nonjudgment (OCEAN; Siegel, 2007). It is hypothesized that any exercise, meditation, or personal development that enhances mindful awareness will decrease negative reactivity and increase positive reactivity, thereby increasing one's capacity to cope and enjoy life.

Openness We know that openness to new experiences is an adaptive personality trait because it opens up more opportunities for learning and personal growth. Openness allows you to be aware of things that you want to avoid because of past experiences or cultural biases (Chapters 12 and 15, this volume). Openness also makes it more likely that we will discern our responsibility to the situation (Frankl, 1946/1985). More important, by being mindful of what is happening here and now, we may be surprised by joy.

Compassion The literature has made it abundantly clear that others matter and that relationships are key to meaning and happiness (Chapters 4, 11, and 16, this volume). The literature also emphasizes the importance of altruism and caring for others as essential for the well-being of individuals and humanity as a whole (Chapters 9, 11, and 13, this volume). A compassionate person seeks to understand without prejudice or hostility what other people are saying (Chapter 12, this volume). In meaning research, self-transcendence or altruism is one of the main avenues to meaning (Wong, 1998b). The essential ingredient for positive relationships and altruism is compassion (Chapters 9 and 18, this volume). In a broader sense, compassion means being kind to all living things as well as to oneself. Compassion enables one to be willingly vulnerable in order to reach out to help others.

Empathy Empathy is related to compassion. We are neurologically programmed to feel other people's emotions. Empathy can also be cultivated by recognizing the universality of existential concerns and human problems. All human beings struggle with predicaments of loneliness, meaninglessness, and fear of death. Empathy allows us to be emotionally and relationally attuned to the people we interact with on a day-to-day basis (Chapters 12, 18, and 19, this volume). Without empathy, we would not be able to bridge the gaps between people.

Acceptance Acceptance is the key to all three regulation systems. For the approach system, we need to accept the limitations of our own abilities and resources before setting life goals. In the avoidance system, we need to accept the reality of negative events that cannot be avoided. According to ABCDE, acceptance is the first necessary step to recovery and healing. In mindful awareness, acceptance also means that we recognize the inevitable presence of negative thoughts and negative emotions (Chapter 12, this volume). This mental preparedness to accept and confront negativity reduces unnecessary suffering and makes it more likely for us to devote our energy toward productive work. Without acceptance, we would have to spend a great deal of time and energy defending ourselves against inevitable negative emotions, thoughts, and experiences (Chapter 10, this volume). In fact, the wisdom of acceptance is one of the main ingredients of tragic optimism (Wong, 2009b).

Nonjudgment A nonjudgmental attitude is related to the previous four elements of mindful awareness. Nonjudgment does not mean that we suspend our cognitive function of appraising whether or not a situation or person is dangerous or harmful, nor does it mean that we lose our moral sense of discriminating between right and wrong (Chapters 12 and 15, this volume). It does mean, however, that at the initial orienting phase we attempt to see and hear what is actually happening without the blinkers of our own biases. When we are first exposed to a situation or a new person, we should observe with mindful awareness and without judgment. This is the most rational and helpful way for us to have a sense of what is going on before forming judgment with respect to adaptive implications and potentials of meaning.

Our ability to make life worth living is compromised when we (a) focus exclusively on the negative aspects of life; (b) focus exclusively on the positive aspects of life (Baumeister, 1989; Baumeister, Bratslavsky, Finkenhaur, & Vohs, 2001; Oettingen & Mayer, 2002); and (c) ignore the "neutral resting" state, a state wherein one is not actively engaged in problem solving or goal striving (Mason et al., 2007). In the resting state, the mind is relaxed, open, exploratory, and orienting to new stimuli but is still responding to whatever happens while it is happening. Mindfulness exercises also help the mind to remain focused and calm, thus reducing agony and over-reactions (Shapiro, Schwartz, & Santerre, 2002; Siegel, 2007).

The Duality Hypothesis

Most people in positive psychology recognize the positive potential of negative events. For example, character strengths and fulfillment often involve overcoming adversities (Chapters 13, 23, and 25, this volume). The duality hypothesis posits that optimal outcomes depend on the interaction between the approach and avoidance systems. A number of studies can be conducted to test the duality hypothesis, namely, that a combination of positive and negative interventions is more likely to yield better outcomes than either positive or negative methods alone. For example, asking people to write about their pleasant and unpleasant life events should lead to more mental health benefits than asking them to write only about either positive or negative events. Similarly, enhancing one's strengths and correcting one's weaknesses will lead to greater improvement than focusing on only strengths or only weaknesses. According to the duality hypothesis, we should move beyond pitching the positive against the negative. The future of positive psychology should focus on how to make positives and negatives work together to yield optimal results (Wong, in press-a).

The Deep-and-Wide Hypothesis

Most psychologists do not realize the full extent of adaptive potentials from confronting and overcoming negative conditions. My research has identified at least four ways whereby frustration can contribute to adaptive success and personal growth (Wong, 1979, 1995).

1. Setbacks or failure can arouse an individual or team members to give their all in order to achieve success.
2. Desperation can lead to ingenuity and resourcefulness. When confronted with a seemingly intractable problem, people tend to dig deeper into their inner resources and come up with ingenious solutions.
3. Prolonged frustration can result in a broader search for alternatives and a major change of life direction.
4. The experience of overcoming progressively more difficult tasks or enduring increasing levels of frustration can result in higher frustration tolerance or a higher breaking point. We can learn generalized behavioral persistence and flexibility in the face of setbacks and adversity through intermittent reinforcement schedules (Amsel, 1992; McCuller, Wong, & Amsel, 1976; Wong, 1995, 2006).

The behavioral mechanisms in various stages of coping with frustration can become the basis for learned dispositions or character traits. Empirical evidence and practical implications of dispositional learning can be found in Amsel (1992) and Wong (1995). These findings are important for developing resilience in children as well as in adults.

The Breaking-Point Hypothesis

Both the duality hypothesis and the deep-and-wide hypothesis imply the existence of a breaking point beyond which negativity is no longer beneficial. For example, when the desire to avoid failure becomes overwhelming, avoidance will replace approach rather than enhance it. Similarly, when the deep-and-wide coping strategy fails to improve the condition, learned helplessness will set in (Wong, 1979, 1995, 2006). Although everyone has a breaking point, individuals can vary a great deal in how much they can tolerate before they become helpless. McCuller, Wong, and Amsel (1976) have shown that through progressive-ratio training, one can greatly increase the amount of frustration animals can tolerate. This finding is also relevant to humans. Wong (2009a) has made the case that Chinese people's capacity for endurance comes from their personal and national history of having to endure and overcome hardships. Learned optimism depends on both a high breaking point and explanatory styles (Peterson, 2000; Selgiman, 1990).

Seery, Holman, and Silver (2010) have documented that a history of moderate amount of adversity leads to better mental health than either a high history or no history of adversity. The U-shaped quadratic relationship between adversity and well-being can be predicted by the breaking-point hypothesis. What does not kill us makes us stronger only when the adversity does not reach the breaking point. An examination of individual data of the Seery et al. study may reveal that some individuals may still enjoy good mental health even after a large amount of prior exposure to adversity.

The Meaning-Mindset Hypothesis

Mindset refers to one's overarching motivations and worldviews. The meaning mindset focuses on the person (Maslow, 1962; Rogers, 1995) as meaning-seeking and meaning-making creatures. It also capitalizes on the human capacity for reflection and awakening (Wong, 2007). It is built on the PURE principle. An enduring passion for living comes from commitment to a higher purpose. Understanding refers to making sense of the self, life, and one's place in the world, as well as the mysteries of life. The ability to articulate one's worldview and assumptions enables us to make positive changes. A sense of responsibility ensures that the individual will behave as an instrumental and moral agent. Joy comes from living meaningfully and authentically, relatively free from circumstances and fleeting emotions.

A meaning mindset also means living a balanced life because meaning comes from several sources, among them achievement, relationships, altruism, spirituality, and justice (Wong, 1998b, 2011). The challenge is to provide both road signs and practical tools for individuals to facilitate their quest for personal transformation and fulfillment.

All great reformers, visionaries, or missionaries—for example, Mohandas Gandhi, Martin Luther King, Jr., Mother Teresa, and Hudson Taylor—have a meaning mindset rather than a happiness mindset. If we could teach people to embrace a meaning mindset, then our society would be better. The main prediction is that individuals who choose a meaning orientation are more likely to experience eudaimonic happiness but less hedonic happiness. Furthermore, they are more likely to be resilient because suffering becomes more bearable when we suffer for a cause.

The meaning mindset is of fundamental importance because it reflects one's philosophy of life, ultimate concern, core values, and worldview and is the overarching motivation in one's life. This mindset is related to character strengths, personal meaning, passion for excellence, moral judgment, altruism, volunteerism, business ethics, religiosity, spirituality, prosocial behaviors, resilience, and all kinds of good things that make life worth living. Training in developing meaning mindset can also serve as an educational tool to combat addiction, violence, and other antisocial behaviors.

For idealists who embrace a meaning mindset, the good life lies in the heroic struggle to realize an ideal. Their life satisfaction is beyond pleasure and pain; it is beyond success and failure. The meaning mindset makes sense of the self and one's place in life throughout the ups and downs of the path one has chosen. Life satisfaction is based not on calculating the ratio between positives and negatives but on beliefs, values, and a whole-hearted dedication to a worthy mission, regardless of the outcome.

We can also predict that meaning-minded individuals are more likely to be motivated by intrinsic rather than extrinsic motivations (Chapter 4, this volume) and by commitment to long-term missions (Chapter 8, this volume). Krause (Chap. 19, p. 426, this volume) explains why a meaning mindset is important for persistence and resilience:

> Having a sense of purpose in life and goals to pursue helps people deal with adversity by enhancing their sense of hope or optimism. A goal or plan instills the belief that no matter how bleak things may seem at the moment, there is still a way to get through these difficulties, and if these goals or plans are executed faithfully, hard times will eventually subside.

Conclusion

The 21st century may be called a century of meaning in which people are struggling to recover a sense of meaning and purpose in the midst of international terrorism and the global financial meltdown. The creation of a new world order and a more cooperative and humane society will demand a grassroots campaign to educate people about the importance of responsible and purposeful living. In this endeavor, this book is intended to provide the framework for meaning-based education.

In an age of anxiety, Rachman (2011) suggests that for positive psychology to resonate with people, it needs to recognizes anxiety as an existential given and emphasize the human capacity for meaning transformation. The dual-system model gets to the heart of the human struggle of trying to move forward to achieve worthy life goals while attempting to overcome external and internal constraints that threaten to make life miserable and hopeless. The dual-systems model provides a conceptual framework to integrate both positive and negative psychology. The central message of the dual-systems model is that too much emphasis on either approach or avoidance can be maladaptive. Life surges forward, driven by the motivations to preserve and expand oneself—two fundamental biological needs. Individuals can survive and flourish better when they manage to meet these basic needs through meaning-based self-regulations. The dual-systems model also integrates psychotherapy with positive psychology in a comprehensive and coherent manner. The interactive dynamics of meaning processes not only address clients' predicaments but also facilitate their quests for happiness.

References

Amsel, A. (1992). *Frustration theory: An analysis of dispositional learning and memory.* New York, NY: Cambridge University Press.

Aristotle. (2004). *Nichomachean ethics* (F. H. Peters, Trans.). New York, NY: Barnes and Noble.

Attenborough, R. (2008). *The words of Gandhi* (Newmarket "Words of" series). New York, NY: Newmarket Press.

Baumeister, R. F. (1989). The optimal margin of illusion. *Journal of Social and Clinical Psychology, 8*, 176–189.

Baumeister, R. F. (1991). *Meanings of life.* New York, NY: Guilford Press.

Baumeister, R. F., Bratslavsky, E., Finkenhaur, C., & Vohs, K. D. (2001). Bad is stronger than good. *Review of General Psychology, 5*, 323–370.

Baumeister, R. F., & Leary, M. R. (1995). The need to belong: Desire for interpersonal attachments as a fundamental human motivation. *Psychological Bulletin, 117*, 497–529.

Bruner, J. S. (1990). *Acts of meaning.* Cambridge, MA: Harvard University Press.

Camus, A. (1991). *The myth of Sisyphus and other essays* (J. O'Brien, Trans.). New York, NY: Vintage Books. (Originally published 1942)

DelleFave, A. (2009). Optimal experience and meaning: Which relationship. *Psychological Topics, 18*, 285–302.

Diener, E., Emmons, R. A., Larsen, R. J., & Griffin, S. (1985). The satisfaction with life scale. *Journal of Personality and Social Psychology, 47*, 1105–1117.

Elliot, E. (1989). *Shadow of the Almighty: The life and testament of Jim Elliot.* New York, NY: HarperCollins.

Ellis, A. (1962). *Reason and emotion in psychotherapy.* Oxford, England: Lyle Stuart.

Ellis, A. (1987). *The practice of rational-emotive therapy.* New York, NY: Springer.

Frankl, V. (1985). *Man's search for meaning.* Boston, MA: Beacon Press. (Originally published 1946)

Fredrickson, B. L. (2009). *Positivity: Groundbreaking research reveals how to embrace the hidden strength of positive emotions, overcome negativity, and thrive.* New York, NY: Crown.

Huta, V. (2009). Eudaimonic well-being. In I. Boniwell & S. David (Eds.), *Oxford handbook of happiness.* New York, NY: Oxford University Press.

Maslow, A. H. (1943). A theory of human motivation. *Psychological Review, 50*, 370–396.

Maslow, A. H. (1962). *Toward a psychology of being.* New York, NY: Van Nostrand.

Mason, M. F., Norton, M. I., Van Horn, J. D., Wegner, D. M., Grafton, S. T., & Macrae, C. N. (2007). Wandering minds: The default network and stimulus-independent thought. *Science, 315*, 393–395.

McCrae, R. R., & Costa, P. T., Jr. (1987). Validation of the five-factor model of personality across instruments and observers. *Journal of Personality and Social Psychology, 52*(1), 81–90. doi:10.1037/0022-3514.52.1.81

McCuller, T., Wong, P. T., & Amsel, A. (1976). Transfer of persistence from fixed-ratio barpress training to runway extinction. *Animal Learning and Behavior, 4*, 53–57.

Oettingen, G., & Mayer, D. (2002). The motivating function of thinking about the future: Expectations versus fantasies. *Journal of Personality and Social Psychology, 83*, 1198–1212.

Pavlov, I. P. (2003). *Conditioned reflexes: An investigation of the physiological activity of the cerebral cortex.* Mineola, NY: Dover. (Originally published 1927)

Peterson, C. (2000). Optimistic explanatory style and health. In J. Gillham (Ed.), *The science of optimism and hope* (pp. 145–162). Philadelphia, PA: Templeton Foundation Press.

Peterson, C., & Seligman, M. E. (2004). *Character strengths and virtues.* New York, NY: Oxford University Press.

Rachman, G. (2011). *Zero-sum future: American power in an age of anxiety.* New York, NY: Simon & Schuster.

Rogers, C. R. (1995). *On becoming a person: A therapist's view of psychotherapy.* Boston, MA: Houghton Mifflin.

Ryan, R. M., & Huta, V. (2009). Wellness as health functioning or wellness as happiness: The importance of eudaimonic thinking. *Journal of Positive Psychology, 4,* 202–204.

Ryan, R. M., Huta, V., & Deci, E. L. (2008). Living well: A self-determination theory perspective on eudaimonia. *Journal of Happiness Studies, 9,* 139–170.

Sartre, J. P. (1990). *Existentialism and human emotions.* New York, NY: Oxford University Press.

Schumaker, J. F. (2007). *In search of happiness: Understanding an endangered state of mind.* Westport, CT: Praeger.

Seery, M. D., Holman, E. A., & Silver, R. C. (2010). Whatever does not kill us: Cumulative lifetime adversity, vulnerablity, and resilience. *Journal of Personality and Social Psychology, 99*(6), 1025–1041.

Seligman, M. E. (1990). *Learned optimism.* New York, NY: Knopf.

Seligman, M. E. (2002). *Authentic happiness.* New York, NY: Free Press.

Seligman, M. E., & Csikszentmihalyi, M. (2000). Positive psychology: An introduction. *American Psychologist, 55,* 5–14.

Shapiro, S. J., Schwartz, G. E. R., & Santerre, C. (2002). Meditation and positive psychology. In C. R. Snyder & S. J. Lopez (Eds.), *The handbook of positive psychology* (pp. 632–645). New York, NY: Oxford University Press.

Sheldon, K. M. (2009). Providing the scientific backbone for positive psychology: A multi-level conception of human thriving. *Psychological Topics, 18,* 267–284.

Shweder, R. A. (1991). Thinking through cultures: Expeditions in cultural psychology. Cambridge, MA: Harvard University Press.

Siegel, D. J. (2007). *The mindful brain: Reflection and attunement in the cultivation of well-being.* New York, NY: Norton.

Waterman, A. S. (2008). Reconsidering happiness: A eudaimonist's perspective. *Journal of Positive Psychology, 3,* 234–252.

Weiner, B. (1975). *Achievement motivation and attribution theory.* Englewood Cliffs, NJ: Silver Burdett.

Wong, P. T. P. (1979). Frustration, exploration, and learning. *Canadian Psychological Review, 20,* 133.

Wong, P. T. P. (1991). Existential vs. causal attributions. In S. Zelen (Ed.), *New models, new extensions of attribution theory* (pp. 84–125). New York, NY: Springer Verlag.

Wong, P. T. P. (1993). Effective management of life stress: The resource-congruence model. *Stress Medicine, 9,* 51–60.

Wong, P. T. P. (1995). A stage model of coping with frustrative stress. In R. Wong (Ed.), *Biological perspectives on motivated activities* (pp. 339–378). Norwood, NJ: Ablex.

Wong, P. T. P. (1998a). Academic values and achievement motivation. In *The human quest for meaning: A handbook of psychological research and clinical applications* (pp. 261–292). Mahwah, NJ: Erlbaum.

Wong, P. T. P. (1998b). Implicit theories of meaningful life and the development of the personal meaning profile. In *The human quest for meaning; A handbook of psychological research and clinical applications* (pp. 111–140). Mahwah, NJ: Erlbaum.

Wong, P. T. P. (2006, February). *The positive psychology of persistence and flexibility*. Retrieved from http://www.meaning.ca/articles06/president/persistenceand flexibility-feb06.htm

Wong, P. T. P. (2007). Positive psychology and a positive revolution. In P. T. P. Wong, M. McDonald, & D. Klaassen (Eds.), *The positive psychology of meaning and spirituality*. Abbotsford, BC: INPM Press.

Wong, P. T. P. (2009a). Chinese positive psychology. In S. Lopez (Ed.), *Encyclopedia of positive psychology* (Vol. 1, pp. 148–156). Oxford, England: Wiley Blackwell.

Wong, P. T. P. (2009b). Viktor Frankl: Prophet of hope for the 21st century. In A. Batthyany & J. Levinson (Eds.), *Existential psychotherapy of meaning: Handbook of logotherapy and existential analysis*. Phoenix, AZ: Zeig, Tucker, & Theisen.

Wong, P. T. P. (2011, January). The good life is a balanced life. *The Positive Living Newsletter*.

Wong, P. T. P. (in press-a). Positive psychology 2.0: Towards a balanced interactive model of the good life. *Canadian Psychology*.

Wong, P. T. P. (in press-b). Reclaiming positive psychology: A meaning-centered approach to sustainable growth and radical empiricism. *Journal of Humanistic Psychology*.

Wong, P. T. P., & Weiner, B. (1981). When people ask "why" questions and the heuristic of attributional search. *Journal of Personality and Social Psychology, 40*, 650–663.

Wong, P. T. P., & Wong, L. C. J. (2005). *The handbook of multicultural perspectives on stress and coping*. New York, NY: Springer.

Yalom, I. D. (1980). *Existential psychotherapy*. New York, NY: Basic Books.

2
The Search for Meaning in Evolutionary Goal-Theory Perspective and Its Clinical Implications

ERIC KLINGER

University of Minnesota

"Felix aims for Honduras" went the newspaper headline. Felix, a Category 5 hurricane, was a swirling mass of gases and vapors, but the headline imbued it with intentionality and purpose. Humans often ascribe these attributes to things that are uncontrolled and in motion. When ascribed to oneself, these attributes of intentionality and purpose are at the core of *meaning* in the sense of the word as used in this book.

The fundamental position of this chapter is that the search for meaning, as that has come to be understood in humanistic psychology, is an inexorable result of the way the human brain is organized. Lack or loss of meaning therefore inherently signals psychological deprivation or disorder. Moreover, the research area that has grown around the phenomenon of search for meaning, while developing important contributions in a number of areas, parallels other research activities that proceed under different names but that similarly probe facets of basic human nature. To an important degree, the language of research on the search for meaning can be mapped onto concept systems of other research traditions.

This chapter will proceed by first examining what is meant by the search for meaning and then arguing that in the sense in which it is used here, the search for meaning is an inevitable outgrowth of human evolution. The chapter then examines some important implications of this view with respect to both basic human functions and certain human disorders.

The Meaning of Meaning

The term *meaning* has been used in so many ways by philosophers, linguists, psychologists, and colloquial speakers that it is necessary to distinguish among them and to clarify how the term is used in this chapter. In doing so, I will make clear that in certain respects even apparently widely different usages of the term are actually related, at least at their etymological roots.

Etymology

Broadly speaking, there are two different thrusts of the term *meaning*. One thrust focuses on intention (in the psychological sense, what an individual means to have happen) and the other on semantics (what a word means). In the words of *Merriam-Webster's Collegiate Dictionary* (1999), the first definition of the verb *to mean* is "to have in the mind as a purpose: INTEND"; and the second definition is "to serve or intend to convey, show, or indicate: SIGNIFY" (p. 720). Similarly, the first definition of the noun *meaning* is given as "the thing one intends to convey by language: PURPORT" or "the thing that is conveyed esp. by language: IMPORT"; and the second definition is "something meant or intended: AIM" (p. 712). These two seemingly quite different meanings of the concept *meaning* are, however, rooted in a common etymological stem: Old High German *meinen*, "to have in mind" (p. 712). In modern German, *meinen* means "to think," in the sense of to opine, but the modern German word *Sinn* carries the meanings of both semantic meaning (sense) and purpose.

This nesting of both senses of meaning in a single word is seemingly not restricted to a single narrow family of languages (German and English, partially derived from German). Czech words for *intend, mean, meaningful, purpose*, and *sense* contain the same common root *mysl*, meaning "mind." The Italian *intendere* means "to understand" (i.e., to perceive meaning), "to hear," "to think" (opine), and "to intend." Thus, representatives of all three of the greatest language families of Europe—the Romance, the Germanic, and the Slavic—have the semantic field around a single word or stem encompass both meaning as signifier and meaning as intention. This dual function is apparently also true in Chinese (Paul T. P. Wong, private communication).

Clearly, the two senses of meaning are related in numerous etymologies, as a result suggesting that meaning in the semantic sense is for humans bound up with intentionality and purpose. In this framework, the meaning of life, or the meaningfulness of a person's life to that person, would then have something to do with purposes. What a word means depends at least in part on what the speaker intended to convey and on the motivational set of the listener. What a life means is what that life purposes.

Philosophical Analysis

Philosophy has a long tradition of analyzing the meaning of meaning (e.g., Johnson, 1987; Loewer & Rey, 1991). In much of that tradition, philosophers were concerned with relating language to the objective reality to which language was presumed to refer. Furthermore, from Aristotle to Locke (Loewer & Rey, 1991) and on to Herbart's theory of apperception (Herbart, trans. 1834), meaning has been understood to involve mental images or "ideas." This understanding has a long and tortuous history, for the detailing of which this chapter is not the appropriate place. Suffice it to say here that modern philosophers have tried to pin meanings of language to the recipients' pragmatic experiences with the referents—a movement generally attributed to Peirce (Smith, 1978)—or to the way in which the language is used (e.g., Wittgenstein; Smith, 1978) or, recently, to the "intentional directedness of human understanding" (Johnson, 1987). Broadening the concept of meaning to things beyond language, including life and lives, Johnson (1987) makes a case that "meaning is a matter of human understanding, regardless of whether we are talking about the meaning of someone's life, the meaning of a historical happening, or the meaning of a word or sentence" (p. 176). Here, again, we find that the linguistic sense of meaning occupies the same semantic spectrum as its sense in the meaning of life.

To some degree consistent with Johnson's emphasis on understanding, Joske (1974/1981) wrote that

> people who ask about the meaning of life ... wish to know whether the world is the sort of place which justifies and gives significance to what might otherwise seem to be the drudgery of a typical human existence. In other words, they are asking whether or not the world confers derivative meaning upon life. (p. 250)

Joske subsequently raises the question of what differentiates a meaningful from a meaningless life. He suggests four "elements of the meaningless ... worthlessness, pointlessness, triviality, and futility" (p. 252). It is important to note that the second element relates to having a purpose and the fourth relates to its realizability. The other two elements relate to the value of the goal: meritorious or not, and degree of importance. Thus, Joske has in effect defined the meaning of life in purposive terms.

Psychological Definitions—Conceptual and Operational

In one of the very few social psychological books devoted to the meaning of life, Baumeister (1991; see also Sommer & Baumeister, 1998) provides a definition that by its breadth can accommodate any other (and a good deal more!): Meaning involves "shared mental representations of possible relationships among things, events, and relationships. Thus, meaning *connects* things" (Baumeister, 1991, p. 15). Later, he appears to broaden the implicit definition of meaning even further to encompass, in effect, all motivation: "Without meaning, behavior is guided by impulse and instinct" (Baumeister, 1991, p. 18). That is, by implication, meaning provides direction and hence intention.

The main impetus for psychological research on the meaning of life originated with the work of Viktor Frankl (1963/1946), for whom the will to meaning was a human universal—indeed, a prerequisite for mental and physical well-being—and was unambiguously defined as the need to perceive one's life, especially one's travails, as making sense in serving some worthy purpose.

The research programs that his writings unleashed have given rise to at least two book-length attempts at theory building (Baumeister, 1991; Klinger, 1977; see also Chapter 14, this volume) and a number of instruments for assessing purposes. These instruments include especially the Purpose in Life (PIL) Test (Crumbaugh & Maholick, 1964); the Life Regard Index (Battista & Almond, 1973; Debats, 1998), which provides separate scores for having a framework for meaning and for fulfillment; a Seeking of Noetic Goals Test (SONG; Crumbaugh, 1977); an unnamed questionnaire and categorization procedure for eliciting varieties of life meanings (DeVogler & Ebersole, 1980); a procedure for rating Meaning In Life Depth (MILD; DeVogler-Ebersole & Ebersole, 1985); a three-item Meaninglessness Scale (Newcomb & Harlow, 1986); the Life Attitude Profile (LAP) (Reker, Peacock, & Wong, 1987), which dimensionalizes the concept into Life Purpose, Existential Vacuum, Life Control, and Will to Meaning; the Personal Meaning Profile (Wong, 1998a; Chapter 17, this volume), and the Meaning in Life Questionnaire (Steger, Frazier, Oishi, & Kaler, 2006), which dimensionalizes the concept into presence of meaning and seeking it. Parallel to these developments, other researchers have evolved the Motivational Structure Questionnaire (Cox & Klinger, 1988, 2011a); the Work Concerns Inventory (Roberson, 1989); the Personal Concerns Inventory and subsequent Personal Aspirations and Concerns Inventory (Cox & Klinger, 2011a); and their immediate ancestor, the Interview Questionnaire (Klinger, 1987b), all of which assess the respondent's current goals.

The remaining sections of this chapter will focus on the evolutionary imperative of meaning and its psychological implications, not just regarding the meaning of life in an abstract, global sense but, more important, with regard to the meaningfulness that individuals find in their own particular lives. (For more on the relationships between global meaning and situational meaning, see Chapter 20, this volume.)

The Imperative of Purpose

The position of this chapter is that the disposition to live purposively is built into the most fundamental architecture of zoological organisms, and the disposition to seek meaning stems straightforwardly from the evolution of purposiveness together with human intellect. This section sketches the argument for that position.

The Evolution of Purpose and Meaning

In the beginning there was presumably the Big Bang, and a few billion years later the first complex organic substances developed the ability to withstand entropy—the tendency for matter to fly apart randomly and thus lose organization and focus—to preserve their existence and chances for procreation. In this struggle against entropy—and against the accidents and perversity of nature—two general strategies emerged as viable, which correspond to the two "kingdoms" of living organisms: sessile beings, which settle wherever they are wafted and remain there until removed; and motile beings, which can alter their location at will. Sessile beings have to depend on their environments to provide them with life's necessities. Huge proportions of these individuals die young, but the strategy has succeeded well at the cost of enormously prolific reproduction, as any inspection of plant life shows. Motile organisms are equipped to escape the limitations of their most immediate environments by actively seeking out life's necessities; and this they must do because their survival depends on it. This strategy characterizes probably all animal species at some life stage. The necessities of life that they seek are what psychologists call goals, from which it becomes apparent that animal life, and with it human life, consists of a virtually continual succession of goal pursuits. Because success at these pursuits is central to animal survival, and because success has in the history of the species generally required sustained, persistent goal striving, it constitutes an imperative of purpose.

This generalization leads to some further important conclusions. One is that within evolutionary theory, every feature of animal organisms must have evolved in the service of goal pursuit. If we designate the systems that most immediately direct goal striving as motivational, we must conclude that all of any zoological organism's biopsychological systems have evolved in support of motivation. This must have been true for anatomy and physiology and for every behavioral system, including cognition. We may conclude that any understanding of cognitive processing is incomplete without an account of its relationship to motivation.

In this view, cognitive processes have a specifiable set of functions. Important among these functions is to process stimuli until they can be channeled into an appropriate brain pathway that leads to an emotional or evaluative response, to activation of associations to one or more of one's goals, and perhaps to further cognitive processing, as in thoughts or dreams, and to taking action. For some kinds of stimuli, nature has provided fairly automatic responses, whereas responses to others depend on experience.

Animal organisms, including humans, are hard-wired to respond with unconditioned responses to certain stimuli (sensation of falling, sudden loud noises, maternal voice and heartbeat, etc.), each class of which is innately linked to an emotional response system and probably—at least incipiently—to an action system. These primary emotional systems, such as joy, fear, and anger, are well known. There are also other systems that humans are biologically prepared to experience, such as the negative "self-conscious" emotions (Lewis, 1993) of embarrassment, pride, shame, and guilt. There are most probably yet other systems that have been little studied or acknowledged, such as those related to wonder, awe, humor, aesthetic appreciation, and the sense of understanding something or having achieved insight. These kinds of emotions seem far removed from the crasser ones but are probably subject to similar principles. They may entail such distinctive cognitive features as reflecting on oneself or emotional distancing (Frijda & Sundararajan, 2007), but these are probably not central to the emotional components themselves. I assume, as a working position, that normal human beings are biologically disposed to experience some degree of each class of emotion, no matter how basic or rarefied, in response to specifiable properties of situations.

However, the great majority of stimuli that humans encounter are not among the innately unconditioned stimuli. One major role of cognitive processing, then, beyond the original sensory reception and apart from problem solving to overcome barriers to goal attainment, is to sort out the ambiguous or confusing stimuli, working them over until they can be dismissed as irrelevant (habituation, extinction of response) or channeled into one of the individual's brain pathways that link the stimuli with emotions and goal pursuits. Near the beginning of a person's life, the ability to make such discriminations is presumably acquired through a process of conditioning and learning, but increasingly people come to interpret stimuli with the help of reflective and critical thinking.

Although this way of casting a major function of cognition—processing stimuli until they can be assigned to one of the individual's emotional, motivational, or action systems—may seem to be overly primitive and mechanical, it is meant to apply to instances that are distinctively human and sophisticated. This approach applies both to simple stimuli and to such complex patterns as life situations, and the cognitions to which it applies include the three classes suggested by Wong (1991): attributional, coping appraisal, and reevaluative. For example, resolving ambiguity or confusion leads people to experience distinctive affective responses. Thus, if a passage in a book seems confusing, that leads to affective discomfort, perhaps enough to motivate the reader to go back over the passage to try to figure it out. When the reader achieves understanding, that moment is accompanied by the classical "aha!" response, an affectively pleasant reaction; and on the basis of that reaction and the cognitive clarification that gave rise to it, the individual now knows how else to react to the passage—with what emotion and with what further goal-directed action.

In other words, any new, unconditioned event that cannot be related to the perceiver's purposes is either eventually regarded as neutral and ignored or, if it is sufficiently obtrusive, becomes a source of discomfort, leading to efforts to cognize its relationship to the perceiver's goals, to the perceiver's purposes. Only then can the new event engage action systems, and hence only then can it acquire adequate meaning of the kind meant by this book.

Goals, Purpose, Meaning

To have a goal is to have a purpose for action, and that purpose provides the meaning for the action. In this view, meaning arises naturally out of commitment to goals and their pursuit. This relationship appears, from a number of studies, to agree with people's subjective assessments of what makes life meaningful. High on their lists are their personal relationships.

To construct the Personal Meaning Profile (Wong, 1998a), the first step was simply to ask people to characterize an ideally meaningful life. These characterizations were then turned into items, which were winnowed to remove redundancies and factor-analyzed. The great majority of the items explicitly or implicitly referred to some kind of goal pursuit. The largest factor to come out of the factor analysis, accounting for 32% of the variance, was labeled "Achievement Striving." The next factor, with 9% of the variance, was labeled "Religion," which included such items, among others, as "Seeks to glorify God" (Wong, 1998a, p. 117), a clear goal pursuit. The third factor was "Relationship," with 5% of the variance. A relationship for most people presumably constitutes at least an implicit goal: to seek, maintain, or improve it. Other, weaker factors related to desirable personal attributes, such as self-confidence, which one may suppose often constitute at least wished-for attributes of the self. Thus, the subjective notion of what makes life meaningful is heavily loaded with whatever people value, which typically also constitute positive goals—that is, things that people seek to attain, do, maintain, or restore.

Similarly, Ebersole (1998) reports on a number of studies, with samples ranging from adolescence to old age, in which participants were asked to describe "the most central personal meaning in their life" (p. 180). Although the groups differed somewhat from one another in ways to be expected from their different age statuses, there was remarkable similarity. Consistent with an earlier finding (Klinger, 1977), the most frequently mentioned class of personal meanings was relationships. Other frequently mentioned classes included service, belief, obtaining something, and health, among others. These classes, again, entail positive goals to attain, do, maintain, or restore something.

Using rather different methods, Little's (1998) Personal Projects Analysis asks respondents to list and rate their current projects (i.e., goal pursuits). Some of the rating dimensions were selected to reflect presumed dimensions of meaning: Importance, Value-Congruence, Self-Identity, and Enjoyment. Summing across these dimensions, Little (1998) reported that the highest meaning scores went to interpersonal projects, again consistent with previous findings. It appears clear, then, that of the various classes of goals that have been investigated, interpersonal relationships of one kind or another are the greatest contributors to people's sense that their lives are meaningful.

Motivational Structure

The Motivational Structure Questionnaire, the Personal Concerns Inventory, and the Personal Aspirations and Concerns Inventory (Cox & Klinger, 2011a) ask respondents to list their current goal pursuits and then characterize each one on a set of scales such as valence, commitment, joy anticipated at goal attainment, probability of success, and time frame. At this stage, the procedure can be considered a form of autobiographic narrative, which has been found to have benefits of its own (e.g., Chapter 18, this volume). When, however, ratings of individual goals are aggregated for a respondent across the different goals that the person has listed, one can derive reasonably reliable summary scores that correspond to the various dimensions (Klinger & Cox, 2011b). We have dubbed the patterning of these scores an individual's *motivational structure* (e.g., Cox & Klinger, 2002; Klinger & Cox, 2011b). Factor analyses of the individual scales have regularly produced a first factor made up principally of commitment, anticipated emotions at goal attainment or failure, and probability of success; we have dubbed scores on this factor *Adaptive Motivational Structure*. Data on the relationship of these measures to sense of meaning in one's life are discussed in a later section, but some of their dimensions are clearly conceptually related to it (see later discussion). Adaptive Motivational Structure has also been found related inversely to alcohol consumption (Cox et al., 2002) and positively to response to treatment with *Systematic Motivational Counseling* (Cox et al., 2003).

In What Sense Is Purpose an Imperative?

It is probably not the case that all or even necessarily most people consciously search for the meaning of their lives. Researchers who have documented the near-universality of having important purposes—from childhood to old age (DePaola & Ebersole, 1995; DeVogler & Ebersole, 1980, 1981, 1983; Ebersole & DePaola, 1987; Klinger, 1977; Taylor & Ebersole, 1993)—have gone about this by asking people to list the things that are important to them. That is, just about everyone has purposes, and in that sense has life meaning, but this is a different case from everyone actively seeking meaning (which is a very different matter; see Steger et al., 2006). In Baumeister's (1991) words, "The meaning of life is a problem for people who are not desperate, people who can count on survival, comfort, security, and some measure of pleasure" (p. 3); and, I would add, it is not a problem for people who for any other reason find themselves persistently engaged in striving for valued goals. The more introspective among them, especially when someone else raises the issue, may well be inclined to articulate for themselves one or more consistent life purposes, but probably most individuals would not otherwise be bothered.

On the other hand, when people find themselves spending inordinate amounts of time in activities they do not value highly or find themselves suffering for no immediately evident good purpose, they are likely to raise the question "What for?" On anecdotal grounds, it appears that this response commonly occurs when people are induced to work largely to avoid punishment rather than for appetitive reasons, as in concentration camps, or when they are working for appetitive goals whose value is extrinsic (as in working largely to earn money or school grades) and the activity or its products are not respected as worthwhile. However, research to date has provided no systematic evidence for delineating the conditions that provoke the question of life's meaning.

It is necessary to add one more qualification. Individuals often ask why, what is the purpose, when they suffer through no wish or deliberate action of their own. A terminally ill patient may lie in bed depressed, pondering the meaning of it all. Deep reflection or counseling may generate a purpose that can be served by the suffering, such as providing an example of dignified dying for the children or an opportunity for scientists to engage in important research on the disease. Clinical and other experiences (e.g., Frankl, 1946/1963) indicate that locating a purpose, even for something that has already taken place, is psychologically beneficial. It relieves depression and helps patients to regain composure in the face of suffering and death (see also Chapter 7, this volume). This happens, not because the suffering is deliberate or becomes somehow pleasant, but because the individual is able to identify an end served by it and hence to identify with it as, willy-nilly, having a purpose (Wong, 1991; Wong & Weiner, 1981; see also Chapters 1, 10, and 23, this volume).

Again, to emphasize and clarify: The human brain cannot sustain purposeless living. It is not designed for that. Its systems are designed for purposive action. When that is blocked, its systems deteriorate, and the emotional feedback from idling these systems signals extreme discomfort and motivates the search for renewed purpose, renewed meaning. This process accounts for Viktor Frankl's (1946/1963; 1969) observation of a *will to meaning*.

The Place of Idleness, Fulfillment, Just Being, and Consummatory Behavior

One emotional system that appears inherently associated with muted or idled goal striving is depressed mood, which can range from disappointment to clinical depression (Klinger, 1975, 1977, 1987a). It is ordinarily activated in response to inexorable loss or failure, an effect that is normally transient except when repeated or when losses are multiple (Wong, 1995). Depressed mood is part of a process of disengaging from hopeless goal pursuits, which is a necessary part of conserving one's resources for adaptive living (Klinger, 1975, 1977). Indeed, being able to disengage is important for mental and physical health as well as for life meaning (see also Wrosch, Miller, Scheier, & de Pontet, 2007; Chapter 24, this volume). Some components of depressive affect may be tied to an involuntary, nonconsummatory idling of action systems, so that whenever and however these are idled, depression ensues.

There is an important qualification here: Idling of action systems is uncomfortable if the idling is involuntary and nonconsummatory. The broad framework of this theory owes much to ethology (Tinbergen, 1969), which long ago divided goal-striving behavior into appetitive and consummatory phases, where consummatory behavior is defined as behavior that, as the name implies, constitutes the goal-consummation sequence, such as eating, drinking, or copulating, whereas appetitive behavior is defined as the goal-striving activity leading to the consummatory behavior. Both are very much part of goal striving.

Stated more broadly, consummatory behavior can be construed as the process of reaping rewards. It includes any experience that is an end in itself, rather than a stepping stone to something else; in other words, it is anything that generates intrinsic satisfaction. It may therefore encompass skiing, sunning oneself at the beach, attending an opera or rock concert, reading a good book, chatting with friends, sleeping, and other forms of natural relaxation and recreation, provided that these activities are not undertaken as means to some other end. They may seem to be the opposite of goal striving and perhaps seem to contradict the generalization that human life is a succession of goal pursuits, but one must remember that goal striving is pointless without enjoyment of the rewards.

The consummatory activity around one goal attainment may well delay the pursuit of another because people, like other zoological organisms, try to prolong the positive affective states that go with consummation. However, that is merely an instance of prolonging the consummatory phase of one goal pursuit at the expense of the appetitive activity toward another. It illustrates the inevitability of occasional conflict among goal pursuits. Sunbathing may seem lazy to someone who would have the sunbather do something else, but engaging in it in no way contradicts the view that all but reflexive action is goal directed. The warm skin sensations of sunbathing, perhaps together with general physical relaxation, are the goal phase of that sequence.

But what is the benefit of subsuming so many sensory and intellectual pleasures under the rubric "consummatory"? Remember, there is no need to think that human wired-in emotions are limited to only the crassest. From surprise to humor, from aesthetic pleasure to awe—yes, and even to the sense of understanding, of things having fallen into place—there is almost certainly a biological basis for what we regard as distinctively human emotions. It makes sense to suppose that these responses are human adaptations that have evolved out of the crasser systems and are still like them in essential ways. And there is indeed an important benefit from bringing these phenomena within an explanatory framework that has proven useful across species and in the study of humans. Not to bring them within such a framework leaves them without linkages, without explanation.

The benefit for scientific explanation arises as follows. By bringing the more rarefied human pleasures into the same framework as other goals, we can construe such pleasures as part of the common affective currency of an individual's motivational economy. Doing so, in turn, sanctions treating them as choices among the other choices that people make, as the source of motivational forces—in Lewin's (1938) sense—capable of entering into conflict with or summating with the other forces, and as goals among the other goals. As argued in a later section, goal pursuits potentiate emotional responses to goal-related cues and hence potentiate cognitive processing of those cues and construct the contents of each individual's consciousness; furthermore, they do so in pursuits of the most ethereal pleasures as much as of the crassest.

The Relationship of This View to Other Formulations

Consummatory behavior falls into a subcategory of purpose that Baumeister (1991) calls "fulfillments" (pp. 33ff), one of two subcategories, the other of which he calls "goals." He defines goals as having extrinsic value. This is an important terminological difference from my use of the term, which defines goals as anything of value (presumably by virtue of evoking affective responses) that an individual has decided to pursue. Goals in my usage can have either extrinsic or intrinsic value; though if their value is extrinsic, they are presumably subgoals in a chain leading to something of intrinsic value. Ultimate goals must carry intrinsic value because by definition there is nothing else to confer value on them. It therefore seems confusing to me to define goals in terms of extrinsic value.

This conceptual analysis also points out a problem with the dichotomy articulated by Ebersole and Quiring (1991), who indicate their agreement with Yalom (1980) that "sometimes the meaning in life is not found in striving but just being" (Ebersole & Quiring, 1991, p. 115). People go to great lengths to "just be," including taking long walks, journeying to the mountains or ocean, undertaking years of meditative training, and doing what is necessary to acquire a variety of psychoactive drugs. People are too often willing to kill others in order to make possible their ways of just being. These states of just being are therefore clearly goal states. They are the rewarding result of manipulating one's own affect by attaining the goals (including substance use) that make one feel better. For many people, these states constitute important sources of life's meaning.

That said, it must also be recognized that a large part of life's pleasure and hence meaning is in the pursuit itself. The human organism is equipped with a variety of affective reactions to properties of pursuing goals, including such positive reactions as pride in effectance (Atkinson, 1957; White, 1959), the experience of "flow" in skilled, integrated behavior sequences (Csikszentmihalyi, 1990; Klinger, 1971), and the excitement of the chase, including the scholar's chase after knowledge, all of which also contribute meaning to many lives.

Baumeister's Four Needs for Meaning

Baumeister (1991; Chapter 14, this volume) posits four needs for meaning that he calls purpose, value, efficacy, and self-worth. It is helpful to have this list because it reminds us of four important facets of goal striving. Furthermore, this conceptual scheme enabled Baumeister to arrive at some intriguing ideas regarding the difficulties of achieving meaning in modern society, such as the paucity of value bases external to the self.

Rather than viewing the four as separate needs, however, it seems preferable to view them as dimensions of a single process. Having purposes presupposes that these will have value of some kind and in varying degree, as well as in varying relation to an individual's self-articulated scale of values. As Joske (1974/1981) also recognized, having goals of low value contributes to meaninglessness. Efficacy—control, impact—refers to the self-perceived aptness with which one pursues one's goals. Goal striving is futile without at least a modicum of efficacy. Hence, it seems reasonable to consider it as yet one more dimension of goal striving. Self-worth in Baumeister's sense is largely tied to social comparisons with others. It is a function partly of self-perceived social status and partly of self-assessment using the normative yardsticks espoused by the reference groups in comparison with which one judges one's own worth. Social status is clearly one kind of goal, the desire for which is at least learned through extensive socialization—experiences with the benefits of high status and the deprivations of low status—and may also have a sociobiological basis. I view it as one kind of purpose rather than as something essentially different.

It is perhaps worth adding that there are many types of goals. The prototypical goal is something positive that someone seeks to attain, but other goals are to keep, restore, do, avoid, escape, get rid of, attack, and find out more about something. In this sense, it is perfectly legitimate to label as the object of a goal something that someone already has if the goal is to keep it, for instance, a relationship or one's health. It is unclear how this diversity of goal types fits into Baumeister's analysis.

The Role of Emotion

Emotion is relevant to goal striving, purpose, and meaning in at least two fundamental ways. First, it constitutes the ultimate system for evaluation. It thus is the basis for value, which in turn determines what people strive for; and it is the internal code for experiencing goal pursuits as going well or ill. Second, it is intertwined with cognitive processing—for example, with attention, recall, thought content, and dream content—and may very well be necessary for quickly noticing and processing events around us and inside us. In this second role, it codetermines people's inner experience and their construals of the world around them. This chapter discusses the first role next and the second role in later sections.

Emotion and Evaluation

Goal striving cannot happen without elaborate systems for relating to the world outside. These systems must include receiving and processing feedback regarding the degree to which the behavior is on track toward its goals. But goal striving necessarily aims beyond present reality, away from what is, out toward what should be. If a feedback mechanism were purely informative about objective external reality, it would be useless for directing behavior because it could report only on what is, and not on movement toward what should be. No amount of sheer information or information processing leads inevitably to evaluation. I may stand in the street calculating that an onrushing truck will obliterate me in 3.6 seconds, but where is the evaluation in this? There is nothing here that provides a sufficient basis for concluding that the event is good or bad. An efficient feedback mechanism needs an evaluative component that goes beyond perceptual transformations of sensory information.

Evaluation is presumably the task of emotion. Emotions are inherently evaluative responses that are tied to fundamental action systems for approach, avoidance, and attack. Whereas the sensorium relays the objective state of affairs and cognition calculates its consequences and implications, emotion relays its significance for the future, whether good or bad, desirable or abhorrent. Emotions also often contain basic schemas for what one should do about something, whether to eat it up or spit it out, whether to flee or attack. In this view, emotion is the indispensable evaluative component of a motivational system.

There is now compelling neuroscientific evidence to support this view. Working with macaque monkeys, Tobler, Fiorillo, and Schultz (2005) found that activity levels of individual dopamine neurons varied monotonically with reward value and also with expectancies, the likelihood of obtaining the reward. That is, these neurons, which were mostly part of the substantia nigra and ventral tegmental area, reflected the bottom line of a Value × Expectancy (or Expected Utility) computation for making choices and decisions, that is, whether to select and pursue this possible goal or that one. Furthermore, the amount of neural activity reflected adaptation to certain reward levels in that if the reward was exactly what had been expected, neural activity remained flat, as if to reflect lack of excitement; if reward was greater than expected, neural activity rose accordingly; and if reward was below expectation, neural activity was suppressed, which one might interpret as disappointment. These reward-sensitive pathways are closely linked in previous evidence to positive affect. Regrettably, the monkeys provided no ratings of their subjective emotional experience, but the inference of emotional involvement seems a reasonably safe one to make.

Working with humans, Knutson, Taylor, Kaufman, Peterson, and Glover (2005) found parallel results using functional magnetic resonance imaging (fMRI). A number of brain structures were active in relation to the valence, magnitude, and probability of anticipated monetary gains and losses. Most clearly, activity in nucleus accumbens reflected the anticipated magnitude of reward, and activity in mesial prefrontal cortex reflected probability of reward and, the authors suggested, most likely also integrated anticipated magnitude (i.e., value) with probability (i.e., expectancy) of reward. Unlike Tobler et al.'s (2005) monkeys, Knutson et al.'s humans did in fact produce ratings. Their emotional arousal ratings correlated significantly with activity in nucleus accumbens. Probability ratings correlated with activity in mesial prefrontal cortex but not with activity in nucleus accumbens. The implications are clear: The human brain evaluates stimuli in brain areas that have long been associated with reward seeking and positive affect.

Emotion and Action

Much research has also documented the close intertwining of emotion and action. As Schneider (1990) and Scherer (1981) have noted, emotional reactions cannot be entirely detached from other information-pickup and information-processing activity, beginning with noticing something, with orientation toward it, and proceeding with continuing evaluation of the object and of the organism's own behavior toward it, that is, whether to pursue it as a goal or not.

Thus, it appears that both cognition and emotion, the two traditional contributors to consciousness, are fundamental outgrowths of the imperative to pursue goals—in short, to live purposively.

Emotion and the Sense That Life Is Meaningful

Inasmuch as brain pathways for emotion, especially positive affect, overlap those associated with evaluation, reward, and goal striving, it may be expected that emotion will also be linked to the sense that one's life is meaningful. An extensive research program by King, Hicks, Krull, and Del Gaiso (2006) has indeed demonstrated this relationship. They showed that (a) measures of positive affect are substantially correlated (with typical coefficients in the .40s and .50s) with measures of life's perceived meaningfulness and purpose; (b) the relationship is concurrent—that is, the positive affect and perceived meaningfulness occur together at particular points in time—but neither positive affect nor meaning in life at one time point predicts increases in the other variable two years later; (c) manipulating participants' mood by having them read happy, tragic, or neutral scenarios influences meaning in life in that participants' sense that life is meaningful is higher after reading happy scenarios than after reading one of the other two; and (d) as compared with people scoring low in positive emotionality, individuals scoring high find meaningful tasks especially meaningful and meaningless tasks especially meaningless.

The implication that King et al. (2006) draw from their findings is that positive affect accounts for most of the variance in the sense of meaningfulness. This relationship might suggest the possibility that the sense of meaningfulness can be reduced to feeling positive affect. There are, however, a number of reasons to doubt this latter implication, including both King et al.'s own original data and the subsequent studies by King and Hicks (see Chapter 6, this volume) that showed positive affect interacting with other variables in its relation to sense of meaningfulness.

To consider the interactions first, King and Hicks (Chapter 6, this volume) reported that positive affect predicted meaning scores for people who had few sources of meaning or who were low in religious commitment or lacked strong, supportive personal relationships, but not for those who scored high on such variables. That is, the high scorers on these measures reported high levels of meaning in their lives regardless of their moods, but the low scorers were more likely to report high levels of meaning if their moods were also high.

Some data, reported here, suggest a possible reason for this finding. These data show that one of the strongest independent predictors of high meaning scores is feeling confident of reaching one's goals. Positive moods render people more optimistic about reaching their goals and perhaps therefore raise meaning scores.

One finding of these data that made it appear as if the sense of meaningfulness can largely be reduced to positive affect was that the participants' ratings of the value and difficulty of their "typical" goals—Emmons's (1999) *personal strivings*—were less strongly related to their life's meaningfulness than was positive affect (King et al., 2006). But a number of other considerations can explain this finding. First, the value and difficulty scores used to characterize participants' typical goals were relatively unreliable; their Cronbach's alpha coefficients of internal consistency of about .60 fell short of acceptable levels of reliability. This lack of reliability would necessarily weaken their correlations with other variables. Second, when affect scores and ratings of goals were analyzed together in a regression for predicting Meaning in Life (MIL) scores, the goal ratings of value and difficulty were related to MIL independently of affect scores. Third, some other variables—extraversion and two of its facets, warmth and assertiveness—correlated with MIL even more strongly than did positive affect, suggesting that sheer affective state may be only part of the story, with dispositional traits being a further part. Fourth, in another study in this program, participants kept track of what they were working on, doing, and thinking about on each of five days. Their thinking about their typical goals was related to their "daily meaning in life" independently of positive affect.

Finally, consider the study in King et al.'s (2006) program in which participants whose mood had been raised experimentally reported greater MIL. The way in which the investigators manipulated participants' moods was to have them read and then write about one of three brief scenarios: reuniting a "child with her parents and being hailed as a hero" (King et al., 2006, p. 188), being responsible for an automobile collision that kills a baby, or making plans for the day. When participants were cautioned about the possible influence of the scenario exercise on their MIL responses, there were no differences in MIL between the groups. When there was no such caution, participants who worked with the positive scenario scored significantly higher than the other two groups. One cannot, however, rule out the possibility that the conceptual content of the scenarios, rather than just the induced moods, influenced MIL responses directly. It would be interesting to attempt a replication of this study using music (or other nonverbal methods) to induce positive mood.

As indicated earlier, it is unsurprising that positive affect is closely related to meaning in life. The valuable findings by King et al. (2006) suggest strongly that positive affect is an important facet of meaning in life, but their and others' data also suggest that it is not the entirety of life's meaningfulness. Frankl (1946/1963) managed to retain a strong sense of meaning in life, and helped others to do so, in the hellish circumstances of Nazi concentration camps. Indeed, Emmons (1999) makes the case that "growth is possible to the degree to which a person creates or finds meaning in suffering, pain, and adversity" (p. 144; see also Emmons, Colby, & Kaiser, 1998). Most likely, achieving meaning in such situations itself evokes positive emotions, and yet the context for this achievement is often highly aversive.

Lukas (1972) asked people in various locations in Vienna, Austria, to name something that gave their life meaning. The places at which the smallest proportion of respondents could name something were the Prater amusement park and the zoo at Schönbrunn. One imagines that they were having a good time, and yet Lukas' measure suggests that they were experiencing a low level of meaningfulness—perhaps empty pleasure obtained in trying to compensate for the missing joy of meaning in their everyday lives. Substance abuse may often act as a similar compensation, and substance abusers may feel similarly empty.

In the very different city of Dallas, Texas, both college students and community adults rated a life low in happiness but high in meaning as at least as desirable as a life high in happiness but low in meaning (King & Napa, 1998). It appears that a sense of life being meaningful is often accompanied by positive affect, but it enriches life beyond the effect of sheer positive affect.

Results from a study by Stuchlíková and Klinger (unpublished data) are in agreement with this position. Using the same four Purpose In Life (PIL) items identified by McGregor & Little (1998) and used by King et al. (2006) to assess meaning, the Personal Concerns Inventory (PCI; Cox & Klinger, 2011a) to assess motivational structure, and the Positive and Negative Affect Scale (PANAS; Watson, Clark, & Tellegen, 1988) to assess affectivity, the researchers found substantial correlations of PIL meaningfulness of life with both positive affect scores (PA; $r(148) = .42$, $p = .000$) and key Personal Concerns Inventory (PCI) variables, especially Adaptive Motivational Structure ($r(148) = .40$, $p = .000$) and one of its components, subjective probability of success ($r(148) = .51$, $p = .000$). Because a trait measure of subjective probability of success can be considered a measure of self-efficacy (Bandura, Adams, & Beyer, 1977; Bandura & Locke, 2003; Baumeister, 1991; Chapter 14, this volume), this strong correlation with PIL meaning scores supports

Baumeister's view that self-efficacy is important in a person's sense of having a meaningful life.

In this study, PA was correlated moderately with the four PIL meaning items ($r = .34$, $p = .000$), but not strongly enough to consider them equivalent variables. Furthermore, controlling for either one of the two predictor variables—PA or Adaptive Motivational Structure—only modestly reduced the correlation of the other predictor variable with PIL meaning (from .40 to .31, and from .42 to .32), with significance of the partial correlations remaining at $p = .000$. Unlike King and Hicks's findings (Chapter 6, this volume) with religious commitment and interpersonal support, there was no appreciable interaction between PA and Adaptive Motivational Structure (or its probability-of-success component) in predicting PIL meaning scores. Regression analyses that included both PA and Negative Affect confirmed that neither motivational structure nor affect substantially accounts for the ability of the other to predict PIL. Together, however, their multiple correlation with PIL scores was .63, thus accounting for a very large proportion of the variance of PIL meaning scores. One may infer that both positive affect and goal-striving patterns are associated independently with the sense of one's life feeling meaningful. (See also Wong, Chapter 1, this volume, on this point.)

Finally, factor analyses, such as those of the items in the PIL Scale (Crumbaugh & Maholick, 1964) and measures of well-being, have found that items that assess happiness load on a different orthogonal factor from those items that assess meaningfulness (McGregor & Little, 1998). Similarly, meaning scores derived from Personal Projects Analysis are poorly correlated with measures of well-being (Little, 1998; see also Chapter 8, this volume, for a review of the relationship between well-being and a sense of one's life having meaning).

Relationships between meaning and affect, however, may be more complex than they seem from relatively global measures of meaning. Working with a large item pool of meaningfulness items, Steger et al. (2006) found two different meaning factors, *Presence* of meaning in one's life and *Seeking* meaning. The Presence scale correlated moderately with measures of positive affect (coefficients in the .40s); the Seeking scale did not, but it correlated .36 with depression. Thus, combining Presence and Seeking items in the same scale could tend to diminish the association of meaning with positive affect. It is relevant to interpreting the results of King et al. (2006) that the items used there to measure meaning were predominantly or entirely Presence items.

Effects of Goal Pursuits on Consciousness and Cognition

Goal-Directed Time-Binding and Current Concerns

Any goal pursuit that is more than momentary requires some kind of underlying brain process that keeps behavior aimed at the goal or that returns behavior to the goal following interruption. This brain process can also be regarded as a goal-specific state that lasts until the goal is either reached or relinquished. I call this process or state a *current concern*. That is, specific to each goal there is, theoretically, an underlying corresponding current concern that remains in force until the goal is reached or relinquished.

In colloquial English the word *concern* connotes something happening in consciousness, but in this theoretical usage the term has the status of a hypothetical construct, referring to a nonconscious brain process. It theoretically does indeed influence the contents of consciousness—what people attend to, recall, and think about—but it does not itself refer to a conscious process. In fact, most of the time that one harbors a long-lasting concern, one's consciousness is on something else.

Effects of Current Concerns

The construct of current concerns—that is, of pursuing a goal—is important here primarily because it is the motivational unit we used to investigate the effects of goal pursuits on consciousness, thought and dream flow, and other cognitive processing. This construct is important for present purposes because it dramatizes the dependence of consciousness—and hence presumably the experience of meaningfulness of life—on goal pursuits.

The first results that we obtained with this construct made clear that knowing participants' current concerns as assessed by interviews and questionnaires, we could predict with statistical significance and large effect sizes which experimentally varied information on tape-recorded narrations our participants would notice, retain, and think about (Klinger, 1978). With an adaptation for the sleep state, we could also predict what they would dream about (Hoelscher, Klinger, & Barta, 1981). Participants spent more time listening to passages related to their own concerns and recalled them and thought about them about twice as often as passages related to someone else's concerns. These results were specific to the stimuli participants had received. When we compared thoughts to taped passages that participants had not yet heard, we found that passages related to the participants' own concerns were only weakly and not significantly better attended to, recalled, or thought about than passages related to another's concerns.

Subsequent investigations established that the effects of current concerns occurred automatically, in the sense of involuntarily and seemingly irresistibly. For instance, we played words or phrases to participants while they were in rapid-eye-movement (REM) sleep and then awakened them a few seconds later for a dream report. Judges blind for conditions rated stimuli related to participants' own concerns as having been incorporated in some way into the dreams about three times as often as stimuli related to someone else's concerns (Hoelscher et al., 1981). In another dream investigation (Nikles, Brecht, Klinger, & Bursell, 1998), presleep instructions to dream about particular topics increased sleepers' dreaming about them when the prescribed topics related to a sleeper's own concerns but not when they related to other participants' concerns.

A very different kind of investigation showed that the effects of concerns on cognitive processing were not only automatic but also extremely quick, occurring within fractions of a second after the onset of a stimulus. For example, Young (1987) gave waking participants a lexical task: Press one of two buttons as quickly as possible to indicate whether a string in the middle of a computer screen is an English word or a nonword string. Off to the side of the screen were groups of lines that participants were instructed to ignore and, indeed, did not recall. However, these lines sometimes contained words related to participants' current concerns. On trials when this occurred, participants' reaction times to the target word were significantly slower than on other trials, which suggests that participants had to process the peripheral words first, even though they were unaware of what they were, which slowed down processing of the more neutral target words. Because such responses take place in fractions of a second, the processing of the seemingly unattended concern-related words must have occurred during the early part of that second.

There have now been numerous other investigations showing effects of current concerns on attention, recall, Stroop-like performance, and dream content (e.g., Bock & Klinger, 1986; Cox, Fadardi, & Pothos, 2006; Nikula, Klinger, & Larson-Gutman, 1993; Riemann, Amir, & Louro, 1995; Riemann & McNally, 1995). For example, Riemann and McNally (1995) gave participants a Stroop-like task to name the ink colors of words that were in some cases related to participants' current concerns. Reaction times to the concern-related words were significantly slower than to the other words. Presumably, again, participants were unintentionally giving processing priority to the content of concern-related words and therefore slowing down by some milliseconds the participants' naming of font colors. Similarly, in studies using the alcohol Stroop (Cox et al., 2006), reaction times for naming the font colors of alcohol-related words or pictures rose in proportion to the participants' customary alcohol intake. In a different paradigm, participants with panic disorder, who heard previously encountered sentences with a white-noise background, judged the white noise as softer when accompanying panic-related sentences rather than neutral sentences, suggesting, again, a higher sensitivity toward (and processing priority for) content related to their own concerns (Amir, McNally, Riemann, & Clements, 1996).

The Role of Emotional Reactions in Concern (or Goal-Pursuit) Effects on Cognition

Meanwhile, investigators in cognitive, clinical, and social psychology were finding emotional effects on cognitive processing that paralleled the findings with concern effects, that is, with the effects of pursuing a goal. Social psychologists working under the rubric of attitudes (e.g., Bargh, Chaiken, Govender, & Pratto, 1992; Fazio, Sanbonmatsu, Powell, & Kardes, 1986) also provided supporting evidence of these effects. Without meaning to understate the complexities of these findings, it is possible to portray the body of results in the following generalizations: If emotionally arousing stimuli are central to a target task—and are therefore at the focus of processing—they facilitate perceptual and attentional responses; if, on the other hand, the emotionally arousing stimuli are incidental to the target task, they distract from the task and slow reaction time. In general, people also retain emotionally arousing stimuli better than others and experience more thoughts triggered by them.

For example, trait-anxious individuals are inclined to spend more time processing threat stimuli, or at least they let their attention rest there longer. Investigations with Stroop-like methods led Ehlers, Margraf, Davies, and Roth (1988) to conclude that compared to normal participants, both clinical and nonclinical panic-disorder patients take longer to name colors of threat words than of neutral words, even though the patients function normally on the standard Stroop. Fox (1994) concluded, among other things, that "a primary function of anxiety is to facilitate the rapid detection of threat (Eysenck, 1992)" (p. 191).

One might go a step further to conclude that the primary function of several emotions is to direct attention to concern-related stimuli. Just as anxious individuals are likely to recall anxiety-related words more than depression-related ones, depressed individuals are likely to recall depression-related more than anxiety-related words (Broadbent & Broadbent, 1988; Gotlib, McLachlan, & Katz, 1988; Ingram, Kendall, Smith, Donnell, & Ronan, 1987; R. J. McNally, Foa, & Donnell, 1989).

In general, words are recalled best when they elicit emotional arousal, an effect that is probably not attributable to participants' more stable dispositions. Thus, patients with generalized anxiety disorder (GAD) behaved cognitively in the expected way, but remitted GAD participants did not (Mogg, Mathews, & Eysenck, 1992). Likewise, depressed patients recalled more negatively toned autobiographic events in their lives than did nondepressed patients, but recovered depressives did not (Lewinsohn & Rosenbaum, 1987). The fact that cognition fluctuates with emotional state over time suggests that emotion, rather than dispositional traits, is the actual mediator of these cognitive differences among people.

The Relationship of Emotional Effects to Current Concerns (or Goal Pursuits)

From all these results, it might seem that cognitive processing is steered by emotional reactions and that current concerns (i.e., goal pursuits) have little to do with it. After all, it is also the case that the emotional arousal value of a word is strongly correlated with its relationship to an individual's current concerns. There are reasons, however, not to dismiss current concerns from a crucial role in cognition, because the nature and focus of emotional responses are probably guided by them. For example, using a dot probe method, Mogg et al. (1992) showed that anxious participants did not react differentially just to any threat words. Rather, the more participants were concerned only about social threats, the longer they attended to words related to social threat but not to those related to bodily dysfunction; and the more participants were concerned about bodily dysfunction, the longer they attended to words related to that but not to words related to social threat. Evidently, what operated here was not just raw emotion taken out of context but emotion directed at specific sources of threat, the kinds of sources that are the foci of aversive goal striving: to avoid injury and illness, for example, or to avoid social rejection and humiliation.

Protoemotions and Cognitive Processing

The patterning of these many data has important implications for theories of both emotion and cognition, as well as for theories of personal meaning. For cognitive theory, the implication is that emotional responses steer cognitive processing, probably at a number of different stages and levels, including during some of the earliest processing steps (Klinger, 1996). This conclusion is consistent with a continuous-flow model of information processing (e.g., Coles, Gratton, Bashore, Eriksen, & Donchin, 1985), but in a way that provides an evaluative role for essentially emotional responses. Continuous-flow theory posits that as cognitive processing unfolds, its results at every phase become available for further use, such as decision making. Primitive evaluations begin to stimulate reactions even as more refined processing continues. Presumably, if the primitive processing portends, for example, an external threat, the individual begins to mobilize for fight or flight (or conciliation, etc.!) even as higher-level, later phase processing continues to confirm or disconfirm and to clarify what it was that was perceived. The data described so far suggest that emotional response of some kind plays a role in this primitive processing.

For theory of emotion, the results suggest that essentially emotional responses are continually active without necessarily involving the autonomic, motoric, and humoral responses or the conscious features that are most often identified with emotion. Emotional responses at this early level, designated here as *protoemotional* responses, theoretically recruit the more traditional response components of emotion only if the reciprocal effects of protoemotional evaluation and cognitive processing pass some kind of threshold of urgency, the nature of which is still unclear (a *sequential-component* theory of emotion).

Finally, for theories of personal meaning, the results indicate that purposes, in the sense of current concerns, affect cognitive processing near its very outset. Purposes thereby color the person's subjective world and the kind of meaning he or she extracts from it. From the evidence described, this impact is not one that takes place deliberatively or necessarily consciously.

Nonetheless, the question of timing is crucial. If the cognitive effects of purposes (achieved via emotional responses) take place early enough, they would virtually foreclose discretionary processing; their effects would become nonoptional, and their ability to shape a person's perception of meaning virtually absolute. It is therefore critical to establish the point in the processing sequence at which motivational and emotional processes exert their influence.

The extent to which this influence occurs near the outset of cognitive processing is indicated by two sets of further investigations of its timing, one set employing near-liminal stimulation and the other set employing evoked cortical potentials. These investigations, which explore the essential biopsychological linkage between purposes and cognition, and hence the shaping of personal meaning, are described in the sections that follow.

Primacy of Emotion in Processing Words

The sequential-component theory of emotion espoused here, which posits a very early involvement of essentially emotional responses in cognition, gains support from investigations using average evoked potentials (EPs; regularities in electroencephalographic responses to particular classes of stimuli) as an approach to protoemotional processes. These investigations have shown that the time course of certain EP components that are linked to emotion is consistent with the concept of protoemotions.

The older EP literature provides little encouragement for such an approach, for EPs have commonly been regarded as reflections of cognitive processes (Coles, Gratton, & Fabiani, 1990). However, recent evidence has related the P300 component (positive deflections in the neighborhood of 300 ms after stimulus onset) and more generally the late positive complex to emotional variables in ways that cast doubt on purely cognitive formulations. The P300 has been shown in numerous investigations to covary with the emotionality of stimuli, both facial expressions and words (e.g., Cuthbert, Schupp, Bradley, Birbaumer, & Lang, 2000; Hajcak & Olvet, 2008; Johnston, Miller, & Burleson, 1986; Kestenbaum & Nelson, 1992; Schupp et al., 2004). In addition, in EP components the difference between emotionally toned and neutral words—especially 240 to 300 ms and 650 to 800 ms (intervals often subsumed under the broad label of P300 or Late Positive Potential)—has been found to be significantly smaller in psychopaths, who are generally regarded as deficient in at least some kinds of emotional response, than in other individuals (Williamson, Harpur, & Hare, 1991). It thus seems reasonable to conclude that early cognitive processing and protoemotional processes may well be intertwined, but that it is the emotional facet that is reflected in the P300.

Taking all the evidence together, there is ample reason to suppose that emotional processes begin to take effect within the first third of a second following stimulus onset. The stimuli that evoke these emotional processes are determined in part by innate response tendencies but predominantly by the goals to which people have become committed, along with the knowledge structures and association pathways linked to those goals. Once processing of the stimulus has begun, both its emotional and goal relevance are processed early at the start of the cognitive-processing sequence—early enough to steer subsequent processing and thereby influence the way in which people consciously experience their worlds. This control over cognition and consciousness is therefore likely to be part of the way in which goal striving influences people's sense that their lives are meaningful.

Personal Coherence, Integration, Religiousness, and Meaning

Everyone has numerous goals, some more important than others, and some possibly in conflict with others. People vary in the extent to which their goals relate to or conflict with one another. For example, some individuals devote themselves almost exclusively to one goal realm, whereas others divide their energies among disparate goals. Such people as Wilhelm Wundt in psychology, Mohandas Gandhi in liberating India, and Mother Teresa in serving the poor were notable for their intense focus on their focal long-term goals, which most of their other goals served as subgoals, that is, as steps toward the focal goal, or *ultimate concern*, to use Emmons's (1999) terminology. Most people invest themselves in a greater variety of pursuits, among them occupational success or service; committed partner relationships; relationships with parents, siblings, and children; recreational and volunteer pursuits; and, often not least, religious or spiritual commitments. These disparate pursuits may or may not be compatible with one another. In some instances, they may conflict, as when recreational pursuits divert energy from family or occupation; in others, they may facilitate each other, as when golf outings cinch business agreements and when support by family or friends eases an individual through occupational stresses.

The extent to which a person's goal pursuits harmonize with one another, along with the perceptions, inner experiences, beliefs, and actions related to them, is what is meant by personality coherence, integration, or integrity (e.g., Cervone & Shoda, 1999b; Emmons, 1999; McGregor & Little, 1998). Indeed, the case can be made that because goals often occur in hierarchies, are often long-lasting, and direct people's perceptions, recall, thought, dreams, and actions, they account for much of the coherence in personality (Grant & Dweck, 1999).

The study of the coherence of personality has burgeoned during the past 20 years (e.g., Cervone & Shoda, 1999a), and it is becoming clear that coherence is an important factor in promoting people's sense that their lives are meaningful. In fact, meaningfulness has been proposed to be the emotional component of a sense of coherence (Korotkov, 1998; see also Chapter 14, this volume). Some measures of this dimension (of "integrity" or "goal coherence") have been found to correlate significantly with PIL scores (McGregor & Little, 1998;

Tix, 2002) but not with happiness scores (McGregor & Little, 1998), a finding that again underscores the distinction between meaning and positive affect.

A number of writers have supposed that religious or spiritual commitments foster having a coherent set of goals and are likely to become ultimate concerns (Emmons, 1999) and provide for meaning in life (Wong, 1998c). Indeed, Tix (2002), with a sample composed mostly of students with religious affiliations, found a significant relationship between intrinsic religiousness and coherence of goals (Vertical Coherence = .26; Horizontal Coherence = .28). The number of religious goals that individuals list as a proportion of their total goals is correlated with having a sense of purpose in life and, hence, a sense that one's life is meaningful (Emmons, Cheung, & Tehrani, 1998; Tix, 2002). Tix (2002) reported significant correlations between PIL scores, which are commonly regarded as a measure of meaning in life, and intrinsic religiousness (.21), self-reported probability of adopting a religious life goal (.22), and the proportion of the person's self-reported strivings that were religious or spiritual (.23). The relationship of intrinsic religiousness with PIL scores was moderated by both sex and age: It was stronger for men than for women and stronger for older than for younger students.

These findings support the belief that commitment to a religion is associated with a greater sense of having a purpose in life and hence a sense of meaning in life. (For links between meaning and religion, see also Chapters 8, 13, 14, and 21, this volume). It is not clear from these data, however, whether having equally strong commitments to other life goals, such as justice or science, might not yield the same kind of association with having a purpose in life. In this connection, Battista and Almond (1973) argued for a "relativistic" theory of meaning, in which having any clear framework within which to structure one's life, along with commitment to attaining important goals within that framework, can—regardless of the nature of the framework or goals—imbue a life with significant meaning.

Moreover, even though PIL scores were correlated in Tix's (2002) study with a number of measures of religiousness, they were correlated much more highly with some other measures, especially Environmental Mastery (.57), Self-Acceptance (.52), and Positive Relations With Others (.47). These, in turn, correlated only weakly (mostly less than .20), although often significantly, with the measures of involvement with religion. This pattern therefore suggests that whatever unique contribution religiousness makes to purpose or meaning in life, it may be weaker than other personal attributes and perhaps no greater than other kinds of commitments. This pattern will have to be examined in future research.

Clinical Implications

There are numerous findings linking a sense of meaninglessness with psychopathology (see Chapter 8, this volume, for an extensive review). The foregoing formulation helps to clarify those links by shedding light on two paths to distress and psychopathology: a life of inadequate goals and a life of excessively aversive goals.

A behavioral system without goals, or with inadequate goals, lacks the prerequisites for its continued healthy functioning. This is because an individual's set of goal pursuits steers attention, perception, cognition, recall, thought content, and emotional responses and, hence, exercises pervasive influence over consciousness. It follows that the absence of adequate goals removes the linchpin of psychological organization. It would lead to desultory, apathetic activity, to much inactivity, and to reduced reactivity to environmental events. Because this is an unhappy state of affairs, it is likely to provoke self-examination, including questions regarding the meaning of one's life. Furthermore, insofar as the person is unable to locate an adequate set of purposes, he or she is likely to resort to other means for improving subjective well-being, for manipulating affect, for example, through substance use and emotionally rousing amusements (Lukas, 1972). The result is a lifestyle at risk for alienation, isolation, and depression.

When an individual's goal pursuits are predominantly aversive, the dominant tone of consciousness is presumably pervaded by negative affect, and the net effect is one of generalized stress with little relief. It is a state most probably marked by worry and other indicators of anxiety, and for some individuals it will lead to physical illness (cf. Ryff & Singer, 1998). Individuals who lack sufficient hope of terminating this state are presumably at risk for antianxiety and possibly other substance use, including cocaine and opiates, and are, in some instances, at risk for violence (Klinger, 1977). Also probable would be self-examination of the kind that leads to questions regarding the meaning of one's life.

Meaning and Psychopathology

A number of investigations have shown associations between meaninglessness and psychopathology, including substance use and depressed mood states, or recreational patterns (see Chapter 8, this volume, for an extensive review). For instance, a sample of psychiatrically disturbed individuals reported less meaningful lives than did others (Crumbaugh & Maholick, 1964). A substantial student sample produced a correlation of –.46 between a rating of their lives' meaningfulness and depression scores (Klinger, 1977). Other investigations have found relationships between scores on the Life Regard Index (LRI), especially its Fulfillment scale, with status as a psychiatric patient and with SCL-90 scales for General Psychological Distress and Depression (Debats, 1998). In a large sample of Chinese adolescents, Shek (1992; Chapter 16, this volume) similarly found scores on the Chinese Purpose in Life Scale (C-PIL) substantially inversely correlated (mostly –.50s) with measures of depression and anxiety, along with lower but still significant inverse correlations with self-report measures of somatic problems. Of the two C-PIL subscales, the Quality of Existence scale related to these measures more strongly than did the Purpose of Existence scale, but even the latter produced significant correlations that were lower by only about .10.

Looking at the relationship with well-being, Reker et al. (1987) found correlations of .55 with LAP Life Purpose ("zest for life, fulfillment, and satisfaction," p. 45) and −.41 with Existential Vacuum ("lack of meaning in life, lack of goals, and free-floating anxiety," p. 45), and these relationships were reasonably consistent for samples over most of the life span (ages 16 to 74). The LRI also predicted changes in well-being and distress over the course of psychotherapy, with individuals who scored higher on LRI Fulfillment before psychotherapy scoring less distressed and happier on retest than was true of those who initially scored lower on LRI Fulfillment (Debats, 1998). There also is a larger, older literature relating meaninglessness to various forms of depression and alienation (reviewed by Klinger, 1977) and relating goal striving or related concepts to depression and happiness (Baumeister, 1991; Klinger, 1977).

Bond and Feather's (1988) Use of Time scale of their Time Structure Questionnaire, which has a correlation of .65 with PIL scores, also correlated in the .50s with measures of self-esteem, −.44 and −.55 with depression (two samples), −.56 and −.68 with trait anxiety, −.37 with state anxiety, −.55 with neuroticism, −.49 with hopelessness, and .27 with reported health (all coefficients significant), among others.

Meaning and Substance Use

Turning to substance use, Newcomb and Harlow (1986) found low-order but significant relationships with meaninglessness (i.e., having no direction, plans, or solutions) in two samples of adolescents and young adults. Even more interesting, the obtained structural models placed meaninglessness as the final mediator of the relationship between substance abuse and the other two factors: Meaninglessness mediated the effects of perceived loss of control (with which meaninglessness was highly correlated) and uncontrollable stressful events. Thus, the sense of meaninglessness here acted as a subjective funnel for the effects of the other factors on substance use.

In a comparison of Czech students and demographically rather similar nonstudent alcoholic patients (Man, Stuchlikova, & Klinger, 1996), the clinical group listed 40% fewer goals, responded as if they needed richer incentives to form strong commitments to goal striving, displayed marginally less average commitment to their goals, and, after researchers partialed out other variables, expressed less ability to influence the course of goal attainment. Although this investigation did not include a measure of meaningfulness, the differences observed are those that relate significantly to it.

A number of studies have indicated that motivational structure—that is, an individual's pattern of goal striving—is associated with alcohol consumption and control over it (Cox et al., 2003; Cox et al., 2002; Fadardi & Cox, 2006). People for whom drinking creates no problems are, of course, uninterested in reducing their intake; but when drinking does create problems, people vary in their ability to control it. One study (Cox et al., 2002) revealed an important determinant of who can and who cannot exercise adequate control. The study data indicate that adaptive motivational structure influences people's tendency or perhaps their ability to control their drinking after they have encountered problems created by their alcohol consumption. Another study (Cox et al., 2003) found that improvements in motivational structure were associated with reduced substance use. Such components of adaptive motivational structure as commitment to goals, joy anticipated upon goal attainment, and subjective probability of success are also those goal-striving variables that are related to finding meaning in one's life.

Meaning-Related Treatment Approaches

It is clear that the meaningfulness of one's life has an extensive association with both happiness and distress, including psychopathology. The precise nature of those links remains to be investigated, but the clinical reports of treatment procedures that focus specifically on meaning (e.g., logotherapy: Frankl, 1969; self-confrontation: Hermans, Fiddelaers, de Groot, & Nauta, 1990; Wong, 1998b; Chapters 22 and 25, this volume) or motivational structure (systematic motivational counseling: Cox et al., 2003; Cox & Klinger, 1988, 2011b; de Jong-Meyer, 2011; Fuhrmann, Schroer, & de Jong-Meyer, 2011) suggest that the motivational restructuring associated with regaining meaning has a causal role in clinical improvement. Rigorous empirical investigations of meaning-related treatments are scarce, but Cox et al. (2003) reported on a demonstration project on traumatically brain-injured patients. In this investigation, patients in two Chicago rehabilitation clinics took the Motivational Structure Questionnaire (MSQ) and received standard rehabilitation treatments, but those in one of these clinics additionally received 12 sessions of systematic motivational counseling (SMC). Both groups were subsequently reassessed with the MSQ, once more in the case of the control group and twice more—at the end of treatment and at follow-up about nine months later—in the case of the SMC group. The SMC group improved in motivational structure over the course of treatment and follow-up and reduced alcohol use and number of substances used, whereas the control group showed no significant changes. Within the SMC group, the extent of reduction in number of substances used correlated firmly with improvement in a number of SMC indices, suggesting that the meaning-related motivational change was responsible for the clinical improvement. A study of group SMC with an alcohol-abusing sample (Fuhrmann et al., 2011) found that group SMC produced improvement equivalent to a program of social skills training but did so more efficiently.

A number of other investigators have attempted brief interventions based on such motivational principles as motivational interviewing (e.g., Miller & Rollnick, 2002), employing client-centered methods for inducing recognition of discrepancies between one's own behavior and one's own ideals or population norms. These methods have shown effects on health behaviors (Resnicow & Rollnick, 2011) and alcohol-drinking behaviors (e.g., A. M. McNally & Palfai, 2003; A. M.McNally, Palfai, & Kahler, 2005).

Conclusion

To conclude, then, it is apparent that goal pursuits influence most of an individual's cognitive processing, emotional responses, and therefore consciousness as well as choices and overt actions. Goal striving appears also to form one of the main determinants of persons' sense that their lives are meaningful. The sense of life's meaningfulness is related inversely to psychopathology and substance use. Treatment procedures aimed at improving motivational structure and the sense of meaningfulness reduce substance use and show promise in alleviating other forms of psychopathology.

Acknowledgments

I thank Heather A. Haas and editor Paul T. P. Wong for perceptive, helpful comments on an earlier draft of this chapter.

References

Amir, N., McNally, R. J., Riemann, B. C., & Clements, C. (1996). Implicit memory bias for threat in panic disorder: Application of the "white noise" paradigm. *Behaviour Research and Therapy*, *34*(2), 157–162.

Atkinson, J. W. (1957). Motivational determinants of risk-taking behavior. *Psychological Review*, *64*, 359–372.

Bandura, A., Adams, N. E., & Beyer, J. (1977). Cognitive processes mediating behavioral change. *Journal of Personality and Social Psychology*, *35*(3), 125–139.

Bandura, A., & Locke, E. A. (2003). Negative self-efficacy and goal effects revisited. *Journal of Applied Psychology*, *88*(1), 87–99.

Bargh, J. A., Chaiken, S., Govender, R., & Pratto, F. (1992). The generality of the automatic attitude activation effect. *Journal of Personality and Social Psychology*, *62*(6), 893–912.

Battista, J., & Almond, R. (1973). The development of meaning in life. *Psychiatry*, *36*, 409–427.

Baumeister, R. F. (1991). *The meanings of life*. New York, NY: Guilford.

Bock, M., & Klinger, E. (1986). Interaction of emotion and cognition in word recall. *Psychological Research*, *48*, 99–106.

Bond, M. J., & Feather, N. T. (1988). Some correlates of structure and purpose in the use of time. *Journal of Personality and Social Psychology*, *55*, 321–329.

Broadbent, D., & Broadbent, M. (1988). Anxiety and attentional bias: State and trait. *Cognition and Emotion*, *2*, 165–184.

Cervone, D., & Shoda, Y. (Eds.). (1999a). *The coherence of personality: Social-cognitive bases of consistency, variability, and organization*. New York, NY: Guilford Press.

Cervone, D., & Shoda, Y. (1999b). Social-cognitive theories and the coherence of personality. In D. Cervone & Y. Shoda (Eds.), *The coherence of personality: Social-cognitive bases of consistency, variability, and organization* (pp. 3–33). New York, NY: Guilford Press.

Coles, M. G. H., Gratton, G., Bashore, T. R., Eriksen, C. W., & Donchin, E. (1985). A psychophysiological investigation of the continuous flow model of human information processing. *Journal of Experimental Psychology: Human Perception and Performance, 11*, 529–553.

Coles, M. G. H., Gratton, G., & Fabiani, M. (1990). Event-related potentials. In J. T. Cacioppo & L. G. Tassinary (Eds.), *Principles of psychophysiology*. New York, NY: Cambridge University Press.

Cox, W. M., Fadardi, J. S., & Pothos, E. M. (2006). The Addiction–Stroop test: Theoretical considerations and procedural recommendations. *Psychological Bulletin, 132*, 443–476.

Cox, W. M., Heinemann, A. W., Miranti, S. V., Schmidt, M., Klinger, E., & Blount, J. (2003). Outcomes of systematic motivational counseling for substance use following traumatic brain injury. *Journal of Addictive Diseases, 22*, 93–110.

Cox, W. M., & Klinger, E. (1988). A motivational model of alcohol use. *Journal of Abnormal Psychology, 97*, 168–180.

Cox, W. M., & Klinger, E. (2002). Motivational structure: Relationships with substance use and processes of change. *Addictive Behaviors, 27*, 925–940.

Cox, W. M., & Klinger, E. (2011a) Measuring motivation: The Motivational Structure Questionnaire and Personal Concerns Inventory and their variants. In W. M. Cox & E. Klinger (Eds.), *Handbook of motivational counseling* (2nd ed., pp. 161–204). Chichester, England: Wiley-Blackwell.

Cox, W. M., & Klinger, E. (2011b) Systematic motivational counseling: From motivational assessment to motivational change. In W. M. Cox & E. Klinger (Eds.), *Handbook of motivational counseling* (2nd ed., pp. 275–302). Chichester, England: Wiley-Blackwell.

Cox, W. M., Schippers, G. M., Klinger, E., Skutle, A., Stuchlíková, I., Man, F., … Inderhaug, R. (2002). Motivational structure and alcohol use of university students with consistency across four nations. *Journal of Studies on Alcohol, 63*, 280–285.

Crumbaugh, J. C. (1977). The Seeking of Noetic Goals Test (SONG): A complementary scale to the Purpose in Life Test (PIL). *Journal of Clinical Psychology, 33*, 900–907.

Crumbaugh, J. C., & Maholick, L. T. (1964). *Manual of instructions for the Purpose-in-Life Test*. Lafayette, IN: Psychometric Affiliates.

Csikszentmihalyi, M. (1990). *Flow: The psychology of optimal experience*. New York, NY: HarperCollins.

Cuthbert, B. N., Schupp, H. T., Bradley, M. M., Birbaumer, N., & Lang, P. J. (2000). Brain potentials in affective picture processing: Covariation with autonomic arousal and affective report. *Biological Psychology, 52*(2), 95–111.

Debats, D. L. (1998). Measurement of personal meaning: The psychometric properties of the Life Regard Index. In P. T. P. Wong & P. S. Fry (Eds.), *The human quest for meaning: A handbook of psychological research and clinical applications* (pp. 237–259). Mahwah, NJ: Erlbaum.

De Jong-Meyer, R. (2011). Systematic motivational analysis as part of a self-help technique aimed at personal goal attainment. In W. M. Cox & E. Klinger (Eds.), *Handbook of motivational counseling* (pp. 349–372). Chichester, England: Wiley-Blackwell.

DePaola, S. J., & Ebersole, P. (1995). Meaning in life categories of elderly nursing home residents. *International Journal of Aging & Human Development, 40*, 227–236

DeVogler, K. L., & Ebersole, P. (1980). Categorization of college students' meaning of life. *Psychological Reports, 46*, 387–390.
DeVogler, K. L., & Ebersole, P. (1983). Young adolescents' meaning in life. *Psychological Reports, 52*, 427–431.
DeVogler-Ebersole, K., & Ebersole, P. (1985). Depth of meaning in life: Explicit rating criteria. *Psychological Reports, 56*, 303–310.
Ebersole, P. (1998). Types and depth of written life meanings. In P. T. P. Wong & P. S. Fry (Eds.), *The human quest for meaning: A handbook of psychological research and clinical applications* (pp. 179–191). Mahwah, NJ: Erlbaum.
Ebersole, P., & DePaola, S. (1987). Meaning in life categories of later life couples. *Journal of Psychology, 121*, 185–191.
Ebersole, P., & Quiring, G. (1991). Meaning in life depth: The MILD. *Journal of Humanistic Psychology, 31*, 113–124.
Ehlers, A. M., Margraf, J., Davies, S., & Roth, W. T. (1988). Selective processing of threat cues in subjects with panic attacks. *Cognition and Emotion, 2*, 201–220.
Emmons, R. A. (1999). *The psychology of ultimate concerns: Motivation and spirituality in personality*. New York, NY: Guilford Press.
Emmons, R. A., Cheung, C., & Tehrani, K. (1998). Assessing spirituality through personal goals: Implications for research on religion and subjective well-being. *Social Indicators Research: Validity theory and the methods used in validation: Perspectives from social and behavioral sciences* [Special issue], *45*(1–3), 391–422.
Emmons, R. A., Colby, P. M., & Kaiser, H. A. (1998). When losses lead to gains: Personal goals and the recovery of meaning. In P. T. P. Wong & P. S. Fry (Eds.), *The human quest for meaning: A handbook of psychological research and clinical applications* (pp. 163–178). Mahwah, NJ: Erlbaum.
Eysenck, M. W. (1992). *Anxiety: The cognitive perspective*. Hove, England: Erlbaum.
Fadardi, J. S., & Cox, W. M. (2006). *Can university students' alcohol-attentional bias and motivational structure predict their alcohol consumption?* Article manuscript submitted for publication.
Fazio, R. H., Sanbonmatsu, D. M., Powell, M. C., & Kardes, F. R. (1986). On the automatic activation of attitudes. *Journal of Personality and Social Psychology, 50*, 229–238.
Fox, E. (1994). Attentional bias in anxiety: A defective inhibition hypothesis. *Cognition and Emotion, 8*, 165–195.
Frankl, V. E. (1963). *Man's search for meaning: An introduction to logotherapy*. New York, NY: Washington Square Press. (Originally published 1946)
Frankl, V. E. (1969). *The will to meaning: Foundations and applications of logotherapy*. New York, NY: New American Library.
Frijda, N. H., & Sundararajan, L. (2007). Emotion refinement: A theory inspired by Chinese poetics. *Perspectives on Psychological Science, 2*, 227–241.
Fuhrmann, A., Schroer, B. M., & deJong-Meyer, R. (2011). Systematic motivational counseling in groups: Promoting therapeutic change through client interaction. In W. M. Cox & E. Klinger (Eds.), *Handbook of motivational counseling* (pp. 303–327). Chichester, England: Wiley-Blackwell.
Gotlib, I. H., McLachlan, A. L., & Katz, A. N. (1988). Biases in visual attention in depressed and nondepressed individuals. *Cognition and Emotion, 2*, 185–200.
Grant, H., & Dweck, C. S. (1999). A goal analysis of personality and personality coherence. In D. Cervone & Y. Shoda (Eds.), *The coherence of personality: Social-cognitive bases of consistency, variability, and organization* (pp. 345–371). New York, NY: Guilford Press.
Hajcak, G., & Olvet, D. M. (2008). The persistence of attention to emotion: Brain potentials during and after picture presentation. *Emotion, 8*(2), 250–255.

Herbart, J. F. (1834). *A text-book in psychology* (M. K. Smith, Trans.). New York, NY: Appleton.

Hermans, H. J., Fiddelaers, R., de Groot, R., & Nauta, J. F. (1990). Self-confrontation as a method for assessment and intervention in counseling. *Journal of Counseling & Development, 69*, 156–162.

Hoelscher, T. J., Klinger, E., & Barta, S. G. (1981). Incorporation of concern- and nonconcern-related verbal stimuli into dream content. *Journal of Abnormal Psychology, 49*, 88–91.

Ingram, R. E., Kendall, P. C., Smith, T. W., Donnell, C., & Ronan, K. (1987). Cognitive specificity in emotional distress. *Journal of Personality and Social Psychology, 53*, 734–742.

Johnson, M. (1987). *The body in the mind*. Chicago, IL: University of Chicago Press.

Johnston, V. S., Miller, D. R., & Burleson, M. H. (1986). Multiple P3s to emotional stimuli and their theoretical significance. *Psychophysiology, 23*(6), 684–694.

Joske, W. D. (1981). Philosophy and the meaning of life. In E. D. Klemke (Ed.), *The meaning of life* (pp. 248–261). New York, NY: Oxford University Press. (Originally published 1974)

Kestenbaum, R., & Nelson, C. A. (1992). Neural and behavioral correlates of emotion recognition in children and adults. *Journal of Experimental Child Psychology, 54*, 1–18.

King, L. A., Hicks, J. A., Krull, J. L., & Del Gaiso, A. K. (2006). Positive affect and the experience of meaning in life. *Journal of Personality and Social Psychology, 90*, 179–196.

King, L. A., & Napa, C., K. (1998). What makes a life good? *Journal of Personality and Social Psychology, 75*, 156–165.

Klinger, E. (1971). *Structure and functions of fantasy*. New York, NY: Wiley.

Klinger, E. (1975). Consequences of commitment to and disengagement from incentives. *Psychological Review, 82*, 1–25.

Klinger, E. (1977). *Meaning and void: Inner experience and the incentives in people's lives*. Minneapolis: University of Minnesota Press.

Klinger, E. (1978). Modes of normal conscious flow. In K. S. Pope & J. L. Singer (Eds.), *The stream of consciousness: Scientific investigations into the flow of human experience* (pp. 225–258). New York, NY: Plenum Press.

Klinger, E. (1987a). Current concerns and disengagement from incentives. In F. Halisch & J. Kuhl (Eds.), *Motivation, intention and volition* (pp. 337–347). Berlin, Germany: Springer.

Klinger, E. (1987b). The Interview Questionnaire technique: Reliability and validity of a mixed idiographic-nomothetic measure of motivation. In J. N. Butcher & C. D. Spielberger (Eds.), *Advances in personality assessment* (Vol. 6, pp. 31–48). Hillsdale, NJ: Erlbaum.

Klinger, E. (1996). Emotional influences on cognitive processing, with implications for theories of both. In J. A. Bargh & P. M. Gollwitzer (Eds.), *The psychology of action: Linking cognition and motivation to behavior* (pp. 168–189). New York, NY: Guilford Press.

Klinger, E., & Cox, W. M. (2011a). Motivation and the goal theory of current concerns. In W. M. Cox & E. Klinger (Eds.). *Handbook of motivational counseling* (pp. 3–47). Chichester, England: Wiley-Blackwell.

Klinger, E., & Cox, W. M. (2011b). The Motivational Structure Questionnaire, Personal Concerns Inventory, and their variants: Psychometric properties. In W. M. Cox & E. Klinger (Eds.), *Handbook of motivational counseling* (pp. 205–232). Chichester, England: Wiley-Blackwell.

Knutson, B., Taylor, J., Kaufman, M., Peterson, R., & Glover, G. (2005). Distributed neural representation of expected value. *Journal of Neuroscience, 25*, 4806–4812.

Korotkov, D. (1998). The sense of coherence. In P. T. P. Wong & P. S. Fry (Eds.), *The human quest for meaning: A handbook of psychological research and clinical applications* (pp. 51–70). Mahwah, NJ: Erlbaum.

Lewin, K. (1938). *The conceptual representation and the measurement of psychological forces.* Durham, NC: Duke University Press.

Lewinsohn, P. M., & Rosenbaum, M. (1987). Recall of parental behavior by acute depressives, remitted depressives, and nondepressives. *Journal of Personality and Social Psychology, 52*, 611–619.

Lewis, M. (1993). Self-conscious emotions: Embarrassment, pride, shame, and guilt. In M. Lewis & J. M. Haviland (Eds.), *Handbook of emotions* (pp. 563–573). New York, NY: Guilford Press.

Little, B. R. (1998). Personal project pursuit: Dimensions and dynamics of personal meaning. In P. T. P. Wong & P. S. Fry (Eds.), *The human quest for meaning: A handbook of psychological research and clinical applications* (pp. 193–212). Mahwah, NJ: Erlbaum.

Loewer, B., & Rey, G. (Eds.). (1991). *Meaning in mind: Fodor and his critics.* Cambridge, MA: Blackwell.

Lukas, E. (1972). Zur Validierung der Logotherapie [Toward the validation of logotherapy]. In V. Frankel, *Der Wille zum Sinn: Ausgewählte Vorträge über Logotherapie* [*The will to meaning: Selected lectures on logotherapy*] (pp. 233–266). Bern, Switzerland: Huber.

Man, F., Stuchlikova, I., & Klinger, E. (1996). *Motivational structure of alcoholic and nonalcoholic Czech males.* Article manuscript submitted for publication.

McGregor, I., & Little, B. R. (1998). Personal projects, happiness, and meaning: On doing well and being yourself. *Journal of personality and social psychology, 74*, 494–512.

McNally, A. M., & Palfai, T. P. (2003). Brief group alcohol interventions with college students: Examining motivational components. *Journal of Drug Education, 33*(2), 159–176.

McNally, A. M., Palfai, T. P., & Kahler, C. W. (2005). Motivational interventions for heavy drinking college students: Examining the role of discrepancy-related psychological processes. *Psychology of Addictive Behaviors, 19*(1), 79–87.

McNally, R. J., Foa, E. B., & Donnell, C. D. (1989). Memory bias for anxiety information in patients with panic disorder. *Cognition and Emotion, 3*, 27–44.

Merriam-Webster's Collegiate Dictionary. (1999). (10th ed.). Springfield, MA: Merriam-Webster.

Miller, W. R., & Rollnick, S. (2002). *Motivational interviewing: Preparing people for change* (2nd ed.). New York, NY: Guilford.

Mogg, K., Mathews, A., & Eysenck, M. (1992). Attentional bias to threat in clinical anxiety states. *Cognition and Emotion, 6*, 149–159.

Newcomb, M. D., & Harlow, L. L. (1986). Life events and substance use among adolescents: Mediating effects of perceived loss of control and meaninglessness in life. *Journal of Personality and Social Psychology, 51*, 564–577.

Nikles, C. D., II, Brecht, D. L., Klinger, E., & Bursell, A. L. (1998). The effects of current-concern- and nonconcern-related waking suggestions on nocturnal dream content. *Journal of Personality and Social Psychology, 75*, 242–255.

Nikula, R., Klinger, E., & Larson-Gutman, M. K. (1993). Current concerns and electrodermal reactivity: Responses to words and thoughts. *Journal of Personality, 61*, 63–84.

Reker, G. T., Peacock, E. J., & Wong, P. T. (1987). Meaning and purpose in life and well-being: A life-span perspective. *Journal of Gerontology, 42*, 44–49.

Resnicow, K., & Rollnick, S. (2011). Motivational interviewing in health promotion and behavioral medicine. In W. M. Cox & E. Klinger (Eds.), *Handbook of motivational counseling* (pp. 591–605). Chichester, England: Wiley-Blackwell.

Riemann, B. C., Amir, N., & Louro, C. E. (1995). *Cognitive processing of personally relevant information in panic disorder*. Unpublished manuscript.

Riemann, B. C., & McNally, R. J. (1995). Cognitive processing of personally-relevant information. *Cognition and Emotion*, *9*, 325–340.

Roberson, L. (1989). Assessing personal work goals in the organizational setting: Development and evaluation of the Work Concerns Inventory. *Organizational Behavior and Human Decision Processes*, *44*, 345–367.

Ryff, C., & Singer, B. (1998). The role of purpose in life and personal growth in positive human health. In P. T. P. Wong & P. S. Fry (Eds.), *The human quest for meaning: A handbook of psychological research and clinical applications* (pp. 213–235). Mahwah, NJ: Erlbaum.

Scherer, K. R. (1981). Wider der Vernachlässigung der Emotionen in der Psychologie [Countering the neglect of emotions in psychology]. In W. Michaelis (Ed.), *Bericht über den 32. Kongreß der Deutschen Gesellschaft für Psychologie in Zürich 1980* [*Report on the 32nd Congress of the German Psychological Society*] (Vol. 1, pp. 304–317). Göttingen, Germany: Hogrefe.

Schneider, K. (1990). Emotionen. In H. Spada (Ed.), *Lehrbuch Allgemeine Psychologie* [*Textbook of general psychology*] (pp. 405–449). Bern, Switzerland: Huber.

Schupp, H. T., Cuthbert, B. N., Bradley, M. M., Hillman, C. H., Hamm, A. O., & Lang, P. J. (2004). Brain processes in emotional perception: Motivated attention. *Cognition & Emotion*, *18*(5), 593–611.

Shek, D. T. (1992). Meaning in life and psychological well-being: An empirical study using the Chinese version of the Purpose in Life Questionnaire. *Journal of Genetic Psychology*, *153*(2), 185–200.

Smith, J. E. (1978). *Purpose and thought: The meaning of pragmatism*. New Haven, CT: Yale University Press.

Sommer, K. L., & Baumeister, R. F. (1998). The construction of meaning from life events: Empirical studies of personal narratives. In P. T. P. Wong & P. S. Fry (Eds.), *The human quest for meaning: A handbook of psychological research and clinical applications* (pp. 143–161). Mahwah, NJ: Erlbaum.

Steger, M. F., Frazier, P., Oishi, S., & Kaler, M. (2006). The Meaning in Life Questionnaire: Assessing the presence of and search for meaning in life. *Journal of Counseling Psychology*, *53*, 80–93.

Taylor, S. J., & Ebersole, P. (1993). Young children's meaning in life. *Psychological Reports*, *73*, 1099–1104.

Tinbergen, N. (1969). *The study of instinct*. Oxford, England: Clarendon Press.

Tix, A. P. (2002). *Moderators and goal-based mediators of the relationship between intrinsic religiousness and mental health* (Doctoral dissertation). University of Minnesota, Minneapolis.

Tobler, P. N., Fiorillo, C. D., & Schultz, W. (2005). Adaptive coding of reward value by dopamine neurons. *Science*, *307*, 1642–1645.

Watson, D., Clark, L. A., & Tellegen, A. (1988). Development and validation of brief measures of positive and negative affect: The PANAS scales. *Journal of Personality and Social Psychology*, *54*(6), 1063–1070.

White, R. W. (1959). Motivation reconsidered: The concept of competence. *Psychological Review*, *66*, 297–333.

Williamson, S., Harpur, T. J., & Hare, R. D. (1991). Abnormal processing of affective words by psychopaths. *Psychphysiology, 28*, 260-273.

Wong, P. T. P. (1991). Existential versus causal attributions: The social perceiver as philospher. In S. L. Zelen (Ed.), *New models, new extensions of attribution theory* (pp. 84–125). New York, NY: Springer-Verlag.

Wong, P. T. P. (1995). A stage model of coping with frustrative stress. In R. Wong (Ed.), *Biological perspectives on motivated activities* (pp. 339–378). Norwood, NJ: Ablex.

Wong, P. T. P. (1998a). Implicit theories of meaningful life and the development of the Personal Meaning Profile. In P. T. P. Wong & P. S. Fry (Eds.), *The human quest for meaning: A handbook of psychological research and clinical applications* (pp. 111–140). Mahwah, NJ: Erlbaum.

Wong, P. T. P. (1998b). Meaning-centered counseling. In P. T. P. Wong & P. S. Fry (Eds.), *The human quest for meaning: A handbook of psychological research and clinical applications* (pp. 395–435). Mahwah, NJ: Erlbaum.

Wong, P. T. P. (1998c). Spirituality, meaning, and successful aging. In P. T. P. Wong & P. S. Fry (Eds.), *The human quest for meaning: A handbook of psychological research and clinical applications* (pp. 359–394). Mahwah, NJ: Erlbaum.

Wong, P. T. P., & Weiner, B. (1981). When people ask why questions and the heuristics of attributional search. *Journal of Personality and Social Psychology, 40*, 650–663.

Wrosch, C., Miller, G. E., Scheier, M. F., & de Pontet, S. B. (2007). Giving up on unattainable goals: Benefits for health? *Personality and Social Psychology Bulletin, 33*, 251–265.

Yalom, I. D. (1980). *Existential psychotherapy*. New York, NY: Basic Books.

Young, J. (1987). *The role of selective attention in the attitude-behavior relationship* (Doctoral dissertation). University of Minnesota, Minneapolis.

3
Creating Meaning Through Making Decisions

SALVATORE R. MADDI

University of California, Irvine

A cardinal assumption of existential psychology is that an individual's personal sense of meaning is the major determinant of mentation and action (e.g., Binswanger, 1963; Boss, 1963; Frankl, 1963). This emphasis has led to a vibrant conceptual and research effort to investigate the biological, cultural, social, familial, and developmental stage sources of personal meaning (e.g., DePaola & Ebersole, 1995; Fabry, 1990; Fry, 1992; Heidrich & Ryff, 1993; Horley, Carroll, & Little, 1988; Parks, Klinger, & Perlmutter, 1988–1989; Reker & Wong, 1988; Ryff & Keyes, 1995; Wong, 1995). Another cardinal assumption of existential psychology is that personal meaning derives from the individual decisions people make every day (Kierkegaard, 1954; Maddi, 1970; May, 1967). One role of this decision-making assumption is to identify the mechanism whereby cultural, social, and familial norms come to influence personal meaning (e.g., Baumeister, Reis, & Delespaul, 1995; Ryff & Keyes, 1995). More important, however, is the implication that through daily decision making, individuals may actually transcend the limitations of norms, thereby achieving more individualistic or subjective meaning (e.g., Fabry, 1988; Frankl, 1963; Kierkegaard, 1954; Lukas, 1990; Maddi, 1970; May, 1967; Sartre, 1956). There is recent research and theory pointing in this direction (e.g., Fry, 1989, 1992; Klinger, 1994, 1995; Palys & Little, 1983; Ryff, 1989; Sheldon & Emmons, 1995; Tweed & Ryff, 1991).

It is one thing to say that daily decisions determine personal meaning, but it is quite another to conceptualize specifically how concrete, everyday thoughts, feelings, and actions actually lead to particular views of self and world. In this, it is especially difficult to understand how the decision-making process sometimes facilitates endorsement of cultural and social norms yet other times leads to their transcendence. To fully understand the pivotal meaning-creating role of decision making requires grounding this process in a complete theory of personality (Maddi, 1997). This chapter attempts to do that by discussing an existential formulation on the core of personality (or what people are all born with), the periphery of personality (or the lifestyle people learn), and the developmental process (how social interaction leads people to differentiate from their shared core into various lifestyles). In the course of this discussion, especially important topics—such as courage or hardiness, existential psychopathology, and the tension between infinite possibility and concrete limitation—are explained in terms of their relevance to finding meaning through decision making.

Before plunging into an existential theory of personality, it would be well to reflect on the decision-making process. Sometimes decisions are made in the mind alone, through rumination and the play of imagination, with actions either being absent or only following later. Thus, people may decide mentally that they no longer love their spouses, but they stay with them anyway, trying all the while to continue acting in a loving way. Other times, decisions are made more impulsively in action with little or no mental consideration, though such consideration can follow after the fact of action. For example, a person may accept a new job in another location as soon as it is offered, without really thinking through all the social, familial, economic, and ecological implications of having done so. Still other times, decisions involve from the very beginning an interplay between mentation and action. In this interplay, you reach a tentative conclusion in your mind, try it out in action, use the feedback to think further, try out the result, and so forth. Also, decisions can be large or small. In a real sense, everything people do in life results from a decision. But it is one thing for individuals to decide not to go to a party because they are too tired, and quite another for them to sell their home. The larger the decision, the greater the impact on personal meaning. But the accumulation of small decisions has a definite role in personal meaning as well. When all is said and done, the major importance existentially is whether the decision (be it mental or behavioral, large or small) points the individuals toward new experience or keeps them in familiar territory (Kierkegaard, 1954; Maddi, 1970; May, 1967).

The Existential Core of Personality

In considering decision making in the context of existential personality theory, the first step is to explicate core assumptions, or views concerning directions and characteristics inherent in human beings. Understanding its core assumptions is necessary if a theory of personality is to be fully coherent (Maddi, 1997). The core assumptions of existential personality theory are that the inherent needs of people are biological, social, and psychological (Fabry, 1990; Fry, 1992; Maddi, 1970). At the biological level are the survival needs for nutrients and safety. At the social level are needs for contact and communication with others. In and of themselves, these biological and social needs do not distinguish humans from other animals. Nor are they unusual to assume. It is the psychological (or mental, cognitive) needs for symbolization, imagination, and judgment that set humans apart and are perhaps a bit more unusual to assume (Maddi, 1970).

Symbolization is the mental act of going beyond the specific characteristics of experiences by categorizing and interpreting them. Imagination is the mental act of combining and recombining categories of experience in a manner that goes beyond the literal ways in which they occur in the external world. Judgment is the mental act of taking an evaluative stance (either ethical or preferential) with regard to literal or imagined experience. That symbolization, imagination, and judgment are inherent psychological needs in humans is assumed on the basis of ubiquity—all cultures include a language (words are collective categories, after all), a mythology (the collective expression of imagination), and a value system (the fruit of collective judgments). Apparently, the human nervous system, which evolved as a fantastic information-processing unit, cannot lie fallow. It requires information to process, as has been shown in the sensory deprivation experiments popular some years ago, and the continuing demonstrations that mental functions need to be stimulated and used in order to develop well and maintain their vitality.

The Inherent Decision-Making Process

Think of the implications of the inherent human tendency to symbolize, imagine, and judge. Humans are not very likely to take stimulus experience at face value. Instead, they will be constantly sorting or interpreting it, resorting and reconsidering it, and determining what they think of all that. If they were only characterized by biological and social needs, then humans would be far likelier to accept the demand characteristics of the external world and their own organisms without reflection or question. They would be an undiscerning part of the world in which they exist. But once the psychological needs are added in, humans are capable of construing their interactions with the social, cultural, and physical world as their own, doing as much, if not more, than the passive, inevitable result of pressures on them. In short, they will recognize that as they go through the days, they are constantly making decisions that affect their lives. It is the content and direction of the decisions that give human lives their special meaning.

Properly understood, the many decisions constituting a life have an invariant form, though they differ widely in content. As to directionality, the decision can project individuals into the future, or secure them in the past (Kierkegaard, 1954; Maddi, 1988; May, 1967). Deciding in a way that secures the past involves humans in using symbolization, imagination, and judgment to construe the ongoing experience as similar to earlier experiences and to find no justification for doing anything other than what was done before. In contrast, deciding in a way that projects one into the future involves humans in using symbolization, imagination, and judgment to construe the ongoing experience as either different or similar to earlier experiences but, in any event, as warranting a course of action that is different from what was done before. Thus, a person may choose the future by either construing the experience as new or as requiring a new response, or both.

The human value of choosing the future is that doing so contributes much more information to be processed than does choosing the past. Choosing the future is an inherently stimulating process because it provokes new observations, insights, and ruminations within oneself and brings new reactions and feedback from others and the physical world. Regularly choosing the past produces an information-starved central nervous system and mind, where everything seems increasingly the same, and cognitive acuity declines. Desperately attempting to overcome this malaise is a reason why some people who regularly choose the past end up continually criticizing and complaining, though they would never risk doing anything to solve the problems they identify. In contrast, regularly choosing the future maintains vitality of physical and mental functioning through a continual flow of new experience. There is ongoing involvement in one's unfolding, developing life. There is also a trend toward transcendence of the herd mentality inherent in the most simplistic, static, and unchanging aspects of cultural values and social norms.

The Inherent Individuality of Living

Another outcome of regularly choosing the future is an increasingly individuated lifestyle.

This lifestyle develops because the resulting continual flow of new experience provides information to be assimilated in a symbolization, imagination, and judgment process that spurs personal development. After all, the end result of vigorous cognitive functioning is a variety of ways of construing an individual's interaction with the world. Specifically, vigorous exercise of symbolization continually increases the number of categories available to apply to experience, of imagination provides a stream of new ideas about what can be done, and of judgment brings many values and preferences into play (Maddi, 1970, 1996). Consequently, as time passes, each person will become more thoughtful, complex, and individualistic through a process of psychological growth.

This process of increasing individuation does not imply scattered formlessness. Indeed, the opposite is true (Maddi, 1988). That decisions are made for the future and involve specific content indicates directionality of thought and behavior. As decisions accumulate, an underlying direction—or what Sartre (1956) called a *fundamental project*—emerges that is more compelling as time goes on. Before long, a hierarchy of goals is developed, with the more concrete and easily achievable ones being instrumental to those that are more abstract, long range, and difficult to realize. But these goals are such that the person is continually in the process of patterned, directional change (Sheldon & Emmons, 1995). As one goal is achieved, the next that is instrumental to the fundamental project becomes salient, and so on. Thus, existential individuation binds together a person's past, present, and future in an ongoing directional process.

Nor does this increasing individuation imply irresponsibility. On the contrary, it is functioning at the level of biological and social needs, without benefit of the psychological needs, that courts irresponsibility. When biological needs operate with minimal psychological input, anything that leads to and constitutes nutrients and safety is pursued, and nothing else is taken into account. Subtlety, taste, and decorum in the search for nutrients and safety are contributed by the individual's psychological needs (Maddi, 1970). When social needs operate with minimal psychological input, anything that leads to and constitutes simple contact and communication is pursued, and nothing beyond that is desired. Transcending contractual relationships into intimate ones requires the contribution made by psychological needs (Fabry, 1990; Fry, 1992; Maddi, 1970; Ryff, Lee, Essex, & Schmutte, 1994). Because they are more committed, intense, and renewing, intimate relationships are more likely to last than are contractual ones (Maddi, 1970). In all these ways, the infusion of biological and social need gratification with psychological need gratification leads toward an individualism that is relationship and culture building rather than irresponsible.

Existential Views on Development and the Periphery of Personality

Although the core assumptions of a personality theory are crucial in disclosing what the position is about, they are too abstract and removed from the specifics of everyday life to permit much application and testing. To engage in empirical evaluation or clinical application of hypotheses requires working with the developmental and peripheral assumptions of a personality theory. In contrast to the inherent, unlearned status of human characteristics referred to in core assumptions, peripheral assumptions concern the lifestyle characteristics learned through developmental processes (Maddi, 1996). It is now time to turn to the developmental and lifestyle aspects of existential psychology.

The continual change associated with existential individuation is hardly an emotionally benign process. Indeed, contemplating or making a decision for the future brings inherent, or ontological, anxiety because of the unpredictability of the uncharted terrain being entered (Kierkegaard, 1954; Maddi, 1970; May, 1950; Tillich, 1952). Perhaps the new experience gained through a future-oriented choice will be disruptive, not nearly as satisfying as expected, or even a failure. Why should one continually push toward such uncertainties? The answer is because the alternative is even worse. Contemplating or making a decision for the past brings with it inherent, or ontological, guilt over the sacrifice of possibility. Only occasionally choosing the past may lead to little more than the rankling thought of what might have been. But ontological guilt accumulates. So regularly choosing the past leads first to stagnation and boredom, subsequently to a sense that one has missed out on a vigorous life, and finally to the conviction that existence is meaningless. In short, choosing the past regularly is a hard way to grow old.

Minimizing choices of the past is all the more important because even in choosing the future individuals cannot pursue all available possibilities. Perhaps in youth someone was drawn to careers in both medicine and architecture. Legitimately choosing the future at all decision points, this person might inevitably have pursued one career and, sadly, left the other aside. Any time possibility is lost, people feel ontological guilt. Therefore, to avoid the sinister syndrome of stagnation, self-recrimination, and meaninglessness resulting from an accumulation of ontological guilt, people must at least avoid choosing the past.

Courage or Hardiness

By regularly choosing the future, is a person damned to a life of overwhelming anxiety? Not necessarily. First, ontological anxiety does not accumulate, except in the unlikely case of choice after choice of the future backfiring in the form of multiple setbacks. Usually, the anxiety associated with each choice of the future recedes when the resulting experience is fulfilling, or at least manageable. And the new information gained through the future-oriented choice has a salutary, enlivening effect despite the concomitant anxiety.

More important, there is a way for persons to minimize ontological anxiety without turning away from future-oriented choices. They need to develop existential courage (Tillich, 1952). As a secular alternative to the earlier theological notion of faith (Kierkegaard, 1954), courage emphasizes self-confidence and self-reliance at times of peril. The more recent concept of hardiness (Kobasa, 1979; Maddi & Kobasa, 1984) constitutes a sufficient concretization of the concept of courage to have led to relevant research in support of this existential formulation (Funk, 1992; Maddi, 1990, 2002; Ouellette, 1993). Now there is a reliable and valid way to measure hardiness (Maddi, 1997, 2002; Maddi & Khoshaba, 2001).

Hardiness emphasizes the three interrelated beliefs about individuals interacting with the world of commitment, control, and challenge. People strong in the commitment component believe that by involving themselves actively in whatever is going on, they have the best chance of finding what is interesting and worthwhile to them. They experience the opposite—being or feeling uninvolved or alienated—as wasteful. People strong in the control component believe that through struggle they can usually influence the outcome of events going on around them. They experience the opposite—being or feeling powerless—as wasteful. People strong in the challenge component believe that what is ultimately most fulfilling is to continue to grow in wisdom through what they learn from experiences, whether these be positive or negative. They experience the opposite—the wish for easy comfort and security—as overly entitled. Conceptualized as positively interrelated, these three Cs (of commitment, control, and challenge) combine additively to yield a hardiness disposition especially helpful in minimizing and tolerating the ontological anxiety of choosing the future.

Hardiness is conceived of as learned in early life, that is, childhood and perhaps some of adolescence. Parent–child interactions are the natural context for learning hardiness (Khoshaba & Maddi, 1999; Maddi, 1997). The child brings to these interactions a pattern of inherent needs and capabilities (core of personality), as do the parents. But the parents have lived long enough to have developed views of themselves, the world, and childrearing (periphery of personality), and these views also influence the parent–child interactions.

In order to build the *commitment* component of hardiness, the majority of the parent–child interactions must help the youngster to feel accepted and encouraged (Kobasa & Maddi, 1977). Children will attempt to satisfy their needs (e.g., for safety and love) and express their potentialities (e.g., mathematical or artistic ability) in many ways (Khoshaba & Maddi, 1999). When parents usually meet efforts with approval and encouragement, the child feels supported enough to view self and world as interesting and worthwhile, and this view is the cornerstone of commitment (Fry & Lupart, 1987). But if parents are regularly hostile, disapproving, or neglectful toward the youngster's expressions, then what is developed is a view of self and world as empty and worthless, which leads to alienation (Emmons, 1995).

In the development of the *control* component of hardiness, it is important to recognize that as youngsters grow, their maturing physical and mental capabilities lead them to try to accomplish many things. In this developmental process, it is best for youngsters when the tasks they encounter are just a bit more difficult than what they can easily perform (Khoshaba & Maddi, 1999; Kobasa & Maddi, 1977). If the task is too easy, then succeeding at it will bring no sense of accomplishment or mastery. Conversely, if the task is too hard, the child is likely to fail and feel powerless. What builds a sense of control is for the youngster's interactions with the world to be characterized by tasks that can be mastered regularly through effort. In order to ensure this, it behooves parents to arrange the child's tasks so that they are always just a bit more difficult than can easily be accomplished.

To build a sense of *challenge*, that third component of hardiness, the child's environment must include frequent changes construed as richness rather than chaos (Khoshaba & Maddi, 1999; Kobasa & Maddi, 1977; Maddi, 1988). In the construal of richness, it helps if the changes are small (e.g., varying tasks around the home, contact with lots of people who talk and act in differing ways) rather than large (e.g., many changes in residence, divorces and remarriages) and if the parents experience changes in their own lives as interesting rather than threatening and convey this sense to the child. If youngsters are regularly encouraged to see changes as interesting possibilities, they will develop a sense of challenge. If, however, children are explicitly or implicitly taught that changes are dire, disruptive losses, then they will develop a sense of threat instead.

By now, there is considerable research showing that hardiness facilitates turning stressful circumstances from potential disasters into growth opportunities. These studies show that hardiness enhances performance, positive emotions, and health despite stresses in working adults and college students (e.g., Maddi, 2002, 2004; Maddi, Harvey, et al., 2006; Maddi, Harvey, Resurreccion, Giatras, & Raganold, 2007; Maddi, Kahn, & Maddi, 1998; Maddi & Khoshaba, 2002). Also, hardiness has emerged in research as a more effective influence on performance and health than is optimism or religiosity (Maddi & Hightower, 1999; Maddi, Brow, Khoshaba, & Vaitkus, 2006).

Managing Ontological Anxiety Through Hardiness

As indicated earlier, making future-oriented decisions brings with it ontological anxiety. The anxiety results from the newness and unpredictablity of the changed circumstances brought about by the decision for the future. Such changed circumstances are legitimately called stressful and elicit the same organismic response as happens with life changes imposed on (rather than chosen by) the person. This pattern of events and reactions is shown in Figure 3.1.

Specifically, the changes produced by future-oriented decisions are unpredictable or disruptive. Appraised as stressful, these changes fuel the mobilization of the fight-or-flight syndrome, the organismic part of which involves

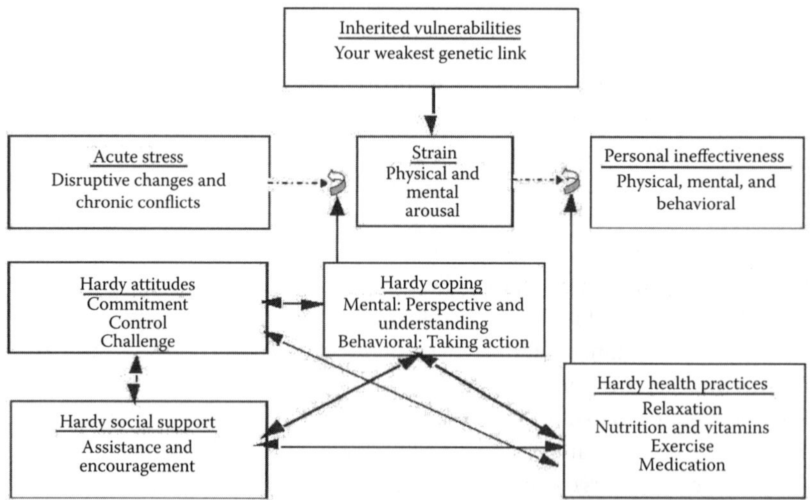

Figure 3.1 The hardiness model. (Copyright © 1993 by the Hardiness Institute, Inc. Reprinted with permission.)

extensive endocrine, nervous, and immune system response, and the mental part of which involves anxiety. As proven by accumulated research (e.g., Selye, 1976), if the mobilization syndrome is too intense and too continual, then the person's risk of wellness breakdown increases.

Wellness breakdown (Maddi, 1994, 1998, 2002) can involve the stress-related, degenerative illnesses (e.g., heart disease, cancer, stroke), characteristic mental illnesses (e.g., phobias, major depression), and performance deteriorations (e.g., inability to concentrate, forgetfulness, self-preoccupation). So people trying to regularly choose the future for existential or developmental reasons had best be strong enough to weather the storm of resulting stressful circumstances, lest they damage themselves in the process.

As shown in Figure 3.1, hardiness is really the key in the system that moderates the effects of stressful circumstances and preserves health. That system can diminish the stress-and-strain effects on the likelihood of wellness breakdown in two ways. One way is through beneficial health practices, which can decrease strain (the fight-or-flight reaction) once it has been provoked by stressors (Maddi, 2002; Maddi & Kobasa, 1984). In this regard, aerobic physical activity; a diet low in fat, sugar, salt, and cholesterol; such relaxation exercises as abdominal breathing; and even prescription medications mimicking the effects of these other health practices can decrease subjective tension and regulate mood and electrochemical balances (Khoshaba & Maddi, 2001). The other way of decreasing the likelihood of wellness breakdown is by coping with disruptive changes and chronic conflicts in a way that decreases their stressfulness. This decrease in the stressfulness of circumstances results in a lessening of the strain reaction, which, in turn, lowers the likelihood of breakdown. To achieve these desired effects, this transformational coping process must include a characteristic mental and action orientation (Maddi, 1987, 1990; Maddi & Khoshaba, 2001). The mental orientation involves achieving a broadened perspective and a deepened understanding of the stressful circumstance so that it does not seem so terrible after all and what can be done to resolve it is sensed. The action orientation involves carrying out a plan that can decisively incorporate the stressful circumstance into an overarching life plan.

The other two components of Figure 3.1 are motivational in nature. For most people, it is difficult to engage on a continuing basis in sound health practices and transformational coping because doing so requires time, effort, persistence, discernment, and acceptance of personal responsibility for the viability of one's life. It is hardiness—that mix of commitment, control, and challenge beliefs—that provides the motivation for regular engagement in transformational coping and sound health practices. Furthermore, hardiness leads to interaction with people by giving and getting assistance and encouragement, those two aspects of social support that also motivate transformational coping and sound health practices.

As shown by the two-sided arrows in Figure 3.1, the stress-resistance factors form a system in protecting persons from overwhelming anxiety and wellness breakdown. Thus, engaging in sound health practices and/or transformational coping can increase hardiness, as can receiving the social support of assistance and encouragement from others. But it is hardiness that motivates people to engage in an existentially effective manner in coping, health practices, and supportive social interaction.

Individualism and Conformism

As implied earlier, the level of hardiness learned in early life is crucial in the development of a person's lifestyle, or periphery of personality (Maddi, 1996). In existential psychology, early development (Khoshaba & Maddi, 1999; Kobasa & Maddi, 1977) takes place when the child is young enough to be relatively unformed by experience and is therefore more strongly influenced by significant others (such as parents) than will ever be true again. If hardiness is learned at this early stage, then a more personally initiated period of later development begins that continues throughout the life span.

The first stage of this later development is *aestheticism*, or *hedonism* (Kobasa & Maddi, 1977), which has emerged through factor-analytic research as an identifiable lifestyle associated with youth (Horley et al., 1988). For the first time, youngsters feel free of parental pressures and rush to explore their freedom. The youngster lives in the moment, making no commitments and accepting none from others. There is little concern for consequences, and responsibilities are minimized. However exhilarating this freedom may be, certain characteristic failure experiences also accumulate. Because no commitments are made or accepted, youngsters often end up feeling alone. Because only the moment is considered, there is little organization of experience into coherent directions. Having the strength of hardiness, youngsters can finally recognize this as insufficient, a failure experience, and learn from it. This learning culminates in the disconfirmation of aestheticism as a way of life.

At this point, the *idealistic* phase of development begins (Kobasa & Maddi, 1977). It is characterized by a perfectionistic insistence that things be completely good or completely bad and that good things last forever. If idealists love, they insist that it be perfect in its manifestations, and this includes professing that it will not end. They require that admired figures, whether politicians or mentors, be completely admirable. Because no one and nothing is perfect, the idealist is inevitably frustrated and disappointed. Having the strength of hardiness, however, leads to recognition of these failed experiences and learning from them. This learning leads to the disconfirmation of idealism as a way of life.

What then emerges is the existential lifestyle ideal of *authenticity* (May, Angel, & Ellenberger, 1958) or *individualism* (Maddi, 1970, 1996), an orientation that continues to deepen throughout the remainder of the life span. Factor-analytic research has identified this "Promethean" lifestyle in mature adults (Horley et al., 1988). The following characteristics are indicative of individualism:

Self-definition: Having a mental life that permits comprehension of and influence over social and biological experiences
Worldview: Believing that society is the creation of its citizens and properly in their service
Functioning: Showing directional change, innovativeness, and continuity over time
Coping: Transforming changes into opportunities by seeking broader perspective and deeper understanding, as well as taking decisive actions
Biological and social experiencing: Showing subtlety, taste, intimacy, and love
Ontological anxiety (or doubt): Experiencing such feelings, though frequent, as a natural concomitant of creating one's own meaning and without undermining the decision-making process
Ontological guilt (or sense of missed opportunity): Having such feelings at a minimum
Failure experiences: Accepting failures as natural and viewing them as opportunities for learning
Experiential evaluation: Emphasizing that an experience is positive if it fits into one's life pattern rather than if it can be expected to last forever

Consider now youngsters who do not develop hardiness in early life. They are best conceived of as never transcending this period of dependency into more self-determined development. Because they are not good at recognizing and learning from failures, they do not enter into or emerge from stages of aestheticism or idealism. And they certainly do not achieve authenticity, or individualism. Instead, they never stop being strongly influenced by the significant others around them, finding little of themselves to work with. They are aptly labeled conformists (Maddi, 1970) and show the following characteristics:

Self-definition: Seeing themselves as nothing more than players of social roles and embodiments of biological needs
Worldview: Perceiving society and biological needs as givens, and therefore universals, thereby leading to materialistic and pragmatic values
Coping: Dealing with changes regressively, involving denial, externalization of blame, and avoidance by such means as distraction, or by fighting back

Biological experiencing: Having fragmented and undifferentiated relationships
Social experiencing: Remaining contractual rather than intimate
Ontological guilt: Having high guilt, expressed in feelings of worthlessness and insecurity, and the vague sense that there must be something more to life
Failure experiences: Considering failures terrible and to be avoided at any cost, making it unlikely that anything can be learned from them
Experiential evaluation: Emphasizing experiences as worthwhile only if they are predictable and can be expected to last forever

Existential Stressors

Individualists and conformists differ sharply in their ability to tolerate stressful circumstances. Indeed, as indicated already, individualists actually encourage stressful changes through choosing the future regularly. But they avoid being debilitated by these self-induced changes through their hardiness (or courage), and its motivation of transformational coping, sound health practices, and activistic social support. In contrast, conformists seldom encounter self-induced changes because they regularly choose the past.

But both individualists and conformists are likely to experience stressful circumstances that are not so much self-induced as imposed by external circumstances. Once again, individualists are likely to weather these externally imposed stressors well, because of their hardiness, transformational coping, and activistic social support. Because conformists are low in hardiness, which results in regressive coping and contractual social relationships, unlike individuals they are especially vulnerable to wellness breakdown in the face of externally imposed stressors.

The major categories of stresses to which conformists are vulnerable are social upheaval, threat of death, and imposed recognition of lifestyle superficiality (Maddi, 1967). Social upheavals can include the trickle-down effects of such things as economic recession, wartime disruption, and the transition from an industrial to an information society. Such social changes are especially stressful to conformists, who have been treating currently constituted society as absolute reality, which implies that it will never change. They have also been treating their biological organism as an absolute reality, almost as if they implicitly believe they will live forever. Thus, the threat of death to themselves or someone closely related is a major stressor.

The recognition of superficiality in their living is, of course, something conformists strenuously avoid. They do not admit failures and bend every effort to avoid stressful problems. They insist that their lives are fine, covering up their feelings of insecurity and worthlessness. So, recognition of the superficiality in their lifestyle will not happen unless it is forced on them by circumstances. A typical circumstance involves spouses, partners, or family members who are suffering sufficiently from the conformists' superficiality to confront them and force the issue. Another circumstance emerges when conformists fail simultaneously in so many arenas of life that there is little or no way to deny or distract themselves from the flood of adverse information.

Existential Sickness

Whereas individualists have hardiness-based resources sufficient to weather the storm of major existential stressors, conformists do not have these resources. Experiencing major existential stressors, conformists are at risk of wellness breakdown in the form of physical illnesses, mental illnesses, or performance and conduct deterioration. What particular form the wellness breakdown takes may involve other factors besides personality (e.g., genetic vulnerabilities, immune system functioning). But existential psychology highlights disorders involving meaninglessness as one likely breakdown product of conformism under stress (Maddi, 1967).

The most severe existential sickness is *vegetativeness* (Maddi, 1967). At the cognitive level, individuals suffering from vegetativeness cannot find anything they are doing or can imagine doing that seems interesting or worthwhile. At the emotional level, vegetativeness involves a continuing state of apathy and boredom, punctuated by periods of depression that become less frequent as the disorder is prolonged. And at the action level, vegetative people show a low level of activity that feels and appears aimless, without any direction. This vegetative pattern has been identified through research and psychotherapy practice concerning personal meaning, where it is usually called depression (Farran, Herth, & Popovich, 1995; Fry, 1989, 1993).

Nihilism is a less severe form of existential sickness because there remains some semblance of meaningfulness in the person's life (Maddi, 1967). But it is paradoxical or antimeaning. At the cognitive level, the nihilist can find meaning only by disconfirming anything that purports to have positive meaning. At the emotional level, nihilism characteristically involves anger, disgust, and cynicism. At the action level, the nihilistic person is competitive and combative, rather than having any self-determined direction (Heidrich & Ryff, 1993).

The least severe form of existential sickness is adventurousness (Maddi, 1967, 1970), in which some basis for positive meaning remains, but only through extreme, risky activities. At the cognitive level, everyday life seems empty, with vitality and importance reserved only for extreme, uncommon experiences. At the emotional level, adventurers are apathetic and bored in ordinary life, feeling excited, afraid, and alive when taking risks. At the action level, people suffering from adventurousness oscillate between lackluster behavior and heroic intensities (Horley et al., 1988).

The Paradox of Limitations on Possibility

Choosing the future as much as possible implies that everything is in the realm of possibility. Each step toward the future brings new experiences that can change the way people think, feel, and act. In this fashion, individuals can engage in a continual process of self-renewal. Exhilarating though this may be to contemplate, it clearly is not completely so. Some things are not possible, at least not now (Maddi, 1988). For example, the physical limitation of anatomy and physiology does not permit childbirth for males. Someone whose legs have been amputated is not going to be a sprinter. It would not be wise to go swimming at the beach in a bathing suit during a North Pole winter. In the social realm, although laws may certainly be broken, doing so is likely to bring punishment. And even some social norms (which have not the status of laws), such as being polite to strangers, may be insistent enough to affect behavior universally. Furthermore, in the more strictly personal realm, some people may have developed in such a way as to value and require only honorable actions. For other people, honor may be unimportant by comparison with making money, with the latter requirement being unshakable. At any given point in time, everyone is a blend of both what is changeable and what is unchangeable in them.

Personality as a Blend of Facticity and Possibility

In a life, that which cannot be changed, at least at present, is its facticity (Sartre, 1956). Existentialists see personality as a blend of facticity and possibility (Kierkegaard, 1954). One source of facticity for persons is what seems unchangeable in their biology (e.g., height, sex), ecology (e.g, climate, geography), and social system (e.g., laws, norms). Even more important than this as a source of facticity is the person's own decision-making process. Whenever people choose the past, they give to their current ways of being (experiencing and understanding) the status of givens in the sense that they implicitly or explicitly regard them as unshakeable truths or at least necessary conditions. Even when one chooses the future, that may have the side effect of contributing to facticity. Imagine making the future-oriented decisions that lead toward a particular career—say, to becoming a psychologist. Though future oriented in the sense of involving new experiences, these decisions may well preclude other possible careers, such as being a lawyer or an architect. As time goes on and the psychology career decisions accumulate into a definite direction, with its commitments and requirements, the other possible careers cease to be possibilities for all intents and purposes. These no-longer-viable career options then become part of one's facticity. Despite wondering whether these careers would have been better, one is no longer in a position to try them.

It is the nature of facticity to haunt individuals in the form of ontological guilt. When people second-guess their lives, wondering what might have been, this bittersweet process expresses their implicit or explicit recognition that through a decision-making pattern, they excluded (rendered as facticity) certain life paths that were originally possibilities. Therefore, the best stance to take in living is to make efforts to maximize possibility and minimize facticity by choosing the future regularly (Maddi, 1988). Indeed, that which appears as a given today may be more amenable to change tomorrow. Laws, norms, convictions, and even physical and environmental limitations may change through human effort or be changed through natural evolution. Space travel, the information superhighway, a democratic form of government, and even sex changes, though barely imagined in the recent past, are now possibilities. They are the result of choosing the future in a process rich with symbolization, imagination, and judgment.

Compensatory Effort

But pushing to maximize possibility by choosing the future does not mean that facticity can be shrunken to nonexistence. In even the most ideal life of individualism, there will be some facticity at any particular point in time. Individuals will not always be able to do what they want when they want to. Indeed, the natural aging process often brings with it increased physical, mental, and social facticity. In the physical realm, powers decline with age, as strength, endurance, vitality, and visual acuity diminish. Mentally, the aging process often brings memory, concentration, and flexibility problems that appear to be physiologically based. Even socially, the death of loved ones, career retirement, and diminished income can increase facticity.

Developmentally speaking, the major problem with facticity is that it may lead to bitterness toward a seemingly recalcitrant world or self-pity as a poor victim. Bitterness and self-pity, if strong and prolonged, can undermine hardiness (Maddi, 1987, 1988). In turn, undermined hardiness robs persons of the vigor and motivation for choosing the future. If this failing of motivation increases the tendency to choose the past, this will only build even greater facticity and ontological guilt. The resulting greater conformism increases vulnerability for various forms of wellness breakdown, including existential sickness. What can be done to avoid this potentially undermining effect of facticity?

The answer is the compensatory effort involved in pushing on to whatever areas of possibility remain, rather than ruing the loss of possibility that inheres in the facticity (Maddi, 1987, 1988). For example, when Sartre's habit of writing manuscripts longhand was disrupted by failing vision, he sought to remain productive and influential by granting more media interviews. Notice that he did not regress to complaining about old age or decide to retire from intellectual work. Rather, he found another productive route to further development through thoughts and their communication. As people age, it is wise for them to plan ahead for ways of compensating for physically, socially, and personally determined transitions or losses. At retirement age, and feeling the effects of physical decline, a patient who had been active in the accounting field designed compensatory effort that worked for him. Good at "fixing things" and interested in how people learn, he planned to give free workshops for children wherein he would show them how to repair their broken toys and equipment. Also relevant is the case of the elderly woman, feeling bereft at the death of her longtime husband, who volunteers at the local settlement house, rather than sitting home alone regretfully.

How can one distinguish facticity from possibility (Maddi, 1988)? Sometimes, as in the case of physical limitation or loss through death, there is little difficulty in determining what is a given. In other cases, however, it may be more difficult to be sure whether a situation really qualifies as a given. For example, in troubled marriages, one or both spouses may have concluded too easily that the problem is that the other cannot or will not change. This view may be a convenient fiction masking the real problem, which may include an unwillingness to confront and change one's own contribution to the problem, an unrealistic view of marriage as perfect union, and a failing of empathy for the other's unhappiness. What is needed in this case is not a misguided acceptance of facticity but vigorous symbolization, imagination, and judgment, the better to choose the future of marriage improvement. Only if and when vigorous, discerning efforts to improve the marriage have failed repeatedly does it make sense to conclude that the mismatch is facticity. And at that point, compensatory effort is called for, whether that leads to divorce or some other mutually acceptable alternative.

Existential Psychotherapy

The overall goal of existential psychotherapy is to facilitate in the client regular choices of the future through vigorous symbolization, imagination (Maddi, 1996). In other words, the therapy fosters the individuation lifestyle. Instrumental to this goal, the therapy needs to increase the client's recognition of the inevitability of choices in life, importance of choosing the future regularly, and role of hardiness (or courage) in mastering ontological anxiety. Further, the therapy must actually build hardiness in the client. The overall goal and instrumentalities mentioned are important in existential psychotherapy regardless of whether the client's presenting problem constitutes conformism alone or is the breakdown product of this nonideal lifestyle into existential sickness of the vegetative, nihilistic, or adventurous sort.

There are a few techniques that are specialized to existential psychotherapy for helping persons recognize the decisions that have led them where they are, take responsibility for those decisions, and engage in corrective, future-oriented decisions. Among them is *paradoxical intention* (Frankl, 1963), in which clients are encouraged to exaggerate their uncontrollable symptoms and in that manner bring them under volitional control. Also used is *dereflection* (Frankl, 1963), in which clients excessively preoccupied with their own painful emotions are encouraged to attend to external circumstances in order to focus outside themselves. When clients seem to believe they are incapable of changing, some existentialists (Binswanger, 1963) greet this view with the insistent question "why?" until the excuses are exhausted and personal responsibility for decision making is taken.

More generally, in attempting to deepen existential insights and related actions, existential psychotherapists rely on a combination of empathic listening and strategic interpretation (Maddi, 1996; Yalom, 1980). The psychotherapeutic stance is both present oriented and confrontational. In emphasizing the present, existential therapy does not ignore the way in which past experience influences people's perception and interpretation of the present. This does not mean, however, that what is happening now is seen as a mere reflection or repeating of some unresolved conflict from the past. Rather, the present is regarded as very real, and the client needs to take responsibility for the present situation rather than using the past as an excuse. This emphasis on the present in doing psychotherapy differentiates the existential approach from Freudian psychoanalysis. In being confrontational, existential psychotherapy aims to force clients to recognize and take responsibility for their ongoing decision-making pattern, and change it if necessary. Thus, the interpretations do not concern unresolved conflicts from the past so much as failures to choose the future when that could be done. This approach differentiates existential psychotherapy from Freudian psychoanalysis on the basis of the nature of interpretations and from a Rogerian client-centered approach on the basis of reliance on confrontations.

In recent years, a training technique for building hardiness has been introduced (Khoshaba & Maddi, 2001; Maddi, 1987, 1996), which can be used for individual clients or small groups (Maddi, 1987, 1996). The first step in this procedure teaches clients how to recognize the small and large, acute and chronic, stressful circumstances in their lives. The second step involves learning the mental skills of transformational coping. To do this, the client works on one current stressful circumstance at a time, with a technique called *situational reconstruction*, in order to construe and consider alternatives to what is actually taking place. Specifically, clients imagine scenarios in which the circumstance could be better and worse than it is and consider what they can do to encourage the better and discourage the worse. Then, reflecting on what they have done, clients try to put the stressful circumstance in a broader perspective and understand it more deeply. If they have difficulty progressing in this task, clients supplement their efforts with a second technique called *focusing* (Gendlin, 1962). Involving a way of turning inward by sensitizing oneself to bodily reactions, focusing is used to explore emotions aroused by the stressful circumstance that may not be fully appreciated by the client and therefore stand in the way of stress resolution. Emotional insights obtained in this way are used to facilitate the ongoing process of transformational coping.

If clients emerge from this mental coping process with broadened perspective and deepened understanding concerning the stressful circumstance, they are ready to take the third, or action, step of transformational coping. This step involves developing and carrying out an *action plan* aimed at transforming the stressful circumstance to advantage through future-oriented decisions.

There is a special case in which no amount of effort through situational reconstruction and focusing works in producing a viable action plan. In this case, the client is permitted to conclude that the stressful circumstance is facticity, and then the coping effort shifts toward *compensatory effort*. Accordingly, clients are encouraged to find another stressful problem to work on that is linked in their minds to the one that cannot be changed. They work on this compensatory problem with the same tools of situational reconstruction and focusing, hoping to arrive at the end point of broadened perspective, deepened understanding, and an action plan to be carried out.

By whichever route, the actions taken engender *feedback*. The sources of feedback are clients' own reactions to themselves as actors, the reactions to clients by observers, and the effects of the actions on the circumstance. The feedback from these sources is the major building block of the hardiness components of commitment, control, and challenge. Typically, clients find that the feedback received from decisive efforts to transform problems into opportunities incline them to feel more involved, influential, and insightful. The training procedure increases hardiness as the entire process described is repeated for the major stressful circumstances in clients' lives.

Recently added to the coping emphasis of hardiness training are techniques for enhancing socially supportive interactions and effective self-care (Khoshaba & Maddi, 2001). As to increasing social support, trainees are put through exercises that involve identifying conflicts with significant others, resolving these conflicts, and replacing them with a pattern of giving and getting assistance and encouragement (Khoshaba & Maddi, 2001). As to effective self-care, to facilitate coping efforts trainees go through exercises involving relaxation, eating, and exercise patterns that moderate arousal levels (Khoshaba & Maddi, 2001). Once again, trainees learn how to use the feedback from these experiences to enhance the hardiness attitudes of commitment, control, and challenge.

Carefully controlled research is accumulating that demonstrates the effectiveness of the hardiness training approach (now called *HardiTraining*) in enhancing the objectively measured performance and health of college students and working adults (Maddi, 1987; Maddi, Harvey, Khoshaba, Fazel, & Resurreccion, 2009; Maddi, Khoshaba, Jensen, Carter, Lu, & Harvey, 2002). Further, the hardiness assessment and training techniques summarized in the foregoing discussion are now available for trainees on the Internet. Specifically, regarding assessment, http://www.HardinessInstitute.com makes available the *HardiSurvey III-R*, a 65-item questionnaire that when completed yields a comprehensive report, with recommendations, concerning one's hardiness attitudes (which constitute the existential courage and motivation to do the hard work of turning stresses to advantage), and hardiness skills (problem-solving coping, socially supportive interactions, and effective self-care). In addition, regarding *HardiTraining*, http://www.HardiTraining.coursehost.com makes available the entire set of training exercises, along with informative case-study examples and self-evaluation procedures. Along with its overall emphasis on hardiness attitudes, this training can also be used to also emphasize hardy coping, hardy social support, and hardy self-care or some combination of these skills.

Suggestions About the Aims and Process of Psychotherapy

As indicated earlier, existential psychotherapy applies to a wide range of emotional and behavioral problems. The approach is particularly relevant, however, to emotional and behavioral expressions of anxiety or depression significant enough to be regarded as psychopathology.

It is, of course, the existential position that some anxiety is endemic to living and is not a reason for psychotherapy. But there is a problem when anxiety becomes so intense that living is grossly disrupted and choosing the future becomes intolerable. In this pattern, the anxious person is also playing it safe behaviorally. This motivation is certainly the case in phobias, obsessive-compulsive patterns, and levels of free-floating anxiety that jeopardize working, family relationships, ability to sleep, and the like. In pathological levels of anxiety, the underlying problem is likely to be insufficient hardiness (existential courage) to tolerate the uncertainty of choosing the future regularly. Here, the client has most likely not yet fallen into the morass of guilt and depression that grows as shrinking from the future solidifies into choosing the past pervasively.

Existential psychologists also believe that all people carry around some ontological guilt because even in a future-oriented life pattern, some paths originally possible were precluded by the paths actually taken. So, occasional bittersweet ruminations over what might have been do not indicate psychopathology and the need for psychotherapy. To the contrary, such ruminations can have a developmentally salutary effect through encouraging reconsideration of ongoing life patterns and decisions. When depression, meaninglessness, and hopelessness mount to the point where behavioral vigor and future-oriented decision making is jeopardized, however, psychotherapy is needed. Sometimes, this level of depression and malaise is indirectly expressed as what was previously called vegetativeness. As also indicated earlier, less severe, more disguised forms of the depression, called existential sickness, are nihilism (with its emphasis on antimeaning) and adventurousness (with its avoidance of boredom through excessive risk taking).

Vegetativeness, nihilism, and adventurousness are serious forms of existential sickness. They reflect a lifetime of choosing the past and the resulting pattern of conformity. But this pattern has been undermined by one or more traumatic events that have stripped the protective conformist coating from around this decision-making limitation. Adventurousness and nihilism express a desperate second line of defense against full recognition of the problem of having chosen the past too much, whereas in vegetativeness there is not even this defensiveness left.

A two-step process is recommended for clients with anxiety or depression pathology. The first step involves their gaining insight into the existential basis of their emotional and behavioral problems. This can usually be facilitated by the therapist through a combination of empathy for the client as a poignant expression of human suffering and strategic interpretations aimed at illuminating the decision-making process that has led to and perpetuates this suffering (Maddi, 1996). Therapists can feel successful in this effort when clients recognize that their lives and the meaning therein are of their own making and that the architect of the good life is future-oriented decision making.

Having achieved insight, clients then need the courage to actually live a life of their own making. This is the second psychotherapeutic step and involves hardiness training (Khoshaba & Maddi, 2001; Maddi, 1987). One way this training helps is by engendering skills of transformational coping that are useful whenever choosing the future leads to disruptive changes that must be turned to advantage in order to manage anxiety sufficiently to derive the benefit from new experiences. Also, clients learn to appraise themselves as approaching interaction with the world with a sense of commitment, control, and challenge. This helps them to avoid alienation, powerlessness, and threat. Finally, hardiness training encourages social interaction patterns of giving and getting assistance and encouragement, rather than overprotection and competition. These changes in coping, self-perception, and social interaction patterns will not only diminish anxiety and depression but also orient the client toward self-renewal.

There are definite signs indicating when the psychotherapeutic process is complete. One sign is that in place of debilitating anxiety or depression is emotional and behavioral vitality. Another sign is the substitution of future-oriented for past-oriented decision making. The capstone is when clients assume responsibility for their own lives despite all the outside pressures that can easily be blamed for what happens to them, accept that they are ultimately alone in their subjectivity despite wonderfully stimulating efforts at intimacy, and face that they will ultimately die despite the heroism involved in creating meaning by choosing the future (Maddi, 2002; Yalom, 1980).

Conclusions

Developing steadily, existential psychology now has extensive positions on personality, development, psychopathology, and psychotherapy. Needless to say, these positions all need to be further elaborated. By now, there is also increasing research on personal meaning; that is, on individual differences in it, its role in structuring life, and ways of changing it (e.g., Baumeister et al.,

1995; Debats, Drost, & Hansen, 1995; DePaola & Ebersole, 1995; Emmons, 1995; Fry, 1992; Korotkov & Hannah, 1994; Maddi, 2002; Midlarsky & Kahana, 1994; Nikula, Klinger, & Larson-Gutman, 1993; Palys & Little, 1983; Ryff & Keyes, 1995; Sheldon & Emmons, 1995; Wong, 1995). The results of such research are taking their place alongside recent insights gained through doing psychotherapy as the impetus for further development of the existential position (Fabry, 1982, 1988; Farran et al., 1995; Fry, 1992; Hermans, 1995; Ishiyama, 1995a, 1995b; Lukas, 1990, 1991; Maddi, 1987; Yalom, 1980). The coming years should be exciting ones in this area.

References

Baumeister, R. F., Reis, H. T., & Delespaul, P. G. (1995). Subjective and experiential correlates of guilt in daily life. *Personality and Social Psychology Bulletin, 21*, 1256–1268.

Binswanger, L. (1963). *Being-in-the-world: Selected papers of Ludwig Binswanger* (J Needleman, Trans.). New York, NY: Basic Books.

Boss, M. (1963). *Psychoanalysis and daseinanalysis* (L. B. Lafebre, Trans.). New York, NY: Basic Books.

Debats, D. L., Drost, J., & Hansen, P. (1995). Experiences of meaning in life: A combined qualitative and quantitative approach. *British Journal of Psychology, 86*, 359–375.

DePaola, S. J., & Ebersole, P. (1995). Meaning in life categories of elderly nursing home residents. *International Journal of Aging and Human Development, 40*, 227–236.

Emmons, R. A. (1995). Emotional conflict and well-being: Relation to perceived availability, daily utilization, and observer reports of social support. *Journal of Personality and Social Psychology, 68*, 947–959.

Fabry, J. (1982). Some practical hints about paradoxical intention. *International Forum for Logotherapy, 5*, 25–29.

Fabry, J. (1988). Dilemmas of today: Logotherapy proposals. *International Forum for Logotherapy, 11*, 5–12.

Fabry, J. (1990). The evolution of noos. *International Forum for Logotherapy, 13*, 67–70.

Farran, C. J., Herth, K. A., & Popovich, J. M. (1995). *Hope and hopelessness: Critical clinical constructs.* Thousand Oaks, CA: Sage.

Frankl, V. E. (1963). *Man's search for meaning: An introduction to logotherapy* (L. Lasch, Trans.). New York, NY: Washington Square Press.

Fry, P. S. (1989). Preconceptions of vulnerability and controls in old age: A critical reconstruction. In P. S. Fry (Ed.), *Psychological perspectives of helplessness and control in the elderly* (pp. 1–39). Amsterdam, The Netherlands: North-Holland, Advances in Psychology.

Fry, P. S. (1992). Major social theories of aging and their implications for counseling concepts and practice: A critical review. *Counseling Psychologist, 20*, 246–329.

Fry, P. S. (1993). Mediators of depression in community-based elders. In P. Cappeliez & R. J. Flynn (Eds.), *Depression and the social environment: Research and intervention with neglected populations* (pp. 369–394). Montreal, QC: McGill-Queen's University Press.

Fry, P. S., & Lupart, J. L. (1987). *Cognitive processes in children's learning: Practical applications in educational practice and classroom management.* Springfield, IL: Thomas.

Funk, S. C. (1992). Hardiness: A review of theory and research. *Health Psychology, 11*, 335–345.

Gendlin, E. T. (1962). *Experiencing and the creation of meaning.* New York, NY: Free Press.

Heidrich, S. M., & Ryff, C. D. (1993). The role of social comparison processes in the psychological adaptations of elderly adults. *Journal of Gerontology, 48*, 127–136.

Hermans, H. J. M. (1995). *The construction of meaning in psychotherapy*. New York, NY: Guilford Press.

Horley, J., Carroll, B., & Little, B. R. (1988). A typology of lifestyles. *Social Indicators Research, 20*, 383–398.

Ishiyama, F. I. (1995a). Culturally dislocated clients: Self-validation and cultural conflict issues and counseling implications. *Canadian Journal of Counseling, 29*, 262–275.

Ishiyama, F. I. (1995b). Use of validation in counseling: Exploring sources of self-validation on the impact of personal transition. *Canadian Journal of Counseling, 29*, 134–136.

Khoshaba, D. M., & Maddi, S. R. (1999). Early experiences in hardiness development. *Consulting Psychology Journal, 51*, 106–116.

Khoshaba, D. M., & Maddi, S. R. (2001). *HardiTraining*. Irvine, CA: Hardiness Institute.

Kierkegaard, S. (1954). *Fear and trembling and the sickness unto death*. Garden City, NY: Doubleday Anchor.

Klinger, E. (1994). On living tomorrow today: The quality of inner life as a function of goal expectations. In Z. Zaleski (Ed.), *Psychology of future orientation* (pp. 97–106). Lublin, Poland: Scientific Society of the Catholic University of Lublin.

Klinger, E. (1995). Effects of motivation and emotion on thought flow and cognition: Assessment and findings. In P. E. Shrout & S. T. Fiske (Eds.), *Personality research, methods and theory: A festschrift honoring Donald W. Fiske* (pp. 257–270). Hillsdale, NJ: Erlbaum.

Kobasa, S. C. (1979). Stressful life events, personality, and health: An inquiry into hardiness. *Journal of Personality and Social Psychology, 37*, 1–11.

Kobasa, S. C., & Maddi, S. R. (1977). Existential personality theory. In R. Corsini (Ed.), *Current personality theory* (pp. 243–275). Itasca, IL: Peacock.

Korotkov, D., & Hannah, T. E. (1994). Extraversion and emotionality as proposed superordinate stress moderators: A prospective analysis. *Personality and Individual Differences, 16*, 787–792.

Lukas, E. (1990). Overcoming the "tragic triad." *International Forum for Logotherapy, 13*, 89–96.

Lukas, E. (1991). Meaning-centered family therapy. *International Forum for Logotherapy, 14*, 67–74.

Maddi, S. R. (1967). The existential neurosis. *Journal of Abnormal Psychology, 72*, 311–325.

Maddi, S. R. (1970). The search for meaning. In M. Page (Ed.), *Nebraska symposium on motivation* (pp. 137–186). Lincoln: University of Nebraska Press.

Maddi, S. R. (1987). Hardiness training at Illinois Bell Telephone In J. Opatz (Ed.), *Health promotion evaluation* (pp. 101–115). Stephens Point, WI: National Wellness Institute.

Maddi, S. R. (1988). On the problem of accepting facticity and pursuing possibility. In S. B. Messer, L. A. Sass, & R. L. Woolfolk (Eds.), *Hermeneutics and psychological theory* (pp. 182–209). New Brunswick, NJ: Rutgers University Press.

Maddi, S. R. (1990). Issues and interventions in stress mastery. In H. S. Friedman (Ed.), *Personality and disease* (pp. 121–154). New York, NY: Wiley.

Maddi, S. R. (1994). The Hardiness Enhancing Lifestyle Program (HELP) for improving physical, mental, and social wellness. In C. Hopper (Ed.), *Wellness lecture series* (pp. 1–18). Oakland: University of California / HealthNet.

Maddi, S. R. (1996). Existential psychotherapy. In S. J. Lynn & J. P. Garske (Eds.), *Contemporary psychotherapies* (2nd. ed., pp. 191–219).Columbus, OH: Charles Merrill.

Maddi, S. R. (1997). *The Personal Views Survey II: A measure of dispositional hardiness.* Lanham, MD: Scarecrow Press.

Maddi, S. R. (1998). Hardiness in health and effectiveness. In H. S. Friedman (Ed.), *Encyclopedia of mental health* (pp. 1–13). San Diego, CA: Academic Press.

Maddi, S. R. (2002). The story of hardiness: Twenty years of theorizing, research, and practice. *Consulting Psychology Journal, 54,* 173–185.

Maddi, S. R. (2004). Hardiness: An operationalization of existential courage. *Journal of Humanistic Psychology, 44,* 279–298.

Maddi, S. R., Brow, M., Khoshaba, D. M., & Vaitkus, M. (2006). The relationship of hardiness and religiosity to depression and anger. *Consulting Psychology Journal, 58,* 148–161.

Maddi, S. R., Harvey, R. H., Khoshaba, D. M., Fazel, M., & Resurreccion, N. (2009). Hardiness training facilitates performance in college. *Journal of Positive Psychology, 4,* 566–577.

Maddi, S. R., Harvey, R. H., Khoshaba, D. M., Lu, J. L., Persico, M., & Brow, M. (2006). The personality construct of hardiness, III: Relationships with repression, innovativeness, authoritarianism, and performance. *Journal of Personality, 74,* 575–598.

Maddi, S. R., Harvey, R. H., Resurreccion, R, Giatras, C. D., & Raganold, S. (2007). Hardiness as a performance enhancer in firefighters. *International Journal of Fire Service Leadership and Management, 1,* 3–9.

Maddi, S. R., & Hightower, M. (1999). Hardiness and optimism as expressed in coping patterns. *Consulting Psychology Journal, 51,* 95–105.

Maddi, S. R., Kahn, S., & Maddi, K. L. (1998). The effectiveness of hardiness training. *Consulting Psychology Journal, 50,* 78–86.

Maddi, S. R., & Khoshaba, D. M. (2001). *HardiSurvey III-R: Test development and Internet instruction manual.* Irvine, CA: Hardiness Institute.

Maddi, S. R., & Khoshaba, D. M. (2002). Hardiness training for resiliency and leadership. In D. Paton, J. M. Violanti, & L. M. Smith (Eds.), *Posttraumatic psychological stress: Individual, group, and organizational strategies for resiliency* (pp. 43–58). Springfield, IL: Charles C. Thomas.

Maddi, S. R., Khoshaba, D. M., Jensen, K., Carter, E., Lu, J. L., & Harvey, R. H. (2002). Hardiness training for high-risk undergraduates. *NACADA Journal, 22,* 45–55.

Maddi, S. R., & Kobasa, S. C. (1984). *The hardy executive: Health under stress.* Homewood, IL: Dow Jones–Irwin.

May, R. (1950). *The meaning of anxiety.* New York, NY: Ronald.

May, R. (1967). *Love and will.* New York, NY: Norton.

May, R., Angel, E., & Ellenberger, H. F. (1958). *Existence: A new dimension in psychiatry and psychology.* New York, NY: Basic Books.

Midlarsky, E., & Kahana, E. (1994). *Altruism in later life.* Thousand Oaks, CA: Sage.

Nikula, R., Klinger, E., & Larson-Gutman, M. K. (1993). Current concerns and electrodermal reactivity: Responses to words and thoughts. *Journal of Personality, 61,* 63–84.

Ouellette, S. C. (1993). Inquiries into hardiness. In L. Goldberger & S. Bresnitz (Eds.), *Handbook of stress: Theoretical and clinical aspects* (2nd ed., pp. 77–100). New York, NY: Free Press.

Palys, T. S., & Little, B. R. (1983). Perceived life satisfaction and the organization of personal project systems. *Journal of Personality and Social Psychology, 44,* 1221–1230.

Parks, C. W., Klinger, E., & Perlmutter, M. (1988–1989). Dimensions of thought as a function of age, gender, and task difficulty. *Imagination, Cognition and Personality, 8,* 49–62.

Reker, G. T., & Wong, P. T. P. (1988). Aging as an individual process: Toward a theory of personal meaning. In T. E. Birren & V. L. Bengtson (Eds.), *Emergent theories of aging* (pp. 214–246). New York: Springer.
Ryff, C. D. (1989). In the eye of the beholder: Views of psychological wellbeing among middle-aged and older adults. *Psychology and Aging, 23*, 195–210.
Ryff, C. D., & Keyes, C. L. M. (1995). The structure of psychological wellbeing revisited. *Journal of Personality and Social Psychology, 69*, 719–727.
Ryff, C. D., Lee, Y. H., Essex, M. J., & Schmutte, P. S. (1994). My children and me: Midlife evaluations of grown children and of self. *Psychology and Aging, 9*, 195–205.
Sartre, J. P. (1956). *Being and nothingness* (H. Barnes, Trans.). New York, NY: Philosophical Library.
Selye, H. (1976). *The stress of life* (2nd ed.). New York, NY: McGraw-Hill.
Sheldon, K. M., & Emmons, R A. (1995). Comparing differentiation and integration within personal goal systems. *Personality and Individual Differences, 18*, 39–46.
Tillich, P. (1952). *The courage to be*. New Haven, CT: Yale University Press.
Tweed, S. H., & Ryff, C. D. (1991.). Adult children of alcoholics: Profiles of wellness amidst distress. *Journal of Studies on Alcohol, 52*, 133–141.
Wong, P. T. P. (1995). The processes of adaptive reminiscence. In B. K. Haight & J. D. Webster (Eds.), *The art and science of reminiscing: Theory, research, methods, and applications* (pp. 23–35). Philadelphia, PA: Taylor & Francis.
Yalom, I. D. (1980). *Existential pyschotherapy*. New York, NY: Basic Books.

4
Motivation, Meaning, and Wellness

A Self-Determination Perspective on the Creation and Internalization of Personal Meanings and Life Goals

NETTA WEINSTEIN

University of Essex

RICHARD M. RYAN and EDWARD L. DECI

University of Rochester

The challenge of pursuing, developing, and maintaining a sense of life's meaning is an undeniable part of human existence. Prominent scholars have suggested that struggling to find meaning in life is centrally important and may be inherent to all people (Binswanger, 1963; Boss, 1963; Frankl, 1978; Klinger, 1977; Reker, Peacock, & Wong, 1987). Frankl (1978) went as far as to propose that seeking meaning is the core motivation for human beings and is crucial not only for well-being but for survival. Such perspectives clearly emphasize that meaning is a central aspect of human development and a defining feature of personhood.

Given the rich literature on human meaning and the postulate of its central importance in living, in this chapter we reflect on this literature from the perspective of self-determination theory (SDT; Deci & Ryan, 2000; Ryan & Deci, 2000b). We believe there are several contributions to be made by investigating meaning through the lens of SDT.

The first concerns the process of *meaning making*. SDT potentially offers insights and hypotheses concerning the motivated processes of assimilation, integration, and symbolization, all processes that are centrally involved in meaning making.

The second issue concerns the social environment that can aid or impair the tendency to assimilate and integrate new meanings. SDT suggests specific social-contextual supports that conduce to a person deeply internalizing meanings, values, and practices, as well as other social-contextual factors that undermine the tendency toward internalization.

A third issue addresses the contents of the meanings or life purposes that people endorse as most important. Research based on SDT has revealed that certain life meanings or purposes are more easily integrated, and thus more likely to foster wellness, than are others. Stated differently, not all meanings or purposes in life, even when strongly personally valued, are likely to be associated with well-being. Moreover, SDT describes some of the social conditions that drive people to buy into compensatory meanings and life goals, to the neglect of others that might be more beneficial.

A fourth issue, although perhaps less often discussed in the meaning literature, concerns whether meaning is itself a basic human need, as has been suggested by some (e.g., Andersen, Chen, & Carter, 2000; Frankl, 1978), and if not, how it relates to those central needs that are posited within SDT as essential to psychological health and well-being. Because SDT has a very specific theory of what constitutes a need, it is interesting to consider how the concept of meaning relates to that conception of needs.

The Meaning of Meaning

Before turning to SDT and its theoretical account of meaning, it is important to take a moment to consider what the term *meaning* conveys. People typically have an intuitive sense that the term *meaning* (or "life meaning") refers to the degree to which individuals have a sense that they are living (or have lived) their lives in meaningful, fulfilling, and satisfying ways. Thus, as they reflect on their lives, they feel a sense that what they have done has been deeply satisfying and worthwhile. Indeed, this is how many writers have either explicitly or implicitly defined the term. Yet it is important to recognize that there is also another conceptual definition of meaning in the literature. Specifically, the concept has also been used to convey that people have a valued *life purpose*. When so used, the term *meaning* indicates that particular goals are important or meaningful to the person, goals that would likely, if achieved, allow the individual to feel that he or she has lived meaningfully. That is, having a purpose can be satisfying and can indeed give meaning to life. The distinction between these two conceptual definitions of meaning is important to keep in mind because different parts of the literature on meaning have tended to use one versus the other of these conceptualizations.

Self-Determination Theory: Motivation and Meaning

SDT (Deci & Ryan, 1985b; Ryan & Deci, 2000b) is an empirically grounded theory of human motivation and personality development. As an organismic theory in the tradition of Goldstein (1939), Rogers (1963), Loevinger (1976), and others, SDT was built upon a general assumption that human beings have a deep-rooted organismic tendency toward self-organization and psychological integration (see Ryan, 1995). Within SDT, integration is considered an inherent growth tendency that is manifest in the phenomena of both intrinsically motivated activities and the internalization and assimilation of ambient social values and practices. Furthermore, empirical findings concerning factors that facilitate or undermine motivation and wellness have led to the SDT proposition that humans share at least three *basic psychological needs*—the needs for competence, autonomy, and relatedness—that must be satisfied for the healthy functioning of these inherent growth and integrative tendencies.

Intrinsic Motivation

According to SDT, humans are liberally endowed with a propensity to actively engage, understand, and master both their inner and outer environments. White (1959) referred to the inherent motivational basis for mastery-oriented activity as *effectance motivation*, which is more commonly called *intrinsic motivation* (Deci, 1975; Harlow, 1950). The concept of intrinsic motivation applies to those activities that are inherently rewarding and thus not dependent on external incentives or pressures for their occurrence. Intrinsic motivation is apparent when people act simply because doing so yields spontaneous experiences of interest and enjoyment. Thus, intrinsic motivation is the chief propellant for play, exploration, and creative acts, as these are typically done because they are interesting or "fun." When intrinsically motivated, individuals willingly expose themselves to new environments, pursue optimal challenges, and develop new skills and knowledge. Because of this deeply evolved, spontaneous form of motivation, individuals are naturally set on a developmental course toward psychological growth.

The importance of postulating intrinsic motivation as an element in human nature is that it specifies one of the central organismic foundations for growth and, accordingly, the development of meaning. In contrast to theories that have argued that meaning and coherence are imputed to the person entirely by the contingencies of reinforcement in the environment (e.g., Skinner, 1953) or imprinted on the persons through cultural transmission (e.g., Markus & Kitayama, 1991), the postulate of intrinsic motivation implies an active element within individuals that energizes exploration, learning, and the making sense of one's surroundings. Studies have found, for example, that when intrinsically motivated, people engage in deeper learning, more creativity, and more persistent mastery attempts, (e.g., Collins & Amabile, 1999; Deci, Schwartz, Sheinman, & Ryan, 1981; Grolnick & Ryan, 1987; Koestner, Ryan, Bernieri, & Holt, 1984). Stated differently, intrinsic motivation plays a critical role in propelling the exploration of people's inner and outer worlds and thus, we suggest, in the processes through which they can create meaning.

Organismic Integration and the Self

Intrinsic motivation is, however, just one aspect of the human tendency toward development and self-organization (e.g., Piaget, 1971; Ryan, 1993, 1995). A second important focus of integration is the deeply evolved and natural human tendency to internalize ambient social mores, beliefs, and practices, and when possible to effectively synthesize these into the self (Rogoff, 2003; Ryan, 1995).

Successful internalization allows people to become more adaptive and integrated into the social world while at the same time experiencing greater coherence in their beliefs, values, and behaviors. Conversely, failures of internalization result in experiences of alienation, conflict, and/or maladaptation (see Ryan, Deci, Grolnick, & La Guardia, 2006). That is, the more individuals are able to effectively assimilate and synthesize social practices and values, the more they will be able to experience a sense of both autonomy and belonging in their interpersonal and cultural contexts (Ryan, 1995) or, as Angyal (1965) would have put it, to experience both autonomy (inner integration, or self-organization) and homonomy (integration into a larger world that transcends the self).

When Integration Is Incomplete: External Regulations and Introjected Meanings

Although there is a general tendency toward assimilation and integration, all too frequently ambient social practices and values to which a person is exposed are not well internalized or integrated. In fact, many social mores, behaviors, and values are imposed or forced on individuals, or in other cases simply "swallowed whole," but not well assimilated. When pressured and controlled, people may enact externally valued behaviors or express socially prescribed meanings simply to gain a sense of approval, avoid guilt or shame, or receive social rewards, all without ever truly accepting the values and behaviors as their own (Deci, Eghrari, Patrick, & Leone, 1994).

The idea that internalization varies in degree is illustrated in Figure 4.1, which displays the SDT model of internalization (see Ryan & Connell, 1989; Vallerand, 1997). On the far left of the figure a complete absence of internalization is apparent in *amotivation*, which applies whenever the person feels either no value for the behavior or no competence to enact it (e.g., feels helpless). To the right, a very impoverished level of internalization is represented as *external regulation*, which is in evidence when social values and practices are controlled by outside rewards and punishments. When externally regulated, people are likely only to act when prompted, rewarded, or controlled, and they

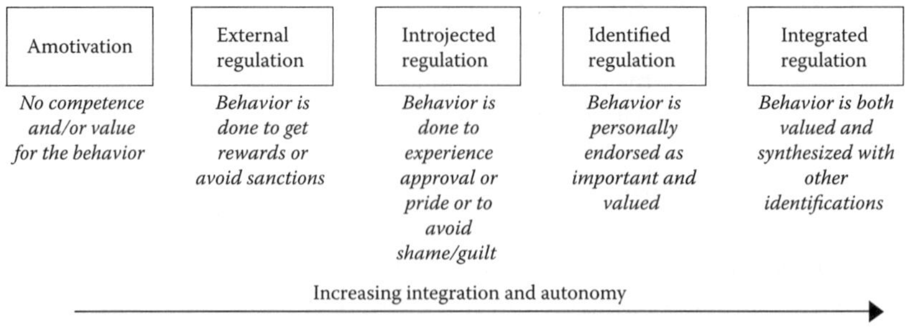

Figure 4.1 The internalization continuum: integration of extrinsic motives and cultural values.

do not "own" the behaviors or values they enact. Somewhat more internalization is evident in *introjected regulation*, which reflects an incomplete internalization of values and regulations. Introjection is typically manifest as an internal pressure to behave in particular ways or to attain certain standards or outcomes in order to maintain feelings of self-worth (Deci & Ryan, 1985b; Ryan & Brown, 2003; Ryan & Connell, 1989). Thus, when introjected, people act to avoid shame or guilt or, oppositely, to feel self-aggrandizement or pride.

When individuals act for external or introjected (i.e., controlled) reasons, the quality of the behaviors and feelings of well-being are inferior to when they have integrated the values and behaviors to a fuller degree. For example, studies have shown that students whose reasons for learning were external or introjected displayed poorer conceptual understanding of the material, had lower positive affect, were less likely to use proactive coping, did more poorly on exams, and reported greater anxiety about failing than did students whose motivation was more fully internalized (Black & Deci, 2000; Ryan & Connell, 1989). With respect to religious practices, Ryan, Rigby, and King (1993) found that churchgoers with introjected motivation for their religious behaviors experienced lower mental health, including greater anxiety, more somatic complaints, more symptoms of depression, and lower self-esteem, than did those individuals with more fully internalized motivation. More recently, a study of depressed clients in psychotherapy with poorly internalized motivation for participating in therapy showed poorer outcomes than did clients with more fully internalized motivation (Zuroff et al., 2007). Even behaviors as specific as New Year's resolutions are less likely to be maintained two months later if the motivation for the resolution was not well internalized (Greenstein & Koestner, 1996).

When regulations have been more fully internalized or integrated, actions emerge more from people's sense of self than from environmental or self-imposed pressures. In Figure 4.1 *identified regulations* represent the idea that people can act from goals and values that they have identified with and that they experience as reflective of the self. Identifications can be further internalized when they are integrated, or brought into coherence with the individual's other values and identified regulatory structures. *Integrated regulation* is, from a theoretical and empirical point of view, nearly as autonomous as intrinsic motivation because it is experienced as emanating from, and endorsed by, the self. In the broadest sense, this means that when the different aspects of personality and experience work harmoniously as a united whole, individuals experience a more profound sense of psychological health and well-being (Allport, 1937; Deci & Ryan, 1991), including greater vitality (Ryan & Frederick, 1997), self-actualization (Shostrom, 1964), and self-esteem (Seeman, 1983). Under these circumstances, we expect that people will experience a greater sense of meaning in their lives—that is, a greater sense that they are or have been living in a fulfilling, satisfying, and worthwhile way.

Promoting Intrinsic Motivation and Integration: Basic Psychological Need Satisfaction

SDT proposes that although people are inherently equipped with the natural tendencies toward intrinsic motivation and integrated internalizations, the robustness of these tendencies is a function of specific supports. In fact, SDT identifies a specific set of nutriments that are necessary for these growth-related processes to function effectively—namely, the satisfaction of the basic psychological needs for competence, autonomy, and relatedness. Specification of these needs occurred empirically, for they seemed necessary to provide a deep and satisfactory interpretation of the results from dozens of social psychological studies on intrinsic motivation and integration (see Deci & Ryan, 2000) in Western, equalitarian cultures as well as Eastern, traditional cultures (e.g., Chirkov, Ryan, Kim, & Kaplan, 2003; Ryan, La Guardia, Solky-Butzel, Chirkov, & Kim, 2005).

The need for *competence* refers to the necessity of people being and feeling effective in acting on the world (White, 1959). This involves the perceptions that their actions will bring about desired outcomes, that they can master challenges, and that they have and will continue to acquire competencies. The social environment supports people's competence by providing positive and constructive feedback and by calibrating activities to be optimally challenging.

The need for *autonomy* refers to the evolved importance to people of experiencing their behavior as self-organized and, therefore, accompanied by a sense of volition and self-endorsement. When that is the case, people experience personal congruence and perceive the locus of causality for their actions to be internal (de Charms, 1968; Ryan & Connell, 1989). The social environment supports people's autonomy by encouraging actions that are in accord with their true selves, as opposed to those that merely serve others' selfish desires or expectations.

The need for *relatedness* refers to the inherent requirement of feeling close and connected to others in the world and of caring for and being cared for by them. Relatedness is reflected in having trusting relationships with significant others and having a sense of belonging to valued groups or organizations. Social environments provide relational supports to people by relating openly and authentically to them and by expressing caring and concern.

Theoretically, SDT sees the natural propensities for intrinsic motivation, internalization, and integration as requiring basic psychological nutriments or need satisfactions in order to be maintained and nourished. When individuals' psychological needs are satisfied, they experience interest, enjoyment, and engagement, and their experience and behavior can become more organized, integrated, and coherent. Numerous studies have shown that basic need satisfaction promotes both intrinsic motivation and integration (e.g., Deci, Koestner, & Ryan, 1999; Ryan & Deci, 2000a). Further, studies have shown that need satisfaction, as it nourishes intrinsic motivation and organismic integration, also leads individuals to a general sense of wellness (e.g., Baard, Deci, & Ryan, 2004). When the environment allows individuals to satisfy their needs, they can begin to pursue a course that is filled with deep feelings of both meaning and aliveness (e.g., Ryan & Frederick, 1997). In this way, basic psychological needs provide nutriments essential for psychological health and well-being. Conversely, when need satisfactions are thwarted, the integrative tendencies reflected in intrinsic motivation and internalization will be negatively impacted; in addition, well-being will be diminished.

For example, Sheldon, Ryan, and Reis (1996) and Reis, Sheldon, Gable, Roscoe, and Ryan (2000) used experience-sampling methods to demonstrate important relations between need satisfaction and well-being, such that on days in which individuals experienced greater psychological need satisfaction they also experienced more well-being, including positive affect and vitality. At the individual-difference level, greater need satisfaction was also related to more well-being. Over extended periods of time, the satisfaction of basic psychological needs has related to such indicators of psychological health as lower anxiety and higher self-esteem and to health in various life domains, including work and home (Baard et al., 2004; Lynch, Plant, & Ryan, 2005).

Perhaps more important with respect to the literature on meaning making is the body of SDT research showing that environments that support the satisfaction of basic needs for autonomy and competence facilitate intrinsic motivation, and those that satisfy all three needs are essential for the promotion of internalization and integration (Deci & Ryan, 2000). This research suggests, as we shall elaborate, that the processes essential to meaning making can be either promoted or forestalled by the social and cultural climates in which an individual is embedded.

Meaning and Self-Determination Theory

Having presented several components of SDT, we now address various issues and questions related to meaning and provide an interpretation of each. Meaning has been described as a "prism of mental representations of expected relations that organizes . . . perceptions of the world" (Heine, Proulx, & Vohs, 2006, p. 88). Similarly, Reker and Wong (1988) suggested that meaning making involves an individual's search for a clear understanding of his or her experiences. The questions we address concern how these self-created frameworks for understanding, coherence, and purpose relate to fundamental motivational processes and the satisfaction of psychological needs.

The Process of Meaning Making

The process of understanding and making connections in the service of synthesizing experiences is essential for growth, well-being, and meaning making. Although different theorists have used distinctive language to describe meaning and the processes that produce it, a common theme is that meaning making is a process of understanding and integration (e.g., Frankl, 1959; Heine et al., 2006; Johnson, 1987; Reker & Wong, 1988). The process of developing meaning arises from people's desire to create the coherence and mastery that allows experiences to fit into place with one another and that provides a sense of purpose and direction, rather than alienation or anomie. This view of meaning making through integration operates in relation to meaning whether defined in terms of having purposes to which one is dedicated or of having an overall sense of one's life being fulfilled and worthwhile, for each requires the bringing together of elements and interpreting them in a coherent and satisfying way. Through examining and integrating one's experiences one can understand how they relate to one's purposes, thus helping to advance the purposes and bringing the experiences into the kind of coherence that gives one's life greater fulfillment.

SDT proposes that the underlying motivation to understand and integrate is a universal characteristic of people, transcending generations and cultures. Everywhere the tendencies toward interested engagement and organismic integration are characteristic of people despite the surface diversity of cultures and belief systems. As people's curiosity is sparked by novel, complex, intriguing possibilities, they pursue those possibilities out of interest, seeking challenges, and exploring themselves within their world. The integrative function works with the experiences, acquired knowledge, and internalized values to facilitate a more elaborated sense of self, along with feelings of having purpose and experiencing personal meaningfulness. Integration further supplies a foundation for autonomous actions, that is, actions that are in accord with underlying values, purposes, and meanings (Ryan & Deci, 2004). In fact, this process of organismic integration is not only a characteristic but also a defining element of the self (Deci & Ryan, 1991; Ryan, 1995).

As described by SDT, then, the meaning-making process is intrinsic to our natures and responsible for helping individuals create what Dittmann-Kohli (1991) called a coherent life course. Thus, it involves making ongoing choices that are in accordance with values, engaging in actions fully, and working to integrate meanings with one's sense of self, which is viewed by other existential thinkers as essential for self-congruity and authenticity (e.g., Camus, 1942; Maslow, 1962). As individuals internalize and integrate new experiences, values, and behaviors, they experience greater internal harmony, purpose, and wholeness (Ryan & Deci, 2001).

An important aspect of meaning making is that it is an active and motivated process of not only externally but also internally focused inquiry. Fry (1998) described this process when suggesting that self-reflection and self-awareness are essential for meaning making and its maintenance. Wong (1998b) similarly stated that people must be inquisitive and open in order to find meaning in their lives. These assertions are shared by SDT, which maintains that it is necessary to explore and question oneself and one's own reactions to the world in order to develop the connections that facilitate autonomy and give meaning to life. Moreover, SDT suggests that meaning will be facilitated by mindfulness, by an open, receptive awareness (Brown & Ryan, 2003). This notion highlights important aspects of the integrative function and the meaning-making process. That is, from the SDT perspective meaning making involves becoming aware of what is occurring within and without and engaging in autonomous, or self-endorsed, activities.

Development, Meaning, and Self-Determination Theory

Understanding and synthesizing, and thus making meaning, is clearly crucial for flourishing and for adaptive, growth-oriented development across the life span (Frankl, 1959; Reker & Fry, 2003; Reker & Wong, 1988). Because this process is sensitive and responsive to new and significant experiences, the directions it takes may repeatedly be changing over time. In other words, to the degree individuals are open and nondefensive (Hodgins & Knee, 2002), they may be reframing and reevaluating their personal meanings with some regularity. In part, this is because people's internal and external environments change through time, and they face a multitude of new challenges to existing beliefs and ways of living. With each experience comes the opportunity to integrate new values, beliefs, affects, or perceptions into one's sense of self. In the SDT view, every experience may be more or less effectively organized so that it is not only internally consistent but also brought into a harmonious relation with other aspects of the self, even ones that are potentially in conflict with it. Thus, it can be expected that given time, individuals who agree to take up the challenge of opening themselves to these experiences will develop an increasingly complex and integrated self.

Considerable research suggests that psychological development does in fact involve a general movement toward greater internalization and autonomy (e.g., C. L. Chandler & Connell, 1987; Ryan & Connell, 1989), and we argue that with internalization and greater autonomy comes a greater sense of meaning. Yet, for the natural integrative process to function effectively with people moving toward greater meaning, they must experience ongoing supports in the form of satisfaction of their basic psychological needs for competence, autonomy, and relatedness (Deci & Ryan, 2000). Conversely, social environments that thwart these basic needs can derail the process of growth and move the individuals away from a course of understanding, creativity, and integrity.

As people experience need supports, their intrinsic activity and integrative tendencies are buttressed and their experience of life meaning are enhanced. Fry (1998) similarly proposed that supportive, sharing relationships and a trusting and accepting atmosphere is important, even necessary, for adolescents to have courage to explore the experiences that make sense or provide meaning (see also Harré 1984; Meacham, 1989). Fry added that children and adolescents must grow up with caregivers who value them, have faith in them, and encourage them to pursue creative and self-expanding tasks. Fry (1998) also proposed that adolescents' sense of personal meaning depends on encouragement for describing, questioning, and doubting their beliefs, values, and experiences—in other words, providing adolescents with a sense of autonomy that leads to self-exploration. Moreover, scholars argue that people must be free to select their own outcomes for a sense of meaningfulness to develop (Antonovsky, 1979; Korotkov, 1998). In short, these views imply what SDT specifies, namely, that conditions supplying satisfaction of autonomy, relatedness, and competence are necessary not only for the development of a true sense of self but also for the development of life meaning.

Conversely, need deprivation is expected to lead to meaninglessness and ill-being. SDT researchers have found that when needs are not met, individuals succumb to a state of *amotivation*. When amotivated, people lack intention and exist in a state of passivity or helplessness, being diminished by a lack of either competence to enact behaviors or a lack of value for acting. Amotivation is associated with poor performance in activities and a variety of ill-being dimensions (Deci & Ryan, 1985b; Ryan et al., 2006). With respect to broader individual differences, amotivation is at the heart of the impersonal causality orientation (Deci & Ryan, 1985a), which is an orientation toward interpreting the environment as conveying incompetence and an inability to attain desired outcomes. It also involves a lack of intentionality and poor self-regulation.

A state similar to the idea of pervasive amotivation in SDT, discussed in the meaning literature, is referred to as an existential vacuum and involves the experience of vegetativeness (Maddi, 1970), hopelessness (Alloy & Clements, 1998), or apathy. In this state, individuals are passive and indifferent without a sense of meaning (Wiesel, 1958). Epistemological loneliness describes a related state in which one's meanings seem contradictory and inconsequential (M. J. Chandler, 1975). The use of the term *loneliness* to describe a sense of meaninglessness highlights the importance of feeling belonging in the world to develop and maintain life meaning. In order to escape the existential vacuum and epistemological loneliness characterized by amotivation and meaninglessness, adolescents need to build relationships with other trustworthy people who will promote the exploration of their own insecurities, fears, and incompetencies (Bugental, 1990; Fry, 1998). In other words, escape from an existential vacuum requires that individuals find environments that satisfy their basic psychological needs so they can feel the support to confront their inner experiences (Zuroff et al., 2007).

Meaning and Need Satisfaction

Recent research within the SDT tradition has begun to examine the relations between life meaning and psychological wellness. For example, the theory suggests that a life purpose would yield well-being to the extent that the purpose is truly need satisfying. To explore these effects, Weinstein, Ryan, and Deci (2008) examined the relations among searching for meaning, need satisfaction, and well-being. Participants completed questionnaires assessing their degree of searching for meaning (Steger, Frazier, Oishi, & Kaler, 2006); satisfaction of the relatedness, competence, and autonomy needs (La Guardia, Ryan, Couchman, & Deci, 2000); and well-being indicators of lack of anxiety (Spielberger, 1983), lack of depression (Radloff, 1977), and life satisfaction (Neugarten, Havighurst, & Tobin, 1961). Results indicated that individuals who were pursuing a purpose in their lives tended to have greater need satisfaction. Pursuing meaning also predicted less anxiety, less depression, and more life satisfaction. As well, need satisfaction predicted less anxiety, less depression, and more life satisfaction. For our present purposes, however, the following point is most critical: When controlling for the effects of need satisfaction, researchers found that pursuing meaning no longer predicted any of these outcomes. That is, need satisfaction mediated the relations between pursuing life meaning and the indicators of well-being. In sum, then, having meaningful pursuits does, in general, tend to be need satisfying and is thus aligned with psychological health and well-being.

In the work just discussed, meaning was assessed with a survey developed by Steger et al. (2006), which defines meaning in terms of having a purpose. With this operationalization, the Weinstein et al. (2008) study indicated that having a purpose tends to promote need satisfaction. Although this relationship is yet to be examined, SDT would also propose that need satisfaction leads to greater meaning in the sense of having a fulfilling and satisfying life. Rather, SDT research has focused on how need satisfaction promotes people's sense of wholeness, self-actualization, and wellness. A large body of empirical studies indicates that when needs are supported these outcomes are enhanced and that when needs are thwarted these outcomes are diminished. Thus, for example, studies have shown links between need satisfaction and mindfulness (e.g., Brown & Ryan, 2003), mental and physical health (V. M. Kasser & Ryan, 1999; Niemiec, Ryan, & Deci, 2009), and cultural integration (e.g., Chirkov, Ryan, & Willness, 2005), among other outcomes that we suggest are collectively indicative of having a life that is meaningful and worthwhile.

Meaning theorists have tended not to explicitly link need satisfaction to meaning, but we now argue that many of the writings of several meaning theorists can be understood as support for the view that experiencing what we identify as competence, autonomy, and relatedness satisfaction is indeed necessary for meaning. For example, Frankl (1965) implicitly highlighted the importance of autonomy need satisfaction when he maintained that personal valuing and caring is essential for the foundation of meaning, adding further that people will experience meaning to the extent that their activities are congruent with this valuing and caring (Frankl, 1978). The concept of personal valuing implies that the values have been well integrated with the self and thus form the basis for autonomous action. Frankl further emphasized that although individuals do not have control over many of the things that happen to them, life meaning is reflected in the freedom they evidence when choosing how to respond to those events. People create meaning, argued Frankl, by making distinctive and personally valued choices, a point echoed by Lukas (1998) and Yalom (1980). In short, to find true meaning, individuals must get to know who they truly are—that is, know what is valuable and important to them—and act in accord with that knowledge (Bugental, 1990).

The literature on meaning also emphasizes that relatedness is a core element in living a meaningful life. Frankl (1959) stated that encounters with other people provide a sense of meaning to individuals, and Wong (1998a) proposed that meaningfulness necessarily involves a relational and communal dimension. In addition, Little (1998) claimed that highly meaningful projects are characterized by a common theme of intimacy or connectedness in diverse forms.

Finally, having a sense of meaning also involves a sense that what one is doing is useful and important (Pines, 1993, 2004). Engagement and effectiveness, or what Frankl (1959) referred to as personal accomplishment, is an important contributor to the meaningfulness of pursuits. Thus, feeling a sense of competence and efficacy is another of the contributors to meaning. In sum, several meaning theorists have proposed, either explicitly or implicitly, that satisfying autonomy, relatedness, and/or competence needs is essential for a meaningful life.

Some empirical work in the area of meaning can also be interpreted as support for the importance of need satisfaction. In studies of caregivers of Alzheimer's patients, Lukas (1998) found that the process of developing ultimate meaning involves finding and enacting intimately held values and beliefs and experiencing deep emotions. As well, Lukas suggested that the experience of community is important for promoting meaning among the caregivers, thus concurring with Fry (1998) who argued that what people find meaningful will typically involve relating to others and enacting the values that they themselves find most important.

Research by King et al. (2003) also supported the importance of autonomy when studying turning points in people with chronic disabilities. They reported that, during difficult times, individuals found a sense of life meaning as they explored their nature and the world around them, thus moving toward self-synthesis and autonomy (Antonovsky, 1979). Additionally, research on Israeli citizens showed that even under conditions of difficult work, people had a sense of meaning that positively impacted their well-being when they felt competent at the work, perceiving themselves as able to make a difference in the world (Pines, 2004). Additional research demonstrated that individuals with chronic conditions derived a sense of meaning from maintaining a perception of competence as they engaged in important activities (King et al., 2003). Finally, Szadejko (2007) demonstrated that individuals who reported greater satisfaction of all three needs for autonomy, competence, and relatedness also experienced greater life meaning with the Lyon and Younger (2005) questionnaire, which tends to define meaning as living one's life in a way that is deeply satisfying and fulfilling.

The need satisfying content of meaning often emerges when asking participants to describe what they find to be meaningful. For example, Ebersole and De Paola (1987) categorized responses from participants who were asked to describe the central meaning in their lives. Their responses most often fell into three categories: relatedness (relationships, service), autonomy (belief, growth, self-understanding), and competence (self-improvement, life work). Wong (1998a) similarly summarized responses from participants describing those things that are meaningful to them in ways consistent with SDT. The relatedness theme was present in responses such as family and friends, love for others, strong ties, knowing you are needed and wanted by others; the competence theme was present in responses such as satisfaction with accomplishments, having knowledge, and striving to see goals actualized; and the autonomy theme was present in responses such as self-knowledge, a healthy self-concept, and following one's dreams.

Because need satisfaction is essential to the experience of meaning, life pursuits or aspirations that are need satisfying are expected to be most meaningful. Thus, the satisfaction of basic psychological needs and the acquisition of meaning are inextricably linked. We derive life meaning when we engage purposes that satisfy our basic psychological needs for autonomy, competence, and relatedness. This, however, brings us to the question of whether all life purposes are likely to lead to the experience of need satisfaction, and thus to a true sense of meaning and well-being.

Self-Determination Theory and the Content of Meaning

Various authors have discussed what it is that individuals find meaningful. One extreme view is that the content of significant pursuits and contexts does not matter for the experience of meaning to occur. When people devote themselves to any pursuit, they can gain meaning from it. For example, a central proposition of the *meaning maintenance model* (Heine et al., 2006), which is referred to as the fluid compensation process, suggests that when people are pursuing a meaningful activity and encounter an obstacle, they could quite easily transfer their attention and energy to another, perhaps distant, activity to compensate for being unable to persist at their initial pursuit. This model suggests that people are inherently pursuing relations or associations among aspects of themselves or between aspects of themselves and the world, and it is implied that associations can be drawn to any particular contents and that they can be equally meaningful. Whatever goal is being pursued can provide meaning, and when access to it is blocked any other goal can take its place.

The *outcome approach* (Dennis, Williams, Giangreco, & Cloninger, 1993) is also broader than is SDT in the contents that can give meaning to individuals, although it outlines particular characteristics necessary for an activity to produce a sense of meaning. Specifically, from this perspective, meaningful pursuits are defined in terms of goals external to people that they wish to accomplish or acquire. For example, meaning may come to people from attaining or maintaining a successful career, a loving relationship, or acquisitively amassing wealth.

The SDT view is quite different from either of these, for it states very specifically what kinds of activities, life pursuits, or attainments will tend to be more beneficial than others. Specifically, the theory maintains that only those activities or goals whose contents are related to satisfaction of basic psychological needs for autonomy, relatedness, and competence will be effective in facilitating a general sense of life meaning. That is, only pursuits that provide basic need satisfaction will be experienced as meaningful when one reflects seriously upon them. Further, SDT has specified one category of life goals that will yield meaning and well-being for people and a second category of life goals that tends not to. We begin by considering the goals or purposes that are associated with greater need satisfaction and thus produce greater meaning, as well as those that tend not to yield need satisfaction and meaning. We then turn to the social-developmental contexts that lead people to compensate for need thwarting by selecting the types of purposes in their lives that turn out not to satisfy needs and yield meaning.

Need Satisfaction and Personal Goals

As we said, some theorists have suggested that any activity will yield meaning for people if the activity is important to them. Indeed, this is a core assumption of most social-cognitive theories (e.g., Bandura, 1996; Heine et al., 2006; Markus & Kitayama, 1991). In these theories virtually any cultural content can be valued, and if so, its attainment will produce well-being. SDT has proposed, however, that some goal pursuits more directly facilitate basic need satisfaction than do others, and thus "not all goals are created equal" (Ryan, Sheldon, T. Kasser, & Deci, 1996).

For example, research by T. Kasser and Ryan (1996) showed that people's life goals or aspirations tend to fall into two broad categories referred to as intrinsic aspirations and extrinsic aspirations. Intrinsic aspirations have been found to include the pursuit of personal growth, health and fitness, close relationships, and community contributions. Extrinsic aspirations include the pursuit of financial success, recognition and fame, and an appealing image. Numerous studies by T. Kasser and Ryan (e.g., 1993, 1996, 2001) and by other investigators (e.g., McHoskey, 1999; Sheldon & Kasser, 1995; Vansteenkiste, Simons, Lens, Sheldon & Deci, 2004) have found that people whose extrinsic aspirations were relatively stronger tended to display less self-actualization and vitality, more depression and anxiety, poorer relationship quality, and poorer performance than was the case for those whose intrinsic aspirations were relatively stronger than their extrinsic aspirations. Research on people's life narratives by Bauer, McAdams, and Sakaeda (2005) showed that people whose life stories emphasized intrinsic aspirations (growth, affiliation, and generativity) displayed greater hedonic and eudaimonic well-being (see Ryan & Deci, 2001) than those whose stories emphasized the extrinsic goals of wealth, status, approval, and physical appearance. Evidence for the positive relation of intrinsic, but not extrinsic, aspirations or purposes to well-being has also been found in samples outside North America (e.g., Ryan et al., 1999).

It is not only the *pursuit* of intrinsic goals that is associated with greater wellness, but also their *attainment*. For example, whereas attaining valued intrinsic aspirations promotes psychological well-being, attaining valued extrinsic aspirations does not, and in some studies the results suggest that it can even contribute to ill-being (Niemiec et al., 2009). Further, the link between aspirations and well-being is mediated by basic need satisfaction. Whereas the pursuit and attainment of intrinsic life goals tend to promote satisfaction of the basic psychological needs and, in turn, psychological wellness, the pursuit and attainment of extrinsic life goals tend to thwart satisfaction of basic psychological needs, resulting in ill-being.

In short, it appears to be only the pursuit and attainment of intrinsic aspirations or purposes and the need satisfaction derived from their pursuits and attainments, that promote well-being and give true meaning to people's lives. As such, this leads us to the hypothesis that not all activities, goals, and purposes that are important to people will necessarily bring benefits to their lives. The activities and pursuits have to be ones that are closely linked to basic psychological need satisfaction.

Intrinsic Versus Extrinsic Aspirations as Predictors of Meaning

A recent study by Weinstein et al. (2008) directly tested the hypothesis that intrinsic aspirations would be more strongly associated with experiencing life meaning than would extrinsic aspirations. Participants reported on both the importance of intrinsic and extrinsic aspirations (T. Kasser & Ryan, 1996) and also the presence of life meaning (Steger et al., 2006). Three factors were derived from the life meaning questionnaire: wanting life meaning, searching for life meaning, and having a clear sense of purpose or meaning in life. The strategy for this study was not to ask individuals what pursuits were meaningful to them but instead to test whether people who strongly espoused intrinsic pursuits reported experiencing a higher sense of meaning in life than did people who strongly espoused extrinsic pursuits. Results showed that the more strongly participants held intrinsic aspirations the more they wanted meaning in life, the more they were searching for meaning, and the more they had a sense of purpose and meaning in life. In contrast, although the strength of people's extrinsic aspirations were positively related to wanting meaning in life and searching for meaning, the strength of extrinsic aspirations was not related to *having* purpose or meaning in life. Further, the results held up for the specific aspirations as well as for the overarching categories of intrinsic and extrinsic aspirations. For example, strongly holding the value for community was significantly positively related to wanting, searching for, and having meaning, whereas strongly holding the value for wealth was related to wanting and searching for meaning but not to having meaning.

It is very interesting that individuals who are strongly focused on intrinsic aspirations are more likely to have a true sense of purpose and meaning in life, but those who are focused on extrinsic aspirations, although they are searching for purpose and meaning in their lives, seem unable to find it. Such findings indicate that holding strong intrinsic values tends to yield greater meaning, in addition to yielding well-being and psychological health, as was shown in other studies. As such, it seems that people can either focus on purposes and goals in life that foster need satisfaction and wellness or they can adopt meanings and goals that do not tend to be need fulfilling and thus are associated with more alienation, anomie, stress, and pathology.

This set of findings is very interesting and supplements the other findings by Weinstein et al. (2008) discussed earlier in the chapter. Specifically, the earlier-discussed findings indicated that when people have a life purpose, they tend to experience need satisfaction and meaning. However, the study just reported makes clear that although having a life purpose tends to facilitate meaning, some life purposes (viz., the extrinsic ones) do not promote experiences of meaningfulness.

Within the meaning literature, many authors have suggested that failure to create meaning in life results in a condition of apathy and aimlessness that depletes the appeal of existence and undermines interest and energy for new and significant experiences (Maddi, 1970). Klinger (1977) stated that without meaning people are apathetic, inactive, and prone to psychopathology. Consistent with these ideas, studies have also shown that when people do have meaning, they tend to experience life satisfaction, positive affect, subjective well-being, mental health, and sensory health (Chamberlain & Zika, 1992; Reker et al., 1987; Zika & Chamberlain, 1992). What we have seen is that SDT adds a moderating consideration to this: We argue that it is only those life meanings that conduce to basic need satisfaction (i.e., intrinsic aspirations and life goals) that foster wellness. Not every meaning a person embraces is beneficial, and some may be empty and compensatory in nature.

The Development of Compensatory, Nonfulfilling Purposes

From the SDT perspective, the development of intrinsic aspirations or goals follows from ongoing satisfaction of the basic psychological needs in people's lives. When children are provided with supports for autonomy, the safety of relatedness, and the scaffolding of competence supports, they are expected to develop the values underlying intrinsic aspirations. Within SDT, an emphasis on extrinsic aspirations is hypothesized to occur when needs for autonomy, competence, and/or relatedness are neglected or thwarted. Indeed, thwarting of needs is expected to foster insecurity, which in turn leads people to seek out compensatory goals (e.g., a focus on material goods or outward appearance), hoping that such goals will ameliorate the insecurities and ill-being that result from need deprivation.

Two SDT studies demonstrated that need satisfaction is associated with the development of intrinsic aspirations whereas need thwarting is associated with the development of extrinsic aspirations. In the first study, T. Kasser, Ryan, Zax, and Sameroff (1995) found, using questionnaires, clinical interviews, and archival data, that when mothers were cold and controlling, their teenage children were more likely to place strong emphasis on the extrinsic goal of wealth rather than the intrinsic goals. This in turn was associated with indicators of poor well-being. Further, a study by Williams, Cox, Hedberg, and Deci (2000) examined high school students' perception of their parents' autonomy supportiveness and found that greater autonomy support from parents was associated with the students' having more intrinsic aspirations, whereas greater control from parents was associated with the students' espousing strong extrinsic aspirations.

The importance of such studies is that they indicate that when basic needs are thwarted individuals will attach themselves to values and purposes that may promise a sense of worth, such as values for wealth, fame, or an attractive external image. But such extrinsic values, goals, and purposes typically do not yield basic need satisfactions, and they indeed may lead people away from activities and purposes that yield need satisfaction and, ultimately, a greater sense of security and meaning.

Is It Useful to Think of Meaning as a Basic Need?

As mentioned earlier, various writers such as Frankl (1978), Andersen et al. (2000), and others have proposed that meaning is a basic human need—perhaps even the most important psychological need. This view suggests that people need to feel a sense that their lives are being lived in ways that are deeply fulfilling and so direct much of their energy toward satisfying this need. This implies that when the individuals have satisfied the need for meaning they will experience psychological wellness—that is, self-actualization, vitality, and health.

SDT takes a different perspective. Generally, we too use the definition of meaning as a reflection of the degree to which people's lives have been well lived and thus yield a deep sense of satisfaction. We suggest that when interpreted in this way, meaning is best thought of as a notable outcome of a fully lived life that is marked by interest, curiosity, and openness. In a sense, this conceptualization suggests that meaning is best understood to be an indicator of wellness. Indeed, satisfaction with life (Diener, Emmons, Larsen, & Griffin, 1985), which is a core component of subjective well-being, is very closely related to life meaning; in fact, the concepts are sometimes used interchangeably. Our view is that life meaning results from satisfaction of the needs for autonomy, competence, and relatedness rather than being a need itself. In preliminary support of this, satisfaction of the three basic needs of SDT does indeed strongly relate to meaning when defined as a general sense of living a worthy life (Szadejko, 2007) although the research does not allow causal interpretations so further evidence about this point is needed.

Thus far, we have argued that the concept of feeling that one's life is meaningful is an outcome of need satisfaction, rather than being a need itself. Further, we suggest that the concept of meaning does not have the qualities of a basic human need. Our definition of the concept of a basic psychological need includes that it must convey *specific content* that people need for growth, integrity, and wellness, thus speaking to the idea of human nature. Stated differently, basic needs must specify the contents that are necessary or essential for all people to be psychologically whole and healthy. The concept of competence contains specific content—it refers to being effective and having an impact on one's environment—and research indicates that it is relates to well-being across cultures, thus suggesting universality (e.g., Deci et al., 2001). The concept of relatedness similarly has specific content—it refers to having connections with others, belonging to groups, being loved and loving others, being cared for and caring for others—and its relation to well-being has been found in many cultures (e.g., Sheldon, Elliot, Kim, & Kasser, 2001). Finally, the concept of autonomy has specific content—it refers to being volitional and endorsing one's actions and to not being heteronomously controlled—and it too has been shown to relate to well-being cross-culturally (e.g., Chirkov et al., 2003). Satisfaction of these needs, we argue, also provides meaning, but meaning itself does not specify any content that yields health and well-being. Rather, meaning results from other contents—for example, from pursuing purposes that allow people to feel autonomous, competent, and related to others.

As described above, the concept of meaning has sometimes been used to convey that people have important goals or purposes. However, we argued in this chapter that meaning is an important experience that arises when individuals pursue intrinsic purposes and are reasonably successful in achieving them. Further, as previously noted, studies have also shown that some life purposes, even when strongly valued, are not associated with psychological well-being. For example, extrinsic goals, even when personally valued, do not meet the essential criteria that define a need. It follows then that, purpose in life, which could include all purposes, does not satisfy the criteria of specifying content or of being invariantly related to well-being. In summary, having a purpose or meaning is not sufficient to define a need, and those meanings and purposes that do foster wellness and strivings are likely characterized by qualities of autonomy, competence, and relatedness.

To summarize, the term meaning has tended to have two somewhat different conceptual and operational definitions in the literature on meaning. When it is treated as a general concept having to do with living one's life in a fulfilling, satisfying, and meaningful way it is best understood to be a powerful indicator of well-being that results from satisfaction of the basic psychological needs. When, however, it is treated as a more specific concept having to do with searching for or pursuing a purpose in life, it is perhaps better understood as a set of goals and activities that to greater or less degrees tend to promote satisfaction of the basic psychological needs and in turn yield well-being and the feeling of living meaningfully.

Meaning and Eudaimonia

Definitions of human well-being have derived from two distinct traditions within psychology, which were discussed at length by Ryan and Deci (2001) in terms of the hedonic and the eudaimonic traditions. The hedonic conception of wellness (Kahneman, 1999) defines well-being in terms of positive experiences and moments of pleasure. The eudaimonic tradition (Waterman, 1993), in contrast, defines wellness in terms of people's realization of their human potentials—such as functioning in ways that are reflective, moral, and focused on "the good."

The literature on meaning is clearly most reflective of the eudaimonic tradition (Little, 1998). That is, most conceptions of meaning reflect the eudaimonic ideal of living in accord with abiding values and pursuing those ends that matter most. An important corollary of this is that meaningful life is one that can be associated not only with being good, but also with feeling good (Ryan, Huta, & Deci, 2008). In fact, the evidence suggests that acting in accord with values actually fosters positive affect and feelings of happiness (Ryan & Deci, 2001).

At the same time that we acknowledge that meaningful pursuits can produce happiness and conduce to well-being, we also want to add that some activities that have no meaning beyond themselves can also lead to happiness and a greater sense of wellness. For example, Huta and Ryan (2007) recently demonstrated that although people who were high in either eudaimonic or hedonic activities experienced some positive well-being outcomes, a life characterized by both types of pursuits seemed to foster the broadest array of positive outcomes. Further, whereas eudaimonic pursuits—those more associated with meaning—were related to a longer-term sense of self-worth and self-actualization, hedonic pursuits seemed especially important for boosting positive affect in the short term and helping to revitalize people, even though these pursuits were not focused on meaningful outcomes. In short, not every behavior we engage in need be meaningful, but were we to lack such activities, overall well-being would indeed be diminished.

Questions of meaning are inherently relational, as they concern the importance and significance of things (Rychlak, 1977), and they nearly always seem to lead individuals to think beyond the moment. But in this regard it is also important to discover the significance not in what is beyond this moment or in what can be done, for there is also the significance of just *being*, of fully residing in the here and now, or being mindful and present (Brown & Ryan, 2003). If there is not intrinsic good in simply being, then there can never be meaning in what can be done.

Conclusion

Life meaning is a complex and fundamental construct that is important in human development. In this chapter we have argued that meaning making is an expression of the integrative propensities inherent in all individuals and that its presence reflects a pervasive tendency towards growth. Meaning making arises from people's intrinsic motivation to explore, understand, and connect their experiences. It also arises as people work to internalize and integrate the non-intrinsically motivated regulations transmitted to them though socialization and culture.

Through intrinsic motivation and integrative activity the self-structure moves towards greater complexity and coherence, which results in psychological health and more volitional and adaptive functioning. Yet in order for this inherent propensity to thrive, environmental nutriments that facilitate and support integration are essential. Specifically, autonomy, relatedness, and competence supports facilitate people's engagement with new environments and new challenges with openness and interest (as opposed to threat and defense) and thus allow richer opportunities for them to create meaning.

When their needs are met, people are more prone to develop and internalize intrinsic life goals, that in turn fosters both enhanced wellness and a sense of meaning. Need thwarting, in contrast, leads to the adoption of compensatory goals and purposes, which are less likely to leave people feeling that they have meaning. This is only to say that not all meanings are created equal and that SDT's conception of need satisfaction helps differentiate "empty" meanings from those that can truly fulfill the individual. In this sense the relations of purposes or meanings to wellness are hypothesized within SDT to be mediated by basic psychological need satisfactions.

The rich literature on meaning speaks to a deep existential truth about human nature. To feel whole and healthy we need to have a sense of purpose and to experience our lives as significant and as valuable. Constructing and internalizing a sense of meaning is thus a formidable developmental project. Although the task of finding meaning is ultimately the responsibility of individuals, it is likely to succeed only when one's family, community and culture provide the requisite nutriments for personal growth and integrity, namely supports for autonomy, competence, and relatedness. These needs underlie this central human quest and provide the signposts on how we can promote and maintain meaning in a universe pervaded by questions and uncertainties.

References

Alloy, L. B., & Clements, C. M. (1998). Hopelessness theory of depression: Tests of the symptom component. *Cognitive Therapy and Research, 22*, 303–335.

Allport, G. W. (1937). *Personality: A psychological interpretation.* New York, NY: Holt.

Andersen, S., Chen, S., & Carter, C. (2000). Fundamental human needs: Making social cognition relevant. *Psychological Inquiry, 11*, 269–275

Angyal, A. (1965). *Neurosis and treatment: A holistic theory.* New York, NY: Wiley.

Antonovsky, A. (1979). *Health, stress, and coping.* San Francisco, CA: Jossey-Bass.

Baard, P. P., Deci, E. L., & Ryan, R. M. (2004). Intrinsic need satisfaction: A motivational basis of performance and well-being in two work settings. *Journal of Applied Social Psychology, 34*, 2045–2068.

Bandura, A. (1996). *Self-efficacy: The exercise of control.* New York, NY: Freeman.

Bauer, J. J., McAdams, D. P., & Sakaeda, A. R. (2005). Interpreting the good life: Growth memories in the lives of mature, happy people. *Journal of Personality and Social Psychology, 88*, 203–217.

Binswanger, L. (1963). *Being-in-the-world.* Selected papers of Ludwig Binswanger (Jacob Needleman, Trans.). New York, NY: Basic Books.

Black, A. E., & Deci, E. L. (2000). The effects of student self-regulation and instructor autonomy support on learning in a college-level natural science course: A self-determination theory perspective. *Science Education, 84*, 740–756.

Boss, M. (1963). *Psychoanalysis and daseinanalysis.* New York, NY: Basic Books.

Brown, K. W., & Ryan, R. M. (2003). The benefits of being present: Mindfulness and its role in psychological well-being. *Journal of Personality and Social Psychology, 84*, 822–848.

Bugental, J. F. T. (1990). Existential-humanistic psychotherapy. In J. K. Zeig & W. M. Munion (Eds.), *What is psychotherapy? Contemporary perspectives* (pp. 189–193). San Francisco, CA: Jossey-Bass.

Camus, A. (1942). *The stranger.* New York, NY: Knopf.

Chamberlain, K., & Zika, S. (1992). Religiosity, meaning in life, and psychological well-being. In J. F. Schumaker (Ed.), *Religion and mental health* (pp. 138–148). New York, NY: Oxford University Press.

Chandler, C. L., & Connell, J. P. (1987). Children's intrinsic, extrinsic and internalized motivation: A developmental study of children's reasons for liked and disliked behaviors. *British Journal of Developmental Psychology, 5*, 357–365.

Chandler, M. J. (1975). Relativism and the problem of epistemological loneliness. *Human Development, 18*, 171–180.

Chirkov, V., Ryan, R. M., Kim, Y., & Kaplan, U. (2003). Differentiating autonomy from individualism and independence: A self-determination theory perspective on internalization of cultural orientations and well-being. *Journal of Personality and Social Psychology, 84*, 97–110.

Chirkov, V. I., Ryan, R. M., & Willness, C. (2005). Cultural context and psychological needs in Canada and Brazil: Testing a self-determination approach to the internalization of cultural practices, identity, and well-being. *Journal of Cross-Cultural Psychology*, 36, 423–443.

Collins, M., & Amabile, T. (1999). Motivation and creativity. In R. J. Sternberg (Ed.), *Handbook of creativity* (pp. 297–312). New York, NY: Cambridge University Press

De Charms, R. (1968). *Personal causation: The internal affective determinants of behavior.* New York, NY: Academic Press.

Deci, E. L. (1975). *Intrinsic motivation.* New York, NY: Plenum Press.

Deci, E. L., Eghrari, H., Patrick, B. C., & Leone, D. R. (1994). Facilitating internalization: The self-determination theory perspective. *Journal of Personality, 62,* 119–142.

Deci, E. L., Koestner, R., & Ryan, R. M. (1999). A meta-analytic review of experiments examining the effects of extrinsic rewards on intrinsic motivation. *Psychological Bulletin, 125,* 627–668.

Deci, E. L., & Ryan, R. M. (1985a). The General Causality Orientations Scale: Self-determination in personality. *Journal of Research in Personality, 19,* 109–134.

Deci, E. L., & Ryan, R. M. (1985b). *Intrinsic motivation and self-determination in human behavior.* New York, NY: Plenum Press.

Deci, E. L., & Ryan, R. M. (1991). A motivational approach to self: Integration in personality. In R. Dienstbier (Ed.), *Nebraska Symposium on Motivation: Vol. 38. Perspectives on motivation* (pp. 237–288). Lincoln: University of Nebraska Press.

Deci, E. L., & Ryan, R. M. (2000). The "what" and "why" of goal pursuits: Human needs and the self-determination of behavior. *Psychological Inquiry, 11,* 227–268.

Deci, E. L., Ryan, R. M., Gagné, M., Leone, D. R., Usunov, J., & Kornazheva, B. P. (2001). Need satisfaction, motivation, and well-being in the work organizations of a former Eastern Bloc country. *Personality and Social Psychology Bulletin, 27,* 930–942.

Deci, E. L., Schwartz, A. J., Sheinman, L., & Ryan, R. M. (1981). An Instrument to assess adults' orientations toward control versus autonomy with children: Reflections on intrinsic motivation and perceived competence. *Journal of Educational Psychology, 73,* 642–650.

Dennis, R. E., Williams, W., Giangreco, M. F., & Cloninger, C. J. (1993). Quality of life as context for planning and evaluation of services for people with disabilities. *Exceptional Children, 59,* 499–512.

Diener, E., Emmons, R., Larsen, R. J., & Griffin, S. (1985). The Satisfaction With Life Scale. *Journal of Personality Assessment, 49,* 71–75.

Dittmann-Kohli, F. (1991). Meaning and personality change from early to late adulthood. *European Journal of Gerontology, 2,* 98–103.

Ebersole, P., & De Paola, S. (1987). Meaning in life categories of later life couples. *Journal of Psychology,* 12, 185–191.

Frankl, V. E. (1959). *Man's search for meaning.* Boston, MA: Beacon Press.

Frankl, V. E. (1965). *The doctor and the soul, from psychotherapy to logotherapy* (2nd ed., R. Winston & C. Winston, Trans.). New York, NY: Knopf.

Frankl, V. E. (1978). *The unheard cry for meaning: Psychotherapy and humanism.* New York, NY: Touchstone Books.

Fry, P. S. (1998). The development of personal meaning and wisdom in adolescence: A reexamination of moderating and consolidating factors and influences. In P. T. P. Wong & P. S. Fry (Eds.), *The human quest for meaning: A handbook of psychological research and clinical applications* (pp. 91–110). Mahwah, NJ: Erlbaum.

Goldstein, K. (1939). *The organism.* New York, NY: American Book.

Greenstein, A., & Koestner, R. (1996). *Success in maintaining new year's resolutions: The value of self-determined reasons.* Paper presented at the International Congress of Psychology, Montreal, Quebec, Canada.

Grolnick, W. S., & Ryan, R. M. (1987). Autonomy in children's learning: An experimental and individual difference investigation. *Journal of Personality and Social Psychology, 52*, 890–898.
Harlow, H. F. (1950). Learning and satiation of response in intrinsically motivated complex puzzle performance by monkeys. *Journal of Comparative and Physiological Psychology, 43*, 289–294.
Harré, R. (1984). *Personal being: A theory for individual psychology*. Cambridge, MA: Harvard University Press.
Heine, S. J., Proulx, T., & Vohs, K. D. (2006). The meaning maintenance model: On the coherence of social motivations. *Personality and Social Psychology Review, 10*, 88–110.
Hodgins, H., & Knee, C. R. (2002). The integrating self and conscious experience. In E. L. Deci & R. M. Ryan (Eds.), *Handbook of self-determination research* (pp. 87–100). Rochester, NY: University of Rochester Press.
Huta, V., & Ryan, R. M. (2007). *Pursuing pleasure versus virtue: The differential and overlapping well-being benefits of hedonic and eudaimonic motives*. Manuscript submitted for publication.
Johnson, M. (1987). *The body in the mind: The bodily basis of meaning, Imagination and reason*. Chicago, IL: University of Chicago Press.
Kahneman, D. (1999). Objective happiness. In D. Kahneman, E. Diener, & N. Schwarz (Eds.), *Well-being: The foundations of hedonic psychology* (pp. 3–25). New York, NY: Russell Sage Foundation.
Kasser, T., & Ryan, R. M. (1993). A dark side of the American dream: Correlates of financial success as a central life aspiration. *Journal of Personality and Social Psychology, 65*, 410–422.
Kasser, T., & Ryan, R. M. (1996). Further examining the American dream: Differential correlates of intrinsic and extrinsic goals. *Personality and Social Psychology Bulletin, 22*, 80–87.
Kasser, T., & Ryan, R. M. (2001). Be careful what you wish for: Optimal functioning and the relative attainment of intrinsic and extrinsic goals. In P. Schmuck & K. M. Sheldon (Eds.), *Life goals and well-being: Towards a positive psychology of human striving* (pp. 115–129). Goettingen, Germany: Hogrefe & Huber.
Kasser, T., Ryan, R. M., Zax, M., & Sameroff, A. J. (1995). The relations of maternal and social environments to late adolescents' materialistic and prosocial values. *Developmental Psychology, 31*, 907–914.
Kasser, V. M., & Ryan, R. M. (1999). The relation of psychological needs for autonomy and relatedness to vitality, well-being, and mortality in a nursing home. *Journal of Applied Social Psychology, 29*, 935–954.
King, G., Cathers, T., Brown, E., Specht, J. A., Willoughby, C., Miller Polgar, J., … Havens, L. (2003). Turning points and protective processes in the lives of people with chronic disabilities. *Qualitative Health Research, 13*, 184–206.
Klinger, E. (1977). *Meaning and void: Inner experience and the incentives in people's lives*. Minneapolis: University of Minnesota Press.
Koestner, R., Ryan, R. M., Bernieri, F., & Holt, K. (1984). Setting limits on children's behavior: The differential effects of controlling versus informational styles on children's intrinsic motivation and creativity. *Journal of Personality, 54*, 233–248.
Korotkov, D. (1998). The sense of coherence: Making sense out of chaos. In P. T. P. Wong & P. S. Fry (Eds.), *The human quest for meaning: A handbook of psychological research and clinical applications* (pp. 51–70). Mahwah, NJ: Erlbaum.
La Guardia, J. G., Ryan, R. M., Couchman, C. E., & Deci, E. L. (2000). Within-person variation in security of attachment: A self-determination theory perspective on

attachment, need fulfillment, and well-being. *Journal of Personality and Social Psychology, 79,* 367–384.

Little, B. R. (1998). Personal project pursuit: Dimensions and dynamics of personal meaning. In P. T. P. Wong & P. S. Fry (Eds.), *The human quest for meaning: A handbook of psychological research and clinical applications* (pp. 193–212). Mahwah, NJ: Erlbaum.

Loevinger, J. (1976). *Ego development.* San Francisco, CA: Jossey-Bass.

Lukas, E. (1998). The meaning of life and the goals of life for chronically ill people. In P. T. P. Wong & P. S. Fry (Eds.), *The human quest for meaning: A handbook of psychological research and clinical applications* (pp. 307–316). Mahwah, NJ: Erlbaum.

Lynch, M. F., Plant, R. W., & Ryan, R. M. (2005). Psychological needs and threat to safety: Implications for staff and patients in a psychiatric hospital for youth. *Professional Psychology, 36,* 415–425.

Lyon, D. E., & Younger, J. (2005). Development and preliminary evaluation of the Existential Meaning Scale. *Journal of Holistic Nursing, 23,* 54–65.

Maddi, S. R. (1970). The search for meaning. In M. Page (Ed.), *Nebraska symposium on motivation* (pp. 137–186). Lincoln: University of Nebraska Press.

Markus, H. R., & Kitayama, S. (1991). Culture and the self: Implications for cognition, emotion, and motivation. *Psychological Review, 92,* 224–253.

Maslow, A. H. (1962). *Toward a psychology of being.* Princeton, NJ: Van Nostrand.

McHoskey, J. W. (1999). Machiavellianism, intrinsic versus extrinsic goals, and social interest: A self-determination theory analysis. *Motivation and Emotion, 23,* 267–283.

Meacham, J. A. (1989). Autonomy, despair and generativity in Erikson's theory. In P. S. Fry (Ed.), *Psychology of helplessness and control in the aged* (pp. 63–98). Amsterdam, The Netherlands: North-Holland.

Neugarten, B. L., Havighurst, R. J., & Tobin, S. S. (1961). The measurement of life satisfaction. *Journal of Gerontology, 16,* 134–143.

Niemiec, C. P., Ryan, R. M., & Deci, E. L. (2009). The path taken: Consequences of attaining intrinsic and extrinsic aspirations in post-college life. *Journal of Research in Personality, 43,* 291–306.

Piaget, J. (1971). *Biology and knowledge.* Chicago, IL: University of Chicago Press.

Pines, A. M. (1993). Burnout: Existential perspectives. In W. B. Schaufeli, C. Maslach, & T. Marek (Eds.), *Professional burnout: Recent developments in theory and research* (33–52). Washington, DC: Taylor & Francis.

Pines, A. M. (2004). Why are Israelis less burned out? *European Psychologist, 9,* 69–77.

Pyszczynski, T., Solomon, S., & Greenberg, J. (2003). *In the wake of 9/11: The psychology of terror.* Washington, DC: American Psychological Association.

Radloff, L. S. (1977). The CES-D Scale: A self-report depression scale for research in the general population. *Applied Psychological Measurement, 1,* 385–401.

Reis, H. T., Sheldon, K. M., Gable, S. L., Roscoe, J., & Ryan, R. M. (2000). Daily well-being: The role of autonomy, competence, and relatedness. *Personality and Social Psychology Bulletin, 26,* 419–435.

Reker, G. T., & Fry, P. S. (2003). Factor structure and invariance of personal meaning measures in cohorts of younger and older adults. *Personality and Individual Differences, 35,* 977–993.

Reker, G. T., Peacock, E. J., & Wong, P. T. (1987). Meaning and purpose in life and well-being: A life-span perspective. *Journal of Gerontology, 42,* 44–49.

Reker, G. T., & Wong, P. T. P. (1988). Aging as an individual process: Toward a theory of personal meaning. In J. E. Birren & V. L. Bengtson (Eds.), *Emergent theories of aging.* (pp. 214–246). New York: Springer.

Rogers, C. (1963). The actualizing tendency in relation to "motives" and to consciousness. In M. R. Jones (Ed.), *Nebraska Symposium on Motivation* (11, 1–24). Lincoln: University of Nebraska Press.

Rogoff, B. (2003). *The cultural nature of human development.* New York, NY: Oxford University Press.

Ryan, R. M. (1993). Agency and organization: Intrinsic motivation, autonomy and the self in psychological development. In J. Jacobs (Ed.), *Nebraska Symposium on Motivation: Developmental perspectives on motivation* (Vol. 40, pp. 1–56). Lincoln: University of Nebraska Press.

Ryan, R. M. (1995). Psychological needs and the facilitation of integrative processes. *Journal of Personality, 63,* 397–427.

Ryan, R. M., & Brown, K. W. (2003). Why we don't need self-esteem: Basic needs, mindfulness, and the authentic self. *Psychological Inquiry,* 14, 71–76.

Ryan, R. M., Chirkov, V. I., Little, T. D., Sheldon, K. M., Timoshina, E., & Deci, E. L. (1999). The American dream in Russia: Extrinsic aspirations and well-being in two cultures. *Personality and Social Psychology Bulletin, 25,* 1509–1524.

Ryan, R. M., & Connell, J. P. (1989). Perceived locus of causality and internalization: Examining reasons for acting in two domains. *Journal of Personality and Social Psychology, 57,* 749–761.

Ryan, R. M., & Deci, E. L. (2000a). Intrinsic and extrinsic motivations: Classic definitions and new directions. *Contemporary Educational Psychology, 25,* 54–67.

Ryan, R. M., & Deci, E. L. (2000b). Self-determination theory and the facilitation of intrinsic motivation, social development, and well-being. *American Psychologist, 55,* 68–78.

Ryan, R. M., & Deci, E. L. (2001). To be happy or to be self-fulfilled: A review of research on hedonic and eudaimonic well-being. In S. Fiske (Ed.), *Annual Review of Psychology* (Vol. 52, pp. 141–166). Palo Alto, CA: Annual Reviews.

Ryan, R. M., & Deci, E. L. (2004). Avoiding death or engaging life as accounts of meaning and culture: A comment on Pyszczynski, Greenberg, Solomon, Arndt, and Schimel (2004). *Psychological Bulletin, 130,* 473–477.

Ryan, R. M., Deci, E. L., Grolnick, W. S., & La Guardia, J. G. (2006). The significance of autonomy and autonomy support in psychological development and psychopathology. In D. Cicchetti & D. J. Cohen (Eds.), *Developmental psychopathology* (pp. 795–849). Hoboken, NJ: Wiley.

Ryan, R. M., & Frederick, C. M. (1997). On energy, personality, and health: Subjective vitality as a dynamic reflection of well-being. *Journal of Personality, 65,* 529–565.

Ryan, R. M., Huta, V., & Deci, E. L. (2008). Living well: A self-determination theory perspective on eudaimonia. *Journal of Happiness Studies, 9,* 139–170.

Ryan, R. M., La Guardia, J. G., Solky-Butzel, J., Chirkov, V., & Kim, Y. (2005). On the interpersonal regulation of emotions: Emotional reliance across gender, relationships, and cultures. *Personal Relationships, 12,* 145–163.

Ryan, R. M., Rigby, S., & King, K. (1993). Two types of religious internalization and their relations to religious orientations and mental health. *Journal of Personality and Social Psychology, 65,* 586–596.

Ryan, R. M., Sheldon, K. M., Kasser, T., & Deci, E. L. (1996). All goals are not created equal: An organismic perspective on the nature of goals and their regulation. In P. M. Gollwitzer & J. A. Bargh (Eds.), *The psychology of action: Linking cognition and motivation to behavior* (pp. 7–26). New York, NY: Guilford Press.

Rychlak, J. F. (1977). *The psychology of rigorous humanism.* New York, NY: Wiley.

Seeman, M. (1983). Alienation motifs in contemporary theorizing: The hidden continuity of classic themes. *Social Psychology Quarterly, 46,* 171–184.

Sheldon, K. M., Elliot, A. J., Kim, Y., & Kasser, T. (2001). What's satisfying about satisfying events? Comparing ten candidate psychological needs. *Journal of Personality and Social Psychology, 80*, 325–339.

Sheldon, K. M., & Kasser, T. (1995). Coherence and congruence: Two aspects of personality integration. *Journal of Personality and Social Psychology, 68*, 531–543.

Sheldon, K. M., Ryan, R. M., & Reis, H. T. (1996). What makes for a good day? Competence and autonomy in the day and in the person. *Personality and Social Psychology Bulletin, 22*, 1270–1279.

Shostrom, E. L. (1964). A test for the measurement of self-actualization. *Educational and Psychological Measurement, 24*, 207–218.

Skinner, B. F. (1953). *Science and human behavior.* New York, NY: Macmillan.

Spielberger, C. D. (1983). *Manual for the State-Trait Anxiety Inventory (STAI).* Palo Alto, CA: Consulting Psychologists Press.

Steger, M. F, Frazier, P., Oishi, S., & Kaler, M. (2006). The Meaning in Life Questionnaire: Assessing the presence of and search for meaning in life. *Journal of Counseling Psychology, 53*, 80–93.

Szadejko, K. (2007, May). *Meaningful life and intrinsic motivation.* Paper presented at the Third International Conference on Self-Determination Theory, Toronto, Ontario, Canada.

Vallerand, R. J. (1997). Toward a hierarchical model of intrinsic and extrinsic motivation. In M. P. Zanna (Ed.), *Advances in experimental social psychology* (Vol. 29, pp. 271–360). San Diego, CA: Academic Press.

Vansteenkiste, M., Simons, J., Lens, W., Sheldon, K. M., & Deci, E. L. (2004). Motivating learning, performance, and persistence: The synergistic effects of intrinsic goal contents and autonomy-supportive contexts. *Journal of Personality and Social Psychology, 87*, 246–260.

Waterman, A. S. (1993). Two conceptions of happiness: Contrasts of personal expressiveness (eudaimonia) and hedonic enjoyment. *Journal of Personality and Social Psychology, 64*, 678–691.

Weinstein, N., Ryan, R. M., & Deci, E. L. (2008). *Life aspirations and the experience of meaning.* Manuscript in preparation.

White, R. W. (1959). Motivation reconsidered: The concept of competence. *Psychological Review, 66*, 297–333.

Wiesel, E. (1958). *Night.* New York, NY: Hill & Wang.

Williams, G. C., Cox, E. M., Hedberg, V., & Deci, E. L. (2000). Extrinsic life goals and health risk behaviors in adolescents. *Journal of Applied Social Psychology, 30*, 1756–1771.

Wong, P. T. P. (1998a). Implicit theories of meaningful life and the development of the personal meaning profile. In P. T. P. Wong & P. S. Fry (Eds.), *The human quest for meaning: A handbook of psychological research and clinical applications* (pp. 111–140). Mahwah, NJ: Erlbaum.

Wong, P. T. P. (1998b). Meaning-centered counseling. In P. T. P. Wong & P. S. Fry (Eds.), *The human quest for meaning: A handbook of psychological research and clinical applications* (pp. 395–436). Mahwah, NJ: Erlbaum.

Yalom, I. D. (1980). *Existential psychotherapy.* New York, NY: Basic Books.

Zika, S., & Chamberlain, K. (1992). On the relation between meaning in life and psychological well-being. *British Journal of Psychology, 83*, 133–145.

Zuroff, D. C., Koestner, R., Moskowitz, D. S., McBride, C., Marshall, M., & Bagby, M. (2007). Autonomous motivation for therapy: A new common factor in brief treatments for depression. *Psychotherapy Research, 17*, 137–147.

5
Meaning and Personality

DAN P. McADAMS
Northwestern University

In 1945, shortly after his release from a Nazi concentration camp, Viktor Frankl spent nine intensive days writing *Ein Psycholog Erlebt das Konzentrationslager*, a psychological account of his three years in Auschwitz, Dachau, and other Nazi prison camps. The original German version bears no name on the cover because Frankl was initially committed to publishing an anonymous report that would never earn its author literary fame. Expanded to include a short overview of "logotherapy" ("therapy of meaning"), the English version of Frankl's book first appeared as *From Death Camp to Existentialism* and finally under its well-known title, *Man's Search for Meaning* (1959/1992). The book detailed Frankl's harrowing experiences as a prisoner of war and described his desperate efforts, and those of many inmates, to sustain hope in the face of unspeakable suffering. Prisoners who lost meaning simply gave up and died at Auschwitz. But those who managed to wrench some semblance of purpose amid the wretchedness maintained at least some chance for survival, Frankl asserted, although luck played a major role as well. Frankl argued that the human quest for meaning is a fundamental human propensity. Under certain extreme conditions, furthermore, finding meaning could make the difference between life and death.

In *Man's Search for Meaning*, and in his earlier *The Doctor and the Soul* (Frankl, 1955), Viktor Frankl helped to usher in a new way to think about human personality. He proposed an *existential psychology of meaning and purpose* that aimed to replace psychoanalysis and behaviorism. As Frankl saw it, Freud's libidinal instincts and Hull's stimulus-response habits were no longer up to the task of explaining why people do what they do and what people really want from life, especially in the wake of the Holocaust and in the midst of the angst and the uncertainty that characterized the postwar years. The human quest for meaning became a central theme in an array of personality theories that began to gain currency in the 1950s and 1960s. Variously termed humanistic, phenomenological, and existential theories, these included broad perspectives on personality offered by Carl Rogers (1951), Abraham Maslow (1954), George Kelly (1955), Ludwig Binswanger (1963), and Rollo May (1967), among others. These theories still have direct impact on research and practice today, and some textbooks (e.g., Ryckman, 2004) still group them together as constituting a broad paradigm for personality study, to be contrasted with psychoanalytic theory and its offshoots, behaviorist and social-learning theories, trait and type approaches, and those theories of personality focused mainly on the biological bases of human behavior.

It would be misleading, however, to conclude that the study of meaning in personality today is confined to those enterprises that call themselves "existential" or "humanistic" or that trace their lineage directly back to Frankl, logotherapy, and the like. In the first decade of the 21st century, the psychological study of meaning is ubiquitous. In a development that would surely have pleased Frankl, psychological theorists, researchers, and therapists of many different persuasions today focus their inquiries and their interventions on how people make meaning in life (e.g., Angus & McLeod, 2004; Bering, 2002; Molden & Dweck, 2006; Neimeyer, 2002; Pals, 2006; Singer, 2004; Wong & Fry, 1998). Some investigators even claim that chimpanzees make meaning, at least in a primitive way (Povinelli & Bering, 2002). When it comes to human personality, one is hard pressed to find a perspective in the current scientific literature that does *not* allow for the prospect of meaning making. The proposition that human beings are largely about the psychological business of making sense out of their own experiences and their interactions in the world is, therefore, an implicit (or in many cases explicit) assumption in many different theories and research programs in personality psychology today (McAdams, 1997, 2006a).

In what follows, I will highlight some of the most important and interesting efforts on the part of theorists and researchers to understand the role of meaning in human personality. My account will be organized according to an emerging integrative framework for personality psychology (Hooker, 2002; McAdams, 1995; McAdams & Pals, 2006; Sheldon, 2004; Singer, 2005). From this perspective, personality may be viewed from three different levels. At the first level, broad *dispositional traits* provide a general sketch of psychological individuality. At the second level, more contextualized *characteristic adaptations* fill in many of the details. At the third level, integrative *life stories* speak to the overall narrative pattern of a life. For any individual, personality is a unique arrangement of (a) dispositional traits, (b) characteristic adaptations, and (c) integrative life stories, evolving in a complex social and cultural context. Human meaning making happens at all three levels of personality, but in different ways.

Level 1: Dispositional Traits

Personality begins with traits. From birth onward, psychological individuality may be observed with respect to broad dimensions of behavioral and emotional style that cut across situations and contexts and readily distinguish one individual from another (Caspi, Roberts, & Shiner, 2005). Through repeated and complex transactions between genes and environments over developmental time, early temperament differences morph into the broad traits of personality that may be observed in adulthood and that go by such names as "extraversion," "dominance," and the tendency toward "depressiveness." Typically assessed by means of self-report scales, dispositional traits account for broad consistencies in behavior across situations and over time. A considerable body of research speaks to the longitudinal continuity of dispositional traits, their substantial heritability, and their ability to predict such important life outcomes as psychological well-being, job success, and mortality (McAdams, 2006a; Ozer & Benet-Martinez, 2006; Roberts & Pomerantz, 2004). Decades of factor-analytic studies conducted around the world suggest, furthermore, that the broad universe of trait dimensions may be organized into about five regions or clusters, now routinely called the Big Five (Goldberg, 1993; McCrae & Costa, 1999). The most well-known conception of the Big Five divides traits into the categories of extraversion (vs. introversion), neuroticism (vs. emotional stability), conscientiousness, agreeableness, and openness to experience.

When it comes to the psychology of meaning, one of the most frequently invoked trait concepts is *hardiness*. In their original conception of hardiness, Kobasa (1979) and Maddi (1998) drew upon existential theory to describe a tendency to strive for meaning and purpose in the face of life's most daunting demands. People with a strong disposition toward hardiness, they argued, welcome *challenges* in life, exert *control* over difficult events, and aim to make lasting *commitments* amid uncertainty and change. A hardy disposition should promote healthy behavior and the ability to cope well with stress. Self-report scales designed to assess individual differences in the three components of hardiness—challenge, control, and commitment—predict corresponding differences in people's responses to stress. For example, Kobasa (1979) found that executives who experienced high levels of stress on the job showed significantly lower levels of physical illness and overall better health if they were high on hardiness compared to individuals low on hardiness. Hardy college students report lower levels of illness than do their peers who are lower in hardiness, regardless of stress level; and lawyers who score high on the commitment scale of hardiness report lower levels of physiological strain (Kobasa, 1982; Kobasa & Pucetti, 1983). Hardiness has also been associated with higher levels of social support, which itself has been linked to better physical and psychological health (Ganellen & Blaney, 1984; Kobasa & Pucetti, 1983). According to Maddi (1998), hardiness helps to promote a wide range of healthy behaviors and attitudes, from dieting to meditation. Hardy attitudes and habits of mind do more than make us happy, however. Following Frankl, Maddi (1998) believes that they also stave off existential despair and help modern people find meaning in life.

Critics have argued that hardiness is not a unitary dispositional construct. For example, Hull, Van Treuren, and Virnelli (1987) insist that challenge, control, and commitment are three very different things. People may show high levels of control in their daily behavior, for instance, but they may not necessarily be predisposed to make enduring commitments or welcome change. Different facets of hardiness appear to predict different outcomes, as well. In light of the emergence of the five-factor model of dispositional traits, it indeed appears that hardiness is something of a hodgepodge—part conscientiousness, part low neuroticism, perhaps part high openness to experience. These well-established trait domains have themselves been shown to link to health and meaning making in important ways. Conscientiousness is a strong predictor of such health-related behaviors as physical exercise, better diet, and lower levels of substance abuse, smoking, and risky sexual practices (Bogg & Roberts, 2004). Conscientiousness also predicts such meaningful, prosocial involvements in the community as church attendance and volunteerism (Lodi-Smith & Roberts, 2007). High levels of openness to experience tend to be associated with preferences for complex and challenging environments (McCrae & Costa, 1997). High levels of neuroticism are a risk factor for a wide range of problems in life, including those implicated in both personal meaning and physical health. People high in neuroticism tend to feel vulnerable and insecure and are more apt than individuals low in neuroticism to report guilt, shame, anguish, despair, and alienation in life.

Surveying the full panoply of Big Five traits reveals a surprisingly powerful connection between meaning and a disposition toward *extraversion*. Traditional conceptions of extraversion have suggested that this trait is mainly about being gregarious and sociable. For example, Jung (1936/1971) argued that extraverts tend to draw energy from people and social relationships, whereas introverts tend to draw energy from the inner life of the mind. As in so many things, however, Jung appears to have been more romantic than right. A substantial body of research now shows that extraversion is just as much about the tendency to pursue rewards and to experience positive emotion as it is about being with people (Smillie, Pickering, & Jackson, 2006; Watson & Clark, 1997). Again and again, studies show that people high in extraversion report more positive emotions in life, even when they are *not* with people (Lucas & Diener, 2001). And high levels of positive emotion tend to be strongly associated with feeling that life has meaning and purpose. Whether considering the short-term effects of a situationally induced experience of positive emotion or considering the long-term effects of trait-based dispositions toward positive emotionality, researchers found that people who are experiencing positive emotion tend to report that their lives feel more meaningful to them, compared to individuals experiencing lower levels of positive emotion (King, Hicks, Krull, & Del Gaiso, 2006). Fredrickson (2001) has argued that positive emotions "build and broaden" a healthy and meaningful life. The dispositional tendency to enjoy life, to find joy and excitement in what life has to offer, may promote the search for meaning; likewise, striving for meaning may cultivate traits of positive emotionality.

In sum, a broad range of dispositional traits in personality, ranging across the Big Five spectrum, appear to have implications for meaning in life. Certain dispositional profiles—high hardiness, for example, high levels of extraversion, conscientiousness, and openness to experience, and low levels of neuroticism—tend to be associated with an overall feeling that life has purpose and value, that one is connected to others and to society in meaningful ways, and that obstacles in life can be overcome. Basic dispositional traits in personality appear to provide *psychological resources* upon which individuals draw in the quest for human meaning. If one is blessed with high levels of extraversion, for example, or a strong conscientiousness trait, one may be better equipped, psychologically speaking, to find ways to make life feel meaningful and purposeful. Precisely what form such meaning making may take, however, can typically not be deduced from traits. One hardy person may find meaning in an activist life of social change. Yet another may find it in the family. A third may believe that the deepest meanings in life come from spiritual longings and religion. A fourth may locate meaning primarily in a life dedicated to work. Dispositional traits can take us only so far in understanding how personality relates to meaning in life. To articulate a more nuanced understanding, one must move from the dispositional sketch provided by personality traits to a second level of personality.

Level 2: Characteristic Adaptations

From middle childhood onward, human beings build a second layer of personality upon the dispositional base, even as that base continues to develop thereafter. Residing at the second level are characteristic adaptations—a wide assortment of motivational, social-cognitive, and developmental constructs that are more specific than dispositional traits and that are contextualized in time, place, and/or social role (McAdams, 2006a; McAdams & Pals, 2006). Included in this list are motives, goals, strivings, personal projects, values, interests, defense mechanisms, coping strategies, relational schemata, possible selves, developmental concerns, and other variables of psychological individuality that speak directly to what people want and do not want (e.g., fear) in life and how they go about getting what they want and avoiding what they do not want in particular situations, during particular times in their lives, and with respect to particular social roles. Characteristic adaptations have typically been the constructs of choice for classic motivational (e.g., Deci & Ryan, 1991; Murray, 1938/2008), social-cognitive (e.g., Mischel & Shoda, 1995), and developmental (e.g., Erikson, 1963; Loevinger, 1976) theories of personality. Whereas broad personality traits provide a dispositional sketch for psychological individuality, characteristic adaptations fill in many of the details.

A great deal of what people mean when they use the word *meaning* can be discerned in the kinds of characteristic adaptations they ultimately develop. For many people, meaning in life is tied up with their most cherished values. Political conservatives and liberals, for example, understand themselves and their worlds in very different ways. Conservatives show higher levels of mortality concerns and greater needs for order and closure than do liberals (Jost, Glaser, Kruglanski, & Sulloway, 2003). Liberals are more likely to say that a moral person should promote justice and alleviate suffering above all else, whereas conservatives are more likely to affirm the values of authority, loyalty, and purity of the self (Haidt, 2007; McAdams et al., 2008). Religious values and interests shape how people the world over make meaning in life. For many people, religious traditions provide a source of ultimate life meaning and purpose (Emmons, 1999). Take religious faith away and life would suddenly be bereft of meaning, many people say.

Among those characteristic adaptations that are most instrumental in shaping life meanings are personal goals and projects (Freund & Riediger, 2006; Little, 1998). Goals and projects are always about the future—the imagined ends for tomorrow that guide behavior today. As situations change, as people grow older, as individuals move from one social role to the next, goals and projects change to meet new demands and constraints. Research suggests that goals in early adulthood often focus on expanding the self and gaining new information, whereas goals in later adulthood may focus more on the emotional quality of ongoing relationships (Carstensen, 1995; Helson, Soto, & Cate, 2006). At any given point in the life course, the content of people's goals reflects important sources of personal meaning. Personality psychologists have examined those sources at the broad levels of motivational categories (e.g., intrinsic vs. extrinsic goals; motives for power, achievement, and intimacy) and with respect to the particularities of a given person–situation ecology. Studies of the former type have found, for example, that intrinsic, growth-oriented goals and strong needs to care for others and make positive contributions to society are often associated with greater psychological well-being and reports of higher life meaning (Bauer & McAdams, 2004a; Emmons, 1999; Kasser & Ryan, 1996). Beyond content, process variables are just as important for life meaning. People tend to feel that their lives are most meaningful when they are making steady progress on their personal goals and when their goals are viewed to be congruent rather than conflicting (Emmons & King, 1988; Little, 1998).

Theories of personality development suggest that what constitutes meaning changes with developmental time. In her highly influential theory of ego development, Loevinger (1976) conceives of the ego as a person's characteristic framework for making meaning of self and society. Young children and individuals at the lowest stages of ego development make sense of the world in terms of their egocentric needs and their primitive calculations of personal hedonism. What is good is what meets my needs; what is bad is what brings me punishment and pain. In the middle stages of her scheme, people mature into a conventional framework for meaning making as they take the perspectives of their self-defining groups and eventually the perspectives of society as a whole. Deep sources of meaning come from one's conformity to society's most cherished scripts for productive and responsible behavior at work, at home, and in the broader societal context. At higher stages, one comes to construct more personalized frameworks of meaning that may defy conventions and incorporate self-evaluated standards and abstract ethical principles. Love, work, family, citizenship—these are all powerful sites for meaning making at almost all stages in Loevinger's scheme. But precisely what these meaningful domains actually mean depends on the stage of ego development wherein one finds oneself at any given point in the life course.

Loevinger (1976) suggested that as one moves up the ego-developmental ladder, one is likely to become more and more concerned with establishing an *identity*. In his theory of psychosocial development, Erikson (1963) located this move within the developmental epoch that now goes by the name of *emerging adulthood* (Arnett, 2000). In the late teens and throughout the 20s, and especially in modern societies, the most pressing psychosocial challenge is to construct and begin to live a coherent and vivifying ego identity. Erikson viewed identity to be a special arrangement of the self. The arrangement functions to integrate disparate roles, goals, needs, fears, skills, and inclinations into a coherent pattern, a pattern that specifies how the emerging adult will live, love, work, and believe in a complex and changing world. The virtue of the identity stage is *fidelity*, Erikson maintained. One must show fidelity to a particular arrangement of selfhood. One must commit oneself to a particular kind of meaningful life. At the very heart of identity, then, is the problem of meaning and purpose in life (McAdams, 1985). What does my life mean in full? Who am I today? How am I different today from what I was in my past? Who will I be in the future? These large questions regarding the meaning of one's life in full developmental time—past, present, and future—cannot be fully answered through dispositional traits and characteristic adaptations. Instead, they require a story of who I am, was, and will be. One way to read Erikson's idea of identity is to see it as an internalized and evolving story of the self that people begin to construct in the emerging adult years (Habermas & Bluck 2000; McAdams, 1985). Beyond dispositional traits and characteristic adaptations, then, lies the realm of narrative identity, wherein life meanings reach their most extended and elaborated forms.

Level 3: Narrative Identity

Even as dispositional traits and characteristic adaptations continue to develop through the emerging adulthood years, a third level of personality surfaces to meet the psychosocial challenge of modern identity. Layered over the Big Five traits and the panoply of goals, motives, projects, fears, strategies, values, and beliefs that heretofore comprised psychological individuality is an emerging narrative identity—an internalized and evolving story of the reconstructed past and imagined future that aims to provide life with unity, coherence, and purpose. For both the self and others, the life story explains how I came to be, who I am today, where I am going in the future, and what I believe my life means within the psychosocial niche provided by family, friends, work, society, and the cultural and ideological resources of my environment. It is a story that distinguishes me from all others and yet shows how I am connected to others as well. It is a story that narrates the evolution of a particular self, but it is a self in cultural context. Every life story says as much about the culture within which a person lives as it does about the person living it. In constructing a life story, people choose from the menu of images, themes, plots, and characters provided by the particular environments to which they are exposed (McAdams, 2006b; Rosenwald & Ochberg, 1992). They make meaning within the milieu of meanings provided by culture. What Frankl called man's search for meaning takes place in an existentially circumscribed arena, wherein certain culturally favored meanings already exist and the individual is challenged to pick and choose and appropriate in order to make a story that makes sense to the self and the social world within which the self is embedded (McAdams, 2006b).

What prompts the emergence of narrative identity in late adolescence and young adulthood? Cognitive factors are surely important. With the advent of what Piaget called formal operational thought, adolescents are now able to take their own lives as objects of systematic reflection (Breger, 1974; McAdams, 1985). Whereas young children can dream about what might someday be, adolescents can think through the possibilities in a hypothetico-deductive manner. They can now ask themselves such questions as these: What is my life really about? Who might I be in the future? What if I decide to reject my parents' religion? How might my life develop if I am gay? This newfound philosophical inclination requires a narrative frame for self-construction. The earliest drafts of narrative identity may take the form of what Elkind (1981) called the *personal fable*, that is, fantastical stories of the self's greatness. But later drafts become more realistic, as reality testing improves and narrative skills become further refined. Habermas and Bluck (2000) have shown how adolescents gradually master the cognitive skills required for constructing a coherent narrative of the self. By the end of their teenaged years, they regularly engage in sophisticated forms of *autobiographical reasoning.* They can link together multiple autobiographical scenes in causal sequences to explain what they believe to be their own development in a given area of life. And they can extract underlying themes that they believe characterize unique aspects of their lives in full.

Social and cultural factors also help to bring narrative identity to the developmental fore at this time. Peers and parents expect adolescents to begin sorting out what their lives mean, both for the future and the past. Given what I have done up to this point in my life, where do I go now? What kind of life should I make for myself? Paralleling the cognitive and emotional changes taking place within the individual are shifts in society's expectations about what the individual, who was a child but who is now almost an adult, should be doing, thinking, and feeling. Erikson (1959) wrote:

> It is of great relevance to the young individual's identity formation that he be responded to, and be given function and status as a person whose gradual growth and transformation make sense to those who begin to make sense to him. (p. 111)

In general, modern societies expect their adolescents and young adults to examine occupational, ideological, and interpersonal opportunities around them and to begin to make some decisions about what their lives as adults are to be about. This is to say, both society and the emerging adult are ready for his or her explorations in narrative identity by the time he or she has, in fact, become an emerging adult. As Erikson (1959) described it:

> The period can be viewed as a psychosocial moratorium during which the individual through free role experimentation may find a niche in some section of his society, a niche which is firmly defined and yet seems to be uniquely made for him. In finding it the young adult gains an assured sense of inner continuity and social sameness which will bridge what he was as a child and what he is about to become, and will reconcile his conception of himself and his community's recognition of him. (p. 111)

For the past 15 years or so, personality psychologists and other social scientists have examined the content, structure, and functions of the narrative identities that people begin to construct in the emerging adulthood years and continue to construct as they move through the adult life course. Researchers have catalogued common narrative forms and themes, connected features of narrative identity to personality traits and characteristic adaptations, examined developmental change in narrative identity, and explored the interpersonal and cultural contexts within which life stories are constructed and performed (McAdams, 2008; McAdams, Josselson, & Lieblich, 2006; McLean, Pasupathi, & Pals, 2007; Singer, 2004; Thorne, 2000). With respect to personal meaning, an important theme in this research is the construction of life narratives in the face of suffering. As Frankl knew, pain and suffering challenge human beings to make sense out of that which seems senseless, random, and tragic. Not surprisingly, therefore, researchers have focused a great deal of attention on the narration of negative events.

Pals (2006) has argued that making sense out of negative events in one's life ideally involves a two-step process. In the first step, the narrator explores the negative experience in depth, thinking long and hard about what the experience feels or felt like, how it came to be, what it may lead to, and what role the negative event may play in one's overall understanding of self. In the second step, the narrator articulates and commits the self to a positive resolution of the event. Pals (2006) warned that one should not pass lightly over Step 1. When it comes to narrative identity, Pals suggested, the unexamined life lacks depth and meaning.

Consistent with Pals (2006), a number of studies have shown that exploring negative life events in detail is associated with psychological maturity. For example, King and her colleagues have conducted a series of intriguing studies wherein they ask people who have faced daunting life challenges to tell stories about "what might have been" had their lives developed in either a more positive or more expected direction. In one study, mothers of infants with Down syndrome reflected upon what their lives might have been like had they given birth to babies not afflicted with Down's. Those mothers who were able to articulate detailed and thoughtful accounts, suggesting a great deal of exploration and meaning making in their processing of this negative life event, tended to score higher on Loevinger's (1976) measure of ego development than did mothers who discounted what might have been (King, Scollon, Ramsey, & Williams, 2000).

In a study of how midlife women respond to divorce, the elaboration of loss in narrative accounts interacted with time since divorce to predict ego development (King & Raspin, 2004). Among women who had been divorced for an extended period of time, vivid and highly elaborate accounts of the married life they had lost were associated with higher ego development at the time of their life telling, and narrative elaboration predicted increases in ego development measured two years later. In a methodologically similar study, King and Smith (2004) found that the extent to which gay and lesbian individuals explored what might have been had their lives followed a more conventional (heterosexual) course predicted high levels of ego development at the time of their life-narrative accounts and increases in ego development two years later.

Narrative studies of life transitions have also shown that self-exploration and elaboration are associated with higher levels of ego development. Bauer and McAdams (2004b) examined narrative accounts from people who had undergone major life changes in either work or religion. People high in ego development tended to construct accounts of these difficult transitions that emphasized learning, growth, and positive personal transformation. The extent to which personal narratives emphasizing self-exploration, transformation, and integration are positively correlated with ego development has also been documented in studies of narrative accounts of life's high points, low points, and turning points (Bauer, McAdams, & Sakaeda, 2005). In another study linking development to narrative processing, McLean and Pratt (2006) found that young adults who used more elaborated and sophisticated forms of meaning making in narrating turning points in their lives tended also to score higher on an overall identity maturity index.

If the first step in making narrative sense of negative life events is exploring and elaborating upon their nature and impact, Step 2 involves constructing a positive meaning or resolution (Pals, 2006). Numerous studies have shown that deriving positive meanings from negative events is associated with life satisfaction and indicators of emotional well-being. For example, King and colleagues demonstrated that attaining a sense of closure regarding negative experiences from the past and/or lost possible selves predicts self-reported psychological well-being among mothers of Down syndrome children (King et al., 2000) and divorced women (King & Raspin, 2004). In her analysis of longitudinal data from the Mills study, Pals (2006) found that coherent positive resolutions of difficult life events at age 51 predicted life satisfaction at age 61 and were associated with increasing ego resiliency between young adulthood and midlife.

Finding positive meanings in negative events is the central theme that runs through McAdams's (2006b) conception of *the redemptive self.* In a series of nomothetic and idiographic studies conducted over the past 15 years, McAdams and colleagues have consistently found that midlife American adults who score especially high on self-report measures of generativity—suggesting a strong commitment to promoting the well-being of future generations and improving the world in which they live (Erikson, 1963)—tend to see their own lives as narratives of redemption (Mansfield & McAdams, 1996; McAdams, Diamond, de St. Aubin, & Mansfield, 1997; McAdams et al., 2001; see also Walker & Frimer, 2007). Compared to their less generative American counterparts, highly generative adults tend to construct life stories that feature redemption sequences in which the protagonist is delivered from suffering to an enhanced status or state. In addition, highly generative American adults are more likely than their less generative peers to construct life stories in which the protagonist (a) enjoys a special advantage or blessing early in life, (b) expresses sensitivity to the suffering of others or societal injustice as a child, (c) establishes a clear and strong value system in adolescence that remains a source of unwavering conviction through the adult years, (d) experiences significant conflicts between desires for agency and power and desires for communion and love, and (e) looks to achieve goals to benefit society in the future. Taken together, these themes articulate a general script or narrative prototype that many highly generative American adults employ to make sense of their own lives. For highly productive and caring midlife American adults, the redemptive self is a narrative model of an especially good and meaningful life.

The redemptive self is a life-story prototype that serves to support the generative efforts of midlife men and women. Their redemptive life narratives tell how generative adults seek to give back to society in gratitude for the early advantages and blessings they feel they have received. In every life, generativity is tough and frustrating work, as every parent or community volunteer knows. But if an adult constructs a narrative identity in which the protagonist's suffering in the short run often gives way to reward later on, he or she may be better able to sustain the conviction that seemingly thankless investments today will pay off for future generations. Redemptive life stories support the kind of life strivings that a highly generative man or woman is likely to set forth.

At the same time, the redemptive self may say as much about American culture and tradition as it does about the highly generative American adults who tend to tell this kind of story about their lives. McAdams (2006b) argued that the life-story themes expressed by highly generative American adults recapture and couch in a psychological language especially cherished, as well as hotly contested, ideas in American cultural history—ideas that appear prominently in spiritual accounts of the 17th-century Puritans, Benjamin Franklin's 18th-century autobiography, slave narratives and Horatio Alger stories from the 19th century, and the literature of self-help and American entrepreneurship from more recent times. Evolving from the Puritans to Emerson to Oprah, the redemptive self has morphed into many different storied forms in the past 300 years as Americans have sought to narrate their lives as redemptive tales of atonement, emancipation, recovery, self-fulfillment, and upward social mobility. The stories speak of heroic individual protagonists—the *chosen people*—whose *manifest destiny* is to make a positive difference in a dangerous world, even when the world does not wish to be redeemed. The stories translate a deep and abiding script of American exceptionalism into the many contemporary narratives of success, recovery, development, liberation, and self-actualization that so pervade American talk, talk shows, therapy sessions, sermons, and commencement speeches. It is as if especially generative American adults, whose lives are dedicated to making the world a better place for future generations, are, for better and sometimes for worse, the most ardent narrators of a general life-story script as Americans as apple pie and the Super Bowl.

Conclusion

What Victor Frankl first described as "man's search for meaning" plays itself out at three different levels of human personality. At the level of dispositional traits, human beings draw upon basic psychological resources to support their efforts to find happiness and meaning amid life's struggles. These resources, however, are not distributed in a random or egalitarian manner. The dispositional traits that group themselves together within the Big Five cluster of neuroticism may breed alienation and undermine people's best efforts to cope with adversity and loss. By contrast, traits associated with extraversion and positive emotionality appear to enhance meaning making and promote positive coping, whereas traits associated with conscientiousness promote positive lifestyle habits that enhance health and make for productive and meaningful work. At the second level of personality, meaning is captured in goals, projects, strategies, and other motivational, social-cognitive, and developmental facets of personality that are contextualized in time, place, and social role. As trait dimensions provide basic resources upon which people draw to construct a meaningful life, the characteristic adaptations at the second level of personality spell out what kinds of meanings people make and the specific areas in life wherein they make them.

The human quest for meaning reaches its developmental and epistemic apex with the construction of narrative identity, a process that begins in the emerging adulthood years. Beyond dispositional traits and characteristic adaptations, life stories convey what people believe their lives mean in full, and in time. Who am I? How did I come to be who I am? Where is my life going? What does my life mean in full? It takes a story to answer the big questions like these. People begin to construct internalized and evolving life stories in the emerging adulthood years, and they continue the process of narrative identity construction for pretty much the rest of their lives. The stories they construct are strongly shaped by culture. Indeed, culture provides the canonical set of images, themes, plots, and characters from which people draw in fashioning their own unique stories—stories that, at the end of the day, say as much about culture as they do about the storytellers themselves.

Recent research suggests that a favored life-narrative form in American society is the redemptive self, a narrative about a gifted and morally steadfast protagonist who journeys forth into a dangerous world, transforms suffering into growth, and aims to leave a positive legacy of the self for future generations. Epitomized in American stories of atonement, liberation, recovery, and upward social mobility, the redemptive self provides a good example of one way that many highly generative American adults make meaning in their lives. Indeed, this kind of story is a very meaningful story for many people, and research suggests that it is a story that promotes a caring and productive adult life, at least among many Americans. But there are many ways to make a meaningful life, many different kinds of meaningful stories of life that can be told and lived. Culture provides a range of possibilities for life-story constructions, and each culture provides its own unique range. Recalling his experiences in the concentration camps, Frankl knew that different prisoners made meaning in different ways. Personality psychology has always affirmed the vast variability of psychological functioning. There are many ways to live a meaningful life and many kinds of stories to tell about it.

References

Angus, L. E., & McLeod, J. (Eds.). (2004). *Handbook of narrative and psychotherapy.* London, England: Sage.

Arnett, J. J. (2000). Emerging adulthood: A theory of development from the late teens through the twenties. *American Psychologist, 55*, 469–480.

Bauer, J. J., & McAdams, D. P. (2004a). Growth goals, maturity, and well-being. *Developmental Psychology, 40*, 114–127.

Bauer, J. J., & McAdams, D. P. (2004b). Personal growth in adults' stories of life transitions. *Journal of Personality, 72*, 573–602.

Bauer, J. J., McAdams, D. P., & Sakaeda, A. (2005). Interpreting the good life: Growth memories in the lives of mature, happy people. *Journal of Personality and Social Psychology, 88*, 203–217.

Bering, J. M. (2002). The existential theory of mind. *Review of General Psychology, 6*, 3–24.

Binswanger, L. (1963). *Being-in-the-world.* New York, NY: Basic Books.

Bogg, T., & Roberts, B. W. (2004). Conscientiousness and health-related behavior: A meta-analysis of the leading behavioral contributions to mortality. *Psychological Bulletin, 130*, 887–919.

Breger, L. (1974). *From instinct to identity: The development of personality.* Englewood Cliffs, NJ: Prentice-Hall.

Carstensen, L. L. (1995). Evidence for a life-span theory of socioemotional selectivity. *Current Directions in Psychological Science, 4*, 151–155.

Caspi, A., Roberts, B. W., & Shiner, R. L. (2005). Personality development: Stability and change. In S. T. Fiske & D. Schacter (Eds.), *Annual review of psychology* (Vol. 56, pp. 453–484). Palo Alto, CA: Annual Reviews.

Deci, E. L., & Ryan, R. M. (1991). A motivational approach to self: Integration in personality. In R. Dienstbier & R. M. Ryan (Eds.), *Nebraska symposium on motivation, 1990* (pp. 237–288). Lincoln: University of Nebraska Press.

Elkind, D. (1981). *Children and adolescents* (3rd ed.). New York, NY: Oxford University Press.

Emmons, R. A. (1999). *The psychology of ultimate concerns: Motivation and spirituality in personality.* New York, NY: Guilford Press.

Emmons, R. A., & King. L. A. (1988). Conflict among personal strivings: Immediate and long-term implications for psychological and physical well-being. *Journal of Personality and Social Psychology, 54*, 1040–1048.

Erikson, E. H. (1959). Identity and the life cycle: Selected papers. *Psychological Issues, 1*, 5–165.

Erikson, E. H. (1963). *Childhood and society* (2nd ed.). New York, NY: Norton.

Frankl, V. E. (1955). *The doctor and the soul: From psychotherapy to logotherapy.* New York, NY: Knopf.

Frankl, V. E. (1992). *Man's search for meaning* (4th ed.). Boston, MA: Beacon Press. (Originally published 1959)

Fredrickson, B. L. (2001). The role of positive emotions in positive psychology: The broaden-and-build theory of positive emotions. *American Psychologist, 56*, 218–226.

Freund, A. M., & Riediger, M. (2006). Goals as building blocks of personality and development in adulthood. In D. K. Mroczek & T. D. Little (Eds.), *Handbook of personality development* (pp. 353–372). Mahwah, NJ: Erlbaum.

Ganellen, R. J., & Blaney, P. H. (1984). Hardiness and social support as moderators of the effects of life stress. *Journal of Personality and Social Psychology, 47*, 156–163.

Goldberg, L. R. (1993). The structure of phenotypic personality traits. *American Psychologist, 48*, 26–34.

Habermas, T., & Bluck, S. (2000). Getting a life: The emergence of the life story in adolescence. *Psychological Bulletin, 126*, 748–769.

Haidt, J. (2007). The new synthesis in moral psychology. *Science, 316*, 998–1001.

Helsen, R., Soto, C. J., & Cate, R. A. (2006). From young adulthood through the middle age. In D. K. Mroczek & T. D. Little (Eds.), *Handbook of personality development* (pp. 337–352). Mahwah, NJ: Erlbaum.

Hooker, K. (2002). New directions for research in personality and aging: A comprehensive model linking levels, structures, and processes. *Journal of Research in Personality, 36*, 318–334.

Hull, J. G., Van Treuren, R. R., & Virnelli, S. (1987). Hardiness and health: A critique and alternative approach. *Journal of Personality and Social Psychology, 53*, 518–530.

Jost, J. T., Glaser, J., Kruglanski, A. W., & Sulloway, F. J. (2003). Political conservatism as motivated social cognition. *Psychological Bulletin, 129*, 339–375.

Jung, C. G. (1971). Psychological typology. In H. Read, M. Fundham, G. Adler, & W. McGuire (Eds.), *The collected works of C. G. Jung* (Vol. 6, pp. 542–555). Princeton, NJ: Princeton University Press. (Originally published 1936)

Kasser, T., & Ryan, R. M. (1996). Further examining the American dream: Well-being correlates of intrinsic and extrinsic goals. *Personality and Social Psychology Bulletin, 22*, 281–288.

Kelly, G. (1955). *The psychology of personal constructs.* New York, NY: Norton.

King, L. A., Hicks, J. A., Krull, J. L., & Del Gaiso, A. K. (2006). Positive affect and the experience of meaning in life. *Journal of Personality and Social Psychology, 90*, 179–196.

King, L. A., & Raspin, C. (2004). Lost and found possible selves, subjective well-being, and ego development in divorced women. *Journal of Personality, 72*, 602–632.

King, L. A., Scollon, C. K., Ramsey, C., & Williams, T. (2000). Stories of life transition: Subjective well-being and ego development in parents of children with Down Syndrome. *Journal of Research in Personality, 34*, 509–536.

King, L. A., & Smith, N. G. (2004). Gay and straight possible selves: Goals, identity, subjective well-being, and personality development. *Journal of Personality, 72*, 967–994.

Kobasa, S. C. (1979). Stressful life events, personality, and health: An inquiry into hardiness. *Journal of Personality and Social Psychology, 37*, 1–11.

Kobasa, S. C. (1982). Commitment and coping in stress resistance among lawyers. *Journal of Personality and Social Psychology, 42*, 707–717.

Kobasa, S. C., & Pucetti, M.C. (1983). Personality and social resources in stress resistance. *Journal of Personality and Social Psychology, 45*, 839–850.

Little, B. R. (1998). Personal project pursuit: Dimensions and dynamics of personal meaning. In P. T. P. Wong & P. S. Fry (Eds.), *The human quest for meaning: A handbook of psychological research and clinical applications* (pp. 193–212). Mahwah, NJ: Erlbaum.

Lodi-Smith, J., & Roberts, B. W. (2007). Social investment and personality: A meta-analysis of the relationship of personality traits to investment in work, family, religion, and volunteerism. *Personality and Social Psychology Review, 11*, 68–86.

Loevinger, J. (1976). *Ego development.* San Francisco, CA: Jossey-Bass.

Lucas, R. E., & Diener, E. (2001). Understanding extraverts' enjoyment of social situations: The importance of pleasantness. *Journal of Personality and Social Psychology, 81*, 343–356.

Maddi, S. R. (1998). Creating meaning through making decisions. In P. T. P. Wong & P. S. Fry (Eds.), *The human quest for meaning: A handbook of psychological research and clinical applications* (pp. 3–26). Mahwah, NJ: Erlbaum.

Mansfield, E. D., & McAdams, D. P. (1996). Generativity and themes of agency and communion in adult autobiography. *Personality and Social Psychology Bulletin, 22*, 721–731.

Maslow, A. (1954). *Motivation and personality*. New York, NY: Harper & Row.
May, R. (1967). *Love and will*. New York, NY: Norton.
McAdams, D. P. (1985). *Power, intimacy, and the life story: Personological inquiries into identity*. Homewood, IL: Dorsey Press.
McAdams, D. P. (1995). What do we know when we know a person? *Journal of Personality, 63*, 365–396.
McAdams, D. P. (1997). A conceptual history of personality psychology. In R. Hogan, J. Johnson, & S. Briggs (Eds.), *Handbook of personality psychology* (pp. 3–29). San Diego, CA: Academic Press.
McAdams, D. P. (2006a). *The person: A new introduction to personality psychology* (4th ed.). New York, NY: Wiley.
McAdams, D. P. (2006b). *The redemptive self: Stories Americans live by*. New York, NY: Oxford University Press.
McAdams, D. P. (2008). Personal narratives and the life story. In O. John, R. Robins, & L. Pervin (Eds.), *Handbook of personality: Theory and research* (3rd ed., pp. 241–261). New York, NY: Guilford Press.
McAdams, D. P., Albaugh, M., Farber, E., Daniels, J., Logan, R. L., & Olson, B. (2008). Family metaphors and moral intuitions: How conservatives and liberals narrate their lives. *Journal of Personality and Social Psychology, 95*, 978–990.
McAdams, D. P., Diamond, A., de St. Aubin, E., & Mansfield, E. D. (1997). Stories of commitment: The psychosocial construction of generative lives. *Journal of Personality and Social Psychology, 72*, 678–694.
McAdams, D. P., Josselson, R., & Lieblich, A. (Eds.). (2006). *Identity and story: Creating self in narrative*. Washington, DC: American Psychological Association Press.
McAdams, D. P., & Pals, J. L. (2006). A new Big Five: Fundamental principles for an integrative science of personality. *American Psychologist, 61*, 204–217.
McAdams, D. P., Reynolds, J., Lewis, M., Patten, A., & Bowman, P. J. (2001). When bad things turn good and good things turn bad: Sequences of redemption and contamination in life narrative, and their relation to psychosocial adaptation in midlife adults and in students. *Personality and Social Psychology Bulletin, 27*, 472–483.
McCrae, R. R., & Costa, P. T., Jr. (1997). Conceptions and correlates of openness to experience. In R. Hogan, J. Johnson, & S. Briggs (Eds.), *Handbook of personality psychology* (pp. 825–847). San Diego, CA: Academic Press.
McCrae, R. R., & Costa, P. T., Jr. (1999). A five-factor theory of personality. In L. Pervin & O. John (Eds.), *Handbook of personality: Theory and research* (2nd ed., pp. 139–153). New York, NY: Guilford Press.
McLean, K. C., Pasupathi, M., & Pals, J. L. (2007). Selves creating stories creating selves: A process model of self-development. *Personality and Social Psychology Review, 11*, 262–278.
McLean, K. C., & Pratt, M. W. (2006). Life's little (and big) lessons: Identity statuses and meaning-making in the turning point narratives of emerging adults. *Developmental Psychology, 42*, 714–722.
Mischel, W., & Shoda, Y. (1995). A cognitive-affective systems theory of personality: Reconceptualizing situations, dispositions, dynamics, and invariance in personality structure. *Psychological Review, 102*, 246–268.
Molden, D. C., & Dweck, C. S. (2006). Finding "meaning" in psychology: A lay theories approach to self-regulation, social perception, and social development. *American Psychologist, 61*, 192–203.
Murray, H. A. (2008). *Explorations in personality*. New York, NY: Oxford University Press. (Originally published 1938)

Neimeyer, R. A. (Ed.). (2002). *Meaning reconstruction and the experience of loss.* Washington, DC: American Psychological Association Press.

Ozer, D. J., & Benet-Martinez, V. (2006). Personality and the prediction of consequential outcomes. In S. Fiske, A. E. Kazkin, & D. L. Schacter (Eds.), *Annual review of psychology* (Vol. 57, pp. 401–421). Palo Alto, CA: Annual Reviews.

Pals, J. L. (2006). Narrative identity processing of difficult life events: Pathways of personality development and positive self-transformation in adulthood. *Journal of Personality, 74,* 1079–1109.

Povinelli, D. J., & Bering, J. M. (2002). The mentality of apes revisited. *Current Directions in Psychological Science, 11,* 115–119.

Roberts, B. W., & Pomerantz, E. M. (2004). On traits, situations, and their integration: A developmental perspective. *Personality and Social Psychology Review, 8,* 402–416.

Rogers, C. R. (1951). *Client-centered therapy.* Boston, MA: Houghton Mifflin.

Rosenwald, G., & Ochberg, R. L. (Eds.). (1992). *Storied lives: The cultural politics of self-understanding.* New Haven, CT: Yale University Press.

Ryckman, R. M. (2004). *Theories of personality* (8th ed.). Belmont, CA: Thomson.

Sheldon, K. M. (2004). *The psychology of ultimate being: An integrative, multi-level perspective.* Mahwah, NJ: Erlbaum.

Singer, J. A. (2004). Narrative, identity, and meaning making across the adult lifespan: An introduction. *Journal of Personality, 72,* 437–459.

Singer, J. A. (2005). *Personality and psychotherapy: Treating the whole person.* New York, NY: Guilford Press.

Smillie, L. D., Pickering, A. D., & Jackson, C. J. (2006). The new reinforcement sensitivity theory: Implications for personality measurement. *Personality and Social Psychology Review, 10,* 320–335.

Thorne, A. (2000). Personal memory telling and personality development. *Personality and Social Psychology Review, 4,* 45–56.

Walker, L. J., & Frimer, J. A. (2007). Moral personality of brave and caring exemplars. *Journal of Personality and Social Psychology, 93,* 845–860.

Watson, D., & Clark, L. A. (1997). Extraversion and its positive emotional core. In R. Hogan, J. Johnson, & S. Briggs (Eds.), *Handbook of personality psychology* (pp. 767–793). San Diego, CA: Academic Press.

Wong, P. T. P., & Fry, P. S. (Eds.). (1998). *The human quest for meaning: A handbook of psychological research and clinical applications.* Mahwah, NJ: Erlbaum.

6 Positive Affect and Meaning in Life

The Intersection of Hedonism and Eudaimonia

LAURA A. KING

University of Missouri, Columbia

JOSHUA A. HICKS

Texas A&M University

> All Goods are disguised by the vulgarity of their concomitants, in this work-a-day world; but woe to him who can only recognize them when he thinks them in their pure and abstract form!
>
> **—William James (1892)**

Happiness is a central theme in many approaches to the Good Life. Drawing on Aristotle's (350 BCE/1998 CE) treatment of happiness in *The Nicomachean Ethics*, psychologists interested in well-being have frequently employed the distinction between hedonism and eudaimonia to understand the many facets of the Good Life (King, Eells, & Burton, 2004). Generally speaking, hedonic well-being is essentially how a person feels about his or her life (Kahneman, Diener, & Schwarz, 1999; Ryan & Deci, 2001). For example, subjective well-being, an indicator of hedonic functioning, is typically defined as one's positive and negative mood coupled with a cognitive evaluation of satisfaction with one's life (Diener, Suh, Lucas, & Smith, 1999). Eudaimonia, in contrast, refers to the extent to which an individual's life is characterized as enacting virtue or organismic values, engagement in meaningful pursuits, or authentic expression of the self (Waterman, 1993). Eudaimonia might be measured by an individual's commitment to intrinsic values or dedication to a life of meaning (Ryan & Deci, 2001).

The two variables at the center of this chapter arguably represent prototypical aspects of these two sides of well-being. Positive affect (PA) is clearly at the very heart of hedonics, essentially a person's subjective feeling states. In turn, meaning in life is emblematic of eudaimonia. A meaningful life might be thought of as representing the greater good of virtuous living. Recently, research has revealed a very strong positive link between PA and the experience of meaning in life (King, Hicks, Krull, & Del Gaiso, 2006). This link might be viewed as a puzzle to be solved or a problem to be explained away. In contrast, the strong relationship between PA and meaning in life might be entertained as an indication of a very real link between the rather quotidian "work-a-day" experience of mood and the grander experience of the Good in life that is the experience of meaning. In this chapter, we consider both of these possibilities. First, we briefly review past research demonstrating the relationship between PA and the experience of meaning in life. We then examine the accumulated evidence relevant to explaining away this relationship. Finally, we set aside the notion that the relationship between PA and meaning in life ought to be explained away and consider the possibility that this relationship is real, adaptive, and important. Understanding the role of PA in the experience of meaning in life may have implications for our very notions of the Good Life itself.

Positive Affect and Meaning in Life

Before summarizing research demonstrating the relationship between PA and meaning in life, it might be helpful to briefly review the definitions and typical measurement methods for these two variables. PA refers to pleasant mood and is often measured using such mood adjectives as *happy*, *joyful*, *pleased*, *enjoyment*, or *fun*. Although the structure of PA has certainly been debated in the mood literature (e.g., Feldman, 1995; Watson & Vaidya, 2003), particularly with regard to the differential role of valence and arousal in PA (e.g., "energetic" vs. "content"), the relationship of affect to meaning in life is not unique to a particular measure of PA.

Defining and measuring PA, then, has not been a particularly challenging endeavor. In contrast, defining and measuring meaning in life presents a potentially greater obstacle. Reviewing the considerable literature on the topic, we adopted the following definition:

> A life is meaningful when it is understood by the person living it to matter in some larger sense. Lives may be experienced as meaningful when they are felt to have significance beyond the trivial or momentary, to have purpose, or to have a coherence that transcends chaos. (King et al., 2006, p. 180)

This grand conceptual definition notwithstanding, meaning in life has often been measured using such self-report questionnaires as the Purpose in Life Test (PIL; Crumbaugh & Maholick, 1964; McGregor & Little, 1998); the Sense of Coherence Scale (SOC; Antonovsky, 1988); and more recently, the Meaning in Life Questionnaire (MLQ; Steger, Frazier, Oishi, & Kaler, 2006). Sample items illustrate the focus of these measures on the respondent's intuitive sense of what meaning in life is, for example, "My personal existence is very purposeful and meaningful" (from the PIL) and "I have a good sense of what makes my life meaningful" (from the MLQ Presence of Meaning subscale). Although some individuals might take issue with the very idea that meaning in life is appropriately measured using self-report, it is worth noting that the large body of evidence supporting the role of meaning in life in health and psychological functioning (Mascaro & Rosen, 2005; Reker, Peacock, & Wong, 1987; Ryff, 1989; Steger & Frazier, 2005; Zika & Chamberlain, 1987, 1992) has used such measures routinely. Although these measures differ in a variety of ways, as was the case with PA, the direction of the relations we have found have not depended on the particular measure used.

As already noted, research has demonstrated a robust positive correlational relationship between PA and meaning in life (King et al., 2006). These correlations range in magnitude from .45 between PA and a composite of PIL and SOC (in a sample of 568 undergraduates) to .80 for PA and the SOC (in a sample of 266 community adults). In addition, extraversion, the personality trait most associated with the experience of PA (Lucas & Baird, 2004), strongly related to self-reported meaning in life (r = .62; King et al., 2006, Study 1).

With regard to the experience of daily life as meaningful, we conducted a five-day diary study in which participants rated their mood, daily activity and thoughts, positive and negative events that may have occurred, and daily meaning in life. Results demonstrated that the strongest predictor of the meaning experienced in a day was the amount of PA experienced that day (King et al., 2006, Study 2).

That the experience of meaning in life is related to feeling good is probably not particularly surprising. Theoretical conceptions of eudaimonia acknowledge that meaningful pursuits are associated with positive hedonic feelings, although these positive feelings are not viewed as an end in themselves (Ryan & Deci, 2001). A great deal of research has shown that meaning in life is, in fact, associated with hedonic well-being concurrently and longitudinally (Mascaro & Rosen, 2005; Reker et al., 1987; Ryff, 1989; Steger & Frazier, 2005; Zika & Chamberlain, 1987, 1992). It is important to note, however, that all this work, as well as that reviewed in the foregoing introduction, has been correlational in nature, leaving open the possibility that the causal arrow might run in the other direction—that is, not simply from meaning in life to happiness but from PA to meaning in life itself.

Indeed, experimental evidence suggests that PA plays a causal role in the experience of meaning in life. Priming participants with words related to PA and experimentally induced PA lead to heightened meaning in life (Hicks & King, 2007; King et al., 2006). Thus, PA not only is a correlate of meaning in life but also enhances the experience of meaning in life. Given the place of meaning in life as a central component of the Good Life, it is perhaps surprising to find that something as presumably transient, trivial, or even "vulgar," in Henry James's terms, as being in a good mood ought to play a role in its achievement. How can these results be made comprehensible?

Explaining the Relationship Away

One way to approach the effects of PA on meaning in life is to focus on ways in which this relationship can be explained, or even explained away. One such approach might focus on the mood as information hypothesis; thus perhaps when judging the meaning in their lives, individuals are simply relying on mood as a shortcut answer to the question. Another approach to explaining the relationship between PA and meaning in life might involve focusing on the mediators or mechanisms that might underlie this relationship. That is, one might assume that the relationship between PA and meaning in life is spurious and may be explained by the shared relations of these two variables with a number of theoretically important "third variables." We now examine the evidence for these two approaches.

Mood as Information

When confronted with such an abstract question as "Is my life meaningful?" it is improbable that one consults all relevant information while forming an answer (Schwarz & Clore, 1996). Instead, it is adaptive to "stop" as soon as enough information that provides a satisfactory answer comes to mind (Schwarz & Clore, 1996). Research has shown that mood can often serve as such a default source of information. According to the mood-as-information hypothesis, people sometimes use their current mood as a source of information when making evaluative judgments of broad life domains (for review, see Schwarz, 2001; Schwarz & Clore, 1983, 1996). That is, rather than taking all possible information into account, an individual might (erroneously) interpret his or her current feelings as relevant to the target such that positive moods lead to more favorable evaluations and negative moods lead to less favorable evaluations (Schwarz & Clore, 1996). It is important to note that mood-as-information effects are theorized to arise when people misattribute their mood as being relevant to the target; when the source of one's mood is made salient, these effects often disappear entirely.

We have directly tested whether mood-as-information effects might also contribute to the relationship between PA and meaning in life (King et al., 2006, Study 5). In this experiment, participants first completed a positive-, negative-, or neutral-mood induction task. Half the participants were then given a mood attribution cue (i.e., they were told that the induction might have influenced their moods), and the other half were given no information about the potential source of their moods. Next, participants completed a standard measure of meaning in life. The results of this study supported the mood-as-information hypothesis. Participants in the positive-mood condition, who were *not* given a mood attribution cue, reported enhanced meaning in life compared to all other groups. In contrast, those in the positive-mood induction condition who were provided with a cue to discount mood showed more tempered meaning in life ratings. These results suggest the relationship between PA and meaning in life might partially derive from the use of mood-as-information heuristic (see also Hicks & King, 2009). At the very least, these results indicate that PA ought to be recognized as a potential nuisance variable in the measurement of meaning in life. From these results, we might conclude that PA ought to be included as a control variable in any study using self-report measures of meaning.

Notably, there are limits to the mood-as-information explanation. For example, in one study we measured mood, then asked individuals to list all the things that made their lives meaningful, and finally asked them to rate their meaning in life (King & Hicks, 2007). From a mood-as-information perspective, the act of listing one's sources of meaning ought to wipe out the effects of mood on meaning-in-life judgments. That is to say, all participants should have been brought down to earth by the listing exercise and should therefore no longer rely on mood as information for this judgment. As such, only a main effect for number of sources listed ought to predict meaning in life.

Although number of sources listed was positively associated with meaning in life, PA also continued to predict meaning in life, even controlling for sources listed. Furthermore, these main effects were qualified by a significant sources X PA interaction: The effect of PA meaning in life was moderated by the number of sources listed. Those individuals who were able to list many different sources reported high levels of meaning in life regardless of mood. Meaning ratings were just as high, however, for individuals who were unable to provide many different reasons why their lives are meaningful if they were in a positive mood. That is, even after a potential threat to the importance of one's existence (i.e., through the inability to list numerous sources of meaning), those individuals still reported enhanced meaning in life if they were in a good mood.

Thus, even in the presence of more realistic evidence that life lacks meaning, PA appears to promote a sense of meaning in life (King & Hicks, 2007). We will return to these provocative moderational results later, but for now we use them to demonstrate that although mood-as-information effects may, as typically interpreted, partially account for the relationship between PA and self-reported meaning-in-life ratings, clearly this explanation cannot fully account for the effect of PA on meaning in life.

Mediational Explanations

The search for potential mediators of the relationship between PA and meaning in life appears to be a reasonable and intuitively appealing solution to this puzzling relationship. PA is a concomitant of many aspects of eudaimonia, and as such it may be that it is through these variables that PA relates to meaning in life. The literature is replete with potential mediators, and here we review the evidence for candidate explanatory variables, including the cognitive effects of PA, the role of PA in motivation and values, and finally social relationship functioning.

Cognitive Mediators

Perhaps that most appealing explanation for the strong relationship between PA and meaning in life is derived from research examining the influence of PA on cognitive processes (e.g., Fredrickson & Branigan, 2004; Gasper & Clore, 2002). For example, according to the broadening-and-build theory of positive emotions (Fredrickson, 1998, 2001), PA leads to a broadened, global attentional focus. That is, PA can bias one to focus on the whole forest instead of just the trees within it. King et al. (2006) argued that this broadened mindset may partially account for the relationship between PA and the experience of meaning in life; in a broadened mindset, it may, for example, be easier to recognize how one's daily activities are connected to a larger framework of meaning. If the experience of meaning in life involves recognizing one's place in some grand scheme, then the broadened attentional focus afforded by PA might foster the ability to see one's life in the Big Picture.

The relationship between PA and creative cognitive processes has also been suggested to account for the link between happiness and the experience of meaning in life. Positive moods have been shown to increase flexibility when categorizing stimuli (Isen, Niedenthal, & Cantor, 1992; Murray, Sujan, Hirt, & Sujan, 1990) and increase performance on divergent thinking tasks (e.g., Isen, Daubman, & Nowicki, 1987), including listing more ideas (Kahn & Isen, 1993), identifying more activities (Fredrickson, 2001), or generating more unique responses (Isen, Johnson, Mertz, & Robinson, 1985). To the extent the PA leads to creativity, being in a positive mood may make it easier to think of one's meaningful daily behaviors, cherished life goals, or important accomplishments. Bringing these types of cognitions to the fore should ultimately enhance one's global meaning-in-life ratings.

A third cognitive path through which PA might enhance the experience of meaning in life is through its promotion of general knowledge structures. Research on mood and cognition demonstrates that PA is associated with the availability and use of general knowledge structures (Bless et al., 1996). People in positive moods often rely on general knowledge structures presumably because this type of processing strategy helps them free up valuable cognitive resources and may enable them to make novel and creative inferences beyond their immediate external circumstances (Bless, 2001; Fiedler & Bless, 2000). Thus, if one's sources of meaning are included in these general knowledge structures, being in a positive mood should make one's important sources of meaning in life (e.g., religious beliefs, philosophy of life, core values) more cognitively accessible. With these sources of meaning made salient, people should be more likely to see, for example, the relevance of their current circumstances to these larger meaning systems.

Unfortunately, to date there is no direct evidence supporting the idea that the relationship between PA and the experience of meaning in life is mediated by these types of cognitive processes. Our research has shown that although traditional measures of broadening are related to PA, they are not related to meaning in life, precluding the possibility that cognitive broadening mediates the relationship between PA and meaning in life (Hicks & King, 2007).

Similarly, creative cognitions do not appear to mediate the relationship between PA and meaning in life either. For example, in the sources-of-meaning study described earlier (King & Hicks, 2007), the lists generated by participants were coded for divergent thinking. Using the Personal Meaning Profile (PMP) as a guideline (Wong, 1998), we coded responses to examine how many different categories of implicit sources of meaning in life were listed (e.g., achievement, relationship, religion). Although our results showed that both PA and the number of sources of meaning listed were unique predictors of meaning in life, there was no indication that cognitive flexibility mediated the relationship between PA and the experience of meaning.

Finally, the results of our studies do not suggest that the use of general knowledge structures can fully account for the strong relationship between the two variables. Thus, PA did not predict, for instance, that individuals generated more sources of meaning, thereby suggesting that PA did not enhance the accessibility of these general structures. Furthermore, (as will be detailed) having religious beliefs (potentially a part of one's general knowledge structures) does not mediate the relationship between PA and meaning in life (Hicks & King, 2008).

Motivational Mediators

Another potential explanation for the relationship between PA and meaning in life rests on the role of PA in motivation. To the extent that mood serves as feedback about goal pursuits (Carver & Scheier, 2007), it might be that the experience of PA indicates that one is making good progress on valued goals, that is, experiencing a life of purpose. However, idiographic goal progress and commitment and daily goal thought and activity do not mediate the relationship between PA and meaning in life in either global or daily measures of these variables (King et al., 2006).

Although idiographic goal pursuit does not mediate the relationship between PA and meaning in life, perhaps higher level values might play a mediational role. Commitment associated with one's religious beliefs, for example, can lead to a life enriched with purpose and meaning (Silberman, 2005). Religion can provide individuals with core beliefs, expectations, and goals, placing the individual's life into a larger, more ultimate context (Batson & Stocks, 2004; Emmons, 2005; Silberman, 2005). Many empirical studies have supported the idea that religion is strongly associated with self-reported meaning in life (e.g., George, Ellison, & Larson, 2002; Hicks & King,

2007; Paloutzian, 1981; Steger & Frazier, 2005). In addition, religious commitment has also been linked to happiness in general (Myers, 1993). Furthermore, the relationship between religious commitment and well-being is itself mediated by meaning in life (Steger & Frazier, 2005). The strong relationships among PA, religious commitment, and meaning in life raises the intriguing possibility that the religious commitment mediates the relationship between PA and meaning in life.

As previously mentioned, in a series of studies, we tested whether religious commitment might mediate the relationship between PA and meaning in life (Hicks & King, 2008). Participants completed measures of religious commitment, PA, and meaning in life. Interestingly, we found that meaning in life completely mediated the relationship between religious commitment and PA (see Steger & Frazier, 2005, for similar findings). Yet, we did not find any evidence that religious commitment accounted for the relationship between PA and meaning in life (Hicks & King, 2008).

Social Mediators

Finally, we have examined whether social relationships might account for the strong association between PA and meaning in life. Strong social bonds are perhaps the most fundamental requirement for health and well-being, including experiencing meaning in life (e.g., Baumeister, 1991; Baumeister & Leary, 1995; Ryan & Deci, 2001; Mikulincer, Florian, & Hirschberger, 2004). Empirical evidence has shown that people almost always mention social relationships when describing what makes their lives meaningful (Ebersole, 1998; Wong, 1998). Self-reported relatedness need satisfaction is positively associated with meaning in life (Steger, Kashdan, Sullivan, & Lorentz, 2008). In turn, social exclusion has been shown to lead to decreases in meaning in life (Stillman et al., 2009; Twenge, Catanese, & Baumeister, 2003).

In addition, research has shown that social functioning is strongly related to PA (Lyubomirsky, King, & Diener, 2005). It has been suggested that PA may actually lead to the more fulfilling social relationships (Lyubomirsky et al., 2005). Perhaps the relationship between PA and meaning in life might be explained by the underlying mechanism of social relationship functioning. If happiness improves the quality of one's relationships, then it is possible that those relationships explain the link between PA and meaning in life.

Recently, we conducted a series of studies to test this possibility. In two studies (Hicks & King, 2009), participants completed measures of social functioning (either relatedness need satisfaction or loneliness) at two separate times during the academic semester. During the second assessment, they also completed measures of PA and meaning in life. In these studies, we did not find any support for the idea that the quality of one's social relationships mediates the association between PA and meaning in life. Instead, we found that naturally occurring PA does not influence meaning ratings if one has strong (and stable) social connections. On the other hand, for those people whose social relationships were less than optimal (i.e., low or unstable), PA was strongly associated with the amount of meaning in life reported.

Of course, the search for mediators underlying the relationship between PA and meaning in life is a continuing process, and future research might strive to incorporate additional potential explanatory mechanisms. In particular, it might be that considering multiple mediators at once will be necessary to illuminate the role of different sources of meaning as well as PA in meaning-in-life judgments. However, at this point, sufficient evidence has accumulated to suggest that potential mediators are likely to emerge instead as moderators of the effects of PA on meaning in life, a finding we now discuss.

An Alternative Account: Moderation

Although we have yet to uncover variables that mediate the relationship between PA and meaning in life, one finding has consistently emerged, namely, that individuals low on variables that have been empirically or theoretically linked to meaning in life tend rely more strongly on their current positive mood when making meaning-in-life judgments. Figure 6.1 depicts a generic version of this interaction. As noted, for the listing of sources of meaning, religious commitment, and the social functioning studies, results showed not mediation but moderation, such that those low on sources of meaning, religious commitment, or social relationship functioning tended to be more reliant on PA in judging meaning in life.

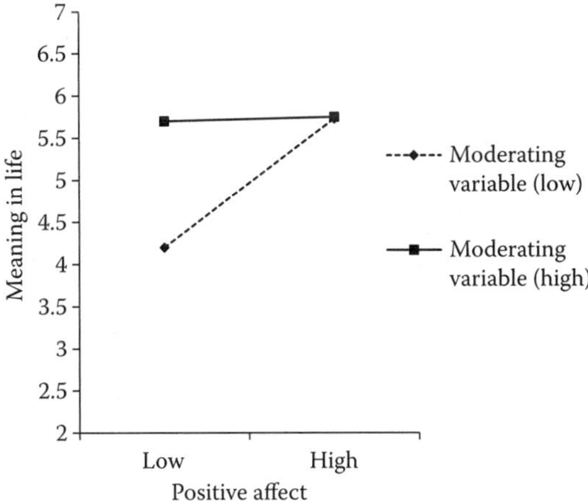

Figure 6.1 Positive affect and meaning. Sample moderators include relatedness need satisfaction (Hicks, Schlegel, & King, 2010), religious commitment (Hicks & King, 2008), and sources of meaning in life (King & Hicks, 2007).

We have found this pattern of interaction in many different studies. For example, although cognitive broadening is not related to meaning-in-life ratings (Hicks & King, 2007), individuals in a broadened mindset are less likely to use their PA as information when making their meaning-in-life judgments. We have argued that one possibility for these intriguing results is that individuals in a broadened mindset are more likely to make more realistic judgments when evaluating life's meaningfulness. Perhaps the Big Picture contains more substantive evidence about meaning in life than does one's positive mood.

Experimental manipulations of mood have produced similar results. In one study, we measured religious commitment and then, one month later, induced either positive or neutral mood before assessing meaning in life. Replicating previous findings (King et al., 2006, Study 5), we found that people in the positive mood condition reported higher levels of meaning in life compared to people in the neutral mood condition. However, this effect was qualified by a two-way interaction such that those who were high in religious commitment reported high levels of meaning in life regardless of their current mood (Hicks & King, 2007). Those individuals low in religious commitment rated their lives as being meaningful if they were in a good mood.

In another study (Hicks, Schlegel, & King, 2010), we found similar results examining an indicator of social functioning as a moderating variable. In this study, participants completed a measure of loneliness prior to the laboratory session. During the laboratory session, we again induced either positive or neutral mood followed by an assessment of meaning in life. We also provided half the participants with a mood attribution cue. We found that participants in the positive-mood condition reported higher levels of meaning in life compared to people in the neutral condition. We also found evidence for moderation such that those who had satisfying relationships (as indicated by reporting low loneliness) reported high levels of meaning in life regardless of their assigned mood or attributional cue condition. For individuals who reported themselves as lonely, PA predicted meaning in life, particularly in the absence of the cue to discount mood.

A similar pattern of moderation emerges using priming paradigms. Priming individuals with cues related to positive sources of meaning renders PA irrelevant to meaning in life. For example, Christians primed with concepts related to heaven are impervious to the effects of mood on meaning in life (Hicks & King, 2008). In addition, priming individuals with positive social relationship words wipes out the effect of PA on meaning in life (Hicks & King, 2009).

These results suggest that individuals may report similarly high levels of meaning in life, but the factors that contribute to the experience of meaning depend on their salience as well as the likelihood that the factors provide affirmative information about life's meaning. When evaluating meaning in life, individuals may consult an array of indicators. One of these is clearly PA, but it exists among a host of other potential sources of meaning. It is important to note that among all the potential sources of meaning in life, PA is often one that suggests that the answer to the existential question of whether life is meaningful is yes. It is also interesting that priming individuals with loneliness led to *enhanced* reliance on PA in meaning-in-life judgments (Hicks et al., 2010). When other sources of meaning fail the individual, mood may emerge as a preferred cue that life remains meaningful.

In sum, potential mediators of the relationship between PA and meaning in life have instead consistently been found to serve as moderators of the relationship. Individuals who are high on a given moderator or primed with positive cues to the moderator do not rely on mood in evaluating their meaning in life. In contrast, individuals low on the moderator or primed with negative cues about the moderator tend to rely heavily on PA as a cue to meaning in life. Thus, PA itself may serve as an affirmative cue that life is meaningful even in the absence of confirmatory evidence from more "meaningful" sources. Perhaps it is time to acknowledge what appears to be a substantive role for the mundane experience of mood in the grand experience of meaning in life.

What If the Relationship Is Real?

Accumulated evidence bears witness to the strong relationship between PA and meaning in life. This relationship does not appear to be fully accounted for by mood-as-information effects, nor do mediators tested to date explain this relationship away. As such, it makes sense to entertain the notion that the relationship between PA and meaning in life might be a real, durable, and potentially adaptive one. Individuals use PA as an indicator that life is meaningful. Understanding the nuances of this relationship might help to illuminate uncharted territory—that place where hedonic and eudaimonic well-being overlap.

Positive Affect and Meaningful Behavior

Theorists have argued and research has shown that many of the most meaningful human behaviors are associated with PA. Csikszentmihalyi (1990) described "flow" as "the state in which people are so involved in the activity that nothing else seems to matter; the experience itself is so enjoyable that people will do it even at a great cost, for the sheer sake of doing it" (p. 4). Experience sampling studies have shown that flow is more likely to occur when people are experiencing positive mood (Csikszentmihalyi & Wong, 1991). In addition, enjoyment is often used as a definitive characteristic of intrinsically motivated behavior (Csikszentmihalyi, Rathunde, & Whalen, 1993; Deci & Ryan, 2000; Ryan, 1995). Altruism and helping are also strongly related to the experience of PA (Batson & Powell, 2003).

Thus, although PA may seem to be a relatively trivial aspect of life, it is routinely paired with the experience of meaning. Experiences that bring us joy are likely to be those experiences that make our lives meaningful. Indeed, it should not be surprising that hedonic experience tracks the experience of eudaimonia; considerable evidence has shown that engagement in intrinsically motivating pursuits shares a strong relationship to enhanced hedonic well-being (King, 2008; Sheldon, 2001). We feel hedonically better when we are engaged in eudaimonia. As Aristotle (350 bce/1998 ce) noted, eudaimonia is the "best, finest and *most pleasant* thing" (emphasis added; p. 4).

The contrast that has been drawn between hedonic and eudaimonic well-being highlights a seeming mistrust of hedonic experience among scholars of psychological functioning (King, 2007). One purpose of maintaining this distinction seems to be to distinguish between individuals who are happy but whose lives lack meaning from those who are experiencing a more "authentic" form of happiness (Seligman, 2002). Our results and those of Sheldon and colleagues (e.g., Sheldon, 2001) indicate that this mistrust is potentially misguided. Indeed, the empirical question might be posed thus: "Are happy people mindlessly experiencing meaning in meaningless activities?" Our results suggest not, as we review next.

Positive Affect and Sensitivity to Meaning

It is important to note that PA does not render all experiences meaningful. Rather, PA might play a role in tuning individuals to the meaning relevance of situations. In one study, we manipulated the meaningfulness of an activity by asking participants to either read a meaningful passage (the meaningful condition) or simply count the number of *e*s in the passage (the meaningless condition; King et al., 2006, Study 6). Although PA was associated with enhanced perceptions of meaning in the meaningful condition, it was also negatively related to the perceived meaning of the meaningless activity. Rather than render all activities meaningful, PA appears to heighten an individual's capacity to discriminate between meaningful versus meaningless experiences. It may be that PA represents a preparedness for meaning such that when in a good mood, individuals have an expectancy for meaning (just as other moods may prepare individuals to be, for instance, scared by a horror film; Martin, Ward, Achee, & Wyer, 1993). PA may allow individuals to become aware of the meaning relevance of experiences during those times when meaning might otherwise go unnoticed. Ironically, meaningful experiences may require some hedonic value for their meaningfulness to be fully appreciated (Yalom, 1982).

Positive Affect, Sources of Meaning, and the Experience of Daily Meaning in Life

Results of a recent daily diary study suggest an interesting substantive role of PA in the experience of meaning in daily life. In that study, participants rated the daily mood, daily meaning in life, and the extent to which their relatedness needs were met each day. Multilevel modeling showed that main effects for PA and daily relatedness need satisfaction were qualified by a significant PA X need satisfaction interaction (Hicks et al., 2010). Of interest is that the direction of this interaction was the opposite of the direction of the interactions presented thus far. That is to say, in previous studies examining global meaning in life and PA and other variables, moderation typically occurred in the negative direction such that PA predicted meaning in life only at low levels of these moderators. In contrast, at the daily level, PA and relatedness need satisfaction interacted to positively predict daily meaning life. On days when relatedness need satisfaction was high, PA actually predicted even higher daily meaning (Hicks et al., 2010).

These results suggest that to some extent, more global-level analyses gloss over the dynamic between PA and sources of meaning on a more micro level. It appears that PA may, at any given moment, play a role in enhancing the experience of meaning provided by more conceptually relevant sources of meaning, lending hedonic reinforcement to these eudaimonic endeavors. Thus PA may be the affective reward that accompanies other relatively costly meaningful behaviors (e.g., flow, altruism). Indeed, PA may play a role in developing, supporting, and maintaining the relations between the experience of meaning in life and these central sources of meaning. If we think of daily mood as the psychological glue that ties us to the events and activities of daily life, PA may serve as a natural meaning barometer or a meaning-detecting lens.

The Mundane and the Grand in Human Functioning and the Good Life

To the extent that the experience of meaning is an adaptive one, it may be for the best that individuals can shift the sources-of-meaning judgments to ensure a positive answer to this existential question. That something as trivial and potentially fleeting as positive mood promotes the grand experience of meaning in life does not devalue that grand experience. Rather, it demonstrates the high importance of the experience of meaning in life. Pleasure is typically paired with behaviors that are necessary for survival; this might be considered evolution's way of ensuring that we engage in the behaviors we must to continue living (de Waal, 1992). Sex and eating are often proffered as examples of survival-relevant activities that are also paired with pleasure. We might add to this list the experience of meaning, which appears itself to be robustly related to pleasure.

Routinely basing one's meaning in life on PA might not be the most effective strategy; but to the degree that PA is commonly paired with meaningful experience, the relationship between PA and the experience of meaning in life is not necessarily a troubling one. Meaning in life or eudaimonia, that side of well-being of which it is a part, need not be viewed as a rarified experience reserved for those who have attained some level of existence beyond the mundane, everyday world that humans typically occupy. Catching a snippet of a beloved piece of music on the radio, chatting with the kids on the way to soccer practice, or sitting down to dinner with friends—these mundane pleasantries may well represent the local experience of meaning. That such simple pleasures might enhance the perception and experience of meaning is not so much a puzzle to be solved as a remarkable aspect of healthy human functioning.

Acknowledgment

Josh Hicks's work on this chapter was supported by the National Institute on Alcohol Abuse and Alcoholism Grant T32 AA13526.

References

Antonovsky, A. (1988). *Unraveling the mystery of health.* San Francisco, CA: Jossey-Bass.

Aristotle. (1998). *Nicomachean ethics* (J. L. Ackrill, J. O. Urmson, & D. Ross, Trans.). New York, NY: Oxford University Press.

Batson, C. D., & Powell, A. A. (2003). Altruism and prosocial behavior. In T. Millon & M. J. Lerner (Eds.), *Handbook of psychology: Vol. 5, Personality and social psychology* (pp. 463–484). Hoboken, NJ: Wiley.

Batson, D. C., & Stocks, E. L. (2004). Religion: Its core psychological functions. In J. Greenberg, S. L. Koole, & T. Pyszczynski (Eds.), *Handbook of experimental existential psychology* (pp. 141–155). New York, NY: Guilford Press.

Baumeister, R. F. (1991). *Meanings of life.* New York: Guilford Press.

Baumeister, R. F., & Leary, M. R. (1995). The need to belong: Desire for interpersonal attachments as a fundamental human motivation. *Psychological Bulletin, 117*, 497–529.

Bless, H. (2001). Mood and the use of general knowledge structures. In L. L. Martin & G. L. Clore (Eds.), *Theories of mood and cognition: A user's guidebook* (pp. 9–26). Mahwah, NJ: Erlbaum.

Bless, H., Clore, G. L., Schwarz, N., Golisano, V., Rabe, C., & Wolk, M. (1996). Mood and the use of scripts: Does a happy mood really lead to mindlessness? *Journal of Personality and Social Psychology, 71*, 665–679.

Carver, C. S., & Scheier, M. F. (2007). Feedback processes in the simultaneous regulation of action and affect. In J. Y. Shah & W. L. Gardner (Eds.), *Handbook of motivation science* (pp. 308–324). New York: Guilford Press.

Crumbaugh, J. C., & Maholick, L. T. (1964). An experimental study in existentialism: The psychometric approach to Frankl's concept of noogenic neurosis. *Journal of Clinical Psychology, 20*, 200–207.

Csikszentmihalyi, M. (1990). *Flow.* New York, NY: Harper & Row.

Csikszentmihalyi, M., Rathunde, K., & Whalen, S. (1993) *Talented teenagers.* New York, NY: Cambridge University Press.

Csikszentmihalyi, M., & Wong, M. M. (1991). The situational and personal correlates of happiness: A cross-national comparison. In F. Strack, M. Argyle, & N. Schwarz (Eds.), *Subjective well-being: An interdisciplinary perspective* (pp. 193–212). Elmsford, NY: Pergamon Press.

De Waal, F. (1992). *Good natured: The origins of right and wrong in humans and animals.* Cambridge, MA: Harvard University Press.

Diener, E., Suh, E. M., Lucas, R. E., & Smith, H. L. (1999). Subjective well-being: Three decades of progress. *Psychological Bulletin, 125*, 276–302.

Ebersole, P. (1998). Types and depth of written life meanings. In P. T. P. Wong & S. P. Fry (Eds.), *The human quest for meaning: A handbook of psychological research and clinical applications* (pp. 179–191). Mahwah, NJ: Erlbaum.

Emmons, R. A. (2005). Striving for the sacred: Personal goals, life meaning, and religion. *Journal of Social Issues, 61*, 731–745.

Feldman, L. A. (1995). Variations in the circumplex structure of mood. *Personality and Social Psychology Bulletin, 21*, 806–817.

Fiedler, K., & Bless, H. (2000). The formation of beliefs and the interface of affective and cognitive processes. In N. H. Frijda, A. S. R. Manstead, & S. Bem (Eds.), *Emotions and beliefs: How feelings influence thoughts* (pp. 144–170). Cambridge, England: Cambridge University Press.

Fredrickson, B. L. (1998). What good are positive emotions? *Review of General Psychology, 2*, 300–319.

Fredrickson, B. L. (2001). The role of positive emotions in positive psychology: The broaden-and-build theory of positive emotions. *American Psychologist, 56*, 218–226.

Fredrickson, B. L., & Branigan, C. (2004). Positive emotions broaden the scope of attention and thought-action repertoires. *Cognition and Emotion, 19*, 313–330.

Gasper, K., & Clore, G. L. (2002). Attending to the big picture: Mood and global versus local processing of visual information. *Psychological Science, 13*, 34–40.

George, L. K., Ellison, C. G., & Larson. D. B. (2002). Explaining the relationships between religious involvement and health. *Psychological Inquiry, 13*, 190–200.

Hicks, J. A., & King, L. A. (2007). Meaning in life and seeing the big picture: Positive affect and global focus. *Cognition and Emotion, 21*, 1577–1584.

Hicks, J. A., & King, L. A. (2008). Mood and religion as information about meaning in life. *Journal of Research in Personality, 42*, 43–57.

Hicks, J. A., & King, L. A. (2009). Positive mood and social relatedness as information about meaning in life. *Journal of Positive Psychology, 4*, 471–482.

Hicks, J. A., Schlegel, R. J., & King, L. A. (2010). Social threats, happiness, and the dynamics of meaning in life judgments. *Personality and Social Psychology Bulletin, 36*, 1305–1317.

Isen, A. M., Daubman, K. A., & Nowicki, G. P. (1987). Positive affect facilitates creative problem solving. *Journal of Personality and Social Psychology, 52*, 1122–1131.

Isen, A. M., Johnson, M. M., Mertz, E., & Robinson, G. F. (1985). The influence of positive affect on the unusualness of word associations. *Journal of Personality and Social Psychology, 48*, 1413–1426.

Isen, A. M., Niedenthal, P. M., & Cantor, N. (1992). An influence of positive affect on social categorization. *Motivation and Emotion, 16*, 65–78.

Kahn, B. E., & Isen, A. M. (1993). The influence of positive affect on variety seeking among safe, enjoyable products. *Journal of Consumer Research, 20*, 257–270.

Kahneman, D., Diener, E., & Schwarz, N. (Eds.). (1999). *Well-being: The foundations of hedonic psychology*. New York, NY: Russell-Sage.

King, L. A. (2008). Interventions for enhancing SWB: The pursuit of happiness. In R. J. Larsen & M. Eid (Eds.), *The science of subjective well-being* (pp. 431–448). New York, NY: Guilford Press.

King, L. A., Eells, J. E., & Burton, C. M. (2004). The good life, broadly defined. In A. Linley & S. Joseph (Eds.), *Positive psychology in practice.* (pp. 35–52). Hoboken, NJ: Wiley.

King, L. A., & Hicks, J. A. (2007, August). *A competition of cues model for the search for meaning in life.* Presented in a Symposium entitled "The Search for Meaning: Social and Clinical Perspectives," Michael Steger, Chair. The American Psychological Association Convention, San Francisco, CA.

King, L. A., Hicks, J. A., Krull, J., & Del Gaiso, A. (2006). Positive affect and the experience of meaning in life. *Journal of Personality and Social Psychology, 90*, 179–196.

Lucas, R. E., & Baird, B. M. (2004). Extraversion and emotional reactivity. *Journal of Personality and Social Psychology, 86*, 473–485.

Lyubomirsky, S., King, L. A., & Diener, E. (2005). The benefits of frequent positive affect: Does happiness lead to success? *Psychological Bulletin, 131*, 803–855.

Martin, L. L., Ward, D. W., Achee, J. W., & Wyer, R. S. (1993). Mood as input: People have to interpret the motivational implications of their moods. *Journal of Personality & Social Psychology, 64*, 317–326.

Mascaro, N., & Rosen, D. H. (2005). Existential meaning's role in the enhancement of hope and prevention of depressive symptoms. *Journal of Personality, 73*, 985–1014.

McGregor, I., & Little, B. R. (1998). Personal projects, happiness, and meaning: On doing well and being yourself. *Journal of Personality & Social Psychology, 74*, 494–512.

Mikulincer, M., Florian, V., & Hirschberger, G. (2004). The terror of death and the quest for love—An existential perspective on close relationships. In J. Greenberg, S. L. Koole, & T. Pyszczynski (Eds.), *Handbook of experimental existential psychology* (pp. 287–304). New York, NY: Guilford Press.

Murray, N., Sujan, H., Hirt, E. R., & Sujan, M. (1990). The influence of mood on categorization: A cognitive flexibility interpretation. *Journal of Personality and Social Psychology*, 59, 411–425.

Myers, D. G. (1993). *The pursuit of happiness.* New York, NY: Morrow.

Paloutzian, R. F. (1981). Purpose in life and value changes following conversion. *Journal of Personality and Social Psychology, 41*, 1153–1160.

Reker, G. T., Peacock, E. J., & Wong, P. T. P. (1987). Meaning and purpose in life and well-being: A life-span perspective. *Journal of Gerontology, 42*, 44–49.

Ryan, R. M. (1995). Psychological needs and the facilitation of integrative processes. *Journal of Personality, 63*, 397–427

Ryan, R. M., & Deci, E. L. (2001). On happiness and human potentials: A review of research on hedonic and eudaimonic well-being. In S. Fiske (Ed.), *Annual review of psychology* (Vol. 52, pp. 141–166). Palo Alto, CA: Annual Reviews.

Ryff, C. D. (1989). Happiness is everything, or is it? Explorations on the meaning of psychological well-being. *Journal of Personality and Social Psychology, 57*, 1069–1081.

Schwarz, N. (2001). Feelings as information: Implications for affective influences on information processing. In L. L. Martin & G. L. Clore (Eds.), *Theories of mood and cognition: A user's handbook* (pp. 159–176). Mahwah, NJ: Erlbaum.

Schwarz, N., & Clore, G. L. (1983). Mood, misattributions, and judgments of well-being: Informative and directive functions of affective states. *Journal of Personality and Social Psychology, 45*, 513–523.

Schwarz, N., & Clore, G. L. (1996). Feelings as phenomenal experiences. In E. T. Higgins & A. Kruglanski (Eds.), *Social psychology: Handbook of basic principles* (pp. 433–465). New York, NY: Guilford Press.

Seligman, M. E. P. (2002). *Authentic happiness.* New York: Free Press.

Sheldon, K. M. (2001). The self-concordance model of healthy goal striving: When personal goals correctly represent the person. In P. Schmuck & K. M. Sheldon (Eds.), *Life goals and well-being: Towards a positive psychology of human striving* (pp. 18–36). Ashland, OH: Hogrefe & Huber.

Silberman, I. (2005). Religion as a meaning system: Implications for the new millennium. *Journal of Social Issues, 61*, 641–663.

Steger, M. F., & Frazier, P. (2005). Meaning in life: One link in the chain from religion to well-being. *Journal of Counseling Psychology, 52*, 574–582.

Steger, M. F., Frazier, P., Oishi, S., & Kaler, M. (2006). The meaning in life questionnaire: Assessing the presence of and search for meaning in life. *Journal of Counseling Psychology, 53*, 80–93.

Steger, M. F., Kashdan, T. B., Sullivan, B. A., & Lorentz, D. (2008). Understanding the search for meaning in life: Personality, cognitive style, and the dynamic between seeking and experiencing meaning. *Journal of Personality, 76*, 199–228.

Stillman, T. F., Baumeister, R. F., Lambert, N. M., Crescioni, A. W., DeWall, C. N., & Fincham, F. D. (2009). Alone and pointless: Life loses meaning following social rejection. *Journal of Experimental Social Psychology, 45*, 686–694.

Twenge, J. M, Catanese, K. R., & Baumeister, R. F. (2003). Social exclusion and the deconstructed state: Time perception, meaninglessness, lethargy, lack of emotion, and self-awareness. *Journal of Personality and Social Psychology, 85*, 409–423.

Waterman, A. S. (1993). Two conceptions of happiness: Contrasts of personal expressiveness (eudaimonia) and hedonic enjoyment. *Journal of Personality & Social Psychology, 64*, 678–691.

Watson, D., & Vaidya, J. (2003). Mood measurement: Current status and future directions. In J. A. Schinka & W. F. Velicer (Eds.), *Handbook of psychology: Research methods in psychology* (Vol. 2, pp. 351–375). Hoboken, NJ: Wiley.

Wong, P. T. P. (1998). Implicit theories of meaningful life and the development of the personal meaning profile. In P. T. P. Wong & S. P. Fry (Eds.), *The human quest for meaning: A handbook of psychological research and clinical applications* (pp. 111–140). Mahwah, NJ: Erlbaum.

Yalom, I. (1982). The "terrestrial" meanings of life. *International Forum for Logotherapy, 5*, 92–102.

Zika, S., & Chamberlain, K. (1987). Relation of hassles and personality to subjective well-being. *Journal of Personality and Social Psychology, 53*, 155–162.

Zika, S., & Chamberlain, K. (1992). On the relation between meaning in life and psychological well-being. *British Journal of Psychology, 83*, 133–145.

7

On the Distinction Between Subjective Well-Being and Meaning in Life

Regulatory Versus Reconstructive Functions in the Face of a Hostile World

DOV SHMOTKIN and AMIT SHRIRA

Tel Aviv University

The Good Life: A Tale of Two Concepts

The human struggle to grasp the elusive nature of the good and well-lived life extends from ancient to modern thought (McGill, 1967; Telfer, 1980). Greek philosophers attempted to grapple the good life through different, often contradictory, formulations. Thus, for those who endorsed sheer hedonism, like Aristippus, the good life is epitomized in the experience of maximum pleasure. A more moderate school of hedonism was established by Epicurus, who advocated restraint in the consumption of pleasure. In contrast, Aristotle championed the optimal actualization of one's potentials, which he termed *eudaimonia*. Referring to excellence and perfection of individuals' virtues and talents, eudaimonia is a meaning-based prescription of the "supreme good" in life, and its attainment may sometimes require anguish rather than pleasure.

This old controversy over whether the good life should primarily be pleasant or meaningful is not merely a philosophical question. It induces profound differences in people's art of living at the personal level (Veenhoven, 2003a) and underlies the rationale of governing people's lives at the social level (Feldman, 2004). Thus, Bentham regarded the fundamental propensity to seek pleasure and avoid pain as a natural key principle that defines the essence of happiness and determines the major role of governments: to provide the greatest happiness to the greatest number of people. In contrast, Kant presented a moralistic view that renounced happiness as the complete good; rather, he regarded the performance of duty, which embodies universally reasoned values, as the categorical imperative. Both Benthanm and Kant, then, depict human beings as striving for certain ultimate ends, be that end happiness (as also proclaimed by such other empiricist philosophers as Hobbes and Locke) or a meaningful perfection of a virtue or ideal (as also central to such idealist and teleological philosophers as Hegel and Schopenhauer). Being desired ends on the route to the good life, both happiness and meaning depend on mental and social institutions, such as communally shared beliefs and legal systems, which regulate the forms and attainability of these ends (Brunner, 2007; Tatarkiewicz, 1976).

In the present chapter, we follow psychological inquiries of happiness and meaning in life that derived from, as well as further elaborated, the aforementioned dilemmas of the philosophical accounts (Ryan & Deci, 2001; Ryff, 1989). Particularly, we propose a psychological view that departs from the tradition that has treated happiness and meaning mainly as end results or outcomes of such antecedent factors as ways of life, psychological dispositions, biographical events, sociodemographic characteristics, and situational factors. As presented here, happiness and meaning constitute two dynamic systems designed to deal with the adverse contingencies of life. With this agentic role, happiness and meaning respectively provide distinct, yet complementary, functions of regulation and reconstruction. In this view, the individual's shaping of the good life must be examined in conjunction with the existential, often dialectical, task of living within a hostile world. Following a preliminary overview, the chapter describes the distinct functions of happiness and meaning in this conceptual framework. Before concluding, in a final section the chapter presents the aftermath of trauma endured by Holocaust survivors as a most pertinent example.

Subjective Well-Being and Meaning in Life: A Preliminary Overview

Happiness, as a popular term, is a synonym of the more research-oriented construct of *subjective well-being* (SWB), which consists of cognitive and affective evaluations that people make about their lives. The former evaluations include long-term judgments of one's general satisfaction with life, whereas the latter include reports on one's immediate experiences of positive and negative affect (Diener, Suh, Lucas, & Smith, 1999; Eid & Larsen, 2008; Kahneman, Diener, & Schwarz, 1999). As a superordinate construct, SWB cannot be captured as mere hedonism, though some parts of SWB reflect hedonistic concerns (Brülde, 2007; Veenhoven, 2003b). Empirical research on SWB emerged during the 1950s in the search for indicators that could monitor quality of life at social and individual levels and has since then amassed an impressive pile of evidence. SWB is connected with heredity and personality and, to a lesser degree, with objective life conditions (DeNeve & Cooper, 1998; Lykken, 1999). Notably, researchers of SWB are bearers of good news: They have found that SWB is a stable characteristic (McCrae & Costa, 1994) but still sensitive to situational clues (Schwarz & Strack, 1999); that most people maintain an above-medium, positive baseline of SWB (Cummins & Nistico, 2002; Diener & Diener, 1996); that people tend to adapt back to their SWB baseline following adversity (Diener, Lucas, & Scollon, 2006; Headey & Wearing, 1989); and that the level of positive affect is relatively independent from that of negative affect (Cacioppo, Gardner, & Berntson, 1999).

As a parallel concept, meaning in life essentially refers to a personal, desirably consonant combination of cognitive schemas that connect different time points and contexts along one's life (Baumeister, 1991; McGregor & Little, 1998). These schemas encompass beliefs (Park, 2010), values (Baumeister, 1991), and goals (Emmons, 1999; Klinger, Chapter 2, this volume). Modern research on meaning in life is even fresher than that of SWB and originates from such eminent humanistic psychologists as Maslow (1968) and Rogers (1961), from existential psychology (Yalom, 1980), and particularly from Frankl's (1963, 1969) seminal theory that attributed humans with an innate drive termed *the will to meaning*.

Recent research has delineated the motivations for meaning (Baumeister, 1991; Baumeister & Vohs, 2002) and its manifestations (Davis, Nolen-Hoeksema, & Larson, 1998; Janoff-Bulman & Yopyk, 2004; Park, 2010). In line with Frankl's assumptions, meaning in life has a vital contribution to adaptation, as evident in the evolutionary advantage of humans through the construction of goal-directed perspectives (Klinger, Chapter 2, this volume) and the universal human tendency to integrate personal experiences into a unified sense of self (Joseph & Linley, 2005). An adaptation model of meaningful life has been formulated in Ryff's (1989; Ryff & Keyes, 1995; Ryff, Chapter 11, this volume) conception of psychological well-being, which refers to positive functioning and life pursuits in the face of challenge. In this conception, meaningful life has both psychosocial and biological underpinnings and thus constitutes an essential part of positive health at large (Ryff & Singer, 1998; Ryff, Singer, & Love, 2004).

Similarly to SWB, findings on meaning are quite encouraging, because most people formulate meaningful life through the adoption of positive assumptions, beliefs, and expectations about themselves and the world around them. Thus, people generally conceive their world as benevolent and predictable, and their self as worthy (Janoff-Bulman, 1992), even if such conceptions have a moderately illusory nature (Taylor & Brown, 1988). This positivity bias in people's meaning in life yields the often found correlation between meaning and SWB despite their being distinct psychological entities (Compton, Smith, Cornish, & Qualls, 1996; Keyes, Shmotkin, & Ryff, 2002; McGregor & Little, 1998; Ring, Höfer, McGee, Hickey, & O'Boyle, 2007; Ryff & Keyes, 1995; Waterman, 1993; Waterman, Schwartz, & Conti, 2008). The correlation between the two constructs may also suggest reciprocally causal links whereby positive affect facilitates advanced cognitive functions and behavioral repertoires, thus fostering psychological growth and meaning making (Fredrickson, 2001; Fredrickson, Tugade, Waugh, & Larkin, 2003; King & Hicks, Chapter 6, this volume), whereas meaningful commitments and purpose in life promote opportunities of satisfaction and happiness (Baumeister, 1991; Emmons, 1999; Steger, Chapter 8, this volume).

The launch of the positive psychology movement (Seligman & Csikszentmihalyi, 2000; Snyder & Lopez, 2002) has facilitated the study of SWB and meaning under the umbrella of positive experience and human flourishing. Thus, unlike polar traditions of certain philosophers mentioned at the outset of this chapter, contemporary psychology increasingly integrates SWB and meaning as major faculties of the good life (Kashdan, Biswas-Diener, & King, 2008; King & Napa, 1998; Ryan & Deci, 2001) and indeed as components within larger networks of qualities of life and arts of life (Veenhoven, 2000, 2003a). This trend has paved the way to a broader examination of human strengths (e.g., engagement, creativity, hope) whose agentic power in life is substantial (Peterson & Seligman, 2004; Seligman, 2002).

Challenging Subjective Well-Being and Meaning: The Hostile-World Scenario

So far, the foregoing considerations lead to the conclusion that most people tend to be happy and to assimilate their life experiences into a global meaning system. Being predominantly happy makes the life of those people pleasant enough, and adhering to a meaning system makes their world worthy enough to live in. This message may come as a surprise when one reflects about the abundant dangers and suffering that engulf people in our world. Large parts of humanity are daily exposed to imminent calamities, among them malnutrition, brutal violence, political oppression, deadly epidemics, natural disasters, and wars. Existence is shaky even for people in developed countries, because they too live under the threat of crime, terrorism, accidents, environmental pollution, illness, aging, and death. Inherent to the human condition are interpersonal conflicts that make many lives anguished through family breakups, social discrimination, and bitter rivalries. In view of the profound and long-lasting impact of these perils, one may be reluctant to accept the portrayal of the favorable life as one's own envisioned future (Gilbert & Wilson, 2007; Lacey, Smith, & Ubel, 2006). Indeed, Baumeister, Bratslavsky, Finkenauer, and Vohs (2001) presented persuasive evidence that "bad is stronger than good," meaning that undesirable, harmful, or unpleasant outcomes have a greater impact than desirable, beneficial, or pleasant ones (for additional evidence, see also Rozin & Royzman, 2001).

Facing the foregoing listed dangers in our world, we each hold an image of the actual or potential threats to our lives or, more broadly, to our individual physical and mental integrity. This image of adversity was termed by Shmotkin (2005) as the *hostile-world scenario* (HWS). Nourished by beliefs about likely catastrophes and inflictions, the HWS functions as a system of appraisal that scans for any potential negative condition or for an even worse condition when a negative one already prevails. Thus, when activated adaptively, the HWS helps us to keep vigilant and prudent in our struggle to remain safe and well, but an extreme HWS generates a continuous sense of survivorship in a disastrous world.

How does one resolve this unsettling contradiction between the intimidating and merciless world on the one hand and the ability of most people to lead generally happy and meaningful lives on the other hand? We argue that the answer lies in the unique attributes of SWB and meaning. Moreover, the different tracks to the good life offered by SWB and meaning present us with varied modi operandi when facing the hostile world and its scenarios. We next dwell on, while also distinguishing between, the special functions of SWB and those of meaning vis-à-vis the HWS.

Regulating the Hostile-World Scenario by Subjective Well-Being

In an attempt to integrate the aforementioned conflicting messages, Shmotkin (2005) proposed a new conceptual framework of SWB. Here, SWB is regarded as a dynamic system whose principal role is to constitute a *favorable psychological environment*, conceived as a positive state of mind that allows an individual to maintain ongoing tasks by regulating the disturbing disruptions caused by the HWS. It should be stated that this favorable psychological environment is not synonymous with other constructs of fitness, such as adjustment and mental health. A favorable psychological environment may lapse in mentally healthy individuals; conversely, mental illness does not preclude all ingredients of well-being (Keyes, 2005, 2007).

SWB acquires its dynamics and flexibility by operating in multiple patterns of activity, defined as *modules*. The modules enumerated by Shmotkin (2005) locate SWB in four major contexts of psychological space and psychological time. These modules include the private domain of self-awareness (experiential SWB), the public domain of self-reports (declarative SWB), the synchronic interaction among dimensions of the self (differential SWB), and the diachronic trajectories of the personal life story along time (narrative SWB). This framework creates profiles of different levels of various SWB components across the distinctive modules. For example, people who convey a similar message of being happy (high declarative SWB) may be incorporated into strikingly different SWB profiles of multiple SWB representations such as private feelings of happiness or unhappiness, interactions between dimensions of positive and negative affect, and perceived trajectories of progression or regression in happiness along time (see also Shmotkin, Berkovich, & Cohen, 2006). We contend that such configurations of SWB provide flexible means in the service of managing the adverse environments of the hostile world (for works on SWB profiles see Busseri, Sadava, Molnar, & DeCourville, 2009; Palgi & Shmotkin, 2010).

Elaborating the aforementioned conception, several SWB–HWS intersections may be suggested. As indicated by the literature, SWB most commonly counteracts the negativity of the HWS. This is done by a positively slanted baseline of SWB, termed the *positivity offset* (Cacioppo et al., 1999), ensuring that people's motivation to approach their environment is stronger than their motivation to avoid it. The encounter with the negative representations of the

HWS requires a considerable mobilization of resources, but people gradually minimize this impact and return to their normal baseline (Taylor, 1991) by using such antidotes as positive affect (Fredrickson, 2001) and positive memories (Walker, Skowronski, & Thompson, 2003). Yet, a caveat against an overly high SWB is in order. An inflated SWB may disavow the HWS and drive people into a risky fool's paradise. Thus, even when SWB is high, it should constantly negotiate with reality to avoid naiveté or excessive repression (e.g., Shedler, Mayman, & Manis, 1993).

At other times, SWB may be temporarily overpowered by the HWS. Such situations may be paramount for survival, when avoidant behavior is necessary (e.g., Cacioppo et al., 1999), but also when approach tendencies fail and there is a need to redirect them (Carver, 2001). Sometimes people may even be motivated to inhibit SWB and to maintain the HWS in order to promote realistic thinking or to protect against future disappointments (Norem & Cantor, 1986; Parrott, 1993). Nevertheless, when SWB is constantly overridden by the HWS, a permanent sense of catastrophe prevails and disrupts adaptive functioning. This condition is especially expected among traumatized individuals (e.g., Herman, 1992), but as evident later, other SWB–HWS intersections may also follow trauma.

SWB and HWS can also cofunction. Here, SWB does not serve to ward off the HWS; rather, SWB lets people benefit from the favorable psychological environment while remaining vigilant for hostile conditions. This strategy may be effective for handling complex situations, where the favorable psychological environment facilitates exploration and manipulation of certain HWS representations (Larsen, McGraw, & Cacioppo, 2001). This cofunctioning also extends to severely stressful situations, where a positive yet disillusioned outlook helps individuals to reach a properly balanced resolution (Folkman & Moskowitz, 2000; Larsen, Hemenover, Norris, & Cacioppo, 2003). Indeed, as discussed later, such a coactivation of SWB and HWS can also characterize certain traumatized individuals who sustain their identity as survivors while leading a normal life.

Finally, it is possible that both SWB and the HWS maintain low activation. Low activation of both positive and negative evaluative processes denotes neutrality (Cacioppo et al., 1999). When transient, this state signals a reduced involvement with the environment, which may provide a relieving withdrawal (Carver, 2001). When lasting, this state reflects a depleted ego with expended regulatory capabilities, practically helping to conserve the remaining resources in order to avoid full exhaustion (Baumeister, Muraven, & Tice, 2000). With little or no positive affect to replenish the depleted ego, a chronic deactivation of both SWB and the HWS signals a general psychic numbing common in posttraumatic distress (Asmundson, Stapleton, & Taylor, 2004; Lifton, 1993).

In sum, SWB is not just an outcome or a by-product of other processes as it is typically addressed in research. Rather, it is an agentic force operating in various modular ways within the mental apparatus of adaptation. By providing people with a positive climate for functioning, whether in everyday self-maintenance or in a higher order self-actualization, SWB has the role to regulate the HWS. Although various intersections between SWB and the HWS bear adaptive functions, the adaptive intersection in the long run is when SWB counteracts the HWS up to an optimal degree. However, such a result may not always be attainable. When SWB fails, redemption may be found by reestablishing meaning in life.

Reconstructing the Hostile-World Scenario by Meaning

Whereas SWB can regulate the HWS, meaning making can actually reconstruct the HWS by creating or revising beliefs, values, and goals (Shmotkin, 2005). As humans are a meaning-seeking species, their meaning systems are geared to process information into schemas that direct behavior at all levels and provide this behavior with purpose, coherence, and justification (Kreitler & Kreitler, 1976).

The aforementioned positivity bias in meaning systems functions to meliorate the HWS by offering favorable interpretations to adverse life contingencies through beliefs that dwell, partly unrealistically, on purpose, control, efficacy, optimism, coherence, and self-worth (Antonovsky, 1987; Baumeister, 1991; Janoff-Bulman, 1992; Taylor & Brown, 1988). Meaning may, however, offer consonant interpretations of the world that do not necessarily follow favorable tracks but, rather, present tragic and pessimistic paradigms of life. Also in this case, meaning may serve adaptation by sharpening and sensitizing the HWS when the latter needs to scan potential adversity and make its implications explicit.

Meaning-making strategies are designed to assimilate the appraisals of actual situations into global beliefs or goals (Park, 2010). Thus, meaning can reconstruct the HWS by imposing an overarching principle that makes the HWS interpretable more adaptively. A simple example where the HWS can be interpreted more leniently is by imposing the principle of "happy end" that prevails in popular conceptions ("all's well that ends well"; "there is no bad without good"), fairy tales, and many movie scripts. More elaborate is the reconstructive function of worldviews and self-esteem according to the *theory of terror management* (Pyszczynski, Greenberg, & Solomon, 1999), which postulates that the fear of death in people's mind is a most potent determinant of behavior. Worldviews and self-esteem produce integrative schemes of meaning that connect the self to immortal values and worth and thus transcend the individual's death.

At other times, there is a need to handle major beliefs and goals concerning situations or events that activate the HWS to such a high degree that one's current conceptions are no longer tenable and need to be revised or even completely replaced. Processes of assimilation or accommodation can affect construals of meaning attributed to one's view of the world or to one's sense of self. These construals may be respectively sorted into *meaning as comprehensibility* versus *meaning as significance* (Janoff-Bulman & Yopyk, 2004), or otherwise into *making sense* versus *finding benefit* (Davis et al., 1998). Both comprehensibility (knowledge about existing threats) and significance (estimated effects of those threats on the self) are required, at least in rudimentary forms, to construct the HWS as an efficient scanner for actual and potential adversity.

Religion is a common unifying framework of meaning as well as a major personal striving (Emmons, 2005) that renders the HWS understandable and bearable by providing a sense of directionality, predictability, and self-worth (Park, 2005). Indeed, in view of the *resource-congruence model*, which posits that coping efficacy depends on whether the coping response is congruent with the nature of the stress (Wong, Reker, & Peacock, 2006), religious ways of coping seem suitable to handle existential crises. Religious coping may involve the reconstructive principle of a just world (Lerner, 1980), positing that the world is basically a just and fair place where people ultimately get what they deserve (Hafer & Bègue, 2005). Religious coping may also involve a complete reframing of meaning related to the HWS, such as the conception that suffering is a sublime act of atonement and self-purification or the notion that suffering is part of a providential, benevolent plan of the world (Hudson, 1996).

Another mechanism is the reconstruction of HWS within rational contours of meaning so that horrible threats are interpretable in terms of controllable behaviors and reasonable calculations. Accordingly, people often address important elements in their HWS by taking precautions against hazards, buying insurance policies, practicing emergency drills, and adopting preventive health behaviors.

The dynamic and flexible nature of the meaning system in updating the HWS is further revealed when one recognizes that the search for meaning is relatively independent from the presence of meaning (Park, 2010; Steger, Frazier, Oishi, & Kaler, 2006). Although it is reasonable that people may not search for meaning when a sense of meaning is present, a state of meaningfulness may not foreclose further attempts to explore current or additional sources of meaning (Steger et al., 2006). However, a sense of meaninglessness may not automatically set in motion the search for meaning. Although this condition is discrepant with the human will to meaning, it is more widespread among traumatized populations than was previously acknowledged (Davis, Wortman, Lehman, & Silver, 2000). This idea will be further elaborated shortly.

As appears in the preceding examples, SWB and meaning function as overlapping modalities (Keyes et al., 2002) and therefore may affect the HWS synergistically. Echoing recent holistic models of the good life (Kashdan et al., 2008), we acknowledge the reciprocal influence between SWB and meaning.

Indeed, a meaningful reconstruction of the HWS can fortify self-perceptions of SWB that in turn help to regulate the HWS; on the other hand, by successfully regulating the HWS, SWB facilitates a better generation and awareness of meaning (King & Hicks, Chapter 6, this volume). We further suggest that SWB and meaning complement each other in the engagement with the HWS. As we shortly demonstrate, the boundaries between SWB and meaning become particularly sharpened by the sequela of trauma (King & Pennebaker, 1998; Shrira, Palgi, Ben-Ezra, & Shmotkin, 2011). In any case, whether SWB and meaning reinforce or complement each other, they have distinct operations that should not be confused: SWB makes actual or potential adversity more manageable by evaluating life as favorable, whereas meaning makes such adversity more interpretable by conceiving life as comprehensible. In these capacities, SWB and meaning are pivotal human resources. We now move on to examine how psychological trauma, when the HWS realizes itself, may put these two resources to the test.

Subjective Well-Being and Meaning Following Trauma: How Holocaust Survivors Regulate and Reconstruct a Chronically Activated Hostile-World Scenario

Psychological trauma is a harsh, often extreme realization of the HWS in personal life. Hence, trauma is a test case for the functionality of both SWB and meaning in life as pivotal components of the good life. As evident from various arguments already presented, SWB and meaning are not easy to sustain in the aftermath of trauma. First, trauma tears people away from the world of normalcy by shattering their fundamental assumptions about leading a worthy life in a benevolent and predictable world (Janoff-Bulman, 1992). Second, it is feasible that the bad impact of the trauma proves stronger than that of many good experiences in the trauma survivor's life (Baumeister et al., 2001). In addition, because loss is more potent than its equivalent gain, trauma may trigger a continuous loss cycle whereby the drainage of resources by the trauma generates further frailty rather than replenishment (Hobfoll, 1989). Also, clinical experience shows that posttraumatic reactions are often fixated in repetitive structures manifesting notorious resistance to cure (Herman, 1992) and are susceptible to reactivation when new events of a reminiscent nature occur (Solomon, 1995). As summed up by Frijda (1988), "The emotional impact of traumatic events never really wanes, it can only be overwritten" (p. 354).

In an apparent contradiction to the foregoing assertions, most trauma survivors manifest resilient functioning (Bonanno, 2004). Some even experience positive outcomes, widely referred to as posttraumatic growth (Calhoun & Tedeschi, 2006; Tedeschi & Calhoun, Chapter 25, this volume), by improving and deepening their perceptions of the self, interpersonal relationships, and philosophy of life. Wong (2008) elaborates on a related state while extending Frankl's model of tragic optimism, explaining how people may acknowledge their pain while clinging to renewed sources of hope. Wong (2008) suggests that hope can be sustained in the midst of calamities by reaffirming the intrinsic value of human life, acknowledging the difficulties one is faced with, transcending self-interest by dedicating oneself to a higher purpose, fortifying spiritual belief, and having the courage to face adversity. Tragic optimism is coupled with a bittersweet, yet more mature, sense of happiness such that it is less conditioned upon external circumstances because the fragility of human existence is already accounted for (King & Hicks, 2007).

The positive evidence on the functioning and rehabilitation of trauma survivors points to the dialectical tasks that those survivors face: reformulating the blurred boundaries between vulnerability and resilience, combining evil and benevolent worlds into a coherent life story, and turning an ineradicable infliction into a challenge of thriving. In order to clarify how SWB and meaning serve as major vehicles for performing these posttrauma tasks, we turn our focus on the case of Holocaust survivors.

The Holocaust has become a prototypic symbol of extreme human loss and suffering perpetrated by an incomprehensibly evil power. Amid the mass extermination of Jews in World War II, survivors of the Holocaust faced the evident imminence of being murdered, suffering systematic degradation and physical torment, losing their families and communities, undergoing disruption of their self-identity, and experiencing the total collapse of fundamental human values. The most extreme and massive nature of these experiences makes the psychological study of Holocaust survivors pertinent to cardinal questions about the limits of human endurance. These questions initiated an array of psychological conceptions (e.g., Antonovsky, 1987; Bettelheim, 1979; Frankl, 1963) and outlined still unresolved issues in subsequent research (Ayalon, 2005; Shmotkin, 2003).

Early research on Holocaust survivors focused on clinical settings, aggregating the survivors' distressful symptoms under the labels of concentration camp syndrome or survivor's syndrome (Chodoff, 1963; Eitinger, 1964; Niederland, 1968) and since the 1980s using the contemporary term *posttraumatic stress disorder* (American Psychiatric Association, 2000). When research focus shifted to the general survivor population, it became evident that a vast majority of survivors showed remarkable adaptive and reintegrative capacities alongside specific impairments and vulnerabilities (e.g., Kahana, Harel, & Kahana, 2005; Shmotkin, Blumstein, & Modan, 2003). Despite their past trauma and losses, many survivors succeeded in regaining self-reliance and fortitude, and they went on to flourish in familial and professional domains (Helmreich, 1992; Lev-Wiesel & Amir, 2003).

A similarly mixed pattern was found with regard to SWB. Thus, studies found survivors as happy as comparisons when using measures of overall SWB (Carmil & Carel, 1986; Landau & Litwin, 2000; Shmotkin & Lomranz, 1998). When each of the affects was measured separately, however, survivors showed more negative affect (Ben-Zur & Zimmerman, 2005). Furthermore, survivors were lower than comparisons on aging-related themes of SWB (Kahana et al., 2005; Shmotkin & Lomranz, 1998) and on narrative-related measures of SWB (Cohen & Shmotkin, 2007; Shrira & Shmotkin, 2008). The integration of these findings testifies that survivors are vulnerable when faced with the various tasks of aging. The general decline, illnesses, and losses that accompany the aging process echo distant traumatic memories and intensify distress (Shmotkin, 2003). The need to review one's life and to narrate a coherent life story poses a laborious challenge for the survivors, who have lived in irreconcilable worlds of normalcy and trauma (Lomranz, 1998, 2005).

Frankl (1963, 1969), a Holocaust survivor himself, argued that survivors could endure the agonizing suffering by rising above the dehumanizing horror and embracing beliefs, values, and goals. As a result of the traumatic experiences, survivors became painfully aware of what was precious and valuable in their lives, and so they further toiled to preserve it. To Frankl, this determination reflected the defiant power of the human spirit. These avenues of meaning generation certainly explain the recovery of large numbers of the Holocaust survivors. Many of the survivors found relief in dwelling on such relatively demarcated themes of meaning as maintaining their self-decency, adhering to their religious faith, or vowing to serve as a voice for those who perished (Shantall, 1999). Another prevalent theme among survivors was the notion that their postwar adjustment and successes served as an ultimate proof that the demonic Nazi plan was thwarted (Kahana et al., 2005).

In other veins, however, studies indicate that clinical groups of survivors had difficulties in reconstructing meaning systems as illustrated, for example, by a fragile assumptive world (Brom, Durst, & Aghassy, 2002). Also, survivors sampled in the community yielded mixed results: Some held negative views about the self and the world, whereas others held views that were similar or even more positive compared to those of comparisons (Brom et al., 2002; Prager & Solomon, 1995). The mixed results seemingly attest to the complex, indeed paradoxical, process by which survivors establish renewed schemas of meaning (Suedfeld, 2003).

The life-narrative framework may be helpful in combining the findings on SWB and meaning in general, and when referring to traumatized people in particular. McAdams, who established a conception of the life story as an essential agent of self-identity, further delineated the narrative identity as a major level of personality that embodies the most extended and elaborated forms of satisfaction and meaning (McAdams, 1993, Chapter 5, this volume). Moreover, the three functions of autobiographical narratives—namely, identity maintenance, instrumental and interpersonal reinforcement (e.g., Cappeliez, O'Rourke, & Chaudhury, 2005)—resonate the three basic psychological needs for autonomy, competence, and relatedness that are highlighted by the self-determination theory as the royal road to the good and healthy life (Weinstein, Ryan, & Deci, Chapter 4, this volume). Also, autobiographical techniques tap the most from narratives when combining an expression of emotions in memories with a critical examination of life, which together promote SWB and meaning (Reker, Birren, & Svensson, Chapter 18, this volume). Narratives are particularly pivotal to SWB and meaning in old age, because narrative elaborations commensurate with the developmental tasks of reconciling and integrating the various periods in one's life (Butler, 1963; Erikson, 1982; Krause, Chapter 19, this volume; Shmotkin & Shrira, in press; Wong & Watt, 1991). Nevertheless, among traumatized people, and especially among traumatized elderly, narrative frameworks may have paradoxical effects. On the one hand, when positive and negative autobiographical events are interwoven into a larger mental framework, both SWB and meaning are fortified (Pennebaker & Chung, 2006; Sommer, Baumeister, & Stillman, Chapter 14, this volume). On the other hand, narrating one's life may invoke horrid memories of past trauma, thus catalyzing considerable distress.

Using their narrative, survivors may derive positive aspects of life (de Vries, Suedfeld, Krell, Blando, & Southard, 2005; Shmotkin et al., 2006; Suedfeld et al., 2005), which in turn facilitate the option to address the past trauma openly and learn to live with the incongruence that it introduces into the narrative (Danieli, 1981; Lomranz, 2005). However, as presented in the following discussion, the beneficial role of self-narrative in integrating SWB and meaning varies according to the way that the survivors approach their trauma.

Narratives of survivors strongly reflect the perceived *temporal status* of the trauma (O'Kearney & Perrott, 2006; Shmotkin & Barilan, 2002) as well as its *verbal disclosure* (Finkelstein & Levy, 2006; Pennebaker, Barger, & Tiebout, 1989). The temporal and verbal elements respectively reflect the regulation of the traumatic experience as part of a developmental (time-bound) trajectory of life and social (verbally dominated) interaction with the environment. These regulatory processes can denote different modes of victimization. In this context, Shmotkin and Barilan (2002) found that different time perspectives serve as modes of coping with the trauma among Holocaust survivors. Some survivors remain enmeshed in their traumatic experience: They experience present threats as the continuation of past persecutions and even prepare themselves for another potential Holocaust. For other survivors, the Holocaust exists as a compartmentalized experience that provides a relative freedom from intrusive traumatic memories. These two basic modes were titled as *Holocaust-as-present* and *Holocaust-as-past*, respectively.

Intersecting the temporal status of the trauma with trauma-related verbal disclosure, Shrira and Shmotkin (2006) delineated four different victimization types. First, there are survivors with *renounced victimization*; these individuals tend to remain distant from the Holocaust at both temporal and verbal levels. Then, there are survivors with a *commemorating victimization*; such survivors frequently relate to their traumatic past, but in a past-oriented, controlled manner. This approach enables them to emphasize the role of the Holocaust as a forging event in their lives and to derive pride from their survivor identity. Survivors with *withdrawn victimization* try to avoid being flooded by the trauma through flattening their Holocaust-related verbal expressions. Unlike their renouncing counterparts, who detach their identity from the trauma, withdrawn survivors are characterized by a general numbness that still signals a continuous, present sense of survivorship. Finally, survivors with *absorbed victimization* recurrently and intrusively experience the trauma while also frequently expressing their misery.

Given that typologies tend to oversimplify complex patterns, it is not assumed that the foregoing types fully account for the range of possible victimization experiences. Nevertheless, we propose this typology because it presumably captures major experiences in ways that reflect how trauma may be regulated both internally and externally. Moreover, the victimization typology reverberates other typologies of survivors (Bettelheim, 1979; Bergmann, 1985; Danieli, 1988; Hantman & Solomon, 2007; Kahana, Kahana, King, Harel, & Seckin, 2008), and, notably, its types embody the aforementioned regulatory and reconstructive operations of SWB and meaning vis-à-vis the trauma-based HWS.

Thus, by distancing themselves from the trauma, renouncing survivors successfully meliorate the HWS through relatively high levels of SWB. Their avoidant strategy (e.g., Shedler et al., 1993), however, also minimizes their conscious engagement with the traumatic experience so that attempts to formulate meaning for this experience are foreclosed. Commemorating survivors preserve cognitive and emotional strategies that dialectically sustain a significant place for the Holocaust in their lives, yet the strategies allow for adaptive functioning. The dedicated and relieving activity of commemoration (e.g., bearing witness to the young generation) produces positive feelings that let SWB cofunction with the terrible HWS involved, while also generating meaning (e.g., disseminating the historic lesson of the Holocaust) that reframes the pertinent HWS by giving it a role in life-long reconstruction processes (Armour, 2003; Lomranz, 2005). This type of victimization is regarded as typically conductive to posttraumatic growth (Tedeschi & Calhoun, Chapter 25, this volume). Finally, the withdrawn, as well as the absorbed, survivors suffer from chronically impaired posttraumatic functioning (Bonanno, 2004). Their fragmented and dissociated traumatic memories preclude reconstruction, sustaining an unsafe view of the world and a fragile view of the self (Gampel, 2000). This split and fragmented existence depletes the withdrawn survivors (Baumeister et al., 2000) and confines them to a numb position (Asmundson et al., 2004), as characterized by a low activation of both SWB and the HWS as well as by extinguished processes of meaning making. On the other hand, absorbed survivors cannot resist being flooded by the trauma, so that their HWS overrides their SWB. Yet, their distress also signals a prolonged but fruitless search for the meaning of the trauma. We are currently conducting a large-scale study to further delineate this typology and test certain relationships between its types and factors of human strength.

Summing up, it seems that SWB and meaning continuously attempt to tackle the chronically activated HWS that follows a severe trauma. The processes involved partly take place in the narrative realm according to options of time perspective (treating the trauma as past or present) and self-disclosure (treating the trauma in private or in public). Through their inclination to certain types of victimization, which actually sketch varieties of the HWS, trauma survivors maintain their negotiation with the good life. In the aftermath of the most hellish circumstances, the novelist and Holocaust survivor Primo Levi phrased his insight thus: "Sooner or later in life everyone discovers that perfect happiness is unrealizable, but there are few who pause to consider the antithesis: that perfect unhappiness is equally unattainable" (1958/1995, p. 17).

Conclusion

Our main purpose in this chapter is to show that the very separation between SWB and meaning in life, along with their reciprocal links, enables people to take multiple paths in dealing with the threats of the surrounding world. We maintain that the scenarios of the hostile world are typically experienced as manageable as a result of the regulatory function of SWB mechanisms and perceived as interpretable through the reconstructive function of meaning-making systems. Extending a previously formulated model on well-being in the face of adversity (Shmotkin, 2005), we further examine how SWB and meaning serve as major assets in people's encounters with trauma. We argue that extreme trauma sets limits to the operative capabilities of SWB and meaning. Hence, a particularly strained and dialectical life is imposed on trauma survivors who cannot surmount the paradox of living in unbridgeable spheres, namely, a sphere that permits growth by the benevolent normalcy of life and one that is governed by the horrific eruption of human evil.

References

American Psychiatric Association. (2000). *Diagnostic and statistical manual of mental disorders* (4th ed., rev.). Washington, DC: Author.

Antonovsky, A. (1987). *Unraveling the mystery of health: How people manage stress and stay well.* San Francisco, CA: Jossey-Bass.

Armour, M. (2003). Meaning making in the aftermath of homicide. *Death Studies, 27*, 519–540.

Asmundson, G. J. G., Stapleton, J. A., & Taylor, S. (2004). Are avoidance and numbing distinct PTSD symptom clusters? *Journal of Traumatic Stress, 17*, 467–475.

Ayalon, L. (2005). Challenges associated with the study of resilience to trauma in Holocaust survivors. *Journal of Loss and Trauma, 10*, 347–358.

Baumeister, R. F. (1991). *Meanings of life.* New York, NY: Guilford Press.

Baumeister, R. F., Bratslavsky, E., Finkenauer, C., & Vohs, K. D. (2001). Bad is stronger than good. *Review of General Psychology, 5*, 323–370.

Baumeister, R. F., Muraven, M., & Tice, D. M. (2000). Ego depletion: A resource model of volition, self-regulation, and controlled processing. *Social Cognition*, *18*, 130–150.

Baumeister, R. F., & Vohs, K. D. (2002). The pursuit of meaningfulness in life. In C. R. Snyder & S. J. Lopez (Eds.), *Handbook of positive psychology* (pp. 608–618). New York, NY: Oxford University Press.

Ben-Zur, H., & Zimmerman, M. (2005). Aging Holocaust survivors' well-being and adjustment: Associations with ambivalence over emotional expression. *Psychology and Aging*, *20*, 710–713.

Bergmann, M. S. (1985). Reflections on the psychological and social function of remembering the Holocaust. *Psychoanalytic Inquiry*, *5*, 9–20.

Bettelheim, B. (1979). *Surviving and other essays*. New York, NY: Knopf.

Bonanno, G. A. (2004). Loss, trauma, and human resilience: Have we underestimated the human capacity to thrive after extremely aversive events? *American Psychologist*, *59*, 20–28.

Brom, D., Durst, N., & Aghassy, G. (2002). The phenomenology of posttraumatic distress in older adult Holocaust survivors. *Journal of Clinical Geropsychology*, *8*, 189–201.

Brülde, B. (2007). Happiness theories of the good life. *Journal of Happiness Studies*, *8*, 15–49.

Brunner, J. (2007). Modern times: Law, temporality and happiness in Hobbes, Locke and Bentham. *Theoretical Inquiries in Law*, *8*, 277–310.

Busseri, M. A., Sadava, S., Molnar, D., & DeCourville, N. (2009). A person-centered approach to subjective well-being. *Journal of Happiness Studies*, *10*, 161–181.

Butler, R. N. (1963). The life review: An interpretation of reminiscence in the aged. *Psychiatry*, *26*, 65–76.

Cacioppo, J. T., Gardner, W. L., & Berntson, G. G. (1999). The affect system has parallel and integrative processing components: Form follows function. *Journal of Personality and Social Psychology*, *76*, 839–855.

Calhoun, L. G., & Tedeschi, R. G. (2006). The foundations of posttraumatic growth: An expanded framework. In L. G. Calhoun & R. G. Tedeschi, (Eds.), *Handbook of posttraumatic growth* (pp. 1–23). Mahwah, NJ: Erlbaum.

Cappeliez, P., O'Rourke, N., & Chaudhury, H. (2005). Functions of reminiscence and mental health in later life. *Aging and Mental Health*, *9*, 295–301.

Carmil, D., & Carel, R. S. (1986). Emotional distress and satisfaction in life among Holocaust survivors—A community study of survivors and controls. *Psychological Medicine*, *16*, 141–149.

Carver, C. S. (2001). Affect and the functional bases of behavior: On the dimensional structure of affective experience. *Personality and Social Psychology Review*, *5*, 345–356.

Chodoff, P. (1963). Late effects of the concentration camp syndrome. *Archives of General Psychiatry*, *8*, 323–333.

Cohen, K., & Shmotkin, D. (2007). Emotional ratings of anchor periods in life and their relation to subjective well-being among Holocaust survivors. *Personality and Individual Differences*, *43*, 495–506.

Compton, W. C., Smith, M. L., Cornish, K. A., & Qualls, D. L. (1996). Factor structure of mental health measures. *Journal of Personality and Social Psychology*, *76*, 406–413.

Cummins, R. A., & Nistico, H. (2002). Maintaining life satisfaction: The role of positive cognitive bias. *Journal of Happiness Studies*, *3*, 37–69.

Danieli, Y. (1981). On the achievement of integration in aging survivors of the Nazi Holocaust. *Journal of Geriatric Psychiatry*, *14*, 191–210.

Danieli, Y. (1988). The heterogeneity of postwar adaptation in families of Holocaust survivors. In R. L. Braham (Ed.), *The psychological perspectives of the Holocaust and of its aftermath* (pp. 109–128). Boulder, CO: Social Science Monographs.

Davis, C. G., Nolen-Hoeksema, S., & Larson, J. (1998). Making sense of loss and benefiting from the experience: Two construals of meaning. *Journal of Personality and Social Psychology, 75*, 561–574.

Davis, C. G., Wortman, C. B., Lehman, D. R., & Silver, R. C. (2000). Searching for meaning in loss: Are clinical assumptions correct? *Death Studies, 24*, 497–540.

DeNeve, K. M., & Cooper, H. (1998). The happy personality: A meta-analysis of 137 personality traits and subjective well-being. *Psychological Bulletin, 124*, 197–229.

De Vries, B., Suedfeld, P., Krell, R., Blando, J. A., & Southard, P. (2005). The Holocaust as a context for telling life stories. *International Journal of Aging and Human Development, 60*, 213–228.

Diener, E., & Diener, C. (1996). Most people are happy. *Psychological Science, 7*, 181–185.

Diener, E., Lucas, R. E., & Scollon, C. N. (2006). Beyond the hedonic treadmill: Revising the adaptation theory of well-being. *American Psychologist, 61*, 305–314.

Diener, E., Suh, E. M., Lucas, R. E., & Smith, H. L. (1999). Subjective well-being: Three decades of progress. *Psychological Bulletin, 125*, 276–302.

Eid, M., & Larsen, R. J. (Eds.). (2008). *The science of subjective well-being*. New York, NY: Guilford Press.

Eitinger, L. (1964). *Concentration camp survivors in Norway and Israel*. Oslo, Norway: Oslo University Press.

Emmons, R. A. (1999). *The psychology of ultimate concerns: Motivation and spirituality in personality*. New York, NY: Guilford Press.

Emmons, R. A. (2005). Striving for the sacred: Personal goals, life meaning, and religion. *Journal of Social Issues, 61*, 731–746.

Erikson, E. H. (1982). *The life cycle completed: A review*. New York, NY: Norton.

Feldman, F. (2004). *Pleasure and the good life: Concerning the nature varieties and plausibility of hedonism*. New York, NY: Oxford University Press

Finkelstein, L. E., & Levy, B. R. (2006). Disclosure of Holocaust experiences: Reasons, attributions, and health implications. *Journal of Social and Clinical Psychology, 25*, 117–140.

Folkman, S., & Moskowitz, J. T. (2000). Positive affect and the other side of coping. *American Psychologist, 55*, 647–654.

Frankl, V. E. (1963). *Man's search for meaning: An introduction to logotherapy*. New York, NY: Washington Square Press.

Frankl, V. E. (1969). *The will to meaning: Foundations and applications of logotherapy.* New York, NY: New American Library.

Fredrickson, B. L. (2001). The role of positive emotions in positive psychology: The broaden-and-build theory of positive emotions. *American Psychologist, 56*, 218–226.

Fredrickson, B. L., Tugade, M. M., Waugh, C. E., & Larkin, R. (2003). What good are positive emotions in crises? A prospective study of resilience and emotions following the terrorist attacks on the United States on September 11th, 2001. *Journal of Personality and Social Psychology, 84*, 365–376.

Frijda, N. H. (1988). The laws of emotion. *American Psychologist, 43*, 349–358.

Gampel, Y. (2000). Reflections on the prevalence of the uncanny in social violence. In A. C. G. M. Robben & M. M. Suarez-Orozco (Eds.), *Cultures under siege: Collective violence and trauma* (pp. 48–69). Cambridge, England: Cambridge University Press.

Gilbert, D. T., & Wilson, T. D. (2007). Prospection: Experiencing the future. *Science, 317*, 1351–1354.

Hafer, C. L., & Bègue, L. (2005). Experimental research on just-world theory: Problems, developments, and future challenges. *Psychological Bulletin, 131*, 128–167.

Hantman, S., & Solomon, Z. (2007). Recurrent trauma: Holocaust survivors cope with aging and cancer. *Social Psychiatry and Psychiatric Epidemiology, 42*, 396–402.

Headey, B., & Wearing, A. (1989). Personality, life events, and subjective well-being: Toward a dynamic equilibrium model. *Journal of Personality and Social Psychology, 57*, 731–739.

Helmreich, W. B. (1992). *Against all odds: Holocaust survivors and the successful lives they made in America*. New York, NY: Simon & Schuster.

Herman, J. L. (1992). *Trauma and recovery*. New York, NY: Basic Books.

Hobfoll, S. E. (1989). Conservation of resources: A new attempt at conceptualizing stress. *American Psychologist, 44*, 513–524.

Hudson, D. W. (1996). *Happiness and the limits of satisfaction*. Lanham, MD: Rowman & Littlefield.

Janoff-Bulman, R. (1992). *Shattered assumptions: Towards a new psychology of trauma*. New York, NY: Free Press.

Janoff-Bulman, R., & Yopyk, D. J. (2004). Random outcomes and valued commitments: Existential dilemmas and the paradox of meaning. In J. Greenberg, S. L. Koole, & T. Pyszczynski (Eds.), *Handbook of experimental existential psychology* (pp. 122–139). New York, NY: Guilford Press.

Joseph, S., & Linley, P. A. (2005). Positive adjustment to threatening events: An organismic valuing theory of growth through adversity. *Review of General Psychology, 9*, 262–280.

Kahana, B., Harel, Z., & Kahana, E. (2005). *Holocaust survivors and immigrants: Late life adaptations*. New York, NY: Springer.

Kahana, B., Kahana, E., King, C., Harel, Z., & Seckin, G. (2008). A multi dimensional view of late life adaptation of trauma survivors: Focus on aged survivors of the Holocaust. *Gerontology: Journal of the Israel Gerontological Society, 34*, 19–34 [Special issue on Holocaust and aging, in Hebrew].

Kahneman, D., Diener, E., & Schwarz, N. (Eds.). (1999). *Well-being: The foundations of hedonic psychology*. New York, NY: Russell Sage Foundation.

Kashdan, T. B., Biswas-Diener, R., & King, L. A. (2008). Reconsidering happiness: The costs of distinguishing between hedonics and eudaimonia. *Journal of Positive Psychology, 3*, 219–233.

Keyes, C. L. M. (2005). Mental illness and/or mental health? Investigating axioms of the complete state model of health. *Journal of Consulting and Clinical Psychology, 73*, 539–548.

Keyes, C. L. M. (2007). Promoting and protecting mental health as flourishing: A complementary strategy for improving national mental health. *American Psychologist, 62*, 95–108.

Keyes, C. L. M., Shmotkin, D., & Ryff, C. D. (2002). Optimizing well-being: The empirical encounter of two traditions. *Journal of Personality and Social Psychology, 82*, 1007–1022.

King, L. A., & Hicks, J. A. (2007). Whatever happened to "what might have been"? *American Psychologist, 62*, 625–636.

King, L. A., & Napa, C. K. (1998). What makes a life good? *Journal of Personality and Social Psychology, 75*, 156–165.

King, L. A., & Pennebaker, J. W. (1998). What's so great about feeling good? *Psychological Inquiry, 9*, 53–56.

Kreitler, H., & Kreitler, S. (1976). *Cognitive orientation and behavior.* New York, NY: Springer.

Lacey, H. P., Smith, D. M., & Ubel, P. A. (2006). Hope I die before I get old: Mispredicting happiness across the adult lifespan. *Journal of Happiness Studies, 7*, 167–182.

Landau, R., & Litwin, H. (2000). The effects of extreme early stress in very old age. *Journal of Traumatic Stress, 13*, 473–487.

Larsen, J. T., Hemenover, S. H., Norris, C. J., & Cacioppo, J. T. (2003). Turning adversity to advantage: On the virtues of the coactivation of positive and negative emotions. In L. G. Aspinwall & U. M. Staudinger (Eds.), *A psychology of human strengths: Fundamental questions and future directions for a positive psychology* (pp. 211–225). Washington, DC: American Psychological Association.

Larsen, J. T., McGraw, P. A., & Cacioppo, J. T. (2001). Can people feel happy and sad at the same time? *Journal of Personality and Social Psychology, 81*, 684–696.

Lerner, M. J. (1980). *The belief in a just world: A fundamental delusion.* New York, NY: Plenum Press.

Levi, P. (1995). *Survival in Auschwitz.* New York, NY: Touchstone. (Originally published 1958)

Lev-Wiesel, R., & Amir, M. (2003). Posttraumatic growth among Holocaust child survivors. *Journal of Loss and Trauma, 8*, 229–237.

Lifton, R. J. (1993). From Hiroshima to the Nazi doctors: The evolution of psychoformative approaches to understanding traumatic stress syndromes. In J. P. Wilson & B. Raphael (Eds.), *International handbook of traumatic stress syndromes* (pp. 11–23). New York, NY: Plenum Press.

Lomranz, J. (1998). An image of aging and the concept of aintegration: Personality, coping, and mental health implications. In J. Lomranz (Ed.), *Handbook of aging and mental health: An integrative approach* (pp. 217–250). New York, NY: Plenum Press.

Lomranz, J. (2005). Amplified comment: The triangular relationships between the Holocaust, aging, and narrative gerontology. *International Journal of Aging and Human Development, 60*, 255–267.

Lykken, D. (1999). *Happiness: What studies on twins show us about nature, nurture, and the happiness set-point.* New York, NY: Golden Books.

Maslow, A. (1968). *Toward a psychology of being* (2nd ed.). New York, NY: Van Nostrand.

McAdams, D. P. (1993). *The stories we live by: Personal myths and the making of the self.* New York, NY: Morrow.

McCrae, R. R., & Costa, P. T., Jr. (1994). The stability of personality: Observations and evaluations. *Current Directions in Psychological Science, 3*, 173–175.

McGill, V. J. (1967). *The idea of happiness.* New York, NY: Praeger.

McGregor, I., & Little, B. R. (1998). Personal projects, happiness, and meaning: On doing well and being yourself. *Journal of Personality and Social Psychology, 74*, 494–512.

Niederland, W. G. (1968). Clinical observations of the "survivor syndrome." *International Journal of Psychoanalysis, 49*, 313–315.

Norem, J. K., & Cantor, N. (1986). Defensive pessimism: Harnessing anxiety as motivation. *Journal of Personality and Social Psychology, 51*, 1208–1217.

O'Kearney, R., & Perrott, K. (2006). Trauma narratives in posttraumatic stress disorder: A review. *Journal of Traumatic Stress, 19*, 81–93.

Palgi, Y., & Shmotkin, D. (2010). The predicament of time near the end of life: Time perspective trajectories of life satisfaction among the old-old. *Aging and Mental Health, 14*, 577–586.

Park, C. L. (2005). Religion as a meaning-making framework in coping with life stress. *Journal of Social Issues, 61*, 707–730.

Park, C. L. (2010). Making sense of the meaning literature: An integrative review of meaning making and its effects on adjustment to stressful life events. *Psychological Bulletin, 136*, 257–301.

Parrott, W. G. (1993). Beyond hedonism: Motives for inhibiting good moods and for maintaining bad moods. In D. M. Wegner & J. W. Pennebaker (Eds.), *Handbook of mental control* (pp. 278–305). Englewood Cliffs, NJ: Prentice Hall.

Pennebaker, J. W., Barger, S. D., & Tiebout, J. (1989). Disclosure of traumas and health among Holocaust survivors. *Psychosomatic Medicine, 51*, 577–589.

Pennebaker, J. W., & Chung, C. K. (2006). Expressive writing, emotional upheavals, and health. In H. S. Friedman & R. C. Silver (Eds.), *Foundations of health psychology* (pp. 263–284). New York, NY: Oxford University Press.

Peterson, C., & Seligman, M. E. P. (2004). *Character strengths and virtues: A handbook and classification*. New York, NY: Oxford University Press.

Prager, E., & Solomon, Z. (1995). Perceptions of world benevolence, meaningfulness, and self-worth among elderly Israeli Holocaust survivors and non-survivors. *Anxiety, Stress, and Coping, 8*, 265–277.

Pyszczynski, T., Greenberg, J., & Solomon, S. (1999). A dual-process model of defense against conscious and unconscious death-related thoughts: An extension of terror management theory. *Psychological Review, 106*, 835–845.

Ring, L., Höfer, S., McGee, H., Hickey, A., & O'Boyle, C. A. (2007). Individual quality of life: Can it be accounted for by psychological or subjective well-being? *Social Indicators Research, 82*, 443–461.

Rogers, C. R. (1961). *On becoming a person: A therapist's view of psychotherapy*. Boston, MA: Houghton Mifflin.

Rozin, P., & Royzman, E. B. (2001). Negativity bias, negativity dominance, and contagion. *Personality and Social Psychology Review, 5*, 296–320.

Ryan, R. M., & Deci, E. L. (2001). On happiness and human potentials: A review of research on hedonic and eudaimonic well-being. *Annual Review of Psychology, 52*, 141–166.

Ryff, C. D. (1989). Happiness is everything, or is it? Explorations on the meaning of psychological well-being. *Journal of Personality and Social Psychology, 57*, 1069–1081.

Ryff, C. D., & Keyes, C. L. (1995). The structure of psychological well-being revisited. *Journal of Personality and Social Psychology, 69*, 719–727.

Ryff, C. D., & Singer, B. (1998). The contours of positive human health. *Psychological Inquiry, 9*, 1–28.

Ryff, C. D., Singer, B., & Love, G. D. (2004). Positive health: Connecting well-being with biology. *Philosophical Transactions of the Royal Society of London, 359*, 1383–1394.

Schwarz, N., & Strack, F. (1999). Reports of subjective well-being: Judgmental processes and their methodological implications. In D. Kahneman, E. Diener, & N. Schwarz (Eds.), *Well-being: The foundations of hedonic psychology* (pp. 61–84). New York, NY: Russell Sage Foundation.

Seligman, M. E. P. (2002). *Authentic happiness: Using the new positive psychology to realize your potential for lasting fulfillment*. New York, NY: Free Press.

Seligman, M. E. P., & Csikszentmihalyi, M. (2000). Positive psychology: An introduction. *American Psychologist, 55*, 5–14.

Shantall, T. (1999). The experience of meaning in suffering among Holocaust survivors. *Journal of Humanistic Psychology, 39*, 96–124.

Shedler, J., Mayman, M., & Manis, M. (1993). The illusion of mental health. *American Psychologist, 48*, 1117–1131.

Shmotkin, D. (2003). Vulnerability and resilience intertwined: A review of research on Holocaust survivors. In R. Jacoby & G. Keinan (Eds.), *Between stress and hope: From a disease-centered to a health-centered perspective* (pp. 213–233). Westport, CT: Praeger.

Shmotkin, D. (2005). Happiness in face of adversity: Reformulating the dynamic and modular bases of subjective well-being. *Review of General Psychology, 9*, 291–325.
Shmotkin, D., & Barilan, Y. M. (2002). Expressions of Holocaust experience and their relationship to mental symptoms and physical morbidity among Holocaust survivor patients. *Journal of Behavioral Medicine, 25*, 115–134.
Shmotkin, D., Berkovich, M., & Cohen, K. (2006). Combining happiness and suffering in a retrospective view of anchor periods in life: A differential approach to subjective well-being. *Social Indicators Research, 77*, 139–169.
Shmotkin, D., Blumstein, T., & Modan, B. (2003). Tracing long-term effects of early trauma: A broad-scope view of Holocaust survivors in late life. *Journal of Consulting and Clinical Psychology, 71*, 223–234.
Shmotkin, D., & Lomranz, J. (1998). Subjective well-being among Holocaust survivors: An examination of overlooked differentiations. *Journal of Personality and Social Psychology, 75*, 141–155.
Shmotkin, D., & Shrira, A. (in press). Happiness and suffering in the life story: An inquiry into conflicting expectations concerning the association of perceived past with present subjective well-being in old age. *Journal of Happiness Studies.*
Shrira, A., Palgi, Y., Ben-Ezra, M., & Shmotkin, D. (2011). How do subjective well-being and meaning in life interact in the hostile world? *Journal of Positive Psychology, 6*, 273–285.
Shrira, A., & Shmotkin, D. (2006). *A thematic analysis of Holocaust-related expressions in life stories of Holocaust survivors.* Paper presented at the National Conference on Health and Life Quality of Holocaust Survivors, Kiriat Sdeh Hateufa, Israel.
Shrira, A., & Shmotkin, D. (2008). Can past keep life pleasant even for old-old trauma survivors? *Aging and Mental Health, 12*, 807–819.
Snyder, C. R., & Lopez, S. J. (Eds.). (2002). *Handbook of positive psychology.* London, England: Oxford University Press.
Solomon, Z. (1995). The pathogenic effects of war stress: The Israeli experience. In S. E. Hobfoll & M. W. de Vries (Eds.), *Extreme stress and communities: Impact and intervention* (pp. 229–246). Dordrecht, Netherlands: Kluwer.
Steger, M. F., Frazier, P., Oishi, S., & Kaler, M. (2006). The meaning in life questionnaire: Assessing the presence of and search for meaning in life. *Journal of Counseling Psychology, 53*, 80–93.
Suedfeld, P. (2003). Specific and general attributional pattern of Holocaust survivors. *Canadian Journal of Behavioural Science, 35*, 133–141.
Suedfeld, P., Soriano, E., McMurtry, D. L., Paterson, H., Weiszbeck, T. L., & Krell, R. (2005). Erikson's components of healthy personality among Holocaust survivors immediately and 40 years after the war. *International Journal of Aging and Human Development, 60*, 229–248.
Tatarkiewicz, W. (1976). *Analysis of happiness.* Warsaw, Poland: Polish Scientific Publishers.
Taylor, S. E. (1991). Asymmetrical effects of positive and negative events: The mobilization-minimization hypothesis. *Psychological Bulletin, 110*, 67–85.
Taylor, S. E., & Brown, J. D. (1988). Illusion and well-being: A social psychological perspective on mental health. *Psychological Bulletin, 103*, 193–210.
Telfer, E. (1980). *Happiness.* New York, NY: St. Martin.
Veenhoven, R. (2000). The four qualities of life: Ordering concepts and measures of the good life. *Journal of Happiness Studies, 1*, 1–39.
Veenhoven, R. (2003a). Arts-of-living. *Journal of Happiness Studies, 4*, 373–384.
Veenhoven, R. (2003b). Hedonism and happiness. *Journal of Happiness Studies, 4*, 437–457.

Walker, W. R., Skowronski, J. J., & Thompson, C. P. (2003). Life is pleasant—And memory helps to keep it that way! *Review of General Psychology, 7*, 203–219.

Waterman, A. S. (1993). Two conceptions of happiness: Contrasts of personal expressiveness (eudaimonia) and hedonic enjoyment. *Journal of Personality and Social Psychology, 64*, 678–691.

Waterman, A. S., Schwartz, S. J., & Conti, R. (2008). The implications of two conceptions of happiness (hedonic enjoyment and eudaimonia) for the understanding of intrinsic motivation. *Journal of Happiness Studies, 9*, 41–79.

Wong, P. T. P. (2008). Viktor Frankl: Prophet of hope for the 21st century. In A. Batthyany & J. Levinson (Eds.), *Anthology of Viktor Frankl's logotherapy* (pp. 67–96). Phoenix, AZ: Zeig, Tucker & Theisen.

Wong, P. T. P., Reker, G. T., & Peacock, E. J. (2006). A resource-congruence model of coping and the development of the Coping Schemas Inventory. In P. T. P. Wong & L. C. J. Wong (Eds.), *Handbook of multicultural perspectives on stress and coping* (pp. 223–283). New York, NY: Springer.

Wong, P. T. P., & Watt, L. M. (1991). What types of reminiscence are associated with successful aging? *Psychology and Aging, 6*, 272–279.

Yalom, I. D. (1980). *Existential psychotherapy.* New York, NY: Basic Books.

8
Experiencing Meaning in Life

Optimal Functioning at the Nexus of Well-Being, Psychopathology, and Spirituality

MICHAEL F. STEGER

Colorado State University and North-West University

The previous edition of *The Human Quest for Meaning* arrived at a watershed moment for meaning-in-life research. Appearing in the same year as Ryff and Singer's (1998) influential treatise on psychological well-being (Ryff and Singer also contributed to *The Human Quest for Meaning*), the two contributions set the stage for innovative, rigorous, mainstreamed, and revitalized empirical inquiry into the nature, origins, and consequences of people's beliefs that their lives are meaningful. Exciting research now is building on a foundation of four decades of work. This body of foundational research is the focus of this chapter. Meaning, by its very nature, appears to be an integrating factor in people's lives, drawing together the threads of their efforts to achieve happiness, withstand distress, and attain transcendence beyond their solitary selves (Steger, 2009). In a parallel fashion, this chapter focuses on providing an overview and a conceptual framework for viewing what the field has learned about the well-being, psychopathology, and spirituality correlates of meaning in life.

Meaning in Life

Plato observed that humans are beings in search of meaning; people automatically coax meaning from their experiences, including the experience of life itself. Meaning is the web of connections, understandings, and interpretations that help us comprehend our experience and formulate plans directing our energies to the achievement of our desired future. Meaning provides us with the sense that our lives matter, that they make sense, and that they are more than the sum of our seconds, days, and years. Comprehending our experience in this way builds the cognitive component of meaning in life. The cognitive component of meaning in life thus refers to the understandings that we develop of who we are, what the world is like, and how we fit in with and relate to the grand scheme of things (Heine, Proulx, & Vohs, 2006; Steger, 2009).

If people grasp these qualities, their comprehension should give them a firm grounding in their life experiences. They will have a strong set of related memories that coalesce into a continuous narrative, defensible theories about how the world works, and the ability to test theories of how they are perceived by others (e.g., self-verification theory; Swann, Rentfrow, & Gunn, 2003). Because of this they should be able to forge links between familiar experiences and new ones, integrating new experiences into the web of associations bringing unity to their lives.

The cognitive component of meaning also may provide a foundation from which people develop the aspirations and identify the pursuits that provide their lives with a sense purpose and mission. This sense of purpose comprises the motivational component of meaning, which is the other half of the conceptual core of meaning in life. In some ways, this motivational component may be most familiar to readers. When a person talks about the meaning of his or her life, it often seems the question relates to what that life is for (what purpose does it serve?) or what that persons will accomplish (what are you going to do with your life?). The value of finding an overarching goal or mission to which one's life can be dedicated has led to the inclusion of purpose in the definition of psychological well-being proposed by Ryff and colleagues (e.g., Ryff, 1989; Ryff & Singer, 1998). Other prominent theories of well-being have similarly prioritized having goals and a sense of purpose (e.g., Emmons, 1986; Klinger, 1977). Others contend that it is important to develop a set of motivations closely aligned with one's authentic self (e.g., Deci & Ryan, 2000; McGregor & Little, 1998; Sheldon & Elliot, 1999; Waterman, 1993). I argue that the goals people develop are most beneficial when they arise naturally from the unique ways they comprehend life; when the cognitive component of meaning provides the springboard for the motivational component.

Together the cognitive (comprehension) and motivational (purpose) aspects of meaning in life distinguish meaning from other psychological constructs (Steger, 2009). By binding together these two important dimensions of human psychological functioning, meaning in life is relevant to a broad range of quality-of-life issues. Although meaning in life derives from comprehension and purpose that are attained at a high level of abstraction, more specific and subsidiary processes are implicated. The cognitive component of meaning in life rests on understanding self, world, and niche, and thus people high in meaning would be expected to be high in those domains as well. From here we may be able to proceed logically down to lower levels of abstraction. For example, people's understanding of their niches implies they understand how they relate to others, how they perform under certain circumstances, and how they respond to certain contextual factors. Continuing this example, people high in meaning may have greater awareness that people sometimes interpret their shyness as aloofness, that they prefer to have clear guidelines and timelines for projects they're working on, and that they become moody on rainy days. It is easy to see why knowledge like this would be beneficial, for people would be able anticipate and regulate their behaviors in adaptive ways. These links have rarely been articulated in a coherent fashion, however, and they have not been tested empirically.

With What Should Meaning in Life Correlate?

A great deal of research has been conducted regarding meaning in life, and it is the purpose of this chapter to provide a review of the major domains of findings. Although some experimental research has been conducted on meaning in life, correlational research comprises the bulk of published meaning-in-life studies. Therefore, this chapter will focus primarily on correlational findings.

On the one hand, there is a wealth of information about how people who say their lives are meaningful characterize other aspects of themselves, their relationships, and their lives. On the other hand, this research can convey the appearance of a lot of activity with little thematic unity. Because of its sheer vastness, it can be difficult to know what has already been reported and to identify linkages across research programs and domains. Viewing meaning in terms of its cognitive and motivational aspects provides a framework for anticipating and understanding much of this research. Further, a useful starting point for bringing order to the mass of findings in the literature is provided by looking at some common, and sensible, families of related variables, namely, well-being, psychological distress, and spirituality.

Both comprehension and purpose suggest ways in which meaning in life could help people foster well-being; resolve, as well as develop future resilience to, psychological distress; and cultivate a sense of spiritual connection with something larger than their momentary experiences. I will briefly discuss three of these: the sense that one's life matters, the articulation of valued and overarching goals, and the feeling that one's life makes sense, transcending the moment.

One of the theoretical characteristics of the comprehension component of meaning is the sense that one's life matters. A life that matters holds value, conceptually connecting meaning with such well-being variables as life satisfaction and self-esteem, in which one's life or self is perceived to hold value in terms of satisfaction, esteem, or worth. Low self-worth is a diagnostic marker for several psychopathological syndromes, including depression. Thus, failure to develop the sense that one's life matters, or losing that perspective, might play a role in the experience of psychological distress. It is possible that people might feel their lives matter in a restricted sense pertaining only to their immediate circumstances (e.g., I matter because I left a nice tip). Even this limited sense of "mattering" would often involve a connection with other people, and we might further expect that people also see their lives mattering in the bigger picture. This sense of mattering may help them see connections between their experience and more grandly encompassing circles of life, akin to what

Allport (1961) called the mature self. As the circles expand to include romantic partners, family and friends, neighborhood, community, social causes, religious movements, humanity, and life, people may transcend the bounds of their momentary existence and gain a sense of spiritual connectedness.

The purpose aspect of meaning also links meaning in life with well-being. Frankl (1963) was a strong advocate for people's need to develop a clear vision of what they are trying to accomplish through their lives and that this vision could answer questions about meaning in their lives. The development and pursuit of goals may be rooted in well-functioning appetitive motivational systems (also known as behavioral approach systems; Carver, Sutton, & Scheier, 2000; Elliott & Thrash, 2002; Gable, Reis, & Elliot, 2002; Gray, 1987). These systems facilitate the acquisition of such sought-after environmental rewards as new relationships, new sources of food, and opportunities for growth, which can all lead to greater meaning in life (Kashdan & Steger, 2007). There is support for links between purpose and well-being on several levels, from immediate intentions to engage in a goal-supporting activity (Gollwitzer, 1999) to the ability to engage in long-term planning (e.g., Little, Salmela-Aro, & Phillips, 2006). A lack of interest and heightened indecisiveness is likewise part of the symptom profile of some psychopathological syndromes, including depression. Such factors may decrease people's abilities to form and pursue goals. Viewed in a longer term sense, goals can provide a trajectory for a person's life. The type of goal orientation intended by the term *purpose* suggests a mission that can motivate persons for long periods of time, organizing their activities toward long-term, highly valued goals. Although such goals do not necessarily require that a mission-driven person be spiritual, they are consistent with a sense of spirituality and the transcendence of mundane daily distractions.

Making sense of one's life should be related to a sense of certainty and self-understanding. Some research indicates that having a clear view of one's self is related to well-being (Campbell, 1990). There may be a link between the sense people makes of their lives and the clarity they achieve in their self-understanding. This link may be achieved through people's life narratives. Psychiatric patients often complain of feeling disoriented, and some intriguing research suggests that even people suffering from schizophrenia benefit from the creation of coherent stories explaining their aberrant experiences. In this research, people with symptomatic schizophrenia reported higher meaning than did post-treatment people with schizophrenia whose delusional symptoms had receded (Roberts, 1991). The power of people's ability to make sense of their experience has inspired an approach to psychological distress known as narrative therapy. Narrative therapy regards clients' psychological problems as an opportunity for clients to rewrite their story, often working to transform their self-images from helpless victim of their disorder to empowered agent of change (Brown & Augusta-Scott, 2007). Finally, being able to make sense of one's life, discern a pattern across one's experiences, and expand awareness beyond the immediate press of the moment should provide a person with a sense of transcendence about his or her experience. People's lives encompass more than what is happening now; their lives instead trace an arc of experience that links past and present circumstances to future prospects and pursuits. People's ability to make sense of their lives should facilitate this sort of transcendence, enabling them to find a meaningful place for the things that happen to them and in the world around them.

The previous discussion attempted to lend some structure to the large number of variables that have been empirically linked with meaning in life. I focused on developing conceptual links between the theoretical elements of meaning in life, comprehension, and purpose, as well as specific aspects of those elements (life matters, is endowed with purpose, and makes sense) and well-being, psychological distress, and spirituality. The scarcity of efforts to delineate the variables meaning should be related to, and the reasons why (i.e., the nomological net; Cronbach & Meehl, 1955), is surprising. Meaning is, at its heart, an integrating factor for people. Meaning pulls together people's ideas about who they are, the kind of world they live in, and how they relate to the people and environments around them. Meaning incorporates these elements into people's aspirations and overarching aims. This is the kind of meaning, philosophers have argued, that helps sustain us through adverse circumstance (see Frankl, 1963).

In the subsequent sections, we will review the literature linking meaning in life with well-being, psychological distress, and spirituality. In the past, it has been common to include the Sense of Coherence Test (SOC; Antonovsky, 1987) among measures of meaning in life. Although there is some evidence that the SOC is strongly related to measures of meaning in life, and the SOC includes a subscale labeled "Meaningfulness," it is somewhat misleading to refer to the SOC, or even the Meaningfulness subscale, as a measure of meaning in life. The SOC was designed to assess a basic coping disposition in which people orient themselves to stressors and challenges in an effective and proactive manner (Antonovsky, 1987; Sammallahti, Holi, Komulainen, & Aalberg, 1996). Thus, the SOC is more similar to such psychological concepts as hardiness (e.g., see Maddi, 2005).

Well-Being

Contemporary meaning-in-life research often draws on psychological theories of well-being, particularly eudaimonic well-being (King, Hicks, Krull, & Del Gaiso, 2006; Steger, Kashdan, & Oishi, 2008). Eudaimonic theories of well-being focus on fully flourishing and achieving one's potential as a human being. Given the focus of these theories on people achieving their optimal levels of functioning, it is no surprise that meaning in life appears in several accounts of eudaimonic well-being. In some theories, meaning or purpose in life is a definitional characteristic of well-being; that is, persons cannot be considered to have achieved well-being if they do not feel that their lives have meaning or purpose (e.g., Ryff & Singer, 1998). In other theories, meaning in life is one of several outcomes, or indicators, expected if an individual has reached his or her potential (e.g., Ryan & Deci, 2001). Even in much broader efforts to define well-being, meaning in life is regarded as a valuable indicator of positive functioning (e.g., Diener & Seligman, 2004). The components considered to be central to the experience of meaning—feeling that life matters, identifying a sense of purpose, and achieving an understanding of one's self and one's life—hold direct implications for well-being.

Beginning with the most basic level of well-being, several studies have linked meaning in life with positive affect and emotions (Chamberlain & Zika, 1988; Kennedy, Kanthamani, & Palmer, 1994; Keyes, Shmotkin, & Ryff, 2002; King et al., 2006; Ryff, 1989; Steger, Frazier, Oishi, & Kaler, 2006; Steger, Kashdan, & Oishi, 2008; Zika & Chamberlain, 1992), including feelings of high morale (Ryff, 1989), love, joy, and vitality (Steger et al., 2006). Links with positive affect have been replicated among elderly American and Taiwanese respondents (Chang & Dodder, 1983). According to a recent meta-analysis, the correlation between meaning in life and positive affect among older adults is .47 (Pinquart, 2002).

Meaning in life is also associated with such positive personality traits as Extraversion (Mascaro & Rosen, 2005; Pearson & Sheffield, 1974a; Schmutte & Ryff, 1997; Steger et al., 2006; Steger, Kashdan, Sullivan, & Lorentz, 2008), Agreeableness (Mascaro & Rosen, 2005; Schmutte & Ryff, 1997; Steger et al., 2006; Steger, Kashdan, Sullivan, et al., 2008), Conscientiousness (Mascaro & Rosen, 2005; Schmutte & Ryff, 1997; Steger et al., 2006; Steger, Kashdan, Sullivan, et al., 2008), and Openness to Experience (Schmutte & Ryff, 1997). These findings have been replicated in a German sample (Schnell & Becker, 2006).

Positive affect and personality traits delineate well-being on a basic level. So too do a variety of broadband measures of wellness. Several studies have reported links between meaning in life and various measures of global happiness in American (Ryff & Keyes, 1995), Dutch (e.g., Debats, 1996; Debats, van der Lubbe, & Wezeman, 1993), and Japanese samples (Steger, Kawabata, Shimai, & Otake, 2008). Also reported are links between meaning in life and psychological adjustment (N. J. Thompson, Coker, Krause, & Henry, 2003), including adjustment among elderly nursing home residents (O'Conner & Vallerand, 1998) and general well-being in American college and adult samples (e.g., Bonebright, Clay, & Ankenmann, 2000; Garfield, 1973; Reker, Peacock, & Wong, 1987; Scannell, Allen, & Burton, 2002; Steger, Kashdan, Sullivan, et al., 2008; Wong, 1998a; Zika & Chamberlain, 1987, 1992), as well as among Chinese adults (Shek, 1995), Korean adolescents (Shin, Lee, & Lee, 2005), community- and institution-dwelling older adults (Fry, 2000; Reker, 2002), and bereaved older adults (Fry, 2001). Finally, meaning in life is positively correlated with quality of life among cancer patients (Brady, Peterman, Fitchett, Mo, & Cella, 1999).

At a somewhat more specific level, several studies (Bonebright et al., 2000; Chamberlain & Zika, 1988; Keyes, Shmotkin, & Ryff, 2002; Ryff, 1989; Ryff & Keyes, 1995; Steger, 2006; Steger & Frazier, 2005; Steger et al., 2006; Steger & Kashdan, 2006; Steger, Kashdan, & Oishi, 2008; Zika & Chamberlain, 1992) have reported a link between meaning in life and life satisfaction—the degree to which people positively evaluate their lives—which is a finding replicated among elderly nursing home residents (O'Conner & Vallerand, 1998).

Just as meaning in life should be related to satisfaction with life, it should be related to satisfaction with self. Indeed, several studies have reported a link between meaning in life and self-esteem in American (Ryff, 1989; Steger, 2006; Steger et al., 2006) and Dutch (Debats, 1996) samples and between meaning in life and self-acceptance (Garfield, 1973; Ryff, 1989; Steger, Kashdan, Sullivan, et al., 2008), self-actualization (Ebersole & Humphreys, 1991; Phillips, Watkins, & Noll, 1974), and positive self-regard (Phillips et al., 1974) among general samples. This relationship between meaning and self-worth has been found among prisoners (Reker, 1977), elderly nursing home residents (O'Conner & Vallerand, 1998), and Chinese students (Shek, 1992). Similar results have been obtained with self-confidence among Dominican nuns in training (Crumbaugh, Raphael, & Shrader, 1970).

An interesting side branch of this work has reported positive relations between meaning in life and other positive, self-empowering traits. This list includes ego resiliency (Tryon & Radzin, 1972) and ego strength among Chinese students (Shek, 1992), internal locus of control (Phillips, 1980; Reker, 1977; Reker & Peacock, 1981; Ryff, 1989), internal health locus of control among people with spinal cord injuries (N. J. Thompson et al., 2003), autonomy (Reid, 1996; Ryff, 1989; Steger, Kashdan, Sullivan, et al., 2008), personal growth (Ryff, 1989; Steger, Kashdan, Sullivan, et al., 2008), self-control (Garfield, 1973), sense of control (Newcomb & Harlow, 1986), ambition in Dutch samples (Debats et al., 1993), personal responsibility among high school students (Furrow, King, & White, 2004), less chance and powerful other locus of control (Ryff, 1989), environmental mastery (Ryff, 1989; Steger, Kashdan, Sullivan, et al., 2008), and a sense of mastery among Chinese students (Shek, 2001).

Individuals who report high meaning in life also appear to report more desirable perspectives and outlooks. For example, meaning in life is related to more positive perceptions of the world (Sharpe & Viney, 1973; Simon, Arndt, Greenberg, Pyszczynski, & Solomon, 1998) and toward life in general among retired academics (Acuff & Allen, 1970) and one's present and future life (Reker, 1977). High-meaning people also report greater future orientation (Reker & Peacock, 1981) as well as more positive future orientations (Steger, Kashdan, Sullivan, et al., 2008), including greater hope and optimism (Mascaro & Rosen, 2005, 2006; Mascaro, Rosen, & Morey, 2004; Steger, 2006;

Steger & Frazier, 2005; Steger et al., 2006). A greater number of present and future strivings have been reported among college students (Simmons, 1980) and cancer patients (S. C. Thompson & Pitts, 1993). Adults high in meaning in life enjoy their work more and report lesser workaholism (Bonebright et al., 2000).

Finally, there is some evidence that people high in meaning in life may be better equipped to manage life's challenges. They report more effective past coping in Dutch (Debats, Drost, & Hansen, 1995) and American (Jim, Richardson, Golden-Kreutz, & Anderson, 2006; Stevens, Pfost, & Wessels, 1987) samples, less avoidance coping and more emotion-focused coping (Edwards & Holden, 2001), more positive emotional regulation in Korean adolescents (Shin et al., 2005).

In summary, there appear to be abundant links between meaning in life and a very wide range of other indicators of well-being. One might be tempted to conclude that life is as empty of suffering as it is full of happiness for people who feel their lives are meaningful. However, in light of rapidly accumulating evidence that positive and negative psychological processes constitute different systems (e.g., Ryff et al., 2006), it is perhaps reckless to assume that because meaning in life is related to more of what is good in life it is also related to less of what is bad. The next section reviews the evidence regarding this latter idea.

Psychological Distress and Psychopathology

One of the most influential ideas to arise from Frankl's (1963) writings was that the attitude one takes toward suffering is a route to meaning. Some suffering may be unavoidable; and being able to endure such suffering in a manner that reduces its damage to the self, relationships, and life goals while also using the suffering to challenge one's priorities, strengthen one's bonds with others, and develop a broader purpose should provide deep meaning for people. From a different perspective, some people have argued that meaning in life may serve as a resource in the face of suffering, providing a buffer from the negative impact of traumatic events, for example (e.g., Steger, Frazier, & Zacchanini, 2008). The relationship between meaning in life and the types of attributions, interpretations, and meaning people develop surrounding specific traumatic events has attracted considerable theoretical attention (e.g., Janoff-Bulman & Yopyk, 2004; Park & Folkman, 1997) but less empirical attention. Nonetheless, an enhanced sense of life's meaning is a commonly observed positive outcome of enduring difficult life events (Tedeschi, Park, & Calhoun, 1998), and the possibilities for testing models of how meaning in life and psychological suffering interact appear rich.

Aside from the possibility that successful coping with psychological distress may facilitate enhanced meaning in life, there are conceptual reasons to expect that people with more meaning in life would report less psychological distress and lower psychopathology. Valuing one's life, having a sense of direction and purpose, and being able to comprehend one's experience seem contradictory to many manifestations of psychological distress.

At a basic level of psychological distress is the experience of negative affect and emotions. Research indicates that meaning in life is inversely related to negative affect and emotions (e.g., Chamberlain & Zika, 1988; Kennedy et al., 1994; Keyes et al., 2002; Steger, Kashdan, & Oishi, 2008; Zika & Chamberlain, 1992), including fear, anger, shame, and sadness (Steger et al., 2006), rumination (Steger, Kashdan, Sullivan, et al., 2008), stress (Flannery & Flannery, 1990; Flannery, Perry, Penk, & Flannery, 1994; Frenz, Carey, & Jorgensen, 1993), and general psychological distress among breast cancer survivors (Vickberg, Bovbjerg, DuHamel, Currie, & Redd, 2000).

Meaning in life is generally inversely related with negative personality traits like neuroticism among Americans (Addad, 1987; Mascaro & Rosen, 2005; Pearson, & Sheffield, 1974a, 1989; Steger et al., 2006; Steger, Kashdan, Sullivan, et al., 2008) and Germans (Schnell & Becker, 2006), as well as psychoticism (Pearson & Sheffield, 1989; Scheier & Newcomb, 1993).

Research also has been conducted on the relationship between meaning in life and symptoms more closely associated with specific psychopathological syndromes. Meaning in life is inversely related to the severity of posttraumatic stress disorder symptoms in the United States (Edmonds & Hooker, 1992) and Spain (Steger, Frazier, & Zacchanini, 2008). One of the most pervasive findings is that meaning in life is inversely related to depression in American (e.g., Crumbaugh & Maholick, 1964; Flannery & Flannery, 1990; Flannery et al., 1994; Harlow, Newcomb, & Bentler, 1986; Lester & Badro, 1991; Lewis, Lanigan, Joseph, & de Fockert, 1997; Mascaro & Rosen, 2005, 2006; Mascaro et al., 2004; Phillips, 1980; Ryff, 1989; Ryff & Keyes, 1995; Scheier & Newcomb, 1993; Simon et al., 1998; Steger et al., 2006; Zika & Chamberlain, 1992) and Dutch (Debats, 1990; Debats et al., 1993) samples, as well as among cancer patients (S. C. Thompson & Pitts, 1993), individuals living with HIV (Lyon & Younger, 2001, 2005), elderly nursing home residents (O'Conner & Vallerand, 1998), Chinese students (Shek, 1992), and "problem students" (Rahman & Khaleque, 1996). According to a recent meta-analysis, the correlation with depression is –.46 among older adults (Pinquart, 2002). Likewise, meaning in life is inversely related to anxiety among American (Flannery & Flannery, 1990; Flannery et al., 1994; Frenz et al., 1993; Mascaro & Rosen, 2005; Scheier & Newcomb, 1993; N. J. Thompson et al., 2003) and Dutch (Debats, 1990; Debats et al., 1993) samples, as well as among Chinese students (Shek, 1992), Dominican nuns in training (Crumbaugh et al., 1970), and people with spinal cord injuries (N. J. Thompson et al., 2003). Meaning in life also is inversely related to hostility, antisociality, and aggression in American (Mascaro et al., 2004; Scheier & Newcomb, 1993; Steger, Kashdan, Sullivan, et al., 2008; N. J. Thompson et al., 2003) and Dutch (Debats, 1990; Debats et al., 1993) samples and aggression among Chinese secondary school students (Shek, Ma, & Cheung, 1994).

Those individuals who report greater meaning in life report less hopelessness in a wide variety of samples (Edwards & Holden, 2001; Gomez & Fisher, 2003; Grygielski, Januszewska, Januszewski, Juros, & Oles, 1984; Harris & Standard, 2001) and are more likely to derogate themselves (Harlow et al., 1986; Scheier & Newcomb, 1993). Cancer patients who report lesser meaning in life also report a wider discrepancy between who they feel they actually are and who they would ideally like to be (Heidrich, Forsthoff, & Ward, 1994). People who report lesser meaning in life report more numerous negative life events (Newcomb & Harlow, 1986) and hassles (Flannery & Flannery, 1990) and more grief in their lives (Edmonds & Hooker, 1992). Unsurprisingly, they report higher levels of suicidal ideation (e.g., Edwards & Holden, 2001; Harlow et al., 1986; Lester & Badro, 1991; Scheier & Newcomb, 1993), although, it is interesting to note, they also report greater fear of death (Durlak, 1972).

People who experience a deficit in meaning in life express a stronger need for psychotherapy (Battista & Almond, 1973). Comparisons between psychiatric or psychotherapy patients and general population samples bear out this relationship, with patients reporting lesser meaning in life (e.g., Crumbaugh & Maholick, 1964; Frenz et al., 1993; Pearson & Sheffield, 1974b). Loss and developmental disruption also appear related to meaning in life, with homeless and at-risk youths (Bearsley & Cummins, 1999) and bereaved parents (Florian, 1989) reporting lower meaning in life. Likewise, members of substance abuse treatment groups, both adults (e.g., Nicholson et al., 1994) and adolescents (Hutzell & Finck, 1994), report lesser meaning in life compared to general samples; meaning in life is inversely correlated with levels of substance use (Harlow et al., 1986; Newcomb & Harlow, 1986; Padelford, 1974; Shean & Fechtmann, 1971) and successful completion of substance abuse treatment (Klinger, 1987). Low-meaning people also report greater sexual frustration (Sallee & Casciani, 1976).

Antisocial behavior is also higher among people low in meaning in life. For example, meaning in life is inversely correlated with problematic or antisocial behavior in Chinese students (Shek, 1997; Shek et al., 1994); and disruptive pre–secondary school students (e.g., Rahman & Khaleque, 1996) report lower levels of meaning in life, as do criminals in the United States (Addad, 1987; Reker, 1977) and New Zealand (Black & Gregson, 1973) and shoplifters (McShane, Lawless, & Noonan, 1991).

There is evidence, however, that therapy has benefits for people in terms of meaning in life, and improvements in meaning have been reported in psychiatric patients at post-treatment versus pretreatment in both psychological (Crumbaugh, 1977; Wadsworth & Barker, 1976; see also Davis & McKearney, 2003) and substance abuse treatment (Waisberg & Porter, 1994).

In summary, a substantial amount of research has been conducted on the link between the experience of meaning in life and the experience of psychological distress and psychopathology. This research supports the contention that across a wide range of indicators, meaning in life is inconsistent with the experience of psychological distress. There is no solid evidence that meaning in life reduces distress or psychopathology, but the evidence reviewed here does seem persuasive in making the case that meaning in life should be considered a part of the overall picture of psychological health and functioning and thus perhaps warrants scrutiny as either an essential outcome variable for therapeutic interventions or the inspiration for new meaning-based interventions (see Wong, 1998b).

Spirituality

To this point, this chapter has surveyed several studies establishing links between meaning in life and positive functioning (well-being) and negative functioning (psychological distress and psychopathology). Spirituality may represent a unique dimension of functioning, irreducible to a simple positive or negative dichotomy. The present use of the term *spirituality* highlights a general sense of transcendence and connection with something larger than one's self. Other accounts of spirituality have identified it as the pursuit of significance in that which is sacred about life (e.g., Pargament, 1997), which is certainly in line with how meaning in life has been conceptualized in this chapter. Spirituality has been suggested as a theoretical source (Emmons, 2003) or augmentative factor (Reker & Wong, 1988) for meaning in life, and this chapter advanced some conceptual links between meaning in life and people's achievement of a sense of transcendence and connection. Because spirituality is somewhat of an umbrella term covering formalized religious experience as well as individual transcendental experience, we will consider all such relevant expressions of spirituality in this section, including religious experience, religiousness, spirituality, and transcendence.

Beginning with people's general, spiritual experiences, previous research has shown that meaning in life is positively related to spiritual satisfaction among the elderly (Gerwood, LeBlanc, & Piazza, 1998) and spiritual well-being and the importance of spirituality among college students (Harris & Standard, 2001). People high in meaning report a larger number of transcendent experiences (Kennedy et al., 1994) and score higher on measures of existential transcendence (Harris & Standard, 2001), cosmic transcendence among Dutch adults (Braam, Bramsen, van Tilburg, van der Ploeg, & Deeg, 2006), sense of universality and spiritual transcendence (Piedmont & Leach, 2002), and self-transcendence (Reker, 1994). They report more transcendent goals (Sharpe & Viney, 1973).

Meaning in life is also positively correlated with intrinsic religiosity (Crandall & Rasmussen, 1975; Soderstrom & Wright, 1977; Steger & Frazier, 2005), with satisfaction among retired academics (Acuff & Allen, 1970; Acuff & Gorman, 1968), and with religious activity (praying, meditating; Steger & Frazier, 2005), the salience of one's religion (Petersen & Roy, 1985), and beliefs in personal monotheism (Molcar & Stuempfig, 1988). Chinese post–secondary school students with religious beliefs reported greater meaning in life (Shek, Hong, & Cheung, 1986). People who have devoted their lives to their religious beliefs also tend to report greater meaning in their lives than do people who have not. This relationship has been found among Anglican (Roberts, 1991) and Dominican nuns (Crumbaugh et al., 1970), as well as among Protestant ministers (Weinstein & Cleanthous, 1996), and recently converted Christians (Paloutzian, 1981).

Although the earliest research on meaning in life and spiritual variables was conducted in the late 1960s, there appears to have been a steady interest in understanding the connections between these two bodies of research. The body of evidence is small but consistent in indicating that people who have more satisfactory religious and spiritual lives also report greater meaning in life. Thus, meaning in life appears connected to transcendence, as well as positive and negative functioning.

Conclusions and Future Directions

Four decades of research have led to the accumulation of an impressive number of variables related to people's experience of meaning in life. Broad measures of well-being and adjustment, life satisfaction, self-worth, self-empowerment broadly construed, depression, anxiety, and differences in meaning among known clinical or behavioral groups have been the subject of the largest number of studies, with at least 10 published reports fitting into each category. Thus, it seems safe to conclude that people who say they lead meaningful lives are also fairly happy, are satisfied with their lives and self, and experience lower levels of psychological distress, psychopathological complaints, substance-related problems, and disruptive behavior.

One problem with this body of research is that it has often accumulated in the absence of a unifying theoretical framework. Various influential theories or prominent empirical reports have been consulted in most of the studies reviewed here, usually for the apparent purpose of laying the groundwork for relatively circumscribed investigations. For example, Frankl's (1963) theory that meaning arises, in part, from people's adaptive endurance of suffering has inspired a number of studies looking at people's coping (e.g., Debats et al., 1995; Steger, Frazier, & Zacchanini, 2008); and Maslow's (1971) theory of self-actualization has inspired research looking at self-worth (e.g., Ebersole & Humphreys, 1991). However, the entire endeavor of meaning in life research would benefit to some degree by developing higher order conceptual models and theoretical frameworks that could integrate the intriguing and often solitary number of findings and provide us better information about the deeper nature of meaning in life as a human experience, leading us to prioritize a future research agenda.

I have attempted to sketch one such model by drawing on the distinct psychological features of meaning in life to identify implications for well-being, psychological distress, and spirituality. Of particular interest were the ideas that meaning in life necessarily involves people feeling their lives matter, making sense of their lives, and determining a broader purpose for their lives. I also suggested that theories about meaning in life could generate hypotheses at lower levels of abstraction. For example, from this approach, we can account for the positive relationship of meaning in life with relatedness (Ryff, 1989; Steger, Kashdan, et al., 2008) by arguing that having high-quality relationships indicates an effective ability to understand how one fits with the world around one. This view is more satisfying than arguing that good relationships are important to meaning in life because they are important for well-being in general. Why? Because the former explanation gleans insight into where meaning comes from and what it does. In contrast, the latter explanation seems to diminish critical distinctions between meaning in life and other well-being variables; as a consequence, those researchers who are less familiar with or interested in meaning in life might dismiss it as being generic and thus unworthy of investigation. Meaning-in-life research has achieved a high degree of visibility and acceptance within the broader spectrum of psychological research as a result of the consistent, dedicated, and rigorous work of many scholars over the past four decades. To continue this legacy will require maintaining the empirical rigor and theoretical innovation that have marked the best of previous scholarship as scholars endeavor to connect the disparate threads of research into an integrated theory of meaning in life.

Acknowledgment

I would like to thank Erica Adams for her help in preparing this chapter.

References

Acuff, G., & Allen, D. (1970). Hiatus in "meaning": Disengagement for retired professors. *Journal of Gerontology*, *25*, 126–128.

Acuff, G., & Gorman, B. (1968). Emeritus professors: The effect of professional activity and religion on "meaning." *Sociological Quarterly*, *9*, 112–116.

Addad, M. (1987). Neuroticism, extraversion, and meaning of life: A comparative study of criminals and non-criminals. *Personality and Individual Differences*, *8*, 879–883.

Allport, G. W. (1961). *Pattern and growth in personality.* New York, NY: Holt, Rinehart & Winston.

Antonovsky, A. (1987). *Unraveling the mystery of health: How people manage stress and stay well.* San Francisco, CA: Jossey-Bass.

Battista, J., & Almond, R. (1973). The development of meaning in life. *Psychiatry*, *36*, 409–427.

Bearsley, C., & Cummins, R. A. (1999). No place called home: Life quality and purpose of homeless youths. *Journal of Social Distress and the Homeless*, *8*, 207–226.

Black, W. A. M., & Gregson, R. A. M. (1973). Time perspective, purpose in life, extraversion and neuroticism, in New Zealand prisoners. *Journal of Social and Clinical Psychology*, *12*, 50–60.

Bonebright, C. A., Clay, D. L., & Ankenmann, R. D. (2000). The relationship of workaholism with work–life conflict, life satisfaction, and purpose in life. *Journal of Counseling Psychology, 47*, 469–477.

Braam, A. W., Bramsen, I., van Tilburg, T. G., van der Ploeg, H. M., & Deeg, D. J. H. (2006). Cosmic transcendence and framework of meaning in life: Patterns among older adults in the Netherlands. *Journal of Gerontology: Social Sciences, 61B(3)*, S121–S128.

Brady, M. J., Peterman, A. H., Fitchett, G., Mo, M., & Cella, D. (1999). A case for including spirituality in quality of life measurement in oncology. *Psycho-oncology, 8*, 417–428.

Brown, C., & Augusta-Scott, T. (Eds.). (2007). *Narrative therapy: Making meaning, making lives.* Thousand Oaks, CA: Sage.

Campbell, J. D. (1990). Self-esteem and clarity of the self-concept. *Journal of Personality and Social Psychology, 59*, 538–549.

Carver, C. S., Sutton, S. K., & Scheier, M. F. (2000). Action, emotion, and personality: Emerging conceptual integration. *Personality and Social Psychology Bulletin, 26*, 741–751.

Chamberlain, K., & Zika, S. (1988). Religiosity, life meaning, and wellbeing: Some relationships in a sample of women. *Journal for the Scientific Study of Religion, 27*, 411–420.

Chang, R. H., & Dodder, R. A. (1983). The Modified Purpose in Life Scale: A cross-national validity study. *International Journal of Aging and Human Development, 18*, 207–216.

Crandall, J. R., & Rasmussen, R. D. (1975). Purpose in life as related to specific values. *Journal of Clinical Psychology, 31*, 483–485.

Cronbach, L. J., & Meehl, P. E. (1955). Construct validity in psychological tests. *Psychological Bulletin, 52*, 281–302.

Crumbaugh J. C. (1977). The Seeking of Noetic Goals Test (SONG): A complementary scale to the Purpose in Life Test (PIL). *Journal of Clinical Psychology, 33*, 900–907.

Crumbaugh, J. C., & Maholick, L. T. (1964). An experimental study in existentialism: The psychometric approach to Frankl's concept of noogenic neurosis. *Journal of Clinical Psychology, 20*, 200–207.

Crumbaugh, J. C., Raphael, M., & Shrader, R. R. (1970). Frankl's will to meaning in a religious order. *Journal of Clinical Psychology, 26*, 206–207.

Davis, C. G., & McKearney, J. M. (2003). How do people grow from their experience with trauma of loss? *Journal of Social and Clinical Psychology, 22*, 477–492.

Debats, D. L. (1990). The Life Regard Index: Reliability and validity. *Psychological Reports, 67*, 27–34.

Debats, D. L. (1996). Meaning in life: Clinical relevance and predictive power. *British Journal of Clinical Psychology*, 35, 503–516.

Debats, D. L., Drost, J., & Hansen, P. (1995). Experiences of meaning in life: A combined qualitative and quantitative approach. *British Journal of Psychology, 86*, 359–375.

Debats, D. L., van der Lubbe, P. M., & Wezeman, F. R. A. (1993). On the psychometric properties of the Life Regard Index (LRI): A measure of meaningful life. *Personality and Individual Differences, 14*, 337–345.

Deci, E. L., & Ryan, R. M. (2000). The "what" and "why" of goal pursuit: Human needs and the self-determination of behavior. *Psychological Inquiry, 11*, 227–268.

Diener, E., & Seligman, M. E. P. (2004). Beyond money: Toward an economy of well-being. *Psychological Science in the Public Interest, 5*, 1–31.

Durlak, J. A. (1972). Relationship between individual attitudes toward life and death. *Journal of Consulting and Clinical Psychology, 38*, 463.

Ebersole, P., & Humphreys, P. (1991). The short index of self-actualization and purpose in life. *Psychological Reports, 69*, 550.

Edmonds, S., & Hooker, K. (1992). Perceived changes in life meaning following bereavement. *OMEGA*, 25, 307–318.

Edwards, M. J., & Holden, R. R. (2001). Coping, meaning in life, and suicidal manifestations: Examining gender differences. *Journal of Clinical Psychology*, 57, 1517–1534.

Elliot, A. J., & Thrash, T.M. (2002). Approach-avoidance motivation in personality: Approach and avoidance temperaments and goals. *Journal of Personality and Social Psychology, 82*, 804–818.

Emmons, R. A. (1986). Personal strivings: An approach to personality and subjective well-being. *Journal of Personality and Social Psychology, 51*, 1058–1068.

Emmons, R. A., (2003). Personal goals, life meaning, and virtue: Wellsprings of a positive life. In C. Keyes & J. Haidt (Eds.), *Flourishing: Positive psychology and the well-lived life* (pp. 105–128). Washington, DC: American Psychological Association.

Flannery, R. B., & Flannery, G. J. (1990). Sense of coherence, life stress, and psychological distress: A prospective methodological inquiry. *Journal of Clinical Psychology, 46*, 415–420.

Flannery, R. B., Perry, J. C., Penk, W. E., & Flannery G. J. (1994). Validating Antonovsky's Sense of Coherence Scale. *Journal of Clinical Psychology, 50*, 575–577.

Florian, V. (1989). Meaning and purpose in life of bereaved parents whose son fell during active military service. *OMEGA*, 20, 91–102.

Frankl, V. E. (1963). *Man's search for meaning: An introduction to logotherapy*. New York, NY: Washington Square Press.

Frenz, A. W., Carey, M. P., & Jorgensen, R. S. (1993). Psychometric evaluation of Antonovsky's Sense of Coherence Scale. *Psychological Assessment, 5*, 145–153.

Fry, P. S. (2000). Religious involvement, spirituality and personal meaning for life: Existential predictors of psychological wellbeing in community-residing and institutional care elders. *Aging & Mental Health, 4*, 375–387.

Fry, P. S. (2001). The unique contribution of key existential factors to the prediction of psychological well-being of older adults following spouse loss. *Gerontologist, 41*, 69–81.

Furrow, J. L., King, P. E., & White, K. (2004). Religion and positive youth development: Identity, meaning, and prosocial concerns. *Applied Developmental Science, 8*, 17–26.

Gable, S. L., Reis, H. T., & Elliot, A. J. (2000). Behavioral activation and inhibition in everyday life. *Journal of Personality and Social Psychology, 78*, 1135–1149.

Garfield, C. (1973). A psychometric and clinical investigation of Frankl's concept of existential vacuum and anomie. *Psychiatry, 36*, 396–408.

Gerwood, J. B., LeBlanc, M., & Piazza, N. (1998). The Purpose-in-Life Test and religious denomination: Protestant and Catholic scores in an elderly population. *Journal of Clinical Psychology, 54*, 49–53.

Gollwitzer, P. M. (1999). Implementation intentions: Strong effects of simple plans. *American Psychologist, 54*, 493–503.

Gomez, R., & Fisher, J. W. (2003). Domains of spiritual well-being and development and validation of the Spiritual Well-Being Questionnaire. *Personality and Individual Differences, 35*, 1975–1991.

Gray, J. A. (1987). *The psychology of fear and stress* (2nd ed.). Cambridge, England: Cambridge University Press.

Grygielski, M., Januszewska, E., Januszewski, A., Juros, A., & Oles, P. (1984). Meaning in life and hopelessness: Interrelationships and intergroup differences. *Polish Psychological Bulletin, 15*, 277–284.

Harlow, L. L., Newcomb, M. D., & Bentler, P. M. (1986). Depression, self-derogation, substance use, and suicide ideation: Lack of purpose in life as a mediational factor. *Journal of Clinical Psychology, 42*, 5–21.

Harris, A. H. S., & Standard, S. (2001). Psychometric properties of the Life Regard Index–Revised: A validation study of a measure of personal meaning. *Psychological Reports, 89*, 759–773.

Heidrich, S. M., Forsthoff, C. A., & Ward, S. E. (1994). Psychological adjustment in adults with cancer: The self as mediator. *Health Psychology, 13*, 346–353.

Heine, S. J., Proulx, T., & Vohs, K. D. (2006). The meaning maintenance model: On the coherence of social motivations. *Personality and Social Psychology Review, 10*, 88–110.

Hutzell, R. R., & Finck, W. C. (1994). Adapting the Life Purpose Questionnaire for use with adolescent populations. *International Forum for Logotherapy, 17*, 42–46.

Janoff-Bulman, R., & Yopyk, D. J. (2004). Random outcomes and valued commitments: Existential dilemmas and the paradox of meaning. In J. Greenberg, S. L. Koole, & T. Pyszczynski (Eds.), *Handbook of experimental existential psychology* (pp. 122–138). New York, NY: Guilford Press.

Jim, H. S., Richardson, S. A., Golden-Kreutz, D. M., & Anderson, B. L. (2006). Strategies used in coping with a cancer diagnosis predict meaning in life for survivors. *Health Psychology, 25*, 763–761.

Kashdan, T. B., & Steger, M. F. (2007). Curiosity and stable and pathways to well-being and meaning in life: Traits, states, and everyday behaviors. *Motivation and Emotion, 31*, 159–173.

Kennedy, J. E., Kanthamani, H., & Palmer, J. (1994). Psychic and spiritual experiences, health, well-being, and meaning in life. *Journal of Parapsychology, 58*, 353–383.

Keyes, C. L. M., Shmotkin, D., & Ryff, C. D. (2002). Optimizing well-being: The empirical encounter of two traditions. *Journal of Personality and Social Psychology, 82*, 1007–1022.

King, L. A., Hicks, J. A., Krull, J. L., & Del Gaiso, A. K. (2006). Positive affect and the experience of meaning in life. *Journal of Personality and Social Psychology, 90*, 179–196.

Klinger, E. (1977). *Meaning and void.* Minneapolis: University of Minnesota Press.

Klinger, E. (1987). The Interview Questionnaire technique: Reliability and validity of a mixed idiographic–nomothetic measure of motivation. In J. N. Butcher & C. D. Spielberger (Eds.), *Advances in personality assessment* (Vol. 6, pp. 31–48). Hillsdale, NJ: Erlbaum.

Lester, D., & Badro, S. (1991). Depression, suicidal preoccupation and purpose in life in a subclinical population. *Personality and Individual Differences, 13*, 75–76.

Lewis, C. A., Lanigan, C., Joseph, S., & de Fockert, J. (1997). Religiosity and happiness: No evidence for an association among undergraduates. *Personality and Individual Differences, 22*, 119–121.

Little, B. R., Salmela-Aro, K., & Phillips, S. D. (2006). *Personal project pursuit: Goals, action, and human flourishing.* Mahwah, NJ: Erlbaum.

Lyon, D. E., & Younger, J. B. (2001). Purpose in life and depressive symptoms in persons living with HIV disease. *Image: Journal of Nursing Scholarship, 33*, 137–141.

Lyon, D. E., & Younger, J. B. (2005). Development and preliminary evaluation of the Existential Meaning Scale. *Journal of Holistic Nursing, 23*, 54–65.

Maddi, S. R. (2005). Hardiness as the key to resilience under stress. *Psychology Review, 11*, 20–23.

Mascaro, N., & Rosen, D. H. (2005). Existential meaning's role in the enhancement of hope and prevention of depressive symptoms. *Journal of Personality, 73*, 985–1014.

Mascaro, N., & Rosen, D. H. (2006). The role of existential meaning as a buffer against stress. *Journal of Humanistic Psychology, 46*, 168–190.

Mascaro, N., Rosen, D. H., & Morey, L. C. (2004) The development, construct validity, and clinical utility of the Spiritual Meaning Scale. *Personality and Individual Differences*, 37, 845–860.
Maslow, A. H. (1971). *The further reaches of human nature.* New York, NY: Viking.
McGregor, I., & Little, B. R. (1998). Personal projects, happiness, and meaning: On doing well and being yourself. *Journal of Personality and Social Psychology*, *74*, 494–512.
McShane, F. J., Lawless, J., & Noonan, B. A. (1991). Personal meaning in the lives of a shoplifting population. *International Journal of Offender Therapy and Comparative Criminology*, *35*, 190–204.
Molcar, C. C., & Stuempfig, D. W. (1988). Effects of world view on purpose in life. *Journal of Psychology*, *122*, 365–371.
Newcomb, M. D., & Harlow, L. L. (1986). Life events and substance use among adolescents: Mediating effects of perceived loss of control and meaninglessness in life. *Journal of Personality and Social Psychology*, *51*, 564–577.
Nicholson, T., Higgins, W., Turner, P., James, S., Stickle, F., & Pruitt, T. (1994). The relation between meaning in life and the occurrence of drug abuse: A retrospective study. *Psychology of Addictive Behaviors*, *8*, 24–28.
O'Conner, B. P., & Vallerand, R. J. (1998). Psychological adjustment variables as predictors of mortality among nursing home residents. *Psychology and Aging*, 13, 368–374.
Padelford, B. L. (1974). Relationship between drug involvement and Purpose in Life. *Journal of Clinical Psychology*, *30*, 303–305
Paloutzian, R. F. (1981). Purpose in life and value changes following conversion. *Journal of Personality and Social Psychology*, *41*, 1153–1160.
Pargament, K. I. (1997). *The psychology of religion and coping.* New York, NY: Guilford Press.
Park, C. L., & Folkman, S. (1997). Meaning in the context of stress and coping. *Review of General Psychology*, *30*, 115–144.
Pearson, P. R., & Sheffield, B. F. (1974a). Purpose-in-life in a sample of British psychiatric out-patients. *Journal of Clinical Psychology*, *30*, 459.
Pearson, P. R., & Sheffield, B. F. (1974b). Purpose-in-life and the Eysenck Personality Inventory. *Journal of Clinical Psychology*, *30*, 562–564.
Pearson, P. R., & Sheffield, B. F. (1989). Psychoticism and purpose in life. *Personality and Individual Differences*, *10*, 1321–1322.
Petersen, L. R., & Roy, A. (1985). Religiosity, anxiety, and meaning and purpose: Religion's consequences for psychological well-being. *Review of Religious Research*, *27*, 49–62.
Phillips, W. M. (1980). Purpose in life, depression, and locus of control. *Journal of Clinical Psychology*, *36*, 661–667.
Phillips, W. M., Watkins, J. T., & Noll, G. (1974). Self-actualization, self-transcendence, and personal philosophy. *Journal of Humanistic Psychology*, *14*, 53–73.
Piedmont, R. L., & Leach, M. M. (2002). Cross-cultural generalizability of the Spiritual Transcendence Scale in India. *American Behavioral Scientist*, *45*, 1888–1901.
Pinquart, M. (2002). Creating and maintaining purpose in life in old age: A meta-analysis. *Ageing International*, *27*, 90–114.
Rahman, T., & Khaleque, A. (1996). The purpose in life and academic behavior of problem students in Bangladesh. *Social Indicators Research*, *39*, 59–64.
Reid, J. K. (1996). Tickets to adulthood? The relationship between life attitudes, death acceptance, and autonomy in adulthood. *Family Therapy*, *23*, 135–149.
Reker, G. T. (1977). The Purpose-in-Life test in an inmate population: An empirical investigation. *Journal of Clinical Psychology*, *33*, 688–693.

Reker, G. T. (1994). Logotheory and logotherapy: Challenges, opportunities, and some empirical findings. *International Forum for Logotherapy, 17*, 47–55.
Reker, G. T. (2002). Prospective predictors of successful aging in community-residing and institutionalized Canadian elderly. *Ageing International, 27*, 42–64.
Reker, G. T., & Peacock, E. J. (1981). The Life Attitude Profile (LAP): A multidimensional instrument for assessing attitudes toward life. *Canadian Journal of Behavioral Science, 13*, 264–273.
Reker, G. T., Peacock, E. J., & Wong, P. T. P. (1987). Meaning and purpose in life and well-being: A life-span perspective. *Journal of Gerontology, 42*, 44–49.
Reker, G. T., & Wong. P. T. P (1988). Aging as an individual process: Toward a theory of personal meaning. In J. E. Birren & V. L. Bengston (Eds.), *Emergent theories of aging* (pp. 214–246). New York, NY: Springer.
Roberts, G. (1991). Delusional belief systems and meaning in life: A preferred reality? *British Journal of Psychiatry, 159* (Suppl. 14), 19–28.
Ryan, R. M., & Deci, E. L. (2001). On happiness and human potentials: A review of research on hedonic and eudaimonic well-being. *Annual Review Psychology, 52*, 141–166.
Ryff, C. D. (1989). Happiness is everything, or is it? Explorations of the meaning of psychological well-being. *Journal of Personality and Social Psychology, 57*, 1069–1081.
Ryff, C. D., & Keyes, C. L. M. (1995). The structure of well-being revisited. *Journal of Personality and Social Psychology, 69*, 719–727.
Ryff, C. D., Love, G. D., Urry, H. L., Muller, D., Rosenkranz, M. A., Friedman, E. M., … Singer, B. (2006). Psychological well-being and ill-being: Do they have distinct or mirrored biological correlates? *Psychotherapy and Psychosomatics, 75*, 85–95.
Ryff, C. D., & Singer, B. (1998). The contours of positive human health. *Psychological Inquiry, 9*, 1–28.
Sallee, D. T., & Casciani, J. M. (1976). Relationship between sex drive and sexual frustration and purpose in life. *Journal of Clinical Psychology, 32*, 273–275.
Sammallahti, P. R., Holi, M. J., Komulainen, E. J., & Aalberg, V. A. (1996). Comparing two self-report measures of coping—The Sense of Coherence Scale and the Defense Styles Questionnaire. *Journal of Clinical Psychology, 52*, 517–524.
Scannell, E. D., Allen, F. C. L., & Burton, J. (2002). Meaning in life and positive and negative well-being. *North American Journal of Psychology, 4*, 93–112.
Scheier L. M., & Newcomb, M. D. (1993). Multiple dimensions of affective and cognitive disturbance: Latent-variable models in a community sample. *Psychological Assessment, 5*, 230–234.
Schmutte, P. S., & Ryff, C. D. (1997). Personality and well-being: Reexamining methods and meanings. *Journal of Personality and Social Psychology, 73*, 549–559.
Schnell, T., & Becker, P. (2006). Personality and meaning in life. *Personality and individual Differences, 41*, 117–129.
Sharpe, D., & Viney, L. (1973). Weltanschauung and the Purpose-in-Life Test. *Journal of Clinical Psychology, 29*(4), 489–491.
Shean, G., & Fechtmann, F. (1971). Purpose in Life scores of student marihuana users. *Journal of Clinical Psychology, 27*, 112–113.
Shek, D. T. L. (1992). Meaning in life and psychological well-being: An empirical study using the Chinese version of the Purpose in Life Questionnaire. *Journal of Genetic Psychology, 153*, 185–200.
Shek, D. T. L. (1995). Marital quality and psychological well-being of married adults in a Chinese context. *Journal of Genetic Psychology, 156*, 45–56.
Shek, D. T. L. (1997). Family environment and adolescent psychological well-being, school adjustment, and problem behavior: A pioneer study in a Chinese context. *Journal of Genetic Psychology, 158*, 113–128.

Shek, D. T. L. (2001). Meanings in life and sense of mastery in Chinese adolescents with economic disadvantage. *Psychological Reports, 88*, 711–712.
Shek, D. T. L., Hong, E. W., & Cheung, M. Y. P. (1986). The Purpose in Life Questionnaire in a Chinese context. *Journal of Psychology: Interdisciplinary and Applied, 121*, 77–83.
Shek, D. T. L., Ma, H. K., & Cheung, P. C. (1994). Meaning in life and adolescent antisocial and prosocial behavior in a Chinese context. *Psychologia, 37*, 211–218.
Sheldon, K. M., & Elliot, M. (1999). Goal striving, need satisfaction, and longitudinal well-being the self-concordance model. *Journal of Personality and Social Psychology, 76*, 482–497.
Shin, J. Y., Lee, Y. A., & Lee, K.-H. (2005). The effects of life meaning and emotional regulation strategies on psychological well-being. *Korean Journal of Counseling and Psychotherapy, 17*, 1035–1057.
Simmons, D. D. (1980). Purpose-in-life and the three aspects of valuing. *Journal of Clinical Psychology, 36*, 921–922.
Simon, L., Arndt, J., Greenberg, J., Pyszczynski, T., & Solomon, S. (1998). Terror management and meaning: Evidence that the opportunity to defend the worldview in response to mortality salience increases the meaningfulness of life in the mildly depressed. *Journal of Personality, 66*, 359–382.
Soderstrom, D., & Wright, E. W. (1977). Religious orientation and meaning of life. *Journal of Clinical Psychology, 33*, 65–68.
Steger, M. F. (2006). An illustration of issues in factor extraction and identification of dimensionality in psychological assessment data. *Journal of Personality Assessment, 86*, 263–272.
Steger, M. F. (2009). Meaning in life. In S. J. Lopez (Ed.), *Handbook of positive psychology* (2nd ed., pp. 679–687). Oxford, England: Oxford University Press.
Steger, M. F., & Frazier, P. (2005). Meaning in life: One link in the chain from religion to well-being. *Journal of Counseling Psychology, 52*, 574–582.
Steger, M. F., Frazier, P., Oishi, S., & Kaler, M. (2006). The Meaning in Life Questionnaire: Assessing the presence of and search for meaning in life. *Journal of Counseling Psychology, 53*, 80–93.
Steger, M. F., Frazier, P., & Zacchanini, J. L. (2008). Terrorism in two cultures: Traumatization and existential protective factors following the September 11th attacks and the Madrid train bombings. *Journal of Trauma and Loss, 13*, 511–527
Steger, M. F., & Kashdan, T. B. (2006). Stability and specificity of meaning in life and life satisfaction over one year: Implications for outcome assessment. *Journal of Happiness Studies, 8*, 161–179.
Steger, M. F., Kashdan, T. B., & Oishi, S. (2008). Being good by doing good: Eudaimonic activity and daily well-being correlates, mediators, and temporal relations. *Journal of Research in Personality, 42*, 22–42.
Steger, M. F., Kashdan, T. B., Sullivan, B. A., & Lorentz, D. (2008). Understanding the search for meaning in life: Personality, cognitive style, and the dynamic between seeking and experiencing meaning. *Journal of Personality, 76*, 199–228.
Steger, M. F., Kawabata, Y., Shimai, S., & Otake, K. (2008). The meaningful life in Japan and the United States: Levels and correlates of meaning in life. *Journal of Research in Personality, 42*, 660–678.
Stevens, M. J., Pfost, K. S., & Wessels, A. B. (1987). The relationship of purpose in life to coping strategies and time since the death of a significant other. *Journal of Counseling and Development, 65*, 424–426.
Swann, W. B., Jr., Rentfrow, P. J., & Gunn, J. S. (2003). Self-verification: The search for coherence. In M. Leary & J. Tangney (Eds.), *Handbook of self and identity* (pp. 367–383). New York, NY: Guilford Press.

Tedeschi, R. G., Park, C. L., & Calhoun, L. G. (1998). Posttraumatic growth: Conceptual issues. In R. G. Tedeschi, C. L. Park, & L. G. Calhoun (Eds.), *Posttraumatic growth: Theory and research on change in the aftermath of crisis* (pp. 1–22). Mahwah, NJ: Erlbaum.

Thompson, N. J., Coker, J., Krause, J. S., & Henry, E. (2003). Purpose in life as a mediator of adjustment after spinal cord injury. *Rehabilitative Psychology, 48*, 100–108.

Thompson, S. C., & Pitts, J. (1993). Factors relating to a person's ability to find meaning after a diagnosis of cancer. *Journal of Psychosocial Oncology, 11*, 1–21.

Tryon, W., & Radzin, A. (1972). Purpose-in-life as a function of ego resiliency, dogmatism, and biographical variables. *Journal of Clinical Psychology, 28*, 544–545.

Vickberg, S. M. J., Bovbjerg, D. H., DuHamel, K. N., Currie, V., & Redd. W. H. (2000). Intrusive thoughts and psychological distress among breast cancer survivors: Global meaning as a possible protective factor. *Behavioral Medicine, 25*, 152–161.

Wadsworth, A. P., & Barker, H. R., Jr. (1976). A comparison of two treatments for depression: The antidepressive program vs. traditional therapy. *Journal of Clinical Psychology, 32*, 445–449.

Waisberg, J. L., & Porter, J. E. (1994). Purpose in life and outcome of treatment for alcohol dependence. *British Journal of Clinical Psychology*, 33, 49–63.

Waterman, A. S. (1993). Two conceptions of happiness: Contrasts of personal expressiveness (eudaimonia) and hedonic enjoyment. *Journal of Personality and Social Psychology*, 64, 678–691.

Weinstein, L., & Cleanthous, C. C. (1996). A comparison of protestant ministers and parishioners on expressed purpose in life and intrinsic religious motivation. *Psychology: A Journal of Human Behavior, 33*, 26–29.

Wong, P. T. P. (1998a). Implicit theories of meaningful life and development of Personal Meaning Profile. In P. T. P. Wong & P. S. Fry (Eds.), *The human quest for meaning: A handbook of psychological research and clinical applications* (pp. 111–140). Mahwah, NJ: Erlbaum.

Wong, P. T. P. (1998b). Meaning-centered counseling. In P. T. P. Wong & P. S. Fry (Eds.), *The human quest for meaning: A handbook of psychological research and clinical applications* (pp. 395–435). Mahwah, NJ: Erlbaum.

Wong, P. T. P., & Fry, P. S. (1998). *The human quest for meaning: A handbook of psychological research and clinical applications.* Mahwah, NJ: Erlbaum.

Zika, S., & Chamberlain, K. (1987). Relation of hassles and personality to subjective well-being. *Journal of Personality and Social Psychology, 53*, 155–162.

Zika, S., & Chamberlain, K. (1992). On the relation between meaning in life and psychological well-being. *British Journal of Psychology, 83*, 133–145.

9
The Meaning of Love

ARTHUR ARON and ELAINE N. ARON

State University of New York at Stony Brook

After some preliminaries, we consider the meaning of love and then turn to how love gives meaning: first, the role of love in giving meaning as love of and by close others; next, the role of love in giving meaning as love of and by one's larger social world (connection and integration in community); then, finally, the role of love in giving meaning as love of and by that which is beyond close others and community. We conclude with some classical views of love to provide continuity with our contemporary science-based thinking.

Some Preliminaries

About Meaning

Based on the various conceptualizations that have been put forward by those researchers who have focused on this issue (as spelled out, for example, in the various chapters of this volume), two key ideas have guided us in this chapter. First, we have focused on meaning in life as a sense of purpose beyond mere survival. By purpose, we mean central motivations or goal orientations. Second, we have also considered meaning in life as referring to one's life being rich and full—that is, deep, significant, and coherent versus shallow, trivial, and disjointed.

About Love

In the next main section, we review briefly the considerable body of scholarly and scientific literature on the nature of love. We want to emphasize at the outset, however, that we are using the term in a very general way to include romantic love, familial love, compassionate love for strangers, love in the more general sense of love of particular objects and activities and values, and even love of God. Our main focus will be on love in the context of close relationships; to a somewhat lesser extent love in the context of community; and then only relatively briefly other kinds of love, particularly at the conclusion of the chapter.

What Is Love?

The meaning of love has been vague for both lay people and scholars. Indeed, Fehr (1988, 2001) suggested that the long-standing philosophical controversies over its meaning and the corresponding diversity of conceptual and operational definitions in the scientific literature are the result of a basic problem. She argued that ordinary people recognize instances of love not by their conforming to some formal definition but, rather, by their family resemblance to a prototypical exemplar (just as people recognize something as a fruit by its similarity to an apple.) Thus, Fehr adapted Mervis and Rosch's (1981) prototype approach to the topic of love.

In one set of studies (Fehr & Russell, 1991), one group of participants freely listed types of love, and then another sample rated each of the most commonly mentioned types on a scale from "1 (extremely poor example of love) to 6 (extremely good example of love)" (p. 428). The most central type of love was maternal love (mean centrality = 5.39), followed by parental love (5.22), friendship (4.96), sisterly love (4.84), romantic love (4.76), brotherly love (4.74), familial love (4.74), sibling love (4.73), affection (4.60), committed love (4.47), love for humanity (4.42), spiritual love (4.27), passionate love (4.00), Platonic love (3.98), self-love (3.79), sexual love (3.76), patriotic love (3.21), love of work (3.14), puppy love (2.98), and infatuation (2.42). Taking a parallel approach in another series of studies focusing on "features" of love, Fehr (1998) first had one sample freely list features, and then another sample rated the most commonly listed ones for centrality to love. The most central features were about caring and intimacy; other features, such as butterflies in the stomach and euphoria, though clearly part of the concept, were more peripheral. In both of these love-prototype research series (Fehr & Russell, 1991; Fehr, 1998), additional studies demonstrated that the more centrally prototypical types and features of love were indeed used by people to recognize instances of love and that these types and features structured processing and memory for love-related information.

One line of research emerging from Fehr's work has focused on generalizability. Fehr's studies were with North American students. However, replications with other age groups and in a number of other societies have produced quite similar results (reviewed in Fehr, 2001). Another line of research emerging from Fehr's prototype work focuses on the latent structure of the prototypical love features. Across seven studies using various factor-analytic methods, A. Aron and Westbay (1996) identified and cross-validated three underlying dimensions of these features: intimacy (which included mainly features with the highest centrality ratings), commitment (mainly the next most central items), and passion (mainly the least central items).

Another approach to how ordinary people understand love has focused on love as a prototypical emotion. Shaver, Schwartz, Kirson, and O'Connor (1987) had participants sort a large list of emotion words into common groupings. Hierarchical cluster analysis of these sortings yielded two overarching grouping of emotions: one for negative emotions, in which the main next-level subordinate clusters were fear, anger, and sadness; and one for positive emotions, in which the main next-level subordinate clusters were joy and love. Within the love subcluster were three further subclusters—one for longing; one for passion, arousal, and similar terms; and one, the largest, that included adoration, affection, fondness, liking, caring, compassion, and so forth.

In sum, although there is considerable variation across approaches, the centerpiece of laypeople's understanding of the word *love* is generally in terms of familial, romantic, or friendship relationships, and emphasizes intimacy, caring, and concern for the one loved. Even though most studies were with college students where romantic love might be especially salient, the passion aspect was most often peripheral or separated. Indeed, people do clearly distinguish romantic love from other types of love. For example, Meyers and Berscheid (1997) asked people to list those whom they "love" (a general term) and to make another list for those with whom they were "in love" (a term seemingly related specifically to romantic love). As expected, the latter list was a small subset of the former.

But what about lay understandings of types of love beyond close relationships, such as compassionate love of strangers and love of humanity? In Fehr and Russell's (1991) prototype analysis, "love for humanity," though not among the most central, was nevertheless rated well above the mean (4.42 on the 1-to-6 scale) as a good example of love. More recently, Fehr and Sprecher (2004) applied a prototype-feature approach specifically to compassionate love. The most central features were the same as those central to love in general, such as trust, caring, and honesty. The prototypical features that were relatively unique to compassionate love were related to unselfishness, putting others first, and sacrificing for others. That is, though these features are also seen in close-relationship contexts of love, they seem especially to come to the fore when people think about compassionate love.

What about love of society, justice, knowledge, and God? When these appear at all in prototype studies, they are rated as relatively peripheral. This rating does not, of course, mean the rated features are trivial for everyone and at all times. It does suggest, however, that for most people, society, justice, and God are not what first come to mind when they think of love. This may be because of the relative rarity of strong experiences of these kinds of love. But it also may be that the word *love* is less often used in this context than are other terms (e.g., patriotism, virtue, faith, devotion).

Before concluding this section, we should also note that scholars have offered more formal definitions. Thus, A. Aron and Aron (1991) defined love as "the constellation of behaviors, cognitions, and emotions associated with a desire to enter or maintain a close relationship with a specific other person" (p. 26).

Lee (1977; see also Hendrick & Hendrick, 2003) distinguished six types of love in the context of romantic relationships: eros (romantic, passionate love), ludus (game-playing love), storge (friendship love), pragma (logical, "shopping-list" love), mania (possessive, dependent love), and agape (selfless love). And Sprecher and Fehr (2005) defined compassionate love as

> an attitude toward other(s), either close others or strangers or all of humanity; containing feelings, cognitions, and behaviors that are focused on caring, concern, tenderness, and an orientation toward supporting, helping, and understanding the other(s), particularly when the other(s) is (are) perceived to be suffering or in need. (p. 630)

The various views and types of love share a key aspect: Valuing and caring for others (Rousar, 1990). Love definitions consistently focus on altruistic behavior in relation to others, including close others. Indeed, in the context of relationships with others, there is a considerable body of evidence that a core difference between those people we love and those people we do not is that we attend to the needs of those whom we love; that is, we have a "communal relationship" with them (e.g., Mills & Clark, 2002). Further, in addition to experiencing love *for* others, there is also a substantial body of data showing that a crucial aspect of love has to do with experiencing love *from* others (e.g., what is sometimes called perceived partner responsiveness; Reis, Clark, & Holmes, 2004).

Ultimately, then, it seems to be the valuing of and concern for the other—and the being valued by and being cared for by the other—that provide whatever benefit love might give, including the extent to which love may give meaning to life. Further, it also seems reasonable that to the extent loving and being loved give benefits in this way (including meaning), it follows that the more intense and more expansive the loving and being loved, the more the benefits (and meaning). It is to these issues we turn next.

Love in the Context of Close Relationships

Evolutionary Foundations

Evolutionary theorists have traditionally emphasized that the purpose of life is survival not of the individual but of the genes. Thus, the fundamental purpose in human life is the creating and raising of offspring, an activity for humans that initially involves selection and focusing of attention on a particular partner, pair bonding and sexual intercourse, attachment to the partner during the time of raising the child, and attachment to the child (and of the child to the parent) during raising of the child and perhaps through the period of the child's selecting a mate with whom to bond (i.e., in most cultures, parents are heavily involved in the mate selection of their offspring, as is the community). Indeed, with regard to pair bonding and as based on an extensive review of the relevant animal and human literature, Fisher (1998) has argued that there are three key mating systems: sexual desire, attraction (selective attention to a particular mate), and attachment (ongoing connection with the mate to facilitate parenting). That is, if purpose beyond our own individual survival is what gives meaning, then clearly we have all evolved so as to find great meaning in these relationships.

The meaningfulness of the bond between parents and children needs little documentation, although the details of the attachment process and of its deep significance to us have been successfully elaborated by researchers, particularly in the context of attachment theory (Bowlby, 1969) and the very large body of research it has generated (e.g., see Cassidy & Shaver, 1999). Indeed, some researchers have argued that adult love is primarily an evolutionary extension of the parent–child bond (Hazan & Diamond, 2000; Miller & Fishkin, 1997); and there is strong evidence that individual differences in attachment experiences in childhood are closely linked to parallel individual differences in adult attachment behavior (Grossmann, Grossmann, & Waters, 2005; Main, 2000; Mikulincer & Shaver, 2007).

Further, from an evolutionary point of view, and particularly from extrapolation from other social species, same-sex alliances (friendships) and extended family solidarity play a significant role in the success of individuals and the ability of their offspring to survive and thrive (e.g., De Waal, 2005). From this point of view, the major human close relationships—romantic, parental, sibling, extended family, and peer friendship—are intensely involved in providing meaning beyond mere survival in that they serve the purpose of carrying on one's genes. We are familiar with this idea of the "selfish gene" (Dawkins, 1989), namely, that we care about and give care to our relatives and their offspring because they will carry on some of our genes. Even if we are not kin, however, the selection for altruism or caring for each other, whether it evolves genetically or culturally—to use Dawkins's term, as a "meme"—occurs in any group where it benefits the majority of members (Sober & Wilson, 1998). And it almost always does benefit everyone, at least in human social groups. So, we have evolved to care about everyone in a particular in-group of ours, including groups of two, and to prefer those who will care about us.

The point is that for a variety of reasons, we have evolved to make caring for each other a central purpose of life, and a purpose that goes beyond ourselves. This view is meant not to reduce caring to "mere biology" but, rather, to see from another perspective why caring for others is central to meaning. We will return to this point again.

Psychological Principles: The Self-Expansion Model

Besides considering this evolutionary perspective, we must take into account the substantial evidence from psychological research with humans that relationships indeed function to provide purpose beyond our own individual survival. To explore this issue, we need to consider the motivational mechanisms associated with love. There are, in fact, several psychological models of love. Most of these models (e.g., Hendrick & Hendrick, 2003; Sternberg, 1998) focus relatively exclusively on romantic love, and mostly on typologies; thus they are of only tangential relevance in the present context. There are, however, three major theoretical approaches that focus on mechanisms and apply to close relationships more generally. One of the most successful and influential such models is attachment theory (e.g., Cassidy & Shaver, 1999), briefly noted earlier. Attachment theory examines the processes through which infants develop mental models of relating to close others that shape, and also are shaped by, later relationships. However, its main focus has been on individual differences in such mental models, and it has only tangentially considered purpose or motivational processes. Thus, other than as an evolutionary force, the attachment model is not of major relevance in the current context. Another successful and influential model is interdependence theory (e.g., Kelley, 1983), including Rusbult's (1983) investment model and related theories focusing on equity (e.g., Walster [Hatfield], Walster, & Berscheid, 1978) and communal and exchange patterns of relationships (Mills & Clark, 2002). However, these models mainly delineate the different ways that rewards and costs function to guide relational life and have much less to say about what makes something rewarding or costly in the first place. Thus, our main focus here will be on a third theoretical approach, the self-expansion model (A. Aron & Aron, 1986). The self-expansion model is particularly relevant to the present context because it has focused quite specifically on people's primary motivations and purposes in the context of relationships and beyond.

The self-expansion model of motivation and cognition in close relationships (A. Aron & Aron, 1986; A. Aron, Aron, & Norman, 2001; A. Aron, Lewandowski, Mashek, & Aron, in press) has two fundamental principles: (a) the *motivational principle* and (b) the *inclusion-of-other-in-the-self principle*. The motivational principle holds that people seek to expand their potential efficacy; that is, the model posits that a major human motive is what has previously been described as exploration, effectance, curiosity, or competence. The inclusion-of-other-in-the-self principle emphasizes that one way in which people seek to expand the self is through close relationships because in a close relationship the other's resources, perspectives, and identities are experienced, to some extent, as one's own; that is, the other is to some extent "included in the self." We first consider the motivational aspect and then turn to the inclusion-of-other aspect.

Self-Expansion Motivation A. Aron et al. (2001; see also A. Aron, Norman, & Aron, 1998; Strong & Aron, 2006) suggest that a central human motive is the desire to expand the self, part of a general motive to enhance one's potential efficacy, which has been postulated in various well-known models of competence motivation, self-efficacy, intrinsic motivation, and self-improvement (e.g., Bandura, 1977; Gecas, 1989; Ryan & Deci, 2000; Taylor, Neter, & Wayment, 1995; White, 1959). Further, rapid expansion of the self, as often occurs when forming a new romantic relationship or the birth of a new child, is posited to result in high levels of excited positive affect, consistent with Carver and Scheier's (1990) analysis of the impact on affective state of rapid movement toward a goal. These abstract ideas can be made more concrete by considering the Self-Expansion Questionnaire (Lewandowski & Aron, 2002) that assesses the degree to which a person experiences a relationship partner as facilitating increased knowledge, skills, abilities, mate value, positive life changes, and novel experiences. Representative items include the following questions: "How much does your partner provide a source of exciting experiences?" "How much has knowing your partner made you a better person?" and "How much do you see your partner as a way to expand your own capabilities?"

Several research programs lend support to hypotheses generated from the motivational aspect of the self-expansion model. For example, one implication is that developing a new relationship expands the self. Thus, A. Aron, Paris, and Aron (1995) tested 325 students five times, once every two and one-half weeks over a 10-week period. At each testing participants answered a number of questions, including items indicating whether they had fallen in love since the last testing, plus a free listing of "who are you today?" As predicted, there was a significantly greater increase in number of self-content domains in the self-descriptions from before to after falling in love as compared to the average changes from before to after other testing sessions for those who fell in love or as compared to typical between-test changes for participants who did not fall in love. In a sense, then, there was a literal expansion of self. Similarly, based on this same line of thinking, Lewandowski, Aron, Bassis, and Kunak (2005) found in a series of surveys and experiments that the more expansion a relationship provided before its dissolution, the greater the contraction of the working self-concept after its dissolution.

Another key implication of the motivational aspect of the model, which has generated a number of studies, is based on the idea that the *process* of rapid expansion is affectively positive (Strong & Aron, 2006). The major line of work developed from this idea has focused on a predicted increase in satisfaction in long-term relationships from joint participation in self-expanding activities. This work emerged from a consideration of the well-documented typical decline in relationship satisfaction after the "honeymoon period" in a romantic relationship, a lowered level that is typically maintained over subsequent years (e.g., Tucker & Aron, 1993). When two people first enter a relationship, there is usually an initial, exhilarating period in which the couple spend hours talking, engaging in intense risk-taking and self-disclosure. From the perspective of the self-expansion model, this initial exhilarating period is one in which the partners are expanding their selves at a rapid rate by virtue of the intense exchange. Once they know each other fairly well, opportunities for further rapid expansion of this sort inevitably decrease. When rapid expansion occurs, there is a high degree of satisfaction; when expansion is slow or nonexistent, there is little emotion or perhaps even boredom. If slow expansion follows a period of rapid expansion, the loss of enjoyable emotion may be disappointing and attributed to deficiencies in the relationship. Indeed, this pattern has been demonstrated in various surveys and in field and lab experiments. For example, in one series of laboratory experiments (A. Aron, Norman, Aron, McKenna, & Heyman, 2000, Studies 3–5), couples in long-term relationships from the community came for what they believed was an assessment session involving questionnaires and being videotaped while interacting. Indeed, that is what happened—they completed questionnaires, participated together in a task that was videotaped, and then completed more questionnaires. However, the questionnaires before the task served as a pre-test, those after, as a posttest, and the task itself was experimentally manipulated so that some couples engaged in an expanding activity (one that was novel and challenging) and those in the control condition engaged in a more mundane activity. (In the expanding activity the partners in the couple was tied together on one side at the wrists and ankles and then took part in a task in which they crawled together on mats for 12 meters, climbing over a barrier at one point while pushing a foam cylinder with their heads. The task was timed and the partners received a prize if they beat a time limit, but the situation was rigged so that they almost made it within the time limit on the first two tries and then just barely made it on the third try.) In all three experiments, as predicted, there was a significantly greater increase in relationship satisfaction for the couples in the expanding condition, whether measured by self-report or by blind analysis of content of pre and post couple verbal interactions.

Yet another line of work emerging from the motivational aspect of the model is based on the idea that early stage passionate love is best conceptualized as a goal-oriented motivational state in which the individual is experiencing an intense desire to merge with the partner (A. Aron & Aron, 1991). That is, the hypothesis is that passionate love is not a distinct emotion in its own right (as has often been hypothesized by emotion theorists), as is sadness or happiness; rather, passionate love can evoke a variety of emotions according to whether and how the desire is fulfilled or frustrated. In support of this view, in one series of seven experiments (Acevedo & Aron, 2004), participants from each of three different cultures and with a variety of procedures checked from a large standard list the emotions they feel when they experience love or one of several emotions. In each study, many more emotions were checked (and with faster response time) in relation to feeling love than in relation to feeling sadness, anger, fear, or happiness; further, many more negative valence items were checked for love than for happiness or other positive emotions used in these studies. A second line of research (Acevedo, Gross, & Aron, 2005) found that as predicted from this model and as is true for such goal-oriented states as hunger, people find it is much more difficult to up-regulate (i.e., increase) feelings of passionate love than they do to up-regulate such emotions as happiness, sadness, or anger. A third line of relevant research has examined the neural correlates of passionate love, the idea being that passionate love should consistently engage brain regions associated with intense reward (i.e., the ventral tegmental area and associated dopamine system) but should be much less consistent across subjects in engaging brain regions associated with specific emotions (i.e., orbital frontal cortex, anterior cingulate cortex, and amygdala). Results of two fMRI studies, one in the United States (A. Aron et al., 2005) and one in China (Xu et al., 2007), have found exactly this pattern. Further, in the U.S. study, where participants completed a standard questionnaire measure of passionate love, the degree of reported passionate love correlated $r = .60$ with activation in the key reward regions; this was an especially striking result, given the considerably restricted range of scores among these participants who were all intensely in love.

In sum, the motivational aspect of the self-expansion model proposes that a major human motive, which occurs in diverse contexts including close relationships, is the desire to expand one's ability to accomplish goals. One can see the evolutionary value in this pursuit being meaningful in the relationship context and also see examples of it all around us in other life domains: People feel it is meaningful to pursue learning, work, athletic competency, and so forth.

Including Others in the Self According to the self-expansion model, this general motivation to expand the self often leads to a desire to enter and maintain a particular close relationship in part because close relationships are an especially satisfying, useful, and human means to self-expansion. Specifically, in a close relationship, each partner includes to some extent in his or her self the other's resources, perspectives, and identities (A. Aron, Mashek, & Aron, 2004). Of course, as noted in the foregoing discussion—and as we will return to at the end of the chapter—people also self-expand in ways besides including others in the self.

With regard to the resources of the other that are potentially included in the self, we are referring to material, knowledge-related (conceptual, informational, and procedural), and social assets that can facilitate the achievement of goals. Perceiving one's self as including a relationship partner's resources refers to perceiving one's self as having access to those resources as if, to some extent, the other's resources were one's own (e.g., "I can do this because my partner will show me how"). This perceived inclusion of another's resources is particularly central from a motivational point of view because it means that the outcomes (i.e., rewards and costs) the other incurs are to some extent experienced as one's own. Thus, for example, helping the other is helping the self; interfering with the other is interfering with the self (e.g., "I'll be quiet while my partner reads the instructions"). This analysis also implies that the other's acquisition and loss of resources are experienced to some extent as if they were happening to one's own resources. In the first direct test of this principle (A. Aron, Aron, Tudor, & Nelson, 1991), participants took part in an allocation game in which they made a series of decisions allocating money to self, best friend, or another person or persons. As predicted, allocations to best friend were consistently similar to those for self, but allocations to people who were not close to others consistently favored self. It is important to note that these results held up whether or not the other would know who was responsible for the allocations. Several other studies using a variety of paradigms and theoretical orientations support the prediction from the model that people react to a close other's outcomes as if the outcomes were their own (e.g., Beach et al., 1998; De La Ronde & Swann, 1998; Gardner, Gabriel, & Hochschild, 2002; McFarland, Buehler, & MacKay, 2001; Medvene, Teal, & Slavich, 2000).

The perspective aspect of inclusion refers to consciously or unconsciously experiencing the world, to some extent, from the partner's point of view. For example, when a long-term married individual attends a ballet, the ballet may be experienced not only through the individual's own eyes but also, as it were, through the spouse's eyes. Thus our model implies that when another person is included in the self, various self-related attributional and cognitive biases should also apply with regard to that other person. Regarding attributional biases, consistent with the predictions of the model, several studies have revealed that the usual actor–observer difference in the tendency to make situational more than dispositional attributions for self compared to others (Jones & Nisbett, 1971) is smaller when the other is someone close to self, such as a best friend or romantic partner (A. Aron et al., 1991; A. Aron & Fraley, 1999; Sande, Goethals, & Radloff, 1988). Perhaps a more dramatic illustration of including a close other's perspective in the self is a series of studies adapting a memory paradigm developed by Lord (1980, 1987). As predicted from his model of self as background to experience, Lord found consistently *fewer* nouns recalled that were imaged with self as compared to nouns imaged with media personalities. In our studies using this paradigm (A. Aron et al., 1991), in addition to self and a person who was familiar but not a close other, participants also imaged nouns with a close other, their mother. Our results replicated Lord's for self and nonclose other. But also, as predicted from our inclusion-of-other-in-the-self model, we found that nouns imaged with the close other were recalled about the same as nouns imaged with self.

The *identity aspect*, as used here, refers to features that distinguish one person from other people and objects; these features are primarily the characteristics, memories, and other traits that locate the person in social and physical space. Thus, for example, our model implies that people may easily confuse their own traits or memories with those of a close other. In relation to the cognitive aspects in general (i.e., perspectives and identities), we have described our model as implying shared cognitive elements of self and close others (A. Aron & Fraley, 1999). Some general support for the notion that in close relationships we include close others in the self can be gleaned from research on "the self-reference effect," an advantage in terms of memory and response time for self-relevant versus other-relevant processing. For example, in a meta-analysis of 126 articles and book chapters on just the memory aspect of the effect, Symons and Johnson (1997) reported a consistent overall better memory for words studied in relation to self than for words studied in relation to other persons. However, consistent with the inclusion-of-other-in-the-self model, they found that the degree to which self-referent and other-referent memory differed was moderated by the relationship to the other. Across the 65 relevant studies, Symons and Johnson found significantly smaller differences between self-reference memory facilitation and other-reference memory facilitation when the other was someone who was close to the self. Thus, being in a close relationship does seem to subvert the seemingly fundamental cognitive distinction between self and other.

Our model also posits, however, that this apparent subversion by close relationships of the self–other distinction is specifically a result of the other becoming "part of the self"; it results from the very structure of the self changing such that the self includes the other in its very make up. For example, the model implies that one's own and a close-other's traits may actually be confused or interfere with each other. To test this idea, we evaluated the patterns of response latencies in making me–not me decisions about traits previously rated for their descriptiveness of self and of spouse; that is, we looked at responses to the question "Does the trait describe me?" (A. Aron et al., 1991). We found that when a trait of the self matched that of the partner (i.e., when the trait was true of both or false of both), me–not me responses were faster and had fewer errors than when a trait was mismatched for self and partner (i.e., when the trait was true for one but false for the other). Using this same response-time paradigm, Smith, Coates, and Walling (1999) replicated the result and eloquently articulated why such patterns may result: "If mental representations of two persons … overlap so that they are effectively a single representation, reports on attributes of one will be facilitated or inhibited by matches and mismatches with the second" (p. 873).

Another series of experiments (Mashek, Aron, & Boncimino, 2003) focused on the model's prediction that people especially confuse information associated with self with information associated with close others. In these studies, participants rated one set of traits for self, a different set of traits for a close other, and still other traits for one or more familiar nonclose others. Participants were then administered a surprise recognition task in which participants were presented with each trait and asked to indicate for which person they had rated it. The focus of the analysis was on confusions—that is, on traits the participant remembered having rated for one person when the traits had actually been rated for a different person. The results were consistent with predictions. For example, if participants did not correctly recognize a trait as having been originally rated for the self, they were significantly more likely to remember it as having been rated for the partner than as having been rated for a media personality. Similarly, if participants did not correctly recognize a trait as having been originally rated for the partner, they were significantly more likely to remember it as having been rated for the self than as having been rated for the media personality. These results were replicated in two follow-up studies and held up after controlling for a variety of potential confounds, among them a greater tendency to see traits in general as having been rated for self, valence and extremity of ratings, and familiarity with and similarity to the close other.

Evidence for the Central Role of Close Relationships in Providing Meaning in Human Life

Does all this matter? That is, do relationships actually affect people's lives in significant ways? We think, first of all, that it is obvious from general experience that relationships are of central importance. There is little in life more wonderful than falling in love (and especially discovering for the first time that a beloved reciprocates our feelings) or having a new child; and there is little in life more distressing than a romantic rejection or betrayal or loss of a child or spouse. Indeed, when looking at obituaries or gravestones, one sees with rare exceptions that the themes are relational. Thus, it is surprising that most scholarly perspectives on life—as spelled out, for example, in the various chapters of first edition of this volume—do not even mention relationships. But when Wong (1998) asked ordinary people to describe what gives meaning to life, relationships turned out to be a major factor, with quite high ratings for their importance in an "ideally meaningful life." Similarly, in Deci and Ryan's initial version of their influential model of fundamental human motives, the self-determination theory (e.g., Deci & Ryan, 2000), there was only autonomy and competence. But over the years, the data forced the researchers to add a third fundamental motive, relatedness. Perhaps we have been overlooking something that was too obvious to be noticed.

If having meaning affects people's quality of life and health, it is very clear that relationships play a major role in these too. Overviews of the relationship literature (e.g., Reis, 2007) consistently point to close relationships as "people's most frequent source of both happiness and distress" (Berscheid & Reis, 1998). Overviews of the well-being literature yield the same conclusions. For example, Sears's (1977) classic review pointed out that retrospective surveys of the sources of life satisfaction list family life satisfaction as number one; a finding that continues to dominate contemporary happiness research (e.g., Lyubormisky, King, & Diener, 2005). Similarly, relationship problems are consistently among people's greatest sources of suffering. For example, in a survey of more than 2,200 Americans, Veroff, Douvan, and Kulka (1981) asked, "What was the last bad thing to happen to you?" Of all respondents, 20% listed an interpersonal problem or conflict and another 30% listed death of a significant other, compared to only 14% listing work or legal problem. In the same vein, Pinsker, Nepps, Redfield, and Winston (1985) reported that 48% of presenting problems among psychotherapy patients were about troubled relationships.

Love in the Context of Community and Social Inclusion

Evolutionary Foundations

Human life is lived, however, not only in the context of close others but in the more general context of community. Our evolutionary origins, like those of most primates, are thought to be in small, face-to-face groups. Belonging to these groups—and benefiting these groups through love for these groups and its members—also seems to be very important to people subjectively, even when there is no genetic relationship. Indeed, even in Western individualistic cultures, belonging is among the most centrally important human motivations in the sense that our self-worth is heavily dependent on it (Baumeister & Leary, 1995). And one's social identity—one's sense of membership in a particular group—plays a major role in shaping our sense of who we are (e.g., Tajfel & Turner, 1986).

Why is this? Although the idea of group selection was once firmly rejected by evolutionary theorists, it has necessarily returned to explain the many instances in which individuals "sacrifice" their lives for the sake of the group in which they live, which results in the group surviving better in competition with other groups (see Sober & Wilson, 1998; Wilson, 2002, 2007). It seems as though altruistic individuals ought to die out if there are any selfish members in the group to take advantage of them. In fact, living in a group in which all or at least some members are altruistic can give the genes of all the members a far greater chance of being passed on, provided groups do compete so that some survive and others do not.

Sober and Wilson (1998) provide the example of an actual poultry-breeding experiment to raise egg production. Of course, over the years the highest egg producers had been selected for breeding, for they were individually the most successful. But they were also the most aggressive. Multiple-hen cages are used for egg production because they are more efficient for feeding and egg gathering than are single-hen cages; but they have come to be the cause of such high rates of stress and aggression that even after beak trimming, annual mortality rates of hens approach 50%, a costly problem. Hence, Muir (1995) tried breeding hens from the *cages* that produced the most eggs regardless of the egg production of the individual hens. Using that approach, annual egg production increased by 160% and aggression and mortality were so low that beak trimming was unnecessary. That is, if eggs represent survival of a hen's genes, then hens in the peaceful cages were, on the average, more successful.

Wilson (e.g., Sober & Wilson, 1998) goes on to apply the idea to humans, namely, that group selection has led to greater pair bonding, reduced aggression, and higher overall rate of survival. As do the other primates, we live in social groups; in our case, the groups that survived were those that kept all their members alive through cooperation and sharing. Human pair bonding and the privacy of the sexual act probably arose in order to reduce competition between males so they could work together without conflict, and the pair bond is especially successful when the partners are willing to sacrifice their lives for each other and their offspring. All this evolved altruism is not dependent on genes. Clearly, humans are willing to sacrifice their lives for those who are not kin. They simply tend to care for others, for humans have become as successful through cooperation as the social insects, which comprise 50% of the insect biomass on the planet. (Look around your highly complex city or community and think bee hive.) Our biomass compared to that of other primates must be rather high as well.

Whereas genetic evolution through group selection has probably ended for humans, cultural evolution through group selection does still occur. Social units, whether families or businesses, small towns or whole countries—that is, whether genetically related or not—tend to survive better if they emphasize cooperation, altruism, sharing, and the general sense that the group is more important than the individual. True, selfishness and individualism have advantages for the individual and sometimes for the group, through inventiveness, for example, but these characteristics cannot be allowed to develop to the point of the groups falling apart.

What about all the cruelty that can occur within groups, in large groups especially? In these cases, there may exist a highly cooperative small group banded around a leader who meets their needs as they meet the leader's needs. If members of this small group then coordinate their efforts and cooperate with each other, they can use violence, for example, to control the larger group and thus promote selfish rather than altruistic ends. But this dynamic means the larger group will be less cooperative and effective in the long run. For leaders to wrest control effectively, however, they must provide a high level of meaning for the members of the small group of enforcers. We see this relationship in situations of mass cruelty promoted to those who must carry it out as having some "higher purpose," such as "ethnic cleansing."

The Psychology of Social Life as Providing Purpose

It seems highly probable that the strong sense of meaning we derive from caring deeply about others even beyond our own kin has been supported through individual and group selection over millennia. Although such natural selection may seem to reduce the meaning of humanitarian love to something based on random mutations and brutal selection, that such selection occurs at all also means it is with us to stay as something so meaningful that we hardly think about it.

Nor, from this perspective, is love separate from work or any other endeavor. That we are writing this chapter and others are writing chapters like it, or constructing buildings, composing music, or struggling to be elected, suggests how important it is to all of us to contribute to the whole. And if some people are paid for their work, that does not diminish the work's importance to a society willing to pay for us to do our piece of the work for the whole. Moreover, if we were to be paid an equal wage for doing something "meaningless" or for contributing something of lasting value to others and to the future of our group or species, we know what humans almost always choose. That is the point of most of the chapters in this book.

There are also other strong theoretical models from social psychology to help us understand love of community, including compassionate love and even love of the various communities to which we belong and the values these communities encompass, whether the communities reflect a profession, one's church, the country as a whole, and so on. One view focuses on the value of holding normative beliefs and ingroup–outgroup distinctiveness. Our own model focuses on extending the self-expansion idea to the social level (e.g., A. Aron, McLaughlin-Volpe, et al., 2004), such as ingroup identification (McLaughlin-Volpe, Aron, Wright, & Lewandowski, 2005; Wright, Brody, & Aron, 2005), including communities as part of the self (e.g., Mashek, Cannaday, & Tangney, 2007), and compassionate love for strangers (Brody, Wright, Aron, & McLaughlin-Volpe, 2008). (Perhaps self-expansion is even the mechanism by which altruism came to exist; that is, it reflects the type of brain structure that was selected for during evolution.)

Specifically, we have suggested that (a) people seek group memberships and social identities in order to expand the self and (b) such group memberships and social identities expand the self because the resources, perspectives, and identities of one's social groups are included in the self. A number of studies have now supported hypotheses based on these ideas. For example, Smith and Henry (1996), extending A. Aron et al.'s (1991) me–not me response-time paradigm to the group level, showed that people's response time to rating traits for applicability to self was faster when traits were similar between self and one's ingroup and slower when traits were different between self and one's ingroup. Tropp and Wright (2001) replicated this effect for a variety of group memberships and using diverse methods. Further, the desire to expand the self through group memberships extends even beyond ingroups. For example, several studies have shown that when one has a friend in another group, one comes to treat that group as if it were one's own (A. Aron & McLaughlin-Volpe,

2001). Most important, under conditions where it is not threatening to do so, one prefers to meet potential friends from other groups (Wright, Aron, & Brody, 2008; Wright, Aron, McLaughlin-Volpe, & Ropp, 1997), presumably because they offer greater potential expansion than does meeting potential friends from within the ingroup. Going outside one's ingroup provides the possibility for the expansion of the sense of ingroup to include more and more people, so that compassion becomes increasingly universal.

Love of Justice and Knowledge; Love of God; Love of Truth, Beauty, and More

We also can think of love in more general terms with regard to its symbolic meaning and the love of such so-called higher objects as love of justice, knowledge, truth, beauty, and God. Such love is not inconsistent with evolutionary approaches, because all these can be seen as having a function in promoting survival of ones genes through promoting better close and group relationships, as noted earlier. Because these kinds of love appear to be so uniquely human, however, and because their links with evolution are relatively less direct, they have mostly been studied in purely psychological or even philosophical terms.

For example, one approach has focused on these phenomena as social values or as extensions of basic social processes. In terms of the concept of love, we would note that in an extensive qualitative study, Ahuvia (1993) found that the same self-expansion principles as apply to close relationships also apply to love of objects and such activities as baseball. At an even more exalted level, Kirkpatrick (1998) found that individual differences in attachment style to close others also predict individual differences in people's beliefs about God. Other researchers have found good success using standard measures of including other in the self when "other" was animals, nature, or even God (e.g., Schultz, Shriver, Tabanico, & Khazian, 2004; Tipsord & Leary, 2004).

Yet another approach focuses on the deeply symbolic meaning of such objects of love. The force of evolution that led us to finding meaning through love is continued in us both through genes and through cultural symbols. Words are symbols, obviously, but there are other symbols with even deeper potential to stir us. Carl Jung (e.g., 1969) and others called these blends of instinct and culture *archetypes*, which are very general templates for behavior, such as attachment between mother and child. From this point of view, archetypes guide behavior both as genetically determined behaviors and as ideas transmitted by words, and especially by powerful images, such as that of the mother and child.

There is no list of archetypes or particular importance to be gained by using the term *archetype*, except that the term itself possesses a certain power to stir us more than does the term *cultural idea*. Furthermore, Jung, who gave the term its extended meaning, did have an important observation about how arechetypes give meaning.

Consider the example of the mother archetype. It works to guide this essential altruistic behavior to the extent that a woman is fully identified with it, and so the archetypes necessarily recruit such identification. The mother archetype more or less takes over a woman's life for a time, as any mother will tell you. In a similar way, the father archetype takes over a man, even without the experience of pregnancy and childbirth. He is fully identified with the father archetype, so that he does not have to decide what he as a father should do, for genes and culture have decided that long ago. No doubt identification with an archetype, as defined here, infuses us with far more direct meaning than do more abstract ideas about cooperation. Archetypes may be a way of thinking about self-expansion beyond our personal self, conceiving us to be a part of something very large and almost eternal.

Also, however, humans benefit from their flexibility, their ability to shift from role to role rather than having to stay in one role, whether the situation calls for it or not, as a social insect might do. It is the central ego or self that switches us from one role to another according to its assessment of the situation. There may or may not be times in our lives when we must be the heroes, healers, children, grandmothers, winners, losers, prophets, prostitutes, victims crying out for help, worshipers of the divine, bereaved crying out for comfort, or any of the other archetypal social roles that have supported the survival of social groups. But when we take up one of these roles, it can happen that this identification continues with too much force or for longer than its usefulness; perhaps we hang on to this identification just because it supplies meaning and purpose to a life that would otherwise lack it and feel less expanded.

Besides engendering the obvious social problems created by someone insisting on being heroic or maternal when it is not useful to them or others, this overidentification has clinical implications as well. For example, one might wonder what is the meaning or purpose of remaining a victim, a person bereaved, or a person defeated past the usefulness of doing so. Then, one realizes that individuals can fall into an archetypal position that is inherent in them simply because when we as humans are victimized, bereaved, or defeated, we need to know how to be that; and so the potential for identifying with that position and finding continued meaning in it is always there once the identification is triggered. Jung thought that harmful autonomous complexes—or in more recent terms, emotional schemas that are dissociated or cannot be regulated—always develop around identification with an archetype. Hence, finding another meaning, another archetype with which to identify, might be one clinical implication of these insights. An even better one might be to strengthen the executive functioning of the self in such a way that it can see the harm in such identification and live in a new relationship to these archetypes.

Do archetypes matter in human life? If the mother and father roles are fostered by being archetypes—for both roles reflect social behaviors with powerful contributions from genes and cultural symbols—then we need not look far to see their significance. That we know so well how to be heroic, dominating, or meekly humble are other examples, each of which gives a meaning to life.

Concordance With Ancient Views of Love and Meaning

Two ancient views of love, one from the East and one from the West, have been particularly influential in our thinking about love and meaning and played substantial roles in the initial shaping of the self-expansion model of love (A. Aron & Aron, 1986, 1991; E. N. Aron & Aron, 1996). Indeed, mystics in nearly every tradition have insisted that all motivation can be reduced to love. In the Eastern traditions, especially in the Upanishads, love is the basis of life, but in a curious way: All love—love of house, love of car, love of spouse, love of child—is said to be directed toward the "Self" (*Brihadaranyaka Upanishad* 4.V.1). Note the capitalization that translators (e.g., George Thibaut) supply. The idea is that the self expands toward knowing or becoming that which includes everything and everyone, the Self. The steps along the way are ones of including one person or thing, then another, then still another. The assumption is that whether the self knows it or not, it seeks this state of having or being everything. Whether there is any real Self is not the question to be addressed here. The question is the heuristic value of assuming that when people love, they are at least sometimes, in some sense, seeking an infinitely expanding self. Indeed, A. Aron, Aron, and Allen (1998) found that those individuals who were most intensely in unrequited love strongly endorsed items suggesting that if only their love was returned, life would be perfect, ideal.

One value of this motivational assumption about seeking to expand the self is that it seems to underlie many of the most consequential theoretical positions on love, from Plato's *Symposium* and Stendhal's *de l'Amour* to such contemporary scientific theorizing as Berscheid and Walster [Hatfield]'s (1978) influential description of passionate love. For example, at the more recent end of this time continuum, Brehm (1988) proposed that "the core of passionate love lies in the capacity to construct in one's imagination an elaborated vision of a future state of perfect happiness" (p. 253). The possible evolutionary advantage of such a capacity, according to Brehm, would be our species' tendency to imagine and yearn for a better world and to try to bring it about.

A major ancient Western influence, Plato also takes love to its ultimate form and meaning. He has been equally influential in our thinking about love and, in terms of the present chapter, about how love gives meaning to life. Here is the way in which Plato (trans. 1953) describes love in the *Symposium*, in Socrates' final speech, supposedly quoting from the mystic Diotima of Mantineia, "a woman wise in this and in many other kinds of knowledge":

> Love may be described generally as the love of the everlasting possession of the good.
>
> ... There is a certain age at which human nature is desirous of procreation—procreation which must be in beauty and not in deformity; and this procreation is the union of man and woman, and is a divine thing; for conception and generation are an immortal principle in the

> mortal creature, and in the inharmonious they can never be.... [A]ll animals ..., in their desire of procreation, are in agony when they take the infection of love, which begins with the desire of union; whereto is added the care of offspring, on whose behalf the weakest are ready to battle against the strongest even to the uttermost ... the mortal nature is seeking as far as is possible to be everlasting and immortal.
>
> [Then] think of the ambition of men, and ... consider how they are stirred by the love of an immortality of fame. They are ready to run all risks greater far than they would have for their children, and to spend money and undergo any sort of toil, and even to die, for the sake of leaving behind them a name which shall be eternal ... for they desire the immortal.
>
> These are the lesser mysteries of love.... For he who would proceed aright in this matter should begin in youth to visit beautiful forms; and first, ... to love one such form only ... and soon perceive that the beauty of one form is akin to the beauty of another; and then ... recognize that the beauty in every form is and the same ... and become a lover of all beautiful forms.... [I]n the next stage, consider that the beauty of the mind is more honourable than the beauty of the outward form.... until he is compelled to contemplate and see the beauty of institutions and laws, and to understand that the beauty of them all is of one family, and that personal beauty is a trifle; and after laws and institutions go on to the sciences, ... create many fair and noble thoughts and notions in boundless love of wisdom; until at last the vision is revealed of a single science, which is the science of beauty everywhere... [W]hen he comes toward the end he will suddenly perceive a nature of wondrous beauty—a nature which in the first place is everlasting, not growing and decaying, or waxing and waning.... He who from these ascending under the influence of true love, begins to perceive that beauty, is not far from the end.

Summarizing all this, Socrates' Diotima concludes (as do we) with "the true order of love":

> Begin from the beauties of earth and mount upwards for the sake of that other beauty, using these as steps only ... from fair forms to fair practices, and from fair practices to fair notions, until from fair notions one arrives at the notion of absolute beauty, and at last knows what the essence of beauty is.... Would that be an ignoble life?

References

Acevedo, B., & Aron, A. (2004, January). *Love: More than just a feeling?* Paper presented at the Annual Meeting of the Society for Personality and Social Psychology, Austin, Texas.

Acevedo, B., Gross, J., & Aron, A. (2005). *Up- and down-regulation of love versus other emotions*. Research in progress.

Ahuvia, A. C. (1993). *I love it! Towards a unifying theory of love across diverse love objects* (Doctoral dissertation). Northwestern University, Evanston, Illinois.
Aron, A., & Aron, E. N. (1986). *Love as the expansion of self: Understanding attraction and satisfaction*. New York, NY: Hemisphere.
Aron, A., & Aron, E. N. (1991). Love and sexuality. In K. McKinney & S. Sprecher (Eds.), *Sexuality in close relationships* (pp. 25–48). Hillsdale, NJ: Erlbaum.
Aron, A., Aron, E. N., & Allen, J. (1998). Motivations for unreciprocated love. *Personality and Social Psychology Bulletin, 24*, 787–796.
Aron, A., Aron, E. N., & Norman, C. (2001). The self expansion model of motivation and cognition in close relationships and beyond. In M. Clark & G. Fletcher (Eds.), *Blackwell handbook of social psychology: Vol. 2. Interpersonal processes*. Oxford, England: Blackwell.
Aron, A., Aron, E. N., Tudor, M., & Nelson, G. (1991). Close relationships as including other in the self. *Journal of Personality and Social Psychology, 60*, 241–253.
Aron, A., Fisher, H., Mashek, D., Strong, G., Li, H., & Brown, L. (2005). Reward, motivation and emotion systems associated with early-stage intense romantic love. *Journal of Neurophysiology, 94*, 327–337.
Aron, A., & Fraley, B. (1999). Relationship closeness as including other in the self: Cognitive underpinnings and measures. *Social Cognition, 17*, 140–160.
Aron, A., Lewandowski, G., Mashek, D., & Aron, E. N. (in press). The self-expansion model of motivation and cognition in close relationships. In J. A. Simpson & L. Campbell (Eds.), *Oxford handbook of close relationships*. New York, NY: Oxford.
Aron, A., Mashek, D., & Aron, E. N. (2004). Closeness, intimacy, and including other in the self. In D. Mashek & A. Aron (Eds.), *Handbook of closeness and intimacy* (pp. 27–41). Mahwah, NJ: Erlbaum.
Aron, A., & McLaughlin-Volpe, T. (2001). Including others in the self: Extensions to own and partner's group memberships. In C. Sedikides & M. B. Brewer (Eds.), *Individual self, relational self, and collective self: Partners, opponents, or strangers?* (pp. 89–109). Philadelphia, PA: Psychology Press.
Aron, A., McLaughlin-Volpe, T., Mashek, D., Lewandowski, G., Wright, S. C., & Aron, E. N. (2004). Including close others in the self. *European Review of Social Psychology, 15*, 101–132.
Aron, A., Norman, C. C., & Aron, E. N. (1998). The self-expansion model and motivation. *Representative Research in Social Psychology, 22*, 1–13.
Aron, A., Norman, C. C., Aron, E. N., McKenna, C., & Heyman, R. (2000). Couples' shared participation in novel and arousing activities and experienced relationship quality. *Journal of Personality and Social Psychology, 78*, 273–283.
Aron, A., Paris, M., & Aron, E. N. (1995). Falling in love: Prospective studies of self-concept change. *Journal of Personality and Social Psychology, 69*, 1102–1112.
Aron, A., & Westbay, L. (1996). Dimensions of the prototype of love. *Journal of Personality and Social Psychology, 70*, 535–551.
Aron, E. N., & Aron, A. (1996). Love and expansion of the self: The state of the model. *Personal Relationships, 3*, 45–58.
Bandura, A. (1977). Self-efficacy: Toward a unifying theory of behavioral change. *Psychological Review, 84*, 191–215.
Baumeister, R. F., & Leary, M. R. (1995). The need to belong: Desire for interpersonal attachments as a fundamental human motivation. *Psychological Bulletin, 117*, 497–529.
Beach, S. R., Tesser, A., Fincham, F. D., Jones, D. J., Johnson, D., & Whitaker, D. J. (1998). Pleasure and pain in doing well, together: An investigation of performance-related affect in close relationships. *Journal of Personality and Social Psychology, 74*, 923–938.

Berscheid, E., & Reis, H. T. (1998). Attraction and close relationships. In S. Fiske, D. Gilbert, & G. Lindzey (Eds.), *Handbook of social psychology* (4th ed., pp. 193–281). Boston, MA: McGraw-Hill.

Berscheid, E., & Walster [Hatfield], E. H. (1978). *Interpersonal attraction* (2nd ed.). Reading, MA: Addison-Wesley.

Brehm, S. S. (1988). Passionate love. In R. J. Sternberg & M. L. Barnes (Eds.), *The Psychology of love* (pp. 232–263). New Haven, CT Yale University Press.

Bowlby, J. (1969). *Attachment and loss: Vol. 1. Attachment.* New York, NY: Basic Books.

Brody, S., Wright, S., Aron, A., & McLaughlin-Volpe, T. (2008). Compassionate love for individuals outside one's social group. In L. Underwood, S. Sprecher, & B. Fehr (Eds.), *The science of compassionate love: Research, theory, and practice* (pp. 283–308). Malden, MA: Blackwell.

Carver, C., & Scheier, M. (1990). Principles of self-regulation, action, and emotion. In E. T. Higgins & R. M. Sorrentino (Eds.), *Handbook of motivation and cognition: Foundations of social behavior* (vol. 2, pp. 3–52.). New York, NY: Guilford Press.

Cassidy, J., & Shaver, P. (Eds). (1999). *Handbook of attachment: Theory, research, and clinical applications.* New York, NY: Guilford Press.

Dawkins, R. (1989). *The selfish gene* (2nd ed.). New York, NY: Oxford University Press.

De La Ronde, C., & Swann, W. B., Jr. (1998). Partner verification: Restoring shattered images of our intimates. *Journal of Personality and Social Psychology, 75*, 374–382.

De Waal, F. (2005). *Our inner ape.* New York, NY: Riverhead.

Fehr, B. (1988). Prototype analysis of the concepts of love and commitment. *Journal of Personality and Social Psychology, 55*, 557–579.

Fehr, B. (2001). The status of theory and research on love and commitment. In G. Fletcher & M. Clark (Eds.), *Blackwell handbook in social psychology: Vol. 2. Interpersonal processes* (pp. 331–336). Oxford, England: Blackwell.

Fehr, B., & Russell, J. A. (1991). The concept of love viewed from a prototypical perspective. *Journal of Personality and Social Psychology, 60*, 425–438.

Fehr, B., & Sprecher, S. (2004, July). *Prototype analysis of the concept of compassionate love.* Paper presented at the International Conference on Personal Relationships, Halifax, Nova Scotia, Canada.

Fisher, H. E. (1998). Lust, attraction and attachment in mammalian reproduction. *Human Nature, 9*(1), 23–52.

Gardner, W. L., Gabriel, S., & Hochschild, L. (2002). When you and I are "we," you are not threatening: The role of self-expansion in social comparison. *Journal of Personality and Social Psychology, 82*, 239–251.

Gecas, V. (1989). Social psychology of self-efficacy. *American Sociological Review, 15*, 291–316.

Grossmann, K. E., Grossmann, K., & Waters, E. (2005). *Attachment from infancy to maturity: The major longitudinal studies.* New York, NY: Guilford Press.

Hazan, C., & Diamond, L. M. (2000). The place of attachment in human mating. *Review of General Psychology, 4*(2), 186–204.

Hendrick, C., & Hendrick, S. S. (2003). Romantic love: Measuring cupid's arrow. In S. J. Lopez & C. R. Snyder (Eds.), *Positive psychological assessment: A handbook of models and measures* (pp. 235–249). Washington, DC: American Psychological Association.

Jones, E. E., & Nisbett, R. (1971). The actor and the observer: Divergent perceptions of the causes of behavior. In E. E. Jones, D. E. Kanouse, H. H. Kelley, R. E. Nisbett, S. Valins, & B. Weiner (Eds.), *Attribution: Perceiving the causes of behavior* (pp. 79–94). Morristown, NJ: General Learning Press.

Jung, C. G. (1969). *The archetypes and the collective unconscious* (2nd ed.). New York, NY: Princeton University Press.

Kelley, H. H. (1983). Love and commitment. In H. H. Kelley, E. Berscheid, A. Christensen, J. H. Harvey, T. L. Huston, G. Levinger, … D. R. Peterson (Eds.), *Close relationships* (pp. 265–314). New York, NY: Freeman.

Kirkpatrick, L. A. (1998). God as a substitute attachment figure: A longitudinal study of adult attachment style and religious change in college students. *Personality and Social Psychology Bulletin, 24*, 961–973.

Lee, J. A. (1977). A typology of styles of loving. *Personality and Social Psychology Bulletin, 3*, 173–182.

Lewandowski, G. W., & Aron, A. (2002). *The Self-Expansion Scale.* Paper presented at the Third Annual Meeting of the Society for Personality and Social Psychology, Savannah, Georgia.

Lewandowski, G. W., Aron, A. P., Bassis, S., & Kunak, J. (2005). *Losing a self-expanding relationship: Implications for the self-concept.* Manuscript under review.

Lord, C. G. (1980). Schemas and images as memory aids: Two modes of processing social information. *Journal of Personality and Social Psychology, 38*, 257–269.

Lord, C. G. (1987). Imagining self and others: Reply to Brown, Keenan, and Potts. *Journal of Personality and Social Psychology, 53*, 445–450.

Lyubomirsky, S., King, L., & Diener, E. (2005). The benefits of frequent positive affect: Does happiness lead to success? *Psychological Bulletin, 131*, 803–855.

Main, M. (2000). Attachment theory. In A. E. Kazdin (Ed.), *Encyclopedia of psychology* (Vol. 1, pp. 289–293). Oxford, England: Oxford University Press.

Mashek, D. J., Aron, A., & Boncimino, M. (2003). Confusions of self and close others. *Personality and Social Psychology Bulletin, 29*, 382–392.

Mashek, D., Cannaday, L., & Tangney, J. (2007). Inclusion of Community in Self Scale: A single-item pictorial measure of community connectedness. *Journal of Community Psychology, 35*, 257–275.

McFarland, C., Buehler, R., & MacKay, L. (2001). Affective responses to social comparisons with extremely close others. *Social Cognition, 19*, 547–586.

McLaughlin-Volpe, T., Aron, A., Wright, S. C., & Lewandowski, G. W. (2005). Inclusion of the self by close others and by groups: Implications of the self-expansion model. In D. Abrams, J. Marques, & M. Hogg (Eds.), *Social inclusion and exclusion* (pp. 113–134). Philadelphia, PA: Psychology Press.

Medvene, L. J., Teal, C. R., & Slavich, S. (2000). Including the other in self: Implications for judgments of equity and satisfaction in close relationships. *Journal of Social and Clinical Psychology, 19*, 396–419.

Mervis, C. B., & Rosch, E. (1981). Categorization of natural objects. *Annual Review of Psychology, 32*, 89–115.

Meyers, S. A., & Berscheid, E. (1997). The language of love: The difference a preposition makes. *Personality and Social Psychology Bulletin, 23*, 347–362.

Mikulincer, M., & Shaver, P. R. (2007). *Attachment in adulthood: Structure, dynamics, and change.* New York, NY: Guilford Press.

Miller, L. C., & Fishkin, S. A. (1997). On the dynamics of human bonding and reproductive success: Seeking windows on the adapted-for human environmental interface. In J. Simpson & D. T. Kenrick (Eds.), *Evolutionary social psychology* (pp. 197–235). Hillsdale, NJ: Erlbaum.

Mills, J., & Clark, M. S. (2002). Viewing close romantic relationships as communal relationships: Implications for maintenance and enhancement. In J. Harvey & A. Wenzel (Eds.), *Close romantic relationships: Maintenance and enhancement* (pp. 13–25). Mahwah, NJ: Erlbaum.

Muir, W. M. (1995). Group selection for adaptation to multiple-hen cages: Selection program and direct responses. *Poultry Science, 75*, 447–458

Pinsker, H., Nepps, P., Redfield, J., & Winston, A. (1985). Applicants for short-term dynamic psychotherapy. In A. Winston (Ed.), *Clinical and research issues in short-term dynamic psychotherapy* (pp. 104–116). Washington, DC: American Psychiatric Association.

Plato. (trans. 1953). *The dialogues of Plato: Translated into English with analyses and introductions* (B. Jowett, Trans.). London, England: Oxford University Press.

Reis, H. (2007, August). *What social psychologists would like to tell clinicians about close relationships.* Presidential address, American Psychological Association Convention, San Francisco, California.

Reis, H. T., Clark, M. S., & Holmes, J. G. (2004). Perceived partner responsiveness as an organizing construct in the study of intimacy and closeness. In D. J. Mashek & A. Aron (Eds.), *Handbook of closeness and intimacy* (pp. 201–225). Mahwah, NJ: Erlbaum.

Rousar, E. E. (1990). *Valuing's role in romantic love.* Unpublished dissertation, California Graduate School of Family Psychology, San Rafael, CA.

Rusbult, C. E. (1983). A longitudinal test of the investment model: The development (and deterioration) of satisfaction and commitment in heterosexual involvements. *Journal of Personality and Social Psychology, 45*, 101–117.

Ryan, R. M., & Deci, E. L. (2000). Self-determination theory and the facilitation of intrinsic motivation, social development, and well-being. *American Psychologist, 55*, 68–78.

Sande, G. N., Goethals, G. R., & Radloff, C. E. (1988). Perceiving one's own traits and others': The multifaceted self. *Journal of Personality and Social Psychology, 54*, 13–20.

Schultz, P. W., Shriver, C., Tabanico, J., & Khazian, A. (2004). Implicit connections with nature. *Journal of Environmental Psychology, 24*, 31–42.

Sears, R. R. (1977). Sources of life satisfaction of the Terman gifted men. *American Psychologist, 32*, 119–128.

Shaver, P., Schwartz, J., Kirson, D., & O'Connor, C. (1987). Emotion knowledge: Further exploration of a prototype approach. *Journal of Personality and Social Psychology, 52*, 1061–1086.

Smith, E., Coats, S., & Walling, D. (1999). Overlapping mental representations of self, in-group, and partner: Further response time evidence and a connectionist model. *Personality and Social Psychology Bulletin, 25*, 873–882.

Smith, E., & Henry, S. (1996). An in-group becomes part of the self: Response time evaluation. *Personality and Social Psychology Bulletin, 22*, 635–642.

Sober, E., & Wilson, D. S. (1998). *Unto others: The evolution and psychology of unselfish behavior*. Cambridge, MA Harvard University Press.

Sprecher, S., & Fehr, B. (2005). Compassionate love for close others and humanity. *Journal of Social and Personal Relationships, 22*, 629–652.

Sternberg, R. J. (1998). *Love is a story: A new theory of relationships*. London, England: Oxford University Press.

Strong, G., & Aron, A. (2006).The effect of shared participation in novel and challenging activities on experienced relationship quality: Is it mediated by high positive affect? In K. D. Vohs & E. J. Finkel (Eds.), *Intrapersonal processes in interpersonal relationships* (pp. 342–359). New York, NY: Guilford Press.

Symons, C. S., & Johnson, B. T. (1997). The self-reference effect in memory: A meta-analysis. *Psychological Bulletin, 121*(3), 371–394.

Tajfel, H., & Turner, J. C. (1986). The social identity theory of inter-group behavior. In S. Worchel & L. W. Austin (Eds.), *Psychology of intergroup relations*. Chicago, IL: Nelson-Hall.

Taylor, S. E., Neter, E., & Wayment, H. A. (1995). Self-evaluative processes. *Personality and Social Psychology Bulletin, 21*, 1278–1287.

Tipsord, J., & Leary, M. (2004, February). *Including others in the self: Extensions to generic people, animals, nature, and god.* Presented at the Society for Personality and Social Psychology, Austin, Texas.

Tropp, L. R., & Wright, S. C. (2001). Ingroup identification as inclusion of ingroup in the self. *Personality and Social Psychology Bulletin, 27*, 585–600.

Tucker, P., & Aron, A. (1993). Passionate love and marital satisfaction at key transition points in the family life cycle. *Journal of Social and Clinical Psychology, 12*, 135–147.

Veroff, J., Douvan, E., & Kulka, R. A. (1981). *Mental health in America: Patterns of help-seeking from 1957 to 1976.* New York, NY: Basic Books.

Walster [Hatfield], E., Walster G. W., & Berscheid, E. (1978). *Equity: Theory and Research.* Boston, MA: Allyn & Bacon.

White, R. W. (1959). Motivation reconsidered: The concept of competence. *Psychological Review, 66*, 297–333.

Wilson, D. S. (2002). *Darwin's cathedral: Evolution, religion, and the nature of society.* Chicago, IL: University of Chicago Press.

Wilson, D. S. (2007). *Evolution for everyone: how Darwin's theory can change the way we think about our lives.* New York, NY: Delacorte Press.

Wong, P. T. P. (1998). Implicit theories of meaningful life and the development of the personal meaning profile. In P. T. P. Wong & P. S. Fry (Eds.), *The human quest for meaning: A handbook of psychological research and clinical applications* (pp. 111–140). Mahwah, NJ: Erlbaum.

Wright, S. C., Aron, A., & Brody, S. (2008). Extended contact and including others in the self: Building on the Allport/Pettigrew legacy. In U. Wagner, L. Tropp, G. Finchilescu, & C. Tredoux (Eds.), *Improving intergroup relations: Building on the legacy of Thomas F. Pettigrew* (pp. 143–159). Malden, MA: Blackwell.

Wright, S. C., Aron, A., McLaughlin-Volpe, T., & Ropp, S. A. (1997).The extended contact effect: Knowledge of cross-group friendships and prejudice. *Journal of Personality and Social Psychology, 73*, 73–90.

Wright, S. C., Brody, S. M., & Aron, A. (2005). Intergroup contact: Still our best hope for improving intergroup relations. In C. S. Crandall & M. Schaller (Eds.), *Social psychology of prejudice: Historical and contemporary issues* (pp. 115–142). Seattle, WA: Lewinian Press.

Xu, X., Aron, A., Fisher, H., Brown, L. L., Cao, G., Feng, T., & Weng, X. (2007, May). *Reward/Motivation systems associated with early stage romantic love in Chinese students: An fMRI study.* Presented at the Neural Systems of Social Behavioral Conference, Austin, Texas.

10
Meaning and Death Attitudes

ADRIAN TOMER

Shippensburg University of Pennsylvania

The main purpose of this chapter is to examine the relationships between the meaning of life and death, on the one hand, and death attitudes as expressed in emotional reactions toward death, on the other hand. Following a short examination of the concept of meaning, the chapter introduces the concept of death attitudes. The next two sections are devoted to an empirically driven discussion of the relationships between different types of death attitudes and between death attitudes and the personal meaning of death. The theories dealing with death attitudes are here somewhat arbitrarily divided into theories of fear (or death rejection) and theories of death acceptance and are examined in the next sections, with special attention to the concept of meaning. The way meaning is being used in coping with the "death of other" is also briefly examined, as is the use of meanings in dealing with death in terminally ill patients. The chapter ends with a discussion of "unified theories" that attempt to account for several types of death attitudes, in an effort to explain, in particular, in the confines of one theoretical framework both fear and acceptance of death.

The Meaning of Meaning of Life and Death

Strictly speaking, meaning is a property of symbols or of acts of communication. Thus one can ask what the meaning of the second sentence of this paragraph is. In another, but related sense, one can enquire about the meaning a writer or a speaker intends to communicate by using a particular formulation, spoken or written. Although meaning, taken in this sense, is a rather complicated topic, things get even murkier when we start talking about the meaning of life. However, I believe a few things are more or less accepted.

First, although meaning of life and the meaning of a sentence are very different, both concepts involve the existence of relationships between parts or connectedness (on this point, see, e.g., Baumeister, 1991). Second, the meaning of life and the meaning of death are interconnected. There are writers arguing, for example, that death makes life more meaningful. Perhaps nowhere is this clearer than when one considers terminally ill patients. To protect and emphasize meaning in terminally ill patients is indeed the cornerstone of meaning-centered psychotherapy (i.e., Greenstein & Breitbart, 2000; Wong, 1998a). Third, when we talk about the meaning of life, we should mean the meaning of a particular life, rather than the meaning of life in general. A fourth commonly made assumption is that meaning of life is not an entity object found in the world in the same way that one can find a treasure; rather, the concept is something a person constructs, makes, or realizes in some way and often is related to having goals, plans, or projects for one's life. Therefore meanings, whatever their ontological status might be, need a human mind to realize them. A fifth idea is that although we can talk about and reflect upon the meaning of life or of parts of life, in many cases we focus on meaning of discrete activities and experiences. Activities may be meaningful by virtue of being in service of some goal. On the other hand, an activity might have meaning in itself, intrinsically. The best examples for an intrinsically meaning activity are perhaps those that can be seen as illustrating the phenomenon of flow (Csikszentmihalyi, 1990, 1993). The person is engaged in this case in an intensive activity and has a sense of widening the boundaries toward the universe around.

The distinction between the meaning of life, in general, and the meaning of specific activities or life events is similar to the distinction Park and colleagues (Park, 2005; Park & Folkman 1997; Wortmann & Park, 2008) make between global meaning and situational meaning. The first includes people's basic goals, assumptions, and expectations from the world, others, and oneself. The situational meaning refers to particular events and interaction between the person and the environment. The person brings the basic beliefs or global meanings to these interactions and uses them to appraise the meaning of an event in processes of primary and secondary appraisal (see Lazarus & Folkman, 1984; also see Folkman, 2001), as well as to search for meaning in an effort to reduce the incongruence between situational meaning and basic beliefs or global meaning (Park & Folkman, 1997). This process of meaning making might involve, therefore, a reappraisal of the event but also, and particularly in the case of such a traumatic event as the death of a close friend or relative (or indeed one's own approaching death), might involve revisions of one's basic beliefs and life goals.

Meaning can be considered an experience (e.g., the experience of joy) or an object of an experience. The distinction between extrinsic and intrinsic meaning emphasizes that some experiences are valuable in themselves. Even then, however, as seen clearly by Frankl, the experience has an object. For example, being directed toward others, happiness or joy is intentional in nature (Frankl, 1946/1969). Similarly, flow is experienced when the person is investing all the skill and energy in pursuing a challenging goal (Csikszentmihalyi, 1990, 1993). Indeed, Csikszentmihalyi sees in this match between challenge and personal skill the key to an understanding of the phenomenon of flow, in particular to the expansion of the self and the sense of transcendence that accompanies it. Following Frankl (1946/1969), we can define three types of sources of meaning: work or creative activity; experiences, particularly those related to loving and being loved; and the individual's attitudes toward his or her limitations, in particular toward suffering. A plumber can create meaning by fixing a faucet. We can experience meaning (or grace, as some would say) by listening to a partita of Johann Sebastian Bach. Or we can realize meaning by choosing our attitudes vis-à-vis our own life events, for example, by focusing on the positive and the beautiful in them rather than dwelling on the negative. Moreover, the third type of meaning, the attitudinal meaning or value, is always possible. Thus, a person whose physical limitations might prevent him or her from realizing creative meaning and who finds even his or her experiential values compromised by pain and disability can, according to Frankl (1946/1969), find meaning in attitudinal values by, for example, becoming a role model for others by sustaining limitations and pain with dignity.

A somewhat different way of developing a typology of meanings is used by Baumeister (1991). An organizational principle here is the level of meaning (somewhat similar to the distinction of *global, situational*) that distinguishes between short-term behaviors and activities and long–range spans of time. Baumeister writes about the need for meaning and, in fact, distinguishes among four needs: purposes (extrinsic or intrinsic), values (as in the phrase *achieving something of value* or *doing the right thing*), being efficacious and in control, and achieving a sense of self-worth. It is arguable that the four needs are reducible to two basic needs: a need to achieve self-esteem or self-worth (see the account of terror management theory discussed later) and the need for growth, for achieving one's potential and exercising and expanding one's skills. From this perspective, formulating goals and abiding by societal standards and values can be considered subservient to the other two needs.

We can also characterize meanings based on their location in time (although all meanings are realized, by definition, in the present). A meaning can be situated in the future as a goal or destination; in the past, as an accomplishment; or in present time as an experience (e.g., an encounter with another human being or even an animal or a tree; see Buber, 1923/1970, 1947/2002) or an ongoing activity of intrinsic value. This formulation has the advantage of showing clearly in what ways death can compromise meaning. It can interrupt the present experience, it can obliterate a project, and it can even question the significance of the past. On the other hand, it was argued that there is no safer place than the past to preserve something (Frankl, 1946/1969). It is also frequently argued that the present cannot be taken away. Even the future can be salvaged, either by a strong religious belief or by "transcending the self" toward a union with the cosmos (e.g., cosmic gerotranscendence; see Tornstam, 1992, 1997).

The present trend toward the development of a positive psychology (e.g., Seligman, 2003; Seligman & Csikszentmihalyi, 2000) places an emphasis on positive subjective experiences, for example, on flow experiences and on techniques that can be used to maximize them. Death certainly makes the process of realization of meaning more difficult but also more imperative. It is also important to remind ourselves that while experiences of meaning are authentic and fulfilling, there are also authentic experiences of lack of meaning. Things might lose their previous sense. We can perceive all of a sudden the world as a place that is not very hospitable to human beings. The physicist Steven Weinberg (1992) writes in *Dreams of a Final Theory*, "More generally, no one has ever discovered any correlation between the importance of *anything* to us and its importance in the laws of nature" (p. 254). We can perceive the reality as completely arbitrary, thrown in front of us full of itself and without purpose and explanation, as it happened to Roquentin in his encounter with a tree root (Sartre, 1938/1965). Indeed, we can perceive ourselves and our life as thrown out and groundless (Heidegger 1927/1996). Death can exacerbate these experiences and, again, may make the realization of meaning both critical and harder to achieve.

Death Attitudes: Definition and Relationships

Death Attitudes

Many of the instruments that measure fear of death were either designed to have a multidimensional structure on theoretical grounds or were shown after the fact to have one. An example of a systematic, theory-grounded development of a multidimensional instrument is Florian's Fear of Personal Death (FPD) Scale (Florian & Kravetz, 1983). The scale is based on a tridimensional model that includes three dimensions: an intrapersonal dimension that includes one's concerns about death, an interpersonal dimension that refers to effects of death in close relationships, and a transpersonal dimension that includes concerns about the postdeath reality or the hereafter (Florian & Kravetz, 1983; see also Mikulincer & Florian, 2008). These dimensions bear similarity to dimensions or factors found in structural analyses of other tools. Thus, the intrapersonal dimension is similar to the fear of nonbeing, reported as one of four factors of the Revised Death Anxiety Scale (RDAS; Thorson & Powell, 1994), and to the fear of being destroyed, one of the eight factors of the Multidimensional Fear of Death Scale (Hoelter, 1979). The multidimensional aspect of fear of death demands precision in the formulation and testing of theoretical models. For example terror management theory and the comprehensive model that will be briefly described take the fear of annihilation as basic.

A further expansion of the concept of death attitudes can be accomplished by considering positive or neutral reactions to death. Such a step was taken by a number of researchers. A cogent approach, theoretically and empirically, was initiated by Paul Wong, who with colleagues designed and tested empirically the Death Attitude Profile–Revised (DAP-R; Wong, Reker, & Gesser, 1994). The measurement of positive death attitudes by Wong and colleagues and by other researchers (see next section) allowed empirical examination of the relationships among various death attitudes. In particular, it allowed researchers to determine the correlations among measures of fear of death and measures of death acceptance.

Correlations Among Death Attitudes

An important step forward toward systematic conceptualization and measurement of a variety of death attitudes was taken by Wong and colleagues (Gesser, Wong, & Reker, 1987–1988; Wong, Reker, & Gesser, 1994), who, as noted in the preceding section, also developed the DAP-R. The DAP-R is based on a number of premises: namely, that (a) death anxiety is multidimensional rather than unidimensional; (b) there is an inverse relationship between fear of death and the ability to find meaning in life, as well as a direct relationship between the degree of meaningfulness in one's life and one's ability to accept death; and (c) fear and acceptance of death should be conceived not as the two poles of one dimension but, rather, as separate dimensions. A person may be anxious and accepting of death at the same time. Consistent with theses views, particularly with (a) and (c), a principal-component analysis of the DAP-R revealed the existence of five dimensions in a sample of about 300 young, middle-aged, and older adults. Two of the dimensions, fear of death and death avoidance, representing "negative" attitudes, were positively correlated ($r = 0.47$). The other three types of attitudes were positive and represented different types of acceptance of death: approach, escape, and remaining neutral. A significant positive correlation existed only between escape acceptance, the acceptance of death as an escape from suffering, and approach acceptance that indicates a positive embracing of death. Even more interesting was the fact that approach acceptance was only moderately or weakly correlated with the two negative dimensions, fear and avoidance ($r = -0.40$ and -0.20, respectively). The finding of low correlations between acceptance and fear was confirmed in other studies. Thus, Ardelt (2008) reported correlations very close to zero between fear and avoidance of death, on the one hand, and approach acceptance or neutral acceptance of death, on the other hand. All death attitudes were measured in this study using the DAP-R (Wong, Reker, & Gesser, 1994), and the sample consisted of 164 older adults living in the community, residing in nursing homes or being patients in hospices. Also, Van Hiel and Vansteenkiste (2007) found a virtually null correlation between acceptance and rejection of one's death in a sample of 92 subjects.

Low or moderate correlations between measures of death anxiety and death acceptance were also reported by Durlak and Kass (1981–1982;

$r = -0.33$); Harding, Flannelly, Weaver, and Costa (2005; $r = -0.35$), Ray and Najman (1974; $r = -0.26$); Tomer and Eliason (2000a; $r = -0.16$ with approach acceptance and −0.26 with neutral acceptance); and Warren (1981–1982; $r = -0.36$). Virtually null correlations were reported by Tomer and Eliason (2005), who found, however, low but significant correlation ($r = -0.22$) between fear of death and neutral acceptance in a sample of college students. Tomer and Eliason (2000a) found negative, significant path coefficients of modest magnitude for the connection between neutral acceptance of death and fear of death in two samples of young and old adults ($r = -0.28$ and −0.35 correspondingly). Consistent with the trend reported here, approach acceptance measured using the DAP-R was not causally connected to fear of death in a latent variables models estimated in a group of about 150 terminally ill hospice patients (Neimeyer, Coleman, Currier, Tomer, & Tooley, 2007).

Meanings of Death and Attitudes Toward Death

The concept of death acceptance, particularly as it is measured by the DAP-R, is strongly connected to the way one conceptualizes death, specifically to the extent to which one believes in an afterlife. There were different attempts to measure the meaning of death for a person. One approach to investigate meaning is to ask people to describe what death means to them. This approach was used by Holcomb, Neimeyer, and Moore (1993), who also used 15 different "death constructs" that were previously developed (Neimeyer, Fontana, & Gold, 1984). The sample consisted of about 500 students from three universities. It is interesting that about 60% of participants described death as meaningful and as allowing a continued existence in an afterlife. In contrast, about 40% described death as involving nonexistence. Death attitudes were measured in this case using the Threat Index and Hoelter Multidimensional Fear of Death Scale (MFODS). It was found that a belief in a continuing existence after death and in death as a purposeful event predicted the score on the fear-of-the-unknown subscale. On the other hand, a perception of death as purposeless and unintelligible and as nonexistence predicted higher fear of the unknown. More insights into the relationship between meanings and attitudes is provided by Cicirelli (1998, 2001). In the later 2001 study, Cicirelli investigated death meanings in two age groups, one of young adults and one of older adults. The Personal Meanings of Death Scale (Cicirelli, 1998), which was used in these studies, measured four dimensions of meaning: Death as Legacy, Death as Afterlife, Death as Extinction, and Death as Motivator (to achieve). Of particular interest is the relationship with fear of death, which was measured using four out of the eight scales of MFODS: fear of the dying process, fear of being destroyed, fear of for significant others, and fear of the unknown. In both age groups, a belief in an afterlife was found to be negatively correlated to the fear of the unknown, whereas a perception of death as involving total extinction was found to be correlated positively to the same fear. The belief in an afterlife was also connected negatively to the fear of being destroyed. In addition to Holcomb, Neimeyer, and Moore (1993) and using a different methodology for measuring meanings (the use of a scale), Cicirelli provided further evidence for the connection between meanings and attitudes. In particular, a view of death as an overture to a new life seems to allow one to fear death less, whereas a view of death as final end might lead to more fear of the unknown. (Admittedly, the last sentence assumes a causal interpretation of correlational results, but such an interpretation seems plausible here.) Evidence consistent with position was also provided by Florian, Kravetz, and Frankel (1984) in a sample composed of nonreligious, moderately religious, and religious Jews in Israel. The religious orthodox Jews who believe in a hereafter were less likely to fear annihilation. On the other hand, they were more likely to fear consequences to family and punishment in the afterlife. Thus, Florian et al.'s study clearly indicates the need to distinguish between different aspects of one's belief as well as between different components of the fear of death.

Notwithstanding the negative correlations between belief in an afterlife and fear, there were also results that showed no connection between the two. Indeed, the results included in the section on death acceptance and fear of death indicated close to null correlations in a number of studies. Other studies have also found little connection. Thus, Rose and O'Sullivan (2002) found no relationship between death anxiety measured using the Templer Death Anxiety Scale and a belief in afterlife in a sample of college students. Consistent with this negative finding was that of Wittkowski (1988): Although finding in a sample of middle-aged German adults that a belief in God was negatively correlated to fear of death in general, Wittkowski found that such belief was not correlated to fear of one's own death.

Also, in an important study based on a sample of about 150 terminally ill patients from a Methodist hospice in Memphis, Neimeyer and colleagues (2007) found that a belief in God—as well as approach acceptance, measured using the DAP-R, so that the approach acceptance dimension indicates a belief in an afterlife—was connected in a structural equation model to escape acceptance, but not to fear of death. Similarly, in a longitudinal study, Wink and Scott (2005) found no linear relations between religiousness and fear of death and dying. Finally, in a quantitative review of the literature, Fortner and Neimeyer (1999) found no reliable relationship between religiosity and death anxiety. Does a belief in an afterlife promote acceptance of death? The Neimeyer et al. (2007) study mentioned earlier found a positive correlation between a belief in God and escape acceptance. Also, Harding et al. (2005) measured death acceptance using Ray and Najman's (1974) acceptance scale, which includes items suggesting either relief from pain, neutral acceptance, or lack of fear and, perhaps, approach acceptance (i.e., "Death is a friend"). In this study, the belief in an afterlife predicted death acceptance even after controlling for demographic characteristics in about 150 parishioners of an Episcopal church in New York City. Another study relevant to this issue included 71 older adults (Falkenhain & Handal, 2003) and measured acceptance using the Klug Death Acceptance Scale (KDAS; Klug & Sinha, 1987), fear using Templer's Death Anxiety Scale, and belief in an afterlife using Osarchuck and Tatz's (1973) Belief in Afterlife Scale. The belief in afterlife correlated −0.10 with death anxiety but 0.48 with death acceptance. This difference between fear (as including a strong emotional component) and acceptance (as being mainly "cognitive") is further addressed in the next section.

Meanings and Attitudes: Different or Similar Constructs?

The foregoing section assumed the distinction between two types of constructs, one representing the way we conceptualize death, and the other being the emotional reaction to it. Relating meanings to attitudes, as if attitudes were a different type of construct, is particularly difficult when one considers acceptance, instead of fear, as the attitude to be related to meaning. Indeed, an acceptance construct might reflect mainly cognitive components; as a result, this construct is likely to correlate highly with other cognitive (belief) constructs. As pointed out by Wong (1998c), a belief in an afterlife, on the one hand, and approach acceptance, on the other hand, are very similar constructs. Moreover, it is possible to think of three personal meanings used by Cicirelli—legacy, motivator, and extinction—as different components of neutral acceptance. Additional work is necessary to separate different constructs and to investigate their internal structure.

Theories of Fear of Death

Becker and Terror Management Theory

An important premise of Becker's (1973) approach in *The Denial of Death* is what he calls "the despair of the human cognition" (p. 269). The despair is related to the fact that human beings want to have a sense of "primary value" (p. 5) to be meaningful, to count in a cosmic sense, to be immortal. Becker calls this desire "man's urge to heroism" (p. 2). Society and culture are systems created to incorporate symbolic structures and meanings that in turn encourage individuals to develop their own individual drive toward heroism and meaning. The tragedy or despair is a result of the individual's mortality that will in due course wipe out any meaning. Faced with the awareness of one's mortal condition, one may fall back on personal heroism, which, as a result, becomes heroism in the face of death. At the same time, heroism becomes a tool for self-esteem enhancement and for the creation of an illusion of immortality. The idea that self-esteem protects one of awareness of one's mortality is a principal postulate of the terror management theory (TMT).

Another main assumption, also based on Becker's approach, is the function of social systems of belief that encourage the individual to accept their prevalent worldviews and to meet their standards of value. Self-esteem thereby becomes dependant on the social system and the person's functioning within the social system. The tight connection between these two assumptions is typically formulated in TMT by presenting the "solution to the problem of death" in the form of a dual-component anxiety buffer consisting of a cultural worldview and of self-esteem that is obtained by adhering to this worldview and by living up to its standards of value (Greenberg, Pyszczynski, & Solomon, 1986; Solomon, Greenberg, & Pyszczynski, 1991). The TMT was supported by an impressive number of studies, many of them confirming the mortality salience hypothesis, which predicted that increase in mortality salience should increase the need of believing in one's worldview (see Pyszczynski, Greenberg, & Solomon, 2003, for a review). The anxiety-buffer hypothesis that predicted that manipulating self-esteem (i.e., strengthening or weakening self-esteem) should have implications in terms of death anxiety (i.e., reducing or increasing the anxiety) is also supported by a large number of studies (for reviews, see Arndt & Goldenberg, 2002; Pyszczynski, Greenberg, Solomon, Arndt, & Schimel, 2004).

Growth and Fear in Becker and Terror Management Theory

Perhaps some of the best parts of *The Denial of Death* are those in which Becker (1973) considers the relationship between what he calls the "twin ontological motives" (p. 159), namely, the urge to lose oneself in the encompassing and transcending universe and the urge to stand out as unique as an eternal and worthy part of this universe. Correspondingly, the drive to immortality is not "a simple reflex of the death-anxiety" but "a reaching out by one's whole being toward life" (p. 152). Similarly, the movement toward identification with a leader, with God, or with one's system of value (transference) can be seen as a way to satisfy both urges—that is, to satisfy one's need to flee or avoid death as well as one's need to grow and expand beyond oneself. The idea of growth is thus introduced by Becker as a primary motivation in itself and as one that will take the individual beyond himself or herself (transcendence). Meaning cannot all be created by the individual. It is rather the case that meaning is established in a process of interconnection with some other that is not me.

Emphasizing the need of individuals to manage terror and under the influence of such psychoanalysts as Rank (1936/1976) and modern theories, in particular self-determination theory (SDT; see Greenberg, Pyszczynski, & Solomon, 1995; Pyszczynski et al., 2004), TMT theorists introduced the idea of dual motivation. The assumption, similar to what we have seen is the case of Becker, is that there are two motivational systems, a defensive one designed to manage terror and a second system that reflects the need for growth and development. The need for growth, as reflected in intrinsic motivation, is evident in those experiences, such as flow, where people are challenged beyond, but not too much beyond, the level of their current skills. An effort at accommodation or integration ensues (see Pyszczynski, Greenberg, & Goldenberg, 2003) with a subsequent change of existent psychological structures and a sense of exhilaration, entirely consistent with the description of the flow phenomenon by Csikszentmihalyi (1990, 1993). Moreover, growth processes satisfy the needs for competence and autonomy that are considered basic in SDT (Deci & Ryan, 2000; Ryan & Deci, 2000) and create self-esteem that is critical in TMT as a buffer against fear of annihilation. TMT theorists view growth processes as eventually generating self-esteem as a product that will in turn alleviate anxiety and by doing so allow integrative growth processes to take place (Pyszczynski, Greenberg, & Goldenberg, 2003). Although TMT accepts the distinction between self-esteem based on intrinsic standards and self-esteem based on extrinsic standards (Pyszczynski et al., 2004), this distinction is less crucial than in SDT. The TMT concedes that self-esteem based on self-determined standards is particularly conducive to growth and development because it requires less defensiveness. Such a sense of self-esteem seems to be particularly compatible with a subjective experience of meaning.

Growth Theories Versus Terror Management Theory

Such growth theories as SDT (Deci & Ryan, 2000; Ryan & Deci, 2000, 2004) as well as Wong's meaning management theory (MMT; Wong, 2008) emphasize growth-related and meaning-processing activities. The quest for meaning and the self-expanding processes are treated not as an antidote to anxiety but, rather, as a manifestation of the drive for challenge, self-expansion or growth, and, particularly in Wong's MMT, as a prerequisite for death acceptance. Although both TMT and SDT theorists accept the primacy of the defensive needs that have to be satisfied before the growth needs, it is still possible to achieve a level of death acceptance even in the presence of relatively high death anxiety. Such a position is also compatible with Firestone's view according to which death anxiety should be seen as natural (Firestone, 1994, p. 237) and accepted as a part of the project of living a fulfilling and meaningful life. Indeed, the counterpart of a growth theory is a "shrinking theory." Firestone in his separation theory (1997; see also Morrant & Catlett, 2008) takes the position that opening oneself to others, in a sense forgetting about oneself and about one's goals, including happiness, is the only way to achieve meaning and, possibly, as a kind of by-product, happiness itself.

The Comprehensive Model of Death Anxiety

The comprehensive model of death anxiety (Tomer & Eliason, 1996, 2000b, 2008) was developed in an attempt to integrate factors that affect the level of death anxiety in individuals. An important point of departure for the model was the somewhat paradoxical finding that death anxiety does not appear to be higher in older persons (Neimeyer et al., 2004). There is indeed evidence for the existence of a quadratic trend with higher level in middle adulthood (Cicirelli, 2002, 2006; Gesser et al., 1987–1988; Kalish, 1977; Neimeyer et al., 2004), although the level of death anxiety levels off and does not show further declines in very old age (Fortner & Neimeyer, 1999) and although the chronically ill do show a higher level of anxiety (Fortner & Neimeyer, 1999).

Similar to a basic TMT assumption, according to the comprehensive model, death anxiety becomes activated when one's personal death becomes salient because of illness, for example, or the death of a close person, or witnessing an accident. The theory postulates the existence of three direct antecedents to death anxiety. These include two types of regret, *past-related regret* and *future-related regret*, as well as a third antecedent representing the way personal death is conceptualized (i.e., meaningfulness of death). The regret constructs are mixtures of cognitive and emotional reactions that people feel when they consider their past and its possible errors of omission (i.e., not doing something that in retrospect should have been done) or commission (i.e., engaging in activities that one regrets afterward) or when they consider their future and the probability of not achieving important life goals. Whereas death salience may directly influence these three determinants of death anxiety, the activation of the three may be mediated by other variables, including beliefs about the world and about oneself, as well as by the coping processes one engages in order to mitigate fear.

Preliminary research on the model provided initial support for some of its propositions. Thus, in samples of both young and old adults, Tomer and Eliason (2000a) found that meaningfulness of life as measured using Antonovsky's (1987) Sense of Coherence Questionnaire was connected to fear of death as measured using the Revised Death Anxiety Scale (Thorson & Powell, 1994). A perception of life as more meaningful was conducive to less fear of nonbeing. Moreover, one's level of religious devotion was a powerful determinant of neutral acceptance in the older (but not the younger) subjects. Also consistent with the model was the finding that salience of death in the older subjects was connected causally to the fear of nonbeing. More recently, estimating a path model in a sample of college students, Tomer and Eliason (2005) found that both past- and future-related regrets were conducive to higher levels of fear of death. The latter study also replicated the finding of a positive relationship between intrinsic religiosity and death acceptance in this group of college students.

A fuller investigation of the comprehensive model was undertaken by Neimeyer et al. (2007) in their study of about 150 terminally ill hospice patients. This study presents a rare opportunity to find out what variables influence death anxiety in a group of people who are very close to the end of their lives. The methodology, structural equation modeling, is particularly adequate to estimate to what extent the empirical data are consistent with the model. Although a complete analysis of the results of the study has still to be completed, a report submitted to the Fetzer Institute (Neimeyer et al., 2007) indicated several findings of particular interest here. Fear of death measured using the DAP-R (Wong et al., 1994) was found here to be affected significantly (standardized beta coefficient of 0.45) by future-related regret as measured by the Multidimensional Fear of Death Scale (MFODS) Fear of Premature Death items. On the other hand, the path from past-related regret to fear did not reach significance. In spite of this negative finding, past-related regret had an indirect effect on fear of death through its association with future-related regret (beta = .58). In addition, stronger past-related regret was associated with a stronger inclination to accept death as an escape from suffering (beta = .35). Moreover, on a more qualitative note, and as reported in the above-mentioned report, the ideas of regret or lack thereof were central in the interviews of the terminally ill, and their relationship to the ability to achieve a sense of peace and acceptance of the inevitable end were unmistakable.

Death Acceptance: Theories and Findings

Meaning Management Theory

The way one thinks about life and death can impact the extent to which one fears and/or accepts death. The idea that one is capable of managing meanings and by doing so able to influence one's emotional reactions to death was developed into a fully fledged theory by Wong (2008). The theory is rooted in existential–humanistic theory, particularly in Frankl's writings, but it also uses cognitive-behavioral processes. Wong distinguishes between three meaning-related activities: meaning seeking, meaning making, and meaning reconstructions. Meaning seeking involves the efforts designed to see events, in particular events of our own life, as causally interconnected and therefore less arbitrary. In addition to this causal attribution is a second type of attribution, called existential, which allows one to see the "silver lining," to make sense of negative events by discovering positive aspects of them. Meaning making refers to activities actively pursued by individuals either to abide by the prevalent cultural values, to develop one's life story, to engage in development of projects, or to engage in personal development by developing and refining one's philosophy of life, systems of values, beliefs, and so on. Paul Wong defines seven sources of meaning, among them achievements, family, love, and religion. Finally, meaning reconstruction is used by Wong to refer to processes of meaning seeking and making following a traumatic event (e.g., death of a spouse or child) that requires one to redefine oneself and to restructure one's life. The development of meaning according to these three processes reflects the need for growth that exists in everybody.

The MMT is certainly in need of empirical confirmation. Several lines of results provide initial support and credence to MMT. One line pointed out by Wong (2008) is research on near-death experience (NDE). Such experiences are frequently associated with such positive effects as increase in feelings of life purpose and spirituality.

The recent literature on bereavement that places an emphasis on processes of meaning disruption and meaning reconstruction provides additional relevant evidence for the MMT. Moreover, findings documenting relatively low fear and high acceptance in older adults, particularly in terminally ill patients, in spite of the nearness of death, also suggest that older adults are able to find and develop ways to deal with their fear and to accept death. It is plausible that these ways are related to the development of a sense of meaning in spite of the proximity of death. The next sections provide short (and incomplete) reviews of the literature in these areas, dealing first with the death of the other and second with the death of oneself.

Acceptance of the Death of the Other

The purpose in this section is not to provide a full literature review of the vast literature connecting loss and meaning making, finding or reconstruction (for a good collection of chapters on this topic see, e.g., Neimeyer, 2001b). Rather, the purpose here is to delineate a few important themes. The idea of making sense of the loss is frequently discussed in the literature on grief. The need and the attempts at making sense are perceived as an important effect of loss. The death of the loved one seems frequently arbitrary, "unjustified," and in this sense meaningless. The need to make sense of the death is a need for providing an interpretation that removes at least some of this arbitrariness and makes the event more consistent with one's worldview (Davis, 2001; Janoff-Bulman, 1989, 1992). It was observed, however, that the loss of meaning that accompanies the death of a loved one is not limited to the arbitrariness of the event. Loss amounts to an impoverishment of oneself. Bereaved persons find their lives suddenly empty, in fact find a large hole within themselves. This emptiness can, however, be a point of departure for the reconstruction of meaning in an effort to increase the cohesiveness of life's narrative (i.e., Neimeyer, Keese, & Fortner, 2000; Wortmann & Park, 2008). Different authors treat this process of reconstruction somewhat differently, but the common elements are unmistakable. Davis (2001), for example, emphasizes that in addition to the process of making meaning in the sense of explaining the loss is meaning making that he calls "finding benefits." The main idea is that sometimes loss is the point of departure for growth, whether the growth is expressed in the development of other relationships, in the development of a new sense of appreciation of the world, or in the development of a sense of competence and strength (Davis, 2001). A dual-process model was proposed also by Stroebe and Schut (2001). In this case, two forms of coping are postulated: loss-oriented coping, which deals with the loss of meaning; and restoration-orientation coping, which deals with reconstruction.

The finding of growth following loss was documented by several authors (e.g., Calhoun & Tedeshi, 2001; Frantz, Farell, & Troley, 2001; Wortmann & Park, 2008). Moreover, if successful, meaning making following loss was found in a number of studies to be conducive to better adjustment (for a review, see Wortmann & Park, 2008).

If meaning making is a major metaphor used to understand bereavement, meaning finding is another metaphor. Whereas meaning making suggests that the person actively modifies or constructs a new world, meaning finding suggests that we discover meanings that present ourselves to us (cf. Attig, 2001). The idea of meaning finding can also be related to the possibility of having positive aspects of loss. The loss of a loved person, with all its poignancy, might shatter our complacency and free us to be receptive again to the world (see also Davis, 2001).

The two topics of dealing with the death of the other and dealing with one's own imminent death meet each other in the case of couples who are facing death of one of the partners. Linda Roberts and colleagues (e.g., Roberts, Wise, & DuBenske, in press) provide preliminary evidence suggesting that consistent with the posttraumatic growth literature, couples facing cancer death undergo transformations that proceed from self-concern to concern for others, including the partner.

In summary, loss, or anticipated loss, brings about a crisis by destroying the cohesiveness of one's life narrative, by destroying or threatening to destroy important meanings of one's life. The attempt to cope with loss and with the destruction of meaning may be more intensive in individuals with a high sense of spirituality or intrinsic religiosity. These individuals might eventually recover a sense of meaning, although they might also initially go through a period of increased spiritual struggle (see Wortmann & Park, 2008).

Acceptance of Death and Meaning of Life in Terminally Ill Patients

The meaning of one's life is an issue of particularly poignancy and urgency for the terminally ill patient. Breitbart (2002) presents in his review evidence suggesting that patients who report high degrees of meaning display positive and adaptive behaviors or feelings, including an ability to tolerate pain, high satisfaction with life, and less depression and hopelessness. Patients report benefiting from their religious and spiritual beliefs. Thus, older HIV-infected adults in a study by Siegel and Schrimshaw (2002) reported, among other things, that their religious and spiritual beliefs offered them strength and comfort, facilitated their finding meaning and accepting the illness, and also reduced their fear of death and self-blame. There is also evidence suggesting that hospice patients who judge themselves to be more spiritual suffer less death anxiety than do other patients who judged themselves to be less spiritual (Ita, 1995). On the other hand, the close end of one's life in conjunction with pain, suffering, and dependency may make one particularly prone to depression and to the loss of meaning. This is the background for development of psychotherapeutic interventions designed to strengthen the individual's sense of meaning (e.g., Breitbart, 2001; Breitbart, Gibson, Poppito, & Berg, 2004; Breitbart & Heller, 2003; Greenstein & Breitbart, 2000). Generally, these attempts tended to focus on the past life of the individual (e.g., as in life-review-based psychotherapies), on the meaning present in the life of the individual, and on the individual's ability to live a purposeful life in spite of suffering and the near end of life. A third possible focus is transcendental meaning, which is sometimes perceived as synonymous with spirituality (e.g., Puchalsky & Romer, 2000). One form of transcendental meaning is that offered by many religions in the form of a hereafter. By comparison, the concept of transcendental meaning is more general and involves the finding of meaning in the dissolution of the self and the perception of this dissolution as an absorption into the cosmic substance of the universe, which is itself perceived as possessing beauty, coherence, and the like. Cosmic gerotranscendence (Tornstam, 1992, 1997) and spiritual transcendence (Piedmont, 1999) and their related measures are the results of efforts to define the concept more rigorously and to operationalize it. An additional measure of spirituality, the Daily Spiritual Experiences Scale (Underwood & Teresi, 2002), was found (Neimeyer et al., 2007) to generate two components, a belief in God component and a transcendence (or transcendental meaning) component. The study has already provided preliminary evidence for the positive role played by transcendental meaning. In this case, a latent variables path analysis showed the transcendence construct to affect positively a measure of acceptance of death. It is interesting to remark, however, that although influencing approach acceptance and (indirectly through approach acceptance) escape acceptance, transcendental meaning was not found to be related to fear of death. This result is consistent with the lack of reliable relationships between religiosity and death anxiety (see Fortner & Neimeyer, 1999). Further distinctions of the concept of spirituality and transcendence (see Piedmont, 2001), as well as more refined ways of measuring death attitudes (see Neimeyer, Moser, & Wittkowski, 2003; Neimeyer, Wittkowski, & Moser, 2004), might shed further light on this issue.

Unified Theories of Death Attitudes

The term *unified* is used here to indicate theories that attempt to explain such multiple death attitudes as fear and acceptance in an integrative way rather than focusing on a particular death attitude. An integrative theory of attitudes toward one's own death in old age was formulated by Wittkowski

(2005) on the basis of Wong's theory of personal meaning (Wong, 1998b, 1998c, 2000) and Tornstam's (1992, 1997) theory of gerotranscendence. A main idea in this approach is the concept of cognitive reframing of life and death. Using cognitive reframing, individuals are able to distance themselves from present life and sources of self-esteem or judgment (as postulated by the theory of gerotranscendence). At the same time, the individuals are moving beyond their present selves (transcendence) by a variety of means that include life review (therefore an emphasis on the past self and an effort to identify oneself with the whole life) and generativity (identification with the future generation). Another source of transcendence includes intrinsic religiosity. This work of reframing can be seen as creation of meaning and spirituality, consistent with Wong's view of spirituality as a dimension of successful aging (Wong, 2000). Wittkowski's model is interesting and, of course, in need of empirical confirmation. The model seems to treat fear of death and death acceptance as poles of the same continuum. In the light of low or modest correlations between fear and acceptance (see earlier discussion), this polarity seems rather unlikely. The model can be modified slightly to accommodate the low correlations by allowing both fear and acceptance to be affected by self-esteem and by reframing, but to different extents. Thus, fear may be affected more by self-esteem (consistent with TMT), whereas acceptance may be more a function of reframing. It is also possible to see acceptance as just one determinant of fear. An attempt in this direction was made by Tomer and Eliason (2005) in extending the comprehensive model to account for death acceptance, in addition to fear. In this case, neutral acceptance was entered as an antecedent of fear and avoidance of death in a model that also included the two types of regret and intrinsic religiosity (as a measure of death meaningfulness) as other possible antecedents. The path analysis found that neutral acceptance predicted fear; in addition, the two types of regret predicted fear and avoidance of death. Obviously, there is a need for further replication of this result.

Another venue toward the achievement of an integrative theory is based on the concept of goal achievements. Indeed we have seen that the concept of meaning is strongly connected to the idea of goal achievements. Achieving important goals, that is, actualizing oneself, may be perceived as a buffer against death anxiety and as facilitating death acceptance. Erikson's (1963) psychosocial theory is consistent with this idea. Yet, it is arguable that death erases accomplishments and that in this sense the accomplished individual has more to lose! Should we expect more or less death anxiety in accomplished individuals? An elegant way out of this conundrum is provided by SDT (Ryan & Deci, 2000; see also Van Hiel & Vansteenkiste, 2007) for SDT distinguishes between intrinsic and extrinsic motivation. The former motivation is behind the tendency to explore and pursue novel avenues and to enhance one's abilities and knowledge. The latter is behind behaviors undertaken for the purpose of attaining a separate goal or outcome. Performing a job activity because it was demanded by the boss is an example of an externally regulated, extrinsic motivation. Trying to do well on a job in order to be rewarded is another example of extrinsic motivation (called introjected regulation). Sometimes people identify and integrate regulations and by so doing experience increased autonomy. According to SDT, intrinsic pursuits and extrinsic but integrated motivations should allow satisfaction of such basic needs as the need for autonomy or competence. Thus, fulfillment of intrinsic aspirations should increase well-being. Conversely, emphasizing extrinsic aspiration, such as wealth or fame, should be connected to decreased well-being. Evidence in this direction was produced (e.g., Kasser & Ryan, 1996; Ryan, Deci, & Grolnick, 1995). A similar relationship should exist, according to Van Hiel and Vansteenkiste (2007), between intrinsic versus extrinsic aspiration and death anxiety and death acceptance. According to Van Hiel and Vansteenkiste, achievement of extrinsic goals should increase death anxiety, whereas achievement of intrinsic goals should promote death acceptance. Indeed, after controlling for extrinsic goal attainment, it was found that intrinsic goal attainment was related to greater acceptance of one's death. At the same time, intrinsic goal attainment was not related to less fear of death, nor was extrinsic goal attainment related to either lower acceptance or greater fear, as predicted. In spite of this only partial confirmation, SDT remains a promising avenue for the investigation of death attitudes in relation to issues of regret and basic life goals.

Conclusions

Virtually all theorists in the field, including not only those who emphasize growth and death acceptance but also those who emphasize their theories of death anxiety recognize the importance played by meaning-related processes (i.e., meaning making or meaning finding) or experiences of meaning. This realization certainly prompted clinically oriented experts from a variety of disciplines to try to develop meaning-based therapies for the terminally ill. At the same time, several methodological and substantive questions are still waiting for an answer. One issue is the extent to which death acceptance should be conceptualized as a type of belief or as a type of emotional reaction to death. It is clear that death acceptance and death anxiety are not the two poles of one continuum. It is possible to formulate theoretical models of death acceptance by elaborating on the relationships between death acceptance and meaning. Paul Wong's MMT is a cogent effort in this direction, one that is in need of further empirical confirmation. Another option is to try to formulate a unified theory. The application of SDT to issues of death anxiety and death acceptance based on the distinction of two types of goals, extrinsic and intrinsic (or two types of meaning), seems to be promising but is also in need of further elaboration and empirical confirmation. One can conclude by saying that any reasonable theory of death attitudes should incorporate in it a subtheory of meaning. SDT and MMT are important steps in this direction.

References

Antonovsky, A. (1987). *Unraveling the mystery of health.* San Francisco, CA: Jossey-Bass.

Ardelt, M. (2008). Wisdom, religiosity, purpose in life, and death attitudes of aging adults. In A. Tomer, G. T. Eliason, & P. T. P. Wong (Eds.). *Existential and spiritual issues in death attitudes* (pp. 139–158). New York, NY: Erlbaum.

Arndt, J., & Goldenberg, J. J. (2002). From threat to sweat: The role of physiological arousal in the motivation to maintain self-esteem. In A. Tesser, J. V. Wood, & D. A. Stapel (Eds.), *Self and motivation: Emerging psychological perspectives* (pp. 43–69). Washington, DC: American Psychological Association.

Attig, T. (2001). Relearning the world: Making and finding meanings. In R. A. Neimeyer (Ed.), *Meaning reconstruction & the experience of loss* (pp. 33–53).Washington, DC: American Psychological Association.

Baumeister, R. F. (1991). *Meanings of life.* New York, NY: Guilford Press.

Becker, E. (1973). *The denial of death.* New York, NY: Free Press.

Breitbart, W. (2002). Spirituality and meaning in supportive care: Spirituality- and meaning-centered group psychotherapy interventions in advanced cancer. *Supportive Care in Cancer, 10,* 272–280.

Breitbart, W., Gibson, C., Poppito, S. R., & Berg, A. (2004). Psychotherapeutic interventions at the end of life: A focus on meaning and spirituality. *Canadian Journal of Psychiatry, 49,* 177–183.

Breitbart, W., & Heller, K. S. (2003). Reframing hope: Meaning-centered care for patients near the end of life. *Journal of Palliative Medicine, 6,* 979–988.

Buber, M. (2002). *Between man and man.* New York, NY: Routledge. (Originally published 1947)

Buber, M. (1970). *I and thou.* New York, NY: Scribner's. (Originally published 1923)

Calhoun, L. G., & Tedeshi, R. G. (2001). Postraumatic growth: the positive lessons of loss. In R. A. Neimeyer (Ed.), *Meaning reconstruction & the experience of loss* (pp. 157–190). Washington, DC: American Psychological Association.

Cicirelli, V. G. (1998). Views of elderly people concerning end-of-life decisions. *Journal of Applied Gerontology, 17,* 187–204.

Cicirelli, V. G. (2001). Personal meanings of death in older adults and young adults in relation to their fears of death. *Death Studies, 25*(8), 663–683.

Cicirelli, V. G. (2002). *Older adults' views on death.* New York, NY: Springer.

Cicirelli, V. G. (2006). Fear of death in mid-old age. *The Journals of Gerontology Series B: Psychological Sciences and Social Sciences, 61,* P75–P81.

Csikszentmihalyi, M. (1990). *Flow: The psychology of optimal experience.* New York, NY: Harper & Row.

Csikszentmihalyi, M. (1993). *The evolving self.* New York, NY: HarperCollins.

Davis, C. G. (2001). The tormented and the transformed: Understanding responses to loss and trauma. In R. A. Neimeyer (Ed.), *Meaning reconstruction & the experience of* loss (pp. 137–155). Washington, DC: American Psychological Association.

Deci, E. L., & Ryan, R. M. (2000). The "what" and "why" of goal pursuits: Human needs and the self-determination of behavior. *Psychological Inquiry, 11,* 227–268.

Durlak, J. A., & Kass, R. A. (1981–1982). Clarifying the measurement of death attitudes: A factor analytic evaluation of fifteen self-report death scales. *Omega: Journal of Death and Dying, 12*, 129–141.

Erikson, E. H. (1963). *Childhood and society* (2nd ed.). New York, NY: Norton.

Falkenhain, M., & Handal, P. J. (2003). Religion, death attitudes, and belief in afterlife in the elderly: Untangling the relationships. *Journal of Religion and Health, 42*, 67–76.

Firestone, R. W. (1994). Psychological defenses against death anxiety. In R. A. Neimeyer (Ed.), *Death anxiety handbook: Research, instrumentation, and application* (pp. 217–241). Washington, DC: Taylor & Francis.

Firestone, R. W. (1997). *Combating destructive thought processes: Voice therapy and separation theory.* Thousand Oaks, CA: Sage.

Florian, V., & Kravetz, S. (1983). Fear of personal death: Attribution, structure, and relation to religious belief. *Journal of Personality and Social Psychology, 44*, 600–607.

Florian, V., Kravetz, S., & Frankel, J. (1984). Aspects of fear of personal death, levels of awareness, and religious commitment. *Journal of Research in Personality, 18*, 289–304.

Folkman, S. (2001). Revised coping theory and the process of bereavement. In M. S. Stroebe, R. O. Hansson, W. Stroebe, & H. Schut (Eds.), *Handbook of bereavement* (pp. 563–584). Washington, DC: American Psychological Association.

Fortner, B. V., & Neimeyer, R. A. (1999). Death anxiety in older adults: A quantitative review. *Death Studies, 23*, 387–412.

Frankl, V. E. (1969). *The doctor and the soul: From psychotherapy to logotherapy.* New York, NY: Bantam Books. (Originally published 1946)

Frantz, T. T., Farell, M. M., & Troley, B. C. (2001). Positive outcomes of losing a loved one. In R. A. Neimeyer (Ed.), *Meaning reconstruction & the experience of loss* (pp. 191–209). Washington, DC: American Psychological Association.

Gesser, G., Wong, P. T. P., & Reker, G. T. (1987–1988). Death attitudes across the life-span: The development and validation of the Death Attitude Profile (DAP). *Omega, 18*, 113–128.

Greenberg, J., Pyszczynski, T., & Solomon, S. (1986). The causes and consequences of the need for self-esteem: A terror management theory. In R. F. Baumeister (Ed.), *Public and private self* (pp. 189–212). New York, NY: Springer-Verlag.

Greenberg, J., Pyszczynski, T, & Solomon, S. (1995). Towards a dual motive depth psychology of self and social behavior. In M. Kernis (Ed.), *Self-efficacy and self-regulation* (pp. 73–99). New York, NY: Plenum Press.

Greenstein, M., & Breitbart, W. (2000). Cancer and the experience of meaning: A group psychotherapy program for people with cancer. *American Journal of Psychotherapy, 54*, 486–500.

Harding, S. R., Flannelly, K. J., Weaver, A. J., & Costa, K. G. (2005). The influence of religion on death anxiety and death acceptance. *Mental Health, Religion & Culture, 8*, 253–261.

Heidegger, M. (1996). *Being and time* (J. Stammbaugh, Trans.). Albany: State University of New York Press. (Originally published 1927)

Hoelter, J. W. (1979). Multidimensional treatment of fear of death. *Journal of Consulting and Clinical Psychology, 47*, 996–999.

Holcomb, L. E., Neimeyer, R. A., & Moore, M. K. (1993). Personal meanings of death: A content analysis of free-response narratives. *Death Studies, 17*, 299–318.

Ita, D. J. (1995). Testing of a causal model: Acceptance of death in hospice patients. *Omega, 32*, 81–92.

Janoff-Bulman, R. (1989). Assumptive worlds and the stress of traumatic events. *Social Cognition, 7,* 113–116.

Janoff-Bulman, R. (1992). *Shattered assumptions: Toward a new psychology of trauma.* New York, NY: Free Press.

Kalish, R. A. (1977). The role of age in death attitudes. *Death Education, 1,* 205–230.

Kasser, T., & Ryan, R. M. (1996). Further examining the American dream: Differential correlates of intrinsic and extrinsic goals. *Personality and Social Psychology Bulletin, 22,* 281–288.

Klug, L., & Sinha, A. (1987). Death acceptance: A two-component formulation and scale. *Omega, 18,* 229–235.

Lazarus, R. S., & Folkman, S. (1984). *Stress, appraisal, and coping.* New York, NY: Springer.

Mikulincer, M., & Florian, V. (2008). The complex and multifaceted nature of the fear of personal death: The multidimensional model of Victor Florian. In A. Tomer, G. T. Eliason, & P. T. P. Wong (Eds.), *Existential and spiritual issues in death attitudes* (pp. 39–64). New York, NY: Erlbaum.

Morrant, C., & Catlett, J. (2008). Separation theory and voice therapy: Philosophical underpinnings and applications to death anxiety across the life span. In A. Tomer, G. T. Eliason, & P. T. P. Wong (Eds.), *Existential and spiritual issues in death attitudes* (pp. 345–373). New York, NY: Erlbaum.

Neimeyer, R. A. (2001a). The language of loss. In R. A. Neimeyer (Ed.), *Meaning reconstruction and the experience of loss* (pp. 261–292). Washington, DC: American Psychological Association.

Neimeyer, R. A. (Ed.). (2001b). *Meaning reconstruction and the experience of loss.* Washington, DC: American Psychological Association.

Neimeyer R. A., Coleman, R., Currier, J. M., Tomer, A., & Tooley, E. (2007). *Self-esteem, spirituality and suffering at the end of life: Toward a comprehensive model of death anxiety.* Report submitted to Fetzer Foundation.

Neimeyer, R. A., Fontana, D. J., & Gold, K. (1984). A manual for content analysis of death constructs. In F. R. Epting & R. A. Neimeyer (Eds.), *Personal meanings of death* (pp. 213–234). Washington, DC: Hemisphere.

Neimeyer, R. A., Keese, N. J., & Fortner, B. V. (2000). Loss and meaning reconstruction: Propositions and procedures. In R. Malkinson, S. Rubin, & E. Witztum (Eds.), *Traumatic and non-traumatic bereavement* (pp. 197–230). Madison, CT: Psychological Press.

Neimeyer, R. A., Moser, R., & Wittkowski, J. (2003). Assessing attitudes toward death: Psychometric considerations. *Omega, 47,* 45–76.

Neimeyer, R. A., Wittkowski, J., & Moser, R. P. (2004). Psychological research on death attitudes: An overview and evaluation. *Death Studies, 28,* 309–340.

Osarchuck, M., & Tatz, S. J. (1973). Effect of fear of death on belief in afterlife. *Journal of Personality and Social Psychology, 27,* 256–260.

Park, C. L. (2005). Religion as a meaning-making framework in coping with life stress. *Journal of Social Issues, 61,* 707–729.

Park, C. L., & Folkman, S. (1997). Meaning in the context of stress and coping. *Review of General Psychology, 1,* 115–144.

Piedmont, R. E. (1999). Does spirituality represent the sixth factor of personality? Spiritual transcendence and the five-factor model. *Journal of Personality,* 67, 985–1013.

Piedmont, R. E. (2001). Spiritual transcendence and the scientific study of spirituality. *Journal of Rehabilitation, 67,* 4–14.

Puchalsky, C. M., & Romer, A. L. (2000). Taking a spiritual history allows clinicians to understand patients more fully. *Journal of Palliative Medicine,* 3, 129–137.

Pyszczynski, T., Greenberg, J., & Goldenberg, J. L. (2003). Freedom versus fear: On the defense, growth, and expansion of the self. In M. R. Leary & J. P. Tangney (Eds.), *Handbook of self and identity* (pp. 314–343). New York, NY: Guilford Press.

Pyszczynski, T., Greenberg, J., & Solomon, S. (2003). *In the wake of 9/11: The psychology of terror.* Washington, DC: American Psychological Association.

Pyszczynski, T., Greenberg, J., Solomon, S., Arndt, J., & Schimel, J. (2004). Why do people need self esteem? A theoretical and empirical review. *Psychological Bulletin, 130,* 435–468.

Rank, O. (1976). *Will therapy and truth and reality.* New York: Knopf. (Originally published 1936)

Ray, J. J., & Najman, J. (1974). Death anxiety and death acceptance: A preliminary approach. *Omega, 5*(4), 311–315.

Roberts, L. J., Wise, M., & DuBenske, L. (in press). Compassionate caregiving in the light and shadow of death. In B. Fehr, S. Sprecher, & L. Underwood (Eds.), *The science of compassionate love: Research, theory and applications.* Blackwell.

Rose, B. A., & O'Sullivan, M. J. (2002). Afterlife beliefs and death anxiety: An exploration of the relationship between afterlife expectations and fear of death in an undergraduate population. *Omega, 45,* 229–243.

Ryan, R. M., & Deci, E. L. (2000). Self-determination theory and the facilitation of intrinsic motivation, social development, and well-being. *American Psychologist, 55,* 68–78.

Ryan, R. M., & Deci, E. L. (2004). Avoiding death or engaging life as accounts of meaning and culture: Comment on Pyszczynski et al. (2004). *Psychological Bulletin, 130*(3), 473–477.

Ryan, R. M., Deci, E. L., & Grolnick, W. S. (1995). Autonomy, relatedness, and the self: Their relation to development and psychopathology. In D. Cicchetti & D. J. Cohen (Eds.), *Developmental psychopathology: Theory and methods* (pp. 618–655). New York, NY: Wiley.

Sartre, J. P. (1965). *Nausea.* Harmondsworth, England: Penguin. (Originally published 1938)

Siegel, K., & Schrimshaw, E. W. (2002). The perceived benefits of religious and spiritual coping among older adults living with AIDS/HIV. *Journal for the Scientific Study of Religion, 41,* 91–102.

Seligman, M. E. P. (2003). The past and future of positive psychology. In C. L. M. Keyes & J. Haidt (Eds.), *Flourishing: Positive psychology and the life well-lived.* Washington, DC: American Psychological Association.

Seligman, M. E. P., & Csikszentmihalyi, M. (2000). Positive psychology: An introduction. *American Psychologist, 55,* 5–14.

Solomon, S., Greenberg, J., & Pyszczynski, T. (1991). A terror management theory of social behavior: The psychological functions of self-esteem and cultural worldviews. In M. P. Zanna (Ed.), *Advances in Experimental Social Psychology:* (Vol. 24, pp. 93–159). New York, NY: Academic Press.

Stroebe, M. S., & Schut, H. (2001). Meaning making in the dual process model of coping with bereavement. In R. A. Neimeyer (Ed.), *Meaning reconstruction & the experience of loss* (pp. 55–73).Washington, DC: American Psychological Association.

Thorson, J. A., & Powell, F. C. (1994). A revised death anxiety scale. In R. A. Neimeyer (Ed.), *Death anxiety handbook* (pp. 31–43). Washington, DC: Taylor & Francis.

Tomer, A., & Eliason, G. (1996). Toward a comprehensive model of death anxiety. *Death Studies, 20,* 343–365.

Tomer, A., & Eliason, G. (2000a). Beliefs about self, life, and death: Testing aspects of the comprehensive model of death anxiety and death attitudes. In A. Tomer (Ed.), *Death attitudes and the older adult* (pp. 137–153). Philadelphia, PA: Taylor & Francis.

Tomer, A., & Eliason, G. (2000b). Attitudes about life and death: Toward a comprehensive model of death anxiety. In A. Tomer (Ed.), *Death attitudes and the older adult* (pp. 3–22). Philadelphia, PA: Taylor & Francis.

Tomer, A., & Eliason, G. (2005). Life regrets and death attitudes in college students. *Omega, 51*, 173–195.

Tomer, A., & Eliason, G. (2008). Regret and death attitudes. In A. Tomer, G. T. Eliason, & P. T. P. Wong (Eds.), *Existential and spiritual issues in death attitudes* (pp. 159–172). New York, NY: Erlbaum.

Tornstam, L. (1992). The quo vadis of gerontology: On the scientific paradigm of gerontology. *Gerontologist, 32*, 318–326.

Tornstam, L. (1997). Gerotranscendence in a broad cross-sectional perspective. *Journal of Aging and Identity, 2*, 17–36.

Underwood, L. G., & Teresi, J. A. (2002). The Daily Spiritual Experience Scale. *Annals of Behavioral Medicine, 24*, 22–34.

Van Hiel, A., & Vansteenkiste, M (2007). *Ambitions fulfilled? The effects of intrinsic and extrinsic goal attainment on ego-integrity, psychological well-being, and attitudes toward death among the elderly.* Manuscript submitted for publication.

Warren, W. G. (1981–1982). Death threats, concern, anxiety, fear and acceptance in death involved and "at risk" groups. *Omega, 12*, 359–372.

Weinberg, S. (1992). *Dreams of a final theory*. New York, NY: Pantheon Books.

Wittkowski, J. (1988). Relationships between religiosity and attitudes toward death and dying in a middle-aged sample. *Personality & individual differences, 9*, 307–312.

Wittkovski, J. (2005). Einstellungen zu Sterben und Todd im höheren und hohen lebensalter: Aspekte der grundlagenforshung [Attitudes toward dying and death in the elderly: Issues of basic research]. *Zeitschrift für Gerontopsychologie & psychiatrie, 18*, 67–79.

Wink, P., & Scott, J. (2005). Does religiousness buffer against the fear of death and dying in late adulthood? Findings from a longitudinal study. *Journals of Gerontology Series B: Psychological Sciences & Social Sciences, 60B*, 207–214.

Wong, P. T. P. (1998a). Meaning-centered counseling. In P. T. P. Wong & P. S. Fry (Eds.), *The human quest for meaning: A handbook of psychological research and clinical applications* (pp. 395–435). Mahwah, NJ: Erlbaum.

Wong, P. T. P. (1998b). Implicit theories of meaningful life and the development of the personal meaning profile. In P. T. P. Wong & P. S. Fry (Eds.), *The human quest for meaning: A handbook of psychological research and clinical applications* (pp. 111–140). Mahwah, NJ: Erlbaum.

Wong, P. T. P. (1998c). Spirituality, meaning and successful aging. In P. T. P. Wong & P. S. Fry (Eds.), *The human quest for meaning: A handbook of psychological research and clinical applications* (pp. 359–394). Mahwah, NJ: Erlbaum.

Wong, P. T. P. (2000). Meaning in life and meaning in death in successful aging. In A. Tomer (Ed.), *Death attitudes and the older adults: Theories, concepts and applications* (pp. 23–35). Philadelphia, PA: Bruner-Routledge.

Wong, P. T. P. (2008). Meaning management theory and death acceptance. In A. Tomer, G. T. Eliason, & P. T. P. Wong (Eds.), *Existential and spiritual issues in death attitudes* (pp. 65–87). New York, NY: Erlbaum.

Wong, P. T., Reker, G. T., & Gesser, G. (1994). Death Attitude Profile–Revised. In R. A. Neimeyer (Ed.), *Death anxiety handbook* (pp. 121–148). New York, NY: Taylor & Francis.

Wortmann, J. H., & Park, C. L. (2008). Religion and spirituality in adjustment following bereavement: An integrative review. *Death Studies, 32*, 703–736.

11
Existential Well-Being and Health

CAROL D. RYFF

University of Wisconsin–Madison

Among the profoundly significant messages of *Man's Search for Meaning* (Frankl, 1946/1992) was the observation that those individuals who maintained a sense that life had meaning and purpose, even amid the horrors of a Nazi concentration camp, survived longer. As a physician, Frankl reflected on this idea in terms of the workings of the body's biological systems and, in particular, immune processes. In this chapter, scientific evidence suggesting that possessing a strong existential well-being is, in fact, accompanied by (and possibly promotes) better biological regulation and better health is examined. This agenda, for which emerging empirical findings are preliminary and partial at best, converges with efforts to foster a perspective on "positive health" that is fundamentally concerned with explicating the physiological substrates of human flourishing (Ryff & Singer, 1998). Thus, rather than define human health as the absence of illness, the positive-health approach begins with the presence of wellness and then probes the neural circuitry and biological processes that underlie it. Probing the inner workings between well-being, the brain, and biology is the essential quest for understanding positive health.

Ten years ago, much of what was offered on this agenda was a promissory note. In the intervening period, considerable research has been generated by a wide group of investigators, research that shows possible health benefits of multiple aspects of well-being. In what follows, I first briefly describe meanings of well-being, noting distinctions between approaches that are more strongly rooted in existential thinking from those derived from other perspectives. Then I review the emergent evidence linking these differing aspects of well-being to diverse biological markers and select assessments of neural circuitry. Bringing life challenge into the formulation, I then summarize the growing evidence that under conditions of adversity, some individuals maintain a strong sense that life is meaningful and worth living and, indeed, grow from the experience. I then probe more deeply to examine whether possessing such a life outlook affords protection against biological risk. Throughout this section, I emphasize future research directions needed to advance scientific understanding of how well-being, particularly its existential varieties, promotes better biological regulation and hence health. The potential of interventions to promote purposeful engagement and self-realization is also part of this future vision.

Varieties of Well-Being: Existential and Otherwise

Numerous prior publications (Diener, 1984; Diener, Suh, Lucas, & Smith, 1999; Kahneman, Diener, & Schwarz, 1999; Keyes, Shmotkin, & Ryff, 2002; Ryan & Deci, 2001; Ryan, Huta, & Deci, 2008; Ryff, 1989; Ryff & Keyes, 1995; Ryff & Singer, 2008) have delineated the various meanings of human well-being, often by examining distant philosophical foundations and then linking them to current empirical indicators. I briefly highlight this large literature with the aim of distinguishing between aspects of well-being that are derived from existential and humanistic conceptions of the human condition, compared with those concerned, not so much with how the external world and its challenges are engaged but with how one feels subjectively, particularly about happiness and contentment in life.

Beginning with the latter, interest in feeling good can be traced philosophically to writings of early Greeks, such as Epicurus, who believed that life's primary purpose was to attain a happiness and tranquility (O'Connor, 1993). Ideas of Epicureanism were closely related to hedonism (also advocated by Aristippus), wherein the goal was to maximize pleasure and minimize pain. Utilitarian philosophy of the 19th century (exemplified by the writings of Hume, Bentham, and Mill) further emphasized the importance of happiness, as well as the larger societal goal of maximizing the greatest amount of it for the largest number of people (see Rosen, 2003).

Following in these philosophical traditions, national survey studies, which became prominent in the United States in the 1960s, put forth key empirical indicators of life quality that asked respondents about their happiness and life satisfaction (Bradburn, 1969; Cantril, 1965; Gurin, Veroff, & Feld, 1960). Decades of survey research followed (e.g., Andrews & Withey, 1976; Bryant & Veroff, 1982; Campbell, Converse, & Rodgers, 1976). Building on this foundation, "subjective well-being" emerged as a key variable in mainstream psychology (Diener et al., 1999; Kahneman et al., 1999). Collectively, this line of inquiry advanced the importance of well-being, defined as happiness and life satisfaction and, among other things, began identifying the factors that influence, or follow from, such subjective feelings.

An alternative view of human well-being, also traceable to the ancient Greeks, was concerned with "eudaimonia," as written about by Aristotle (1925, trans.) in the *Nichomachean Ethics* (350 BC; see Ryff & Singer, 2008). Concerned with ethical guidelines for how to live, Aristotle began with the fundamental question "What is the highest of all goods achievable by human action?" His first answer is that it was not amusement, nor relaxation, nor satisfying appetites, nor money making, nor political power. In fact, he likened the pursuit of contentment to a life "suitable to beasts." Rather, he asserted that the highest human good was "activity of the soul in accordance with virtue." By this he meant achieving the best that is in us, each according to personal disposition and talent. Thus, growth toward one's true or best nature was the essence of eudaimonism for Aristotle and was exemplified by two prominent Greek imperatives—know thyself and become what you are (see also Norton, 1976, for a comprehensive distillation of Hellenic eudaimonism).

Striving to realize one's true potential reappeared centuries later in formulations of humanistic psychology that also put a premium on the growth and self-realization of the individual (Allport, 1961; Maslow, 1968; Rogers, 1962; Ryan & Deci, 2001). Existential psychology, in contrast, drew on somewhat different philosophical foundations (e.g., Kirkegaard, Nietzsche, Sartre, Camus), which were less upbeat in tone and instead emphasized the human struggle to find meaning in a world that was meaningless, absurd, or even horrific (e.g., Frankl, 1946/1992).

Such distant ideas, along with their early Greek predecessors, also influenced empirical studies of well-being in the current era. For example, research on self-determination theory is consistent with a eudaimonic approach in emphasizing the pursuit of intrinsic goals, behaving autonomously, and acting with awareness (Ryan, Huta, & Deci, 2008). Shmotkin and Shrira (Chapter 7, this volume) embrace both hedonic (subjective well-being) and eudaimonic (meaning-in-life) approaches, arguing that each offers important insight for how one deals with a hostile world. Specifically, in dealing with the adverse contingencies of life, subjective well-being facilitates regulatory processes that make things manageable, while meaning in life facilitates reconstructive processes that make things interpretable.

My formulation of psychological well-being (Ryff, 1989; Ryff & Singer, 2008) draws on the aforementioned eudaimonic perspective as well as later humanistic and existential views to articulate multiple aspects of well-being, which are subsequently linked to biological processes and health. Six distinct dimensions have been the focus of inquiry: *autonomy*, which emphasizes the individual's capacity to be self-determining and independent, even if it means going against conventional wisdom; *environmental mastery*, which refers to the capacity to manage everyday life and create a surrounding context that fits with personal needs and values; *personal growth*, which involves seeing oneself as developing through time and thereby realizing personal potential; *positive relations with others*, which pertains to interpersonal well-being, that is, having close, satisfying ties to others; *purpose in life*, wherein one has a sense of direction in life and sees meaning in one's present and past life; and *self-acceptance*, which involves positive self-regard that includes awareness of both personal strengths and limitations.

These six dimensions and their theoretical underpinnings have been extensively detailed elsewhere (Ryff & Singer, 2008). Suffice it to say, they represent points of convergence in many prior formulations of positive human functioning, including humanistic and existential formulations, along with other perspectives from life-span developmental psychology (Bühler, 1935; Bühler & Massarik, 1968; Erikson, 1959; Neugarten, 1968, 1973) and clinical psychology (Jahoda, 1958; Jung, 1933). Some dimensions are obviously existential, such as purpose in life and personal growth, although maintaining a sense of mastery vis-à-vis a difficult world or feeling autonomous in the face of outside pressures also exemplify well-being vis-à-vis the exigencies of daily life. Similarly, the capacity to nurture strong relationships with others and a positive view of oneself also constitute effortful accomplishments. Thus, striving and honing strengths in the face of challenge is a recurrent theme of eudaimonic well-being (see also Ryff & Singer, 2003). It is worth noting that Bertrand Russell made the same point about hedonic well-being—namely, it is something for which one must strive and work hard, hence his title *The Conquest of Happiness* (1930/1958).

Whatever approach to well-being one adopts as a guide for scientific research or a philosophy by which to live, a relevant question is whether those who possess such qualities of well-being (hedonic, eudaimonic, or both), derive health benefits from their subjective experience. The extent to which well-being is salubrious (i.e., health promoting) is the question to which I now turn.

Well-Being and Biology: The Positive Health Agenda

Four topics are covered in this section. The first summarizes evidence linking positive affect (closely linked to the foregoing formulation of hedonic well-being) to health, including morbidity, mortality, symptoms, and various biomarkers. The second describes recent findings linking various aspects of eudaimonic well-being to diverse biological systems. The third examines linkages between well-being and brain assessments. The final section examines well-being as a possible moderator (compensatory or buffering influence) of adverse experience on health. Most scientific evidence to date is correlational in nature, although some studies have used laboratory mood inductions and others have employed longitudinal designs to offer refinements in understanding causal directionality.

A recent review (Pressman & Cohen, 2005) summarized evidence showing that high positive affect (measured in terms of general feelings of happiness, joy, contentment, excitement, and enthusiasm) is linked with lower morbidity and increased longevity as well as reduced health symptoms and pain. Physiological correlates were also examined in experimental studies where positive affect was induced as well as in naturalistic studies. Health-protective responses were more evident in the latter. For example, positive emotional style (e.g., calm, happiness, vigor) over one month was associated with better endocrine function, showing lower levels of cortisol, epinephrine, and norepinephrine (Cohen, Doyle, Turner, Alper, & Skoner, 2003; Polk, Cohen, & Doyle, 2005). With regard to immune measures, higher trait positive affect was also linked with higher levels of antibody production (Marsland, Cohen, Rabin, & Manuck, 2006), and positive emotional style was found to predict resistance to illness after experimental exposure to rhinovirus or influenza A virus (Cohen, Alpen, Doyle, Treanor, & Turner, 2006). Steptoe and colleagues (Steptoe, Gibson, Hamer, & Wardle, 2006; Steptoe, Wardle, & Marmot, 2005) also found that positive affect, assessed by aggregating momentary experiences of happiness over a working day, was inversely related to cortisol output and heart rate. When exposed to mental stress in the laboratory, happier individuals were also found to have lower inflammatory response (plasma fibrinogen) and lower blood pressure.

Research on eudaimonic well-being and biology has also emerged in recent years. Older women with higher levels of purpose in life, personal growth, and positive relations with others showed lower cardiovascular risk (lower glycosylated hemoglobin, lower weight, lower waist–hip ratios, higher "good" HDL cholesterol) and better neuroendocrine regulation (lower salivary cortisol throughout the day; Ryff et al., 2006; Ryff, Singer, & Love, 2004). The link between lower cortisol and eudaimonic well-being was also evident in a Swedish study (Lindfors & Lundberg, 2002). With regard to inflammatory factors, those individuals with higher levels of interpersonal well-being (positive relations with others) and purpose in life were shown to have lower levels of interleukin-6 (IL-6) and its soluble receptor (sIL-6r) (Friedman, Hayney, Love, Singer, & Ryff, 2007; Friedman et al., 2005). The link between relational well-being and better biological regulation converges with growing evidence that quality ties to significant others and related emotions are prominent in understanding variations in health (Ryff & Singer, 2000, 2001).

Psychological well-being has also been connected to research on the brain and, more specifically, research on affective neuroscience (Davidson, 2003, 2004). Well-being has been linked with asymmetric activation of the prefrontal cortex, for example, with greater left than right prefrontal activation associated with higher levels of both hedonic and eudaimonic well-being (Urry et al., 2004). Only eudaimonic well-being, however, revealed a link to EEG asymmetry that persisted after adjusting for hedonic well-being. The hedonic link, in contrast, was no longer evident after adjusting for eudaimonic well-being. Using functional magnetic resonance imaging, van Reekum et al. (2007) further documented that those with higher eudaimonic well-being had slower response to aversive stimuli and reduced amygdala activation as well as greater activation of the ventral anterior cingulate cortex. The latter possibly helps explain what parts of the brain are recruited to minimize the impact of negative stimuli, thereby constituting beginning strides in delineating mechanistic underpinnings of well-being.

Growing interest has been shown in how well-being possibly serves as a moderating influence—that is, providing a buffer or protective factor against the negative effects of adverse experience on biology and health. Such inquiries build on prior work pointing to the importance of optimism, hope, and positive expectations in the face of health challenges (Leedham, Meyerowitz, Muirhead, & Frist, 1995; Scheier & Carver, 1992; Taylor, Kemeny, Reed, Bower, & Gruenewald, 2000). Indeed, unrealistic optimism about health predicted longer survival among HIV-positive men (Reed, Kemeny, Taylor, Wang, & Visscher, 1994). At the level of biological processes, our work has shown that older women with poor sleep efficiency (i.e., defined as time asleep divided by time in bed) had higher levels of IL-6 (Friedman et al., 2005). However, if they had the compensating influence of good social relationships, their levels of IL-6 were comparable to those individuals with high sleep efficiency. We also found that those with poor social relationships had lower IL-6 if they have the compensating benefits of good sleep, suggesting that each variable might serve to protect against low levels of the other.

In predicting glycosylated hemoglobin (also known as HbAlc), which is a marker of glycemic control pertinent to diabetes and cardiovascular disease, we also found that older women with lower levels of income showed greater increments in HbAlc across time (Tsenkova, Love, Singer, & Ryff, 2007) after controlling for sociodemographic and health factors. These effects were, however, moderated by purpose in life, personal growth, and positive affect. The pattern of effects underscored amplification of the negative: That is, those individuals showing the greatest cross-time negative increments in HbAlc had the combined disadvantage of low income and low well-being. It is important to note that for those subjects with high well-being, levels of HbAlc did not differ depending on economic status. In a related study, we have also documented that low positive affect also magnifies the negative effect of low problem-focused coping on cross-time levels of HbAlc (Tsenkova, Dienberg Love, Singer, & Ryff, 2008).

These examples underscore the ways in which well-being, by its presence, might serve to ameliorate the adverse effects of other factors on biology or might, by its absence, serve to exacerbate the negative effects of adverse experience on biology. Such questions point toward studies of the organism under challenge. This perspective invokes a much larger literature to which I now turn. Fewer of these studies are explicitly concerned with biology, but they point to promising directions for such inquiry.

Resilience in the Face of Adversity, Biological Underpinnings, and Interventions

Our previous work briefly noted the topic of resilience, which we have defined as the capacity to maintain (or regain) high well-being in the face of adversity (Ryff, Singer, Love, & Essex, 1998). Extensive literatures now address resilience in children, in the face of poverty or parental psychopathology, as well as resilience in later life, amid health challenges and loss of roles and significant others (Luthar, Cicchetti, & Becker, 2000; Masten, 1999; Ryff & Singer, 2002; Staudinger, Marsiske, & Baltes, 1995). A related literature addresses posttraumatic growth (Tedeschi et al., 1998) and underscores possible gains in self-perceptions, ties to others, and life philosophies that follow in the aftermath of trauma.

Our studies have focused on such diverse challenges as caregiving, community relocation, living with chronic health conditions, living with an alcoholic parent or spouse, and experiencing major depression (Heidrich & Ryff, 1993; Kling, Seltzer, & Ryff, 1997; Kwan, Love, Ryff, & Essex, 2003; Singer, Ryff, Carr, & Magee, 1998). Across all these, the evidence documents that some individuals are able to maintain, or regain, high levels of eudaimonic well-being as they negotiate such challenges. Similarly, in the context of the large literature on social inequalities in health (Adler, Marmot, McEwen, & Stewart, 1999), we have also shown that many such socioeconomically disadvantaged individuals nonetheless have high well-being (Markus, Ryff, Curhan, & Palmersheim, 2004). Further, despite the realities of racism, we have documented that many minority respondents have notably high eudaimonic well-being relative to their majority counterparts (Ryff, Keyes, & Hughes, 2003). Whether this kind of well-being in the face of challenge—the essence of resilience—is beneficial for biological regulation and health is less understood, although we have demonstrated that among men and women with persistently low economic standing from childhood to adulthood, those who had persistently high positive social relationships with significant others were less likely to have high allostatic load (a multisystem summary index of biological risk) in midlife compared to those who were both economically and psychosocially disadvantaged across time (Singer & Ryff, 1999). Understanding brain and biological processes that underlie such positive functioning in the face of challenge is the larger scientific frontier to which I now turn.

Charney (2004) has elaborated numerous possible mechanisms of resilience at psychobiological levels. Specifically, he delineates eleven neurochemical response patterns to acute stress involving cortisol, dehydroepiandrosterone (DHEA), corticotrophin-releasing hormone (CRH), locus coeruleus-norepinephrine system, neuropeptide Y, galanin, dopamine, serotonin (5-HT), benzodiazepine receptors, testosterone, and estrogen. Although many of these have been previously associated with psychopathology, Charney connects them to neural mechanisms of reward and motivation processes (hedonia, optimism, and learned helplessness), fear responsiveness (effective behaviors despite fear), and adaptive social behavior (altruism, bonding, and teamwork)—all relevant characteristics of resilience and hence valuable targets for future inquiry.

Dienstbier's (1989) formulation of "physiological toughness" is also relevant for understanding, at a mechanistic level, a pattern of arousal that works in combination with effective psychological coping to comprise positive physiological reactivity. Such toughness is characterized by low sympathetic nervous system (SNS) arousal base rates combined with strong, challenge-induced SNS-adrenal-medullary arousal, with resistance to brain catecholamine depletion and suppression of pituitary adrenal-cortical responses. Probing the connections between these patterns and related psychosocial strengths in the face of challenge is a much needed direction in the neurobiology of resilience. I note, however, that one of the key difficulties in studying the biology of resilience is that most biomarker data collection takes place after a challenge occurs. Without baseline prior assessments it is difficult to say, from the perspective of biological systems, exactly what are the indicators of resilience.

A notable exception is a study of U.S. Special Forces and Navy Seals in training who undergo severe stressful challenges (National Center for PTSD, 2005). These individuals are selected for special training and could be expected to show high levels of resilience. In a training session involving mock prisoner-of-war camp settings and accompanying psychological and physical stressors, biomarkers were collected (pre-, during-, and postchallenge). During the initial interrogation phase, cortisol, norepinephrine, and neuropeptide Y levels were found to substantially increase. Neuropeptide Y has been found in animal challenge studies to counteract the effects of norepinephrine, thereby restoring the animal to prechallenge levels. A sustained neuropeptide Y response relative to norepinephrine was seen in both the U.S. Special Forces and Navy Seals in the prisoner-of-war camp study, thereby leading to a return, postchallenge, of norepinephrine to the prechallenge levels. A further interaction showed a high and sustained DHEA response relative to the cortisol response. This resulted in a high DHEA-to-cortisol ratio, which pointed to the capacity of DHEA to counteract the cortisol elevations in the face of a highly stressful challenge.

The foregoing biological responses are suggestive of what could be hypothesized to characterize resilient individuals who do well in the face of many forms of challenge. Identifying these biological responses does not by itself, however, provide linkage to the well-being characteristics of resilient persons. Moving in this direction, the study of U.S. Special Forces and Navy Seals was supplemented by a study of 750 Vietnam War veterans who were prisoners of war and did not develop posttraumatic stress disorder (PTSD) or depression (National Center for PTSD, 2005). This inquiry contained extensive psychological assessments. Ten critical elements characterized these resilient veterans: (a) optimism, (b) altruism, (c) having a set of moral beliefs that could not easily be changed, (d) faith and spirituality, (e) a sense of humor, (f) having a role model as a basis for drawing strength, (g) having social supports from family or close friends in the period following release from prison, (h) an ability to face fear, (i) having a sense of purpose and meaning in life, and (j) having had training to develop resilience by meeting and overcoming challenges. Thus, the combined story is that of linkages between successful adaptation to stressful challenge, related biological substrates, and psychological characteristics reflective of existential well-being, as emphasized throughout this chapter.

Turning to the question of interventions, a key question is whether well-being can be promoted and enhanced, particularly among those individuals who do not naturally possess such life outlooks. Here I note the literature on prevention of relapse among people who suffer from recurrent depression or anxiety disorders. This is the work of Fava and colleagues (Fava, 1996; Fava, Rafanelli, Grandi, Conti, & Belluardo, 1998; Fava & Ruini, 2003), which involves "well-being therapy" based on connections to the previously described formulation of eudaimonic well-being. The goal of the therapist is to lead the patient from an impaired to a high level on the six dimensions of psychological well-being (i.e., autonomy, environmental mastery, personal growth, positive relations with others, purpose in life, and self-acceptance).

The therapy itself consists of a short-term protocol that extends over eight sessions, which may take place every week or every other week. The duration of each session may range from 30 to 50 minutes. The technique emphasizes self-observation, by means of keeping a structured daily diary, and interaction between patient and therapist about the diary entries. Sessions are in three phases: First is an initial phase focused on identifying, from daily experience, episodes of positive well-being and setting them in a situational context, no matter how short lived they were. Next are intermediate sessions, where the patient is encouraged to identify thoughts and beliefs leading to premature interruption of well-being. In contrast to standard cognitive-behavioral therapy, the trigger for self-observation in well-being therapy is the client's positive feelings and experiences instead of the distress. Final sessions allow monitoring of the course of episodes of well-being, which in turn allows the therapist to realize specific impairments in well-being dimensions and pay particular attention to them.

Fava et al. (2006) carried out an assessment of well-being therapy in a randomized trial of 40 patients with recurrent depression who had previously been treated with antidepressant drugs. Patients were randomly assigned to either cognitive-behavioral treatment of residual symptoms supplemented by well-being therapy and lifestyle modification or clinical management. In both groups, antidepressant drugs were tapered or discontinued. A six-year follow-up was undertaken. During this period no antidepressant drugs were used unless a relapse occurred. Cognitive behavioral therapy supplemented with well-being therapy and lifestyle modification resulted in a significantly lower relapse rate (40%) after six years than did the clinical-management group (90%).

This trial requires replication on a larger sample. However, the results suggest that the sequential use of cognitive-behavioral therapy, supplemented by well-being therapy and lifestyle modification after pharmacological cotherapy may improve the long-term outcome among those suffering from recurrent major depression. The question that arises, pertinent to neurobiology, is what does well-being therapy do to the brain? For this, I note evidence on structural plasticity in the brain, referred to as remodeling of dendrites in the hippocampus, which is at present investigated only in animal studies. In rats, cognitive-restraint stress (CRS) causes retraction and simplification of dendrites in the CA3 region of the hippocampus, a process which is reversible (McEwen, 1999). Well-being therapy could possibly promote such reversals in persons who would otherwise be prone to recurrent depression. In rats, a reduction in richness of dendrites in the hippocampus is reversible if CRS is terminated at the end of three weeks (McEwen, 2005). A human analogue might be that early application of well-being therapy following effective pharmacological treatment and staged withdrawal may stimulate enrichment of dendritic networks. The tentative nature of this proposal is obvious, given the need for noninvasive studies in humans that demonstrate dendrite remodeling, an agenda for which the requisite technology remains to be developed. Thus, the full scope of scientific linkages suggested here is well down the road, although I am encouraged by the pace of empirical advances occurring over the past decade. To reiterate the opening observations—when I wrote this chapter ten years ago, there was essentially no literature on the neurobiology of well-being or resilience.

Summary

The objective of this chapter has been to distill current approaches to the study of human well-being and explicate their linkages to biology for the purpose of probing whether having high existential or hedonic well-being promotes better health. Although much of the evidence is correlational in nature, making it difficult to discern causal directionality, a growing body of research documents that higher well-being is linked with lower stress hormones, lower inflammatory response, better immune function, and lower cardiovascular risk. How well-being is instantiated in neural circuitry is also under investigation, with recent findings suggesting possible mechanisms whereby certain parts of the brain serve to reduce activation of other structures when the organism is confronted with negative stimuli.

The growing literature on resilience sharpens the foregoing inquiries by bringing challenge and adversity into the scientific formulation. Thus, it is well-being in the face of life's difficulties that is the essential scientific focus. This was, of course, the starting point for Frankl's (1946/1992) seminal work. His observations about those who prevail and, indeed, survive in contexts of overwhelming trauma remain a persistent focus of scientific inquiry. More than a half century later, much more is known about characteristics of individuals who are resilient in the confrontation of chronic and acute life challenges, as well as about individuals who, in fact, grow and are strengthened in the wake of adverse experience. Fortunately, individuals with expertise in complex biological systems and neuroscience now also enter into these investigations, such that underlying mechanistic processes (e.g., how certain neurochemical factors modulate or offset the negative influence of others) are now coming into focus. Thus, the time is auspicious for pushing forward the frontiers of existential well-being and health.

Perhaps most important, studies are emerging that suggest well-being itself can be promoted and advanced, including among those people who least frequently experience it. Thus, the scientific agenda described herein is broad in scope and comes with intriguing possibilities for improving the human condition—both as it is subjectively experienced and as it is internally processed by the brain and the body.

References

Adler, N. E., Marmot, M. G., McEwen, B. S., & Stewart, J. (1999). *Socioeconomic status and health in industrialized nations: Social, psychological, and biological pathways* (Vol. 896). New York, NY: New York Academy of Sciences.

Allport, G. W. (1961). *Pattern and growth in personality*. New York, NY: Holt, Rinehart, & Winston.

Andrews, F. M., & Withey, S. B. (1976). *Social indicators of well-being: America's perception of life quality*. New York, NY: Plenum Press.

Aristotle. (1925). Nicomachean ethics (W. D. Ross, Trans.). In R. McKeon (Ed.), *Introduction to Aristotle*. New York, NY: Modern Library.

Bradburn, N. M. (1969). *The structure of psychological well-being*. Chicago, IL: Aldine.

Bryant, F. B., & Veroff, J. (1982). The structure of psychological well-being: A sociohistorical analysis. *Journal of Personality & Social Psychology, 43*, 653–673.

Bühler, C. (1935). The curve of life as studied in biographies. *Journal of Applied Psychology, 43*, 653–673.

Bühler, C., & Massarik, F. (Eds.). (1968). *The course of human life*. New York, NY: Springer.

Campbell, A., Converse, P. E., & Rodgers, W. L. (1976). *The quality of American life: Perceptions, evaluations, and satisfactions*. New York, NY: Russell Sage Foundation.

Cantril, H. (1965). *The pattern of human concerns*. New Brunswick, NJ: Rutgers University Press.

Charney, D. S. (2004). Psychobiological mechanisms of resilience and vulnerability: Implications for successful adaptation to extreme stress. *American Journal of Psychiatry, 161*(2), 195–215.

Cohen, S., Alpen, C. M., Doyle, W. J., Treanor, J. J., & Turner, R. B. (2006). Positive emotional style predicts resistance to illness after experimental exposure to rhinovirus or influenza A virus. *Psychosomatic Medicine, 68*, 809–815.

Cohen, S., Doyle, W. J., Turner, R. B., Alper, C. M., & Skoner, D. P. (2003). Emotional style and susceptibility to the common cold. *Psychosomatic Medicine, 65*, 652–657.

Davidson, R. J. (2003). Affective neuroscience and psychophysiology: Toward a synthesis. *Psychophysiology, 40*, 655–665.

Davidson, R. J. (2004). Well-being and affective style: Neural substrates and Biobehavioural correlates. *Philosophical Transactions of the Royal Society* (London), *359*, 1395–1411.

Diener, E. (1984). Subjective well-being. *Psychological Bulletin*, *95*, 542–575.

Diener, E., Suh, E. M., Lucas, R. E., & Smith, H. L. (1999). Subjective well-being: Three decades of progress. *Psychological Bulletin*, *125*(2), 276–302.

Dienstbier, R. A. (1989). Arousal and physiological toughness: Implications for mental and physical health. *Psychological Review*, *96*, 84–100.

Erikson, E. H. (1959). Identity and the life cycle: Selected papers. *Psychological Issues*, *1*, 1–171.

Fava, G. (1996). The concept of recovery in affective disorders. *Psychotherapy & Psychosomatics*, *65*, 2–13.

Fava, G. A., Rafanelli, C., Grandi, S., Conti, S., & Belluardo, P. (1998). Prevention of recurrent depression with cognitive behavioral therapy. *Archives of General Psychiatry*, *55*, 816–821.

Fava, G., & Ruini, C. (2003). Development and characteristics of a well-being enhancing psychotherapeutic strategy: Well-being therapy. *Journal of Behavior Therapy & Experimental Psychiatry*, *34*, 45–63.

Fava, G., Ruini, C., Rafanelli, C., Finos, L., Conti, S., & Grandi, S. (2006). Six-year outcome of cognitive behavioral therapy for prevention of recurrent depression. *American Journal of Psychiatry*, *161*, 1872–1876.

Frankl, V. E. (1992). *Man's search for meaning: An introduction to logotherapy* (I. Lasch, Trans.). Boston, MA: Beacon Press. (Originally published 1946)

Friedman, E. M., Hayney, M. S., Love, G. D., Singer, B. H., & Ryff, C. D. (2007). Plasma interleukin-6 and soluble IL-6 receptors are associated with psychological well-being in aging women. *Health Psychology*, *26*(3), 305–313.

Friedman, E. M., Hayney, M. S., Love, G. D., Urry, H. L., Rosenkranz, M. A., Davidson, R. J.,… Ryff, C. D. (2005). Social relationships, sleep quality, and interleukin-6 in aging women. *Proceedings of the National Academy of Sciences*, *102*, 18757–18762.

Gurin, G., Veroff, J., & Feld, S. (1960). *Americans view their mental health: A nationwide interview survey*. Oxford, England: Basic Books.

Heidrich, S. M., & Ryff, C. D. (1993). Physical and mental health in later life: The self-system as mediator. *Psychology & Aging*, *8*(3), 327–338.

Jahoda, M. (1958). *Current concepts of positive mental health*. New York, NY: Basic Books.

Jung, C. G. (1933). *Modern man in search of a soul* (W. S. Dell & C. F. Baynes, Trans.). New York, NY: Harcourt, Brace & World.

Kahneman, D., Diener, E., & Schwarz, N. (Eds.). (1999). *Well-being: The foundations of hedonic psychology*. New York, NY: Russell Sage Foundation.

Keyes, C. L. M., Shmotkin, D., & Ryff, C. D. (2002). Optimizing well-being: The empirical encounter of two traditions. *Journal of Personality & Social Psychology*, *82*(6), 1007–1022.

Kling, K. C., Seltzer, M. M., & Ryff, C. D. (1997). Distinctive late-life challenges: Implications for coping and well-being. *Psychology & Aging*, *12*(2), 288–295.

Kwan, C. M. L., Love, G. D., Ryff, C. D., & Essex, M. J. (2003). The role of self-enhancing evaluations in a successful life transition. *Psychology & Aging*, *18*(1), 3–12.

Leedham, B., Meyerowitz, B. E., Muirhead, J., & Frist, W. H. (1995). Positive expectations predict health after heart transplantation. *Health Psychology*, *14*, 74–79.

Lindfors, P., & Lundberg, U. (2002). Is low cortisol release an indicator of positive health? *Stress & Health: Journal of the International Society for the Investigation of Stress*, *18*(4), 153–160.

Luthar, S. S., Cicchetti, D., & Becker, B. (2000). The construct of resilience: A critical evaluation and guidelines for future work. *Child Development, 71*, 543–562.

Markus, H. R., Ryff, C. D., Curhan, K. B., & Palmersheim, K. A. (2004). In their own words: Well-being at midlife among high school–educated and college-educated adults. In O. G. Brim, C. D. Ryff, & R. C. Kessler (Eds.), *How healthy are we? A national study of well-being at midlife* (pp. 273–319). Chicago, IL: University of Chicago Press.

Marsland, A. L., Cohen, S., Rabin, B. S., & Manuck, S. B. (2006). Trait positive affect and antibody response to hepatitis B vaccination. *Brain, Behavior, & Immunity, 20*, 261–269.

Maslow, A. H. (1968). *Toward a psychology of being* (2nd ed.). New York, NY: Van Nostrand.

Masten, A. S. (1999). Resilience comes of age: Reflections on the past and outlook for the next generation of research. In M. D. Glantz & J. L. Johnson (Eds.), *Resilience and development: Positive life adaptations* (Vol. 14, pp. 281–296). Dordrecht, Netherlands: Kluwer Academic.

McEwen, B. S. (1999). Stress and hippocampal plasticity. *Annual Reviews of Neuroscience, 22*, 105–122.

McEwen, B. S. (2005). Glucocorticoids, depression, and mood disorders: Structural remodeling in the brain. *Metabolism: Clinical & Experimental, 54*(Suppl. 1), 20–23.

National Center for PTSD. (2005). *Resilience & recovery: 16th annual report*. Washington, DC: Department of Veterans Affairs.

Neugarten, B. L. (1968). The awareness of middle age. In B. L. Neugarten (Ed.), *Middle age and aging* (pp. 93–98). Chicago, IL: University of Chicago Press.

Neugarten, B. L. (1973). Personality change in late life: A developmental perspective. In C. Eisodorfer & M. P. Lawton (Eds.), *The psychology of adult development and aging* (pp. 311–335). Washington, DC: American Psychological Association.

Norton, D. L. (1976). *Personal destinies: A philosophy of ethical individualism*. Princeton, NJ: Princeton University Press.

O'Connor, E. (1993). *The essential Epicurus*. New York: Prometheus Books.

Polk, D. E., Cohen, S., & Doyle, W. J. (2005). State and trait affect as predictors of salivary cortisol in healthy adults. *Psychoneuroendocrinology, 30*(3), 261–272.

Pressman, S. D., & Cohen, S. (2005). Does positive affect influence health? *Psychological Bulletin, 131*(6), 925–971.

Reed, G. M., Kemeny, M. E., Taylor, S. E., Wang, H.-Y., & Visscher, B. R. (1994). Realistic acceptance as a predictor of decreased survival time in gay men with AIDS. *Health Psychology, 13*, 299–307.

Rogers, C. R. (1962). The interpersonal relationship: The core of guidance. *Harvard Educational Review, 32*(4), 416–429.

Rosen, A. (2003). Evidence-based social work practice: Challenges and promises. *Social Work Research, 27*(4), 197–208.

Russell, B. (1958). *The conquest of happiness*. New York, NY: Liveright. (Originally published 1930)

Ryan, R. M., & Deci, E. L. (2001). On happiness and human potentials: A review of research on hedonic and eudaimonic well-being. *Annual Review of Psychology, 52*, 141–166.

Ryan, R. M., Huta, V., & Deci, E. L. (2008). Living well: A self-determination theory perspective on eudaimonia. *Journal of Happiness Studies, 9*(1), 139–170.

Ryff, C. D. (1989). Happiness is everything, or is it? Explorations on the meaning of psychological well-being. *Journal of Personality & Social Psychology, 57*(6), 1069–1081.

Ryff, C. D., & Keyes, C. L. M. (1995). The structure of psychological well-being revisited. *Journal of Personality & Social Psychology, 69*(4), 719–727.

Ryff, C. D., Keyes, C. L. M., & Hughes, D. L. (2003). Status inequalities, perceived discrimination, and eudaimonic well-being: Do the challenges of minority life hone purpose and growth? *Journal of Health & Social Behavior, 44*(3), 275–291.

Ryff, C. D., Love, G. D., Urry, H. L., Muller, D., Rosenkranz, M. A., Friedman, E. M.,... Singer, B. (2006). Psychological well-being and ill-being: Do they have distinct or mirrored biological correlates? *Psychotherapy & Psychosomatics, 75*, 85–95.

Ryff, C. D., & Singer, B. H. (1998). The contours of positive human health. *Psychological Inquiry, 9*(1), 1–28.

Ryff, C. D., & Singer, B. H. (2000). Interpersonal flourishing: A positive health agenda for the new millennium. *Personality and Social Psychology Review: Personality and Social Psychology at the Interface: New Directions for Interdisciplinary Research* [Special issue], *4*(1), 30–44.

Ryff, C. D., & Singer, B. H. (Eds.). (2001). *Emotion, social relationships, and health.* New York, NY: Oxford University Press.

Ryff, C. D., & Singer, B. H. (2002). Ironies of the human condition: Well-being and health on the way to mortality. In L. G. Aspinwall & U. M. Staudinnger (Eds.), *A psychology of human strengths: Perspectives on an emerging field* (pp. 271–287). Washington, DC: American Psychological Association.

Ryff, C. D., & Singer, B. (2003). Thriving in the face of challenge: The integrative science of human resilience. In F. Kessel & P. L. Rosenfield (Eds.), *Expanding the boundaries of health and social science: Case studies in interdisciplinary innovation* (pp. 181–205). New York, NY: Oxford University Press.

Ryff, C. D., & Singer, B. H. (2008). Know thyself and become what you are: A eudaimonic approach to psychological well-being. *Journal of Happiness Studies, 9*(1), 13–39.

Ryff, C. D., Singer, B. H., & Love, G. D. (2004). Positive health: Connecting well-being with biology. *Philosophical Transactions of the Royal Society of London Series B, 359*, 1383–1394.

Ryff, C. D., Singer, B. H., Love, G. D., & Essex, M. J. (1998). Resilience in adulthood and later life: Defining features and dynamic processes. In J. Lomranz (Ed.), *Handbook of aging and mental health: An integrative approach* (pp. 69–96). New York, NY: Plenum Press.

Scheier, M. F., & Carver, C. S. (1992). Effects of optimism on psychological and physical well-being: Theoretical overview and empirical update. *Cognitive Therapy & Research, 16*, 201–228.

Singer, B. H., & Ryff, C. D. (1999). Hierarchies of life histories and associated health risks. In N. E. Adler & M. Marmot (Eds.), *Socioeconomic status and health in industrial nations: Social, psychological, and biological pathways* (Vol. 896, pp. 96–115). New York, NY: New York Academy of Sciences.

Singer, B. H., Ryff, C. D., Carr, D., & Magee, W. J. (1998). Life histories and mental health: A person-centered strategy. In A. Raftery (Ed.), *Sociological methodology* (pp. 1–51). Washington, DC: American Sociological Association.

Staudinger, U. M., Marsiske, M., & Baltes, P. B. (1995). Resilience and reserve capacity in later adulthood: Potentials and limits of development across the life span. In D. Cicchetti & D. Cohen (Eds.), *Developmental psychopathology: Band 2. Risk, disorder and adaptation* (pp. 801–847). New York, NY: Wiley.

Steptoe, A., Gibson, E. L., Hamer, M., & Wardle, J. (2006). Neuroendocrine and cardiovascular correlates of positive affect measured by ecological momentary assessment and by questionnaire. *Psychoneuroendocrinology, 32*, 56–74.

Steptoe, A., Wardle, J., & Marmot, M. (with McEwen, B. S.). (2005). Positive affect and health-related neuroendocrine, cardiovascular, and inflammatory processes. *PNAS: Proceedings of the National Academy of Sciences of the United States of America, 102*(18), 6508–6512.

Taylor, S. E., Kemeny, M. E., Reed, G. M., Bower, J. E., & Gruenewald, T. L. (2000). Psychological resources, positive illusions, and health. *American Psychologist, 55*, 99–109.

Tedeschi, R. G., Park, C. L., & Calhoun, L. G. (Eds.). (1998). *Posttraumatic growth: Positive changes in the aftermath of crisis.* Mahwah, NJ: Erlbaum.

Tsenkova, V. K., Dienberg Love, G., Singer, B. H., & Ryff, C. D. (2008). Coping and positive affect predict longitudinal change in glycosylated hemoglobin. *Health Psychology, 27*(Suppl. 2), S163–S171.

Tsenkova, V. K., Love, G. D., Singer, B. H., & Ryff, C. D. (2007). Socioeconomic status and psychological well-being predict cross-time change in glycosylated hemoglobin in older women without diabetes. *Psychosomatic Medicine, 69*(8), 777–784.

Urry, H. L., Nitschke, J. B., Dolski, I., Jackson, D. C., Dalton, K. M., Mueller, C. J.,... Davidson, R. J. (2004). Making a life worth living: Neural correlates of well-being. *Psychological Science, 15*(6), 367–372.

Van Reekum, C. M., Urry, H. L., Johnstone, T., Thurow, M. E., Frye, C. J., Jackson, C. A.,... Davidson, R. J. (2007). Individual differences in amygdala and ventromedial prefrontal cortex activity are associated with evaluation speed and psychological well-being. *Journal of Cognitive Neuroscience, 19*(2), 237–248.

12

Relational Buddhism

A Psychological Quest for Meaning and Sustainable Happiness

MAURITS G. T. KWEE

Taos Institute

The quest for happiness has always been a central topic in the Buddhist tradition since its inception some 2,600 years ago. As expounded by the historical Buddha in his way, known as *Dharma*, the focus is on practical methods to liberate human beings from emotional suffering as imposed by existential misery as a result of "the slings and arrows of outrageous *mis*fortune." The Buddha provided his students with a number of meditation practices enabling freedom from attachments through modifying activities, which meaningful intentional activity, or *Karma*, one is not always aware of. Most notable and currently well known is the technique of *mindfulness meditation*, meant to awaken the mind, thereby enabling the individual to become aware of the *Dependent Origination* of correlated fluctuations of what the Buddha summarized as *Body/Speech/Mind* phenomena (thus spelled to communicate the wholeness of the referents to which the concept alludes). Functionally interlinked, they manifest as feeling, thought, and action on the intrapersonal level and in *Relational Interbeing* (elaborated later) on the interpersonal level. The essence of mindfulness is not to prescribe morality but to train introspection, that is, to observe and describe preconceptual experience (i.e., before a conceptual subject–object dualistic division sets in), in order to be aware of Dependent Origination and Karma, whose daily rebirths depend on a willy-nilly choosing and interpersonal relating.

The pinnacle of the Buddha's training method is to instill the embodied social practices of loving kindness (or warm friendliness), empathic compassion (which is not pity), and shared joy (which is not laughing at someone). These practices come to maturity in equanimity or even-minded balance (which is not indifference) through meditation in action (which is not navel staring). These practices have the potential to provide sustainable happiness, a graceful, blissful happiness of being at ease within oneself and with significant others despite existential suffering. Thus, from a Buddhist point of view, meaning is derived from warm friendliness, compassionate caring, and harmonious relationships in balance with oneself in order to eventually secure everyone's enjoyment of a relative sane and happy life on the planet. This Buddhist variant of positive psychology is based on the ubiquitous principle of Dependent Origination, which accommodates the negative in life by discarding as a pseudo issue the dichotomy of positive versus negative values. Balancing the yin-and-yang, Buddhist psychology offers within its scope the idea that happiness is a relative quality that codependently originates with unhappiness and that therefore it cannot possibly exist in an absolute sense or in isolation.

In striving to cater to the masses, pious and "sky-god" devotional habits and rituals have crept into the pristine Dharma, which began as a nontheistic discipline declaring that the existence or nonexistence of a god is anathema. Thus, when the Dharma was encountered and thoroughly studied by Western scholars in the 19th century, it was categorized in Western terminology and inferred as a religion and a metaphysical philosophy; whereas in today's terminology, it can also be classified, and more appropriately so, as an applied psychology. Buddhist psychology matches best with relatively sane people seeking wisdom who, in the absence of severe psychopathology, advertently wish to deal with existential neurosis, which is a type of emotional suffering resulting from the adversities of life itself (e.g., illness, aging, death, and birth). The first to recognize that the Dharma is a secular psychology was C. Rhys Davids (1900), who wrote on Buddhist psychology based on a Pali scriptural text, a small part of the higher teachings known as the *Abhidhamma*, the third canonical book written by numerous anonymous scholars post the Buddha until the fifth century. Since then the Dharma is also viewed as a psychology; however, until today only by a minority. Recently Buddhist psychology came out of this fringe position to become accepted by mainstream psychologists (e.g., Gyatso & Beck, 2006; Kwee & Ellis, 1997; Kwee, Gergen, & Koshikawa, 2006).

The present account reformulates the Dharma as a 21st-century New Buddhist Psychology. Going beyond the psychology of the *Abhidhamma*, this new Buddhism is a social, clinical, and neuropsychology based on a social constructionist view of the Dharma that reconstitutes the mind as a manifestation of relationships. In the framework of a *Relational Buddhism*, it emphasizes the empty nature of *Transcendental Truth* and expounds Relational Interbeing, which corroborates the Buddhist *not-self*. Grounded in an understanding that relational processes stand prior to the very concept of the individual, the psychology of social construction turns out to concur with the Dharma. In developing a relational account of human activity, this chapter provides tools to redefine and re-vision ingrained religious and metaphysical views of the Dharma. (Extended accounts can be found in Kwee, 2008; Kwee & Kwee-Taams, 2006a, 2006b; the main tenets in this chapter are derived from Kwee, 2010).

Dharma and Psychology

From a Buddhist perspective, the greatest progress in psychology as a science is the unveiling of illusions blurring our daily lives. Illusions are ubiquitous, part of human nature, and mostly beyond our control. Well known are the various optical illusions (e.g., Müller-Lyer, 1894). At this point in evolution, self-deception is inherent in the human condition as a result of our limited and sometimes deficient mental apparatus. For instance, healthy people tend to underestimate the likelihood for future injury or illness that runs counter to the known statistics (unrealistic optimism), whereas depressed individuals seem to have a more realistic outlook toward risks (realistic pessimism). Generally, one is biased to becoming truncated by the positive illusion of optimism, which is not disadvantageous per se: Viewing oneself in a favorable manner is a sign of well-being (Taylor, 1989).

A traditional understanding of positivity—that is, a dual or polar understanding of what is positive—is that it coexists with negativity like the flip side of one coin (P. T. P. Wong, personal communication). However, what is considered to be positive or negative is, on deeper reflection, far from static. As one man's meat could be another man's poison, for example, for what is positive depends on the dynamics of relativity. Thus, positivity as a dualistic construction is an illusion. Existing by the grace of negativity, positivity is an abstraction that is personal, relative, and seemingly irreducible to neurology. To avoid an illusory positive, a Buddhist view proposes to "see things as they become," a seeing that strips off all illusions, including I, me, and mine self-identifications considered to be false. Less known but probably having a big impact on our trade is that the Dharma views "true self" as an illusion. Such self has to be unmasked to make a science of Buddhist psychology possible at all. Peeling away the "false self" layer by layer by digging into it deeper and deeper and putting aside conditionings and instincts, both Buddhist psychology and mainstream psychology could not find a nucleus or essence of a true self. Brain research fails to detect a CEO mastermind or some homunculus (Feinberg, 2000). Even though thought and affect have their equivalents in functional hard-wired processes in diversely activated and widely distributed areas of the brain, there is nobody and nothing of a static substance inside behind our eyeballs. It is therefore appropriate to say "*it* senses, feels, thinks, behaves," and so on, similar to "it rains," as advised in mindful awareness meditation. The fruit of mindfulness is the ability to see penetratingly and understand thoroughly that emptiness is in the core of true self. This ability is called an *awakening* to Buddhahood. Awakening is fostered by cultivating "pure" perception, which precedes "intuitive" perception and "reasoned" perception. It was in the interface of the latter two types of perception that Kahneman (2003) conducted his cognitive-behavioral research on decision making, for which he was awarded a joint Nobel Prize in Economics.

Buddhist psychology makes a distinction between a relative and an ultimate level of reality. The existence of a relative or "provisional" self as an abstract construction is not denied; neither is the referential use of the term *self* incorrect (as in *myself* or *oneself*). The Buddha used the metaphor of the lute to elucidate self's emptiness. Music can be produced only by the unique combination of its constituents, the strings, box, and bow. Thus, the whole is more than the sum of its parts. In the same vein, a mind deconstructed in its modalities (i.e., feeling, thinking, doing) disintegrates like a decomposed body. It is like a chariot that is nothing but a temporary assemblage of its constituent components. Where does inherent essence or quality reside if a bike is torn apart in its 10,000 pieces? Such is also the fate of a self that is composed of modalities when deconstructed. Emptiness is what ultimately underlies the illusion of self where one's identifications with a name, birthday, or passport provide the magic of solid continuity where there is none. To contend the ultimate, the Buddha expounded the wisdom of the "Three Empirical Marks of Existence" (Kwee, 2003):

1. The world is in a flux of impermanence whereby nothing remains the same; thus the true nature of things is empty.
2. Constituting Body/Speech/Mind, the self—existing in impermanence—lacks inherent existence and is thus also empty.
3. Because of craving for permanence and perfection and the concomitant behaviors of grasping and clinging, existential neurosis emanates.

The Buddha started his quest by deeply empathizing with existential suffering and its causes, contended that they can cease, discovered how to cease painful emotions, and pointed on top at the cultivation of what is known as the prime Buddhist values: genuine kindness, compassion, and joy. Whereas positive psychology seeks happiness by living a hedonic, engaged, and meaningful life, a Buddhist perspective adds something more; Kwee (1990) submitted what has become a foundational tenet of positive psychology:

> Up until now, psychological interventions and psychotherapy were mainly directed at eliminating negative conditions rather than promoting positive experiences, let alone spirituality. If psychology wishes to prevent and treat disease effectively, it will be necessary to develop new methods and instruments. (pp. 14–15)

Buddhist psychology thus preceded positive psychology in making the shift from negativity, or being problem-centered and working to repairing damage, toward positivity, emphasizing appreciation and enlarging assets through meditation in action.

Research in positive psychology pointed out that the eudaimonic life, that is, one that is engaged and meaningful, is significantly satisfying ($p < 0.001$;

Seligman, 2004); whereas the hedonic life is only marginally satisfying. Hedonic pleasures—ecstasy, rapture, orgasm, thrills, and the like—habituate like chocolate. Joy ensued from winning a lottery does not warrant lasting happiness. Prolongation of happiness requires not only dishabituation and amplification by skillfully spacing, varying, and savoring but also mindfulness. The inclusion of the latter is not surprising considering its favorable outcome (e.g., Baer, 2003; Grossman, Niemann, Schmidt, & Walach, 2004; Shigaki, Glass, & Schopp, 2006; Toneatto & Nguyen, 2007). From a Buddhist perspective, the Disney-like pleasure of raw feeling (momentary thrills) is relative and to be enjoyed but not grasped or clung to. If the temporariness and inherent lack of satisfaction of hedonism are not understood, craving and greed are its consequences. These are hindrances in striving toward the authentic happiness that will naturally appear if one is truly liberated from hoarding and attachment. Contentment, the middle ground between joy and sorrow, reflects the Buddhist way of life that concurs with "chaironic happiness," a term coined by Wong (http://www.meaning.ca), which, in contrast to hedonic and eudaimonic happiness, is not related to positive events or personal virtue but refers to happiness amid adversities.

The Buddha: A Psychologist?

Needless to say, "psychology" and "psychologist" were concepts that did not exist in the Buddha's time. Psychology as a science emerged out of religion and philosophy and is based on Descartes' 17th-century artificial split of mind and body. This discipline formally started in 1879, when Wundt opened the first psychological laboratory in Germany. There is an interesting analogy with the present status of the Dharma, which even today is usually regarded only as a religion and a metaphysical philosophy or, at best, as a philosophical psychology, whereas it might better be inferred as a combined applied social, clinical, and neuropsychology. At this juncture in history, we are on the verge of transforming the Dharma from *Theravada* (the teaching of the Elders, one of 18 early Buddhist schools extant; practiced in Sri Lanka and Southeast Asia) and *Mahayana* (the "great" vehicle that allowed metaphysics to slip through the back door; practiced in the Himalayas and northern Asia), into a *Neoyana* (a term to denote the new vehicle of contemporary psychology) within the framework of the Buddha's "skillful method" (*Upayakaushalya*), which allows the Dharma to adjust itself to changing mentalities across times and cultures. Upaya legitimizes the Dharma's past variegated appearances as a religion and as a philosophy as well as its present manifestation as a psychology. Indeed, seeds of psychology can be traced in various passages of the Buddha's discourses (http://www.metta.lk).

The Buddha dealt with self (or rather not-self), which is a core subject in psychology. Unlike the proliferation of self psychologies, Buddhist psychology is the only not-self psychology to date. This could well become a foundation to establish a unified science of psychology, similar to what has been established in the exact sciences, where we find one science of physics, chemistry, and biology. As in the "Three Empirical Marks of Existence," the Buddha observed that suffering develops as a result of existence's pervasive impermanence and that the illusion of a perfect self, the I, me, and mine, comes about by clinging to a nonfoundational, empty concept. Because one's craving for permanence and grasping for perfection are in vain, the Buddhist advice is to detach from an eternal self or soul and to admit a self only as a provisional device. Such a relative or empirical self serves a practical purpose; it acts as an index in daily life as does, for instance, having a name or an ID card. The Buddhist awakening implies the in-depth understanding that ultimately, there is no self. Whatever one says about an identified I, me, mine, or self, it cannot ever be the same in the next moment of a flux. Self is thus empty and cannot be something else than an airy, reified abstraction that cannot be captured in a nonabiding world. Awakening to not-self does not imply that one becomes an out-of-orbit, aimless, and vegetating organism without any desires; on the contrary, "empty of self," one preferably leads a life full of affect. It is incumbent to admonish practitioners not to confuse their clients, who may be plagued by a distorted self-image or self-concept, by focusing on not-self. As exemplified in the following anecdote (Kwee & Holdstock, 1996), the Buddha's life was lived conventionally as well:

> Once, the Buddha spent a rainy night in a tavern. The inn-keeper was an opponent of the Dharma. To test the Buddha he gave him a room with a leaking roof. When the Buddha asked for another room, the keeper sarcastically asked: "How can a little bit of water disturb someone who has conquered all suffering?" The Buddha smiled and countered: "Indeed, a little water means nothing for someone who has conquered suffering, but if I want to sleep I don't want to swim."

Another pointer indicating that the Buddha is a psychologist and that his Dharma can be inferred as an applied psychology is the illness metaphor in the awareness of the *4-Ennobling Realities*: namely, (a) there is suffering, to be understood (diagnosis); (b) suffering is a consequence of ignorance, to be abandoned (cause); (c) there is a way out of suffering, to be realized (prognosis); and (d) this exit comprises an *8-Fold Balanced Practice*, to be cultivated (therapy). This eightfold practice is indicated here as "balanced" view, intention, speech, action, living, effort, mindfulness, and attention. The metaphorical illness refers to a *dis*-ease of the mind rather than to a physical disorder, and the cure is not the prescription of medication but the practice of meditation in order to act, think, and feel wholesomely (Kwee & Holdstock, 1996). The prime *dis*-eases alluded to in the Dharma are the three poisons greed, hatred, and ignorance (on the working of the psyche), which are to be *dis*-solved by increasing the positive qualities of kindness, compassion, and joy through daily balanced practice guided by a keen teacher.

The Buddha's holistic notion of Body/Speech/Mind concurs with the view of a 21st-century mental health professional who endorses the World Health Organization's definition of a human being as a bio-, psycho-, and social system (Engel, 1977). Karma (as noted earlier, intentional and meaningful action) impacts anyone's Body/Speech/Mind as cause and as effect and requires to be dealt with in a "this-worldly" manner. After all, according to the Buddha, "in this fathom-long living body with perceptions and thoughts lays the world, the arising and cessation of the world" (http://www.metta.lk). Obviously, by "the world" is meant not the world out there (in the Buddha's era of the iron age conceived as flat) or somewhere in the beyond but the world within the meditator's psyche with its data, called *dharmas*, the smallest units of experience, which include "perceivables" and "thinkables" continuingly entering our sense doors. These units are observable in mindfulness meditation. Because the Buddha dealt with the psyche and its concomitants, his applied psychology will strike the reader as his prime topic. Furthermore, the Buddha not only discarded religion by discarding the god delusions of Brahmin, the Hindu holy men, but also definitely showed no interest in metaphysics (http://www.metta.lk):

> The eyes and forms, the ears and sounds, the nose and smells, the tongue and tastes, the body and tangible things, the mind and mental objects.... If someone should set this "All" aside and proclaim another "All", it would be just talk.... Because this would be beyond the limits of his abilities.

It is a historical datum that the Buddha presented his Dharma as a non-theistic response, contending neither theism nor atheism, to polytheistic Brahmanism (better known by its colonial name Hinduism). In his criticism, the Buddha was quite humorous. In a discourse in *Tevijja Sutta* (http://www.metta.lk), a Brahman named Vasettha discussed the Hindu teachings of the Vedas about the union with Brahma (the Creator) with the Buddha, who asked him whether he or his teacher or his teacher's teacher even back seven generations had ever seen Brahma. Vasettha's denial sparked the Buddha's derision of the opponent's logic by comparing his behavior with that of a person loving a lady on sight but not knowing her name, complexion, dwelling, descent, or looks. In his discourses, the Buddha expounded not other-worldliness but this-worldliness and did not satisfy seekers of an eternalistic "all" or annihilatory "nothing." Keeping a middle way ("neither all, nor nothing"), the Buddha did not formulate a "final truth" but rather offered an understanding of how the mind works in order to help fellow human beings liberate themselves from existential suffering.

From Philosophy to Psychology

The Buddha is renowned for such classic unanswered questions as these: "Is the world and this universe eternal or finite?" "Are the soul and the body identical?" or "Will a liberated person exist or not exist after death?" According to the Buddha, these metaphysical questions will not lead to meaning. They will likely lead to speculation and generate religious issues that are not conducive to liberation or happiness. Following this reasoning, for the Buddha dogma and creed are anathema, as are the concepts of the soul, transmigration, and reincarnation, because all these can neither be confirmed nor denied.

In the *Kalama Sutta*, the Buddha conveyed a charter of free inquiry (http://www.metta.lk):

> Do not believe on rumours or hearsay, because it is reported to be good, ancient or practiced by tradition ... because it is in the scriptures or because of logic, inference or metaphysics [or] ... because the speaker appears believable or you are shown the testimony of an old sage. Do not believe in what is fancied, because it is extraordinary, it must have been inspired by a god or other fancy being ... because of presumption or custom of many years inclines you to take it as true [or] ... just because of someone's reputation and authority or because he is a guru.

Thus, the Dharma is a discipline of free inquiry, a set of practices for students who take nothing on blind faith and who do not own a personal holy figure or impersonal godhead. If the Buddha's words are inferred as hypotheses, the Dharma suggests using a method akin to research. The Buddhist community was and still is studious, rather than religious in the Western meaning of the word. Consequently, it is against all forms of theism. Brahmins are not involved in religious practices, and god is simply not a subject matter. The term *nontheistic* not only means neither theistic nor atheistic, nor even something in the middle, but also is a nonconceptual embodied experience of emptiness. Meaning is constructed on the basis of this emptiness, which is also a scaffold to practice the revered Buddhist prosocial spirit. Thus, the Dharma is neither gnostic (i.e., god can be known) nor agnostic (i.e., god cannot be proven). God is simply irrelevant in the Dharma. The pan-Buddhist view acknowledges that the Buddha did not establish a religion, did not contend to be a godly or omniscient manifestation (i.e., a messiah, savior, or prophet), and did not derive inspiration from any deity or other external power. Nor did the Buddha claim to be other than a fallible human being. He discouraged not only rituals but also his adherents' wish to worship him. By not exceeding the interpersonal realm, the Buddhist spirit does not hover in the sky. To reiterate, Buddhism comprises down-to-earth kindness, compassion, and joy to be cultivated in meditative equanimity: To be spiritual is to be social. In other words, to be prosocial, which requires lots of energy and effort, is spiritual enough.

Regardless of the metaphysical beliefs cherished by Mahayana Buddhists, a New Buddhist Psychology is not concerned with the cosmological order of the universe. It shows more allegiance with the pan-Buddhist views, based on the Buddha's pristine contentions, which is almost exclusively concerned with the nitty-gritty of ceasing human existential suffering (by deconstruction onto emptiness) and the quest for how to come to meaning (by reconstruction of the prosocial and positive values). The unadulterated interest is in developing an art of skillful responsiveness to the human predicament, which is a down-to-earth artisan's approach comparable to the approach of a horse trainer. The Buddha was focused on sensing, feeling, thinking, doing, and relating—that is, on what is effective to buoy contentment and to alleviate anguish. Therefore, one might ask whether the Buddha was perhaps a psychologist *avant la lettre*? The scriptures refer to the Buddha's psychological insight on the mental effects of meditation, as in the *Sallatha Sutta*. If hit by an arrow, the untrained mind touched by bodily pain grieves and laments, whereas the skilled meditator will not be distraught. The untrained mind experiences two kinds of pain: a bodily pain and a mental pain. Such a mind feels pains as if hit by two arrows. But the meditator, if touched by bodily pain, grieves and laments not. The meditator feels only bodily pain, not mental pain, as if hit by just one, not by a second arrow. In another narrative on a man shot by a poison arrow (of greed, hate, and ignorance), the Dharma is depicted not as a navel-staring philosophy but as an applied psychology. The man would die if instead of treating his greed or hatred immediately one would first quiz the archer's name, caste, home, arrow's type, and so on. (http://www.metta.lk).

Viewing the Dharma as a psychology is a paradigm shift comparable to that experienced by Western psychology in its evolution to become a science. William James (1842–1910), the founding father of American psychology, was one of the first individuals who recognized the psychology that inheres in the Dharma, and he agreed with the notion of Karma, the interplay of intentional and meaningful cognition-affect and manifest interpersonal behavior. He also acknowledged that compared to what we ought to be, we are only half awake. James (1890) broke new ground for psychology by addressing the functional value of mindful awareness that operates in the space of "pure" (preconceptual) perception:

> And the faculty of voluntarily bringing back a wandering attention, over and over again, is the very root of judgment, character, and will. No one is *compos sui* if he have it not. An education which should improve this faculty would be the education *par excellence*. But it is easier to define this ideal than to give practical directions for bringing it about. (p. 424)

In 1904, James had the (later) monk Anagarika Dharmapala teach in one of his lectures at Harvard, on which occasion he allegedly told the man from Sri

Lanka to take his chair. After the lecture (apparently on the modalities of sensation, emotion, thought, behavior, and awareness), James declared that this was the psychology everybody would be studying 25 years hence. After James, it was Maslow (in the 1950s) who recognized that the Dharma is a psychology.

Dharma as Contemporary Psychology

Western civilization, from its first encounter with the Dharma, molded Buddha's ideas into Western categories. The Dharma does not exactly belong to religion, according to De la Vallée Poussin (1869–1938), or to philosophy, according to Stcherbatsky (1866–1942). As mentioned earlier, C. Rhys Davids (1857–1942) found out that the Buddha dealt with psychology and psychological issues. In Davids's footsteps two other books saw printer's ink: *The Principles of Buddhist Psychology* (Kalupahana, 1987) and *An Introduction to Buddhist Psychology* (M. de Silva, 1979). These three authors—Davids, Kalupahana, and M. de Silva—are philosophers, not psychologists per se, although the latter also practices as a Buddhist therapist. Worth mentioning are the seminal writings by three vanguard psychologists: Kwee (1990), Mikulas (1978), and P. de Silva (1984), who linked the Dharma with cognitive-behavior therapy. It was only recently that Kwee and Kwee-Taams (2006b), who stand on the shoulders of these giants, offered a contemporary psychological account of the core Dharma that not only builds on but goes beyond the archaic *Abhidhamma*.

The account offered by Kwee and Kwee-Taams (2006b), a New Buddhist Psychology, respects rather than excludes all previous Buddhist traditions by reformulating the quintessence of the Theravada (originally a four-centuries-old oral tradition whose scriptures in Pali, called *suttas*, exceed the size of the Bible 10 times) and the much later Mahayana (a written tradition in Sanskrit, whose scriptures, called *sutras*, exceed the size of the Bible 50 times). All scriptures have been written by anonymous authors living in communities of brotherhoods as from the first century BCE. The historical suttas and the later metaphysical sutras narrate the Buddha's discourses, which rest on the Dharma's basic tenets. Obviously, the Mahayana writings, although composed in a discourse format, cannot be the Buddha's pristine words. Nevertheless, all Buddhist scriptures comprise commonly shared insights into pan-Buddhist core principles, acknowledged by all denominations, through which if intensely gauged and deeply understood, an awakening à la the Buddha might be accrued (see Table 12.1; the reader is referred to Kwee, 2010, for a full discussion of these 15 subjects).

A key practice is mindfulness, phrased here as a metonym: "There is no way to mindfulness, mindfulness is the way." Mindfulness is a striving at awakening to Dependent Origination and at choosing for wholesome Karma by cultivating a sharp awareness by being attentive and remembering to watchfully observe in a receptive, focused, and compassionate way the

Table 12.1 Pan-Buddhist Core Concepts, Terms, and Themes of Buddhist Psychology

1. Four Noble Truths, here called the *4-Ennobling Realities* (as social constructions)
2. Eightfold Path, here called the *8-Fold Balanced Practice* (of relational processes)
3. Skandhas, the psychological modalities of mind or self: feeling, thought, and action
4. Ultimate not-self of "emptiness" and the "provisional self" for everyday life
5. Karma: intentional, meaningful thought or feeling and concomitant action
6. Dharmas: the smallest "units of experience" ("perceivables" and "knowables")
7. Sixth sense: the mind's eye that perceives dharmas during mindful awareness
8. Experience of Nirvana: a state or trait of extinguished unwholesome thought-affect
9. Three poisons: greed, hatred, and ignorance on self-illusions and god delusions
10. Immeasurables: social meditations to augment kindness, compassion, and joy
11. Three empirical marks of existence: suffering, impermanence, and not-self
12. Dependent Origination (of Relational Interbeing): a pivotal causality hypothesis
13. Twelve meditations, with mindfulness (observe and watch) as the general factor
14. Foundations of mindfulness: the fluctuations of body/feelings and mind/thoughts
15. *Patthanas*: 24 functional conditions and relations linking feeling, thought, and action

stimuli entering consciousness through the senses and any feeling, thinking, or doing passing in the spaces of Body/Speech/Mind. Thereby, one is noticing receptively (i.e., free of intentional interference) as the internal stimuli are attended to in a neutral mode (i.e., free from interpretations and evaluations), while surfing from now to now without any direct goal (i.e., free from craving, grasping, and clinging), in "suchness" like a mirror. Mindful awareness is sine qua non for the 12 meditations, eventually meant to transform Karma, which attend the body (its breathing, behaviors, repulsiveness, elements, decomposing, and feelings) and the mind (its hindrances, aggregates, sense bases, awakening, the 4-Ennobling Realities, and the 8-Fold Balanced Practice).

Contemporary Buddhist psychology covers Body/Speech/Mind, encompassing the three levels of existence discerned by the Buddha. In present-day terms, these three layers require scrutiny through research in social, clinical, and neuropsychology. At the neuropsychological level, Austin (2009) reviewed studies from a Zen Buddhist perspective. Typically, the interest is in the topography of meditation and awakening (Hanson, 2009). Also of interest, however, are such subjects as that of the EEG study on the "free won't" of habitual responses (Libet, 2004); the neuroprosthetics technology study using implanted brain–computer interfaces to show that the mind's conation is capable of manipulating a cursor to command fresh behaviors (e.g., drawing or operating a TV remote control; *Nature, 442*);

and the search for the Buddha's *sixth sense*—the notion of the mind or brain that perceives the mind—in terms of neuroplasticity and dynamic brain circuitries (Varela, Lachaux, Rodriguez, & Martinerie, 2001). Yet other neuropsychological studies have involved the neuroimaging of not-self, the idea of "perceiving without perceiver" (see http://www.weizman.ac.il); the neurological correlates of awakening, supposedly the left prefrontal area connected to the left amygdala, specialized in positive affect (Davidson et al., 2003); and the offsetting of age-related cortical thinning attributable to meditation (Lazar et al., 2005). Notwithstanding the interesting findings, the present social constructivist Buddhist purview cautions for any claims of truth based on neuroscience. It is doubtful whether the cortical data accrued by techniques of brain scanning of reason and emotion will exceed the usual speculative guesswork and could really open up the human mind to inspection.

On the clinical front, research on mindfulness is accumulating through the growing interest of mental health professionals (Baer, Smith, & Allen, 2004; Bishop et al., 2004; Didonna, 2009; Germer, Siegel, & Fulton, 2005; Kelly, 2008; Shapiro & Carlson, 2009; Wallace & Shapiro, 2006). The practice of mindful awareness implies both a technique and a result of a nondual observing of dharmas (with small *d*). Since its inception in 1979, Kabat-Zinn's mindfulness-based stress reduction approach has been researched to such an extent that the American Psychological Association's predicate "probably efficacious" applies. It has proven to be a valuable clinical component and adjunct in the treatment of chronic pain, anxiety disorders, binge eating, fibromyalgia, psoriasis, cancer, coronary artery disease, depression, obesity, criminality, and nonclinical stress (e.g., De Vibe, 2006; Giommi, 2006; Kabat-Zinn, 2003, 2009; Kristeller & Jones, 2006). Relapse prevention studies on mindfulness-based cognitive therapy, found to be effective in ex-patients with three previous depressive periods, have lead to the acceptance of mindfulness-based stress reduction among cognitive-behavior therapists (Kuyken et al., 2008; Ma & Teasdale, 2004; Segal, Williams, & Teasdale, 2002; Teasdale, 2000). Without vilifying or belittling the impact of these findings in sparking mainstream psychologists' interest in meditation as an intervention, it is of concern, from a New Buddhist Psychology point of view, that by earning the status of a pill, these "Buddhist Lite" approaches are drifting away from the Dharma as a Buddhist teaching.

The Dharma and cognitive-behavioral therapy had a confluence at a historical summit in 2005—101 years later than James predicted—at the Fifth International Congress of Cognitive Psychotherapy / Ninth World Congress on Constructivism, when the 14th Dalai Lama had a meeting of minds with A. T. Beck, the founder of cognitive therapy. On this occasion Buddhist psychology and psychologists were accepted in mainstream psychology (Kwee et al., 2006). The confluence was further evidenced by the invited presence of the Transcultural Society for Clinical Meditation, which was well represented by eight symposia on Buddhist psychology. It is worth noting that much earlier another founder of cognitive-behavioral therapy, the late Albert Ellis, declared rational emotive behavior therapy's allegiance with the Dharma (Kwee & Ellis, 1998; see also Christopher, 2003, and http://transcultural.meditation.googlepages.com/home).

Dharma and Social Construction

Uncovering "things as they become," a Mahayana school named after the Flower Garland Sutra (Hua-yen), the only school originated in China started by Fa-tsang in the seventh century, postulates notions strongly resembling those of social construction. The sutra reveals that the metaphysical realm is empty through a Lucy-in-the-Sky-With-Diamonds tale on a quest for wisdom through a developmental journey to awaken and become a Buddha.

> Sudhana (Good Wealth), a young rich merchant's son, followed the Bodhisattva (a Buddha-to-be) of Wisdom's advice and set out to learn the blissful course of conduct. During his wanderings far and wide, he encountered 53 teachers/friends (like a monk, physician, banker, king, brahmin, animal, slave, merchant, fool, boatman, boy, prostitute, and queen) symbolizing phases, principles, and virtues. Moving forward he discovered that life in itself is a teaching as each meeting is an enchanting educational adventure, meaningful to discover practices, dedications, contemplations, and meditations. Then, after a journey full of danger, after he gave up striving to attain or not attain Buddhahood, he met, high on a steep mountain, the Future Buddha from whom he learned to understand generosity, and who made him merge with the Bodhisattva of Virtue in radiating interconnectedness of "Indra's Jewel Net" that reciprocally mirrors appearing images in each diamond at every crossing of the net symbolizing the infinite interconnectedness of all beings. He then vowed to practice loving kindness, compassion, and joy, and to dedicate his life to benefit humanity. Ecstatic, Sudhana is able to see with an increased blissful clarity "the reality of things as they become in Dependent Origination." Becoming equal to Virtue and all aspects of wisdom and compassion and delightfully experiencing the interpenetration of all beings on earth, he whispered: "[T]here is no other, we are Interbeing" (the entrance of one into all and all into one, the non-obstruction of all phenomena, the non-duality of all Buddhas). But this was not yet the end. Climbing further, he finally arrived at the Cosmic Buddha's "Tower of the Highest Wisdom." Standing in front of the door to enter this top room, he held his breath and opened the portal to find out that the universe is an empty bubble beyond dual projections and binary conceptions. (Cleary, 1993)

In full, humans are biochemical, sensing, moving, thinking, emoting, and relational beings in Dependent Origination, whose minds usually function at the prerational, irrational, and rational levels, but rarely at the postrational level, which denotes wisdom. It is on this wisdom level that we are able to see and understand that to be means to be related. Life means being interconnected and socially embedded: there is no other way. Thrown from birth onward into a social web, we humans find it is impossible to be self-contained. Anything that we can conceive of is injected with interpersonal meaning. Although we often take our being embedded in bonds for granted, interrelatedness remains from the cradle to the grave. Ensued from a history of interdependency, even our individual private worlds of dharmas are encapsulated in an inextricable relational network. Looking outside to the social realm, we see mirrors of our inner worlds. Looking inside to the private realm, as if in wall-gazing meditation, we see the relational everywhere. And although we are dancing alone in the room, the interpersonal dimension remains omnipresent. Because we are intricately related to each other, it is safe to conclude that even anything appearing in the mind's closed privacy is a social construction. In such envisioning, human beings are subsumed under a sublime metaorder of the interpersonal. This metavision necessitates a view of reality as a collaborative practice and an existential stance of caring responsibility for each other.

The metaphor of "Indra's Jewel Net" is particularly appealing to social constructionists who regard the individual psyche and its contents (i.e., feeling, thinking, and behaving) as atomistic elements. Although not dismissed, "elemental" views lack the capacity to satisfactorily explain the vicissitudes of human functioning embedded in relationship. As in the Buddhist vision, Gergen (2000) deconstructs the binary inner–outer, I–other, and replaces it with a socially coconstructed relational self that necessarily repudiates the "individual self behind the eyeballs" as an explanatory entity. Given "unobstructed" mutual identity penetration, each individual is interconnected with other individuals. Change in one individual results in a relative change in all other individuals through a web of interconnected relationships. Individuals can exist only in the context of relationships; thus, to be is to *inter*-be and to act is to *inter*-act. If from womb-to-tomb relationships precede the notion of the single person, the mind is not contained under the skin but is bound to be extended and reconstituted as a reflection of interpersonal process.

The New Buddhist Psychology's love affair with social construction is centered round Relational Interbeing and mounts in what we have called Relational Buddhism. This offers a social constructivist perspective of the Dharma and Buddhist psychology. Focusing on interactions, the binary you–me collapses. It crumbles in emptiness. Relational Interbeing necessitates the emptiness of solitary selves, which is the Buddha's psychological proposition par excellence. Endorsing the view that an individual is a manifestation of a relationship and not an isolated independent being, Buddhist psychology conceives of persons as empty of the purely private. Even private thinking cannot be solipsistic because such thinking ensues from a history of language and long-lasting relationships. The relational perspective does not discard psychobiology but, rather, completes the picture of the human being as a Body/Speech/Mind system. Relational Interbeing is neither within body nor within mind but in its members' encounter and dialogue. For Relational Interbeing to become, the members must necessarily move as if in a dance.

From both the Buddhist nonindependent and social constructionist codependent perspectives, self is an atomistic agency, bounded, segregated, and alienated from the profound reality of Interbeing (*Gandavyuha Sutra*; Thich, 1998) or Relational Being (Gergen, 2009a, 2009b). Relational Interbeing, as it is called here, is a milestone next to emptiness on the road of awakening to Dependent Origination. In the present quest for meaning, it is the understanding and realization of our human interconnectedness that will, by superseding individual separation, lead to sustainable happiness. The future of global intimacy is bright if we are able to move on to collaborative practice of social construction. Social construction stems from the discipline of social psychology and at its start has nothing to do with the Dharma. However, by discarding Transcendental Truths and embracing the reality of the relational as standing prior to the concept of the individual, social construction definitely bears Buddhist marks.

Thus, not only Relational Interbeing comes to be, but so does reality in general (in Dependent Origination of collaborative practice). Both are defined by what the particular social group believes they are. In other words, reality is not a solipsistic matter. Not located within biology or psyche, it exists in the social experience: 2 + 2 = 4 because we agree. Because reality is constructed between communicating people, it may be perceived as true in one community but untrue in another one. Beyond community there is thundering silence. The notions of truth and absolute reality are at best provisional tools that are historically, culturally, and linguistically coconstructed by people and negotiated in a dance of meaning. Data are human constructs and thus intersubjective and relative—space, time, and culture bound—even if scientifically unveiled as facts. Vico (1668–1744) already contended that facts are fabricated and constructed (*verum ipsum factum*). In a world of impermanence and imperfection, data and facts are conceivable as narratives to be amended and replaced by more adequate constructions going forward.

Toward a New Buddhist Psychology

"If you call this a stick, you affirm; if you call it not a stick, you negate: Beyond affirmation and negation what would you call it?" (Ta-hui, 12th c.). This is a famous *kung-an*, a Chinese word signifying a case of "jurisprudence" that has proven its utility to awaken (provide an "aha" experience). It is better known by its Japanese translation, *koan*, a kind of paradoxical riddle that cannot be solved by reason or language. Language is an instrument that functions as a map and is itself an active form of life within relationship. From a social constructivist perspective, theories are not telling us how the world really is but are a medium to participate in a relationship. Using language, we are eventually unable to tell the truth about the Buddha, the Dharma, or social construction. What matters is to be aware of the constructed and gaming character of language, including the language of social construction (Gergen & Hosking, 2006). Unable to escape the social predicament of the local culture, all that one can conceive is a polyvocal narrative. This notion also applies to science as well as to the Dharma as a religion, philosophy, or psychology.

In Wittgensteinian terms, Dharma qua religion applies the "language game of religion," which inheres in intrinsic rules applied to a family of terms from which each word derives its meaning and out of which corresponding affect and behavior emanate. In the same vein, a Dharma that uses philosophical terminology adheres to the rules of the "language game of philosophy," implying a fabric of relational stance and actions into which it is woven. The present proposition—to view the Dharma as a psychology—requires rules and actions of a "language game of psychology"; this language utilizes words inhering in particular meanings and functions in the psychological idiom. These words are tools that help to structure conceptualizations of reality in a psychological way. Obviously, the Dharma's psychological language game differs from other language games. Wittgenstein (1953), on whose work social construction leans heavily, claimed that words derive meaning from their use in language games: Words by themselves have no intrinsic meaning. Meaning is socially, not privately, constructed actively by members of a community who develop ways of speaking to serve their needs as a group. From a language-game perspective, absolute meanings do not exist. Consequently, science is as much linguistic and social as it is scientific. Buddhist cosmology is, against the backdrop of emptiness, an exotic language game that though still appealing to many might have outlived its usefulness. For instance, in the Buddhist "cosmos game," the world is played as a flat mandala, analogous to the thesis that the world is round. This notion is neither true nor false in terms of representational value. It is practical to play it round when flying from New York to New Delhi and useful to play it flat when walking on Wall Street (cf. Gergen, 2009a).

The Dharma as a psychology tries to be the top game in town. If we agree on the proposition that psychology's language game is most apt to serve 21st-century "free-thinking" humanity, it is imperative to rid the Dharma of the religious and metaphysical idioms that hamper its development as a psychology. It is an arduous task to unlearn old vocabularies and to adopt psychological interpretations of selected keywords, as proposed next (Kwee, 2010).

1. *Dharma*: As disseminated by the Buddha, dharma is a modus vivendi rooted in meditation practice toward emptiness and friendliness. It is not a religion that alludes to a creator, supernatural beings, and worshipping rituals; nor is it a philosophy, a theorized belief system on metaphysics, ontology, ethics, or politics. Colonial scholars trying to catch its meaning looked for a convenient category within their own vocabulary and molded the god-*less* soteriology into a concept implying inaccurate notions: Buddh-*ism*. However, this Eurocentric fabrication has no classical Indian semantic equivalent. Considering that there is no Western equivalent for the Buddhist Dharma either, the term seems to be better off if untranslated. In the absence of an exact Buddhist meaning, the term *Buddhism* might then be used as a storehouse containing every existing manifestation of the Buddhist Dharma. Thus, in this view Relational Buddhism refers to a relational reconceptualization of the Buddhist Dharma in its totality. Note well that Dharma with a capital *D* is differentiated from dharma with a lower-case *d* denoting the smallest unit of experience appearing as social constructions in protean versatility and changeable in form and content: perceivables (verbalized sensations) and thinkables (verbalized thoughts).
2. *Duhkha*: Duhkha (or suffering)—a loose translation that is not, per se, incorrect—arises from nonsatisfaction or discontentment that is not a moral punishment or sacrifice. It is dependently originating in existential impermanence that is the result of the human condition of aging, illness, death, and birth, and of not getting what one craves; life is imperfect and full of gnawing imbalances. Duhkha is omnipresent. Even if one is joyous and happy, there is a disquieting uncertainty to be endured regarding what the next moment will bring. This uncertainty gives rise to unsteadiness and uneasiness, here called *dis*-ease. Life does not spin around smoothly when adversity is met. Duhkha is a daily state of being that is stuck through bearing agony, affliction, anger, angst, anguish, anxiety, aversion, discomfort, despair, frustration, hunger, grief, lamentation, misery, pain, sadness, sorrow, stress, and the like. Duhkha likely perpetuates and augments itself, and it may become cyclical (*Samsara*) by the daily recurrence or "rebirths" of negative affective episodes. Life does not spin around smoothly when adversity is met. Sustainable happiness is hence necessarily chaironic, or experienced amid adversity (http://www.meaning.ca).

3. *Skandhas*: Usually translated as "aggregates" or "heaps," Skandhas are viewed here as congruent to the BASIC modalities of psyche (Kwee, 1998; Kwee & Lazarus, 1986). This acronym stands for behavior (referring to body), affect (motivation), sensation (perception), imagery (vision), and cognition (conception), all of which appear in consciousness as perceivables (the visible, hearable, smellable, tasteable, and touchable) and as thinkables (conceivables, imaginables, memories, dreams, illusions, and delusions). Craving results in grasping and clinging onto illusory certainties and eventually in their piling in the BASIC modalities of which one can be mindfully aware. Mindfulness might sharpen awareness of the Dependent Origination, arising, subsiding, and ceasing of daily emotional episodes by recognizing the modalities involved, their interplay and firing order. Such emotions as fear, anger, sadness, or joy move in a flux in conjunction with biological and relational processes, and they imply their cyclical rebirths if not processed well. Altogether, the atomistic modalities constitute the "provisional self" that is subject to the conditioned habit of attachment. On the ultimate level, this I, me, and mine of self is empty, which is obvious when the provisional self's nature as a reified abstraction is understood. BASIC's emptiness implies that there is no soul in the machine with which to identify. Known as the Buddhist "all and everything," the Skandhas are a down-to-earth dismissal of transmigration and reincarnation (both viewed here as Tibetan atavisms).
4. *Buddhist lore*: A psychological perspective discards the common literal exegesis of the Buddhist lore—for instance, of *The Six Realms* and of the demon *Mara*—viewing them instead as mental projections of inner states. Thus, the "realm of the gods" stands for bliss–pride, "demi-gods" stand for envy–struggle, "animals" for greed–ignorance, "hell fires" for hate–anger, "hungry ghosts" for craving–grasping, and "humans" for doubting–clinging as well as for the potential of awakening. Instead of a seducing demon, *Mara* symbolizes the Buddha's overcoming his four inner enemies of awakening: the five nonhuman realms mentioned earlier, the fear of death, the illusion of self or soul, and the delusions of god and celestial beings.
5. *Enlightenment*: A translation of *bodhi*, enlightenment is a term tasting Eurocentric if alluding to the 18th-century European Age of Enlightenment. Based on Cartesian then-modernist thought, people came to believe in the light of reason and timeless truths and to uphold the supremacy of rational–empirical and logical–positivistic science. In contrast, however, the Buddhist enlightenment stems from *budh*, meaning "to be wakeful and aware of, " that is, not asleep or ignorant. Although the Dharma may elucidate,

illuminate, and enlighten, it does so by means of "heartfelt understanding," rather than through the thinking mind (to be mindfully observed). The potential for bodhi inheres in everyone and simply needs uncovering, as in the smelting process that separates gold from ore.

6. *Nirvana*: Nirvana (from *nir* [(un)] and *vana* [binding]) is often erroneously inferred as a tangible paradise in the hereafter as conceived in the Abrahamic religions of the early translators. The metaphysics of the beyond, however, is at odds with a teaching of emptiness. In effect, Nirvana means coolness as a result of the extinction of unwholesome emotions inspired by the three poisons of greed or grasping and hatred or clinging engendered by ignorance or craving and their cognitive, affective, emotive, behavioral, and interpersonal ramifications. Whereas greed inheres in anxiety (fear of shortage) and sadness (grief of loss), hatred inheres in anger (other-blame) and depression (self-blame). Nirvana may also refer to the smiling contentment and happiness as an epiphenomenon while on the path. Nirvana as a state or trait disrupting Duhkha's rebirth is temporary when "hot" arousal keeps arising and enduring when death quenches the Samsara cycle.
7. *Buddhist ethics*: We are advisably skeptical of Buddhist ethics suggesting a Western type of formalistic theory. Instead, we suggest, the Dharma is best described as a morality without ethics (e.g., the moral standards of Robin Hood differ from the sheriff's). The social constructivist nonfoundational morality of collaborative practice is an appropriate reconceptualization of a moral view rooted in differing interpersonal values and conduct. Because words such as *must* and *should* are anathema in the Buddhist pursuit of free inquiry, Dharma's morality is based on interpersonal motivation. And as there is no morality without relationship, for the focus is on the relational process itself in reflective negotiation and transformational dialogue, to use social constructivist terminology. This is exemplified in fairy-tale-like allegories (*Jataka* stories) where the Buddha as a Bodhisattva allegedly lied and killed in certain life circumstances.

Closing Remarks

Viewing the Dharma as a modus vivendi based on Buddhist psychological insights as contended here is not a matter of course. Its acceptance depends on the culture one lives by and requires a paradigm shift in conceptualizing the Dharma (Gergen, 2000; Kwee, 2007). The New Buddhist Psychology of Relational Buddhism concurs with the social constructionist view that truth and reality are a cultural–historical narrative, a thesis that is conceptually dislocating. Few people are prepared to go along with such a wrenching view.

However, for both Buddhists and social constructionists who are adventurous, innovative, and resilient, the horizons are exciting if one dares to go ahead by

1. Challenging the belief in Cartesian-style knowledge, which separates body and mind and gives an account of reality based on rationality, testability, and objectivity as *the* absolute truth
2. Questioning the permanence of reality and the immutability of truth (e.g., of holy books or cities); recognizing that the metaprocess of communality accrues intelligible coconstructions, not Transcendental Truths
3. Viewing empirical data as fabricated social constructions based on local agreements that lack everlasting foundations; recognizing that science, a relevant narrative about reality, is not the "eternal truth"
4. Pointing at the limitation of the positivist approach in finding timeless truths (while endorsing the indexing value of quantitative research) and valuing qualitative research as immediate social action

A social constructivist New Buddhist Psychology deconstructs and reconstructs. It deconstructs by making transparent the taken-for-granted delusion of the existence of a god (instilled through indoctrination) and the illusion of an unchangeable self. Although these concepts are habitually viewed as real or true, they are social constructions. In order to deconstruct illusions, language needs to be disillusioned. Language creates a picture of provisional reality, but it cannot ever fully represent or express ultimate emptiness that can only be experienced. Language is to be understood as socially constructed maps serving a human purpose. Although deconstructing has a liberating effect, for it frees us from the automatisms of conditioning and literalization, reconstructing and alternative practices are still needed. The social constructionist way of reconstructing implies that we keep on seeing how daily realities owe their existence to relationships and interacting networks. From this and the insight in the processes and potentials of Relational Interbeing comes forth the social constructionist practice to consequently appreciate and mutually accept each other (though not necessarily approving someone's unwholesome behaviors). Both practices consider care for relationships as the most worthy value. The Buddhist caring of relationships is operationalized in the social meditations.

Loving kindness, empathic compassion, and shared joy practiced in meditative equanimity form the alpha and omega of Buddhist action. These practices have existed since the Buddha's time, some 100 generations ago. One can find instructions for these immeasurables, as they are called, in any Buddhist handbook; they aim to immeasurably multiply the Buddhist core social affects. A radical application in daily life is pursued until there is enough love to go round in the world. Recently it was shown that Tibetan monks who permeate themselves with kindness and compassion (an empathic understanding and an unconditional readiness to help) on a long-term basis (more than 10,000 hours) alter the structure and functioning of their brains (Lutz et al., 2004). They show gamma wave synchrony, high-frequency oscillations (40 Hz), indicating that the brain integrates ongoing processes by transient varieties of widely distributed parallel processes of neuronal networks into highly ordered cognitive and affective functions (perception, attention, learning, and memory). This induced synaptic activity changes across different scales of the brain. The data suggest neuroplasticity. Contemplative practices, involving temporal integrative mechanisms, seem able to induce lasting neural change (as does the ability of aerobics to sculpt the muscles), thus upgrading the brain to improved cognitive-emotional achievements.

The Nirvana of emptiness and the extinction of unwholesome craving are not sufficient in themselves. Meaning is derived from the daily practice of the social meditations. Thus, awakening—the experience that Duhkha has ceased—is just the beginning to be better able to help others. Because Karma, or meaningful intentional action, starts with emotions, emotionality, and emotional vicissitudes, evidence-based cognitive, affective, and behavioral or interactional tactics implemented through collaborative practice in interpersonal relationships, which include Buddhist meditation, belong to the most straightforward scenarios to work toward positive affect and eventually happiness. Such might be called a self-applied Karma transformation. It is of interest that the concept of intentional activity recently appeared in positive psychology's happiness literature, without, however, alluding to Karma (Lyubomirsky, 2008). Research suggests that sustainable happiness is determined by these three factors: a genetic set-point (50%), circumstantial factors (10%), and intentional activity (40%). The latter offers a window of opportunity for happiness, which from a social constructionist's view is necessarily relational. Humans are equipped with an idiosyncratic genetic set-point for happiness. This is comparable to a set-point for weight or height, which is hardly modifiable. People with high set-points will find it easier to be happy, whereas people with low set-points will have to work harder to achieve and maintain happiness under similar conditions. Long-term overall circumstances include demographics such as age, health, education, money, country, religion, or marital status. Although these factors matter, they determine but a small percentage of happiness, do not impact long-lasting happiness, and deliver only short-lived boosts of happiness. Happy people make things happen, and their activity spins off a by-product that is happiness over and above the genetic set range and life circumstances.

Granted, there are different strokes for different folks, and Karma transformation is not particularly suitable for the faint-hearted. The faint-hearted would rather profit from a list of dos and don'ts of a holy book, heavenly ethics, or hellish morality and from the metaphysics for saints and sinners. For the mature, however, who have the capacity to freely think, pick, and choose, who wishes to decide for themselves in joint collaboration, and who does not want to blindly follow holy dead men and their rules, there is a psychological roadmap that might generate sustainable happiness for all in interrelatedness.

References

Austin, J. H. (2009). *Selfless insight.* Cambridge, MA: MIT Press.

Baer, R. (2003). Mindfulness training as a clinical intervention: A conceptual and empirical review. *Clinical Psychology: Science & Practice, 10*, 125–143.

Baer, R. A., Smith, G. T., & Allen, K. B. (2004). Assessment of mindfulness by self-report: The Kentucky Inventory of Mindfulness Skills. *Assessment, 11*, 1–16.

Bishop, S. R., Lau, M., Shapiro, S., Carlson, L., Anderson, N. D., Cameron, J.,... Devins, G. (2004). Mindfulness: A proposed operational definition. *Clinical Psychology: Science & Practice, 11*, 230–241.

Christopher, M. S. (2003). Albert Ellis and the Buddha: Rational soul mates? A comparison of rational emotive behavior therapy (REBT) and Zen Buddhism. *Mental Health, Religion & Culture, 6*, 283–293.

Cleary, T. (1993). *The flower ornament scripture.* Boston, MA: Shambala.

Davidson, R .J., Kabat-Zinn, J., Schumacher, J., Rosenkranz, M., Muller, D., Santorelli, S. F.,... Sheridan, J. F. (2003). Alteration in brain and immune function produced by mindfulness meditation. *Psychosomatic Medicine, 65*, 564–570.

de Silva, M. W. P. (1979). *An introduction to Buddhist psychology* (1st ed.). London, England: Palgrave Macmillan.

de Silva, M. W. P. (2005). *An introduction to Buddhist psychology* (4th ed.). London, England: Palgrave Macmillan.

de Silva, P. (1984). Buddhism and behaviour modification. *Behaviour Research & Therapy, 22*, 661–678.

De Vibe, M. (2006). Mindfulness and health intervention. In M. G. T. Kwee, K. J. Gergen, & F. Koshikawa (Eds.), *Horizons in Buddhist psychology: Practice, research & theory* (pp. 197–208). Taos, NM: Taos Institute.

Didonna, F. (Ed.).(2009). *Clinical handbook of mindfulness.* New York, NY: Springer.

Engel, G. L. (1977). The need for a new medical model, *Science, 196*, 129–136.

Feinberg, T. E. (2000): *Altered egos: How the brain creates the self.* New York, NY: Oxford University Press.

Gergen, K. J. (2000). *The saturated self: Dilemmas of identity in contemporary life.* New York, NY: Basic Books.

Gergen, K. J. (2009a). *An invitation to social construction* (2nd ed.). London, England: Sage.

Gergen, K. J. (2009b). *Relational being: Beyond the individual and community.* Oxford, England: Oxford University Press.

Gergen, K. J., & Hosking, D. M. (2006). If you meet social construction along the road: A dialogue: A dialogue with Buddhism. In M. G. T. Kwee, K. J. Gergen, & F. Koshikawa (Eds.), *Horizons in Buddhist psychology: Practice, research & theory* (pp. 299–314). Chagrin Falls, OH: Taos Institute.

Germer, C. K., Siegel, R. D., & Fulton, P. R. (Eds.). (2005). *Mindfulness and psychotherapy.* New York, NY: Guilford Press.

Giommi, F. (2006). Mindfulness and its challenge to cognitive-behavioral practice. In M. G. T. Kwee, K. J. Gergen, & F. Koshikawa (Eds.), *Horizons in Buddhist psychology: Practice, research & theory* (pp. 209–224). Taos, NM: Taos Institute.

Grossman, P., Niemann, L., Schmidt, S., & Walach, H. (2004). Mindfulness-based stress reduction and health benefits: A meta-analysis. *Journal of Psychosomatic Research, 57*, 35–43.

Gyatso, T. (Dalai Lama), & Beck, A. T. (2006). Himalaya Buddhism meets cognitive therapy: The Dalai Lama and Aaron T. Beck in dialogue, narrated by Marja Kwee-Taams and Maurits Kwee. In M. G. T. Kwee, K. J. Gergen, & F. Koshikawa (Eds.), *Horizons in Buddhist psychology: Practice, research & theory* (pp. 27–48). Taos, NM: Taos Institute.

Hanson, R. (2009). *Buddha's brain: The practical neuroscience of happiness, love, and wisdom.* Oakland, CA: New Harbinger.

James, W. (1890). *Principles of psychology.* New York, NY: Holt.

Kabat-Zinn, J. (2003). Mindfulness-based stress reduction (MBSR). In M. G. T. Kwee & M. K. Kwee-Taams (Eds.), *A tribute to Yutaka Haruki* [Special issue]. *Constructivism in the Human Science, 2*, 73–106.

Kabat-Zinn, J. (2009). Foreword. In F. Didonna (Ed.), *Clinical handbook of mindfulness* (pp. xxv–xxxiii). New York, NY: Springer.

Kahneman, D. (2003). A perspective on judgement and choice: Mapping bounded rationality. *American Psychologist, 58*, 697–720.

Kalupahana, D. (1987). *The principles of Buddhist psychology.* Albany, NY: SUNY.

Kelly, B. D. (2008). Buddhist psychology, psychotherapy and the brain: A critical introduction. *Transcultural Psychiatry, 45*, 5–30.

Kristeller, J., & Jones, J. (2006). A middle way: Meditation in the treatment of compulsive eating. In M. G. T. Kwee, K. J. Gergen, & F. Koshikawa (Eds.), *Horizons in Buddhist psychology: Practice, research & theory* (pp. 85–100). Taos, NM: Taos Institute.

Kuyken, W., Byford, S., Taylor, R. S., Watkins, E., Holden, E., White, K., … Teasdale, J. D. (2008). Mindfulness-based cognitive therapy to prevent relapse in recurrent depression. *Journal of Consulting & Clinical Psychology, 76*, 966–978.

Kwee, M. G. T. (1990). *Psychotherapy, meditation, & health: A cognitive-behavioural perspective.* London, England: East-West.

Kwee, M. G. T. (1998). On consciousness and awareness of the BASIC-I.D. In M. M. DelMonte & Y. Haruki (Eds.), *The embodiment of mind* (pp. 21–42). Delft, Netherlands: Eburon.

Kwee, M. G. T. (2003). NeoZEN: A deconstructing process into non-self. In M. G. T. Kwee & M. K. Kwee-Taams (Eds.), *A tribute to Yutaka Haruki* [Special issue]. *Constructivism in the Human Sciences, 8*, 181–203.

Kwee, M. G. T. (2008). The social construction of a new Buddhist psychology (A tribute in memory of Michael J. Mahoney). *Constructivism in the Human Sciences, 12*(1 & 2), 143–168.

Kwee, M. G. T. (Ed.). (2010). *New horizons in Buddhist psychology: Relational Buddhism for collaborative practitioners.* Chagrin Falls, OH: Taos Institute.

Kwee, M. G. T., & Ellis, A. (1997). Can multimodal and rational emotive behavior therapy be reconciled? *Journal of Rational-Emotive & Cognitive-Behavior Therapy, 15*, 95–133.

Kwee, M. G. T., & Ellis, A. (1998). The interface between rational emotive behavior therapy and Zen. *Journal of Rational-Emotive & Cognitive Behavior Therapy, 16*, 5–44.

Kwee, M. G. T., Gergen, K. J., & Koshikawa, F. (Eds.). (2006). *Horizons in Buddhist psychology: Practice, research & theory.* Taos, NM: Taos Institute.

Kwee, M. G. T., & Holdstock, T. L. (Eds.). (1996). *Western and Buddhist psychology: Clinical perspectives.* Delft, Netherlands: Eburon.

Kwee, M. G. T., & Lazarus, A. A. (1986). Multimodal therapy: The cognitive-behavioral tradition and beyond. In W. Dryden & W. L. Golden (Eds.), *Cognitive-behavioral approaches to psychotherapy* (pp. 320–356). New York, NY: Harper & Row.

Kwee, M. G. T., & Kwee-Taams, M. K. (2006a). Buddhist psychology and positive psychology. In A. Delle Fave (Ed.), *Dimensions of well-being: Research and intervention* (pp. 565–582). Milano, Italy: Franco Angeli.

Kwee, M. G. T., & Kwee-Taams, M. K. (2006b). A new Buddhist psychology: Moving beyond Theravada and Mahayana. In M. G. T. Kwee, K. J. Gergen, & F. Koshikawa (Eds.), *Horizons in Buddhist psychology: Practice, research & theory* (pp. 435–478). Chagrin Falls, OH: Taos Institute.

Lazar, S. W., Kerr, C. E., Wasserman, R. H., Gray, J. R., Greve, D. N., Treadway, M. T., ... Fischl, B. (2005). Meditation experience is associated with increased cortical thickness. *Neuroreport, 16*, 1893–1897.

Libet, B. (2004). *Mind-time.* Cambridge, MA: Harvard University Press.

Lutz, A., Greischar, L. L., Rawlings, N. B., Ricard, M., & Davidson, R. J. (2004). Long term meditators self induce high-amplitude gamma synchrony during mental practice. *Proceedings of the National Academy of Science, 101*, 16369–16373.

Lyubomirsky, S. (2008). *The how of happiness: A scientific approach to getting the life you want.* New York, NY: Penguin Press.

Ma, H. S. W., & Teasdale, J. (2004). Mindfulness-based cognitive therapy for depression: Replication and exploration of differential relapse prevention effects. *Journal of Consulting & Clinical Psychology, 72*, 31–40.

Mikulas, W. L. (1978). Four Noble Truths of Buddhism related to behavior therapy. *The Psychological Record, 28*, 59–67.

Müller-Lyer, F. C. (1894). Über kontrast und konfluxion. *Zeitschrift für Psychologie, 9/10*, 1–421.

Rhys Davids, C. A. F. (Trans.). (1900). *A Buddhist manual of psychological ethics.* London, England: Royal Asiatic Society.

Segal, Z. V., Williams, J. M. G., & Teasdale, J. D. (2002). *Mindfulness-based cognitive therapy for depression.* New York, NY: Guilford Press.

Seligman, M. E. P. (2004). Positive psychology and positive intervention. In *Book of Abstracts: 2nd European Conference on Positive Psychology.* Milano, Italy: Archipelago.

Shapiro, S. L., & Carlson, L. E. (2009). *The art and science of mindfulness: Integrating mindfulness into psychology and the helping professions.* Washington, DC: American Psychological Association.

Shigaki, C. L., Glass, B., & Schopp, L. (2006). Mindfulness-based stress reduction in medical settings. *Journal of Clinical Psychology in Medical Settings, 13*, 209–216.

Taylor, S. E. (1989). *Positive illusions: Creative self-deception and the healthy mind.* New York, NY: Basic Books.

Teasdale, J. D. (2000). Mindfulness-based cognitive therapy in the prevention of relapse and recurrence in major depression. In Y. Haruki & K. T. Kaku (Eds.), *Meditation as health promotion: A lifestyle modification approach* (pp. 3–18). Delft, Netherlands: Eburon.

Thich Nhat Hanh. (1998). *Interbeing: Fourteen guidelines for engaged Buddhism.* Berkeley, CA: Parallax Press.

Toneatto, T., & Nguyen, L. (2007). Does mindfulness meditation improve anxiety and mood symptoms? A review of the controlled research. *Canadian Journal of Psychiatry, 52*, 260–266.

Varela, F, Lachaux, J.-P., Rodriguez, E., & Martinerie, J. (2001). The brainweb phase synchronization and large-scale integration. *National Review of Neuroscience, 2,* 229–239.

Wallace B. A., & Shapiro, S. L. (2006). Mental balance and well-being: Building bridges between Buddhism and Western psychology. *American Psychologist, 61,* 690–701.

Wittgenstein, L. (1953). *Philosophical investigations.* New York, NY: Macmillan.

II
Research

13
Character Strengths and the Life of Meaning

CHRISTOPHER PETERSON and NANSOOK PARK
University of Michigan

The new field of positive psychology is defined as the scientific study of what makes life most worth living, so in one sense, positive psychology *is* the study of ultimate meaning (Peterson, 2006). Central figures in the psychological study of meaning—like Viktor Frankl (1959), Carl Rogers (1961), Abraham Maslow (1970), and Rollo May (1953)—are among the individuals upon whose shoulders contemporary positive psychologists stand.

Damon, Menon, and Bronk (2003) noted the similarity in particular between Frankl's approach to meaning and the general premises of positive psychology. Both hold that that higher human characteristics are neither produced by nor derived from more basic needs or drives: According to Frankl (1959), "Man's search for meaning is a primary force in his life and not a 'secondary rationalization' of instinctual drives" (p. 121). Indeed, "the most basic assumption that positive psychology urges is that human goodness and excellence are as authentic as disease, disorder, and distress. Positive psychologists are adamant that these topics are not secondary, derivative, illusory, epiphenomenal, or otherwise suspect (Peterson, 2006, p. 5).

Yet unlike Frankl, positive psychologists do not regard the search for or presence of meaning as necessarily the highest goals or purposes of existence. Meaning is one of several components of the psychological good life, and whether it is the most important—for someone or for everyone—is regarded by positive psychologists as an empirical question that hinges on how meaning is defined and measured as well as on the causes and consequences to which it may be linked by research.

When positive psychologists discuss meaning, they sometimes draw on the specific proposal of Seligman (2002) that a life of *meaning* is one in which people feel connected to something external to and larger than themselves.[1] This vision of meaning overlaps with previous discussions that relate meaning to goals (Emmons, 1986; Klinger, 1977; Little, 1983) and to Antonovsky's (1979) notion that meaning results when the demands of the external world are deemed worthy of investment. It is also similar to the self-transcendent dimensions of meaning distinguished by Wong (1998) and to Damon, Menon, and Bronk's (2003) definition of purpose as the general intention to accomplish something of significance beyond the self.

When Seligman (2002) proposed the life of meaning as one of the routes to authentic happiness, he compared and contrasted it with two other routes: the life of pleasure (i.e., hedonism; J. Watson, 1895) and the life of engagement (i.e., flow; Csikszentmihalyi, 1990). Peterson, Park, and Seligman (2005b) devised a self-report measure of the endorsement of these different approaches to happiness. They found that all three—meaning, pleasure, and engagement—were individually associated with life satisfaction but that orientations to engagement and to meaning had stronger links. There were hints in their data that a *full life*, that is, a life wherein a person is simultaneously oriented to pleasure, engagement, and meaning, is the most satisfying. And the results were clear that an empty life, marked by low scores of all these orientations, is linked to extreme dissatisfaction.

One of the central concerns of positive psychology is good character, that is, such positive traits as curiosity, kindness, and teamwork; thus the question arises about the relationship between strengths of character and a life of meaning. By definition, character is socially and morally valued. Seligman (2002) hypothesized that *any* strength of character, when exercised on a regular basis, contributes to the psychological good life and by implication to the life of meaning.

Park, Peterson, and Seligman (2004) showed that certain strengths of character—namely, curiosity, gratitude, hope, love, and zest—are robustly associated with life satisfaction among adults, more so than such other strengths of character as judgment, creativity, and love of learning; and Peterson (2006) interpreted these findings as showing that the heart matters more than the head when one's concern is with the psychological good life. Given the Western world's emphasis, at least since the time of Aristotle, on intellectual and mental abilities, these are intriguing results. Assuming that we want our children to be happy (Noddings, 2003), they imply that parents and schools should encourage the emotional strengths that tie people together

[1] Seligman (2002) argued that a life is more versus less meaningful depending on how "large" that external something might be. This formulation is only reasonable as an approximate metaphor. Surely, the governor of Rhode Island and the governor of California both have meaningful lives as public servants, yet would one want to say that the former individual has a less meaningful life than the latter individual?

as much as the cognitive skills that allow individual accomplishment (Bacon, 2005). What good is critical thinking if not accompanied by uncritical caring?

In the present contribution, we describe new data that bear directly on the issue of how character strengths might be associated with a life of meaning. This research employed the Orientation to Happiness Scale developed by Peterson, Park, and Seligman (2005b) and Steger, Frazier, Oishi, and Kaler's (2006) measure that divides the construct of meaning into two components: the *presence of meaning* and the *search for meaning*. To introduce our study, we first provide some background on how positive psychologists have approached good character.

The VIA Project

The VIA (Values in Action) Classification of Strengths is an ongoing project meant to complement the *Diagnostic and Statistical Manual* (DSM) of the American Psychiatric Association (1994) by focusing on what is right about people and specifically about the strengths of character that make the good life possible (Peterson & Seligman, 2004). Peterson and his colleagues followed the example of DSM and its collateral creations by proposing a classification scheme and devising ways of assessing its entries. The VIA Classification is the first and arguably most ambitious project deliberately developed from the perspective of positive psychology (Seligman, Steen, Park, & Peterson, 2005).

The VIA Classification recognizes the components of good character as existing at different levels of abstraction. *Virtues* are the core characteristics valued by moral philosophers and religious thinkers: wisdom, courage, humanity, justice, temperance, and transcendence. These six broad categories of virtue emerge consistently from historical surveys (Dahlsgaard, Peterson, & Seligman, 2005). Perhaps these are universal, grounded in biology through an evolutionary process that selected for these predispositions toward moral excellence as means of solving the important tasks necessary for survival of the species.

Character strengths are the psychological ingredients that define the virtues. Said another way, they are distinguishable ways of displaying one or another of the virtues. For example, the virtue of wisdom can be achieved through such strengths as curiosity, love of learning, judgment, and creativity, as well as through what we call perspective—having a "big picture" on life. These strengths are similar in that all involve the acquisition and use of knowledge, but they are also distinct. The VIA Classification approaches character strengths as dimensional traits—individual differences—that exist in degrees.

Criteria for Character Strengths

Entries for the VIA Classification were generated by reviewing pertinent literatures that addressed good character—from psychiatry, youth development, character education, religion, philosophy, organizational studies, and of course psychology. From the many candidate strengths identified, the list was winnowed by combining redundancies and applying the following criteria:

1. A strength needs to be manifest in the range of an individual's behavior—thoughts, feelings, and/or actions—in such a way that it can be assessed. In other words, a character strength should be trait-like in the sense of having a degree of generality across situations and stability across time.
2. A strength contributes to various fulfillments that comprise the good life, for the self and for others. Although strengths and virtues no doubt determine how an individual copes with adversity, our focus is on how they fulfill an individual. In keeping with the broad premise of positive psychology, strengths allow the individual to achieve more than the absence of distress and disorder. They "break through the zero point" of psychology's traditional concern with disease, disorder, and failure to address quality-of-life outcomes (Peterson, 2000).
3. Although strengths can and do produce desirable outcomes, each strength is morally valued in its own right, even in the absence of obvious beneficial outcomes. To say that a strength is morally valued is an important qualification because there exist individual differences that are widely valued and contribute to fulfillment but still fall outside the classification. Consider intelligence or athletic prowess. These talents and abilities are cut from a different cloth than are such character strengths as bravery or kindness. Talents are valued more for their tangible consequences (acclaim, wealth) than are character strengths. Someone who "does nothing" with a talent like a high IQ or physical dexterity risks eventual disdain. In contrast, we never hear the criticism that a person did nothing with his or her hope or honesty. Talents and abilities can be squandered, but strengths and virtues cannot.
4. The display of a strength by one person does not diminish other people in the vicinity but, rather, elevates them. Onlookers are impressed, inspired, and encouraged by their observation of virtuous action. Admiration is created, but not jealousy, because character strengths are the sorts of characteristics to which all can and do aspire. The more people surrounding us who are kind, or curious, or humorous, the greater our own likelihood of acting in these ways.
5. As suggested by Erikson's (1963) discussion of psychosocial stages and the virtues that result from their satisfactory resolutions, the larger society provides institutions and associated rituals for cultivating strengths and virtues. These can be thought of as simulations:

trial runs that allow children and adolescents to display and develop a valued characteristic in a safe (as-if) context in which guidance is explicit.

6. Yet another criterion for a character strength is the existence of consensually recognized paragons of virtue. Paragons of character display what psychologists call a cardinal trait, and the ease with which people can think of paragons in their own social circles gives the lie to the claim that virtuous people are either phony or boring (Wolf, 1982). Certainly, the virtuous people we each know are neither. In one of the preliminary strategies of validating assessment strategies, Peterson and Seligman (2004) asked research assistants to nominate people of their acquaintance who were paragons of virtue and prevail upon them to complete our measures. No one had any difficulty thinking of appropriate respondents.
7. A final criterion is that the strength is unidimensional and not able to be decomposed into other strengths in the classification. For example, the character strength of "tolerance" meets most of the other criteria enumerated but is a complex blend of critical thinking, kindness, and fairness. The character strength of "responsibility" seems to result from persistence and teamwork. And so on.

Character Strengths

When the foregoing criteria were applied to the candidate strengths identified through literature searches, what resulted were 24 positive traits organized under six broad virtues (see Table 13.1). There are, of course, other positive traits that we might wish to encourage among people—ambition, autonomy, and patience, to name but a few—and their absence in the classification reflects the judgment that these are not as universally valued as the included entries.

Assessment of Character Strengths

What distinguishes the VIA Classification from previous attempts to articulate good character is its simultaneous concern with assessment. Most philosophers emphasize that virtuous activity involves choosing virtue in light of a justifiable life plan. In more psychological language, this characterization means that people can reflect on their own virtues and talk about them to others. They may, of course, be misled and/or misleading, but virtues are not the sort of entities that are in principle outside the realm of self-commentary.

Our measurement work has been deliberately broad. To date, we have devised and evaluated several different methods: (a) *focus groups* to flesh out the everyday meanings of character strengths among different groups (Steen, Kachorek, & Peterson, 2003); (b) *self-report questionnaires* suitable for adults and young people (e.g., Park & Peterson, 2006c; Peterson, Park, & Seligman, 2005a); (c) *structured interviews* to identify what we call signature

Table 13.1 VIA Classification of Strengths

1. Wisdom and knowledge
    - Creativity: thinking of novel and productive ways to do things
    - Curiosity: taking an interest in all of ongoing experience
    - Open-mindedness: thinking things through and examining them from all sides
    - Love of learning: mastering new skills, topics, and bodies of knowledge
    - Perspective: being able to provide wise counsel to others
2. Courage
    - Honesty and authenticity: speaking the truth and presenting oneself in a genuine way
    - Bravery: not shrinking from threat, challenge, difficulty, or pain
    - Perseverance: finishing what one starts
    - Zest: approaching life with excitement and energy
3. Humanity
    - Kindness: doing favors and good deeds for others
    - Love: valuing close relations with others
    - Social intelligence: being aware of the motives and feelings of self and others
4. Justice
    - Fairness: treating all people the same according to notions of fairness and justice
    - Leadership: organizing group activities and seeing that they happen
    - Teamwork: working well as a member of a group or team
5. Temperance
    - Forgiveness: forgiving those who have done wrong
    - Modesty: letting one's accomplishments speak for themselves
    - Prudence: being careful about one's choices; not saying or doing things that might later be regretted
    - Self-regulation: regulating what one feels and does
6. Transcendence
    - Appreciation of beauty: noticing and appreciating beauty, excellence, and/or skilled performance in all domains of life
    - Gratitude: being aware of and thankful for the good things that happen
    - Hope: expecting the best and working to achieve it
    - Humor: liking to laugh and joke; bringing smiles to other people
7. Spirituality and religiousness
    - Having coherent beliefs about the higher purpose and meaning of life

strengths; (d) *informant reports* of how target individuals rise to the occasion (or not) with appropriate strengths of character (e.g., courage in the face of fear; open-mindedness when confronting difficult decisions; hope when encountering setbacks; and so on); (e) *case studies* of nominated paragons of specific strengths (e.g., Peterson & Seligman, 2004); (f) a *content analysis* procedure for assessing character strengths from unstructured descriptions of self and others (Park & Peterson, 2006a); and (g) strategies for scoring positive traits from such *archived material* as obituaries. These latter methods will greatly extend the reach of future studies to allow the investigation of good character among the quick, the dead, the famous, and the otherwise unavailable. Furthermore, they will allow longitudinal studies to be mounted retrospectively, so long as suitable verbal material for content analyses has been left behind, a strategy described as the *time machine method* (Peterson & Seligman, 1984).

Space does not permit a detailed description of what has been learned about the reliability and validity of these different methods for assessing strengths of character. Suffice it to say that we have successfully established the internal consistency of our questionnaire scales and their test–retest stability over several months. We have investigated the validity of our methods for assessing positive traits with the known-groups procedure and more generally by mapping out their nomological nets. We also note ongoing attempts to devise interventions to change character strengths (Park & Peterson, 2008), based on Kurt Lewin's adage that one good way to understand a phenomenon is to try to change it. To the degree that interventions successfully target specific character strengths as we measure them, we will have compelling evidence that they indeed are discrete individual differences captured by our assessment strategies. Although these different methods will likely converge in the strengths they identify within given individuals, we emphasize that each method will also provide unique information about good character (cf. Hedge, Borman, & Birkeland, 2001). Indeed, the relevant data at hand suggest convergence but not redundancy.

To develop and validate measures, we did *not* rely on college student samples. Although we of course believe that young adults have strengths of character, we were persuaded by previous thinkers from Aristotle to Erik Erikson that good character is most apt to be found among those who are mature, who have done more than rehearse work and love.

To reach a wide range of adults, we placed questionnaires online (http://www.authentichappiness.org). Critical to the appeal of this method, we believe, is that upon completion of the measures, respondents are given instant feedback about their top five strengths. In addition to expediting our research, this strategy has taught us something about character: Being able to put a name to what one does well is intriguing and even empowering.

If it is meaningful to generalize across our 500,000+ respondents, the typical person we have studied is a middle-aged adult who has attended college, has held various jobs, and is married or living as such. Females are over-represented by a 2–3:1 margin. The majority of the respondents are from the United States; the remainder are mostly from English-speaking nations, but also represented are research participants from the rest of the world. Among U.S. respondents, the ethnic makeup of our samples approximates that of the nation as a whole, with a tilt toward European Americans.

These research subjects are hardly a representative sample of the U.S. or world population, but we would like to stress the diversity of our respondents across virtually all demographic contrasts (other than computer literacy). Recently, researchers have shown that Internet studies typically enroll more diverse samples than do conventional studies using psychology subject pool samples at colleges or universities and that they are as valid as traditional research methods (Gosling, Vazire, Srivastava, & John, 2004; Kraut et al., 2004). In any event, our concern has been with what is common across respondents from different groups and not what is unique, and we believe that the commonalities we have discovered are both striking and real.

Our Internet surveys have paid the dividend of a diverse sample, but we have additionally sought to establish the cross-cultural generality (or not) of our constructs by deliberately surveying people from different nations and cultures about their recognition and valuing of different strengths of character, using focus groups for nonliterate samples (e.g., Biswas-Diener, 2006). And our colleagues around the world have begun serious translations of our inventories into Chinese, French, German, Hindi, Italian, Japanese, Korean, Portuguese, Spanish, and Urdu. These projects are in progress, although preliminary data are consistent with the premise of universality.

Given the range of classified traits, we are able to offer nuanced conclusions about their differential universality. Even within a given nation or culture, there is good reason for researchers to assess a number of different strengths. We believe that good character is comprised of a family of positive traits and that no one person will show all or even most of them (Walker & Pitts, 1998).

Character Strengths and Meaning

How are strengths of character related to measures of meaning? Available to us were responses from a large Internet sample of adults to surveys about character, meaning, and well-being.[2] Specifically, participants completed the Values in Action Inventory of Strengths (VIA-IS; Peterson, Park, & Seligman, 2005a), which yields scores for each of the 24 character strengths of interest to us; the Orientation to Happiness Scale (Peterson, Park, & Seligman, 2005b), which measures the endorsement of pleasure, engagement, and meaning as routes to happiness; the Meaning in Life Questionnaire (Steger et al., 2006), which assesses both the presence of meaning and the search for meaning; the Satisfaction With Life Scale (SWLS; Diener, Emmons, Larsen, & Griffin, 1985), which assesses overall satisfaction with life as it has been lived; the Positive and Negative Affect Schedule (PANAS; Watson, Clark, & Tellegen, 1988); and the Center for Epidemiological Studies Depression Scale (CES-D; Radloff, 1977).

---

[2] Some of these data were reported by Peterson, Ruch, Beerman, Park, and Seligman (2007).

This was an exploratory study, but we had some general hypotheses. Based on past research, we expected an orientation to meaning and the presence of meaning to be positively associated with life satisfaction and positive affect and negatively associated with depression and negative affect. Although one could argue as did Seligman (2002) that any and all character strengths contribute to a life of meaning, we nonetheless expected that the strengths of character associated with life satisfaction—curiosity, gratitude, hope, love, and zest—would be the ones most strongly linked to an orientation to meaning and the presence of meaning, as would such strengths as perspective and religiousness (Steger & Frazier, 2005). Finally, in keeping with the findings of Steger and colleagues, we expected that the search for meaning would show smaller associations with most strengths of character and measures of well-being. Indeed, given that people usually search for meaning when it is absent in their lives, these associations with well-being might even be negatives ones.

Sample

The sample consisted of many thousands of adult respondents who completed one or more of the measures of interest on the Authentic Happiness website (http://www.authentichappiness.com) between September 2002 and December 2005. Respondents registered on the website and provided demographic information. Then, they completed measures of their choosing. Accordingly, sample size varied across measures (see Table 13.2), although in each of the analyses reported here, the degrees of freedom exceeded 4,000.

Respondents received immediate feedback about their scores relative to other respondents, and this feature seemed to motivate participants. Respondents presumably came to the website to learn more about positive psychology and themselves. Questionnaires on this website were presented only in English. For the relatively small number (~5%) of respondents who completed a measure more than once, only the first set of scores was used for the analyses reported here.

Most respondents were from the United States (61%), although respondents were from almost 200 different nations, notably the United Kingdom (7%), Canada (6%), Australia (4%), and New Zealand (1%). There were more females than males (71% vs. 29%). The typical age of respondents was 40 years of age, with a range across the adult years. The typical level of educational attainment for respondents was a few years of college, ranging from less than high school to postbaccalaureate. Relative to the U.S. and world populations as a whole, respondents were highly educated, and most had college degrees (66%).

Measures

Values in Action Inventory of Strengths The VIA-IS is a face-valid questionnaire that uses 5-point Likert-style items to measure the degree to which respondents endorse items reflecting the 24 strengths of character in our

Table 13.2 Correlates of Meaning

	Mean (SD)	Orientation to Meaning	Presence of Meaning	Search for Meaning
Orientation to happiness ($N = 29{,}987$)				
Pleasure	3.12 (.86)	0.17***	0.17***	−0.05***
Engagement	3.09 (.74)	0.44***	0.43***	−0.14***
Meaning	3.50 (.94)	—	0.67***	−0.04
Meaning in life ($N = 10{,}099$)				
Presence	23.5 (8.1)	0.67***	—	−0.33***
Search	24.8 (7.5)	−0.14***	−0.33***	—
Life satisfaction ($N = 61{,}494$)	21.3 (7.5)	0.41***	0.57***	−0.31***
PANAS ($N = 62{,}998$)				
Positive affect	28.8 (8.3)	0.44***	0.51***	−0.16***
Negative affect	15.8 (6.6)	−0.19***	−0.33***	0.19***
Depressive symptoms ($N = 13.343$)	17.4 (13.6)	−0.32***	−0.52***	0.28***
Character strengths ($N = 283{,}576$)				
Religiousness	3.47 (.89)	0.66*	0.61***	−0.07***
Gratitude	3.90 (.62)	0.54***	0.51***	−0.10***
Hope	3.60 (.68)	0.50***	0.62***	−0.23***
Zest	3.57 (.66)	0.48***	0.58***	−0.21***
Perspective	3.77 (.55)	0.48***	0.46***	−0.09***
Love	3.91 (.60)	0.46***	0.50***	−0.16***
Curiosity	3.97 (.56)	0.45***	0.46***	−0.14***
Leadership	3.75 (.55)	0.41***	0.31***	−0.03
Bravery	3.66 (.61)	0.39***	0.37***	−0.11***
Social intelligence	3.76 (.56)	0.39***	0.37***	−0.06***
Kindness	3.96 (.53)	0.38***	0.30***	−0.04
Forgiveness	3.64 (.66)	0.35***	0.30***	−0.08***
Teamwork	3.69 (.55)	0.35***	0.30***	−0.06***
Fairness	3.99 (.50)	0.35***	0.22***	−0.03
Beauty	3.78 (.68)	0.34***	0.23***	0.07***
Honesty	3.96 (.48)	0.33***	0.31***	−0.11***
Creativity	3.76 (.60)	0.31***	0.24***	0.01
Learning	3.83 (.65)	0.30***	0.22***	0.02
Perseverance	3.62 (.67)	0.29***	0.37***	−0.14***
Humor	3.81 (.63)	0.29***	0.30***	−0.11***
Judgment	3.96 (.52)	0.29***	0.22***	−0.01
Self-regulation	3.29 (.63)	0.27***	0.32***	−0.11***
Prudence	3.47 (.58)	0.21***	−0.20***	−0.03
Modesty	3.39 (.63)	0.11***	0.08***	0

These are partial correlations that control for age, gender, and education; ***$p < .001$.

character classification (from 1 = "very much unlike me" to 5 = "very much like me"). There are 10 items per strength. For example, the character strength of hope is measured with items that include "I know that I will succeed with the goals I set for myself." The strength of gratitude is measured with such items as "At least once a day, I stop and count my blessings." Responses were averaged across the relevant items to provide scores for each of the 24 character strengths.

Details concerning the reliability and validity of the VIA-IS are presented elsewhere (Park & Peterson, 2006b). Briefly: (a) all scales have acceptable reliabilities (as > .70); (b) test–retest correlations for all scales over a four-month period are substantial (*rs* > .70) and in almost all cases approach their internal consistencies; (c) scores are skewed to the right but have coefficients of variation ranging from .15 to .25, implying acceptable variability; (d) self-nomination of strengths correlate substantially (*rs* > .5) with the matching scale scores; and (e) ratings by friends or family members of a respondent's top strengths correlate moderately (*rs* ≅ .3) with the matching scale scores for most of the 24 strengths, implying that the VIA-IS reflects something more than just self-perception.

Orientation to Happiness Scale The Orientation to Happiness Scale is an 18-item measure that consists of six items measuring the degree to which one endorses each of three orientations to happiness: engagement (e.g., "I am always very absorbed in what I do"); pleasure (e.g., "Life is too short to postpone the pleasures it can provide"); and meaning (e.g., "I have a responsibility to make the world a better place"). Each item required a respondent to answer on a 5-point scale the degree to which the item applies (1 = "very much unlike me" through 5 = "very much like me"). Scores are averaged across the relevant items to yield scores reflecting the endorsement of engagement, pleasure, and meaning as routes to happiness. Peterson, Park, and Seligman (2005b) showed that these three subscales are reliable (as ≅ .70) and for the most part empirically distinct.

Meaning in Life Questionnaire The Meaning in Life Questionnaire is a 10-item measure that consists of five items indicating the presence of meaning (e.g., "I understand my life's meaning") and five items measuring the search for meaning (e.g., "I am always looking to find my life's purpose"). Participants respond to each item on a 7-point scale (from 1 = "absolutely untrue" to 7 = "absolutely true"). Scores are summed separately for the two components of meaning. These subscales are reliable and stable (Steger et al., 2006). They are negatively correlated but distinct.

Satisfaction With Life Scale The SWLS of Diener, Emmons, Larsen, and Griffin (1985) consists of five items that measure the individual's evaluation of satisfaction with his or her life in general (e.g., "I am satisfied with my life" and "If I could live my life over, I would change almost nothing"). Respondents select one of seven options (ranging from "strongly disagree" to "strongly agree") for each question. Responses are summed to provide a total life satisfaction score. Research has established excellent psychometric properties for the SWLS (Diener, 1994). The measure is highly reliable and has a large network of sensible correlates. Although SWLS scores are typically skewed toward the right, meaning that most respondents are relatively happy, in most samples there is nonetheless a range in life satisfaction.

Positive and Negative Affect Schedule The PANAS is a 20-item measure of experienced affect, positive and negative (Watson, Clark, & Tellegen, 1988). It asks respondents to rate on 5-point scales (from 1 = "very slightly or not at all" to 5 = "extremely") adjectives describing dominant moods during the past week. Scores are created by summing positive affect items (e.g., "inspired") and negative affect items (e.g., "scared") separately. The PANAS is demonstrably reliable and valid, and the evidence is particular strong that positive affect and negative affect are independent factors.

Center for Epidemiological Studies Depression Scale A self-report scale, CES-D (Radloff, 1977) contains 20 items symptomatic of depression, responded to on 0–3-point scales. Scores are summed, and high scores indicate a greater level of depression. The CES-D was designed to avoid the problem of some depression scales of overemphasizing somatic items that frequently characterize nondepressed older persons or persons with disabilities. Respondents indicate the extent to which they have experienced the symptoms over the past week.

Results

We first looked at demographic correlates of the study's major measures. Consistent with past research, women were more likely than men to endorse such character strengths as appreciation of beauty (r = 0.17), gratitude (r = 0.20), kindness (r = 0.18), and love (r = 0.16) but less likely to endorse creativity (r = −0.13). There were no substantive gender differences with respect to any of the measures of meaning (all rs < 0.06). Older respondents reported a greater orientation to meaning (r = 0.06) and to engagement (r = 0.14) and less of an orientation to pleasure (r = −0.18). Older respondents also reported more positive affect (r = 0.16) and less negative affect (r = −0.16). Older respondents were somewhat more likely than younger respondents to report the presence of meaning (r = 0.08) and less likely to indicate that they were searching for meaning (r = −0.13). More educated respondents reported less of an orientation to pleasure (r = −0.14), a greater orientation to meaning (r = 0.15), greater presence of meaning (r = 0.14), and less depression (r = −0.13).

We then examined the intercorrelations among the meaning measures, controlling for age, gender, and level of education (see Table 13.2). Because of the large sample size, virtually all these partial correlations were statistically significant, so we limit our attention to those notable on theoretical grounds. As Steger, Frazier, and Oishi (2006) found, the presence of meaning and the search for meaning were negatively and moderately associated ($r = -0.33$). Orientation to meaning was positively and strongly associated with the presence of meaning ($r = 0.67$) but minimally associated the search for meaning ($r = -0.04$). Interestingly, an orientation to engagement was also positively associated with the presence of meaning ($r = 0.42$), raising questions about directions of implied causality. Being highly engaged in what one does may lead to a sense that one's life is meaningful, but having a sense of meaning seems just as likely to lead to engagement in whatever it is that one is doing.

Table 13.2 also shows correlations between the measures of well-being and character strengths and the different indices of meaning, again controlling for age, gender, and level of education. These data were coherent and much as expected. Both an orientation to meaning and the presence of meaning were positively associated with life satisfaction and positive affect and negatively associated with depression and negative affect. The strengths of character most highly associated with life satisfaction were strongly linked to an orientation to meaning and the presence of meaning: curiosity, gratitude, hope, love, and zest. Also highly associated with meaning were the strengths of religiousness, perspective, leadership, bravery, and social intelligence. The character strength correlates of the search for meaning tended to be more modest and negative, with hope (partial $r = -0.23$) and zest (partial $r = -0.21$) showing the strongest associations.

Discussion

This study showed that meaning is associated with strengths of character, some more so than others. That an orientation to meaning and the presence of meaning were strongly correlated with the character strengths that previous research linked to life satisfaction is not surprising, given that "meaning" is an important component of the psychological good life. However, these meaning measures were also associated with strengths of character not so highly predictive of life satisfaction, specifically religiousness, perspective, leadership, bravery, and social intelligence.

Indeed, the strongest character correlate of meaning in the present sample was religiousness. Religious beliefs are not the only perspective with which to frame a life of meaning, but they certainly provide an important one (Emmons, 1999). The majority of the respondents were from the United States, and the United States is a relatively religious country (Inglehart & Norris, 2004). Further research needs to take a more explicit cross-national focus to see if this result also holds in such more secular countries as those of Northern Europe (cf. Peterson, Ruch, Beerman, Park, & Seligman, 2007).

The VIA Classification defines perspective as the ability to offer wise counsel to others, and the VIA-IS operationalizes bravery with a number of items that entail going against the social grain to express unpopular opinions. The presence of meaning in one's life would be expected to have close links with both of these strengths. Social intelligence and leadership allow a person to contribute to an external good, so their strong associations with the meaning measures also make sense.

Limitations of the present study include its cross-sectional design, which precludes causal conclusions, and its reliance on self-report measures. The individual's own point of view is of course relevant to understanding meaning and, for that matter, strengths of character, but issues of social desirability and other response sets can be raised. Alleviating some of these concerns is that both the Meaning of Life Questionnaire and the VIA-IS have been validated against informant reports.

Earlier in this chapter, we praised Internet samples because they yield diverse respondents. However, the careful reader may have noticed from the means in Table 13.2 that the typical research participant in our study was not especially happy. Life satisfaction scores on average were several scale points lower than what is usually found in non-Internet samples (Veenhoven, 2006), and CES-D scores placed many respondents in the moderately depressed range (Myers & Weissman, 1980). Positive psychology rhetoric holds that the field is interested in moving people from +2 to +5 (Seligman, 2002), but those individuals who take the time to complete online positive psychology measures often reside south of neutral. In retrospect, how could this not be? We need to recognize the special nature of our Internet sample and more generally the constituency of positive psychology among the general public.

Peterson, Park, and Seligman's (2005b) orientation-to-meaning subscale was highly associated with Steger and colleague's (2006) presence-of-meaning subscale, suggesting that they tap the same construct and providing further construct validity for each measure. Orientation to meaning was essentially independent of the search for meaning, underscoring the importance of the distinction by Steger and colleagues between the presence versus the search for meaning.

The present data showed that the search for meaning was associated with somewhat lower life satisfaction, greater depression, less positive affect, and more negative affect. As Steger et al. (2006) observed, one is more likely to search for meaning when one is dissatisfied (cf. King, Hicks, Krull, & Del Gaiso, 2006). It is also conceivable that a search for meaning—at least if futile—leads to dysphoria.

Is the search for meaning therefore undesirable? Given Frankl's (1959) emphasis on the search for meaning, and similar views by Maddi (1970),

Crumbaugh (1977), and others, this conclusion needs to be examined carefully. The Meaning in Life Questionnaire is one of the first measures to distinguish the presence of meaning from the search for meaning, so the relevant data are just starting to appear. That the search for meaning is moderately associated with negative feelings does not in itself mean that the search for meaning is undesirable. One way to find meaning is to search for it, and this search may be neither easy nor particularly pleasant (Baumeister & Vohs, 2005). Although longitudinal data are needed to support a developmental claim, it is of note that in our sample, older respondents were somewhat more likely to report the presence of meaning in their lives and somewhat less likely to be searching for it. Older respondents were also less oriented to pleasure and more oriented to meaning and to engagement.

Steger et al. (2006) observed that the presence of meaning does not preclude the search for further meaning. Indeed, they proposed that when both exist, a person should fare especially well. Their two scales are negatively associated, but not so highly that presence and search cannot coexist. We therefore wondered how these two components of meaning might interact with respect to life satisfaction.

We computed a multiple regression predicting life satisfaction. We entered demographics (age, education, and gender) in the first block, presence and search for meaning (both centered) in the second block, and their product in the third block. The overall regression was significant, $R^2 = .36$, $F = 587$, $p < .001$, and significant beta coefficients in the final model were age (−0.09), education (0.09), presence of meaning (0.58), search for meaning (−0.14), and, most interesting, the interaction (0.07). To interpret this interaction, we split the sample into four groups according to the presence-of-meaning scores; then, within each subsample we calculated the correlation between search for meaning and life satisfaction (controlling for age, education, and gender). As Figure 13.1 shows, these partial correlations were negative except among the

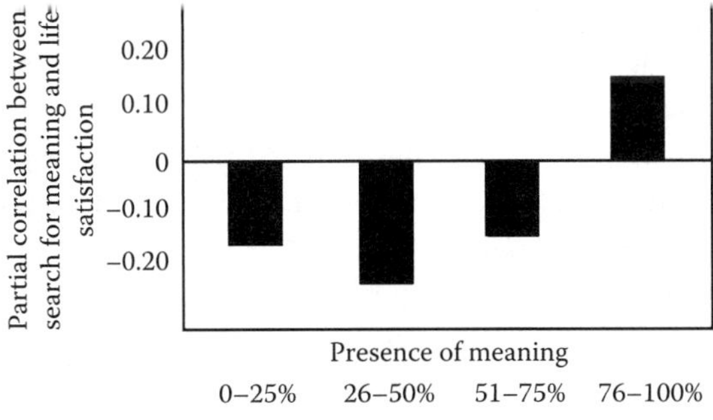

Figure 13.1 Life satisfaction as a function of the search for meaning among respondents differing in the presence of meaning. These are partial correlations controlling for age, gender, and level of education. All partial correlations are significant at $p < .001$.

top quarter of respondents, where the partial correlation was positive. Said another way, the search for meaning is associated with lower satisfaction except for those people who have already found meaning; for the latter, the ongoing search represents value-added vis-à-vis a satisfied life.

Conclusions

The field of positive psychology is conventionally divided into the study of positive emotions, positive traits, and enabling institutions (Peterson, 2006). The study of meaning spans these areas and is therefore of central concern to positive psychology. Although the research described here approached meaning as an individual difference—a positive trait—meaning is strongly linked to feelings and for many individuals goes hand in hand with the venerable institution of religion. Positive psychologists stress that their interest extends beyond "happiness" yet routinely use life satisfaction or happiness measures as the chief outcome of interest (e.g., Seligman, Steen, Park, & Peterson, 2005). Perhaps measures of meaning should be employed as well.

Psychometrically sound measures of meaning now exist that avoid such obvious confounds as item overlap with putative outcomes. Even so, strong associations between measures of meaning and well-being remain, showing that the presence of meaning is an excellent marker of the good life. Could anyone say with sincerity that his or her life is without meaning or purpose but nonetheless a good one?

The study of meaning has a sustained lineage within psychology, and positive psychologists would be wise to heed the available lessons from this work. First, positive psychologists cannot ignore the negative—stress and challenge—in understanding what it means to live well. What is most troubling in life can set the stage for what is most fulfilling. Consider that complex emotional experiences often blend the positive and negative; that optimism is most apparent when people confront setbacks and failures; that crisis reveals strengths of character; that ongoing challenge is a prerequisite to experience flow in the moment and to achieve something important in a lifetime; and so on (Peterson, 2006).

Second, although stores overflow with self-help books describing simple steps toward lasting happiness, there is no corresponding genre for how to attain a meaningful life. Those who study meaning recognize that there are no effortless steps for attaining it, and positive psychologists should be similarly modest in their claims and stick close to the conclusions that data actually allow. Research implies that meaning can emerge from internalized religion, from charitable work, and from community involvement, but all entail a full-fledged lifestyle as opposed to a one-shot intervention. Given the robust links between certain strengths of character and a life of meaning, perhaps another route to a meaningful life lies through good character.

Again, we stress that the cultivation of character requires ongoing work (Park & Peterson, 2008).

In the beginning of this chapter, we raised the question whether meaning is the most important aspect of human existence and suggested that this is, at least in part, an empirical question. Accumulating evidence presented in this volume and elsewhere builds a strong case for the importance of meaning. We have previously written that a three-word summary of positive psychology is possible: Other people matter (Peterson, 2006). Perhaps a two-word summary will someday be equally apt: Meaning matters.

References

American Psychiatric Association. (1994). *Diagnostic and statistical manual of mental disorders* (4th ed.). Washington, DC: Author.

Antonovsky, A. (1979). *Health, stress, and coping.* San Francisco, CA: Jossey-Bass.

Bacon, S. F. (2005). Positive psychology's two cultures. *Review of General Psychology, 9,* 181–192.

Baumeister, R. F., & Vohs, K. D. (2005). The pursuit of meaningfulness in life. In C. R. Snyder & S. J. Lopez (Eds.), *Handbook of positive psychology* (pp. 608–618). New York, NY: Oxford University Press.

Biswas-Diener, R. (2006). From the equator to the North Pole: A study of character strengths. *Journal of Happiness Studies, 7,* 293–310.

Crumbaugh, J. C. (1977). The Seeking of Noetic Goals Test (SONG): A complementary scale to the Purpose in Life Test (PIL). *Journal of Clinical Psychology, 33,* 900–907.

Csikszentmihalyi, M. (1990). *Flow: The psychology of optimal experience.* New York, NY: HarperCollins.

Dahlsgaard, K., Peterson, C., & Seligman, M. E. P. (2005). Shared virtue: The convergence of valued human strengths across culture and history. *Review of General Psychology, 9,* 203–213.

Damon, W., Menon, J., & Bronk, K. C. (2003). The development of purpose during adolescence. *Applied Developmental Science, 7,* 119–128.

Diener, E. (1994). Assessing subjective well-being: Progress and opportunities. *Social Indicators Research, 31,* 103–157.

Diener, E., Emmons, R. A., Larsen, R. J., & Griffin, S. (1985). The Satisfaction With Life Scale. *Journal of Personality Assessment, 49,* 71–75.

Emmons, R. A. (1986). Personal strivings: An approach to personality and subjective well-being. *Journal of Personality and Social Psychology, 51,* 1058–1068.

Emmons, R. A. (1999). *The psychology of ultimate concerns: Motivation and spirituality in personality.* New York, NY: Guilford Press.

Erikson, E. (1963). *Childhood and society* (2nd ed.). New York, NY: Norton.

Frankl, V. E. (1959). *Man's search for meaning: An introduction to logotherapy.* Boston, MA: Beacon.

Gosling, S. D., Vazire, S., Srivastava, S., & John, O. P. (2004). Should we trust web-based studies? A comparative analysis of six preconceptions about Internet questionnaires. *American Psychologist, 59,* 93–104.

Hedge, J. W., Borman, W. C., & Birkeland, S. A. (2001). History and development of multisource feedback as a methodology. In D. W. Bracken, C. W. Timmreck, & A. H. Church (Eds.), *The handbook of multisource feedback* (pp. 15–32). San Francisco, CA: Jossey-Bass.

Inglehart, R., & Norris, P. (2004). *Sacred and secular: Religion and politics worldwide.* New York, NY: Cambridge University Press.

King, L., Hicks, J. A., Krull, J. L., & Del Gaiso, A. (2006). Positive affect and the experience of meaning in life. *Journal of Personality and Social Psychology, 90,* 179–196.

Klinger, E. (1977). *Meaning and void: Inner experience and the incentives in people's lives.* Minneapolis: University of Minnesota Press.

Kraut, R., Olson, J., Banaji, M., Bruckman, A., Cohen, J., & Couper, M. (2004). Psychological research online: Report of board of scientific affairs' advisory group on the conduct of research on the Internet. *American Psychologist, 59,* 105–117.

Little, B. R. (1983). Personal projects: A rationale and method for investigation. *Environment and Behavior, 15,* 273–309.

Maddi, S. R. (1970). The search for meaning. In M. Page (Ed.), *Nebraska symposium on motivation* (pp. 137–186). Lincoln: University of Nebraska Press.

Maslow, A. H. (1970). *Motivation and personality* (2nd ed.). New York, NY: Harper & Row.

May, R. (1953). *Man's search for himself.* New York, NY: Norton.

Myers, J., & Weissman, M. (1980). Use of a self-report symptom scale to detect depression in a community sample. *American Journal of Psychiatry, 137,* 1081–1084.

Noddings, N. (2003). *Happiness and education.* New York, NY: Cambridge University Press.

Park, N., & Peterson, C. (2006a). Character strengths and happiness among young children: Content analysis of parental descriptions. *Journal of Happiness Studies, 7,* 323–341.

Park, N., & Peterson, C. (2006b). Methodological issues in positive psychology and the assessment of character strengths. In A. D. Ong & M. van Dulmen (Eds.), *Handbook of methods in positive psychology* (pp. 292–305). New York, NY: Oxford University Press.

Park, N., & Peterson, C. (2006c). Moral competence and character strengths among adolescents: The development and validation of the Values in Action Inventory of Strengths for Youth. *Journal of Adolescence, 29,* 891–905.

Park, N., & Peterson, C. (2008). The cultivation of character strengths: Teaching the psychological good life. In M. Ferrari & G. Poworowski (Eds.), *Teaching for wisdom* (pp. 59–78). Mahwah, NJ: Erlbaum.

Park, N., Peterson, C., & Seligman, M. E. P. (2004). Strengths of character and well-being. *Journal of Social and Clinical Psychology, 23,* 603–619.

Peterson, C. (2000). The future of optimism. *American Psychologist, 55,* 44–55.

Peterson, C. (2006). *A primer in positive psychology.* New York, NY: Oxford University Press.

Peterson, C., Park, N., & Seligman, M. E. P. (2005a). Assessment of character strengths. In G. P. Koocher, J. C. Norcross, & S. S. Hill III (Eds.), *Psychologists' desk reference* (2nd ed., pp. 93–98). New York, NY: Oxford University Press.

Peterson, C., Park, N., & Seligman, M. E. P. (2005b). Orientations to happiness and life satisfaction: The full life versus the empty life. *Journal of Happiness Studies, 6,* 25–41.

Peterson, C., Ruch, W., Beerman, U., Park, N., & Seligman, M. E. P. (2007). Strengths of character, orientations to happiness, and life satisfaction. *Journal of Positive Psychology, 2,* 1–8.

Peterson, C., & Seligman, M. E. P. (1984). Causal explanations as a risk factor for depression: Theory and evidence. *Psychological Review, 91,* 347–374.

Peterson, C., & Seligman, M. E. P. (2004). *Character strengths and virtues: A handbook and classification.* New York, NY: Oxford University Press.

Radloff, L. S. (1977). The CES-D Scale: A self-report depression scale for research in the general population. *Applied Psychological Measurement, 1*, 385–401.
Rogers, C. R. (1961). *On becoming a person*. Boston, MA: Houghton Mifflin.
Seligman, M. E. P. (2002). *Authentic happiness*. New York, NY: Free Press.
Seligman, M. E. P., Steen, T. A., Park, N., & Peterson, C. (2005). Positive psychology progress: Empirical validation of interventions. *American Psychologist, 60*, 410–421.
Steen, T. A., Kachorek, L. V., & Peterson, C. (2003). Character strengths among youth. *Journal of Youth and Adolescence, 32*, 5–16.
Steger, M. F., & Frazier, P. (2005). Meaning in life: One link in the chain from religiousness to well-being. *Journal of Counseling Psychology, 52*, 574–582.
Steger, M. F., Frazier, P., Oishi, S., & Kaler, M. (2006). The Meaning in Life Questionnaire: Assessing the presence of and search for meaning in life. *Journal of Counseling Psychology, 53*, 80–93.
Veenhoven, R. (2006). *World database of happiness, distributional findings in nations*. Retrieved from www.worlddatabaseofhappiness.eur.nl (Accessed October 20, 2006).
Walker, L. J., & Pitts, R. C. (1998). Naturalistic conceptions of moral maturity. *Developmental Psychology, 34*, 403–419.
Watson, D., Clark, L. A., & Tellegen, A. (1988). Development and validation of brief measures of positive and negative affect: The PANAS scales. *Journal of Personality and Social Psychology, 54*, 1063–1070.
Watson, J. (1895). *Hedonistic theories from Aristippus to Spencer*. New York, NY: Macmillan.
Wolf, S. (1982). Moral saints. *Journal of Philosophy, 79*, 419–439.
Wong, P. T. P. (1998). Implicit theories of meaningful life and the development of the Personal Meaning Profile. In P. T. P. Wong & P. S. Fry (Eds.), *The human quest for meaning: A handbook of psychological research and clinical applications* (pp. 111–140). Mahwah, NJ: Erlbaum.

14
The Construction of Meaning From Life Events

Empirical Studies of Personal Narratives

KRISTIN L. SOMMER
City University of New York

ROY F. BAUMEISTER
Florida State University

TYLER F. STILLMAN
Southern Utah University

The relentless human propensity to interpret all events and experiences has encouraged many thinkers throughout the ages to conclude that a fundamental need or drive for meaning is an innate part of the human mind. Small children endlessly ask "why?" in response to adult generalizations and explanations. Teenagers question what they have learned from parents and authorities by way of forming their own conclusions. Adults analyze the nuances of their spouses' acts as well as the grand import or causal implications of national events, from politics to sports. People may ruminate for years to search for meaning behind unfathomable events; they turn to scientific experts, poets, or religious leaders to give meaning to the incomprehensible.

Yet how is the quest for meaning structured, and what can satisfy it? Our approach to this question has been to collect first-person narratives of people's everyday life events, such as minor interpersonal conflicts and romantic heartbreak. We then compare different perspectives on similar events. For example, as we will describe, people who have their hearts broken offer stories about unrequited love that differ in systematic ways from the stories told by people who played the role of rejector and broke someone else's heart. Such comparisons offer a key to understanding the interpretive activity of the human mind. If the events are roughly the same in an objective sense, then the systematic differences between the groups of stories reflect how the individual's interpretation is shaped by perspective, motivation, and bias.

Narratives are particularly instructive as a method of studying the human drive for meaning. McAdams (1993) has argued that self-knowledge is created, organized, and stored in the form of narratives. In other words, the things people know and feel about themselves and others are based not on trait terms but on stories. McAdams further argues that answering the grand question "Who am I?" is best answered by telling one's life story. Narratives can be a rich source of information about personal meaning and a valuable tool in understanding the human drive for meaning.

Our central argument is that people seek meaning in ordinary events along the same lines that they seek meaning in life generally. That is, the same factors that guide the effort to make sense out of life in general (so as to have a meaningful life) shape the daily efforts to make sense out of individual experiences. Baumeister (1991) proposed that the human quest for a meaningful life is shaped by four needs for meaning, and we will invoke these same needs to explain the meaning-making activities of everyday life (see Baumeister & Newman, 1994).

First, people need a *sense of purpose* in life. That is, people want to perceive their current activities as relating to future outcomes, and so current events draw meaning from possible future circumstances. Purposiveness includes meeting objective goals and reaching a state of subjective fulfillment. Second, people desire *feelings of efficacy*. That is, they seek to interpret events in ways that support the belief that they have control over their outcomes and that they can make a difference in some important way. Third, people want to view their actions as having *positive value* or as being morally justified. Fourth, people want a sense of *positive self-worth*. They seek ways of establishing that they are good, admirable, worthy individuals with desirable traits.

People are most happy when these needs for meaning are satisfied (Baumeister, 1991). However, it is not enough to conclude simply that one has a sense of purpose, efficacy, value, and self-worth. Rather, these conclusions must derive logically from the evidence drawn from one's own life experiences. People must find a way to make sense of events whose implications contradict their understanding of what makes life meaningful. This drive to make sense of life events involves such processes as searching for a higher purpose in negative or tragic life events, presenting the self in ways that enhance feelings of moral rectitude, construing a connection or coherency among outcomes that are truly unpredictable, and reinterpreting ego threats in ways that reflect positively on the self.

The drive for purpose, efficacy, value, and self-worth may be explored through use of autobiographical narratives in which individuals describe the events preceding and following important life outcomes. Evidence for personal meaning often appears under conditions in which one or more of the needs for meaning are thwarted. Life stories communicate a wealth of information regarding the ways in which people counteract the loss of meaning. Much of the evidence presented in this chapter is thus based on the personal accounts of individuals who have experienced such negative or anxiety-inducing events as interpersonal conflicts or unexpected changes in lifestyle. The findings generally reveal that the construction of narratives provides individuals with an opportunity to restructure events in memory in ways that reflect positively on the self and add a sense of coherence and stability to what would otherwise be viewed as a random and unpredictable world.

Four Needs for Meaning

Life stories often reflect more than one type of meaning. That is, several needs for meaning may be threatened or satisfied by a single event. For instance, a virtuous person may be proud of having the ability to uphold a high standard of moral principles. Any event that subsequently tarnishes the person's character or calls into question the person's integrity could then cause a drop in perceived efficacy, value, or self-worth or perhaps all three. As another example, a highly successful author who suddenly finds himself incapable of completing a book might lose both a sense of efficacy and a sense of purpose in life.

There is evidence that negative events cause a decrease in multiple needs for meaning. One such negative event that can be experimentally administered is interpersonal rejection. Williams (1997, 2002) has argued that social rejection harms multiple human needs and, in particular, renders people less able to make sense of their lives. One way of manipulating interpersonal rejection (or acceptance) in the laboratory involves Cyberball, an interactive ball-tossing computer game in which participants are assigned to be either included or excluded by what they perceive as fellow students (Williams, Cheung, & Choi, 2000). In fact, there are no other students—the computer includes or excludes participants by controlling the behavior of the on-screen characters ostensibly controlled by other students.

Following interpersonal rejection using the Cyberball program, participants report an extensive reduction in the perceived meaningfulness of life (Stillman et al., 2009). Specifically, those rejected report an increase in the perceived meaninglessness of life, as measured by the Kunzendorf No Meaning Scale (Kunzendorf & McGuire, 1994; Kunzendorf, Moran, & Gray, 1995–1996). Items on this scale reflect all four of Baumeister's (1991) proposed needs for meaning. For instance, "Life has no meaning or purpose" (purposiveness); "All strivings in life are futile and absurd" (efficacy and control); "It does not matter whether I live or die" (value and justification); "I just don't care about myself any more" (self-worth). Thus, negative events can disrupt meaning broadly. Given the fundamental human drive to form close relationships (Baumeister & Leary, 1995; Buss, 1990), a loss in meaning might be particularly evident following social exclusion. In short, although purpose, efficacy, value, and self-worth represent distinctly different types of meaning, a single event (e.g., succeeding or failing at a goal) can affect more than one type of meaning. The boundaries between these different types of meanings can be blurred.

Needs for meaning may also conflict with one another. Thus, for example, one may wish to derogate a rival in efforts to increase self-worth but simultaneously feel concerned about losing respect (value) in the eyes of others. Under these circumstances, there are no clear criteria for determining in an a priori fashion which need will predominate. Later stories about such events, however, typically relate the relative import of each need through the narrator's description of the actions taken. Using the previous example, one may suppress the desire to denigrate an adversary in an attempt to appear decent and good to others, but then one may subsequently suffer a loss in self-esteem because of the lost opportunity to assert one's superiority. Or, one may aggress toward the rival and increase one's sense of worth but then lose face in the eyes of others. The narrator's description of the event and his or her reaction to the event together convey the strength of each need and the process by which meaning is restored.

A single life story may therefore be taken as supporting the existence of one or more meanings proposed by Baumeister (1991). For clarification purposes, the research findings discussed here are presented according to whether they offer main support for the need for purpose, efficacy, value, or self-worth (though the overlap among these needs should become apparent). This framework has proven useful for organizing a wide range of stories based on everything from seemingly trivial circumstances (e.g., a short-lived argument with a spouse) to life-altering situations (e.g., becoming a quadriplegic; Baumeister & Newman, 1994).

Need for Purpose: Objective Goals and Subjective Fulfillments

A sense of purpose probably comes closest to everyday conceptions of life's meaning (see Frankl, 1959/1976; see also Chapter 2, this volume, for the etymology and evolution of purpose). To believe in life's purpose is to believe that one is here for a reason, whether that reason is chosen by oneself, assigned by society, or decreed by divine powers. People have a sense of purpose in life when they perceive that their current behaviors are linked to future, desired outcomes. This form of meaning can be found through the pursuit of both objective goals and more subjective states of fulfillment. Undergoing years of education in an effort to secure a satisfying job would be an example of planning one's life around an objectively determined goal. The everyday drudgery and poverty of student life may be more meaningful and purposeful to students when the distant goal of being a knowledgeable being with good credentials is kept in mind.

Not all purposes are objective goals; some are subjective states of fulfillment (Baumeister, 1991). Indeed, although most students seem to have specific career goals or ambitions that they are pursuing, we like to think that some are motivated by the intrinsic desire for understanding and knowledge. More obviously, people are sometimes driven by the quest for happiness or for spiritual salvation, and these future states can likewise shape how people interpret their events. Indeed, some major religions have proposed that salvation is not to be expected until after death, and yet the most important meaning of one's current life and activities is in relation to that state of fulfillment to be attained after death.

One role religion plays is to put the events of life in the context of a quest for future spiritual salvation. As such, religion has provided a sense of purpose to the lives of many people throughout history. The positive ways in which religion provides purpose to life are less striking and less easily observed relative to the carnage and devastation that have resulted from extremist religious ideologies. Nevertheless, those individuals who seek a life purpose through the practice of religion or spirituality demonstrate a variety of benefits relative to those who seek meaning elsewhere. A partial list of the benefits include such health benefits as improved immune function, reduced depression, lower blood pressure, and delayed mortality (Townsend, Kladder, Ayele, & Mulligan; 2002). Religion and spirituality also increase relationship satisfaction (Fincham, Beach, Lambert, Stillman, & Braithwaite; 2007; Mahoney et al., 1999) and lower the risk of divorce (Booth, Johnson, Branaman, & Sica; 1995; Clydesdale, 1997; Fergusson, Horwood, & Shannon, 1984). Successfully dealing with the process of aging also corresponds with spiritual and religious practice (Koenig, Smiley, & Gonzales, 1988; see also Chapter 1, this volume).

Throughout history, religion has shaped how people view their life purpose in dramatically different ways (e.g., martyrdom, helping the needy, or escaping from suffering). Religious teachings cause people to give their money to strangers voluntarily, go without food, abstain from sexual activity, even kill themselves and others. Why would humans voluntarily perform activities that seemingly work against the biological imperatives of survival and reproduction? Baumeister (2005) argues that evolution shaped humans for culture. That is, humans are biologically designed to absorb and participate in large systems of meaning, such as religion (or democracy, conservation movements, etc.). As a result, the purpose people see in life varies substantially as a function of their participation in religion.

It appears that actual achievement is less important for a sense of purpose than is the process of working toward one's goals. People do not become permanently satisfied upon reaching some goal or fulfillment state. Indeed, Baumeister (1991) coined the term *myth of fulfillment* to refer to the contrast between popular notions of fulfillment, which are generally permanent, and actual experiences of fulfillment, which tend to be transient. In Western culture, the popular notion of passionate, romantic love is a striking example of the myth of fulfillment because the image celebrated by novels, movies, poetry, and other sources promises undying love, whereas the empirical evidence suggests that such feelings typically drop off substantially after a few months or years.

The mythical nature of fulfillment is suggested by the fact that the process of approaching it is often equally important as, or more important than, the fleeting moments of bliss. This notion can be appreciated by considering narratives of fulfilling sexual experiences. Baumeister (1988, 1989) examined stories drawn from magazines that solicit and publish narratives about masochism in efforts to understand the appeal of this somewhat bizarre sexual practice. These stories were characterized by elaborately detailed descriptions regarding the sequence of events preceding fulfillment. Stories emphasized the process of being tied up, whipped, or otherwise subjugated by others, whereas the momentary fulfillment of orgasm often received a relatively brief or cursory mention. Evidently, engaging in masochism and further relating this experience to others are unfulfilling to the degree that they lack focus on the specific events leading to physical pleasure. Also, though not limited to stories about masochism, the simple act of relating one's experiences to others may allow a person to exaggerate the perceived degree of fulfillment he or she derived from the experience (Baumeister & Newman, 1994).

The idea that a sense of purpose in life is characterized by a chronic pursuit of higher meaning is further illustrated in the life stories of people who have suffered major negative life events. Thompson and Janigian (1988) argued that people search for meaning when negative life events call into question beliefs that the world is orderly and that life has a purpose. Negative events are thus not evaluated in isolation but interpreted according to one's life scheme or storylike representation of the self. Both positive and negative outcomes are imbedded in a larger mental framework for how one's life should unfold. The acquisition of personal meaning involves a series of steps and, in this sense, has an underlying structure.

Janoff-Bulman and Wortman (1977) interviewed paraplegic and quadriplegic individuals who had recently become paralyzed. As one might expect, the majority of respondents indicated that their victimization was the worst thing in the world that could have happened to them. In fact, the degree of self-blame for their victimization was higher than one would expect from an objective view of the circumstances under which the accidents occurred. The stories that participants generated, however, reflected more than the participants' simple need to view themselves as having some degree of control over events. Instead, these accounts focused on the higher purposes served by the victimizations. For example, when describing how they answered their own questions of "why me?" over half the victims generated stories that linked their fate to a higher sense of purpose, for instance, a newfound appreciation for life. Individuals often made comparisons between their former and present selves and focused on what they had learned from the experience rather than dwelling on their new disabilities. Others who could not generate a clear benefit of their paralysis found solace in the conclusion that "God had a reason." Either way, victims best adapted to their new set of circumstances when they viewed their fates as predetermined and as being linked to future, desirable end-states.

Similarly, Taylor (e.g., Meyer & Taylor, 1986; Taylor, 1983; Taylor & Levin, 1976; Wood, Taylor, & Lichtman, 1985) spent several years investigating the processes by which people cope with negative life events. Her analysis revealed that three hallmarks of successful adjustment are finding meaning in an experience, which corresponds roughly to the need for purpose; maintaining mastery over the environment (i.e., self-efficacy); and maintaining self-esteem through self-enhancing evaluations, which includes perceiving one's actions as good and just. Taylor examined autobiographical accounts of victimization and concluded that successful coping is linked directly to the perception that negative events serve a higher purpose (Taylor, 1983). For example, she found that over half of breast cancer victims reported that their illnesses caused them to reappraise their lives. This result included a reported increase in self-knowledge and a tendency to derive greater satisfaction from current relationships. Negative setbacks thus appear to threaten feelings of purpose, which in turn instigate the need to view misfortune as being linked to future, positive outcomes—in this case, a greater appreciation for life.

The need for purpose thus drives people to attain objective goals and also pursue more idealized states of fulfillment. Purpose as meaning is not contemplated with respect to one's current situation but, rather, conceived according to the possibility of some future state of affairs. Narrative thought is a preferred form of mental representation here because it preserves the temporal order of events, which is a central aspect of purpose. Life stories also provide researchers with an excellent resource for understanding how individuals cope with negative life events, specifically, by revealing narrators' tendencies to view their victimization as linked to some positive outcome. By viewing a negative outcome as precursor for something positive, people can better cope with tragedy and maintain a sense of purpose in life.

Need for Efficacy and Control

The second need for meaning is that of efficacy or control. People want to believe that they make a difference and that they are capable of bringing about specific outcomes. Efficacy is thus related to purpose; the latter reflects the need to view one's actions as related to future outcomes, and the former entails the perception that one can achieve these outcomes. Mentally representing efficacious behavior in narrative form is beneficial in that it preserves critical information regarding the necessary steps toward goal attainment. As noted earlier, perceiving a logical connection between events enhances predictability.

Murray and Holmes (1994) devised a creative method for exploring how people restructure past events in ways that allow them to maintain a sense of efficacy in their romantic relationships. These researchers asked people to generate narratives about their partners' previous behaviors that facilitated or disrupted the development of intimacy in the relationship. Prior to writing these stories, half the participants were told that engaging in conflict is healthy or good for the relationship, whereas the remaining half were informed that conflict is bad for the relationship. The results showed that narrators reported higher levels of conflict in their relationships when they believed conflict was good as opposed to bad. In addition, partners' dispositional tendencies toward conflict avoidance were interpreted in a manner consistent with the perceived benefits of conflict. When narrators believed that initiating conflict was good, they made excuses for their partners' conflict avoidance and emphasized the partners' other virtues. Conversely, when narrators perceived conflict to be bad, they downplayed the negative implications of their partners' tendencies to initiate conflict and minimized the importance of interpersonal differences. It thus appears that people want to view themselves as effectively engaging in behaviors that are predictive of relationship success. This perception contributes to a sense of stability, predictability, and control in the relationship.

Research examining the lay perception of free will is consistent with a need for efficacy in the construction of meaning (Stillman, Baumeister, & Mele, in press). In one study, all participants provided narratives concerning an important experience in their lives. Half of the participants were further instructed that the experience should be about a time they controlled an action that they felt was freely chosen by them. For example, one narrator proudly described a time that despite her fears of retaliation, she summoned the courage to demand that a loud, rude customer leave the restaurant she was managing. In contrast, the other half of participants were instructed to write about an important event in which they had not freely chosen the experience. One narrator described missing an important appointment and being sick because "my friends dragged me to the bar and made me drink. They made me drink a lot because they said I was in a bad mood." As suggested by these examples, free-will narratives were characterized by more positive outcomes than were the unfree narratives, according to raters who were blind to condition. Raters likewise scored the free-will narratives as substantially more positive in mood (with condition accounting for 37% of the variance in mood). Narrators were also more likely to describe behaviors that were consistent with their own moral code when prompted to write about events they believe they controlled. Thus, when participants were asked to provide narratives of meaningful life events for which they viewed themselves as responsible, the event outcomes were positive, the narratives pleasant in mood, and the behaviors upright and moral relative to those participants who were asked to describe meaningful events over which they did not perceive control. In short, varying efficacy and control resulted in narratives that differed widely in personal meaning.

The need for efficacy is further demonstrated in narratives in which people describe successful versus unsuccessful attempts at life change (Heatherton & Nichols, 1994). The contents of these stories are valuable indicators of efficacy because they reflect not only individuals' perceptions of control over day-to-day events but also their abilities to effect positive, large-scale changes in their lives. Heatherton and Nichols found that compared to individuals who experienced failed attempts at life change, those who described successful attempts perceived greater degrees of behavioral control and personal responsibility for their outcomes. Failure narratives evidenced a higher rate of external attributions and were more likely to include statements attesting to the difficulty of change. Successful change stories, conversely, were more dramatic; they often portrayed the narrator as one who was faced with many challenges and much suffering but nevertheless was able to overcome these difficult obstacles and achieve happiness. Success accounts also revealed a higher incidence of identity change. Narrators who achieved change despite difficult obstacles reported a newfound knowledge or understanding of the self. Narrators who reported failure attempts reported little change in identity and instead tended to cling to their former roles. Success stories also were linked to a reappraisal of life goals, which in turn were associated with a perceived shift in life meaning. This finding relates back to the idea that people who finally achieve desirable end-states will then form new goals as a means of maintaining a sense of purpose in their lives.

One instance that involves an especially difficult change in one's life is that of divorce. A large literature on interpersonal relationships shows that people are very reluctant to break close attachments (see Baumeister & Leary, 1995, for a review). It is of little surprise, then, that the dissolution of a marriage results in a variety of negative emotional outcomes, including confusion, regret, anger, negative affect, and decreases in self-esteem (Spanier & Castro, 1979). Another outcome might be a lost sense of efficacy. The findings of Murray and Holmes (1994), discussed earlier, suggest that efficacy may be disrupted by divorce because individuals are confronted with the fact that things did not go the way they planned. In fact, other qualitative research suggests that this is indeed the case. Gray and Silver (1990) interviewed divorced couples and compared spouses' perceptions of events related to the marital breakup. The researchers found that both male and females assumed a relatively greater proportion of responsibility for the breakup than they assigned to their partners. Further, the greater the control given to one's former spouse, the poorer one's own subsequent level of psychosocial adjustment. Distorted illusions of control over negative events thus appeared to facilitate adaptation to change. These findings reinforce the notion that a sense of efficacy promotes healthy adjustment to difficult life circumstances.

Taken together, the evidence drawn from life stories suggests that people want to view themselves as capable of bringing about positive outcomes.

When life circumstances threaten a sense of efficacy, individuals will reflect upon past events in a biased fashion and overestimate their own degree of control over events. Often this reflection involves exaggerating the number of obstacles to successful change in attempts to make one's achievements appear even more impressive. Finally, efficacy facilitates healthy, emotional adaptation to negative life events.

It is important to note that declarations of control often become superseded by other needs, mainly those for self-worth and value. Recall that individuals who experienced failed attempts at life change denied responsibility for their current outcomes and emphasized their difficulties in trying to change (Heatherton & Nichols, 1994). Negative outcomes were thus characterized by the absence, rather than presence, of self-efficacious behaviors. Here, admitting to responsibilities for one's own failure likely posed a threat to self-esteem. Concerns for efficacy may thus become overridden by needs to maintain a positive sense of self-worth. In a similar vein, narratives about both anger and unrequited love revealed a pattern of externalizing blame for others' negative consequences (Baumeister, Stillwell, & Wotman, 1990; Baumeister, Wotman, & Stillwell, 1993). In these stories, needs to portray one's actions as morally right and justified necessitated denying responsibility for events.

Need for Value and Justification

A third need for meaning is the desire to view one's actions as good and just. A person wants to be able to reflect upon past behaviors as being right or morally justified. For example, inflicting harm on others is a clear violation of societal standards of right and wrong. Evidence suggesting a need for value often comes from stories about events in which individuals may be perceived as having brought harm to another. Narrators present the sequence of events in ways that absolve them of responsibility for others' negative outcomes.

The need to see one's actions as justified can be seen in narratives about anger. Baumeister et al. (1990) asked people to write two stories, one about an instance in which they angered another and one which someone angered them. These narratives were subjected to in-depth content analyses and compared on the frequency of specific story characteristics. The researchers found a series of systematic differences between the way the transgressors and the way the victims described such transgressions. First, transgressors downplayed the bad consequences, often by asserting that the victim's anger was completely unjustified. Any bad consequences were discussed only in the presence of other information suggesting that the transgressors had good intentions and did not anticipate that their actions would bring the other harm. Transgressors reported attempts to apologize or to compensate for the misdeed.

Second, transgressors presented mitigating circumstances, suggesting that they had a right to act the way they did. Third, transgressors externalized blame in attempts to minimize their own responsibilities for any negative consequences incurred by the victim. Last, transgressors exhibited a pattern of temporal bracketing; that is, any harm doing was considered to be "in the past" and as having no negative implications for the current self. This view was in stark contrast to the perspective of victims, who continued to view the transgressor negatively and saw the past incident as reflecting poorly on the current relationship.

Further evidence for a need for value comes from research on the lay perceptions of free will described earlier (Stillman et al., in press). Participants who were asked to describe an instance in which they did something important that was freely chosen by them provided narratives that differed substantially from those who were asked to describe an event they did not control. Those individuals who wrote about events they controlled were more likely to write about morally upright actions (according to the narrators themselves) relative to those who wrote about events they did not control. For instance, one narrator in the free-will condition wrote about her organization of a charity soccer tournament. In contrast, a narrator in the unfree condition wrote about causing her brother lasting emotional pain by refusing his help. Thus, when people wrote about actions for which they take responsibility, their narrations described good and just behavior; but when they wrote about actions for which they did not take responsibility, they were more likely to write about doing something hurtful.

Narratives about unrequited love also demonstrate a need for value (Baumeister & Wotman, 1992; Baumeister et al., 1993). Baumeister et al. (1993) asked people to describe experiences in which they were the object of another's unsolicited affection and also times when they were rejected by a potential lover. Consistent with norms against hurting others, rejectors often felt guilty for bringing emotional pain to the would-be lover. Guilt is aversive emotion that results directly from viewing one's own actions as bad or hurtful (Baumeister, Reis, & Delespaul, 1995; Baumeister, Stillwell, & Heatherton, 1994). The allusions to guilt suggest that people worry that breaking someone's heart is wrong and hence in need of justification.

Sure enough, rejectors filled their narratives with comments that might help justify their acts. They denied intention to cause harm and indeed often reported playing a passive role (which would minimize their responsibility). Many insisted that they had done nothing to encourage the other's affection, a fact that would indeed reduce or eliminate their guilt. They often reported that they had tried to be explicit, clear, and considerate in discouraging the would-be lover's interest in them.

Some rejectors even conceived of themselves as victims when repeated attempts to thwart the advances of the other proved futile. In their accounts, the would-be lover was the irrationally persistent actor in the situation, whereas they were the innocent bystander who was helpless to bring the unpleasant situation to an end. As Baumeister and Newman (1994) suggested, claiming the victim status provides a sort of moral immunity. The victim role carries with it the advantage of receiving sympathy from others and thereby prevents the unrequited love episode as impugning one's character. Perceived victimization also provides a method of reducing guilt.

Thus, value as meaning presents itself in autobiographical accounts where one's integrity is called into question. As a way to restore meaning, the narrator devises a story that masks his or her faults and elevates feelings of moral superiority. Restructuring one's memory for a threatening event therefore provides an individual with the opportunity to reaffirm the self-concept, restoring the belief that one's actions are good and conform to conventional standards of right and wrong.

Need for Self-Worth

The last need for meaning, self-worth, involves both the desire to view one's own traits and abilities favorably and to elicit positive recognition from others. Most often, people speak of *feelings* of self-worth, which might be understood as the relative frequency of positive and negative emotions that result from the appraisal of one's personal qualities.

Threats to self-worth become apparent when examining the would-be lover's perspective in stories of unrequited love (Baumeister et al., 1993). Relative to the rejectors, "victims" of unrequited love suffered disproportionately large decrements in self-esteem. Interpersonal rejection, after all, implies that one is unworthy of another's attention or affections. In fact, some research and theory suggests that perceptions of one's appeal to others may be the underlying cause of low self-esteem (Baumeister & Leary, 1995; Leary, Tambor, Terdal, & Downs, 1995). Would-be lovers demonstrated various patterns of reducing the negative implications of rejection for their self-worth. First, the would-be lover tended to denigrate the romantic interest of the rejector, often by emphasizing his or her own superiority over the rival and describing the target's choice of the rival over oneself as irrational and incomprehensible. Second, would-be lovers sometimes included in their narratives information about current romantic partners as a way to refute the conclusion that the narrators were not desirable. Thus, individuals describing their unrequited love for another constructed their narrative in ways that buffered threats to their self-worth.

Similar evidence for self-worth comes from life stories about success and failure (Baumeister & Ilko, 1995). Participants in this study provided autobiographical accounts of their greatest success and greatest failure experiences. In addition, half the respondents believed that they would later read their stories aloud to an audience. Evidence for self-esteem needs was furnished by two sets of findings. First, failure narratives written by individuals chronically low in self-esteem evidenced higher rates of temporal bracketing, or the tendency to relegate failures to the past. Temporal bracketing separates the present self from past behaviors and thereby allows individuals to admit past failure while simultaneously rejecting the notion that this failure reflects negatively on the current self. This finding is consistent with other research showing that low (compared to high) self-esteem individuals are mainly concerned with self-protection, sustaining any positive self-feelings they do have (Tice, 1991). High-self-esteem individuals were, as a result of their overwhelmingly positive evaluation of themselves, less threatened by past failure and thus showed fewer needs to bracket off failure events from the present.

The second set of findings involved the assumed credit for success under public versus private conditions. When individuals believed they would be communicating their success stories to their peer groups, they included substantial information regarding the help and support they received from others. Sharing credit for success is a way to appear modest and further uphold norms (values) against self-aggrandizement. Once self-presentational concerns were removed, however, individuals abandoned all false modesty and readily described themselves as responsible. They downplayed any help or support from other people and instead reserved all the credit for themselves. Exaggerating credit for their successes enabled respondents to maximize feelings of self-worth and thereby reap more benefits from the process of constructing their narratives.

Qualitative work by Tangney (see Tangney, 1995, for a review) provides evidence for esteem-protection strategies among shamed individuals. Shame can be distinguished from guilt along several dimensions, the main one being the perceived implications of the emotion-eliciting event for the self. Whereas guilt entails a devaluation of a specific behavior (e.g., interpersonal transgression), shame reflects a global devaluation of the entire self (e.g., Tangney, 1992). Guilt is associated with feelings of remorse or regret, whereas shame is accompanied by more intense feelings of pain, powerlessness, and a "shrinking of the self" (Lindsay-Hartz, De Rivera, & Mascolo, 1995). Autobiographical accounts of guilt and shame experiences show that guilty people admit to their wrongdoings and report such subsequent reparative behaviors as apologies or compensation. Shamed individuals, in contrast, show a pattern of avoiding blame and tend to externalize responsibility for negative events (Tangney, 1995). These findings are consistent with other empirical evidence revealing that shamed individuals tend to avoid public scrutiny and exhibit retaliative, defensive responses to ego threats by lashing out at disapproving others (Tangney, Wagner, Fletcher, & Gramzow, 1992). Thus, unlike guilty individuals, shamed individuals respond to their own moral transgressions by devaluing the self, which in turn activates attempts to regain self-worth by minimizing blameworthiness and aggressing toward disapproving others.

Finally, Taylor's (1983) theory of cognitive adaptation, presented earlier, underscores the significance of positive self-worth for positive emotional and psychological adjustment to negative life events. Interviews with breast cancer patients revealed that only a minority of respondents (17%) reported any negative effects of their illness (Wood et al., 1985). Further, the majority of women engaged in downward comparison by concluding that they were coping as well or better than other women who suffered the same illness (Wood et al, 1985). Downward comparison is well established as an effective self-enhancing strategy (Wills, 1981). Even the women who were objectively worse off comforted themselves with the idea that they were not dying or experiencing a lot of pain. Thus, the literature suggests that major illnesses pose an important threat to feelings of self-worth and resultant cognitive efforts to escape feelings of low self-regard engender successful adaptation to these illnesses.

Self-worth therefore emerges as an important form of personal meaning. People want to feel good about themselves and believe that they are worthy of others' attention and affections. Threatened self-worth is succeeded by defensive attempts to bolster one's image such as by externalizing responsibility for negative outcomes or comparing oneself with those who are worse off. Failure to counteract threat leads to negative affect, perceptions of inferiority, and unhappiness.

Often attempts to regain self-worth conflict with other needs for meaning, most often needs for efficacy or control. Under some circumstances, such as those in which the outcome is negative for another person, one would rather feel guilty and still maintain the perception of control over events than to relinquish control. The evidence suggests, however, that people will avoid claiming control over events that hold long-term implications for their character. One example involves attributions among rape victims. Rape carries a negative stigma. Internal attributions of control that typically characterize personal misfortunes (e.g., Janoff-Bulman & Wortman, 1977) may reinforce this stigma and thereby intensify feelings of low self-regard. This proposition is supported by research showing that high levels of characterological and behavioral self-blame for rape is associated with poorer adjustment (Meyer & Taylor, 1986). It appears, then, that efficacy needs diminish when self-blame is associated with a sense of deservingness for negative outcomes.

Conclusion

The personal quest for a meaningful life can be analyzed into four separate needs for meaning. People who have a sense of purpose, a sense of efficacy, a set of values that justify their actions, and a basis for positive self-worth generally find life meaningful (Baumeister, 1991). The same four needs for meaning probably shape the way people interpret individual events in their lives, and the systematic distortions or biases that shape autobiographical stories probably reflect these four needs.

References

Baumeister, R. F. (1988). Masochism as escape from self. *Journal of Sex Research, 25*, 28–59.

Baumeister, R. F. (1989). *Masochism and the self.* Hillsdale, NJ: Erlbaum.

Baumeister, R. F. (1991). *Meanings of life.* New York, NY: Guilford Press.

Baumeister, R. F. (2005). *The cultural animal: Human nature, meaning, and social life.* New York, NY: Oxford University Press.

Baumeister, R. F., & Ilko, S. A. (1995). Shallow gratitude: Public and private acknowledgments of external help in accounts of success. *Basic and Applied Social Psychology, 16*, 191–209.

Baumeister, R. F., & Leary, M. R. (1995). The need to belong: Desire for interpersonal attachments as a fundamental human motivation. *Psychological Bulletin, 117*, 497–529.

Baumeister, R. F., & Newman, L. S. (1994). How stories make sense of personal experiences: Motives that shape autobiographical narratives. *Personality and Social Psychology Bulletin, 20*, 67–90.

Baumeister, R. F., Reis, H. T., & Delespaul, P. A. E. G. (1995). Subjective and experiential correlates of guilt in daily life. *Personality and Social Psychology Bulletin, 21*, 1256–1268.

Baumeister, R. F., Stillwell, A., & Heatherton, T. F. (1994). Guilt: An interpersonal approach. *Psychological Bulletin, 115*, 243–267.

Baumeister, R. F., Stillwell, A., & Wotman, S. R. (1990). Victim and perpetrator accounts of interpersonal conflict: Autobiographical narratives about anger. *Journal of Personality and Social Psychology, 59*, 994–1005.

Baumeister, R. F., & Wotman, S. R. (1992). *Breaking hearts: The two sides of unrequited love.* New York, NY: Guilford Press.

Baumeister, R. F., Wotman, S. R., & Stillwell, A. (1993). Unrequited love: On heartbreak, anger, guilt, scriptlessness, and humiliation. *Journal of Personality and Social Psychology, 64*, 377–394.

Booth, A., Johnson, D. R., Branaman, A., & Sica, A. (1995). Belief and behavior: Does religion matter in today's marriage? *Journal of Marriage and Family, 57*, 661–671.

Buss, D. M. (1990). The evolution of anxiety and social exclusion. *Journal of Social and Clinical Psychology, 9*, 196–210.

Clydesdale, T. T. (1997). Family behaviors among early U.S. baby boomers: Exploring the effects of religion and income change, 1965–1982. *Social Forces, 722*, 605–636.

Fergusson, D. M., Horwood, L. J., & Shannon, F. T. (1984). A proportional hazards model of family breakdown. *Journal of Marriage and the Family, 46*, 539–549.

Fincham, F. D., Beach, S. R. H., Lambert, N., Stillman, T. F., & Braithwaite, S. (2007). *Do spiritual connections enhance relationship satisfaction? The role of prayer.* Manuscript under review.

Frankl, V. E. (1976). *Man's search for meaning.* New York, NY: Pocket Books.

Gray, J. D., & Silver, R. C. (1990). Opposite sides of the same coin: Former spouses' divergent perspectives in coping with their divorce. *Journal of Personality and Social Psychology, 59*, 1180–1191.

Heatherton, T. F., & Nichols, P. A. (1994). Personal accounts of successful versus failed attempts at life change. *Personality and Social Psychology Bulletin, 20*, 664–675.

Janoff-Bulman, R., & Wortman, C. B. (1977). Attributions of blame and coping in the "real world": Severe accident victims react to their lot. *Journal of Personality and Social Psychology, 35*, 351–363.

Koenig, H. G., Smiley, M., & Gonzales, J. A. P. (1988). *Religion, health, and aging: A review and theoretical integration.* Westport, CT: Greenwood Press.

Kunzendorf, R. G., & McGuire, D. (1994). *Depression: The reality of "no meaning" versus the delusion of "negative meaning."* Unpublished manuscript; *No Meaning Scale* and *Negative Meaning Scale* published in Kunzendorf, Moran, & Gray's (1995–1996) appendices.

Kunzendorf, R. G., Moran, C., & Gray, R. (1995–1996). Personality traits and reality-testing abilities, controlling for vividness of imagery. *Imagination, Cognition, and Personality, 15*, 113–131.

Leary, M. R., Tambor, E. S., Terdal, S. K., & Downs, D. L. (1995). Self-esteem as an interpersonal monitor: The sociometer hypothesis. *Journal of Personality and Social Psychology, 68*, 518–530.

Lindsay-Hartz, J., De Rivera, J., & Mascolo, M. F. (1995). Differentiating guilt and shame and their effects on motivation. In J. Tangney & K. W. Fischer (Eds.), *Self-conscious emotions: The psychology of shame, guilt, embarrassment, and pride* (pp. 274–300). New York, NY: Guilford Press.

Mahoney, A., Pargament, K. I., Jewell, T., Swank, A. B., Scott, E., Emery, E., & Rye, M. (1999). Marriage and the spiritual realm: The role of proximal and distal religious constructs in marital functioning. *Journal of Family Psychology, 13*, 1–18.

McAdams, D. P. (1993). *The stories we live by: Personal myths and the making of the self.* New York, NY: Morrow.

Meyer, B., & Taylor, S. E. (1986). Adjustments to rape. *Journal of Personality and Social Psychology, 50*, 1226–1234.

Murray, S. L., & Holmes, J. G. (1994). Storytelling in close relationships: The construction of confidence. *Personality and Social Psychology Bulletin, 20*, 650–663.

Spanier, G. B., & Castro, R. F. (1979). Adjustment to separation and divorce: A qualitative, analysis. In G. Levinger & O. C. Males (Eds.), *Divorce and separation: Context, causes, and consequences* (pp. 211–227). New York, NY: Basic Books.

Stillman, T. F., Baumeister, R. F., Lambert, N. M., Crescioni, A. W., DeWall, C. N., & Fincham, F. D. (2009). Alone and without purpose: Life loses meaning following social exclusion. *Journal of Experimental Social Psychology, 45*, 686–694.

Stillman, T. F., Baumeister, R. F., & Mele, A. R. (in press). Free will in everyday life: Autobiographical accounts of free and unfree actions. *Philosophical Psychology.*

Tangney, J. P. (1992). Situational determinants of shame and guilt in young adulthood, *Personality and Social Psychology Bulletin, 18*, 199–206.

Tangney, J. P. (1995). Shame and guilt in interpersonal relationships. In J. P. Tangney & K. W. Fisher (Eds.), *Self-conscious emotions: The psychology of shame, guilt, embarrassment, and pride* (pp. 114–139). New York, NY: Guilford Press.

Tangney, J. P., Wagner, P. E., Fletcher, C., & Gramzow, R. (1992). Shamed into anger? The relation of shame and guilt to anger and self-reported aggression. *Journal of Personality and Social Psychology, 62*, 669–675.

Taylor, S. E. (1983). Adjustment to threatening events: A theory of cognitive adaptation, *American Psychologist, 38*, 1161–1173.

Taylor, S. E., & Levin, S. (1976). *The psychological impact of breast cancer: Theory and practice.* San Francisco, CA: West Coast Cancer Foundation.

Thompson, S. C., & Janigian, A. S. (1988). Life schemes: A framework for understanding the search for meaning. *Journal of Social and Clinical Psychology, 7*, 260–280.

Tice, D. M. (1991). Esteem protection or enhancement? Self-handicapping motives and attributions differ by trait self-esteem. *Journal of Personality and Social Psychology, 60*, 711–725.

Townsend, M., Kladder, V., Ayele, H., & Mulligan, T. (2002). Systematic review of clinical trials examining the effects of religion on health. *Southern Medical Journal, 95*, 1429–1434.

Williams, K. D. (1997). Social ostracism. In R. M. Kowalski (Ed.), *Aversive interpersonal behaviors* (pp. 133–170). New York, NY: Plenum Press.

Williams, K. D. (2002). *Ostracism: The power of silence.* New York, NY: Guilford Press.

Williams, K. D., Cheung, C. K. T., & Choi, W. (2000). CyberOstracism: Effects of being ignored over the Internet. *Journal of Personality and Social Psychology, 79*, 748–762.

Wills, T. A. (1981). Downward comparison principles in social psychology. *Psychological Bulletin, 90*, 245–271.

Wood, J. V., Taylor, S. E., & Lichtman, R. R. (1985). Social comparison in adjustment to breast cancer. *Journal of Personality and Social Psychology, 49*, 1169–1183.

15

Autobiographical Memory and Personal Meaning

Stable Versus Flexible Meanings of Remembered Life Experiences

DENISE R. BEIKE

University of Arkansas

TRAVIS S. CRONE

University of Houston–Downtown

> Memory is what makes our lives.... Our memory is our coherence, our reason, our feeling, even our action. Without it, we are nothing.
>
> —**Luis Buñuel (1983)**

Understanding the human quest for personal meaning is a difficult pursuit, complicated by questions about the form and functions of meaning, and even its ontological status. As experimental psychologists studying basic social and cognitive processes, we leave the more philosophical questions to other contributors to this volume. Whatever its form, function, or veridicality, meaning is discovered (or constructed) by human beings. Thus the quest for meaning employs the same human hardware and software available for more mundane tasks such as perception, memory, language, and reasoning. We therefore situate our quest for understanding meaning in basic research on memory and emotion. We focus on the question of how, specifically, people turn the raw material of remembered life experiences into the ephemeral quality of meaning.

We begin with a postulate: In order to experience meaning in life, one must be able to conceptualize and remember the living one has done. As Buñuel eloquently put it, lives are made up of memories; thus the everyday experiences that compose life should be grist for the mill of personal meaning. The search for meaning therefore requires recollecting life experiences, or *autobiographical memory.* In the process of calling up and reflecting upon autobiographical memories, people can come to a sense of meaning in life.

Memories might contribute to the sense of meaning in life by one of several possible processes. One possibility is that remembered experiences are woven into a life story, or narrative, which expresses the individual's sense of his or her life's emotional high and low points, overarching emotional themes, and emotional trajectory (Bluck & Habermas, 2000; McAdams, 1996). To the extent that the life story that arises from autobiographical memories is perceived as coherent, credible, and suggestive of involvement in the larger world, the life comprised by that story is perceived as meaningful (McAdams, 1996). This approach relies on the notion of narrative coherence and the concept of key emotional episodes or *self-defining memories* that play starring roles in the narrative. Such memories provide a stable anchor for understanding the self and one's life across time; they provide firm footholds in a sea of emotions, conflict, and stress. Highly emotional memories in a narrative yield a stable but, as we wll argue, constrained sense of meaning.

An alternative possibility, to be developed in this chapter, is that perspective rather than coherence determines meaning. To the extent that individual life experiences can be recollected with a healthy sense of perspective or distance from the experience, the life comprised of those memories is perceived as meaningful. This approach relies on the notion of emotional distance and the concept of *psychological closure* experienced during recollection. Such memories provide flexibility in understanding the self and one's life across time; they provide raw materials to be shaped to suit current needs. Unemotional memories yield a flexible and, as we will argue, profound sense of meaning.

Thus, what memories tell us about our lives depends on whether they are recollected with a sense of emotional distance. Both emotional and unemotional memories contribute to a sense of meaning in life. But the less emotional the memory, the more novel and creative the ways in which it can be viewed, and therefore the greater the sense of meaning. We support this view with evidence from basic and applied research on autobiographical memory. We conclude with a discussion of the implications of our view.

Meaning Comes From Memory

Meaning in life has been defined as "denot[ing] reflections on, and/or ways of experiencing, contexts of meanings in relation to human life in general, to one's own individual life, or to parts of the latter" (Auhagen, 2000, p. 38). Empirically, one way to investigate what people reflect on or experience as meaningful is simply to ask people to name the sources of meaning in their own lives. The most common source of meaning identified by this empirical approach is interpersonal relationships, followed by personal growth, beliefs, and obtaining goals. The relative emphasis on growth, beliefs, and goals varies over development (Ebersole, 1998).

Another method for investigating meaning is to identify peak life experiences and discover what aspects those experiences have in common.

Self-determination theory posits that the ability to make true and independent choices (autonomy), the experience of mastery (competence), and healthy relationships with others (relatedness) are the basic driving forces in human motivation (Deci & Ryan, 2000). We might therefore expect people to thrive after (and thereby find meaning in) life experiences that fulfill basic psychological needs. The most important needs identified in such an approach are autonomy, competence, relatedness, and self-esteem (Sheldon, Elliot, Kim, & Kasser, 2001).

Yet another method (particularly congruent with our approach) is to examine the subtexts of people's accounts of their life experiences. Narratives of life experiences have been found to express four primary aspects of meaning in life. These narratives reflect purpose, value and justification, efficacy in goal pursuit, and self-worth (Baumeister & Wilson, 1996; Sommer & Baumeister, 1998). These various approaches therefore converge on several common aspects that are critical to meaning in life. One important aspect of meaning relates to goal progress, another aspect of meaning relates to relationships, and a third relates to a sense that the self is valued. Not coincidentally, these three aspects of meaning map well onto the three central functions of autobiographical remembering: a directive function (goal progress), a social function (relationships), and an identity function (self-worth; Conway, 2003). Autobiographical memory therefore seems to fulfill the very aspects of meaning that are most important to people.

Memory, Narrative, and Meaning

Yet the mere fact that autobiographical memories are a source of meaning in life does not explain how these memories contribute to a sense of meaning. Most autobiographical memory researchers have approached the idea of meaning in memories from a narrative perspective. In practice, this approach is usually focused on the narrative quality of autobiographical memory, including the formation, upkeep, themes, and elements of the life story. As Adler (1931) put it, a person's life story or narrative is "a story he repeats to himself to warn or comfort him, to keep him concentrated on his goal, to prepare him … to meet the future" (73–74). The life story expresses the most important themes in personality, and helps to provide a sense of identity (McAdams, 1996). It also provides meaning by virtue of the inferences people draw from their narrated experiences (Singer, 2004).

The life story has been conceptualized as a schema expressing the autobiographical relationship among single events (Bluck & Habermas, 2000). This schema serves as an overarching organizational structure for creation of a narrative that abides by temporal, cultural, thematic, and causal coherence rules. By connecting the current self with the self found in autobiographical memories, the life story schema makes explicit the unitary nature of one's life and provides a sense of a continuous and stable self over time.

A satisfying and meaningful life story is therefore composed of a coherent narrative, which provides both temporal and causal explanations for events. Moreover, a satisfying life story should be grounded in a moral context that is understood by the society in which the story is being told. Coherent and morally grounded self-narratives provide a sense of stability. These well-defined narratives place the self contextually in space and time and integrate the person's life experience and self-concept, thereby providing a sense of a self with purpose (McAdams, 2006).

A well-functioning life narrative should therefore provide a stable sense of meaning and purpose. Indeed, in a three-year longitudinal study, the life narratives of college students and recent graduates were stable over time on measures of emotional tone and conceptual complexity. Despite this stability, developmental changes were evident as personal growth and narrative complexity increased with time (McAdams et al., 2006). Thus, life narratives show the crucial property of stability, yet still allow for development over time. In these ways, life narratives likely contribute to the overall sense of coherence of one's existence (Korotkov, 1998).

A life narrative is composed, in part, of important experiences called *self-defining memories*. These personally significant memories are high points or key scenes in the life story. They represent mile markers on the journey toward self-discovery and understanding (Singer & Moffitt, 1991–1992). Self-defining memories can arouse emotion that is similar in type and intensity to the original experience (Schwartz, Weinberger, & Singer, 1981). The emotion aroused by self-defining memories is partly a consequence of the rememberer's goal progress. The more goal attainment the rememberer reports, the more positive affect he or she will experience when recollecting self-defining memories (Moffitt & Singer, 1994).

As do all autobiographical memories, self-defining memories fulfill the need to have an experience-near record of goal progress as well as a more abstract self-coherence (Conway, Singer, & Tagini, 2004). Autobiographical memories unite cognitions, affect, and goals into a goal-driven construct known as the *working self*. The working self is able to track goal progress over time through the principle of adaptive correspondence and is simultaneously able to ground current goal pursuit in the context of the person's life through the principle of self-coherence.

When people become concerned with abstract self-coherence, self-defining memories are preferentially activated. Self-defining memories fulfill this need for self-coherence, and thereby provide a stable sense of meaning, because they preserve the state of the working self at a given point in time (Conway et al., 2004), namely, the high points in the life story. Therefore, the most accessible memories from any given time span in one's life relate to the Eriksonian stage most likely to be operative at the time of event occurrence (Conway & Holmes, 2004). That is, memories from the teen years are most likely to concern identity, and those of the middle adult years are the most likely to concern generativity. Conway and Holmes conclude that these highly accessible memories are self-defining memories encoded in a particular state of the working self at that time. Preserving such memories allows one to see the challenges one has met throughout life, as well as those one has faced and failed to meet.

A sense of stability results because self-defining memories maximize both coherence (identity) and correspondence (accuracy). Only those individuals who are well-adjusted (i.e., securely attached) have self-defining memories that both correspond with the present view of the self and are fully fleshed out with likely accurate details. If there is too much emotion or too little, either correspondence or coherence will suffer. In order for the individual to be healthy, and even to recover from posttraumatic stress disorder, efforts toward coherence must be balanced by efforts toward correspondence. Thus, not all self-defining memories serve the purpose of stability, only those that have the proper degree of emotion (Conway et al., 2004).

To summarize, the experiences that happen to the self and that are perceived as meaningful reflect the motives of the self, thereby forging a sense of identity. The life story provides a thematic ordering to one's life and thereby provides a sense of coherence and stability, that is, meaning. Experiences that entail overarching goals at various points in one's life are preserved best, and these self-defining memories later serve as mile markers on the recalled journey through life. Self-defining memories are highly emotional because they are both personally significant and tightly linked to goal progress (Blagov & Singer, 2004; Moffitt & Singer, 1994). These highly emotional memories placed in a coherent life narrative therefore make sense of life and provide a stable source of meaning over time.

Individual Memories and Meaning

The research on autobiographical memories in a life narrative has significantly increased our understanding of how people gain a sense of meaning from their memories (Singer, 2004). But the focus on life narratives and self-defining memories in recent autobiographical memory research should not obscure two important facts. First, not all memories fit readily into a single coherent life narrative; and second, not all autobiographical memories are self-defining. Yet even when an individual autobiographical memory is neither critical to the coherence of the life narrative nor self-defining, it can still be a source of meaning. To understand personal meaning, it is therefore necessary to examine not only the life narrative but also individual event memories outside of a life story context.

The key scenes that compose a life narrative are rare, whereas individual life event memories outside a narrative are numerous. Unless a person is a devoted gourmet, for example, his or her experience eating lunch yesterday is unlikely to be self-defining or to cohere in any profound way with his or her life narrative. Nonetheless, a person can produce a memory of this or one of hundreds of other experiences when searching his or her autobiographical memory. Fifty or more memories are routinely produced in a session of autobiographical memory in response to cues (e.g., Denkova, Botzung, Scheiber, & Manning, 2006; J. A. Robinson, 1976). Yet, a person routinely produces only a dozen or so self-defining memories or key scenes (e.g., Blagov & Singer, 2004; McAdams et al., 2006). Memories of individual events might therefore be more important for meaning than are self-defining memories within a life narrative because there are so many more individual events.

In addition, individual events might be more important for meaning because they, rather than the entire life narrative, are usually the focal point when recollecting one's life. The life narrative does play an important role in autobiographical recollection. The search for an individual autobiographical memory usually begins by identifying a potential portion of the life story (a lifetime period; Conway et al., 2004; Haque & Conway, 2001). This lifetime period is used as part of a retrieval model, aiding in the search for general events (common activities) that occurred in that period of life, events that are in turn used to search for episodic memories of a specific experience from which to construct the autobiographical memory (Conway & Pleydell-Pearce, 2000; Conway et al., 2004). Pieces of the life narrative are therefore intimately involved in every generative recollection of an autobiographical memory.

But the goal of autobiographical remembering is usually to arrive at a specific event memory rather than to construct or to relate an entire life narrative. For example, of 24 items assessing reasons for autobiographical remembering, one of the least frequently endorsed items was "When I want to see if my life has an overall theme" (Bluck, Alea, Habermas, & Rubin, 2005). The most frequently endorsed items referred to relating individual experiences (e.g., "When I want to strengthen a friendship by sharing old memories with friends").

A moment's reflection may convey the difference in the two goals. Try to think of the last time you told your entire life story to yourself, or (even less likely) told your life story to someone else. (For many of us, it may be difficult to envision the audience who would have the patience to sit through such a story). Now think of the last time you related a specific event memory. Every day, we think and tell about funny experiences, upsetting experiences, experiences that taught a lesson, experiences that convey juicy gossip, and so on, often beginning with "Have I told you about the time when …?" These everyday stories are about individual events, not life as a whole. In summary, individual life event memories (and not the entire life story narrative) are memory's building blocks for the sense of meaning in life. They are more numerous than the self-defining memories that compose a life narrative, and they are more often the goal of acts of autobiographical remembering.

Not only are self-defining memories and life narrative recollection infrequent, but they are also atypical in another way. Self-defining memories are characterized by a high level of emotion, which is the exception rather than the rule in autobiographical memory (Beike, 2007). Although the bulk of our memories are devoid of emotion, they need not be devoid of meaning. We will present evidence that suggests quite the contrary—the less emotional the memory, the more meaningful it is.

Moreover, the meaning of self-defining memories comes largely from their encapsulation of the prevalent themes in the life narrative and therefore personality (McAdams, 1996). Self-defining memories are seen as meaningful when they highlight themes that are already central to the rememberer (Moffitt & Singer, 1994). Reminding us of important themes in a stable life story, however, is only one way in which memories may provide a sense of meaning. A memory may also provide a sense of meaning when we are able to step back from an experience and examine it from a new and more distanced perspective. That is, memories become meaningful when we are able to take a wide-angle rather than a telephoto view of them. We will present evidence that suggests the more distanced the perspective on a memory, the more meaningful it is.

Lack of Emotion in Most Autobiographical Memories

Self-defining memories and key scenes in life narratives are highly emotional, which makes them unusual. Most autobiographical memories are constructed with the emotional portion suppressed or inhibited (Conway, 2005; Conway & Pleydell-Pearce, 2000; Conway et al., 2004; Philippot, Schaefer, & Herbette, 2003). Emotions must be suppressed because remembering experiences with their concomitant emotions would disrupt the pursuit of current goals, for which autobiographical memory serves a vital role. During autobiographical remembering, the past self must be separable from the present self who is pursuing goals (Conway et al., 2004). Suppression of emotion is one way to provide this separation.

Most people do not believe that autobiographical memories involve suppression of emotion. In fact, 82% of over 200 university students and faculty surveyed believed that they usually remember and reexperience emotions when they recollect life experiences (Beike, 2007). But a good deal of evidence shows that emotions are neither well remembered nor reexperienced. The best evidence for the lack of emotion in autobiographical memories is people's own ratings of the intensity of their memories. Most memories are rated as neutral or mildly positive (Conway, 1990).

More evidence for the lack of emotion in autobiographical memories is that emotion words are slower to elicit autobiographical memories than are other words (Beike, Adams, & Wirth-Beaumont, 2007; Conway & Bekerian, 1987); the memories they do elicit tend to be unusually recent (J. A. Robinson, 1976). Additional evidence for the lack of emotion comes from brain-imaging studies using PET scans or fMRI. When recollecting autobiographical memories, especially if those memories are temporally distant, people show no increased activity in the amygdala, which normally responds readily to emotional stimuli (Maguire & Frith, 2003; but cf. Greenberg et al., 2005). Yet another piece of evidence for the lack of emotion in autobiographical memory is that the intensity of emotional response to most autobiographical memories fades with time, a pattern called the fading affect bias (Walker, Skowronski, Gibbons, Vogl, & Thompson, 2003).

In fact, recollecting autobiographical memories with a great deal of emotional content is associated with poor psychological adjustment. For example, dysphoric people retain emotion rather than experiencing fading of emotion during autobiographical recollection (Walker et al., 2003). Emotion is integrated with, rather than made distinct from, nonemotional aspects of a stressful memory among those who have not yet recovered from the experience (Boals & Klein, 2005). Emotion during recollection is therefore not a sign of health and adjustment, as 87% of Beike's (2007) survey respondents believed. Instead, recollecting experiences with a great deal of emotion may indicate rumination or brooding (Lyubomirsky, Caldwell, & Nolen-Hoeksema, 1998; Martin & Tesser, 1996). Rumination is evoked by problematic goal progress, so a memory that brings to mind incomplete goals will also arouse negative emotion (Martin & Tesser, 1996, 2006). Rumination is also motivated by a lack of insight (Lyubomirsky & Nolen-Hoeksema, 1993). Ruminators are searching for missing meaning, not reflecting upon its presence, when they reminisce. It is actually healthier not to search actively for meaning after stressful experiences (Davis, Wortman, Lehman, & Silver, 2000). Emotion during recollection should be rare because well-adjusted people do not ruminate excessively on their experiences.

Suppression of emotion during recollection is therefore both common and beneficial. This suppression of emotion leads to a sense of psychological closure on a remembered experience (Beike et al., 2007; Beike & Wirth-Beaumont, 2005). Only the few memories for which people report low closure are highly emotional memories. For example, emotion words effectively cue low-closure (but not high-closure) memories (Beike et al., 2007). Also, people report more intense emotion when recalling low-closure memories and recollect more diverse emotions as part of the memory (Beike & Wirth-Beaumont, 2005). Moreover, affect does not fade for low-closure memories (Ritchie et al., 2006). To summarize, because lack of emotion is normative, emotional self-defining memories in a life narrative are atypical memories and therefore exemplify only one way in which people derive meaning from their memories.

The Problem With Emotion in Memories

As is clear from the research on life narrative and self-defining memories, the quest for meaning in part entails overlaying basic personality motives and themes onto memories of life experiences. A second way of engaging in the quest for meaning is holding the experience at arm's length in order to reflect upon it. The first process has been called *learning lessons* about the specific incident, and the second has been called *gaining insight*, which requires stepping back from the incident to see it in perspective (Thorne, McLean, & Lawrence, 2004). Only about 15% of self-defining memories are told with an explicit reference to insight (Thorne et al., 2004), leaving open the question of what kind of meaning people usually gain from self-defining memories. We hypothesize that the more typical unemotional memories would be more likely than self-defining memories to provide insight because unemotional memories provide greater emotional distance.

In general, a distanced cognitive perspective provides a greater sense of meaning. When thinking about one's possible success in the future, for example, seeing the scene from a distanced third-person rather than an intimate first-person perspective leads to an increased sense of the meaningfulness of the goals being pursued (Vasquez & Buehler, 2007). Greater meaning occurs because the distanced point of view provides a more abstract construal of an event, which is more focused on the meaning (why) rather than the process (how) of that event (Fujita, Henderson, Eng, Trope, & Liberman, 2006).

Self-defining memories have the disadvantage that they "may lack an appropriate distance from ongoing experience" (Conway et al., 2004, p. 511). In fact, the more specific (the less abstract and distanced) the description of a self-defining memory, the less likely it is to have integrative meaning (Blagov & Singer, 2004). It is difficult to achieve a sense of meaning when one is too firmly embedded in the details to see the experience through different lenses.

Self-defining memories may interfere with gaining the necessary distance as a result of their emotional nature. When emotion is aroused, it alters—even constrains—further thoughts and judgments (Bower, 1981). For example, people in an unhappy (compared to a neutral) emotional state remember less pleasant memories (Miranda & Kihlstrom, 2005) and make more negatively toned judgments (Forgas & Locke, 2005). People in an unhappy state also have lowered expectations for the future (Johnson & Tversky, 1983); and they are less persistent at tasks, especially if the task is to be continued until it is no longer enjoyable (Martin, Ward, Achee & Wyer, 1993). In contrast, people in a happy state remember more pleasant memories, make more positively toned judgments, have more optimistic expectations, and persist longer.

Beyond simple effects of pleasant and unpleasant emotions, there are more emotion-specific effects on thoughts and judgments (Levine & Pizarro, 2004). Fear, as a discrete emotion, is associated with an appraisal of threat. Imagine a person who brings to mind an autobiographical memory for a time her house was burglarized. Each time she recollects the burglary, she experiences a significant degree of fear. This fear will likely constrain her interpretation of the event such that the meaning she assigns it will involve threat to the self. She is unlikely to be able to see the experience as, for example, a reminder that material goods are replaceable and unimportant. Other specific emotions might constrain the meaning assigned to a memory in different ways. Anger increases approach tendencies toward the person who has interfered with goal progress (Berkowitz & Harmon-Jones, 2004). Guilt decreases approach tendencies until an opportunity for reparation occurs (Amodio, Devine, & Harmon-Jones, 2007). Thus, the presence of anger or guilt in the memory of a life experience will direct the rememberer toward meanings congruent with these action tendencies.

In short, the problem with emotional memories is that the emotion does not allow the rememberer to gain the perspective needed to assign it an updated meaning. Consider the case of relationship dissolution. Many people experience a once-painful breakup in retrospect as "the best thing that ever happened to me," perhaps when the ending of the first relationship allows one to find a happier relationship with a new love. Yet if the sadness of the breakup were well preserved and reexperienced with the memory, it would be difficult to construe the experience as beneficial. The strong emotion would activate similarly gloomy meanings of the experience upon recollection. Furthermore, correcting for this biased interpretation is difficult. The interpretations assigned to experiences are rapid and automatic, and they occur without the awareness of having applied an interpretation (Balcetis & Dunning, 2006).

An experience remembered with little emotion places fewer constraints on meaning. An initially crushing blow can be seen as a meaningful turning point toward happiness if one can shed the emotion that narrows the variety of meanings that can be applied. Lemons are made into lemonade, autobiographically speaking, because perspective can be gained. This sense of perspective is what allows us to see our memories more positively with the passage of time (Kennedy, Mather, & Carstensen, 2004; Miranda & Kihlstrom, 2005).

How Diminished Emotion Allows Meaning

Several lines of evidence support our claim that diminished emotion provides the perspective necessary to obtain life meaning. There is a good deal of direct evidence that diminished emotion and a more distanced perspective in memory go together. For example, memories recalled from an observer (third-person) perspective lead to less emotional response than those recalled from a field (first-person) perspective (Berntsen & Rubin, 2006; J. A. Robinson & Swanson, 1993). Similarly, reporting an unpleasant experience by distancing oneself from the experience yet trying to understand it leads to the least negative emotional response (Kross, Ayduk, & Mischel, 2005).

Unfortunately, there is little direct evidence that diminished emotion and increased meaning go together. For example, in self-defining memories, the degree of affect aroused by the memory is unrelated to integrative meaning (Blagov & Singer, 2004). But one suggestive piece of evidence comes from an intriguing study of the process of deriving meaning from a difficult-to-process experience: observing artworks. Participants were interviewed immediately after having viewed an art show, then again five months later. At each time, they were asked whether they experienced an emotion when remembering a particular artwork, and they were asked to describe the artwork. The memory descriptions were coded for thematic integration, meaning that a theme was mentioned in the description and linked to elements in the artwork. For example, one participant described an artwork as being about mother-and-child relationships because it contrasted large bodies, representing motherhood, with small heads, representing childhood (Medved, Cupchik, & Oatley, 2004). Thematic integration is therefore an indication of finding meaning in the artwork.

Over time, greater fading of affect co-occurred with increased meaning. The percentage of participants who reported having an emotion associated with the memory for the artwork dropped from 80% to 65% after five months. The percentage of participants whose memory indicated integration (finding meaning) in the artwork increased from 33% to 56% after five months. Over time, emotion decreased and meaning increased. Although the researchers reached a different conclusion based on the relationship of emotion to meaning within each time period (Medved et al., 2004), the temporal pattern indicates that the dissociation of emotion from a memory enables discovery of meaning.

To provide more direct evidence of the link between diminished emotion in an autobiographical memory and increased meaning, we conducted an experiment. We compared the effects of recollecting self-defining (usually emotional) memories to recollecting closed (usually unemotional) memories. Seventy-seven participants (mostly University of Arkansas undergraduate students) were assigned to one of four recall conditions. One fourth of the participants were asked to think of an unpleasant self-defining memory. A self-defining memory was described as being at least a year old, clearly remembered, important to understanding who you are as an individual, leading to strong feelings, frequently recalled, and linked to other similar memories (Blagov & Singer, 2004). One fourth of the participants were asked to think of an unpleasant closed memory. A closed memory was described as being at least a year old, feeling behind you or resolved, understood well, and not necessarily still being important to your life (Beike & Wirth-Beaumont, 2005).

We focused on unpleasant memories because they evoke more sense-making and meaning-making efforts. The memories described by participants were rated by two coders according to Singer and Blagov's system (2000), in terms of their specificity (a single event lasting less than a day, a temporally extended series of scenes, or a generic recurrent type of event; α = .53) and integrative meaning (an explicit statement of what the experience means about the self or the world was present or absent in the event description; α = .65).

To determine whether the mere act of remembering led to a sense of meaning, these two recall conditions were compared with a condition in which participants recollected an experience that involved the self on some level but would not typically be considered a true autobiographical memory. To this end, one fourth of participants were asked to recall the most recent television program they had watched (or if they did not watch television recently, the most recent book or magazine they had read). All three recall groups—self-defining, closed, or television—were then asked to rate the importance, unpleasantness, date, and closure (Beike & Wirth-Beaumont, 2005) of the experience they had reported. The remaining one fourth of participants were not asked to recall an experience but simply completed the dependent measures.

The first dependent measure was affect, used to determine whether self-defining memories indeed aroused significant affect. We used Blagov and Singer's (2004) list of 12 positive and negative affect words and asked participants to what extent they were currently experiencing each affective state (happy, angry, surprised, ashamed, disgusted, guilty, interested, contempt, proud, embarrassed, afraid, and sad).

The next dependent measure was designed to address a specific facet of the sense of meaning in life. We were less interested in the *content* of meaning they found in life (e.g., Ebersole, 1998; Wong, 1998) than in the *confidence* with which they ascribed meaning to life. To best capture this confidence in meaning, we chose to measure the extent to which participants felt they clearly understood the self and clearly understood the meaning of life. The self-clarity scale (Campbell et al., 1996) was used, and a modification of it developed to address life meaning. For example, an item on the self-clarity scale is "In general, I have a clear sense of who I am and what I am." Our modification to measure clarity of meaning was "In general, I have a clear sense of the nature of the world and the meaning of life." Both scales demonstrated adequate reliability (self-clarity α = .87; life meaning clarity α = .77). Similarly phrased items have been found to relate to an overall sense of meaning (Wood & Conway, 2006).

In addition, we added two items that specifically addressed the role memories played in uncovering meaning. These were "When I think about my experiences, I often discover important truths about myself" and "When I think about my experiences, I often discover important lessons about life." We also included two measures of well-being to determine whether any effects on clarity of meaning were simply a result of elevated well-being. We measured self-esteem (Rosenberg, 1965; α = .89) and satisfaction with life (Diener, Emmons, Larsen, & Griffin, 1985; α = .80).

Table 15.1 Properties and Effects of Memories

	Memory Type			
	Self-Def	Closed	TV	None
Property	(n = 17)	(n = 20)	(n = 21)	(n = 19)
Single event (n)	6	11		
Integrative meaning (n)	10	1***		
Year of occurrence	2000_a (1.2)	2001_a (1.1)	2007_b (1.1)***	
Importance	6.2_a (0.4)	4.3_b (0.4)	2.8_c (0.4)***	
Unpleasantness	6.5_a (0.3)	6.8_a (0.3)	2.0_b (0.3)***	
Closed book	3.2_a (0.4)	5.3_b (0.4)	4.0_{ab} (0.4)**	
Positive emotion	2.2 (0.2)	2.0 (0.2)	2.3 (0.2)	2.5 (0.2)
Negative emotion	**2.0_a (0.2)**	1.7_{ab} (0.1)	1.4_b (0.1)	1.6_{ab} (0.1)**
Self-clarity	3.2_{ab} (0.2)	3.4_{ab} (0.2)	2.9_a (0.2)	3.5_b (0.2)**
Meaning clarity	3.5 (0.1)	3.3 (0.1)	3.2 (0.1)	3.4 (0.1)
Discover truths about self	3.9 (0.2)	4.3 (0.2)	3.8 (0.2)	3.9 (0.2)
Discover lessons about life	3.9_{ab} (0.2)	**4.3_a (0.2)**	3.7_b (0.2)	4.0_{ab} (0.2)*
Self-esteem	5.3 (0.3)	5.7 (0.2)	5.1 (0.2)	5.6 (0.2)
Satisfaction with life	4.5 (0.3)	5.3 (0.3)	4.6 (0.3)	4.8 (0.3)

Emotion ratings, clarity ratings, and discovery item ratings range from 1 to 5, and other ratings range from 1 to 7. Standard error of the mean is given in parentheses. Means with different subscripts within a row differ at $p < .06$ by post hoc tests using Bonferroni's correction. Means in bold differ from other means in that row by planned contrast ($p < .02$). *univariate $p < .07$; **univariate $p < .05$; ***univariate p or $\chi_2 < .001$.

The results are presented in Tables 15.1, 15.2, and 15.3. Table 15.1 shows that self-defining and closed memories were similar in specificity, recency, and unpleasantness, and their content was quite similar as well (mostly romantic, academic, and family experiences). Thus, self-defining and closed memories were not about substantively different initial experiences. They

Table 15.2 Simultaneous Regression Analysis of Clarity of Meaning in Life

	Meaning Clarity		
Predictors	**B**	**SE B**	**β**
(Constant)	1.60	0.47***	
Positive emotion	−0.01	0.07	−0.01
Negative emotion	0.01	0.10	0.01
Self-esteem	0.29	0.08	0.50***
Satisfaction with life	−0.07	0.07	−0.15
Discover truths about self	−0.17	0.09	−0.26*
Discover lessons about life	0.30	0.10	0.42**

F (6, 70) = 4.87, $p < .0004$, $r^2 = 0.30$; *$p < .07$; **$p < .05$; ***$p < .001$.

Table 15.3 Simultaneous Regression Analysis of Self-Clarity

	Self-Clarity		
Predictors	**B**	**SE B**	**β**
(Constant)	0.70	0.55	
Positive emotion	−0.05	0.90	−0.05
Negative emotion	0.03	0.12	0.02
Self-esteem	0.40	0.09	0.54**
Satisfaction with life	0.07	0.08	0.10
Discover truths about self	−0.28	0.11	−0.33*
Discover lessons about life	0.31	0.12	0.33*

F (6, 70) = 8.66, $p < .0000005$, $r^2 = .43$; *$p < .05$; **$p < .001$.

differed only in their closure and their importance. Table 15.1 shows that the effects of self-defining and closed memories were also quite similar. Neither aroused significant positive affect, neither affected well-being, and neither led to an enhanced sense of clarity of the self or the meaning of life.

However, there were some important differences between self-defining and closed memories, which support our contention that less emotion in an autobiographical memory leads to more flexible meaning. First, recollecting a self-defining memory (compared to the other three conditions) led to the highest negative affect, as predicted. Second, a self-defining memory was more likely to include an explicit statement of meaning. Finally, recollecting a closed memory (compared to the other three conditions) led people to report that they discovered more important lessons about life (i.e., gained more insight) from their memories.

These few differences reveal the differing ways in which emotional and unemotional memories provide a sense of meaning. Self-defining memories, affording emotional arousal, are tagged with a particular meaning that is stored with the memory (see also Thorne et al., 2004). Closed memories, affording emotional distance, are not tagged with a particular meaning but instead allow the rememberer to discover meaningful life lessons by reflecting on the experience. Moreover, as shown in Tables 15.2 and 15.3, this sense of discovery predicted a clearer sense of self and a clearer sense of meaning in life. Thus, recollection of a single closed memory indirectly increased participants' clarity of meaning.[1] Because well-being was not affected by recollecting either type of memory and because the regression analyses took well-being into account, the influence of autobiographical memory on meaning in life

[1] It is of interest that discovering truths about the self (rather than life) predicted less self-clarity and meaning clarity in the regression analyses. One explanation for this unexpected pattern is that discovering truths about the self may lead to self-awareness, which in turn reduces self-clarity and meaning clarity.

shown in Tables 15.1, 15.2, and 15.3 was not simply a result of an enhanced sense of well-being.

Therefore, the primary distinction between self-defining and closed autobiographical memories is the degree of emotion they evoke, not the types of experiences they record. Closed memories evoke less emotion, providing emotional distance that yields a flexible (rather than a previously assigned) sense of meaning. The evidence from our experiment and other research does not specify the temporal or causal sequence in which diminished emotion, distance, and meaning take place. Our conjecture is that emotion reduction during remembering is the first and necessary step. After emotion reduces, a sense of closure is attained; then a novel meaning of the experience can be discovered, thereby improving well-being.

We see the reduction in emotion as the first step for two reasons. First, emotion is quite transient in memory (Levine & Safer, 2002; Odegard & Lampinen, 2004; M. D. Robinson & Clore, 2002). Second, autobiographical remembering activates mechanisms to inhibit and suppress emotion (Conway, Pleydell-Pearce, & Whitecross, 2001; Philippot et al., 2003). Thus, we propose that the process of finding meaning from individual life experiences can occur only after a reduction of emotion in memory.

The Role of Emotional and Unemotional Memories in Meaning

The results of the experiment demonstrate that self-defining memories, as emotional pieces of a life narrative, are tagged with a lesson or insight, a potential source of meaning. Closed memories, as unemotional single-event recollections, are not tagged but, rather, lead to a sense of having discovered meaning through the act of reflection upon the memory. We theorize that this difference is a result of the differing degree of distance provided by self-defining and closed memories. Both types of memories contribute to the sense of meaning in life, but in different ways and at different times. Self-defining memories provide a ready lesson, but the lesson is constrained in content by the emotion inherent in remembering. Closed memories provide no prepackaged lesson, but they do require a moment's reflection to enable the rememberer to discover the meaning of this experience.

Under certain circumstances, people need the ready lessons that come with emotional self-defining memories and the life narrative they comprise. Self-defining memories are particularly meaningful when they preserve stories of the struggle to attain goals (Conway et al., 2004; Thorne et al., 2004). Therefore, self-defining memories and the life narrative may provide particular comfort to people in times of duress or uncertainty (Blagov & Singer, 2004) when they need assurance that past struggles have often turned out well. Self-defining memories may also be the primary memory source of meaning for older adults who are in the process of life review. Older adults reviewing their lives strive to create an integrated life story with a profound sense of meaning. As a consequence, older adults are more likely than younger adults to integrate recollected life experiences into a narrative of the self (Pasupathi & Mansour, 2006).

Under other circumstances, people need flexibility and a sense of discovering meaning from their memories, both of which occur after recollection of emotionally pallid closed autobiographical memories. Therefore, closed memories may be an important source of meaning when people have time to reflect and are open to seeing new options, such as when contemplating the possibility of a career change or a relationship commitment. When recollected with a sense of closure, experiences can be seen as part of one's life, yet in the past. They can therefore be viewed with the wisdom acquired through having lived life.

Throughout this chapter we have set the concept of emotional, self-defining memories in a themed life story against the concept of unemotional, free-floating closed memories in order to highlight their differences. But self-defining memories and closed memories have more commonalities than differences, as the results of our experiment clearly showed. Both self-defining and closed memories are at least somewhat emotional, given their mere association with the self. Both self-defining and closed memories are part of the life narrative, for the life story schema is implicitly involved in every instance of autobiographical remembering (Conway & Pleydell-Pearce, 2000; Conway et al., 2004). Therefore, both self-defining and closed memories must cohere with the life story at some level (see also Beike & Landoll, 2000). The difference is one of degree rather than kind.

Compared to self-defining memories, closed memories are less emotional and less directly related to a life narrative. They are the plain, banal stuff of everyday use. Lest we take our unemotional memories for granted, though, it is important to remember what they do for us. Closed memories allow us to discover meaning in experiences, rather than reminding us of meanings we assigned years ago. By allowing emotions to fade, by gaining a sense of closure, and by seeing the experience from an emotional distance, we unlock the ability to draw novel and potentially more sophisticated insights from individual remembered experiences. These insights add to our autobiographical intelligence, enabling each of us to live a more meaningful life.

References

Adler, A. (1931). *What life could mean to you.* New York, NY: Grosset and Dunlap.

Amodio, D. M., Devine, P. G., & Harmon-Jones, E. (2007). A dynamic model of guilt: Implications for motivation and self-regulation in the context of prejudice. *Psychological Science, 18,* 524–530.

Auhagen, A. E. (2000). On the psychology of meaning of life. *Swiss Journal of Psychology, 59,* 34–48.

Balcetis, E., & Dunning, D. (2006). See what you want to see: Motivational influences on visual perception. *Journal of Personality and Social Psychology, 91,* 612–625.

Baumeister, R. F., & Wilson, B. (1996). Life stories and the four needs for meaning. *Psychological Inquiry, 7,* 322–377.

Beike, D. R. (2007). The unnoticed absence of emotion in autobiographical memory. *Social and Personality Compass, 1*, 392–408.

Beike, D. R., Adams, L. P., & Wirth-Beaumont, E. T. (2007). Incomplete inhibition of emotion in specific autobiographical memories. *Memory, 15*, 375–289.

Beike, D. R., & Landoll, S. L. (2000). Striving for a consistent life story: Cognitive reactions to autobiographical memories. *Social Cognition, 18*, 292–318.

Beike, D. R., & Wirth-Beaumont, E. T. (2005). Psychological closure as a memory phenomenon. *Memory, 13*, 574–593.

Berkowitz, L., & Harmon-Jones, E. (2004). Toward an understanding of the determinants of anger. *Emotion, 4*, 107–130.

Berntsen, D., & Rubin, D. C. (2006). Emotion and vantage point in autobiographical memory. *Cognition and Emotion, 20*, 1193–1215.

Blagov, P. S., & Singer, J. A. (2004). Four dimensions of self-defining memories (specificity, meaning, content, and affect) and their relationships to self-restraint, distress, and repressive defensiveness. *Journal of Personality, 72*, 481–512.

Bluck, S., Alea, N., Habermas, T., & Rubin, D. C. (2005). A tale of three functions: The self-reported uses of autobiographical memory. *Social Cognition, 23*, 91–117.

Bluck, S., & Habermas, T. (2000). The life story schema. *Motivation and Emotion, 24*, 121–147.

Boals, A., & Klein, K. (2005) Cognitive-emotional distinctiveness: Separating emotions from non-emotions in the representation of a stressful memory. *Memory, 13*, 638–648.

Bower, G. H. (1981). Mood and memory. *American Psychologist, 36*, 129–148.

Campbell, J. D., Trapnell, P. D., Heine, S. J., Katz, I. M., Lavallee, L. F., & Lehman, D. R. (1996). Self-concept clarity: Measurement, personality correlates, and cultural boundaries. *Journal of Personality and Social Psychology, 70*, 141–156.

Conway, M. A. (1990). *Autobiographical memory: An introduction*. Buckingham, England: Open University Press.

Conway, M. A. (2003). Commentary: Cognitive-affective mechanisms and processes in autobiographical memory. *Memory, 11*, 217–224.

Conway, M. A. (2005). Memory and the self. *Journal of Memory and Language, 53*, 594–628.

Conway, M. A., & Bekerian, D. A. (1987). Organization in autobiographical memory. *Memory and Cognition, 15*, 119–132.

Conway, M. A., & Holmes, A. (2004). Psychosocial stages and the accessibility of autobiographical memories across the life cycle. *Journal of Personality, 72*, 461–480.

Conway, M. A., & Pleydell-Pearce, C. W. (2000). The construction of autobiographical memories in the self-defining memory system. *Psychological Review, 107*, 261–288.

Conway, M. A., Pleydell-Pearce, C. W., & Whitecross, S. E. (2001). The neuroanatomy of autobiographical memory: A slow cortical potential study of autobiographical memory retrieval. *Journal of Memory and Language, 45*, 493–524.

Conway, M. A., Singer, J. A., & Tagini, A. (2004). The self and autobiographical memory: Correspondence and coherence. *Social Cognition, 22*, 491–529.

Davis, C. G., Wortman, C. B., Lehman, D. R., & Silver, R. C. (2000). Searching for meaning in loss: Are clinical assumptions correct? *Death Studies, 24*, 497–540.

Deci, E. L., & Ryan, R. M. (2000). The "what" and "why" of goal pursuits: Human needs and the self-determination of behavior. *Psychological Inquiry, 11*, 227–268.

Denkova, E., Botzung, A., Scheiber, C., & Manning, L. (2006). Implicit emotion during recollection of past events: A nonverbal fMRI study. *Brain Research, 1078*, 143–150.

Diener, E., Emmons, R. A., Larsen, R. J., & Griffin, S. (1985). The Satisfaction With Life Scale. *Journal of Personality Assessment, 49*, 71–75.

Ebersole, P. (1998). Types and depth of written life meanings. In P. T. P. Wong & P. S. Fry (Eds.), *The human quest for meaning: A handbook of psychological research and clinical applications* (pp. 179–191). Mahwah, NJ: Erlbaum.

Forgas, J. P., & Locke, J. (2005). Affective influences on causal inferences: The effects of mood on attributions for positive and negative interpersonal episodes. *Cognition and Emotion, 19*, 1071–1081.

Fujita, K., Henderson, M. D., Eng, J., Trope, Y., & Liberman, N. (2006). Spatial distance and mental construal of social events. *Psychological Science, 17*, 278–282.

Greenberg, D. L., Rice, H. J., Cooper, J. J., Cabeza, R., Rubin, D. C., & LaBar, K. S. (2005). Co-activation of the amygdala, hippocampus and inferior frontal gyrus during autobiographical memory retrieval. *Neuropsychologia, 43*, 659–674.

Haque, S., & Conway, M. A. (2001). Sampling the process of autobiographical memory construction. *European Journal of Cognitive Psychology, 13*, 529–547.

Johnson, E. J., & Tversky, A. (1983). Affect, generalization, and the perception of risk. *Journal of Personality and Social Psychology, 45*, 20–31.

Kennedy, Q., Mather, M., & Carstensen, L. L. (2004). The role of motivation in the age-related positivity effect in autobiographical memory. *Psychological Science, 15*, 208–214.

Korotkov, D. (1998). The sense of coherence: Making meaning out of chaos. In P. T. P. Wong & P. S. Fry (Eds.), *The human quest for meaning: A handbook of psychological research and clinical applications* (pp. 51–70). Mahwah, NJ: Erlbaum.

Kross, E., Ayduk, O., & Mischel, W. (2005). When asking "why" does not hurt: Distinguishing rumination from reflective processing of negative emotions. *Psychological Science, 16*, 709–715.

Levine, L. J., & Pizarro, D. A. (2004). Emotion and memory research: A grumpy overview. *Social Cognition, 22*, 530–554.

Levine, L. J., & Safer, M. A. (2002). Sources of bias in memory for emotions. *Current Directions in Psychological Science, 11*, 169–173.

Lyubomirsky, S., Caldwell, N. D., & Nolen-Hoeksema, S. (1998). Effects of ruminative and distracting responses to depressed mood on retrieval of autobiographical memories. *Journal of Personality and Social Psychology, 75*, 166–177.

Lyubomirsky, S., & Nolen-Hoeksema, S. (1993). Self-perpetuating properties of dysphoric rumination. *Journal of Personality and Social Psychology, 65*, 339–349.

Maguire, E. A., & Frith, C. D. (2003). Lateral asymmetry in the hippocampal response to the remoteness of autobiographical memories. *Journal of Neuroscience, 23*, 5302–5307.

Martin, L. L., & Tesser, A. (1996). Some ruminative thoughts. In R. S. Wyer Jr. (Ed.), *Advances in social cognition* (Vol. 9, pp. 1–47). Hillsdale, NJ: Erlbaum.

Martin, L. L., & Tesser, A. (2006). Extending the goal progress theory of rumination: Goal reevaluation and growth. In L. J. Sanna & E. C. Chang (Eds.), *Judgments over time: The interplay of thoughts, feelings, and behaviors* (pp. 145–162). New York, NY: Oxford University Press.

Martin, L. L., Ward, D. W., Achee, J. W., & Wyer, R. S. (1993). Mood as input: People have to interpret the motivational implications of their moods. *Journal of Personality and Social Psychology, 64*, 317–326.

McAdams, D. P. (1996). Personality, modernity, and the storied self: A contemporary framework for studying persons. *Psychological Inquiry, 7*, 295–321.

McAdams, D. P. (2006). The problem of narrative coherence. *Journal of Constructivist Psychology, 19*, 109–125.

McAdams, D. P., Bauer, J. J., Sakeada, A. R., Anyidoho, N. A., Machado, M. A., Magrino-Failla, K., ... Pals, J. L. (2006). Continuity and change in the life story: A longitudinal study of autobiographical memories in emerging adulthood. *Journal of Personality, 74*, 1371–1400.

Medved, M. I., Cupchik, G. C., & Oatley, K. (2004). Interpretive memories of artworks. *Memory, 12*, 119–128.

Miranda, R., & Kihlstrom, J. F. (2005). Mood congruence in childhood and recent autobiographical memory. *Cognition and Emotion, 19*, 981–998.

Moffitt, K. H., & Singer, J. A. (1994). Continuity in the life story: Self-defining memories, affect, and approach/avoidance personal strivings. *Journal of Personality, 62*, 21–43.

Odegard, T. N., & Lampinen, J. M. (2004). Memory conjunction errors for autobiographical events: More than just familiarity. *Memory, 12*, 288–300.

Pasupathi, M., & Mansour, E. (2006). Adult age differences in autobiographical reasoning in narratives. *Developmental Psychology, 42*, 798–808.

Philippot, P., Schaefer, A., & Herbette, G. (2003). Consequences of specific processing of emotional information: Impact of general versus specific autobiographical memory priming on emotion elicitation. *Emotion, 3*, 270–283.

Ritchie, T. D., Skowronski, J. J., Wood, S. E., Walker, W. R., Vogl, R. J., & Gibbons, J. A. (2006). Event self-importance, event rehearsal, and the fading affect bias in autobiographical memory. *Self and Identity, 5*, 172–195.

Robinson, J. A. (1976). Sampling autobiographical memory. *Cognitive Psychology, 8*, 578–595.

Robinson, J. A., & Swanson, K. L. (1993). Field and observer modes of remembering. *Memory, 1*, 169–184.

Robinson, M. D., & Clore, G. L. (2002). Belief and feeling: Evidence for an accessibility model of emotional self-report. *Psychological Bulletin, 128*, 934–960.

Rosenberg, M. (1965). *Society and the adolescent self-image*. Middletown, CT: Wesleyan University Press.

Schwartz, G. E., Weinberger, D. A., & Singer, J. A. (1981). Cardiovascular differentiation of happiness, sadness, anger, and fear following imagery and exercise. *Psychosomatic Medicine, 43*, 343–364.

Sheldon, K. M., Elliot, A. J., Kim, Y., & Kasser, T. (2001). What is satisfying about satisfying events? Testing 10 candidate needs. *Journal of Personality and Social Psychology, 80*, 325–339.

Singer, J. A. (2004). Narrative identity and meaning making across the adult lifespan: An introduction. *Journal of Personality, 72*, 437–459.

Singer, J. A., & Blagov, P. S. (2000). *Classification system and scoring manual for self-defining autobiographical memories*. Paper presented at the meeting of the Society for Applied Research on Memory and Cognition, Miami Beach, Florida.

Singer, J. A., & Moffitt, K. H. (1991–1992). An experimental investigation of specificity and generality in memory narratives. *Imagination, Cognition, and Personality, 11*, 233–257.

Sommer, K. L., & Baumeister, R. F. (1998). The construction of meaning from life events: Empirical studies of personal narratives. In P. T. P. Wong & P. S. Fry (Eds.), *The human quest for meaning: A handbook of psychological research and clinical applications* (pp. 143–161). Mahwah, NJ: Erlbaum.

Thorne, A., McLean, K. C., & Lawrence, A. M. (2004). When remembering is not enough: Reflecting on self-defining memories in late adolescence. *Journal of Personality, 72*, 513–542.

Vasquez, N. A., & Buehler, R. (2007). Seeing future success: Does imagery perspective influence achievement motivation? *Personality and Social Psychology Bulletin, 33,* 1392–1405.

Walker, W. R., Skowronski, J. J., Gibbons, J. A., Vogl, R. J., & Thompson, C. P. (2003). On the emotions that accompany autobiographical memories: Dysphoria disrupts the fading affect bias. *Cognition and Emotion, 17,* 703–723.

Wong, P. T. P. (1998). Implicit theories of meaningful life and the development of the Personal Meaning Profile. In P. T. P. Wong & P. S. Fry (Eds.), *The human quest for meaning: A handbook of psychological research and clinical applications* (pp. 111–140). Mahwah, NJ: Erlbaum.

Wood, W., & Conway, M. (2006). Subjective impact, meaning making, and current and recalled emotions for self-defining memories. *Journal of Personality, 74,* 811–845.

16
Life Meaning and Purpose in Life Among Chinese Adolescents
What Can We Learn From Chinese Studies in Hong Kong?

DANIEL T. L. SHEK

The Hong Kong Polytechnic University

With cognitive maturity that enables adolescents to think in abstract terms and explore future possibilities, adolescents commonly ask many questions about life. Included are questions such as these: What is the meaning of life? What is a meaningful life? Why do we exist? What should we accomplish in life? These questions commonly fall within the scope of "meaning of life" or "purpose in life," which addresses three interrelated issues, including meaning of life (e.g., what life signifies and personal reasons as well as importance of existence), meaningfulness of life (e.g., whether life is worth living or is purposeful), and purpose in life (e.g., life goals, life purpose, things one wants to be accomplished, ideals to be attained).

The importance of meaning of life in adolescent behavior is clearly reflected in human history. For example, in the 1930s, young people supported Hitler in Nazi Germany when they believed that building an ethnically superior Germany was their life mission. During the Cultural Revolution in Communist China in the 1960s, the Red Guards fiercely fought against "enemies" of the proletarians when they saw that building a Communist utopia was their sacred life goal. In the contemporary world, many young people with material affluence abuse such psychotropic substances such as Ecstasy and Ketamine when they perceive that life is meaningless and confused. Nevertheless, despite the importance of meaning in life in our understanding of adolescent development (Benson, Roehlkepartain, & Rude, 2003), there is a huge research gap in this area in the developmental sciences (King & Boyatzis, 2004) and clinical literature (Wong & Fry, 1998).

With specific reference to the Chinese culture, surprisingly few research studies have been conducted to examine the issue of meaning of life in Chinese adolescents (Shek, 1995a). Using *purpose in life* and *Chinese* as search terms, computer search of the PsycINFO in July 2007 showed that there were only 32 citations. Similarly, computer search using *purpose in life* and *Chinese* and *adolescents* showed that there were only 12 citations. In short, the Chinese literature on meaning of life in Chinese adolescents is extremely thin. Besides, computer search showed that most of the existing studies indexed in PsycINFO were conducted in Hong Kong and published scientific studies conducted in other Chinese communities, such as mainland China and Taiwan, were almost nonexistent.

This chapter attempts to give an overall picture about research studies examining meaning of life in Chinese adolescents in Hong Kong. There are several sections in this chapter. First, assessment tools of life meaning and purpose in life in Chinese adolescents in Hong Kong will be presented. Second, profiles about meaning of life in Chinese adolescents and the related sociodemographic correlates are described. Third, research findings on the relationship between purpose in life and developmental outcomes in Chinese adolescents, including psychological symptoms and problem behavior, are outlined. Fourth, existing studies pertinent to the relationships between family processes and adolescent purpose in life are reviewed. Fifth, meaning of life in Chinese adolescents experiencing life adversity is examined. Finally, conceptual, methodological, and practical limitations of the existing studies are discussed and future research directions are outlined. In this chapter, meaning in life refers to personal reasons for existence, perceived worth of life, and life goals. The terms *meaning in life* and *purpose in life* will be used interchangeably in this chapter.

Assessment of Life Meaning and Purpose in Life

Two main approaches have been used to assess life meaning and purpose in life in Chinese adolescents. With reference to surveys conducted by social scientists (mainly sociologists and social work researchers), meaning in life was commonly assessed by single items or questions. In the study of young people's outlook on life (The Hong Kong Federation of Youth Groups, 1997), three questions asking about the life aspirations of young people were included: (a) the respondent's ranking of the importance of six things in life, including wealth, family, health, friends, social status and peace of mind; (b) areas of life that the respondents would like to achieve most of the time when they are aged 35 (achievement including knowledge, career, social status, power, making money, a happy marriage, having children, ability to contribute to society, and a livelihood that gives one nothing to worry about); and (c) perceived factors that determine one's ability to achieve one's life goals (including one's own effort, help from other people, coordination of all aspects, luck, and God's will). These items were used again in a follow-up study of The Hong Kong Federation of Youth Groups (2000). Similarly, in the Indicators of Social Development Project (Lau, Lee, Wan, & Wong, 2005), one question was used to assess the respondents' perception of the most important ingredient for a happy life, including health, peace of mind, money, having filial children, freedom, love, marriage and family, career, material enjoyment, and serving society and others.

On the other hand, researchers have used psychological scales comprising multiple items to assess the construct of meaning of life or purpose in life. The most commonly used measure is the Chinese version of the Purpose in Life Questionnaire (Chinese PIL). The PIL was designed to quantify existential meaning perceived by an individual (Crumbaugh, 1968; Dufton & Perlman, 1986), and evidence has been accumulated on its reliability and validity. There are 20 items in the PIL, which covers different aspects of purpose in life, including (a) whether one perceives that life is boring, exciting, empty, worth living, meaningful, refreshing, confusing, under control, and a source of pleasure; (b) whether one has life goals and made related progress; (c) whether one would choose not to exist in this world or consider suicide; (d) whether one would enjoy retirement life and is prepared for death; and (e) one's perception of human nature and one's sense of responsibility. The Chinese PIL was modeled after the Western literature (Crumbaugh, 1968; Shek, 1986, 1988).

A survey of the literature shows that the Chinese PIL possessed acceptable psychometric properties. Based on 2,150 Chinese secondary school students, Shek (1986, 1988) showed that the items in the Chinese PIL were internally consistent. In another study based on 500 Chinese college students, the reliability of the Chinese PIL was high. Utilizing a longitudinal research design, Shek (1999a, 1999b, 1999c) showed that the Chinese PIL was reliable at different times and across time. Regarding the validity of the Chinese PIL, research findings showed that the Chinese PIL scores were concurrently (Shek, 1992) and longitudinally (Shek, 1999a) related to different measures of psychological symptoms and positive mental health indicators, thus providing support for its construct validity. Finally, factor-analytic findings revealed that two dominant dimensions emerged from the Chinese PIL (Shek, 1988). These include the Quality of Existence subscale (Items 1, 2, 5, 6, 8, 9, 11, 12, 16, and 19) and the Purpose of Existence subscale (sum of Items 3, 4, 13, 17, 18, and 20).

Another general measure of meaning in life is the Chinese version of the Existential Well-Being Scale (EXIST). Formed as part of the Spiritual Well-Being Scale, EXIST was constructed by Paloutzian and Ellison (1982) to assess life direction and satisfaction. There are 10 items in the scale. The respondent is invited to determine the extent to which (a) he or she feels that life is pleasurable, gratifying, healthy, enjoyable, good, conflicting in nature, meaningful, and anxiety provoking with reference to the future; and (b) he or she has a life direction and some life goals.

There are several studies showing that the EXIST possessed acceptable psychometric properties. Based on 500 Chinese college students, Shek (1993) showed that the EXIST was internally consistent and the scores were associated with other measures of psychological well-being, including the Chinese PIL. In a series of studies examining the relationships between family functioning and adolescent psychological well-being, Shek (2003c) showed that EXIST was reliable in different samples and the scale was associated with other measures of psychological well-being, including trait anxiety, mastery, life satisfaction, and self-esteem. Further evidence supporting the reliability and validity of the scale could be seen from the cross-sectional and longitudinal studies on adolescents experiencing economic disadvantage (Shek, 2003a, 2005a; Shek et al., 2001).

In addition to the foregoing general measures of meaning of life in adolescents are subscales assessing purpose in life, which is also intrinsic to some of the generic measures of adolescent development. In the Chinese Positive Youth Development Scale developed by Shek, Siu, and Lee (2007) are subscales assessing 15 positive youth development constructs, including bonding, resilience, social competence, emotional competence, cognitive competence, behavioral competence, moral competence, self-determination, self-efficacy, spirituality, beliefs in the future, clear and positive identity, recognition for positive behavior, prosocial involvement, and prosocial norms. In the subscale measuring spirituality, seven items modeled after the items in the Chinese PIL were examined. In the Outlook on Life Scale (Lau & Lau, 1996), four items were used to form the subscale assessing how the respondents viewed their own lifestyles, including whether (a) life is meaningless, (b) life is worth living, (c) life is full of fun and joy, and (d) one lives a positive life. In the Person–Social Development Self-Efficacy Inventory (PSD-SEI) developed by Yuen et al. (2006), there is an Interest and Life Goals subscale that assesses the existence of life goals and related plans for goal attainment in Chinese adolescents.

Finally, the Chinese Beliefs About Adversity Scale (CBA) was developed to assess how Chinese people make sense when facing life with adversity (Shek, 2004, 2005a; Shek et al., 2001). There are nine items in this scale, including the following items: (a) "Chi de ku zhong ku, fang wei ren shange ren" (hardship increases stature); (b) "Hao chou ming sheng cheng" (whether a life is good or bad depends on fate); (c) "You zhi zhe shi jing cheng" (when there is a will, there is a way); (d) "Zhi yao you heng xin, tie zhu mo cheng zhen" (If you work hard enough, you can turn an iron rod into a needle); (e) "Ren qong zhi duan" (poverty stifles ambition); (f) "Jiang qin bu zhuo, qin jian nai ku" (diligence is an important factor to overcome poverty); (g) "Ren ding sheng tian" (man is the master of his own fate); (h) "Zhi zu chang le" (a contented person is always happy); and (i) "Jiang xiang ben wu zhong, nan er dang zi qiang" (man is not born to greatness, he achieves it by his own effort). Reliability analyses showed that this scale was reliable at a specific time and across time in different samples. The CBA scores were also significantly associated with other measures of psychological well-being.

Profiles and Sociodemographic Correlates of Meaning of Life in Chinese Adolescents

The profiles on meaning of life in Chinese adolescents in Hong Kong can be inferred from several social surveys in Hong Kong. The outlook on life among young people in Hong Kong was examined in a social survey conducted by The Hong Kong Federation of Youth Groups (1997). The findings on the life aspirations of young people showed that respondents ranked the importance of several things in life in the following order: family, health, friends, peace of mind, wealth, and social status. Regarding the question "In which area of life do you hope you will have achieved most by the time you are 35 years old?", results are as follows: career (66.1%), a happy marriage (8.9%), making money (5.9%), social status (4.2%), having children (3.0%), knowledge (1.4%), and a livelihood that gives me nothing to worry about (1.1%). Whereas most respondents believed that they could achieve their ideals by themselves (75.9%), others believed that luck or God's will (5.5%), help of others (3.1%), and coordination of all aspects (5.2%) determined their ability to achieve their life goals.

In a follow-up study of the outlook on life among young people in Hong Kong, similar findings were reported (The Hong Kong Federation of Youth Groups, 2000). For the life aspirations of young people, results showed that respondents ranked the importance of several items in life in the following order: health, family, friends, wealth, peace of mind, and social status. An integration of the findings of both surveys suggested that family and health were the two most important goals of life in Chinese adolescents. Regarding the question "In which area of life do you hope you will have achieved most by the time you are 35 years old?", the responses were as follows: career (66.1%), a happy marriage (9.3%), knowledge (3.7%), a livelihood that gives me nothing to worry about (3.7%), making money (2.7%), having children (1.1%), and social status (1.0%). Results also showed that whereas more males regarded career as an important life goal, more adolescent girls regarded a happy marriage as an important life goal. In addition, the significance of career was positively related to educational attainment. Whereas most of respondents believed that they could achieve their ideals by themselves (66.5%), others believed that luck or God's will (10.8%), help of others (2.1%), and coordination of all aspects (7.9%) determined their ability to achieve their life goals. Compared with the 1997 survey, however, the findings showed that while there was a significant reduction in the number of participants believing that one's effort would lead to the achievement of life goals, the proportion of adolescents who believed in God's will and luck increased throughout time. One possibility for this change is that as Hong Kong experienced the Asian financial crisis in 2000, human effort was rather minute in altering life under such unstable financial conditions.

In the study of youth trends in Hong Kong, several questions were used by The Hong Kong Federation of Youth Groups (2008) to understand the life outlook of Chinese adolescents in Hong Kong. With reference to the item "suicide is unacceptable," 75.5% of the respondents agreed to the item and 1.5% were undecided. Regarding the item "religion is important to my life," 62.1% of the respondents disagreed and 1.9% were undecided. Finally, 83.6% of the respondents disagreed that their lives were negative and 0.4% were undecided. Based on the foregoing findings, the researchers concluded that the life outlook of young people in Hong Kong was generally positive in nature.

The profiles of purpose in life based on validated measures of meaning of life were also reported. Based on the responses of Chinese secondary school students to the Chinese PIL, Shek (1986) reported that the mean total score of Chinese students was comparatively lower than that of the Western subjects. A similar finding was obtained in a sample of postsecondary school students by Shek, Hong, and Cheung (1987), who observed that more than one fifth of the subjects felt bored and confused about life and had seriously thought about suicide. In an attempt to understand purpose in life among university students, Shek (1993) showed that although the mean total PIL score was higher than that derived from secondary school students, it was still lower than that of the Western subjects reported in the literature.

Regarding the sociodemographic correlates of meaning in life in Chinese adolescents, the related research findings are generally equivocal and the effect sizes were small (Chou, 2000). Regarding gender differences in meaning of life in Chinese adolescents, although Shek reported that adolescent boys displayed a higher level of Chinese PIL scores than did Chinese girls (1986, 1989b), gender differences were not found in other studies (1993, 1999c). Concerning age differences in purpose in life, whereas Shek (1986) showed that age was positively related to purpose in life in secondary school students, Shek (1993) found that there was no relationship between age and Chinese PIL scores.

The existing research findings also showed that adolescent meaning in life was not strongly related to economic disadvantage. Shek et al. (2001) showed that existential well-being in adolescents receiving welfare was not different from that based on adolescents not receiving welfare. A different picture emerged, however, when perceived economic stress and future economic worry as correlates of adolescent meaning of life were focused upon. Shek (2003b) showed that higher levels of economic stress based on ratings obtained from parents and adolescents were generally related to lower levels of adolescent existential well-being in 229 families receiving welfare. Relative to current economic stress perceived by adolescents, future economic worry perceived by adolescents was more strongly related to the existential well-being of Chinese adolescents with economic disadvantage. In short, the picture on the sociodemographic correlates of Chinese adolescent life meaning is not clear.

Purpose in Life and Adolescent Developmental Outcomes

Frankl's (1988) conceptualization about human nature is based on the premise of "will to meaning" (p. 43). The basic thesis proposed by Frankl is that when there is a vacuum in existence, mental problems come in to "fill the vacuum." When a person fails to find meaning in life and a state of vacuum of perceived meaning in personal existence (i.e., existential vacuum) is present, he or she is confronted by "existential frustration," which is characterized by the feeling of boredom (Crumbaugh, 1968). Although the occurrence of existential vacuum does not necessarily lead to noogenic neuroses, it was contended that existential vacuum is an etiological factor of psychopathology. Based on such reasoning, it is expected that purpose in life is causally related to adolescent developmental outcomes. In a review of the relationships between meaning in life and well-being, psychopathology, and spirituality, Steger (Chapter 8, this volume) shows that people experiencing greater life meaning report greater well-being, less psychopathology, and more positive experience of spirituality. There are also research findings showing that life meaning is intimately related to adjustment in older people (Krause, Chapter 19, this volume) and cancer survivors (Park, Chapter 23, this volume).

There are research findings showing that purpose in life was associated with psychological symptoms. Based on 2,150 Chinese secondary school students' responses to the Chinese PIL, Shek (1992) showed that the total Chinese PIL, Quality of Existence (QEXIST) subscale, and Purpose of Existence (PEXIST) subscale scores were significantly related to other instruments assessing psychiatric symptoms indexed by the General Health Questionnaire, Beck Depression Inventory, and the State-Trait Anxiety Inventory. Relative to PEXIST scores, QEXIST scores were found to be more predictive of psychological symptoms. Participants with different existential status (defined by high vs. low levels of QEXIST and PEXIST) also displayed different levels of psychological symptoms. Based on the responses of 500 Chinese college students, Shek (1993) found that the Chinese PIL scores were significantly associated with general psychological problems, trait anxiety, depression, and hopelessness. Furthermore, participants with different existential status also displayed different levels of psychological symptoms.

There are also longitudinal data showing the relationship between purpose in life and psychological symptoms over time. In a longitudinal study examining psychological well-being and parenting behavior, Shek (1999b) showed that lower PIL scores were associated with higher levels of psychiatric morbidity and hopelessness. Similarly, Shek (1998d) reported that whereas Time 1 general psychological symptoms did not predict Time 2 purpose in life, Time 1 purpose in life did predict Time 2 general psychological symptoms.

Other research findings show that besides being associated with psychiatric symptoms, meaning in life was also related to positive mental health measures: Shek (1992) reported that the Chinese PIL scores were positively related to measures of ego strength and self-image; Shek (1993) showed that the Chinese PIL scores were related to measures of self-esteem, life satisfaction, and existential well-being; Shek (1999b, 1998d) showed that the Chinese PIL scores were concurrently and longitudinally associated with self-esteem and life satisfaction. In a series of studies, Shek (2001a, 2003b, 2004, 2005a) reported that the Existential Well-Being Scale scores were positively related to life satisfaction, mastery, and self-esteem. Shek, Siu, and Lee (2007) also showed that the Spirituality subscale scores of the Chinese Positive Youth Development Scale were positively associated with other positive youth development constructs, including bonding, resilience, social competence, emotional competence, cognitive competence, behavioral competence, moral competence, self-determination, self-efficacy, beliefs in the future, clear and positive identity, recognition for positive behavior, prosocial involvement, and prosocial norms. These findings are generally consistent with the views of Ryff and Singer (1998) that sense of meaning and sense of self-realization are two key components of positive mental health, where meaning in life provides the necessary inner resources to fuel optimal functioning.

There are also research findings showing that meaning in life was related to prosocial behavior and antisocial behavior. In the study conducted by Shek, Ma, and Cheung (1994), the Chinese version of the Purpose in Life Questionnaire was administered to 790 Chinese secondary school students, along with other instruments assessing their antisocial and prosocial behavior. The results showed that the Quality of Existence and Purpose of Existence subscales of the Chinese PIL scores were correlated significantly with all measures of antisocial and prosocial behavior, with those having higher C-PIL scores showing less antisocial behavior and more prosocial behavior. The results also showed that relative to Quality of Existence subscale scores, Purpose of Existence subscale scores were found to be more predictive of antisocial and prosocial behavior measures. The research findings are consistent with Frankl's (1963) notion that meaning in life is intimately related to psychological symptoms as indexed by antisocial behavior. The findings also suggest that purpose in life is associated with positive social behavior as indexed by prosocial behavior.

Finally, research findings revealed that meaning in life was associated with problem behavior. In the study conducted by the Narcotics Division (1994), substance abusers and control subjects could be differentiated in terms of the C-PIL scores at the total scale, subscale, and item levels. Generally speaking, substance abusers displayed lower meaning of life indexed by the Chinese PIL measures than did the control participants. The Chinese Existential Well-Being Scale scores were also negatively related to substance abuse (Shek,

1997a). In another study, the Spirituality subscale scores of the Chinese Positive Youth Development Scale were negatively associated with substance abuse, delinquency, and behavioral intention to engage in high-risk behavior, including consumption of alcohol, smoking, consumption of illicit drugs, engagement in sexual behavior, and gambling.

Family Processes and Adolescent Meaning of Life

Fry (1998) explicitly stated that "it is through supportive and sharing relationships within a trusting and accepting atmosphere that the adolescent gains the courage to explore what experiences make sense or provide meaning even in the face of doubts" (p. 98), thus highlighting the role of intimate relationships in the development of adolescent purpose in life. Within the family context, two types of family experiences may shape meaning of life in adolescents: dyadic family processes (e.g., parent–child relationship and marital quality of the parents, Shek, 2000) and systemic family attributes (e.g., family functioning and communication patterns).

There are several cross-sectional studies showing that the quality of parenting was positively related to adolescent meaning of life indexed by the Chinese PIL. Shek (1989a) reported that parental-treatment-style scores were positively related to Chinese PIL scores in 2,150 secondary school students. Similarly, Shek (1993) found that parenting quality was positively related to Chinese PIL scores in 500 Chinese college students. Based on 429 adolescents, research findings showed that parenting quality indexed by global parenting and specific parenting measures were positively related to Chinese PIL scores (Shek, 1995b, 1997a). In a sample of Chinese adolescents with low academic achievement, Shek, Chan, and Lee (1997) also showed that parenting qualities were positively related to the Chinese PIL scores.

Several cross-sectional studies have showed that parenting attributes were related to adolescent meaning of life indexed by the Existential Well-Being Scale (Shek, 2002e). In a series of studies examining the relationship between family processes and adolescent development, Shek (2002c) showed that positive parenting attributes (e.g., parental support and involvement) were related to existential well-being in several samples. In a sample of 1,519 Chinese secondary school students, Shek et al. (2001) also reported that more positive parenting qualities were positively related to adolescent existential well-being scores. In another study based on Chinese adolescents experiencing economic disadvantage, Shek (2002b) showed that positive parenting attributes based on the modified Paternal Parenting Scale and Maternal Parenting Scale were related to higher existential well-being.

There are also longitudinal research findings showing that parenting characteristics were related to adolescent life meaning. In a longitudinal study examining the relationships between perceived parenting characteristics and adolescent psychological well-being in a sample of Chinese adolescents

($N = 378$), Shek (1999b) showed that global parenting styles and specific parenting behavior were concurrently related to purpose in life at Time 1 and Time 2; longitudinal and prospective analyses (Time 1 predictors predicting Time 2 criterion variables) suggest that the relations between parenting characteristics and adolescent purpose in life were bidirectional in nature. Results showed that the strength of association between perceived parenting characteristics and purpose in life was stronger in female than in male adolescents. Shek (2003a) also examined the relationship between parenting behavior and existential well-being in 199 adolescents experiencing economic disadvantage over time. Results showed that parenting characteristics were concurrently and longitudinally related to existential well-being, although the effect sizes of the correlation coefficients were not high. Shek (1999a) further showed that the association between perceived parenting behavior and adolescent psychological well-being was stronger in adolescents with a lower sense of purpose in life than in those with a higher level of purpose, thus suggesting that a higher sense of purpose in life provides a buffer against the impact of negative parenting behavior on adolescent well-being.

In addition, there are studies showing that parent–adolescent conflicts are related to meaning in life in Chinese adolescents. Based on a sample of Chinese secondary school students with low academic achievement ($N = 365$), Shek, Chan, and Lee (1997) showed that parent–adolescent conflict was negatively related to Chinese PIL scores. In another study, Shek (1997c) examined the association between parent–adolescent conflict and adolescent adjustment in 429 Chinese adolescents using children's and parents' reports of parent–adolescent conflict. Results generally showed that parent–adolescent conflicts based on ratings obtained from different sources were significantly related to purpose in life. Similarly, longitudinal findings (Shek, 1998b) showed that parent–adolescent conflict based on ratings obtained from different sources were concurrently and longitudinally related to purpose in life, and the findings suggest that the relationships between parent–adolescent conflict and adolescent psychological well-being were bidirectional in nature. Shek (2002c) further showed that both parental support and parental conflict were related to existential well-being. Multiple regression analyses showed that parental support was a stronger determinant of adolescent purpose in life.

Based on several quantitative and qualitative measures of paternal and maternal parenting characteristics (including adolescents' perceptions of and satisfaction with parenting styles, perceived parent–adolescent conflict, perceived frequency of parent–adolescent communication and related feelings, and perceived parent–adolescent relationship), Shek (1999c) showed that the questionnaire and interview measures at each time could be grouped into two stable factors: Paternal Parenthood Qualities and Maternal Parenthood Qualities. Although both factors generally had significant concurrent and longitudinal correlations with adolescent purpose in life, Parental Parenthood

Qualities at Time 1 predicted changes in adolescent purpose in life at Time 2, whereas Maternal Parenthood Qualities at Time 1 did not. Adolescent purpose in life at Time 1 was found to predict changes in Maternal Parenthood Qualities but not Paternal Parenthood Qualities at Time 2. Relative to Maternal Parenthood Qualities, Paternal Parenthood Qualities were generally found to exert a stronger impact on adolescent purpose in life.

Based on a study of 199 Chinese adolescents with economic disadvantage in Hong Kong, Shek (2005c) reported that perceived parental parenthood qualities (indexed by perceived parenting styles, support and help from parents, and conflict and relationship with parents) were related to adolescent existential well-being. Longitudinal correlation analyses showed that whereas Paternal Parenthood Qualities at Time 1 predicted adolescent existential well-being at Time 2, Maternal Parenthood Qualities at Time 1 predicted adolescent substance abuse and delinquency at Time 2. Partial correlation and multiple regression analyses showed that whereas Paternal Parenthood Qualities predicted changes in adolescent adjustment over time, Maternal Parenthood Qualities did not. In contrast, adolescent adjustment did not predict any changes in perceived parental parenthood qualities over time.

Finally, there are research findings showing that family functioning is related to adolescent meaning in life (Shek, 1997b, 1998c, 2002b). There are several cross-sectional studies showing that family functioning was related to adolescent life meaning. Utilizing the Chinese Self-Report Family Inventory, Shek (2003c) showed that family functioning was positively related to existential well-being in a convenient sample (N = 361), clinical sample (N = 281), nonclinical sample (N = 451), and community sample (3,649). Based on the Chinese Family Assessment Device, Shek (2003c) showed that the Existential Well-Being Scale scores were positively related to the total and subscale scores of the Chinese Family Assessment Device. Utilizing the Chinese Family Awareness Scale, Shek (2002d) reported that the scale scores were positively related to the total scores of the Existential Well-Being Scale. Shek (2002a) also demonstrated that life meaning indexed by the Existential Well-Being Scale was positively related to the Chinese Family Assessment Instrument.

There are other studies showing that meaning in life was associated with family functioning over time. Using children's and parents' reports of family functioning (N = 378), Shek (1998d) showed that family functioning based on ratings obtained from different sources were concurrently and longitudinally related to purpose in life at Time 1 and Time 2. Similarly, Shek (1998a) further showed that adolescent and parent discrepancies in perceptions of family functioning were concurrently and longitudinally related to adolescent purpose in life at Time 1 and Time 2; further, the longitudinal analyses suggest that relations between discrepancies in perceptions of family functioning and adolescent purpose in life were bidirectional.

In a sample of 199 adolescents experiencing economic disadvantage, Shek (2005b) showed that perceived family functioning was concurrently related to measures of adolescent existential well-being at Time 1 and Time 2. Longitudinal and prospective analyses (Time 1 predictors predicting Time 2 criterion variables) suggest that the relations between perceived family functioning and adolescent existential well-being and problem behavior were bidirectional. The longitudinal linkages between family functioning and adolescent existential well-being were found to be stronger in Chinese adolescent girls than in Chinese adolescent boys with economic disadvantage.

Meaning in Life in Chinese Adolescents Experiencing Adversity

According to Korotkov (1998), meaningfulness is a core construct in the sense of coherence. Consistent with this notion, there are research findings suggesting that meaning in life is an important factor in helping adolescents to face adversity. Utilizing the Chinese Beliefs About Adversity Scale, Shek (2004) examined the relationship between beliefs about adversity and adjustment in Chinese adolescents ($N = 1{,}519$). Results showed that adolescents with stronger endorsement of positive Chinese beliefs (or weaker endorsement of negative Chinese beliefs) about adversity generally had better psychological well-being and school adjustment and less problem behavior. Although adolescents' degree of agreement with Chinese cultural beliefs about adversity was generally associated with adolescent adjustment, this relationship was stronger in adolescents with economic disadvantage than in adolescents without economic disadvantage.

In another study based on 229 Chinese families experiencing economic disadvantage, Shek, Tang, et al. (2003) showed that adolescents with stronger endorsement of positive Chinese beliefs about adversity generally displayed better psychological well-being and school adjustment and less problem behavior. Maternal, but not paternal, endorsement of Chinese beliefs about adversity was related to adolescent adjustment. Parental, but not adolescent children's, endorsement of Chinese beliefs about adversity, was related to the parent's own psychological adjustment. The strengths of association between endorsement of Chinese beliefs about adversity and psychological well-being were similar in the fathers, mothers, and adolescent children samples. No significant differences were found among fathers, mothers, and adolescent children on their endorsement of Chinese beliefs about adversity.

Finally, Shek (2005a) examined the relationships between Chinese cultural beliefs about adversity and psychological well-being and problem behavior in 199 Chinese adolescents with economic disadvantage. Results showed that endorsement of Chinese cultural beliefs about adversity was concurrently related to measures of adolescent psychological well-being (existential well-being, mastery, life satisfaction, self-esteem, and general psychiatric morbidity) and problem behavior (substance abuse and delinquency) at Time 1 and Time 2. Partial correlation and multiple regression analyses showed that whereas Chinese beliefs about adversity at Time 1 predicted changes in developmental outcomes at Time 2 (except self-esteem), developmental outcome variables at Time 1 did not predict changes in endorsement of Chinese cultural beliefs about adversity at Time 2. The findings suggest that identification with Chinese cultural beliefs about adversity is an important factor that influences the psychosocial adjustment of Chinese adolescents experiencing economic disadvantage.

Research findings on meaning in life in adolescents with and without economic disadvantage based on two studies were reported by Shek et al. (2003). In Study 1, the relationship between meaning in life indexed by the Existential Well-Being Scale and adjustment of adolescents with and without economic disadvantage was examined in 1,519 Chinese adolescents. Results showed that adolescents with higher scores in the Existential Well-Being Scale had better psychological well-being and school adjustment and less problem behavior (including substance abuse and delinquency), and the relationship was stronger in adolescents with economic disadvantage than in adolescents without economic disadvantage. In Study 2, life meaning in 12 Chinese adolescents with economic disadvantage was explored by means of qualitative interviews. Results showed that poor adolescents derived life meaning from different sources and that money was not an important factor in the origin of life meaning in poor adolescents. Adolescents who placed greater emphasis on the importance on money tended to have poorer psychosocial adjustment. Adolescents who felt their lives to be controlled by fate rather by themselves generally showed poorer adjustment.

Adopting a qualitative methodology, Shek, Lam, Lam, and Tang (2004) engaged in qualitative interviews to study the perceptions of present, ideal, and future lives among 12 Chinese adolescents experiencing economic disadvantage. Results showed that most of the adolescents evaluated their present lives positively. They also had positive perceptions of their future lives, although negative feelings were also associated with such perceptions. Although money did not play an important role in the adolescents' perceptions of present lives, future lives, life goals, and ideal careers, economic sufficiency emerged as a major theme from the perspective of their ideal lives. Further, although adolescents with better psychosocial adjustment appeared to evaluate their present lives more positively than did adolescents with relatively poorer psychosocial adjustment, there were no differences between the two groups in terms of their views on ideal and future lives.

Existing Research Gaps and Future Research Directions

What are future research directions as far as the study of life meaning and purpose in life in Chinese adolescents is concerned? Conceptually speaking, although the present review shows that ecological factors in individual, interpersonal, and familial contexts are related to purpose in life, there are several conceptual gaps. First, although Frankl's (1963, 1988) theory posits that purpose in life influences developmental outcomes, how the developmental outcomes influence the development of purpose in life is far from clear (i.e., bidirectional influences between purpose in life and developmental outcomes). Obviously, accumulation of research findings in this area would help to enrich Frankl's idea on the role of existential vacuum in human behavior. In view of the findings of Wrosch, Scheier, Miller, and Carver (Chapter 24, this volume) that reengagement in other meaningful goals will take place when the original life goals are unattainable, it would be theoretically stimulating to examine the role of adaptive self-regulative processes related to unattainable life goals. Future studies on conceptualization, assessment, and treatment of discrepancies in meaning (Slattery and Park, Chapter 22, this volume) would also be interesting.

Second, based on the ecological model, further studies should be conducted to examine how individual factors (e.g., religiosity and values), family factors (e.g., global parenting vs. specific parenting practice; behavioral control and psychological control), and social factors (e.g., endorsement of Chinese superstitious beliefs) are related to adolescent purpose in life. This research direction is consistent with the argument of Fry (1998) that "whether adolescents' life meaning and wisdom will grow and unfold from being relatively straightforward to being mature and complex will depend invariably on the presence or absence of a number of other intervening and moderating influences and contextual factors" (p. 93). With reference to the work of Peterson and Park (Chapter 13, this volume), it would be theoretically interesting to look at the relationships among life meaning, character building, and religiousness. The work of Shmotkin and Shrira (Chapter 7, this volume) also shows the common as well as the unique nature of life meaning and subjective well-being.

Third, although the present review highlights the importance of family processes in adolescent purpose in life, further work is needed to examine how specific family processes and related experiences are related to adolescent purpose in life. For example, it would be interesting to study how the purpose in life of the parents is related to that of their adolescent children. Aron and Aron (Chapter 9, this volume) also point out the achievement of life meaning through love in close relationships.

Finally, given that the concept of meaning in life and the associated concepts have mainly been imported from the West, indigenous concepts and theories about meaning in life in relation to different Chinese religions and philosophies (e.g., Confucianism, Buddhism, Taoism) should be developed and investigated. For example, Kwee (Chapter 12, this volume) attempts to look at meaning and happiness among adversity based on New Buddhist Psychology. In Confucian thought, a life is meaningful if one can sacrifice oneself to promote the well-being of the collective entity. In the Buddhist thoughts, meaning of life can be achieved only if we transcend the illusions of the material world. In the Taoist thoughts, meaning of life can be understood only in terms of one's harmony with the universe. Obviously, the values underlying these religious and philosophical systems are in sharp contrast to the emphases on achievement and material possession in Hong Kong. As such, more research should be conducted to examine the conception of life meaning in Chinese adolescents and their life goals (Shek, 2001b).

Methodologically speaking, there are several research directions that deserve our attention. First, except for a few attempts (e.g., the Chinese Beliefs About Adversity Scale), instruments assessing purpose in life in Chinese adolescents are mostly translated Western measures (Ho & Ho, 2007). It is not uncommon for social scientists to use "imported" Western concepts to study Chinese behavior and phenomena, yet it is important to reflect on whether such imported concepts really can capture Chinese meaning of life phenomena. Essentially, the issue that should be addressed is whether an "emic" or "etic" approach should be used to examine purpose in life in Chinese adolescents. Following the earlier argument on the need to examine indigenous Chinese concepts on meaning in life, it would be helpful if indigenous Chinese measures on meaning in life in Chinese adolescents could be devised. Unfortunately, as pointed out by Shek, Chan, and Lee (2005), the Chinese literature on psychosocial assessment tools is thin, and there is an obvious need to strengthen it.

Second, most of the existing studies investigating the antecedents and consequences of meaning in life are cross-sectional studies. Although cross-sectional studies can help to identify the correlates of meaning in life, causal relationships involved cannot be clearly established. With reference to the comment of Shek, Chan, and Lee (2005) that there are very few longitudinal quality-of-life studies in the Chinese culture, it is obvious that more longitudinal studies should be carried out. Furthermore, longitudinal studies are necessary to test the pivotal hypothesis of logotherapy that meaning in life is an antecedent of adolescent developmental outcomes.

Third, this literature review reveals that with a few exceptions, quantitative methods have primarily been used to study meaning of life in Chinese adolescents. Although the postpositivistic approach represents the dominant research paradigm in social science research, its limitations should be duly acknowledged (Ho & Ho, 2007). Furthermore, it is noteworthy that qualitative methods have been used in the literature to examine purpose in life (Ebersole, 1998). Methodologically, it would be illuminating if qualitative research adopting constructionist orientations could be carried out in future. The use of qualitative research can be regarded as particularly useful to look at the "insider" rather than "outsider" accounts of Chinese purpose in life and the related phenomena. However, a thorny issue that qualitative researchers should pay attention to is how the quality of qualitative family studies can possibly be enhanced (Shek, Tang, & Han, 2005).

Fourth, comparative studies should be conducted to examine the topic of meaning in life in Chinese adolescents in different communities. If a research study is claimed to be universally valid, it must be generalizable to different participants at different times in different places. Generally speaking, there are two levels at which comparative meaning of life studies should be carried out. First, findings based on Chinese adolescents are compared to findings obtained from non-Chinese adolescents. Second, because China is a big country and there are regional differences involving different ethnic groups, studies involving Chinese adolescents from different parts of China are also important; that is, there should be comparative studies within the Chinese contexts. Given that the literature on meaning in life in Chinese adolescents is dominated by research studies in Hong Kong, there is a need to replicate the related findings in other Chinese communities.

Practically speaking, because purpose in life plays an important role in human functioning (Maddi, 1998), it is important to explore how meaning-centered counseling strategies and techniques (Wong, 1998; Wong, Chapter 28, this volume) could be applied to promote the development of Chinese adolescents. For example, Reker, Birren, and Svensson (Chapter 18, this volume) propose autobiographical methods to restore, maintain, and enhance personal meaning. Fry (1998) argued, "Adolescents trained in the early stages for acquiring a disposition of hardiness will move more effectively toward achieving a mature meaning for life and a positive sense of self-definition" (pp. 108–109). Accordingly, programs that attempt to promote adolescent purpose in life through hardiness training should be designed. Besides, there are programs that attempt to promote purpose in life in Chinese adolescents. For example, in the project entitled Positive Adolescent Training Through Holistic Social Programs (Project P.A.T.H.S.), units that attempt to promote life meaning of Chinese adolescents have been developed. Although the existing evaluation findings suggest that the program can facilitate the search for life meaning among Chinese adolescent in Hong Kong (Shek, 2006), systematic and rigorous evaluation research efforts are indispensable. Obviously, evaluation of programs with the aim of facilitating the search of life meaning among Chinese adolescents is another important future research direction.

In sum, several conclusions can be highlighted from the present review. First, the literature on meaning in life in Chinese adolescents is extremely thin. Except some studies in Hong Kong, which were mainly conducted by the author, published studies in China and Taiwan are almost nonexistent. Second, although some Chinese measures on adolescent life meaning are available, most of them are imported from the West and indigenously developed measures are few. Third, although some studies have generated profiles on life meaning and life goals among Chinese adolescents in Hong Kong, the related findings are not conclusive. In particular, the use of single-item or -question social surveys casts serious doubt on the validity of the findings. Fourth, there is evidence showing that life meaning in Chinese adolescents is related to indicators of psychological well-being, prosocial behavior, antisocial behavior, and problem behavior. In addition, although there is support for the thesis that meaning in life is causally linked to adolescent developmental outcomes, bidirectional influences among the two domains are also observed. Fifth, dyadic family processes (including marital quality of the parents, parenting attributes, and parent–adolescent conflict) and systemic family functioning are related to adolescent life meaning. Sixth, there are research findings suggesting that positive meaning about life adversity can help Chinese adolescents experiencing economic disadvantage to cope with the related adversity. Finally, conceptual, methodological, and practical gaps in the existing studies are discussed and future research directions are outlined.

Acknowledgments

This work was financially supported by the Research Grants Council of the Government of the Hong Kong Special Administrative Region, Hong Kong (Grant CUHK4293/03H), and Wofoo Foundation Limited.

References

Benson, P. L., Roehlkepartain, E. C., & Rude, S. P. (2003). Spiritual development in childhood and adolescence: Toward a field of inquiry. *Applied Developmental Science, 7*, 205–213.

Chou, K. L. (2000). Intimacy and psychosocial adjustment in Hong Kong Chinese adolescents. *Journal of Genetic Psychology, 16*, 141–151.

Crumbaugh, J. C. (1968). Cross-validation of purpose in life test based on Frankl's concepts. *Journal of Individual Psychology, 24*, 74–81.

Dufton, B. D., & Perlman, D. (1986). The association between religiosity and the Purpose in Life Test: Does it reflect purpose or satisfaction? *Journal of Psychology and Theology, 14*(1), 42–48.

Ebersole, P. (1998). Types and depth of written life meanings. In P. T. P. Wong & P. S. Fry (Eds.), *The human quest for meaning: A handbook of psychological research and clinical applications* (pp. 179–191). Mahwah, NJ: Erlbaum.

Frankl, V. E. (1963). *Man's search for meaning: An introduction to logotherapy*. New York, NY: Pocket Books.

Frankl, V. E. (1988). *The will to meaning: Foundations and applications of logotherapy*. New York, NY: New American Library.

Fry, P. S. (1998). The development of personal meaning and wisdom in adolescence: A reexamination of moderating and consolidating factors and influences. In P. T. P. Wong & P. S. Fry (Eds.), *The human quest for meaning: A handbook of psychological research and clinical applications* (pp. 91–110). Mahwah, NJ: Erlbaum.

Ho, D. Y. F., & Ho, R. T. H. (2007). Measuring spirituality and spiritual emptiness: Toward ecumenicity and transcultural applicability. *Review of General Psychology, 11*, 62–74.

The Hong Kong Federation of Youth Groups. (1997). *Young people's outlook on life*. Hong Kong: Hong Kong Federation of Youth Groups.

The Hong Kong Federation of Youth Groups. (2000). *Young people's outlook on life (II)*. Hong Kong: Hong Kong Federation of Youth Groups.

The Hong Kong Federation of Youth Groups. (2008). *Youth trends in Hong Kong, 2004–2006*. Hong Kong: Hong Kong Federation of Youth Groups.

King, P. E., & Boyatzis, C. J. (2004). Exploring adolescent spiritual and religions development: Current and future theoretical and empirical perspectives. *Applied Developmental Science, 8*, 2–6.

Korotkov, D. (1998). The sense of coherence: Making sense out of chaos. In P. T. P. Wong & P. S. Fry (Eds.), *The human quest for meaning: A handbook of psychological research and clinical applications* (pp. 51–70). Mahwah, NJ: Erlbaum.

Lau, S., & Lau, W. (1996). Outlook on life: How adolescents and children view the lifestyle of parents, adult and self. *Journal of Adolescence, 19*, 293–296.

Lau, S. K., Lee, M. K., Wan, P. S., & Wong, S. L. (2005). *Indicators of social development: Hong Kong, 2004*. Hong Kong: Hong Kong Institute of Asia-Pacific Studies, Chinese University of Hong Kong.

Maddi, S. R. (1998). Creating meaning through making decisions. In P. T. P. Wong & P. S. Fry (Eds.), *The human quest for meaning: A handbook of psychological research and clinical applications* (pp. 3–26). Mahwah, NJ: Erlbaum.

Narcotics Division. (1994). *Report on survey of young drug abusers*. Hong Kong: Narcotics Division, Hong Kong Government.

Paloutzian, R. F., & Ellison, C. W. (1982). Loneliness, spiritual well-being and the quality of life. In L. A. Peplau & D. Perlman (Eds.), *Loneliness; A sourcebook of current theory, research and therapy*. New York, NY: Wiley.

Ryff, C. D., & Singer, B. (1998). The role of purpose in life and personal growth in positive human health. In P. T. P. Wong & P. S. Fry (Eds.), *The human quest for meaning: A handbook of psychological research and clinical applications* (pp. 213–235). Mahwah, NJ: Erlbaum.

Shek, D. T. L. (1986). The Purpose in Life Questionnaire in a Chinese context: Some psychometric and normative data. *Chinese Journal of Psychology, 28*(1), 51–60.

Shek, D. T. L. (1988). Reliability and factorial structure of the Chinese version of the Purpose in Life Questionnaire. *Journal of Clinical Psychology, 44*(3), 384–392.

Shek, D. T. L. (1989a). Perceptions of parental treatment styles and psychological well-being in Chinese adolescents. *Journal of Genetic Psychology, 150*(4), 403–415.

Shek, D. T. L. (1989b). Sex differences in the psychological well-being of Chinese adolescents. *Journal of Psychology, 123*(4), 405–412.

Shek, D. T. L. (1992). Meaning in life and psychological well-being: An empirical study using the Chinese version of the Purpose in Life Questionnaire. *Journal of Genetic Psychology, 153*(2), 185–200.

Shek, D. T. L. (1993). Meaning in life and psychological well-being in Chinese college students. *International Forum for Logotherapy, 16*(1), 35–42.

Shek, D. T. L. (1995a). Mental health of Chinese adolescents in different Chinese societies. *International Journal of Adolescent Medicine and Health, 8*(2), 117–155.

Shek, D. T. L. (1995b). The relation of family environments to adolescent psychological well-being, school adjustment and problem behavior: What can we learn from the Chinese culture? *International Journal of Adolescent Medicine and Health, 8*(3), 199–218.

Shek, D. T. L. (1997a). Family environment and adolescent psychological well-being, school adjustment, and problem behavior: A pioneer study in a Chinese context. *Journal of Genetic Psychology, 158*(1), 113–128.

Shek, D. T. L. (1997b). The relation of family functioning to adolescent psychological well-being, school adjustment, and problem behavior. *Journal of Genetic Psychology, 158*(4), 467–479.
Shek, D. T. L. (1997c). The relation of parent–adolescent conflict to adolescent psychological well-being, school adjustment, and problem behavior. *Social Behavior and Personality, 25*(3), 277–290.
Shek, D. T. L. (1998a). A longitudinal study of Hong Kong adolescents' and parents' perceptions of family functioning and well-being. *Journal of Genetic Psychology, 159*(4), 389–403.
Shek, D. T. L. (1998b). A longitudinal study of the relations between parent–adolescent conflict and adolescent psychological well-being. *Journal of Genetic Psychology, 159*(1), 53–67.
Shek, D. T. L. (1998c). A longitudinal study of the relations of family functioning to adolescent psychological well-being. *Journal of Youth Studies, 1*(2), 195–209.
Shek, D. T. L. (1998d). Adolescent positive mental health and psychological symptoms: A longitudinal study in a Chinese context. *Psychologia, 41*(4), 217–225.
Shek, D. T. L. (1999a). Meaning in life and adjustment amongst early adolescents in Hong Kong. *International Forum for Logotherapy, 22*(1), 36–43.
Shek, D. T. L. (1999b). Parenting characteristics and adolescent psychological well-being: A longitudinal study in a Chinese context. *Genetic, Social and General Psychology Monographs, 125*(1), 27–44.
Shek, D. T. L. (1999c). Paternal and maternal influences on the psychological well-being of Chinese adolescents. *Genetic, Social and General Psychology Monographs, 125*(3), 269–296.
Shek, D. T. L. (2000). Parental marital quality and well-being, parent–child relational quality, and Chinese adolescent adjustment. *American Journal of Family Therapy, 28*(2), 147–162.
Shek, D. T. L. (2001a). Meaning in life and sense of mastery in Chinese adolescents with economic disadvantage. *Psychological Reports, 88*(3), 711–712.
Shek, D. T. L. (2001b). Resilience in adolescence: Western models and local findings. In Chinese Y.M.C.A. (Ed.), *Centennial conference on counseling in China, Taiwan and Hong Kong* (pp. 3–21). Hong Kong: Chinese Y.M.C.A. of Hong Kong.
Shek, D. T. L. (2002a). Assessment of family functioning in Chinese adolescents: The Chinese Family Assessment Instrument. In N. N. Singh, T. H. Ollendick, & A. N. Singh (Eds.), *International perspectives on child and adolescent mental health* (Vol. 2, pp. 297–316). Amsterdam, Netherlands: Elsevier.
Shek, D. T. L. (2002b). Family functioning and psychological well-being, school adjustment, and problem behavior in Chinese adolescents with and without economic disadvantage. *Journal of Genetic Psychology, 163*(4), 497–502.
Shek, D. T. L. (2002c). Interpersonal support and conflict and adjustment of Chinese adolescents with and without economic disadvantage. In S. P. Shohov (Ed.), *Advances in psychology research* (Vol. 18, pp. 63–82). New York, NY: Nova Science.
Shek, D. T. L. (2002d). Psychometric properties of the Chinese version of the Family Awareness Scale. *Journal of Social Psychology, 142*(1), 61–72.
Shek, D. T. L. (2002e). The relation of parental qualities to psychological well-being, school adjustment, and problem behavior in Chinese adolescents with economic disadvantage. *American Journal of Family Therapy, 30*(3), 215–230.
Shek, D. T. L. (2003a). A longitudinal study of parenting and adolescent adjustment in Chinese adolescents with economic disadvantage. *International Journal of Adolescent Medicine and Health, 15*(1), 39–49.

Shek, D. T. L. (2003b). Economic stress, psychological well-being and problem behavior in Chinese adolescents with economic disadvantage. *Journal of Youth and Adolescence, 32*(4), 259–266.

Shek, D. T. L. (2003c). Family functioning and psychological well-being, school adjustment, and substance abuse in Chinese adolescents: Are findings based on multiple studies consistent? In S. P. Shohov (Ed.), *Advances in psychology research* (Vol. 20, pp. 163–184). New York, NY: Nova Science.

Shek, D. T. L. (2004). Chinese cultural beliefs about adversity: Its relationship to psychological well-being, school adjustment and problem behavior in Hong Kong adolescents with and without economic disadvantage. *Childhood, 11*(1), 63–80.

Shek, D. T. L. (2005a). A longitudinal study of Chinese cultural beliefs about adversity, psychological well-being, delinquency and substance abuse in Chinese adolescents with economic disadvantage. *Social Indicators Research, 71*(1–3), 385–409.

Shek, D. T. L. (2005b). A longitudinal study of perceived family functioning and adolescent adjustment in Chinese adolescents with economic disadvantage. *Journal of Family Issues, 26*(4), 518–543.

Shek, D. T. L. (2005c). Paternal and maternal influences on the psychological well-being, substance abuse, and delinquency of Chinese adolescents experiencing economic disadvantage. *Journal of Clinical Psychology, 61*(3), 219–234.

Shek, D. T. L. (2006). Effectiveness of the Tier 1 Program of the project P.A.T.H.S.: preliminary objective and subjective outcome evaluation findings. *The Scientfic-WorldJOURNAL*, 6, 1466–1474. doi:10.1100/tsw.2006.238

Shek, D. T. L., Chan, L. K., & Lee, T. Y. (1997). Parenting styles, parent–adolescent conflict and psychological well-being of adolescents with low academic achievement in Hong Kong. *International Journal of Adolescent Medicine and Health, 9*(4), 233–247.

Shek, D. T. L., Chan, Y. K., & Lee, P. (Eds.). (2005). *Social Indicators Research Series: Vol. 2. Quality of life research in Chinese, Western and global contexts*. Dordrecht, the Netherlands: Springer.

Shek, D. T. L., Hong, E. W., & Cheung, M. Y. P. (1987). The Purpose in Life Questionnaire in a Chinese context. *Journal of Psychology, 121*(1), 77–83.

Shek, D. T. L., Lam, M. C., Lam, C. M., & Tang, V. (2004). Perceptions of present, ideal, and future lives among Chinese adolescents experiencing economic disadvantage. *Adolescence, 39*(156), 779–792.

Shek, D. T. L., Ma, H. K., & Cheung, P. C. (1994). Meaning in life and adolescent antisocial and prosocial behavior in a Chinese context. *Psychologia, 37*(4), 211–218.

Shek, D. T. L., Siu, A., & Lee, T. Y. (2007). The Chinese Positive Youth Development Scale: A validation study. *Research on Social Work Practice, 17*, 380–391.

Shek, D. T. L., Tang, V. M. Y., & Han, X. Y. (2005). Evaluation of evaluation studies using qualitative research methods in the social work literature (1990–2003): Evidence that constitutes a wake-up call. *Research on Social Work Practice, 15*(3), 180–194.

Shek, D. T. L., Tang, V., Lam, C. M., Lam, M. C., Tsoi, K. W., & Tsang, S. K. M. (2003). The relationship between Chinese cultural beliefs about adversity and psychological adjustment in Chinese families with economic disadvantage. *American Journal of Family Therapy, 31*(5), 427–443.

Shek, D. T. L., Tsoi, K. W., Lau, P. S. Y., Tsang, S. K. M., Lam, M. C., & Lam, C. M. (2001). Psychological well-being, school adjustment and problem behavior in Chinese adolescents: Do parental qualities matter? *International Journal of Adolescent Medicine and Health, 13*(3), 231–243.

Wong, P. T. P. (1998). Meaning-centered counseling. In P. T. P. Wong & P. S. Fry (Eds.), *The human quest for meaning: A handbook of psychological research and clinical applications* (pp. 395–435). Mahwah, NJ: Erlbaum.

Wong, P. T. P., & Fry, P. S. (Eds.). (1998). *The human quest for meaning: A handbook of psychological research and clinical applications*. Mahwah, NJ: Erlbaum.

Yuen, M. T., Hui, E., Lau, S. Y., Gysbers, N. C., Leung, T., Chan, R., & Shea, P. (2006). Assessing the psycho-social development of Hong Kong Chinese adolescents. *International Journal for the Advancement of Counseling, 28*, 317–330.

17

Meaning-in-Life Measures and Development of a Brief Version of the Personal Meaning Profile

MARVIN J. MCDONALD

Trinity Western University

PAUL T. P. WONG

Trent University

DANIEL T. GINGRAS

Inquiry into the meaning of life goes back to antiquity from Lao Tzu (trans. 1913) to King Solomon (Ecclesiastes, New International Version). There is also a long and venerable tradition in psychology of exploring the meaning of human existence (Adler, 1931/1958; Frankl, 1963/1985; James, 1902; Jung, 1933; May, 1958) and self-actualization (Maslow, 1962; Rogers, 1980). However, empirical studies of meaning have been very recent (Wong & Fry, 1998). Psychologists have long theorized about the functions of meaning in human adaptation and flourishing, but the development of instruments to measure meaning in life has been hampered by the difficulty of operationally defining the meaning construct.

Personal Meaning Defined

Reker and Wong (1988) define personal meaning as the "cognizance of order, coherence and purpose in one's existence, the pursuit and attainment of worthwhile goals, and an accompanying sense of fulfillment" (p. 221). Wong (1989) defines personal meaning as an individually constructed cognitive system, which endows life with personal significance. This meaning system, according to Wong's (1998) implicit theories research, consists of five components: affective, motivational, cognitive, relational, and personal (i.e., personal characteristics and status in life). Dittmann-Kohli (1991) made a compelling case that the personal meaning system is most important with respect to one's overall functioning. He states:

> It is a dynamic, centralized structure with various sub-domains. It is conceived as a cognitive map that orients the individual in steering through the life course. The personal meaning system comprises the categories (conceptual schemes) used for self and life interpretation. It is a cognitive-affective network containing person-directed and environment-directed motivational cognitions and understandings, like goal concepts and behavior plans, conceptions of character and competencies, of internal processes and mechanisms, various kinds of standards and self-appraisals. (as cited in Wong & Fry, 1998, p. 368)

Frankl (1963) emphasizes the motivational dimension of meaning. He asserts that the "will to meaning" is a significant and universal human motive. Human are not merely biological, social, and psychological beings but also spiritual beings capable of transcending physical limitations through meaning and spirituality (Chapter 28, this volume). Frustration of the will to meaning leads to an "existential vacuum" characterized by a sense of meaninglessness, boredom, apathy, or indifference.

Other motivational perspectives encompass broader psychological needs (Baumeister, 1991) and intrinsic goals (Emmons, 2005). Needs contribute to a sense of meaning when these needs are related to hope and purpose in future-oriented goal striving. Baumeister's major needs related to subjective fulfillment—purpose, value, self-efficacy, and self-worth—map well on Wong's four components of meaning: purpose, understanding, responsibility, and enjoyment.

Goals reflect a concrete plan to meet certain needs through action, commitment, and engagement. Emmons (2005) conceptualizes meaning in people's lives in terms of pursuits of personally significant goals: "Development of goals that allow for a greater sense of purpose in life is one of the cornerstones of well-being" (p. 734). Emmons's four areas of meaningful pursuit are work, intimacy, spirituality, and transcendence, which cover much of the same terrain as Wong's (1998) seven sources of meaning. According to Emmons (2005), personal goals are the units of a meaningful life. He further suggests that it is not just the attainment of goals but also the pursuit of them that makes life meaningful. However, a goal approach to meaning is incomplete because philosophical views, personal beliefs, and self-knowledge are also important for one's sense of meaning. Wong's seven sources of meaning incorporate needs, goals, and cognitive components of meaning systems.

The struggle to discover and realize meaning continues throughout life. From the life-span perspective, values shift and so do the sources of meaning (Baumeister, 1991; Erickson, 1963; Jung, 1971; Thurnher, 1975). The task of rebuilding a meaning subsystem is never-ending because of the ever-changing self and dwindling opportunities. Individuals not only try to maintain a sense of continuity and coherence in the face of change but also attempt to compensate multiple losses that come with advancing age.

Sources of Meaning

Individuals may differ in what makes life meaningful; but on the basis of prior research, Reker and Wong (1988) have identified the following major sources of meaning: (a) meeting such basic needs as food, shelter, and safety; (b) leisure activities or hobbies; (c) creative work; (d) personal relationships (family or friends); (e) personal achievement (education or career); (f) personal growth (wisdom or maturity); (g) social and political activism (e.g., the peace movement or antipollution campaigns); (h) altruism; (i) enduring values and ideals (truth, goodness, beauty, and justice); (j) traditions and culture, including heritage or ethnocultural associations; (k) legacy (leaving a mark for posterity); and (l) religion. These sources of meaning encompass different levels of needs, from basic biological needs to transcendental, spiritual needs.

According to Schnell (2010), "Sources of meaning represent generalized and relatively stable orientations towards life ... [S]ources of meaning motivate commitment, give direction to life, and increase its significance" (pp. 353–354). They do so because each source reflects basic needs, corresponding life goals, and the four components of the meaning structure: purpose, understanding, responsible action, and enjoyment (Chapter 1, this volume). Thus, the Personal Meaning Profile (PMP) represents a comprehensive assessment of one's meaning in life rather than a global subjective assessment of life as meaningful.

According to Westerhof, Bohlmeijer, and Valenkamp (2004), sources of meaning can come from (a) within the person (character traits, personal growth and achievement, self-acceptance, pleasure, fulfillment, tranquility), (b) relationships (sense of connectedness, intimacy, quality relationships, altruism, service, communal consciousness), (c) physical integrity (functioning, health, appearance), (d) activities (work, leisure, hedonistic activities), and (e) material needs (possessions, financial security, meeting basic needs). Beyond these five general sources of meaning, however, there is also a need for a holistic, philosophical view of life consisting of values and beliefs, ideals, humanistic concerns, religion, culture, and existential themes.

Personal Meaning Scales

The Purpose in Life (PIL) Test was developed by Crumbaugh and Maholick (1964) and inspired by Frankl's logotherapy. It is a 20-item, 7-point attitude scale that assesses the degree to which an individual experiences a sense of meaning or purpose in life. Although it has been widely used, it has been criticized for blending a few distinct factors (Dyck, 1987; Yalom, 1980).

The Seeking of Noetic Goals (SONG; Crumbaugh, 1977) and the Life Attitude Profile (LAP; e.g., Reker & Peacock, 1981; Reker, Peacock, & Wong,

1987) were also designed to measure meaning in life. The SONG is a 20-item attitude scale that focuses on the motivation to find meaning in life. The LAP is a 49-item multidimensional measure of life attitudes, assessing both the presence and absence of positive meaning and purpose. Both instruments are based on Frankl's conceptions of will to meaning and the existential vacuum.

The Sense of Coherence (SOC) Scale was developed by Antonovsky (1983), a medical sociologist who challenged the pathogenic orientation (i.e., the disease model) and advocated the salutogenic orientation. The SOC is a 29-item, 7-point Likert scale consisting of three subscales: Comprehensibility, Manageability, and Meaningfulness. Sense of coherence as measured by these three subscales has been shown to be important in predicting health and well-being (Korotkov, 1998). The SOC focuses on the cognitive component of meaning.

The Life Regard Index (LRI) was developed by Battista and Almond (1973). The LRI is a 28-item Likert scale designed as a measure of personal meaning independent of a priori conceptions of the "true nature" of personal meaning. Battista and Almond take the relativistic perspective that everyone has his or her own beliefs regarding what is meaningful. The LRI consists of two subscales: The Framework subscale measures whether an individual has the framework for developing a personal meaning system or a set of life goals. The Fulfillment subscale indicates the extent to which these goals are fulfilled; this scale may, however, be confounded with the outcome measure of life satisfaction.

Development of the Personal Meaning Profile

The PMP is a 57-item instrument intended to measure people's perceptions of personal meaning in their lives. The construction of the PMP began by studying people's own understanding of what constitutes a meaningful life by employing an implicit theories approach (Wong, 1998). Implicit theories are "laypeople's conceptions and beliefs about various psychological constructs as compared to more formal models developed by psychologists" (p. 111). This bottom-up approach allows researchers to understand people's ideas without imposing on them the researchers' own theoretical biases.

Participants were drawn from various walks of life. They were asked to describe what, in their minds, constituted an ideally meaningful life or ideally good life if money were not an issue. Their written responses were analyzed, condensed, and catalogued into a list of 102 items. Content analysis of these items revealed that they could be grouped into five categories of psychological functions: cognitive, motivational, affective, relational, and personal.

The next step in the development of the PMP was to determine how many of the 102 items identified in the previous study were characteristic of (a) an ideally meaningful life and (b) of themselves. The participants rated each item on a scale ranging from 1 (*extremely uncharacteristic*) to 9 (*extremely characteristic*), with 5 indicating undecided for both the ideal and self-ratings. Items that were rated less than 6.0 were considered not to be characteristic of an ideally meaningful life. Using this standard, a total of eight items fell below the cut-off point, most of which had to do with religious beliefs and practices (e.g., "Seeks to glorify God"), though two items related to hedonic pursuits (i.e., "Satisfies all one's wants" and "Seeks pleasures") also fell below the cut-off point. Participants were also asked to complete an eight-item Perceived Personal Meaning (PPM) Scale developed by Wong (1998) to serve as a criterion measure. Steger, Frazier, Oishi, and Kaler's (2006) Presence of Meaning subscale is very similar to Wong's PPM. The PPM includes such items as "My life as a whole has meaning," "My entire existence is full of meaning," and "I led a meaningful life in the past." Self-ratings were significantly correlated with ideal ratings as well as the PPM.

A third study was then conducted to determine whether people from different age groups have differing implicit theories of meaning as well as to determine the prototypical structure of ideal ratings through exploratory factor analysis. This study used a sample of 289 subjects divided into three age groups. The young adult group (18–29) consisted of 96 participants (46 males, 50 females), the middle-age group (30–59) consisted of 107 participants (49 males, 58 females), and the elderly group (60+) consisted of 86 participants (43 males, 43 females). A total of 43 redundant and unrepresentative items from the original list of 102 were dropped for having low item–total correlations or falling below the cut-off point of 6.0 in any age group. Many of these items were such personal characteristics as "Has intelligence," "Has talents," and "Has a good education"; these items were too general to load on any unique factor. Principle components extraction and varimax rotation of the remaining items resulted in a nine-factor solution, consisting of Achievement striving, Religion, Relationship, Fulfillment, Fairness, Self-confidence, Self-integration, Self-transcendence, and Self-acceptance.

A fourth study was performed using a sample of 335 participants (153 males, 182 females). Principle components analysis with varimax rotation resulted in eight factors: Achievement striving, Religion, Fulfillment, Relationship, Self-transcendence, Intimacy, Self-acceptance, and Fair treatment, with a total of 58 items. Following this study, the Fulfillment factor and all affect-related items were eliminated to avoid confounding with outcome measures.

One weakness of the original PMP was that the Intimacy, Self-acceptance, and Fair treatment subscales did not have enough items to achieve acceptable Cronbach's alpha. Therefore, new items were added to the three factors, resulting in a 57-item version. Preliminary research on this version of the PMP resulted in a seven-factor solution, with Intimacy once again being separate from Relationship. In addition, some stylistic changes were made to improve the clarity of some items, and some alterations to the instructions were made.

Preliminary studies showed encouraging reliability for the 57-item PMP. The overall Cronbach's alpha coefficient was .93. The alpha values of the subscales were as follows: Achievement (.91), Religion (.89), Self-transcendence (.84), Relationship (.81), Intimacy (.78), Fairness (.54), and Self-acceptance (.54). Test–retest reliability over a three-week period was .85.

Use of the Personal Meaning Profile in Research

Since 1998, the PMP has been used in a variety of settings and with different populations. For example, it has been used in research on organizational-industrial psychology (Du Buisson-Narsai, 2009; Markow & Klenke, 2005; McConnell, 1998; Wilk, 2000), career and vocational counseling (Kernes & Kinnier, 2008; Stolte, 2006), populations suffering from physical disabilities (Emmons, 2005), stress and trauma (Gall, Basque, Damasceno-Scott, & Vardy, 2007; Leung, Vroon, & Steinfort, 2003; Pan, Wong, Chan, & Joubert, 2008; Pan, Wong, Joubert, & Chan, 2008; Weibe, 2001), depression (Mascaro & Rosen, 2008; Mascaro, Rosen, & Morey, 2004), substance abuse and addiction (Corner, 2003; Jappy, 2001; Robertson, 1997), and aging (Weiler, 2001), as well as in high school settings (DeLazzari, 2000; Rathi & Rastogi, 2007), on populations of various religious and spiritual orientations (Crosby, 2000; Emmons, 2005; Gall et al., 2007; Gallant, 2001; Klaassen & McDonald, 2002), and cross-culturally (Corner, 2003; Pan, Wong, Chan, et al., 2008; Pan, Wong, Joubert, & Chan, 2007; Pan, Wong, Joubert, et al., 2008; Rathi & Rastogi, 2007). The main reason for the broad appeal of the PMP is that it incorporates all major sources of meaning. Therefore, some subscales, such as Self-transcendence (Markow & Klenke, 2005) and Self-acceptance (Gall et al., 2007), are used in their own rights.

Correlations With Positive and Negative Effects

The PMP has been used to examine a wide variety of associations with positive and negative constructs of health and well-being. DeLazzari (2000) found that scores on the PMP were better than emotional intelligence at predicting life satisfaction among high school students. Working in the context of spiritual leadership, Markow and Klenke (2005) found that the self-transcendence source of meaning was significantly correlated with a sense of calling and that a sense of calling was predictive of organizational commitment. A Dutch translation of the PMP administered to cancer patients was found to be positively correlated with psychological well-being and negatively correlated to distress (Jaarsma, Pool, Ranchor, & Sanderman, 2007). Hope (2006) examined secondary traumatic stress in the caregivers of persons who suffered trauma and found that meaning in life contributed to higher levels of well-being in caregivers.

Simms (2005) investigated the contribution of personal meaning, hardiness, and optimism to mental health and well-being. Results showed that 239 participants completed the PMP, Maddi and Khoshaba's (2001) Personal Views Survey III–Revised (PVS-III-R), Scheier, Carver, and Bridges's (1994)

Life Orientation Test–Revised (LOT-R), the Scales of Psychological Well-Being (SPWB; Ryff, 1989), and Diener, Emmons, Larsen, and Griffin's (1985) Satisfaction With Life Scale (SWLS). An exploratory principle components analysis obtained a five-factor solution of mental health and well-being, accounting for 67% of the total variance. The five factors were Subjective well-being, Personal growth, Hardiness, Personal meaning, and Positive relationship.

The PMP has also been found to be positively correlated with measures of perceived well-being (Reker & Wong, 1984), spiritual well-being (Lang, 1994; Robertson, 1997), hope (Mascaro & Rosen, 2005), meaning of work (Giesbrecht, 1997), affective and normative organizational commitment (Du Buisson-Narsai, 2009), and reduced impact of childhood sexual abuse in adulthood (Gall et al., 2007, using Self-acceptance subscale). Gingras (2009) found significant positive correlations between all subscales of the PMP and Flanagan's Quality of Life Scale (Burckhardt, Anderson, Archenholtz, & Hagg, 2003). Mascaro (2006) found that whereas meaning had a positive influence on depression over a two-month period, people who scored low in meaning suffered from greater increases in depressive symptoms in response to increased stress levels. The PMP has also been found to be negatively correlated with depression and depressive symptoms (Mascaro & Rosen, 2008; Wong, 1998), job stress measures (Giesbrecht, 1997), and Derogatis and Melisaratos's (1983) Brief Symptom Inventory (Robertson, 1997). Research with the PMP also shows that meaning of life is related to reduced impact of acculturative stress on positive affect (Pan, Wong, Chan, et al., 2008) and increased life satisfaction (Pan, Wong, Joubert, et al., 2008) and, further, that it mediates the relationship between acculturative stressors and negative affect (Pan et al., 2007). In addition, Rempel (2005) found that the PMP was related to various perceptions of God in older adults.

Correlates With Other Meaning Measures

The psychometric properties of PMP continue to accumulate. PMP correlates positively with such other major measurements of meaning as Reker and Peacock's (1981) LAP (Wong, 1998), Crumbaugh and Maholick's (1969) PIL (Robertson, 1997), Mascaro et al.'s (2004) Spiritual Meaning Scale (SMS; Mascaro, 2006), and Battista and Almond's (1973) LRI (Mascaro, 2006).

The most complete study of the correlates of PMP with other meaning measures was conducted by Mascaro (2006). He investigated the relationships between the PMP, the Framework subscale of the LRI-Revised, and the SMS with depressive symptoms as measured with the Beck Depression Inventory–II, the Depression Anxiety Stress Scales (DASS) depression scale, and the Personality Assessment Inventory (PAI) depression scale. Mascaro (2006) also investigated hope as measured with the Herth Hope Scale, the Adult State Hope Scale, and the Beck Hopelessness Scale. Participants were given these measures at the initial assessment, at the one-month interval, and again at the

Table 17.1 Concurrent Correlations Between the PMP and Other Scales

Scale	*r*
Spiritual Meaning Scale	0.76***
Revised Life Regard Index	0.65***
Undergraduate Stress Questionnaire	–0.09
DASS-depression	–0.56***
PAI-depression	–0.64***
Beck Depression Inventory–II	–0.58***
Beck Hopelessness Scale	–0.62***
Adult State Hope Scale	0.70***
Herth Hope Scale	0.81***
Internal Locus of Control	0.43***

***$p < .001$.

two-month interval. Table 17.1 summarizes the Pearson correlations between the various measures and the PMP reported in the final assessment (Mascaro, 2006, p. 34).

Recent Measures on Meaningful in Life

Since 1998, several new measures have been published. This section examines how these newer tests are related to the PMP. Bellin (in press) has provided a helpful review of the literature on meaning measures.

Multidimensional Life Meaning Scale

Recently, Edwards (2007) developed the Multidimensional Life Meaning Scale (MLMS) based on factor analysis of several existing meaning measures, including the PIL Scale (Crumbaugh & Maholick, 1969), the LRI (Battista & Almond, 1973), the PMP (Wong, 1998), the LAP-R (Reker & Peacock, 1981), and the Sources of Meaning Profile (SOMP; Reker & Wong, 1988). She discovered 10 "super" factors: Achievement, Framework/Purpose, Religion, Death acceptance, Interpersonal satisfaction, Excitement/Fulfillment, Giving to the world, (Lack of) Existential vacuum, Intimacy, and Control. PMP items accounted for all seven Achievement items, five of six Religion items, all seven Interpersonal satisfaction items, all three Intimacy items, and one item from PMP's Self-transcendence subscale in the Giving to the world factor.

The Sources of Meaning and Meaning in Life Questionnaire

The Source of Meaning and Meaning in Life (SoMe) Questionnaire was developed by Schnell (2009, 2010; Schnell & Becker, 2006). It includes 26 sources of meaning (ultimate meanings), which can be categorized into four dimensions: (a) Self-transcendence, (b) Self-actualization, (c) Order, and (d) Well-being and communality. It is of interest that the 26 factors overlap with the PMP;

for example, Religiosity and Spirituality are the same as the PMP's Religion subscale. In fact, SoMe covers six of the seven sources of meaning of the PMP, excluding only the Fair treatment subscale. In addition to the sources of meaning, SoMe incorporates two independent scales that measure Meaningfulness and a Crisis of Meaning. Schnell (2009) defines the term *meaningfulness* as "a fundamental sense of meaning, based on an appraisal of one's life as coherent, significant, directed, and belonging" (p. 487). *Crisis of meaning* is "judgement of one's life as empty, pointless and lacking meaning" (p. 487). The main contribution of SoMe is that it can measure presence of meaning and the search for meaning separately.

Spiritual Meaning Scale

Mascaro et al. (2004) conceptualized meaning in terms of three related constructs: personal meaning, implicit meaning, and spiritual meaning. They believed that the former two were measured by the LRI Framework and PMP respectively, while spiritual meaning required a new measuring instrument. They defined spiritual meaning as, "the extent to which an individual believes that life or some force of which life is a function has a purpose, will, or way in which individuals participate" (p. 847). They developed the 14-item Spiritual Meaning Scale (SMS). They demonstrated that the SMS, LRI Framework, and PMP were able to predict mental health variables (i.e., hope, depression, anxiety, and antisocial features) beyond the Big Five personality factors. The three measures of meaning were also significantly correlated with each other.

Our initial reaction to Mascaro et al. (2004) was that the three meaning constructs may not clearly differentiate the conceptual and empirical levels because the PMP was developed as a measure of personal meaning, although it used implicit theories methodology. Also, PMP contains a religious and spiritual source of meaning.

Edwards (2007) points out the problem of confound or overlap between the SMS and the other two measures of meaning. She observes that the items included in the SMS are quite similar to the items used in the other two measures (e.g., "Life is inherently meaningful," "I see a special purpose for myself in this world"). She concludes that "it may be difficult to truly parcel out spiritual meaning from one's overall sense of meaning in life" (2007, p. 61). In spite of the aforementioned limitations, the SMS comes close to capturing Frankl's (1963/1985) concept of suprameaning. Mascaro (2006) implies that it is something transcendental, transpersonal, and independent of the individual. Thus, spiritual meaning implies that a complete personal framework about the meaning of life cannot be limited to a system of goals:

> Spiritual meaning is not conceptualized as a mere construct of the individual but as something that inheres in existence itself. It is a capital "M" Meaning around which one can form a small "m", personal meaning....

> [S]piritual meaning as belief that life or some force of which life is a function has a purpose, will, or way in which individuals participate. (Mascaro, 2006, pp. 8–9)

In their study, Mascaro et al. (2004) used a longitudinal design and structural equation modeling with a sample of 574 undergraduate students in order to predict depression by the multidimensional existential meaning composed of the SMS, the LRI Framework subscale, and the PMP. They reported that existential meaning was negatively correlated to levels of depression over a two-month period. Given the moderate to large correlations between the three measures of meaning, the composite measure seems to be a more reliable and valid measure of existential meaning than either measure alone.

The Meaning in Life Questionnaire

Steger et al. (2006) define the term *meaning* as "the sense made of, and significance felt regarding, the nature of one's being and existence. This definition allows respondents to use their own criteria for meaning" (p. 81). Their Meaning in Life Questionnaire (MLQ) is a 10-item scale that is composed of two relatively orthogonal five-item subscales: Presence (MLQ-P) and Search (MLQ-S). The Presence subscale measures a subjective sense that one's life is meaningful, whereas "Search for Meaning measures the drive and orientation toward finding meaning in one's life" (p. 85).

Based on the content of the Search subscale, it indeed reflects Frankl's idea of will to meaning as a primary motivation, but it falls short of affirming the belief that there is always meaning to be found in life regardless of the circumstances. As Wong pointed out in Chapter 1, this volume, it is difficult to interpret the score of the Search subscale without knowing which search stage the person is in because the score could be related to a crisis in meaning as measured by Schnell's (2010) SoMe, and it could also reflect the human tendency to continue to make sense of life and seek deeper significance even when the individual already enjoys a meaningful life.

The Schedule for Meaning in Life Evaluation

Fegg, Kramer, L'hoste, and Borasio (2008) developed a respondent-generated instrument for the assessment of individual meaning in life. In the Schedule for Meaning in Life Evaluation (SMiLE), respondents are asked to list three to seven areas that provide meaning to their lives before rating the current level of importance and satisfaction of each area. Then, "the listed MiL areas were assigned to a posteriori categories" (p. 360). It is not clear, however, how the final list of categories was created based on participants' answers; nor is it clear how individually generated responses were sorted into these fixed categories. The categories of meaning in life, such as Family, Friends, Work, Religiosity, and Altruism, are similar to Intimacy, Relationship, Achievement, and

Religion of the PMP. The main limitation of this schedule is that it demands too much cognitive effort for respondents, especially when they are in palliative care, to generate areas of meaning in life and rate their importance and satisfaction in each area.

Meaningful Life Measure

Morgan and Farsides (2009) developed a new meaning measure, the Meaningful Life Measure (MLM), based on selected items from three existing popular meaning measures: LRI, PIL, and Ryff's Psychological Well-Being Purpose subscale (SPWB-P). Factor analysis yielded five factors: Exciting life, Accomplished life, Principled life, Purposeful life, and Valued life. These five factors resemble the PURE component of meaning (Wong, 2010). The purpose component is represented by Purposeful life and Valued life; understanding is represented by Principled life; responsibility represented by Accomplished life; and enjoyment represented by Exciting life. The MLM is useful for examining the antecedents and consequences of *specific* components of personal meaning. For example, the Principled life seems to capture the importance of having a philosophy of life and personal value system in living the good life. However, MLM does not seem to be a comprehensive measure of the meaning construct because it focuses almost exclusively on the purpose dimension of the meaning.

Comparison Groups for the Personal Meaning Profile and Development of the Personal Meaning Profile B

The PMP has been used in a variety of research over the last decade, proving to be useful internationally and in many different fields of investigation. Descriptive information is first provided in this section for comparison purposes in future research. To further extend the usefulness of the PMP, a short-form was developed. The PMP-B, the short form, contains the same seven subscales as the original, but each subscale now contains only three items for a total of 21 items. From a research and clinical perspective, a shorter version of the PMP is desirable for circumstances in which the long version is either inappropriate or impractical (e.g., severe time constraints or participants who are ill or enfeebled). Developers of the short form hope that with the availability of a quick, effective assessment tool, the PMP-B, scholars will be encouraged to engage in further research involving personal meaning in life.

Table 17.2 summarizes 12 theses and dissertations that used the PMP over the last decade and whose data was made available to the authors for the present analyses. These samples were combined to provide responses from a range of participants from different backgrounds, ages, and outlooks. As noted in Table 17.2, a subgroup of the combined sample (N = 1,212) provided comparable information on age and gender. Table 17.3 summarizes demographic information for the combined group.

Table 17.2 The Sources of Samples for the PMP-B

Source	Sample Size	Sample Description
1. Corner (2003)	472	Young adults in Australia between the ages of 18 and 24, including participants in treatment for substance dependence ($n = 59$) and university students ($n = 398$) from diverse backgrounds
2. Crosby (2000)	56	Adults in an online study on mystical experiences
3. Daum & Wiebe (2003)	168	First-semester university students surveyed three times during one term
4. DeLazzari (2000)	154	Private high school students in Grades 9 and 12
5. Gallant (2001)	393	University students from private and public institutions
6. Haag (2000)	29	University students who took a stress management course
7. Klaassen & McDonald (2002)	160	University students in a private institution in a study on identity achievement
8. Leung, Vroon, & Steinfort (2003)	30	Adults in an online study on attitudes toward suffering
9. McConnell (1998)	44	Women working in clerical positions, including ministry-oriented employment ($n = 18$) and secular employment ($n = 22$)
10. Weibe (2001)	67	Professional counselors in a study of vicarious traumatization
11. Weiler (2001)	118	Seniors living in the community in British Columbia
12. Wilk (2000)	192	Clergy ($n = 94$) and managers ($n = 97$) in a study of occupational stress

The combined sample size was 1,883. Information on gender and/or age was unavailable for Samples 1, 4, and 8 and for 15 additional cases scattered among the remaining samples. If these cases are omitted, the combined sample totalled 1,212. Other than Sample 1, all the samples consisted largely of Anglophone Canadians. The online studies also included a substantial proportion of participants from the United States.

Analyses of relationships between gender and age for PMP scores in the composite sample were conducted to explore possible relationships between important personal background features and the PMP. Table 17.4a summarizes significant effects for PMP subscales overall, showing small effects for the overall group (2% to 6% effect size). For descriptive purposes, Table 17.5

Table 17.3 Demographics

Subcategories	Frequency
Relationship status	
Single	404
Married	291
Widowed	32
Divorced	30
Cohabiting	10
Separated	5
Remarried	10
Other	10
Subtotal	792
Missing	420
Total	1,212

Subcategories	Frequency
Education	
University student	213
Less than university	621
BA/BSc	151
Postbachelor's	148
Other	14
Subtotal	1,147
Missing	65
Total	1,212

presents the mean scores of each gender for each of the seven subscales of the PMP. Very small gender (<1%) and age (1%) differences (and a Gender × Age interaction is 1%) in PMP total scores were statistically significant because of the large sample size, but the total score shows substantially smaller correlations than the subscales scores, because subscale distinctiveness is washed out in the total score.

Table 17.4b summarizes the small differences in effects of PMP by gender, age group, and Gender × Age interactions for separate subscales. Subscale comparisons showed small main effects for gender (Relationship: female > male, 3% effect size) and for age (Self-acceptance: older adults high and young adults low, 5%; Fair Treatment: middle-aged adults low and older adults high, 3%). Small interactions for Intimacy (3%) and Religion (4%) were similar: Males reported higher meaning levels in older cohorts, whereas females reported fairly high levels at each of the different ages. See Figures 17.1, 17.2, 17.3, and 17.4 for graphic descriptions of the interaction between

Table 17.4a Significant Effects for PMP Subcategories

		F	*p*	η^2
Gender	Wilks's lambda	8.08	< .001	0.045
Age group	Wilks's lambda	10.62	< .001	0.058
Gender by age group interaction	Wilks's lambda	2.95	< .001	0.017

Table 17.4b Significant Differences in Effects of PMP

		df	*F*	*p*	η^2
Gender	Religion	1	1.07	0.301	0.001
	Relationship	1	36.44	0.000	0.029
	Intimacy	1	7.45	0.006	0.006
	Total	1	4.29	0.039	0.004
Age groups	Achievement	3	4.28	0.005	0.011
	Self-transcendence	3	3.95	0.008	0.010
	Self-acceptance	3	22.58	0.000	0.053
	Religion	3	8.15	0.000	0.020
	Intimacy	3	4.94	0.002	0.012
	Fair treatment	3	10.59	0.000	0.026
	Total	3	4.87	0.002	0.012
Age group by gender interaction	Self-transcendence	3	3.91	0.009	0.010
	Religion	3	7.75	0.000	0.019
	Intimacy	3	5.67	0.001	0.014
	Total	3	4.04	0.007	0.010

All effect sizes greater than 1% are presented. Intimacy, Religion, and Total effects for gender are listed to help clarify the results reported for age and interaction effects.

gender and age for selected PMP scores. Although these small effects are not theoretically significant for many applications, they are presented here for comparison purposes when potentially subtle patterns might be important for specific research or clinical projects or when selected populations are being addressed.

Table 17.5 Gender Mean Differences for Mean Subcategories

	Gender Means	
	Female	**Male**
Achievement	5.241	5.083
Relationship	5.209	4.918
Self-transcendence	5.427	5.314
Self-acceptance	5.243	5.228
Religion	5.561	5.651
Intimacy	5.557	5.315
Fair treatment	5.316	5.283

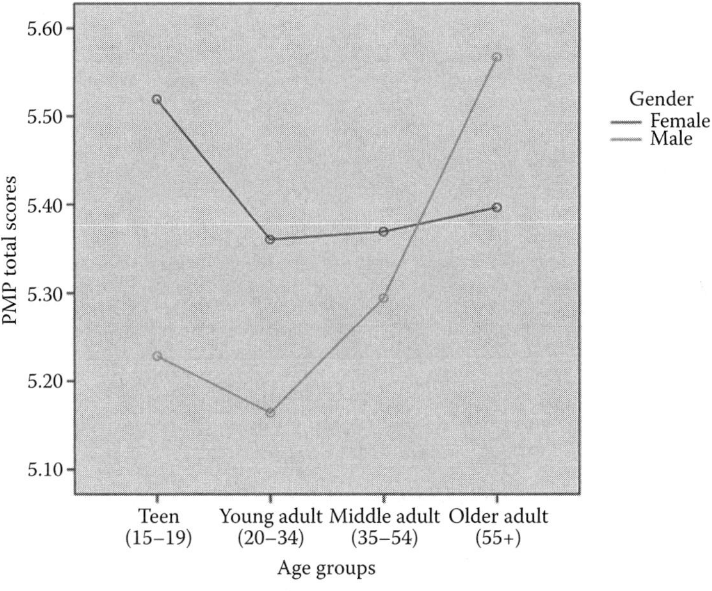

Figure 17.1 Interaction of age and gender for total PMP scores. Scores range from 1.0 to 7.0.

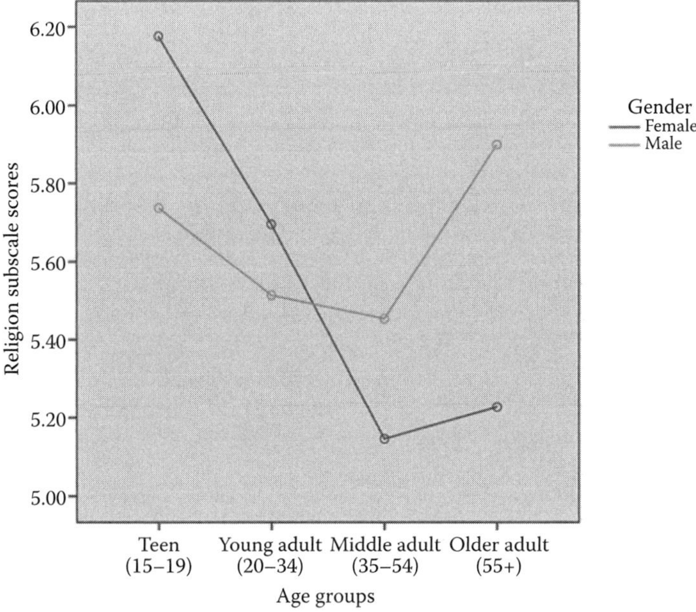

Figure 17.2 Age and gender interactions for PMP religion subscale. Scores range from 1.0 to 7.0.

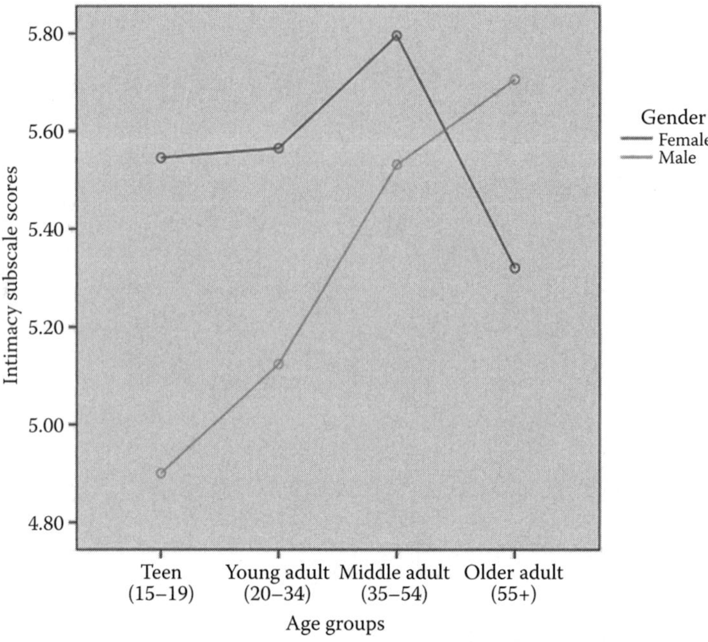

Figure 17.3 Age and gender interactions for Intimacy subscale scores. Scores range from 1.0 to 7.0.

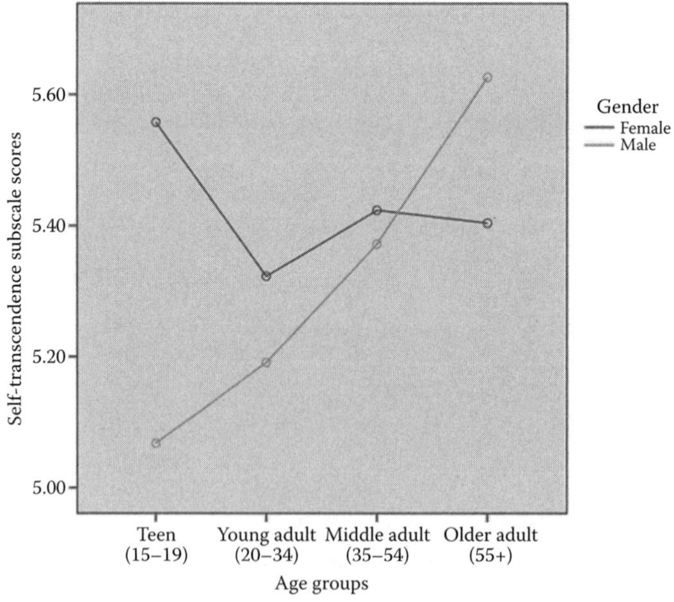

Figure 17.4 Age and gender interactions for self-transcendence subscale scores. Scores range from 1.0 to 7.0.

Development of the Personal Meaning Profile B

An item-level principle components analysis (PCA) was employed in the composite data set to select items for a brief version of the PMP (PMP-B). Several criteria were used to confirm the proper number of dimensions to be retained: Eigen values before and after oblique rotation, percentage of total variance accounted for by each component and by the overall set of components, item communality after extraction, presence of at least three items that loaded primarily on a specific component, and conceptual relationships among the items. The PMP yields correlated subscales, so oblique rotations (Promax) were obtained and loading patterns in the pattern and structure matrices were examined. When items were deleted, close approximations to simple structure emerged that showed strong cross-loadings among the subscales. The extraction of seven components for a reduced subset of 21 items yielded a clear subscale structure for the PMP-B and accounted for 72% of the total variance of those items. The results are presented in the pattern matrix shown in Table 17.6.

A strong approximation to simple structure is evident in Table 17.6, with only one item, Item 57, showing a minor cross-loading on another subscale. The structure matrix showed the same clear pattern of primary loadings of items while also reflecting correlations among the subscales. The correlation matrix among the subscales for the combined group of 1,212 respondents is presented in Table 17.7, demonstrating clear discrimination among the subscales. Also shown in Table 17.7, the internal consistency (Cronbach's alpha) of the subscales is excellent for three-item subscales, with only one subscale yielding a reliability coefficient below .70. The corresponding alpha for the 21-item PMP-B total score is .84. Test–retest reliability for a five-week period showed stability for each subscale (see Table 17.7) and for the total score of the PMP-B, $r(123) = .73$. The correlation between the PMP and PMP-B total scores was .95; the correlations between corresponding subscales ranged from .84 to .95.

A PCA was conducted on a combined group (Samples 1, 4, and 8 from Table 17.2) to check for the stability of the component structure of the PMP-B. This combined sample includes high school students in Canada and university students in Australia, including a large proportion of immigrants from diverse backgrounds. The results demonstrated clear stability of the subscale structure for the PMP-B.

Concluding Discussion

Past studies on theory-based dimensions of the meaning in life (Reker & Peacock, 1981; Reker & Wong, 1988) have been limited to psychologists' own theoretical ideas. Studies on respondents' self-reports of what makes life meaningful (see Ebersole, 1998) are also limited by the constraints of the

Table 17.6 Pattern Matrix of the PMP-B

Item No.	Component						
	Religion	Intimacy	Fair Treatment	Relationship	Self-Transcendence	Achievement	Self-Acceptance
33	.919						
52	.911						
20	.906						
43		.923					
38		.833					
11		.762					
56			.845				
35			.830				
55			.778				
28				.859			
42				.824			
27				.780			
15					.887		
2					.824		
49					.743		
21						.910	
24						.755	
47						.668	
46							.876
36							.818
57						.334	.554

All loadings less than .30 have been omitted.

Table 17.7 Correlations and Reliabilities of the Subscales of the Personal Meaning Profile–Brief Form

Subscale	1	2	3	4	5	6	7
1. Achievement	—	.39	.07	.50	.29	.26	.35
2. Relationship		—	.14	.39	.28	.34	.43
3. Religion			—	.29	.18	.11	.13
4. Self-transcendence				—	.26	.26	.30
5. Self-acceptance					—	.17	.36
6. Intimacy						—	.27
7. Fair treatment							—
Cronbach's alpha	.75	.75	.92	.76	.66	.80	.78
Test–retest	.63	.78	.86	.73	.62	.78	.64
Correlations between PMP and PMP-B subscales	.84	.89	.93	.87	.87	.95	.92

Subscale intercorrelations are all statistically significant, $p < .001$, $N = 1{,}212$. Test–retest reliability coefficients were obtained over a five-week period from first-year university students in a variety of courses (Sample 3 in Table 17.2, $n = 125$).

respondents' present life circumstances. The implicit theories approach is able to minimize the aforementioned limitations and provides a rich and comprehensive picture of what makes life worth living.

The major factors of the PMP, such as Religion, Relationship, Achievement, and Self-transcendence, have been identified by prior research (e.g., Ebersole, 1998; Reker & Wong, 1988). Self-acceptance has been identified by Ryff and Singer (1998) as one of the components of psychological well-being. Wong's prior research identified Self-acceptance as one of the two components of existential coping (Wong, 1993; Wong, Reker, & Peacock, 2006). Self-acceptance is a necessary attitude to soften the blow of negative events and avoid unnecessary frustration when achievement striving fails to materialize because of one's deficiency. One may conclude that accepting what one cannot change is a sign of wisdom necessary for meaningful living. Another interesting finding is that Fair treatment has emerged as an important source of personal meaning. This finding highlights society's responsibility to promote justice, fairness, and equal opportunities. It seems warranted to conclude that it would be very difficult for individuals to enjoy a fully meaningful life in an unjust, discriminating, and oppressive society.

Everybody is seeking something to make life better. The key is to know what people are after. Their pursuit may lead to disillusion; or worse still, they may be driven by fatal desires. Therefore, for both practical and theoretical purposes, we need to know whether people are striving for something that indeed makes life worth living. The main advantage of the PMP is that it identifies the sources of meaning seeking, which have been scientifically linked to well-being.

Another advantage of the PMP is that it provides at least four different indices of meaning seeking: magnitude, breadth, depth, and balance. The total PMP score is an index of magnitude—the greater the score, the more successful a person is in approximating the ideally meaningful life. The number of sources involved indicates the breadth of meaning seeking; thus, individuals who seek meaning from all the sources of the PMP have a broader basis than those who derive meaning from only one or two of these sources. The relative difference in factor scores reflects balance. For example, if individuals score extremely high in Achievement but very low in all other factors, they lack balance in meaning seeking. The depth factor measures the level of meaning to which one moves from the basic level of self-seeking to higher levels of values that transcend the personal self (Reker, Peacock, & Wong, 1987).

In sum, the seven sources of meaning of the PMP, in addition to the initial Fulfillment/Positive affect factor, cover all the components of well-being and happiness (Ryff & Singer, 1998; Seligman, 2011). Furthermore, these sources of meaning can also be understood in terms of the PURE structure and functions of meaning (Wong, 2010). Therefore, PMP-B can be employed for research and clinical purposes if one is interested in discovering the key components of meaning systems and their psychological correlates in different populations. For example, meaning in life has recently become a central theme in palliative care (Breitbart & Heller, 2003), and the results of the PMP-B can be effectively explored to enhance the appropriate areas of patients' personal meaning and well-being.

Appendix: Personal Meaning Profile B

This questionnaire measures people's perception of personal meaning in their lives. Generally, a meaningful life involves a sense of purpose and personal significance. However, people often differ in what they value most, and they have different ideas as to what would make life worth living. The following statements describe potential sources of a meaningful life. Please read each statement carefully and indicate to what extent each item characterizes your own life. You may respond by circling the appropriate number according to the following scale:

1	2	3	4	5	6	7
Not at all			Moderately			A great deal

For example, if going to parties does not contribute to your sense of personal meaning, you may circle 1 or 2. If taking part in volunteer work contributes quite a bit to the meaning in your life, you may circle 5 or 6.

Baumeister, R. F. (1991). *Meanings of life.* New York, NY: Guilford Press.

Bellin, Z. (in press). The quest to capture personal meaning in psychology. *International Journal of Existential Psychology and Psychotherapy.*

Breitbart, W., & Heller, K. (2003). Reframing hope: Meaning-centered care for patients near the end of life. *Journal of Palliative Medicine, 6,* 979–988.

Burckhardt, C. S., Anderson, K. L., Archenholtz, B., & Hagg, O. (2003). The Flanagan Quality of Life Scale: Evidence of construct validity. *Health and Quality of Life Outcomes, 1*(53). doi:10.1186/1477-7525-1-59

Corner, T. L. (2003). *Personal meaning and youth substance use* (Unpublished doctoral dissertation). Macquarie University, Sydney, Australia.

Crosby, J. M. (2000). *Mystical experiences, depression, well-being, and meaning* (Unpublished master's thesis). Trinity Western University, Langley, BC, Canada.

Crumbaugh, J. C. (1977). The Seeking of Noetic Goals Test (SONG): A complementary scale to the Purpose in Life Test (PIL). *Journal of Clinical Psychology, 33,* 900–907.

Crumbaugh, J. C., & Maholick, L. T. (1964). An experimental study on existentialism: The psychometric approach to Frankl's concept of noogenic neurosis. *Journal of Clinical Psychology, 20,* 200–201.

Crumbaugh, J. C., & Maholick, L. T. (1969). *Manual of instructions for the Purpose in Life Test.* Munster, IN: Psychometric Affiliates.

Daum, T. L., & Wiebe, G. (2003). *Locus of control, personal meaning, and self-concept before and after an academic critical incident* (Unpublished master's thesis). Trinity Western University, Langley, BC, Canada.

DeLazzari, S. A. (2000). *Emotional intelligence, meaning, and psychological well being: A comparison between early and late adolescence* (Unpublished master's thesis). Trinity Western University, Langley, BC, Canada.

Derogatis, L. R., & Melisaratos, N. (1983). The brief symptom inventory: An introductory report. *Psychological Medicine, 13,* 595–605.

Diener, E., Emmons, R. A., Larsen, R. J., & Griffin, S. (1985). The Satisfaction With Life Scale. *Journal of Personality and Social Psychology, 47,* 1105–1117.

Dittmann-Kohli, F. (1991, July). *Dimensions of change in personal meaning in young and elderly adults.* Paper presented at the 11th Biennial Meeting of the International Society for the Study of Behavioural Development (ISSBD).

Du Buisson-Narsai, I. (2009). *The relationship between personal meaning, sense of coherence and organisational commitment* (Unpublished doctoral dissertation). University of South Africa, Pretoria, South Africa.

Dyck, M. J. (1987). Assessing logotherapeutic constructs: Conceptual and psychometric status of the Purpose in Life and Seeking of Noetic Goals tests. *Clinical Psychology Review, 7,* 439–447.

Ebersole, P. (1998). Types and depth of written life meaning. In P. T. P. Wong & P. S. Fry (Eds.), *The human quest for meaning: A handbook of psychological research and clinical application* (pp. 237–259). Mahwah, NJ: Erlbaum.

Edwards, M. J. (2007). *The dimensionality and construct valid measurement of life meaning* (Unpublished doctoral dissertation). Queen's University, Kingston, ON, Canada.

Emmons, R. A. (2005). Striving for the sacred: Personal meaning, life meaning, and religion. *Journal of Social Issues, 61*(4), 731–745.

Erikson, E. H. (1963). *Childhood and society.* New York, NY: Norton.

Fegg, M. J., Kramer, M., L'hoste, S., & Borasio, G. D. (2008). The Schedule for Meaning in Life Evaluation (SMiLE): Validation of a new instrument for meaning-in-life research. *Journal of Pain and Symptom Management, 35*(4), 356–564.

It is important that you answer honestly on the basis of your ow ences and beliefs.

1. I believe I can make a difference in the world. 1 2
2. I have someone to share intimate feelings with. 1 2
3. I strive to make this world a better place. 1 2
4. I seek to do God's will. 1 2 3
5. I like challenge. 1 2 3
6. I take initiative. 1 2 3
7. I have a number of good friends. 1 2 3
8. I am trusted by others. 1 2 3
9. I seek to glorify God. 1 2 3 4
10. Life has treated me fairly. 1 2 3 4
11. I accept my limitations. 1 2 3 4
12. I have a mutually satisfying loving relationship. 1 2 3 4
13. I am liked by others. 1 2 3 4 5
14. I have found someone I love deeply. 1 2 3 4 5
15. I accept what cannot be changed. 1 2 3 4 5
16. I am persistent and resourceful in attaining my goals. 1 2 3 4 5
17. I make a significant contribution to society. 1 2 3 4 5
18. I believe that one can have a personal relationship with God. 1 2 3 4 5 6
19. I am treated fairly by others. 1 2 3 4 5 6
20. I have received my fair share of opportunities and rewards. 1 2 3 4 5 6
21. I have learned to live with suffering and make the best of it. 1 2 3 4 5 6

Scoring Key

1. *Achievement*: 5, 6, 16
2. *Relationship*: 7, 8, 13
3. *Religion*: 4, 9, 18
4. *Self-transcendence*: 1, 3, 17
5. *Self-acceptance*: 11, 15, 21
6. *Intimacy*: 2, 12, 14
7. *Fair treatment*: 10, 19, 20

References

Adler, A. (1958). *What life should mean to you.* New York, NY: Capricorn Books. (Originally published 1931)

Antonovsky, A. (1983). The sense of coherence: Development of a research instrument. *Newsletter and Research Report of the W. S. Schwartz Research Center for Behavioral Medicine, 1*, 11–22.

Battista, J., & Almond, R. (1973). The development of meaning in life. *Psychiatry, 36*, 409–427.

Frankl, V. E. (1985). *Man's search for meaning.* New York, NY: Pocket Books. (Originally published 1963)

Gall, T., Basque, V., Damasceno-Scott, M., & Vardy, G. (2007). Spirituality and the current adjustment of adult survivors of childhood sexual abuse. *Journal for the Scientific Study of Religion, 46*(1), 101–117.

Gallant, C. M. (2001). *Existential expeditions: Religious orientations and personal meaning* (Unpublished master's thesis). Trinity Western University, Langley, BC, Canada.

Giesbrecht, H. A. (1997). *Meaning as a predictor of work stress and job satisfaction* (Unpublished master's thesis). Trinity Western University, Langley, BC, Canada.

Gingras, D. T. (2009). *Living well in spite of chronic pain: Meaning in life and quality of life in a sample of chronic pain sufferers* (Unpublished honor's thesis). Tyndale University College, Toronto, ON, Canada.

Haag, A. M. (2000). *The contribution of existential coping to stress management* (Unpublished master's thesis). Trinity Western University, Langley, BC, Canada.

Hope, N. L. (2006). *When caring hurts: The significance of personal meaning for well-being in the presence of secondary traumatic stress* (master's thesis). Trinity Western University, Langley, BC, Canada.

Jaarsma, T. A., Pool, G., Ranchor, A. V., & Sanderman, R. (2007). The concept and measurement of meaning in life in Dutch cancer patients. *Psycho-Oncology, 16*, 241–248.

James, W. (1902). *The varieties of religious experience: A study of human nature.* London, England: Longmans, Green.

Jappy, A. J. (2001). *Christian vs. eclectic spiritual intervention in alcohol and drug addiction recovery* (Unpublished master's thesis). Trinity Western University, Langley, BC, Canada.

Jung, C. G. (1933). *Modern man in search of a soul* (W. S. Dell & C. F. Baynes, Trans.). San Diego, CA: Harcourt Brace Jovanovich.

Jung, C. G. (1971). The stages of life. In R. F. C. Hill (Ed. and Trans.), *The portable Jung.* New York, NY: Viking.

Kernes, J. L., & Kinnier, R. T. (2008). Meaning in psychologists' personal and professional lives. *Journal of Humanistic Psychology, 48*(2), 196–220.

Klaassen, D. W., & McDonald, M. J. (2002). Quest and identity development: Re-examining pathways for existential search. *International Journal for the Psychology of Religion, 12*, 189–200.

Korotkov, D. (1998). The sense of coherence: Making sense out of chaos. In P. T. P. Wong & P. S. Fry (Eds.), *The human quest for meaning: A handbook of psychological research and clinical application* (pp. 237–259). Mahwah, NJ: Erlbaum.

Lang, J. M. (1994). *Does religiosity provide a buffer against uncontrollable life stress?* (Unpublished honor's thesis). Trent University, Peterborough, ON, Canada.

Lao Tzu. (1913). *Tao Te Ching "The Canon of Reason and Virtue"* (D. T. Suzuki & Paul Carus, Trans.). Retrieved from http://www.yellowbridge.com/general/invoke.php?u=http://www.sacred-texts.com/tao/crv/

Leung, M., Vroon, E. J., & Steinfort, T. (2003). *Life Attitudes Scale: Development and validation of a measurement of the construct of tragic optimism* (Unpublished master's thesis). Trinity Western University, Langley, BC, Canada.

Maddi, S. R., & Khoshaba, D. M. (2001). *Personal Views Survey III-R: Internet instruction manual.* Newport Beach, CA: Hardiness Institute.

Markow, F., & Klenke, K. (2005). The effects of personal meaning and calling on organizational commitment: An empirical investigation of spiritual leadership. *International Journal of Organizational Analysis, 13*, 8–27.

Mascaro, N. (2006). *Longitudinal analysis of the relationship of existential meaning with depression and hope* (Doctoral dissertation). Texas A&M University, College Station, Texas.

Mascaro, N., & Rosen, D. H. (2005). Existential meaning's role in the enhancement of hope and prevention of depressive symptoms. *Journal of Personality, 73*(4), 985–1014.

Mascaro, N., & Rosen, D. H. (2008). Assessment of existential meaning and its longitudinal relations with depressive symptoms. *Journal of Social and Clinical Psychology, 27*(6), 576–599.

Mascaro, N., Rosen, D. H., & Morey, L. C. (2004). The development, construct validity, and clinical utility of the Spiritual Meaning Scale. *Personality and Individual Differences, 37*(4), 845–860.

Maslow, A. (1962). *Toward a psychology of being.* New York, NY: Van Nostrand.

May, R. (1958). The origins and significance of the existential movement in psychology. In R. May, E. Angel, & H. F. Ellenberger (Eds.), *Existence* (pp. 3–36). Northvale, NJ: Jason Aronson.

McConnell, K. J. (1998). *The role of meaning and ministry in job satisfaction* (Unpublished master's thesis). Trinity Western University, Langley, BC, Canada.

Morgan, J., & Farsides, T. (2009). Measuring meaning in life. *Journal of Happiness Studies, 10*(2), 197–214.

Pan, J., Wong, D. F. K., Chan, C. L. W., & Joubert, L. (2008a). Meaning of life as a protective factor of positive affect in acculturation: A resilience framework and a cross-cultural comparison. *International Journal of Intercultural Relations, 32*(6), 505–514.

Pan, J., Wong, D. F. K., Joubert, L., & Chan, C. L. W. (2007). Acculturative stressor and meaning of life as predictors of negative affect in acculturation: A cross-cultural comparative study between Chinese international students in Australia and Hong Kong. *Australian and New Zealand Journal of Psychiatry, 41*(9), 740–750.

Pan, J., Wong, D. F. K., Joubert, L., & Chan, C. L. W. (2008b). The protective function of meaning of life on life satisfaction among Chinese students in Australia and Hong Kong: A cross-cultural comparative study. *Journal of American College Health, 57*(2), 221–231.

Rathi, N., & Rastogi, R. (2007). Meaning in life and psychological well-being in pre-adolescents and adolescents. *Journal of the Indian Academy of Applied Psychology, 33*(1), 31–38.

Reker, G. T., & Peacock, E. J. (1981). The Life Attitude Profile (LAP): A multidimensional instrument for assessing attitudes toward life. *Canadian Journal of Behavioural Science, 13*, 64–73.

Reker, G. T., Peacock, E. J., & Wong, P. T. (1987). Meaning and purpose in life and well-being: A life span perspective. *Journal of Gerontology, 42*, 44–49.

Reker, G. T., & Wong, P. T. P. (1984). Psychological and physical well-being in the elderly: The Perceived Well-Being Scale (PWB). *Canadian Journal on Aging, 3*, 23–32.

Reker, G. T., & Wong, P. T. P. (1988). Aging as an individual process: Toward a theory of personal meaning. In J. E. Birren & V. L. Bengston (Eds.), *Emergent theories of aging* (pp. 214–246). New York, NY: Springer.

Rempel, E. J. (April, 2005). Concept of God and personal meaning: Investigating the perspective of older adults. *Proceedings of the National Conference on Undergraduate Research (NCUR), 2005.* Washington and Lee University, Virginia Military Institute, Lexington, Virginia. Retrieved from http://www.newtonchannel.com/academics/undergrad_research/files/63/Elizabeth_Rempel2005.pdf

Robertson, C. R. (1997). *The role of meaning, purpose in life and spiritual well being in the process of addiction recovery & treatment* (Unpublished master's thesis). Trinity Western University, Langley, BC, Canada.

Rogers, C. R. (1980). *A way of being.* New York, NY: Houghton Mifflin.

Ryff, C. D. (1989). Scales of psychological well-being. *Journal of Personality and Social Psychology, 57,* 1069–1081.

Ryff, C. D., & Singer, B. (1998). The role of purpose in life and personal growth in positive human health. In P. T. P. Wong & P. S. Fry (Eds.), *The human quest for meaning: A handbook of psychological research and clinical applications* (pp. 237–259). Mahwah, NJ: Erlbaum.

Scheier, M. F., Carver, C. S., & Bridges, M. W. (1994). Distinguishing optimism from neuroticism (and trait anxiety, self-mastery, and self-esteem): A re-evaluation of the Life Orientation Test. *Journal of Personality and Social Psychology, 67,* 1063–1078.

Schnell, T. (2009). The Sources of Meaning and Meaning in Life Questionnaire (SoMe): Relations to demographics and well-being. *Journal of Positive Psychology, 4*(6), 483–499.

Schnell, T. (2010). Existential indifference: Another quality of meaning in life. *Journal of Humanistic Psychology, 50*(3), 351–373.

Schnell, T., & Becker, P. (2006). Personality and meaning in life. *Personality and Individual Differences, 41*(1), 117–129.

Seligman, M. (2011). *Flourish: A visionary new understanding of happiness and well-being.* New York, NY: Free Press.

Simms, S. M. (2005). *Making lemonade out of life's lemons: Factors of mental health and well-being* (Unpublished master's thesis). Trinity Western University, Langley, BC, Canada.

Steger, M. F., Frazier, P., Oishi, S., & Kaler, M. (2006). The Meaning in Life Questionnaire: Assessing the presence of and search for meaning in life. *Journal of Counseling Psychology, 53,* 30–93.

Stolte, M. (2006). Assets and barriers to finding employment. *Canadian Journal of Counselling, 40*(2), 96–109.

Thurnher, M. (1975). Continuities and discontinuities in value orientation. In M. F. Lowenthal, M. Thurnher, & D. Chiriboga (Eds.), *Four stages of life* (pp. 176–200). San Francisco, CA: Jossey-Bass.

Weibe, R. L. (2001). *The influence of personal meaning on vicarious traumatization in therapists* (Unpublished master's thesis). Trinity Western University, Langley, BC, Canada.

Weiler, P. D. (2001). *Aging with success: Theory of personal meaning as a model of understanding death attitudes* (Unpublished master's thesis). Trinity Western University, Langley, BC, Canada.

Westerhof, G. J., Bohlmeijer, E., & Valenkamp, M. W. (2004). In search of meaning: A reminiscence program for older persons. *Educational Gerontology, 30*(9), 751–766.

Wilk, D. A. (2000). *An exploratory study of meaning and occupational stress experienced by clergy and managers* (Unpublished master's thesis). Trinity Western University, Langley, BC, Canada.

Wong, P. T. P. (1989). Personal meaning and successful aging. *Canadian Psychology, 30*(3), 516–525.

Wong, P. T. P. (1993). Effective management of life stress: The resource-congruence model. *Stress Medicine, 9,* 51–60.

Wong, P. T. P. (1998). Implicit theories of meaningful life and the development of the Personal Meaning Profile (PMP). In P. T. P. Wong & P. S. Fry (Eds.), *The human quest for meaning: A handbook of psychological research and clinical applications* (pp. 111–140). Mahwah, NJ: Erlbaum.

Wong, P. T. P. (2010). Meaning therapy: An integrative and positive existential psychotherapy. *Journal of Contemporary Psychotherapy, 40*(2), 85–93.

Wong, P. T. P., & Fry, P. S. (Eds.). (1998). *The human quest for meaning: A handbook of psychological research and clinical applications.* Mahwah, NJ: Erlbaum.

Wong, P. T. P., Reker, G. T., & Peacock, E. (2006). The resource-congruence model of coping and the development of the Coping Schemas Inventory. In P. T. P. Wong & L. C. J. Wong (Eds.), *Handbook of multicultural perspectives on stress and coping* (pp. 223–283). New York, NY: Springer.

Yalom, I. D. (1980). *Existential psychotherapy.* New York, NY: Basic Books.

18

Restoring, Maintaining, and Enhancing Personal Meaning in Life Through Autobiographical Methods

GARY T. REKER

Trent University

JAMES E. BIRREN and CHERYL M. SVENSSON

University of Southern California

The aim of this chapter is to explore the adaptive value of autobiographical methods in restoring, maintaining, and enhancing a sense of personal meaning in the lives of adults, particularly older adults. Of interest are such autobiographical methods as reminiscence, life review, and guided autobiography that involve an active reconstruction of the past as a basis for achieving meaningful integration with the present and optimistic projection into the near future. Four specific objectives are addressed. First, following a brief introduction, the main autobiographical methods are described in terms of content, structure, and function. Second, a number of theoretical speculations on the link between autobiographical methods and meaning and purpose in life are presented. Third, drawing on both quantitative and qualitative studies, the relevant empirical literature on the effects of these methods in restoring, maintaining, and enhancing a sense of personal meaning in the lives of community-residing and institutionalized older adults is reviewed and evaluated. Finally, drawing on personal experiences, the authors provide an anecdotal account of how the specific method of guided autobiography impacted their lives and how it reaffirmed their conviction that a meaningful life can be discovered and created no matter what the circumstances. It is concluded that one outcome of autobiographical methods—the discovery and creation of personal meaning—facilitates two key meaning-making processes, namely, transcendence (rising above) and transformation (cognitive restructuring).

Autobiographical Methods

Contemporary authors find it useful to divide autobiographical methods into three broad categories: reminiscence, life review, and guided autobiography (Haight & Haight, 2007). *Reminiscence* is defined as a descriptive process of recollecting past experiences and life events. The process is usually spontaneous. *Life review* is defined as the process of review and evaluation of one's life that can result in resolution, reconciliation, atonement, integration, and serenity. Life review encourages reflection and can be either spontaneous or structured. *Guided autobiography* is defined as the process of reconstructing the past and integrating it with the present using thematic topics that are significant to individuals over the life course such as family, career, health, sex role development, experience with death, and meaning in life. Guided autobiography is a structured, systematic process that includes three main elements: (a) short lectures on topics related to developmental psychology and autobiography, (b) the writing of brief autobiographical essays, and (c) the exchange of life stories in a small-group environment (Birren & Cochran, 2001).

One of the stumbling blocks in the field of autobiographical methods has been the proliferation of a wide variety of definitions and little consensus in terms of how "the process of recollecting one's past" ought to be conceptualized. Indeed, prior to Butler's (1963) contribution, reminiscence in the elderly was regarded as a symptom of psychological dysfunction. Researchers focused on reminiscence frequency and its impact on mental health. Butler (1996) preferred the term *life review* to describe a normal developmental task of the later years characterized by the return of memories and past conflicts, which can result in psychological growth but may also contribute to psychological dysfunction. In 1976, Birren introduced the term *guided autobiography*, a topical approach to the collection of autobiographical data (Birren & Hedlund, 1987). Although different in content and structure, guided autobiography can be described as life review conducted in a systematic manner.

Birren (Birren & Birren, 1996) is well known for the statement "You don't know where you are going unless you know where you have been" (p. 299). It is the latter part of the statement that has played a pivotal role in Birren's interest and drive to construct a method that would allow an individual to explore his or her past life. That method is known as guided autobiography, a structured review of one's life as lived with the goal of achieving temporal integration, conflict resolution, reconciliation, ego integrity, generativity, and wisdom. Guided autobiography is one of several autobiographical methods that have been used in the past for the purpose of promoting an overall sense of psychological, physical, and emotional well-being in adults across the entire life span (Birren & Birren, 1996; Birren & Cochran, 2001; Birren & Hedlund, 1987; DeVries, Birren, & Deutchman, 1990). Related approaches include but are not limited to structured reminiscence, reminiscence therapy (Fry, 1991; Haight, 1991; Spector-Eisenberg, 1988), and life review (Butler, 1963, 1996). Although the common theme and focus of these methods is on the past life and memory processes, they are not synonymous but, rather, differ in a number of important ways.

Two features are common to autobiographical methods: (a) all make use of the past and (b) all involve memory processes. There are also some differences. One distinction between reminiscence and life review is that the former, though potentially restorative and generative and thus therapeutic, is nonevaluative. This distinction may not hold, however; several researchers have identified a number of types, styles, and functions of reminiscence. For example, in a qualitative analysis of reminiscence content in the elderly, Wong and Watt (1991) distinguished six types: integrative, instrumental (problem focused), transmissive, narrative (storytelling), escapist (defensive), and obsessive (ruminations). The integrative type is closely associated with the life review, which means that life review can be regarded as one type of reminiscence. Kovach (1991) talks about two styles of reminiscences referred to as validating and lamenting reminiscences. Validating reminiscences include positive self-appraisals, choices, joys, social connections, and past-to-present comparisons. Validating reminiscences can function to maintain and enhance a sense of meaning in life. Lamenting reminiscences are described as analytical and evaluative in order to resolve, reorganize, and reintegrate unresolved issues from the past. These can function to assist with meaning restoration. Webster (1993) identified eight functions of reminiscence, namely, boredom reduction, death preparation, identity, problem solving, conversation, intimacy maintenance, bitterness revival, and teach/inform. Inspired by the writing of Cohen (1998), Cappeliez and O'Rourke (2002a) proposed a broader classification scheme for the functions introduced by Wong and Watt (1991) and Webster (1993). These are the *intrapersonal* functions (e.g., integrative, death preparation, identity); *interpersonal* functions (e.g., narrative, intimacy maintenance), and *knowledge-based* functions (e.g., instrumental, transmissive). More recently, Cappeliez, Guindon, St. Jean, and Pelletier (2005) have formulated and tested a comprehensive model of the functions of reminiscence that describes the links between the intrapersonal, interpersonal, and knowledge-based functions, dimensions of psychological functioning, and specific outcomes. They subsequently introduced a reformulation of their model based on ongoing investigations of the relationship between the functions of reminiscence and health (Cappeliez & O'Rourke, 2006). In the context of this chapter, the addition of problem solving (plans, goals, and coping with life crises) to the identity and death preparation functions, as instances of *positive self-functions*, touches on issues of self-efficacy, life's meaning, coherence, and continuity of the self and thus are more conducive to the restoration, maintenance, or enhancement of meaning and purpose in life.

Life review and guided autobiography share similar features in that both are proactive in fostering a critical examination of lives, in challenging inconsistencies, and in assessing the quality of lives. Regarding program delivery, reminiscence and life review can be conducted in a one-on-one or in a group context. Guided autobiography, however, relies more on the group process and the sharing of life stories with others, referred to as *developmental exchange*. The concept of developmental exchange offers a distinction between guided autobiography and the methods of reminiscence and life review. While reminiscence and life review tend to be primarily cognitive and analytical, guided autobiography, through developmental exchange, has a greater potential to facilitate the activation and expression of emotional memories that when shared with others leads to the formation of strong affective bonds among group members.

Personal Meaning in Life

Personal meaning is concerned with the meaning in life. It is related to such constructs as value, purpose, coherence, and belief system. When we ask, "What is the meaning in life?" we are asking: "What is worth living for? What is the purpose in life?" Such questions call for value judgments and cannot be answered apart from one's belief system or worldview. Reker and Wong (1988) define personal meaning as the cognizance of order, coherence, and purpose in one's existence (reflecting a cognitive component), the pursuit and attainment of worthwhile goals (reflecting a motivational component), and an accompanying sense of fulfillment (reflecting an affective or emotional component). This conceptualization of personal meaning has been operationalized by the Life Attitude Profile (LAP; Reker & Peacock, 1981) and the Life Attitude Profile–Revised (LAP-R; Reker, 1992).

The LAP (Reker & Peacock, 1981) is a multidimensional measure consisting of seven life attitude dimensions: life purpose (having a mission in life, life goals, sense of direction, zest for life, fulfillment), will to meaning (striving to find concrete meaning in existence, an appreciation of life beyond the immediate given), future meaning (acceptance of future potentialities, determination to make the future meaningful), life control (freedom to make life choices, exercise of responsibility, perception of control over life events), death acceptance (acceptance of death as a natural aspect of life, absence of anxiety about death), existential vacuum (lack of purpose, lack of goals, apathy, alienation, feelings of indifference, free-floating anxiety), and goal seeking (desire to seek new goals, search for new and different experiences, to be on the move). Factor analysis of the LAP dimensions revealed three distinct higher order factors labeled Striving for Meaning (existential vacuum, goal seeking, will to meaning), Noological Actualization (life purpose, life control, will to meaning), and Existential Transcendence (death acceptance, future meaning to fulfill). A subsequent refinement of the scale (the LAP-R) resulted in the collapsing of the will-to-meaning and future-meaning dimensions into one, labeled coherence. Life control was relabeled choice/responsibleness to better reflect the item content. Factor analysis of the LAP-R also identified three higher order factors, namely, Found Meaning (purpose, coherence, choice/responsibleness), Search for Meaning (existential vacuum, goal seeking), and Death Acceptance.

In our opinion, the core function of autobiographical methods is to address the general question of how we give our lives meaning. Some of the meaning that we give our lives is through connection with our past, some is by bringing the past into the present, and some is by projecting the past and present into the future in a new way. The process is dynamic, analytical, and constructive. Being-in-the-world means knowing where you have been, fully experiencing the meaning of the moment in the here and now, and having an acute awareness of what is possible in the future. It is our premise that autobiographical methods play a key role in the restoration, maintenance, and enhancement of meaning and purpose in life. Meaning restoration may be achieved through the processes of transformation and cognitive restructuring; meaning maintenance aims to retain a sense of continuity and coherence in self-identity; and meaning enhancement aims to promote self-awareness, self-disclosure, and alternative views of self and life in general. What ensues from having meaning and purpose in life is an improved quality of life, increased self-esteem, a heightened sense of well-being, a sense of serenity, and greater wisdom.

Theoretical Speculations on the Link Between Autobiographical Methods and Meaning in Life

Reker and Chamberlain (2000), in an edited book entitled *Exploring Existential Meaning*, speculate that autobiographical methods, particularly the life review process, may be interwoven with their existential theory of personal meaning. Both methods and theory ask the same questions about life: "What is the purpose of my life?" "Is there meaning in my life?" "What is worth living for?" "How do events in my life fit into a larger context?" Answers to these questions can be explored and found through the life review process, culminating in the restoration, maintenance, and enhancement of a sense of meaning and purpose in life. Within the field of nursing, Kovach (1991) proposed a model in which reminiscence is seen as "a source of self-referent knowledge, which influences a person's self-worth. It views reminiscence as a process of acquiring personal existential meaning and as a mechanism for adapting to stress" (p. 14).

A number of authors have theorized about the potential of autobiographical methods in restoring, maintaining, or enhancing a sense of personal meaning in life. In a discussion of life review as psychotherapy, Butler (1996) noted:

> There is a moral dimension to the life review because one looks evaluatively at one's self, one's behaviour, one's guilt. One stands in judgment

> of the life one has led. Atonement, expiation, redemption, reconciliation, and *meaning in life* [italics added for emphasis] are powerful potential positive outcomes of the life review. (p. 56)

In a chapter of a book exploring aging and biography, Birren and Birren (1996) summarized a number of positive outcomes in research and practice with guided autobiography. Among the list of outcomes is "greater sense of meaning in life." In fact, Birren explicitly acknowledges this potential by incorporating the topic of meaning in life into his method of guided autobiography. The writing and sharing of the details of one's life by group members has the potential effect of raising the participant's level of conscious awareness of what was, is, and will in the future become meaningful. Furthermore, within the context of family life education, Brian deVries et al. (1990) note that as applied to guided autobiography, "the unique features of this approach—its guided nature and the group process—have special potential for … assisting in the search for meaning in one's life" (p. 6).

Webster and McCall (1999) implicitly acknowledge the potential of reminiscence for "meaning restoration" through two reminiscence functions: Identity and Death Preparation. According to Webster and McCall (1999) the Identity function measures "how we use our past in an existential manner to discover, clarify and crystallize important dimensions of our sense of who we are" (p. 77). The Death Preparation function "assesses the way we use our past when thoughts of our own mortality are salient and may contribute to a sense of closure and calmness" (p. 76). This view suggests that one benefit of the Identity and Death Preparation functions is to restore, maintain, or enhance meaning and purpose in life.

An advocate of the importance of personal meaning in promoting health and successful aging, Wong (1989) identified the integrative type of reminiscence as playing an important role in the maintenance of a sense of meaning in the face of illness, pain, and personal death.

For Kenyon, Clark, and deVries (2001), meaning making is seen as an integral part of the narrative process of telling our life stories. In that sense, *restorying* is meaning making in the context of past and present experiences and personal choice. At each restorying moment, an old meaning is transformed into a new one, taking the individual to a higher and deeper level of understanding and thus toward self-transcendence and ordinary wisdom. Kenyon (1996) states, "Therefore, what is needed here, and what can be provided through storytelling, is access to new stories, new wrinkles in established patterns; in other words, new sources of meaning." (p. 32). In effect, meaning restoration is the core process within the narrative approach.

Finally, a web search that included the key words *reminiscence, guided autobiography, life review*, and *meaning in life* identified a large number of sources linking autobiographical methods to personal meaning. Although many of these sources describe linkages at the theoretical and conceptual levels, it is nevertheless amazing how frequently and consistently a sense of meaning and purpose in life is described as either "an integral part of" or "a benefit of" autobiographical methods.

Studies of Autobiographical Methods and Meaning in Life

A good example of how meaning and purpose in life forms an integral part of the method of guided autobiography is a qualitative study conducted by Hedlund (1987). Hedlund used grounded-theory methodology to examine how participants in guided autobiography develop meaning in life as reflected through their autobiographical accounts. She identified several key sources of meaning in life, namely, personal growth and development, personal relationships, career, belief, service to others, and pleasure. Her inductive methodology gave rise to five testable hypotheses: First, the contents of childhood experiences are related to the contents of meaning in life in adulthood. Second, meaning in life is formulated in early adolescence and young adulthood. Third, the earliest source of meaning in life focuses on issues of personal growth and development. Fourth, once issues of personal development have been resolved, meaning in life remains stable across adulthood. Fifth and finally, with increasing age, the content of meaning in life moves toward sources external to the self.

Hedlund's (1987) observations are intriguing in that they help to explain why older adults tend to recall a disproportionately large number of autobiographical events, referred to as the *reminiscence bump*, from the late adolescent–early adulthood period. Although there have been other explanations offered for the reminiscence bump (e.g., see Rubin, Rahhal, & Poon, 1998; Schroots, van Dijkum, & Assink, 2004), there is a large degree of convergence on a developmental interpretation. Emerging adulthood (15 to 25 years) is an active time of goal setting, life planning (e.g., education, career), and identity development. A meaning-based explanation for the bump phenomenon is consistent with the views of Cappeliez, Guindon, et al. (2005), who proposed that memories within the bump are accessible and salient because they relate to the development of goals and personal identity and that older adults use these memories to construct a purposeful, coherent, and consistent self. In testing this hypothesis, Cappeliez, O'Rourke, and Chaudhury (2005) found that for a group of older women memories from the bump period (a) contained a high proportion of events in the education and work domains, (b) were characterized by a higher degree of emotional content, and (c) contained a stronger emphasis on self compared to recent past memories. Moreover, an analysis of the dream content of these women showed that dreams with temporal reference to the bump period contained a higher proportion of content related to personal goals, wishes, and ideals compared to dreams with content related to the recent past (Cappeliez, 2008;

Cappeliez et al., 2005). Finally, when dreams were coded in terms of Wong's (1995) six reminiscence types, a high proportion of bump dreams (70%) were integrative, whereas recent past dreams were more evenly distributed among the six types (Cappeliez, 2008). Thus, for older adults, personal memories from the reminiscence bump constitute a benchmark and play a central organizing role in autobiographical knowledge. They function to maintain self-consistency and a sense of personal meaning in later life.

Empirical studies on the benefit of autobiographical methods in restoring, maintaining, or enhancing personal meaning in life are few. A thorough review of the literature by Haight (1991) points to life satisfaction, self-esteem, depression, morale, psychological well-being, activity level, mental stimulation, anxiety, and ego integrity as the most common outcome measures in published research and reports. Direct reference to meaning and purpose in life is noticeably absent from the list, suggesting that at least prior to 1991, personal meaning had received little attention. Since 1991, personal meaning continues to receive little attention as a researchable outcome variable. This lack of attention is puzzling in view of the numerous theoretical speculations that link autobiographical methods to meaning and purpose in life. Of the outcome measures that have received attention, ego integrity is of particular interest in the present context precisely because Erikson (1963) saw the positive resolution of his final stage as reflecting a basic acceptance of one's life as having been inevitable, appropriate, and, in short, meaningful. Therefore, studies examining the impact of autobiographical methods on ego integrity can provide indirect evidence in support of the construct of meaning in life.

One such correlational study was conducted by Taft and Nehrke (1990). Thirty nursing home residents (15 males, 15 females), average age 84.0 years, from west-central Wisconsin were administered a 13-item reminiscence questionnaire developed by Romaniuk and Romaniuk (1981). The participants were asked to choose yes, no, or not sure to indicate whether they used reminiscence in the way described by each item. Factor analysis of the items revealed three primary functions of reminiscence: to teach or entertain, to solve problems, and to conduct a life review. Two additional questions were asked about the frequency of reminiscence: (a) When you are with others (interpersonal), how often do your conversations turn to past experiences? and (b) When you are alone (intrapersonal), how often do your thoughts turn to past experiences? Ratings were on a 5-point Likert scale ranging from "a few times a year" to "several times a day." An overall reminiscence frequency score was also calculated. Ego integrity was measured with a 10-item, 7-point Likert scale based on Erikson's (1963) description of behaviors and attitudes of the two alternative solutions to the final stage of development—ego integrity or despair.

The results of the correlational analysis are presented in Figure 18.1. As can be seen, reminiscence frequency showed little association with ego integrity,

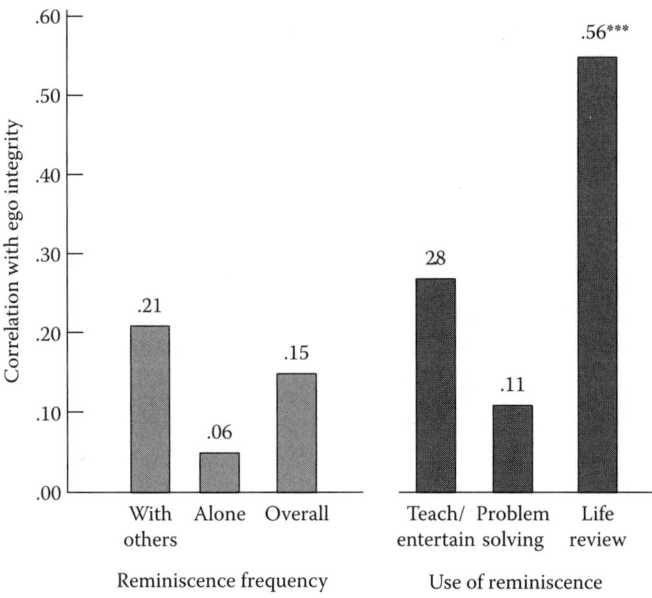

Figure 18.1 The relation of reminiscence frequency and function to ego integrity. N = 30; ***$p < .001$. (Adapted from Taft, L. B., and Nehrke, M. F., *International Journal of Aging and Human Development*, 30, 189–196, 1990.)

sharing less than 1% (reminiscing alone) to slightly over 4% (reminiscing with others) of the variance. Of the three reminiscence functions, only life review was significantly related to ego integrity, sharing 31% of the variance. Two important conclusions can be drawn from these findings. First, the function that reminiscence serves in promoting ego integrity is more important than the frequency of reminiscence activity. Second, it is the life review type of reminiscence, involving analysis and reintegration, that contributes most to the attainment of ego integrity and thus to the maintenance of personal meaning in life. In speculating about the lower association of teach/entertain and problem solving to ego integrity (8% and 1% of the variance, respectively), Taft and Nehrke (1990) suggest that teach/entertain may be related more to Erikson's stage of generativity/stagnation, whereas the problem-solving function may be more relevant to the intimacy/isolation stage.

A number of empirical studies have investigated reminiscence frequency and the use of reminiscence functions as a vehicle for restoring a sense of meaning and purpose in life. Older adults confronted with perceived or societal alienation, role loss, physical declines, and/or chronic illness and who are thus "existentially challenged" may find that their past provides a basis from which a sense of personal meaning may be extracted. In one such study, Quackenbush and Barnett (1995) assessed the extent to which community-residing older adults, average age 73.5 years, reflect on their "past in an effort to enhance self understanding or to establish a sense of meaning" (p. 172). Reminiscence affect (positive and negative) was also assessed. The primary goal was to relate the reminiscence function of enhancement of self-understanding to the personality trait of introversion/extraversion and the life attitude of existential vacuum (the absence of meaning and purpose in life). They found that existential vacuum was positively related to a tendency to engage in reminiscence in an effort to enhance self-understanding ($r = .22, p < .05$). Given the correlational nature of the study, however, the direction of influence is open to speculation as is the possibility of a third variable explanation. In addressing these issues, Quackenbush and Barnett (1995) suggested that either a frustrated need for meaning (i.e., existential vacuum) elicits enhancement of self-understanding or that enhancement of self-understanding elicits the experience of an existential vacuum insofar as the reviewer may begin to question his or her current sources of personal meaning. It is also possible that a third "personality" variable (e.g., introspectiveness), defined as the tendency to focus on thoughts and feelings about the self, elicits both the experience of an existential vacuum and engagement in the reminiscence function of enhancing self-understanding.

In a similar vein, in a study of 140 community-based and nursing home residents, average age about 71 years, Fry (1991) found that frequency of reminiscence was negatively correlated with purpose in life, life control, and future meaning (indicators of found meaning) but was positively correlated with existential vacuum and goal seeking (indicators of the search for meaning). The results are presented in Figure 18.2. Fry (1991) suggested that "older individuals still struggling to find concrete meaning in personal existence are likely to resort more frequently to reminiscence activity" (p. 323).

Cappeliez and O'Rourke (2002a) examined the extent to which personality traits and existential concerns predicted frequency of reminiscence and reminiscence functions, as measured by Webster's (1993) Reminiscence Functions Scale. The ability of existential concerns to predict reminiscence frequency and function is of special significance. Based on the theoretical argument, made by several authors cited earlier—namely, that reminiscence plays a crucial role in the search for meaning, in the establishment of a sense of identity, and in fostering a sense of coherence—it was expected that measures of these existential constructs would predict both the frequency of reminiscence and its various uses, particularly the use of the intrapersonal functions, although Cappeliez and O'Rourke did not offer such a specific hypothesis.

Eighty-nine community-residing older adults (66% women), average age 67 years, range 57–92, took part in the study. The NEO Five Factor Inventory (NEO-FFI; Costa & McCrae, 1992) was used to measure personality; the Life Attitude Profile–Revised (LAP-R: Reker, 1992) was used to measure existential

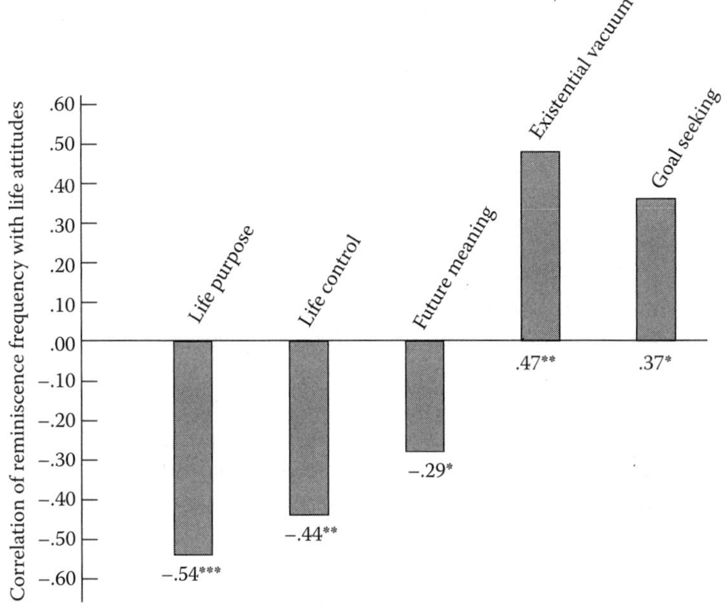

Figure 18.2 The association of reminiscence frequency with meaning in life. N = 140; $*p < .05$; $**p < .01$; $***p < .001$. (Adapted from Fry, P. S., *International Journal of Aging and Human Development*, 33, 311–326, 1991.)

concerns; and the Reminiscence Functions Scale (RFS; Webster, 1993) was used to measure reminiscence functions. Using hierarchical regression analysis, with personality traits entered first, followed by the existential variables, Cappeliez and O'Rourke (2002a) found that the combination of personality traits and life attitudes predicted total frequency of reminiscence and four intrapersonal functions of reminiscence: boredom reduction, death preparation, identity, and bitterness revival. The same variables did not predict the interpersonal or the knowledge-based functions. Once personality traits were taken into account, goal seeking added significant predictive power for total reminiscence frequency and the four intrapersonal functions. Specifically, a lack of desire to achieve new goals, to be on the move, and to seek new challenges added to the prediction. In addition, existential vacuum was a significant predictor of the death preparation function of reminiscence, suggesting that a sense of apathy, alienation, and lack of direction triggers the use of reminiscence to prepare for death. Cappeliez and O'Rourke (2002a) concluded, "Taken together, these results portray a more frequent reminiscer as one who values memories over new challenges and who seeks in memories, rather than in planned actions, materials to fight boredom and lack of stimulation and to reflect about death and old conflicts" (p. 121). Their findings are consistent with the notion that the experience of existential vacuum, lack of goals, and an overall sense of meaninglessness is a main motive for certain types of reminiscence activity.

In an interesting extension of the previous study, Cappeliez and O'Rourke (2002b) performed a cluster analysis on the scores of four intrapersonal functions of reminiscence (boredom reduction, death preparation, identity, and bitterness revival). Three distinct clusters were identified: negative reminiscers, infrequent reminiscers, and meaning seekers. Of interest are the *meaning seekers*, those individuals who on the basis of personality traits, life attitudes, and stress were characterized in terms of greater use of reminiscence for boredom reduction, death preparation, and identity and showed a greater tendency toward openness to experience compared to individuals in the other two clusters. Cappeliez and O'Rourke (2002b) came to several conclusions: "First, meaning seekers use reminiscence to fill a void of stimulation in their current life…. Second, they reminisce for the purpose of establishing and maintaining a coherent sense of self and life meaning and coping with thoughts of one's mortality" (p. 263).

So far, the empirical evidence has been correlational in nature, leaving us open to a number of alternative explanations for the various findings. Controlled studies that assess cause–effect relationships are needed to determine the influence of autobiographical methods on meaning and purpose in life. In one of a very few experimental studies, Spector-Eisenberg (1988) examined the effect of reminiscence therapy on meaning in life in institutionalized older adults residing in three separate nursing homes in West Los Angeles, California. Sixty volunteer participants were randomly assigned to one of three groups: individual reminiscence therapy, current events placebo, and pretest–posttest control. Nine participants did not complete the study, leaving 17 (mean age, 85 years) in the reminiscence group; 18 (mean age, 85 years) in the placebo group; and 16 (mean age, 82 years) in the control group.

The individualized reminiscence therapy consisted of 10 weekly 45-minute interviews conducted by a counselor–student research assistant. Interviews were structured in that the counselor presented a specific topic to be explored each week. For example, the topic for the first week was "happiest time." The interview began as follows: "Today, I would like you to think back into your past and try to recall the happiest time of your life and tell me about it." All interviews were tape-recorded. Other topics included memories of parents, siblings, own children, school and early childhood, the most difficult time, and favorite era.

The current events placebo was structured in a similar manner. Weekly topics included thoughts and feelings about the nursing staff, activities engaged in, food served at the nursing home, who comes to visit, opinions regarding the current president, current health status, friends at the nursing home, relationship with doctors, the nuclear age, and society's treatment of the elderly.

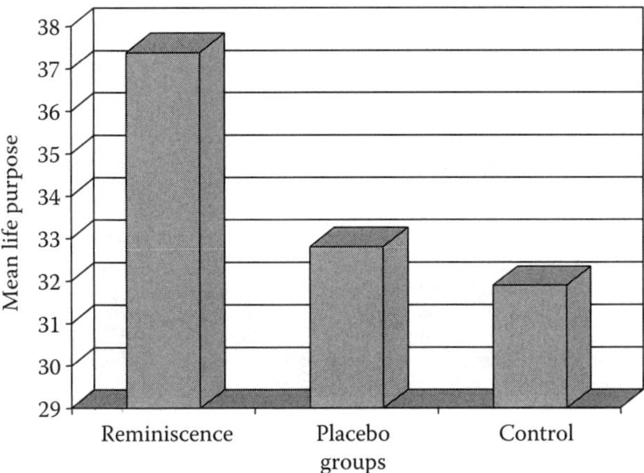

Figure 18.3 Life purpose (adjusted for pretest scores) as a function of reminiscence and control groups. (Adapted from Spector-Eisenberg, W., *The Influence of Structured Reminiscence on Meaning and Purpose in Life in the Institutionalized Elderly* [Doctoral dissertation], University of California, Los Angeles, 1988.)

Shortly before and immediately after the 10-week treatment program, all participants completed a modified version of the Life Attitude Profile (LAP; Reker & Peacock, 1981). The modification involved changing the item stem to a question format (interrogatory format). For example, "I have discovered a satisfying life purpose" was changed to "Have you discovered a satisfying life purpose?" This modification made it much easier for the nursing home participants to understand the items and to respond appropriately. The LAP items were read to all participants, and the responses were recorded by the counselor.

The results for life purpose are shown in Figure 18.3. The posttest results, adjusted for pretest scores, revealed a statistically significant difference ($p = .014$) for the Life Purpose dimension in favor of the reminiscence group compared to both the placebo and the pretest–posttest controls. No statistically significant differences were found for the latter two groups. Life Purpose refers to having life goals; having a mission in life; having a sense of direction from the past, in the present, and toward the future; and having experienced fulfillment. In addition, although not statistically significant by conventional standards, there was a tendency for the reminiscence group to score higher on the Life Control ($p = .117$) and the Future Meaning ($p = .173$) dimensions compared to the attention placebo and pretest–posttest control group (see Figures 18.4 and 18.5). Life Control refers to having the freedom to make life choices and taking responsibility for one's actions. Future Meaning refers to future fulfillment, the acceptance of future potentialities, and positive expectations concerning oneself and one's future life.

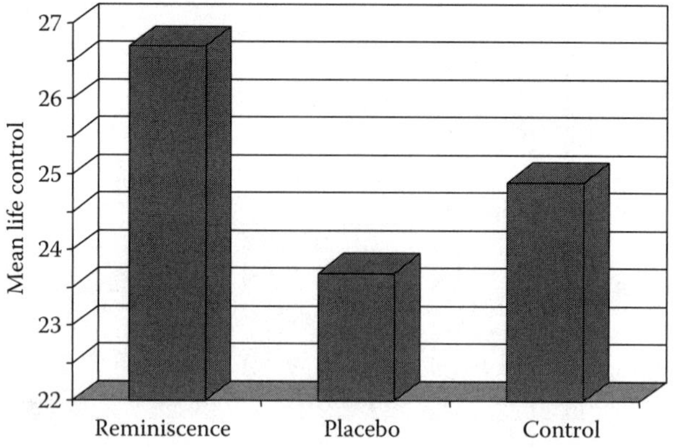

Figure 18.4 Life control (adjusted for pretest scores) as a function of reminiscence and control groups. (Adapted from Spector-Eisenberg, W., *The Influence of Structured Reminiscence on Meaning and Purpose in Life in the Institutionalized Elderly* [Doctoral dissertation], University of California, Los Angeles, 1988.)

In a quasi-experimental study, Georgemiller and Maloney (1984) examined the effect of a structured reminiscence program on pre–post measures of meaning in life, religiosity, self-esteem, and attitudes toward death. Thirty-four older adults (mean age, 75 years), recruited from five Chicago-area senior adult centers, took part in a life review workshop consisting of seven weekly meetings of 90 minutes each. Participants also completed a posttreatment workshop evaluation form. A control group of 29 subjects was matched on age, sex, and activity (e.g., card playing, sewing, envelope stuffing) during the life review time period. The structured life review consisted of mini-lectures

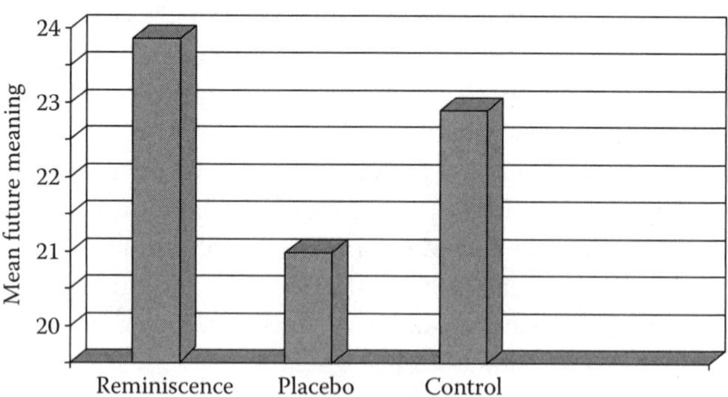

Figure 18.5 Future meaning (adjusted for pretest scores) as a function of reminiscence and control groups. (Adapted from Spector-Eisenberg, W., *The Influence of Structured Reminiscence on Meaning and Purpose in Life in the Institutionalized Elderly* [Doctoral dissertation], University of California, Los Angeles, 1988.)

followed by a group sharing of autobiographical vignettes on a variety of themes (e.g., significant crises in my life, experience with death, development of beliefs and values). The only significant finding was that the life review group decreased in denial of death. Clinical observations and responses to the workshop evaluation pointed to dramatic benefits for some participants and an increase in social reminiscence, good feelings, and improved self-understanding in others. The findings are in line with the existential perspective that individuals who show less fear of death and who are able to confront their own mortality see their lives as more fulfilling and meaningful (Wong, Reker, & Gesser, 1994). Thus, a decrease in denial of death would support the death preparation function of reminiscence as a vehicle for enhancing a sense of meaning and purpose in life.

Westerhof, Bohlmeijer, and Valenkamp (2004) designed a reminiscence program, Searching for Meaning in Life, for Dutch elderly subjects to stimulate personal meaning (including sources of personal meaning) and to decrease depressive symptoms. The program consisted of 12 sessions of 2.5 hours each. Themes addressed cognitive and motivational processes as well as different sources of meaning in life (e.g., first memories and early scents, norms and values, activities, meaning of life and spirituality, life-span and turning points, and identity). Fifty-seven older adults (mean age, 66 years; range, 50–81) received the reminiscence intervention. A comparison group of 57 participants matched on age, gender, educational level, marital status, and employment status were drawn from the larger representative Dutch Aging Survey. Personal meaning was assessed before and after intervention in both groups; depression was assessed before and after but only in the intervention group. Difference scores on depression between pre- and postintervention were used to split the group into three: upper tertile (large improvement), middle tertile (small improvement), and lower tertile (no improvement). The results showed that at pretest, the intervention group was more negative and more focused on self compared to the comparison group, indicating that the participants in the program initially comprised a self-preoccupied group with impoverished meaning. Following intervention, the personal meaning profile was more positive with regard to self-evaluations and evaluations of social relations but still below that of the comparison group. Most notable, the subgroup that showed the largest improvement in depression scores showed the largest change in positive meaning attributed to the self and social relations; those individuals with no improvement or those with small improvement in depression showed little change in personal meaning. Given that no control group was used in this study, the before and after differences in depression and personal meaning may not be attributable to the intervention itself. The systematic pattern of results do, however, provide some evidence that a structured reminiscence program for older adults can alleviate depression and promote personal meaning in life.

Thus, individualized structured reminiscence with community-residing and institutionalized older adults appears to be a viable tool for increasing perceived meaning and purpose in life. More experimental studies need to be conducted with different samples, different reminiscence formats, and different types of reminiscence functions before firm conclusions can be drawn.

The results of quantitative studies provide important information regarding the impact that autobiographical methods may have on such subsequent outcomes as meaning and purpose in life. Such findings do not, however, fully address the underlying processes of meaning making per se. Herein lies the strength of the narrative approach. The earlier work of Kaufman (1986) and Gubrium (1993) with community-residing and institutionalized older adults are good examples of how the narrative approach helps us understand the depth and significance of storytelling as a meaning-making activity.

Schiff and Cohler (2001) demonstrated the usefulness of the narrative approach in identifying the underlying processes of meaning making in a qualitative study of Holocaust survivors and how they narrate their past and assign meaning to it. Three-hour-long in-depth interviews on a wide range of topics (e.g., life before the war; ghetto and camp experiences, feelings of loss) were tape-recorded and transcribed for 20 Nazi concentration camp survivors (13 women, 7 men). The emphasis was on the survivors' interpretations of survival. In about half the interviews, survivors found meaning in what happened in the past by relying on current meaning and projecting that meaning backward into time. Schiff and Cohler note that "by this motion of reading the afterward into the before, the narrative of survival thus attains wholeness or purpose" (p.133). Moreover, they found that for many survivors, purpose is found and also negated, meaning is found but so is meaninglessness, coherence is found but so is incoherence. These tendencies appear to coexist rather than cancel each other out. Schiff and Cohler (2001) comment:

> We argue that it is significant that two contradictory interpretations arise and that sometimes they appear together. Indeed, remembering a troubled past may be more complex than we had previously theorized. Our understanding of these narratives points to what Jacob Lomranz (1995) has called the "paradoxical self" which survivors appear to inhabit. Survivors function very well in certain areas of their lives and thoughts and in other places poorly; there is a sense of *putting together* along with *pulling apart.* (p. 134)

Their findings illuminate how a troubled past can be given meaning after the fact. Their findings also clearly reveal the paradoxical nature of human thought, feeling, and action that cannot be easily revealed through structured, externally interpreted approaches.

That being said, it remains important to validate the process of meaning making through autobiographical methods by demonstrating that it leads to expected changes in the individual's personal meaning system. A central feature of the will to meaning is to preserve one's identity and to promote a sense of coherence. Individuals strive to find unity in their lives by ensuring that their differentiated selves remain integrated. The question of whether guided autobiography could enhance awareness of the self was first explored by Reedy and Birren (1980). In a pre–post assessment of 45 participants in a 10-session guided autobiography program, the real, ideal, and social-image components of the self were found to move closer together. Moreover, participants' views of generalized others moved more closely to their own views of self. In the absence of a control group, however, firm conclusions regarding the effectiveness of guided autobiography in promoting self-awareness and integration cannot be drawn. More controlled outcome studies are needed to follow up on these promising leads.

In one such study, Spanish researchers Botella and Feixas (1992–1993) provide a convincing demonstration of how the method of guided autobiography can lead to a reconstruction of the personal meaning system of older participants. A small sample of eight older adults, average age 68 years, took part in 10 guided autobiography group sessions for 1.5 hours each week over a three-month period. Their approach was similar to Birren and Cochran's (2001) guided autobiography but was specifically adapted for use with older adults in that it included only a short sensitizing lecture about each topic (30 minutes) followed by group discussion (60 minutes). Ten individuals with similar demographic characteristics formed a pre–post control group. The degree of reconstruction was assessed in both groups through the administration of George Kelly's repertory grid at the initial and final sessions. The repertory grid is a procedure in which significant people in the participant's life (including actual self, ideal self, and social-image self) are rated on a number of elicited constructs (e.g., caring vs. callous) using a 5-point Likert-type scale. Results showed that the guided autobiography group underwent significant reconstruction of their construing of past life experiences compared to the control group. Furthermore, the self-system of the guided autobiography group revealed a significant reduction in the distance between ideal versus actual self and ideal versus social-image self compared to the control group. A significant difference was not found for actual self versus social-image self. Although preliminary, these findings suggest that participation in guided autobiography can lead to significant positive changes in the reconstruction and meaningful integration of past life experiences.

Personal Autobiographical Reflections and Meaning in Life

Personal autobiographical reflection may offer additional insight into how the method of guided autobiography could lead to a reconstruction of one's personal meaning system. According to Birren, guided autobiography assists in the exploration of the inside of lives. The goal is not to effect purposeful change but to provide individuals the opportunity to express their existential or experiential selves. There are no externally imposed value-centered notions about what should be changed. Thus, guided autobiography "is *not* therapy … Nevertheless, it often can be therapeutic" (Birren & Cochran, 2001, p. 9 [italics in original]).

Of the various components of guided autobiography, the sharing of experiences with others in the group, known as the *developmental exchange*, is a potentially powerful tool for eliciting and working through the emotions attached to personal memories. Thornton and Collins (2007) describe the exchange process as a transformative learning experience in which participants "learn to re-experience life events and understand their lives from a new perspective" (p. 1). Based on the responses of 38 older participants to the question "What am I learning?" Thornton and Collins found that in relation to meaning in life, nearly all participants reported expanded meaning structures and alternative expressions of meaning.

Resolving Survivor Guilt: Assigning Meaning Backward

In the summer of 1985, the first author (Gary Reker) had the opportunity to participate in a two-week guided autobiography course organized and conducted by James Birren at the University of Southern California. The participants comprised a mixture of young, early middle-, and late-middle-aged adults. Each day was structured along a traditional format: a short lecture on topics related to developmental psychology and autobiography, a brief sensitizing session to introduce the topic for the next class, the exchange of life stories in a small-group environment, and the writing of a two-page autobiographical essay on a selected topic as a homework assignment. Resolving survivor guilt is his story on the theme "The History of Your Experiences With or Ideas About Death."

> Initially, I intellectualized everything and found it difficult to deal with my emotional side. As others in the group began to share their past experiences, I witnessed a great deal of emotional material being offered in the developmental exchange, which turned out to be a good laxative for my "emotional constipation."
>
> When I was a teen-ager my best friend was killed in a car-train collision. He had just left my house to go home to get his ice skates (it was New Years Day, 1961). He needed his skates because minutes earlier we witnessed two girls on whom we had crushes, head for the local pond to skate. We were both in the car as he backed out of our driveway. However, I had forgotten something in the house but Dewey was in a rush to get his skates so he let me out and he drove off. He lived only about a mile from our house. He never came back. Half an hour later I phoned his house but he had not arrived. Knowing that Dewey was a

bit of a prankster, I figured that he decided to go to the pond without me. I left on my own figuring that I would catch up with him at the pond. I never saw him.

When I returned home later that afternoon, I was told Dewey had been killed at the railway crossing near his home and dragged by the train for about ¼ of a mile. Thinking that I had been with him, my family and the police had been looking for me along the railway tracks. Ever since that day, I have wondered why I was spared. I should have been with him and perhaps could have prevented the accident from happening by spotting the train in time.

This was the experience with death that I reconstructed in the guided autobiography class in 1985. I recall that on that day, a lot of bottled-up emotional material was shared with the class. I literally broke down emotionally. However, the support received from the group was overwhelming and led eventually to a resolution of "survivor guilt" that I had harbored for so many years. It was the group process that helped me to attach new meaning to the emotional memory associated with the unfortunate accident and the loss of my best friend. That emotional memory remains vivid today even though the actual facts of the memory of the accident may have dimmed over time. The method of guided autobiography, particularly the component of developmental exchange, reaffirmed my belief on the benefit of this approach in restoring, maintaining, and enhancing a sense of meaning and purpose in life.

Expanded Horizons: The Meaning of Compassion

The third author (Cheryl Svensson) has been a guided autobiography facilitator for several years. Finding the true meaning of compassion is her story on the theme "The History of Your Experiences With or Ideas About Death."

> My personal "ah-hah" experience came during my own guided autobiography class, when I was writing and sharing on the theme death. As it happens, I have an up-close and personal relationship with death from a very early age. My father was killed in a car accident when I was twelve years old. At that time in my life, I felt that the sun rose and set on my father. There was no one who could ever take his place for me. The car accident had been a deadly one; my father had been driving, but also in the car were my aunt, my sister-in-law, and my four-year-old niece. They were hit head-on by a drunk driver, and everyone but my sister-in-law was killed instantly.
>
> With a sudden and unexpected tragedy like this, many, many people are affected by the loss of lives. My sister-in-law remained in a coma in the hospital for weeks … not knowing her only child was dead. Aunts,

> uncles, cousins, siblings, children, friends … all were there to grieve and mourn the untimely loss of lives. But even so, I felt "alone." I felt that no one else could possibly feel as bereft, abandoned, alone in grief as I did. I never allowed another in … not my mother, brothers or sister … to share in the sorrow, to help understand the tragedy and to go on. I wore the loss and sorrow as my own armor … and burden.
>
> It was not until I was sharing my writing on this event in my small group that light began to shine in. One member of the group, a widow, innocently said after I finished reading, "Oh … that must have been terrible for your mother." I had never before put myself in my mother's place to possibly imagine how it must have been for her … a stay-at-home mom with two children to raise … alone … and to lose her husband at only 50 years of age.
>
> The weight of nearly forty years carrying the burden of unshared grief began to dissipate. I realized, it was not only about me and my loss; there were so many others who shared in my grief … and still do.
>
> Through this, I learned the true meaning of compassion … with others as well as with myself. I was able to step outside my own perspective and see and share the joys and sorrows of existence with others.

In her role as a facilitator of guided autobiography, Cheryl Svensson also gained new meanings and wisdom from listening to the shared stories of others. She puts it this way:

> I have learned something from all of them who have willingly shared their life story. Many participants in GAB [guided autobiography] classes have reported new insights that have resulted in life changing behaviors after reading their stories in the small group. It appears that the dynamics of writing, reading, and getting feedback from other trusted members, heightens self-learning. To illustrate, one older woman included a reference in her writings to her ex-husband who had left her and their three small children, for another woman, years before. Near the end of the class, after she had examined her values, she understood, "No one was to blame" … for what had happened. Rather, she realized that her values had been completely different from her ex-husband and they never should have married in the first place. She was then free to let go of the anger and resentment she had carried for decades.

Exploring the Inside of Lives: Transformative Learning

The second author (James Birren) is the pioneer of the guided autobiography approach. His story is a story of what he has learned from the many life stories told by participants of guided autobiography since its inception over 30 years ago.

I have learned much from listening to the stories of lives by the people who lived them. I have become convinced that the histories of individual lives have much to add to our social and behavioral sciences as well as increasing the appreciation of what people have lived through. Life stories provide the details of historical events from the bottom up, from the details of everyday life as they fit into the "top down histories" of wars, depressions, prosperities, and natural environmental events. For example, at age 16 one person had a scholarship to the Julliard School of Music in New York. Then a tornado blew away the family house in St. Louis and she had to return home from New York to help the family but she never got back to music again. She told the details of this life story at age 75. For another participant, growing up on a farm during the Great Depression of the 1930s was described by one person as having "a good life." There was much to eat and parents traded things with their neighbors.

Such differences in the details of lives led me to the view that the study of the personal accounts of lives and their interpretations by the people that lived them represent an important addition to the behavioral and social sciences. They supplement the knowledge gained from laboratory research and designed studies. Listening to life stories has led me to face the paradox that, as individuals, we are so different in the experiences of growing up and growing old, yet we also emerge as being so much the same as we reveal our emotions and feelings about the past. I have learned that studying individual differences and similarities can be enhanced by analysis of the narratives of individuals.

Participation in an autobiography group has taught me that there are several benefits. Listening to the life stories of other persons primes or releases memories that may be long forgotten. All persons have large stores of memories that are just below the level of spontaneous recall. Hearing the life story of another person results in a frequent response, "Oh, what you just said reminds me of something that happened to me." Listening to others has primed my memories about many things such as school, work, family, and health.

Another benefit of listening to the life stories of others is a growing realization that beneath our public surfaces we are similar. This leads to an increasing acceptance or attachment of other persons. I find that autobiography groups often want to continue and have frequent reunions to share their lives. New friendships grow out of sharing our life stories.

Another outcome of sharing our life stories in a group is the release of energy for new activities. Telling our life story is not an end or conclusion. It commonly leads to answering the implicit question, "Where do I want to go from here?" Volunteering for public service, learning a new skill like painting, writing or other activities are frequent next steps in participating in an autobiography group.

> I have learned that getting out my memoirs in a group, adding up my memories help me to decide who I am and where I want to go. It also leaves my life story for family and friends for them to learn what I have learned from life.
>
> Guided autobiography has taught me that adding up one's life often leads to new perspectives that fit into the concept of wisdom. Wisdom requires experience to provide a basis for today's and tomorrow's decisions. Telling one's life story and listening to the life stories of others releases wisdom for our use and the use of our followers.

Conclusion

Taken together, the theoretical speculations, the quantitative and qualitative findings, and the testimonial of personal reflection point to the potential of autobiographical methods in restoring, maintaining, and enhancing a sense of meaning and purpose in life. Two key meaning-making processes, transformation and transcendence, are activated through autobiographical inquiry. Transformation results in changes in thoughts, feelings, and actions. Transformational processes do not change one's experiences or situations; rather, they impact the way one relates to personal experiences and situations (i.e., a change in perspective taking). One outcome of transformational processes is a restructured and expanded worldview and a widening and deepening of one's personal identity. Individuals undergoing a transformational experience are able to transform old meanings into new ones and project those meanings forward, thereby taking them to broader and deeper levels of understanding and the real meaning of life.

Transcendence is a meaning-making process in which individuals climb above or go beyond the experiences or situations presented to them in life. By rising above the contradictions, absurdities, and conflicts that characterize the human condition, individuals become more aware of where they have been, who they are, and where they are going. One outcome of transcendence processes is the expansion of one's horizon and the ability to "see the bigger picture," accompanied by a sense of connectedness with self, with others, and with all living things.

Three directives are offered for future research. First, in order to enhance a sense of meaning and purpose in life, more emphasis needs to be placed on facilitating the recall of "emotional" memories, particularly among elderly residing in institutions and nursing homes. Examples include the use of music-based life review (e.g., Ashida, 2000; Bennett & Maas, 1988) and spiritual life review (e.g., Melia, 2003), both of which contain a strong affective component. Second, in addition to assessing outcomes, more research is needed to understand the underlying meaning-making processes inherent in life review, reminiscence, guided autobiography, and narrative approaches. Third, future applications of autobiographical methods need to tailor the different functions of reminiscence to the achievement of meaning in life at various transition points across the life span.

References

Ashida, S. (2000). The effect of reminiscence music therapy sessions on changes in depressive symptoms in elderly persons with dementia. *Journal of Music Therapy, 37*, 170–182.

Bennett, S. L., & Maas, F. (1988). The effect of music-based life review on the life satisfaction and ego integrity of elderly people. *British Journal of Occupational Therapy, 5*, 433–436.

Birren, J. E., & Birren, B. A. (1996). Autobiography: Exploring the self and encouraging development. In J. E. Birren, G. M. Kenyon, J. E. Ruth, J. J. F. Schroots, & T. Svensson (Eds.), *Aging and biography: Explorations in adult development* (pp. 283–299). New York, NY: Springer.

Birren, J. E., & Cochran, K. N. (2001). *Telling the stories of life through guided autobiography groups*. Baltimore, MA: Johns Hopkins University Press.

Birren. J. E., & Hedlund, B. (1987). Contributions of autobiography to developmental psychology. In N. Eisenberg (Ed.), *Contemporary topics in developmental psychology* (pp. 394–415). New York, NY: Wiley.

Botella, L., & Feixas, G. (1992–1993). The autobiographical group: A tool for the reconstruction of past life experience with the aged. *International Journal of Aging and Human Development, 36*, 303–319.

Butler, R. N. (1963). The life review: An interpretation of reminiscence in the aged. *Psychiatry, 26*, 65–76.

Butler, R. N. (1996). Life review. In J. E. Birren (Ed.), *Encyclopedia of gerontology: Vol. 1. A–K*. New York, NY: Academic Press.

Cappeliez, P. (2008). An explanation of the reminiscence bump in the dreams of older adults in terms of life goals and identity. *Self and Identity, 7*, 25–33.

Cappeliez, P., Guindon, M., St. Jean, G., & Pelletier, I. (2005, June). *Reminiscence bump in memories and dreams, and the theme of identity*. Poster presented at the Annual Meeting of the Canadian Psychological Association, Montreal, QC, Canada.

Cappeliez. P., & O'Rourke, N. (2002a). Personality traits and existential concerns as predictors of the functions of reminiscence in older adults. *Journal of Gerontology: Psychological Sciences, 57B*, P116–P123.

Cappeliez. P., & O'Rourke, N. (2002b). Profiles of reminiscence among older adults: Perceived stress, life attitudes, and personality variables. *International Journal of Aging and Human Development, 54*, 255–266.

Cappeliez, P., & O'Rourke, N. (2006). Empirical validation of a model of reminiscence and health in later life. *Journal of Gerontology: Psychological Sciences, 61B*, P237–P244.

Cappeliez, P., O'Rourke, N., & Chaudhury, H. (2005). Functions of reminiscence and mental health in later life. *Aging & Mental Health, 9*, 295–301.

Cohen, G. (1998). Aging and autobiographical memory. In C. P. Thompson, D. J. Herrmann, D. Bruce, J. D. Reed, D. G. Payne, & M. P. Toglia (Eds.), *Autobiographical memory: Theoretical and applied perspectives* (pp. 105–123). Hillsdale, NJ: Erlbaum.

Costa, P. T., & McCrae, R. R. (1992). *Revised NEO Personality Inventory (NEO-PI-I) and the NEO Five Factor Inventory (NEO-FFI) professional manual*. Odessa, FL: Psychological Assessment Resources.

DeVries, B., Birren, J. E., & Deutchman, D. E. (1990). Adult development through guided autobiography: The family context. *Family Relations, 39*, 3–7.
Erikson, E. H. (1963). *Childhood and society*. New York, NY: Norton.
Fry, P. S. (1991). Individual differences in reminiscence among older adults: Predictors of frequency and pleasantness ratings of reminiscence activity. *International Journal of Aging and Human Development, 33*, 311–326.
Georgemiller, R., & Maloney, H. N. (1984). Group life review and denial of death. *Clinical Gerontologist, 2*, 37–49.
Gubrium, J. (1993). *Speaking of life: Horizons of meaning for nursing home residents*. Hawthorne, NY: Aldine de Gruyter.
Haight, B. K. (1991). Reminiscing: The state of the art as a basis for practice. *International Journal of Aging and Human Development, 33*, 1–32.
Haight, B. K., & Haight, B. S. (2007). Reminiscence. In J. E. Birren (Ed.), *Encyclopedia of gerontology* (2nd ed., pp. 418–424). New York, NY: Academic Press.
Hedlund, B. L. (1987). *The development of meaning in life in adulthood*. Unpublished doctoral dissertation, University of Southern California, Los Angeles.
Kaufman, S. R. (1986). *The ageless self: Sources of meaning in late life*. Madison: University of Wisconsin Press.
Kenyon, G. (1996). The meaning/value of personal storytelling. In J. E. Birren, G. M. Kenyon, J.-E. Ruth, J. J. F. Schroots, & T. Svensson (Eds.), *Aging and biography: Explorations in adult development* (pp. 21–38). New York, NY: Springer.
Kenyon, G., Clark, P., & deVries, B. (Eds.). (2001). *Narrative gerontology: Theory, research, and practice*. New York, NY: Springer.
Kovach, C. (1991). Reminiscence: Exploring the origins, processes, and consequences. *Nursing Forum, 26*, 14–20.
Melia, S. P. (2003). *Spiritual life review: Sources of meaning in late life*. Workshop presented at the International Reminiscence and Life Review Conference, Vancouver, BC, Canada.
Quackenbush, S. W., & Barnett, M. A. (1995). Correlates of reminiscence activity among elderly individuals. *International Journal of Aging and Human Development, 41*, 169–181.
Reedy, M. N., & Birren, J. E. (1980). *Life review through autobiography*. Poster session at the Annual Meeting of the American Psychological Association, Montreal, QC, Canada.
Reker, G. T. (1992). *Manual of the Life Attitude Profile–Revised*. Peterborough, ON: Student Psychologists Press.
Reker, G. T., & Chamberlain, K. (Eds.). (2000). *Exploring existential meaning: Optimizing human development across the life span*. Thousand Oaks, CA: Sage.
Reker, G. T., & Peacock, E. J. (1981). The Life Attitude Profile (LAP): A multi-dimensional instrument for assessing attitudes towards life. *Canadian Journal of Behavioural Science, 13*, 164–273.
Reker, G. T., & Wong, P. T. P. (1988). Aging as an individual process: Toward a theory of personal meaning. In J. E. Birren & V. L. Bengtson (Eds.), *Emergent theories of aging* (pp. 214–246). New York, NY: Springer.
Romaniuk, M., & Romaniuk, J. G. (1981). Looking back: An analysis of reminiscence functions and triggers. *Experimental Aging Research, 7*, 477–489.
Rubin, D. C., Rahhal, T. A., & Poon, L. W. (1998). Things learned in early adulthood are remembered best. *Memory and Cognition, 26*, 3–19.
Schiff, B., & Cohler, B. J. (2001). Telling survival backwards: Holocaust survivors narrate the past. In G. Kenyon, P. Clark, & B. deVries (Eds.), *Narrative gerontology: Theory, research, and practice* (pp. 113–136). New York, NY: Springer.

Schroots, J. J. F., van Dijkum, C., & Assink, M. H. J. (2004). Autobiographical memory from a lifespan perspective. *International Journal of Aging and Human Development, 58*, 91–115.

Spector-Eisenberg, W. (1988). *The influence of structured reminiscence on meaning and purpose in life in the institutionalized elderly* . (Doctoral dissertation). University of Southern California, Los Angeles, California.

Taft, L. B., & Nehrke, M. F. (1990). Reminiscence, life review, and ego integrity in nursing home residents. *International Journal of Aging and Human Development, 30*, 189–196.

Thornton, J. E., & Collins, J. B. (2007, October). *The developmental exchange as reflected in learning outcomes of guided autobiography.* Paper presented at the Transformative Learning Conference, Albuquerque, New Mexico.

Webster, J. D. (1993). Construction and validation of the Reminiscence Functions Scale. *Journal of Gerontology: Psychological Sciences, 48*, P256–P262.

Webster, J. D., & McCall, M. E. (1999). Reminiscence functions across adulthood: A replication and extension. *Journal of Adult Development, 6*, 73–85.

Westerhof, G. J., Bohlmeijer, E., & Valenkamp, M. W. (2004). In search of meaning: A reminiscence program for older adults. *Educational Gerontology, 30*, 751–766.

Wong, P. T. P. (1989). Personal meaning and successful aging. *Canadian Psychology, 30*, 516–525.

Wong, P. T. P. (1995). The process of adaptive reminiscences. In B. K. Haight & J. D. Webster (Eds.), *The art and science of reminiscing: Theory, research, methods, and applications* (pp. 23–36). Washington, DC: Taylor & Francis.

Wong, P. T. P., Reker, G. T., & Gesser, G. (1994). The Death Attitude Profile–Revised: A multidimensional measure of attitudes towards death. In R. A. Neimeyer (Ed.), *Death anxiety handbook: Research, instrumentation, and application* (pp. 121–148). Washington, DC: Taylor & Francis.

Wong, P. T. P., & Watt, L. M. (1991). What types of reminiscence are associated with successful aging? *Psychology and Aging, 6*, 272–279.

19
Meaning in Life and Healthy Aging

NEAL KRAUSE
University of Michigan

The purpose of this chapter is to examine the relationship between meaning in life and health among older adults. Although there is no agreed-upon definition of meaning in life, the one proposed by Reker (1997) provides a useful point of departure. He argues that a sense of meaning involves having a sense of purpose, order, and direction in life, as well as the belief that there is a reason for one's own existence.

Researchers from all the major social and behavioral sciences have argued for decades that people have a compelling need to find a sense of meaning in life. For example, noted psychiatrist Victor Frankl (1946/1984) maintained that "man's search for meaning is the primary motivation in his life" (p. 121). The same notion is evident in the work of sociologist Peter Berger (1967), who argued that there is "the human craving for meaning that appears to have the force of instinct" (p. 22). And Abraham Maslow (1968), a former president of the American Psychological Association, captured the essence of this view when he pointed out that "the human needs a framework of values, a philosophy of life ... in about the same sense that he needs sunlight, calcium, and love" (p. 206).

Although any number of issues could be explored in the study of meaning, four form the cornerstone of the current chapter. The discussion in this chapter begins by exploring whether the need to derive a sense of meaning becomes increasingly important as people grow older. Following this, a series of issues involving the measurement of meaning in life are evaluated. Next, factors that bolster and maintain an older person's sense of meaning are examined. Informal social relationships figure prominently in this respect. Finally, one way in which meaning may influence health and well-being is investigated. In particular, the potentially important role that meaning may play buffering or offsetting the pernicious effects of stress is assessed in detail.

Age-Related Change in Meaning in Life

Although there are few rigorous empirical studies in the literature, there has been considerable discussion about whether a sense of meaning in life becomes increasingly important as people grow older. Some investigators maintain that sense of meaning figures more prominently in the lives of older rather than younger people, whereas other researchers argue that meaning making is a lifelong process.

Meaning Becomes More Important With Age

The heightened importance of meaning in late life is reflected in the work of Settersten (2002), who observes, "The most pervasive discomfort in late life may not be the fear of destitution or even the fear of poor health, but rather an awareness ... that ... life can become empty of meaning" (p. 70). The reason why meaning may be especially important for older people may be found in three sources: Two sources are based primarily on developmental principles. whereas the third has to do with the fear of impending death.

The first explanation for why meaning may become especially important in late life is found in Erikson's (1959) widely cited theory of life course development. He divided the life span into eight stages, with each stage posing a unique developmental challenge. The final stage, which is typically encountered in late life, is characterized by the crisis of integrity versus despair. This is a time of deep introspection, when older people review their lives and try to reconcile the inevitable gap between what they set out to do and what they were actually able to accomplish. Viewed more broadly, this means that as people grow older, they try to weave the stories of their lives into a more coherent whole. Ultimately, the goal of this process is to imbue life with a deeper sense of meaning. But if this developmental challenge is not resolved successfully, Erikson (1959) maintained, the individual is likely to slip into despair.

Research by Tornstam (1997) provides another reason for expecting meaning to become increasingly important with advancing age. His theory of gerotranscendence specifies that as people grow older, they experience a major shift in the way they view the world. More specifically, this shift is characterized by a move away from a materialistic and pragmatic view of the world to a more cosmic and transcendent view. The cosmic dimension involves an exploration of one's own inner space and, consistent with the work of Erikson (1959), a search for greater integrity. The process of gerotranscendence also involves a desire for maintaining fewer, but more meaningful, social relationships as well as a greater preference for, and appreciation of, solitude. Although Tornstam (1997) does not cast his theory explicitly within the context of meaning in life, the emphasis on introspection, integrity, and the desire for deeper social relationships touches on issues that are closely akin to it. Consequently, it is not surprising to find that Braam and his colleagues report that Tornstam's Gerotranscendence Scale is substantially and positively correlated with a measure of meaning in life (Braam, Bramsen, van Tilburg, van der Ploeg, & Deeg, 2006).

Unlike the developmental theories of Erikson (1959) and Tornstam (1997), research on terror management approaches age-related change in the importance of meaning from a different perspective. As Martens, Goldenberg, and Greenberg (2005) argue, unconscious concerns about death enhance the need to view the world as a meaningful place. Because older adults are typically closer to death than are younger individuals, terror management theory predicts older people should have a greater need to find meaning in life. Although it is not widely known, Erikson was also aware of this possibility. His views on death and meaning may be found in a volume of his unpublished papers that was edited by Hoare (2002). In this book, Hoare reports that Erikson believed that older people "can no longer repress death, they harbor fears of 'spiritual meaninglessness,' and the sense of depleted time, 'accentuates issues of nonbeing'" (p. 82). Hoare goes on to point out that Erikson believed that this sense of dread instills in older people a "wish to fuse with another, with God, with the cosmos, or with one's 'innermost self'" (p. 82).

Meaning Making Is a Lifelong Process

In contrast to the work that has been presented so far, other investigators maintain that the search for meaning does not become increasingly important with advancing age. Instead, these researchers argue that meaning making is a lifelong process that is important at every point in the life course. Support for this alternative perspective may be found in the work of Staudinger (2001). Embedded in Erikson's (1959) theory is the notion that a person derives a sense of meaning (i.e., integrity) through a careful review of how his or her life has been lived. This idea makes a good deal of sense because it is difficult to see how an individual can find a sense of meaning without some sort of life review. Although Erikson's (1959) theory specifies that this life review occurs late in life, Staudinger (2001) argues that it may instead take place at any time during adulthood. This perspective is consistent with the view of Reker and Chamberlain (2000), who maintain that "the will to meaning is a continuous process, triggered by changing circumstances, shifting value orientations, and renewed aspirations" (p. 2; see also McAdams, 1996). Perhaps this is one reason why empirical research fails to demonstrate that the life review takes place solely in old age (Merriam, 1993).

A key challenge for scholars involves finding a way to reconcile the seemingly different views of the relationship between aging and meaning in life. One explanation that makes good sense is provided by Staudinger (2001). She suggests that even though adults of all ages engage in a life review, the content or nature of this life review changes as people grow older. More specifically, Staudinger (2001) argues that for younger adults, the life review is focused more on the future and is conducted in order to set new goals and help implement plans. In contrast, she proposes, the life review for older people involves looking backward and reflecting on what has happened in the past instead of what might happen in the future. Although a sense of meaning in life clearly involves much more than a life review, the broader issue identified by Staudinger (2001) is intuitively pleasing: Meaning is important to everyone, but the content and nature of what constitutes a meaningful life is likely to change as people move through the life course. This perspective also has clear implications for the way meaning in life is measured because it suggests that different measures may be needed for people at different points in the life course. It is for this reason that issues involving the measurement of meaning are discussed next.

Measuring Meaning in Late Life

A number of investigators have developed scales to assess meaning in life (e.g., Pohlmann, Karin, Gruss, & Joraschky, 2006; Reker & Peacock, 1981; Steger, Frazier, Oishi, & Kaler, 2006; Wong, 1998). However, none of these instruments were designed specifically for use with older adults. If the nature of meaning in life changes as people grow older, then it is important for researchers to devise scales that capture these age-related changes. Krause (2004) made one of the few attempts to develop this type of measure. The discussion in the next section describes the conceptual underpinnings of the components of his scale and briefly reviews empirical work on the factor structure of this battery of items. Following this is a detailed examination of two measurement issues that confront all scales that assess meaning. The first issue involves something that is known as factorial invariance over time; the second has to do with the potential confounding between scales that assess meaning and measures of psychological well-being, especially depression.

Scales That Assess Meaning Among Older People

Based on the pioneering work of Battista and Almond (1973), Krause (2004) devised a scale of meaning in life that is composed of four dimensions: having values, a sense of purpose, goals, and the ability to reconcile the past. Reviewing the conceptual foundation of each component helps to further clarify the nature of meaning in life.

Values provide the basis for behavioral guidance. When the utility and worthiness of specific thoughts and actions are not clear, values provide a basis for selecting from different options by giving the assurance that personal choices are, in the words of Baumeister (1991), right, good, and justifiable. Simply put, a sense of meaning in life arises when people believe they are doing the right thing.

Although clearly linked to values, a sense of purpose is conceptually distinct. It has to do with believing that one's actions have a set place in the larger order of social life and that one's behavior fits appropriately into a larger, more important social whole. This notion was captured succinctly some time ago by Cooley (1927), who observed, "A man can be content to live and strive without the promise of either happiness or immortality, if only he feels that something worthy, some part of the great whole, is being accomplished in him" (pp. 229–230). Values are codes or standards that define which thoughts and actions are appropriate, whereas a sense of purpose carries evaluative connotations that arise from the successful implementation or execution of actions that comply with underlying values.

A sense of meaning also involves expectations for the future and is often manifested in the form of goals for which people strive. Goals help individuals organize current activities and provide a conduit for focusing and implementing energies, efforts, and ambitions. Even though goals are oriented toward the future, they also provide more immediate rewards by reinforcing and building upon the sense of accomplishment a person may already have derived. Cooley (1927) captured the essence of this view in his discussion of plans, which are closely akin to goals. He argued that

> able men plan and strive not as being discontented now, but because they need to continue the hope and sense of achievement they already have. They bring the future into the scene to animate the present.... Our plans are our working hopes and among our chief treasures." (p. 205)

Earlier, the work of Erikson (1959) was reviewed to show that a sense of meaning arises, in part, by looking back over one's life and attempting to reconcile what one set out to do with one's actual accomplishments. A similar emphasis on reviewing the past was evident in Staudinger's (2001) discussion of the life review among older people. Assessing whether older people have been able to reconcile things that have happened in the past may, therefore, capture one of the relatively unique aspects of meaning in late life. It is for this reason that the scale developed by Krause (2004) contains a dimension assessing the ability to reconcile the past.

A subsequent empirical evaluation of these four components of meaning by Krause (2004) reveals that they are strongly correlated with a higher order factor that reflects a general or overall sense of meaning in life. This study further revealed that the items in this scale have good psychometric properties (i.e., good reliability). Unfortunately, deriving psychometrically sound measures of meaning does not go far enough because other challenging measurement issues arise during the task of scale construction.

Confronting the Problem of Factorial Invariance Over Time

Although the scale devised by Krause (2004) may have contributed to the literature, there are two important measurement issues that face this, as well as any other, index of meaning in life. The first has to do with something that methodologists call factorial invariance over time. Researchers have argued for decades that data that have been gathered at more than one point in time are preferable to data from cross-sectional studies. Longitudinal data are valued more highly because they allow investigators to address one (but not all) of the key requirements for demonstrating causality. More specifically, longitudinal data make it possible to see if the proposed cause precedes the hypothesized effect in time (Morton, Hebel, & McCarter, 2001). Cast within the context of the current chapter, this means, for example, that longitudinal data allow an investigator to see if meaning in life at a baseline interview is associated with change in health over time or whether health at the baseline interview is associated with change in meaning over time.

Unfortunately, the study of change in meaning over time introduces a potential methodological pitfall. In order to determine if true change has occurred in meaning over time, researchers must be sure that questions assessing meaning in life are interpreted by study subjects in the same way at both interviews. If the items are not interpreted in the same way, then change in scores on scales that assess meaning can arise from not one but two reasons: Either true change has taken place in meaning, or scores on scales that assess meaning have changed because study participants do not interpret the items in the same way at baseline and follow-up interviews. This dilemma is known as the problem of factorial invariance over time (Bollen, 1989).

One way to assess factorial invariance over time is to see if the elements of the measurement model (i.e., the factor loadings and measurement error terms) change over time. Tests of this issue, which are conducted in a confirmatory factor-analytic framework, are based on the following rationale. If the meaning of study measures does not change over time, then respondents should answer the same questions in the same way at the baseline and follow-up surveys. If they answer the same questions in the same way, then the covariances among the items that assess meaning should be the same at both points in time. And if this is true, then the factor loadings and measurement error terms that are derived from these covariances should be the same as well.

There appears to be only one study in the literature that has tested for factorial invariance over time in items assessing meaning in late life (Krause, 2007a). These analyses reveal that the measurement structure of items assessing meaning in life changes over time, suggesting that study subjects are not interpreting the items in the same way. But there is a plausible theoretical explanation for these results. Recall that Reker and Chamberlain (2000), as well as McAdams (1996), view meaning making as a lifelong process. Similar views are found in the work of Staudinger (2001). If this notion is true, then the way meaning is understood and manifest should change continuously as well. And if it does, then it is not surprising to find that subjects do not respond to measures of meaning consistently over time. So, rather than being a methodological problem per se, change in the underlying nature of meaning may instead reveal a fundamental characteristic of this core construct.

Although change may be an endemic property of meaning, this characteristic puts researchers in a difficult position if they wish to study change in meaning over time. Unfortunately, there is no way to conclusively resolve this vexing problem. One strategy provides a useful point of departure, however. Given a sufficiently large number of items to assess meaning, it is possible that subjects will view some indicators in the same way over time, but not others. To the extent this is true, investigators can compare results of analyses that have been performed with and without indicators whose meaning changes over time to see if substantive study conclusions are altered (see Rensvold & Cheung, 1998, for a detailed discussion of the statistical challenges involved in this type of analysis).

Issues Involving Measurement Confounding

Several investigators have studied the relationship between meaning in life and depression among older people (e.g., Reker, 1997). These studies reveal that older people who have found a sense of meaning in life tend to report fewer symptoms of depression than do elders who have not been able to derive a sense of meaning in life. Although these findings are noteworthy, they present a potentially troubling measurement problem. More specifically, there is some evidence that measures of meaning may be confounded with measures of depression. Moreover, this problem may be especially evident when working with older adults. Evidence of this may be found in a recent volume by Dan Blazer (2002), who is a leading geriatric psychiatrist. In this book, Blazer notes that "meaninglessness is especially important in the manifestation of late life depression" (p. 179).

The problem identified by Blazer (2002) creates potential challenges for the way in which findings from research on meaning and depression in late life are interpreted. But it also may affect the way investigators view results from studies of meaning and physical health status. Researchers have known for some time that physical and mental health problems are comorbid (e.g., Cohen & Rodriguez, 1995). If measures of meaning in life reflect little more than symptoms of depression and research finds that meaning is associated with physical health, then the results may reveal little more than the well-known relationship between mental and physical health problems rather than the influence of meaning in life per se.

There are three ways to address this vexing problem. The first involves drawing logical conclusions from available data. Although it is not hard to see why people who are depressed would have difficulty believing their lives are meaningful, it does not necessarily follow that all people who are struggling to find a sense of meaning in life are, therefore, also depressed. Evidence of this notion may be found by turning to the bivariate correlations reported by

Reker (1997) in his study of meaning and depression in late life. He reports that the correlation between meaning and depressive symptoms in a sample of community dwelling adults is $r = .37$ ($p < .001$). This study further reveals that the correlation between meaning and depression for a sample of institutionalized elders is $r = .52$ ($p < .001$). Although a significant relationship between the two constructs is clearly present in these data, the correlations are far from perfect. Moreover, the fact that there is 27% shared variance at best between the constructs suggests that a number of people who have not found meaning in life do not have high depression scores.

The second way to confront the problem of measurement confounding has to do with the way items are selected to assess meaning in life. More specifically, researchers should make an effort to avoid indicators that reflect affect or other psychological emotions. For example, the Revised Life Regard Index (Debats, 1998) contains the following item: "I really feel good about my life" (p. 250). Careful reflection reveals that this item does not necessarily capture meaning per se; instead, it reflects an affective state that is presumably associated with having found a sense of meaning in life (i.e., it is something that is "caused" by meaning). If researchers feel it is important to include this type of measure in their scales, however, then it would probably be best to conduct a sensitivity analysis by comparing findings from analyses that estimate the relationship between meaning and depression with and without potentially confounded indicators in the scale that assesses meaning.

The third way to address the issue of measurement confounding has to do with the implementation of a specific kind of data-analytic strategy. This strategy involves estimating a cross-lagged latent variable model that contains identical measures of meaning and depression that have been assessed at two points in time. Consistent with the discussion of assessing causality that was provided earlier, an investigator can then estimate whether meaning at the baseline is associated with change in depression or whether depression at the baseline interview is associated with change in meaning over time (see Kessler & Greenberg, 1981, for a detailed discussion of cross-lagged models).

A preliminary assessment of this type of cross-lagged model was made by Krause (2007a). The findings from this study suggest that greater meaning at the baseline is significantly associated with a decline in depression over time, but depressive symptoms at the baseline were not significantly related to change in meaning over time. Viewed broadly, these results provide some preliminary evidence that meaning in life may not be confounded with symptoms of depression in late life. But these findings should be viewed cautiously because Kessler and Greenberg (1981) convincingly demonstrate that data from at least three waves of interviews are needed to more fully disentangle the temporal ordering between two constructs (e.g., meaning and depression).

Exploring the Sources of Meaning in Late Life

As a number of investigators have pointed out, there are many potential sources of meaning in life. For example, Reker (1991) identifies a long list of possibilities, including occupations, creative activities, leisure activities, material possessions, and social or political causes. But a range of other psychosocial factors may come into play as well. For example, a study by Schnell and Becker (2006) suggests that personality traits may influence a person's ability to find a sense of meaning in life. More specifically, their research indicates that extraverted individuals are more likely than introverts to believe their lives are meaningful. It is obviously not feasible to examine all potential sources of meaning in a single chapter. Instead, the discussion in the next section places an emphasis on two specific sources primarily because the theoretical rationale for linking them with meaning is compelling and because they are especially relevant for the study of older people. These sources of meaning are social relationships and religion.

Social Relationships and Meaning Among Older Adults

In her insightful work on the sources of meaning in life, Debats (1999) points out that personal relationships are the most frequent source of meaning in life. Similar views are expressed by King (2004), who argues that people often find significant meaning in the relationships they forge with others. These observations are consistent with longstanding sociological precepts, which specify that instead of arising from within the individual, a sense of meaning is a social product that emerges during the process of interacting with significant others. The essence of this perspective was captured some time ago by Berger and Pullberg (1965), who noted, "Now the human enterprise of producing the world is not comprehensible as an individual project. Rather, it is a social process: *men together* engage in constructing a world, which then becomes a common dwelling. Indeed, since sociality is a necessary element of human being, the process of world production is necessarily a social one" (p. 201; emphasis in the original). Similar views are expressed by Baumeister (1991), who observes that "although life's meaning is quintessentially personal and individual, meaning itself is fundamentally social. Without culture—including language, value, and personal relationships—life could not have much in the way of meaning" (p. 9).

Although social relationships may be an important source of meaning for individuals of all ages, there is some evidence they may be especially important in late life. In order to see why this may be so, it is helpful to turn to Carstensen's (1992) theory of socioemotional selectivity. According to this perspective, as people go through late life, they become increasingly aware they have relatively little time left to live. This prompts a shift in the nature of the social relationships they try to maintain. In particular, older adults develop a greater preference for emotionally meaningful social relationships and they disengage from more peripheral social ties. Recall that a similar age-related shift in relationship preferences was posited by Tornstam (1997). The shift toward deeper and more emotionally close relationships in the work of Carstensen (1992) and Tornstam (1997) is especially relevant for the study of meaning in life because it seems unlikely that older people would be willing to discuss deeply personal issues involving meaning in life with casual acquaintances. Instead, such discussions are more likely to take place in the safety of more intimate social relationships. Taken as a whole, this research suggests that if deep personal relationships are an important source of meaning and if close personal ties become increasingly important with age, then greater insight into the origin of meaning in late life should be found by studying the social ties that are maintained by older people.

Although significant others may be an important source of meaning in life, it is not clear precisely what social network members do to help older people find a sense of meaning in life. Deriving a sense of meaning is often hard work because it requires a good deal of insight, persistence, introspection, and the ability to grapple with abstract issues. As a result, it is not surprising to find that older people turn to trusted others to verify their own conclusions about meaning in their lives, learn from similar experiences of significant social network members, and rely on close others to help them sort through difficult issues.

The proposition that social support is an important source of meaning in life, therefore, makes a good deal of sense, but evaluating this relationship empirically is not as simple as it may seem because researchers have known for some time that social relationships comprise a complex, multidimensional domain (Krause, 2006). As a result, it is difficult to know which specific type or dimension of social relationships plays the most important role in the meaning-making process. Unfortunately, there has been relatively little empirical research on the interface between multiple dimensions of social relationships and meaning in life, especially with samples composed of older people.

A recent study by Krause (2007b) represents one of the first attempts to evaluate the impact of multiple measures of social ties on change in meaning during late life. Three key components of social relationships were examined in this study: Enacted support, negative interaction, and anticipated support. Enacted support is defined as the actual provision of emotional, tangible, and informational assistance by family members and close friends (Barrera, 1986). In contrast, negative interaction is defined as unpleasant social encounters that are characterized by disagreements, criticism, rejection, and the invasion of privacy (Rook, 1984). Excessive helping as well as ineffective helping are sometimes included under the broad rubric of negative interaction as well. Finally, anticipated support is a subjective measure that reflects the belief that significant others will provide assistance in the future should the need arise (Wethington & Kessler, 1986).

These three dimensions of social relationships were included in the study by Krause (2007b) for the following reasons. First, when social network members provide enacted support, they are doing much more than giving emotional, tangible, and informational help. In the process, more subtle messages are conveyed to the support recipient. In particular, enacted support makes older support recipients feel they are valued and esteemed, and this feeling helps them believe they have a set place in the wider social order. Simply put, receiving support from significant others makes older people feel they belong. Carrier (1965) captured the essence of this construct when he observed that the person who feels he belongs "sees himself as taking part in his group; he identifies with it, he participates in it, he receives motivation from it; in a word, he is in a state or disposition of interaction with the group, which understands, inspires, and welcomes him" (p. 58). Being included in a larger, welcoming group imbues life with a sense of order and purpose and, in the process, helps older people find a deeper sense of meaning in life.

If positive exchanges bolster a sense of meaning in life, then perhaps negative interaction erodes or compromises the process of meaning making in late life. Some insight into this issue may be found by turning to the basic tenets of expectancy theory (Olson, Roese, & Zanna, 1996). Cast within the context of social interaction, expectancies are beliefs about how other people will think, feel, and act in the future. These expectancies are important because social interaction would be difficult unless people believe they can predict what others will do. As Rook and Pietromonaco (1987) point out, most individuals encounter more positive than negative exchanges during the course of daily life. This positive interaction creates the impression (i.e., the expectancy) that social relationships will continue on a positive course. But when negative interaction is encountered instead, it can shatter these expectancies, often stunning the recipient. As Olson, Roese, and Zanna (1996) observe, disconfirmation of expectancies can be a significant source of psychological distress. But it may do more than this. The expectancies surrounding social relationships provide a sense that the social world is an orderly and predictable place. When negative interaction arises, these key expectancies can be dispelled. As well, the resulting loss of predictability and order may threaten an older person's sense of meaning in life.

As discussed earlier, having plans and goals for the future is an important component of meaning. Older people are likely to feel more confident about their ability to attain their goals and plans if they believe that social network members stand ready to help should the need arise. It is for this reason that a strong sense of anticipated support should be an important source of meaning in late life.

Three major findings emerged from the longitudinal study by Krause (2007b). First, the data suggest that greater anticipated support at the baseline interview is associated with an increase in meaning over time. Enacted support also had a beneficial effect on meaning in life, but this effect operates indirectly through anticipated support. More specifically, the findings reveal that greater enacted support is associated with more anticipated support and that greater anticipated support, in turn, tends to bolster an older person's sense of meaning over time. Finally, the results involving negative interaction were complex. In particular, the findings indicate that more negative interaction is associated with a diminished sense of meaning at the baseline survey, but similar effects on change in meaning over time fail to emerge from the data. Taken as a whole, these results confirm that social relationships do, indeed, influence meaning in life and do so in a number of different ways.

Religion and Meaning in Late Life

A number of investigators have argued that one of the primary functions of religion is to help people find a sense of meaning in life (e.g., Baumeister, 1991; Park, 2005; Spilka, Hood, Hunsberger, & Gorsuch, 2003). Cooley (1927) highlighted this vitally important function of religion when he posed the following question: "In what sense is faith an impulse in human nature? In the sense that we need to respect our own endeavors, and hence to believe in something that will give reality and meaning to them" (p. 230). A similar observation was made by Clark (1958), who noted that "religion more than any other human function satisfies the need for meaning in life" (p. 419; see also Pargament, 1997).

Religion may be an especially important factor to study in the genesis of meaning in late life because research consistently shows that older adults are more deeply involved in religion than are younger people. For example, this work suggests that compared to younger people, older adults attend church more often, read the Bible more frequently, pray more often, and are more likely to believe that religion is very important in their lives (Barna, 2002; Gallup & Lindsay, 1999). If religion is an important source of meaning in life and if older people are more deeply involved in religion than younger people, it follows that the meaning-making function of religion should be especially evident in late life.

If religion helps older people find a sense of meaning in life, then it is important to learn more about how this happens. However, research on this issue is complicated by the fact that religion is a complex conceptual domain that encompasses a number of different factors. For example, the Fetzer Institute, National Institute on Aging Working Group (1999) identified 12 main dimensions of religion. As a result, it is difficult to know which aspects of religion play a role in helping older people find a sense of meaning in life. Although a number of factors are likely to come into play, the purpose of the discussion in this section is to argue that social relationships that arise in the church may have something to do with it.

Theoretical justification for the notion that social relationships in the church are a potentially important source of meaning comes from two sources. The first is found in Berger's widely cited volume *The Sacred Canopy* (1967). In this work, Berger argues that a sense of meaning in life, or nomos, is "built up in the consciousness of the individual by conversation with significant others" (p. 16). Similar views are found in the comprehensive theory of religion that was devised by Stark and Finke (2000). The notion of religious explanations figures prominently in their work. Religious explanations are religious models of reality, or religious worldviews, that are designed to guide thoughts and influence behavior. As this definition reveals, there appears to be a good deal of conceptual overlap between religious explanations and meaning in life. Consistent with the observations of Berger (1967), these investigators propose that religious meaning arises from interaction with fellow believers. More specifically, Stark and Finke (2000) argue, "An individual's confidence in religious explanations is strengthened to the extent that others express their confidence in them" (p. 107). Taken together, the insights provided by Berger (1967) and Stark and Finke (2000) suggest that if the purpose of religion is to help people find a sense of meaning in life, then this goal is achieved to a significant extent through social interaction with like-minded religious others.

The interface between church-based social relationships and a religious sense of meaning in life was investigated recently by Krause (2008). Before turning to the substantive issues and findings from this study, however, it is important to briefly discuss how meaning was measured. This research focused specifically on religious meaning, which is defined as the process of turning to religion in an effort to find a sense of purpose in life, a sense of direction, and a sense that there is a reason for one's existence. The difference between religious meaning and a general sense of meaning in life is perhaps best illustrated by turning to the way these constructs have been measured. Wong (1998) created a scale called the Personal Meaning Profile. This index contains the following item that reflects a general sense of meaning in life: "I have a purpose and direction in life." In contrast, the religious meaning scale derived by Krause (2008) contains the following counterpart to this indicator: "My faith gives me a sense of direction in life." If the goal of a study is to show that social relationships in the church influence meaning, then it makes sense to focus on measures that specifically reflect a religiously based sense of meaning in life.

Two types of church-based support were examined in the longitudinal survey by Krause (2008). The first was spiritual support. This support is defined as assistance that is provided in order to increase the religious commitment, beliefs, and behavior of a fellow church member. This type of support may be provided in a number of ways. For example, people at church may share their own religious experiences with fellow church members, or they may show them how to apply religious principles in daily life. If a core function of religion is to promote a sense of meaning in life and if fellow church members encourage each other to adopt religious teachings and beliefs, then it seems likely that spiritual support from coreligionists should be an important source of religious meaning in life.

The second type of support that was examined in the study by Krause (2008) is emotional support from fellow church members. In contrast to spiritual support, explicit religious overtones are less evident in this type of assistance. Instead, emotional support involves the provision of a more general sense of empathy, caring, love, and trust. There were two reasons for including this type of support in the study. First, this type of assistance was examined because research conducted in secular settings revealed that emotional support from family members and close friends is associated with a greater sense of meaning in life (Krause, 2004). Second, church-based emotional support is important because it helps people appreciate how the ties they have developed with others integrate them into a larger social whole (i.e., the church), thereby fostering a sense of belonging, purpose, and ultimately, meaning in life.

The findings from the study by Krause (2008) suggest that emotional and spiritual support from fellow church members both tend to bolster a sense of religious meaning in late life. But of the two, spiritual support appears to exert the strongest effect.

Taken as a whole, a common theme cuts across the research that has been reviewed on the sources of meaning in late life. In particular, the data suggest that in secular as well as religious settings, significant others play an important role in helping older people derive a sense of meaning.

Meaning in Life and the Stress Process

Knowing how a sense of meaning arises is important, but by itself that knowledge does not go far enough because a deeper understanding requires that careful attention be paid to how sense of meaning functions as well. Although meaning may influence an older person's quality of life in a number of ways, the discussion in this section focuses on the potentially important health-enhancing function of meaning. This is an important issue because research consistently shows that older adults consume a disproportionately large amount of the nation's health care resources (U.S. Department of Health and Human Services, 2004). Knowing the factors that influence health in late life may, therefore, form the basis for devising interventions aimed at containing rapidly escalating health care costs.

A small but rapidly growing body of research suggests that people who have developed a deep sense of meaning in life tend to enjoy better physical health (Krause, 2004; Parquart, 2002) and better mental health (Krause, 2007a; Nygren et al., 2005; Reker, 1997) than do individuals who have not been able to find that life is meaningful. It is not entirely evident, however, how the potential health-related benefits of meaning arise. Although there are likely to be a number of important mechanisms, one is of special interest in the current chapter. More specifically, this chapter later examines research that suggests that meaning in life enhances older people's sense of health and well-being because it helps them cope more effectively with the stressful events in their lives. But as this discussion will reveal, the interface between stress and meaning is complex, and a better understanding of it requires that three closely related issues be considered carefully. When viewed together, these issues depict a process that unfolds over time. The first issue deals with the notion that the deleterious effects of stress arise, in part, because stress tends to erode an older person's sense of meaning in life. The second issue specifies that when stress creates deficits in meaning, older people turn to significant others who help them regain the sense that their lives have meaning. Once this restoration of meaning has been accomplished, the third issue is concerned with how a renewed sense of meaning in life acts as a potent coping resource that offsets or buffers the pernicious effects of stressful life events.

Researchers have known for some time that stressful experiences can erode a person's sense of meaning in life. Evidence of this may be found, for example, in Janoff-Bulman's (1992) well-known volume *Shattered Assumptions*. In this work, Janoff-Bulman maintains that significant life events shatter individuals' belief that the world is a meaningful place by violating their sense of trust and leading them to question whether the world is a benevolent and just place.

Further evidence that stress may erode a sense of meaning in life is provided by Krause (2004). He shows how undesirable life events tend to erode the major components of meaning that were reviewed earlier. More specifically, Krause (2004) maintains that the occurrence of an unwanted event in life (e.g., a divorce, the loss of a job) often signals a person's inability to successfully comply with key role expectations and norms. As a result, the stressor may sever the link between the individual and the values he or she regard highly. Stress may also deprive people of a sense of purpose because their inability to fulfill role obligations may make them feel they no longer fit into the wider social order that previously embraced them, for they are no longer contributing to it. Krause (2004) further argues that stressors may force older people to admit that goals to which they previously aspired are either no longer attainable or, at the very least, difficult to reach, thereby depriving them of the social compass that energizes the present, fills them with hope, and illuminates the path into the future. Finally, stress may complicate the process of appraising and evaluating the past because it presents older people with undeniable evidence of their inability to pursue the path they hoped their lives would take.

Although stress may deplete an older person's sense of meaning in life, research further reveals that many individuals do not respond to unpleasant life events in a passive way. Instead, many older adults take active steps to set things right by seeking assistance from close others (Eckenrode & Wethington, 1990). Although family members and close friends may help older people deal with stress in a number of ways, at least part of their supportive efforts may be focused on helping an older adult find a renewed sense of meaning in life. Krause (2004) suggests several ways in which this may happen. For example, significant others may help restore a sense of meaning in life by reminding a stressed elder that many other people are also unable to live up to their values and that it is still possible to get back on track by pursuing cherished values with a renewed sense of commitment and dedication. In addition, as Frankl (1946/1984) pointed out, significant others may help stress victims find a new sense of purpose in their suffering by helping them see that adversity is often necessary for personal development. Moreover, close social network members may help stressed elders rediscover, renew, and reestablish goals and plans by helping them develop a clear sense of what needs to be done next to confront the stressor and restore a sense of balance in life (Caplan, 1981). Finally, support providers may help older adults work through and reconcile disappointments associated with unwanted events. By listening to and advising elders as they process and work through their problems, significant others may help them reconcile things that have happened in the past.

Preliminary support for the notion that significant others may replenish a sense of meaning that has been diminished by stressful life events is provided by Krause (2004). His research suggests that even though stress tends to erode a sense of meaning in life, high levels of emotional support from family members and close friends completely offset these noxious effects by restoring and maintaining an older person's sense of meaning in life.

Having one's sense of meaning restored with the help of significant others is important because researchers have argued for some time that a strong sense of meaning in life is a potent antidote that buffers the noxious effects of stress on physical and mental health. The intellectual roots of this perspective may be found in Frankl's (1946/1984) research. He maintains that "suffering ceases to be suffering at the moment it finds a meaning" (p. 135). Instead of arguing that meaning is merely one of several useful coping resources, Frankl (1946/1984) argued that it may be the most important of all: "There is nothing in the world, I would venture to say, that would so effectively help one survive even the worst conditions as the knowledge that there is meaning in one's life" (p. 126). A strikingly similar view was expressed by Carl Jung. He maintained that "suffering that is not understood is hard to bear, while on the other hand it is often astounding to see how much a person can endure when he understands the why and the wherefore. A philosophical or religious view of the world enables him to do this, and such views prove to be, at the very least, psychic methods of healing if not salvation" (as quoted in Jacobi & Hull, 1953, p. 252).

Unfortunately, neither Frankl (1946/1884) nor Jung (Jacobi & Hull, 1953) provided fully articulated models that specify precisely how a sense of meaning in life helps people cope more effectively with stress. In fact, this gap in the knowledge base is still evident today. As Park and Folkman (1997) point out, "The whole area of meaning is currently poorly understood and not well-integrated with other mainstream approaches to stress and coping" (p. 116). Fortunately, Park and Folkman provide a number of useful theoretical insights into the potential stress-buffering properties of meaning in life. Although it is not possible to review all the mechanisms they discuss, three that are especially important are discussed next. The first involves the way in which a strong sense of meaning helps people feel they have experienced personal growth in the face of adversity, the second arises from benefits that are enjoyed by people who have found a sense of meaning through religion, and the third has to do with the sense of hope or optimism that is fostered by a strong sense of meaning in life.

Park and Folkman (1997) propose that people with stable life philosophies often perceive highly stressful situations as challenges rather than threats. When difficult times are viewed as challenges, people are more likely to regard them as vehicles for achieving personal growth. This perspective is supported by a rapidly growing literature that suggests that people who face even the most traumatic events in life often emerge from them believing they are better off than before the event was encountered (Tedeschi, Park, & Calhoun, 1998). In fact, Tedeschi and Calhoun (2004) recently claimed, "The evidence is overwhelming that individuals facing a wide variety of very difficult circumstances experience significant changes in their lives that they view as highly positive" (p. 3). Some of these positive changes are identified by McMillen (1999). He reviews research showing that adversity helps some people either develop new coping skills or realize they have coping skills that they were not aware they possessed. In addition, stressful events make people more empathic to the plight of others who are in need, thereby motivating them to assist individuals who have experienced similar kinds of difficulties. Finally, adversity may make people more appreciative of the help they have received from family members and close friends, thereby strengthening informal support networks. Finding new personal strengths and skills, helping others who are in need, drawing closer to valued others—all may help offset the physical and mental health problems associated with stressful events.

Park and Folkman (1997) also note that the stress-buffering properties of meaning in life may be especially evident among people who derive a sense of meaning in life through religion. More specifically, individuals who are deeply involved in religion often believe that adverse experiences are part of God's plan for deepening their faith and ultimately improving the quality of their lives. This belief may impart a sense that things are under control, and this heightened feeling of God-mediated control may, in turn, reduce the noxious effects of stress (Krause, 2005). But this is not the only way in which religious meaning may help offset the noxious effects of stress. Koenig (1994) argues that when people become more deeply involved in religion, their priorities shift, and the importance of secular things like personal possessions and personal abilities decline. As a result, losses arising in secular areas of life have a diminished impact and become less threatening because these material things are no longer at the core of a person's sense of meaning in life.

Beyond religious influences, having a sense of purpose in life and having goals to pursue help people deal with adversity by enhancing their sense of hope or optimism. A goal or plan instills the belief that no matter how bleak things may seem at the moment, there is still a way to get through these difficulties; and, further, that if these goals or plans are executed faithfully, hard times will eventually subside (see Feldman & Snyder, 2005, for a detailed discussion of the interface between hope and meaning in life). The importance of maintaining a sense of hope is demonstrated forcefully in a compelling 30-year longitudinal study by Peterson and his colleagues (Peterson, Seligman, & Vaillant, 1994). Their research reveals that people who are more optimistic tend to live longer than individuals who are more pessimistic. The sense of pessimism among people who have not found a sense of meaning in life is perhaps nowhere more evident than in the work of Schopenhauer, a classic 19th-century philosopher. In his widely cited essay "The Vanity of Existence," he concluded that life is meaningless and that, therefore, all that is left is "annihilation—this is nature's unambiguous declaration that all striving of the will is essentially in vain" (p. 39; as quoted in Klemke, 2000). It is not difficult to see why persons with this view of life would be unlikely to take active steps to confront the stressors in their lives. Even though a credible case can be made to support the notion that meaning in life buffers the deleterious effects of stress on health, relatively few studies have evaluated this proposition empirically. Some investigators have found support for this hypothesis, but a good deal of this work has been done with either younger adults (e.g., Edwards & Holden, 2002) or samples of older people who have not been selected at random (e.g., Smith & Zautra, 2004). In contrast, research using a nationally representative sample of older people (Krause, 2007a) reveals that a strong sense of meaning in life tends to offset the noxious effects of traumatic life events on depressive symptoms. Clearly, more empirical work is needed to probe more deeply into the ways in which meaning in life may help older people cope more effectively with the stressors that arise in their lives.

Conclusions

The central role of meaning in life was captured succinctly by Jung, who observed, "The least of things with a meaning is always worth more in life than the greatest of things without it" (p. 285; as quoted in Jacobi & Hull, 1953). Yet the amount of empirical research that has been done on meaning of life does not appear to be commensurate with the core place that sense of meaning appears to occupy in life. There are a number of reasons for this. Chief among them are problems arising from efforts to stake out the content domain of meaning in life and devise sound measures of this elusive construct. Such problems in conceptualization and measurement are compounded by two additional challenges. First, as Reker and Chamberlain (2000) observe, the content and fundamental nature of meaning may change with time. As discussed earlier, this changeability raises the possibility that meaning in life may not be interpreted in the same way by older and younger people. For example, reconciling things that have happened in the past may be a more important facet of the meaning-making process for older than for younger adults. But the notion that reconciling the past is particularly important for elderly people has not been confirmed empirically with carefully designed longitudinal studies that assess change in meaning across successive birth cohorts.

A second major problem facing those who wish to study meaning arises from the possibility that regardless of the content of meaning, the overall importance of leading a life that is meaningful may increase as people grow older. Although evidence presented earlier appears to refute this notion, more rigorous empirical research is called for because current studies focus primarily on the life review. Even though the life review is an integral part of meaning making, this process involves far more than life review. Researchers need to conduct studies that assess whether having a sense of values, purpose, and goals becomes more important with advancing age. This work may reveal, for example, that having values is more important in late life, but setting goals is not as important as it might be for younger adults. Viewed from a broader perspective, these issues point to a compelling need to more deeply infuse research on meaning with a life course perspective (Mortimer & Shanahan, 2004).

In the process of examining fundamental issues about the nature of meaning in life, more attention should be given to the factors that link a sense of meaning with physical and mental health. Several potentially important constructs have been identified in this chapter, including a sense of belonging as well as feelings of hope and optimism. More empirical work is needed with these constructs. As well, a number of other potentially important mechanisms that have not been discussed up to this point merit further inquiry. Researchers have known for some time that stress exerts an adverse effect on health and well-being because it erodes an older person's sense of personal control and his or her feelings of self-worth (Krause, 2003). Yet the potential role that meaning may play in restoring these core coping resources does not appear to have been examined in studies of older people. It seems reasonable to argue, for example, that having goals (one component of meaning) is an important prerequisite for developing a strong sense of personal control. It also seems likely that a person who feels that he or she has a sense of purpose in life is subsequently likely to experience an elevated sense of self-worth (see Baumeister, 1991, for a detailed theoretical discussion of the interface between meaning in life, control, and self-esteem).

If meaning plays a critical role in shaping health and well-being, then researchers need to learn more about how a sense of meaning in life arises. A major emphasis has been placed in the current chapter on the role played by significant others in the meaning-making process. But a host of unanswered questions remain about the influence of significant others. So far, most empirical work has focused primarily on emotional support, anticipated support, and negative interaction with social network members. But such research does not exhaust all the ways in which significant others may help an older person find a sense of meaning in life. One promising lead may be found in the largely overlooked notion of companionship. Rook (1987) defines companionship as social relationships that involved shared activities that are undertaken primarily for the intrinsic goal of enjoyment. Yet, as an intriguing paper by Cocking and Kennett (1998) reveals, companionship may involve far more than this. The researchers maintain that companions share mutual interests and make a concerted effort to emulate the desirable qualities they see in each other. But one facet of companionship appears to be especially relevant for the study of meaning in life. Cocking and Kennett argue that "it is the value we assign to the hopes and concerns we share with each other … and the fact that we choose to talk to each other about what matters to us that contributes to the growth of intimacy between us" (p. 518). The parallels between the role of values in companionship and meaning making are striking. Unfortunately, research on the potential relationship between companions and meaning in life has yet to appear in the literature primarily because good empirical measures of companionship have yet to be devised. Doing so should be a high priority in the future.

The challenges that await those researchers who wish to explore meaning in life are daunting, yet the payoff from conducting this type of research is commensurate with the effort that must be expended to do it well. One hopes that the conceptual and methodological issues explored in this chapter bring the questions that must be addressed into sharper focus, thereby encouraging others to delve more deeply into issues that lie at the very heart of life itself.

Acknowledgments

The research reviewed in this chapter was supported by two grants from the National Institute on Aging (RO1 AG009221; RO1 AG014749).

References

Barna, G. (2002). *The state of the church, 2002.* Ventura, CA: Issachar Resources.

Barrera, M. (1986). Distinctions between social support concepts, measures, and models. *American Journal of Community Psychology, 14,* 413–425.

Battista, J., & Almond, R. (1973). The development of meaning in life. *Psychiatry, 36,* 409–427.

Baumeister, R. F. (1991). *Meanings of life.* New York, NY: Guilford Press.

Berger, P. L. (1967). *The sacred canopy: Elements of a sociological theory of religion.* New York, NY: Anchor Books.

Berger, P. L., & Pullberg, S. (1965). Reification and sociological critique of consciousness. *History and Theory, 4,* 196–211.

Blazer, D. (2002). *Depression in late life* (3rd ed.). New York, NY: Springer.

Bollen, K. A. (1989). *Structural equations with latent variables.* New York, NY: Wiley.

Braam, A. W., Bramsen, I., van Tilburg, T. G., van der Ploeg, H. M., & Deeg, D. J. (2006). Cosmic transcendence and the framework of meaning in life: Patterns among older adults in the Netherlands. *Journal of Gerontology: Social Sciences, 61B,* S121–S128.

Caplan, G. (1981). Mastery of stress: Psychosocial aspects. *American Journal of Psychiatry, 138,* 413–420.

Carrier, H. (1965). *The sociology of religious belonging.* New York, NY: Herder and Herder.

Carstensen, L. L. (1992). Social and emotional patterns in adulthood: Support for socioemotional selectivity theory. *Psychology and Aging, 7,* 331–338.

Clark, W. H. (1958). *The psychology of religion.* New York, NY: Macmillan.

Cocking, D., & Kennett, J. (1998). Friendship and the self. *Ethics, 108,* 502–527.

Cohen, S., & Rodriguez, M. S. (1995). Pathways linking affective disturbances and physical disorders. *Health Psychology, 14,* 374–380.

Cooley, C. H. (1927). *Life and the student.* New York, NY: Knopf.

Debats, D. L. (1998). Measurement of personal meaning: The psychometric properties of the Life Regard Index. In P. T. P. Wong & P. S. Fry (Eds.), *The human quest for meaning: A handbook of psychological research and clinical applications* (pp. 237–259). Mahwah, NJ: Erlbaum.

Debats, D. L. (1999). Sources of meaning: An investigation of significant commitments in life. *Journal of Humanistic Psychology, 39,* 30–57.

Eckenrode, J., & Wethington, E. (1990). The process and outcome of mobilizing social support. In S. Duck (Ed.), *Personal relationships and social support* (pp. 83–103). Newbury Park, CA: Sage.

Edwards, M. J., & Holden, R. R. (2002). Coping, meaning in life, and suicidal manifestations: Examining gender differences. *Journal of Clinical Psychology, 59,* 1133–1150.

Erikson, E. (1959). *Identity and the life cycle.* New York, NY: International University Press.

Feldman, D. B., & Snyder, C. R. (2005). Hope and the meaningful life: Theoretical and empirical associations between goal-directed thinking and meaning in life. *Journal of Social and Clinical Psychology, 24,* 401–421.

Fetzer Institute, National Institute on Aging Working Group. (1999). Multidimensional measurement of religiousness/spirituality for use in health research. Kalamazoo, MI: John E. Fetzer Institute.
Frankl, V. E. (1984). *Man's search for meaning.* New York: Washington Square Press. (Originally published 1946)
Gallup, G., & Lindsay, D. M. (1999). *Surveying the religious landscape: Trends in U.S. beliefs.* Harrisburg, PA: Morehouse Publishing.
Hoare, C. H. (2002). *Erikson on development and adulthood: New insights from unpublished papers.* New York, NY: Oxford University Press.
Jacobi, J., & Hull, R. F. C. (1953). *C. G. Jung: Psychological reflections.* Princeton, NJ: Princeton University Press.
Janoff-Bulman, R. (1992). *Shattered assumptions: Towards a new psychology of trauma.* New York: Free Press.
Kessler, R. C., & Greenberg, D. (1981). *Linear panel analysis: Models of quantitative change.* New York, NY: Academic Press.
King, G. A. (2004). The meaning of life experiences: Application of a meta-model to rehabilitation sciences and services. *American Journal of Orthopsychiatry, 74,* 72–88.
Klemke, E. D. (2000). *The meaning of life* (2nd ed.). New York, NY: Oxford University Press.
Koenig, H. G. (1994). *Aging and God: Spiritual pathways to mental health in midlife and later years.* New York, NY: Haworth Press.
Krause, N. (2003). The social foundations of personal control in late life. In S. Zarit, L. I. Pearlin, & K. W. Schaie (Eds.), *Societal impacts on personal control in the elderly* (pp. 45–70). New York, NY: Springer.
Krause, N. (2004). Stressors in highly valued roles, meaning in life, and the physical health status of older adults. *Journal of Gerontology: Social Sciences, 59B,* S287–S297.
Krause, N. (2005). God-mediated control and psychological well-being in late life. *Research on Aging, 27,* 136–164.
Krause, N. (2006). Social relationships in late life. In R. H. Binstock & L. K. George (Eds.), *Handbook of aging and the social sciences* (pp. 181–200). San Diego, CA: Academic Press.
Krause, N. (2007a). Evaluating the stress-buffering function of meaning in life among older people. *Journal of Aging and Health, 19,* 792–812.
Krause, N. (2007b). A longitudinal study of the social underpinnings of meaning in life. *Psychology and Aging, 22,* 456–469.
Krause, N. (2008). The social foundation of religious meaning in life. *Research on Aging, 30,* 395–427.
Martens, A., Goldenberg, J. L., & Greenberg, J. (2005). A terror management perspective on ageism. *Journal of Social Issues, 61,* 223–239.
Maslow, A. H. (1968). *Toward a psychology of being.* New York, NY: D. Van Nostrand.
McAdams, D. P. (1996). *The stories we live by: Personal myths and the making of the self.* New York, NY: Guilford Press.
McMillen, J. C. (1999). Better for it: How people benefit from adversity. *Social Work, 44,* 455–468.
Merriam, S. B. (1993). Butler's life review: How universal is it? *International Journal of Aging and Human Development, 37,* 163–175.
Mortimer, J. T., & Shanahan, M. J. (2004). *Handbook of the life course.* New York, NY: Springer.
Morton, R. F., Hebel, J. R., & McCarter, R. J. (2001). *A study guide to epidemiology and statistics* (5th ed.). Gaithersburg, MD: Aspen.

Nygren, B., Alex, L., Jonsen, E., Gustafson, Y, Norberg, A., & Lundman, B. (2005). Resilience, a sense of coherence, purpose in life and self-transcendence in relation to perceived physical and mental health among the oldest old. *Aging & Mental Health, 9*, 354–362.

Olson, J. M., Roese, N. J., & Zanna, M. P. (1996). Expectancies. In E. T. Higgins & A. W. Kruglanski (Eds.), *Social psychology: Handbook of basic principles* (pp. 211–238). New York, NY: Guilford Press.

Pargament, K. I. (1997). *The psychology of religion and coping: Theory, research, and practice.* New York, NY: Guilford Press.

Park, C. L. (2005). Religion and meaning. In R. F. Paloutzian & C. L. Park (Eds.), *Handbook of the psychology of religion and spirituality* (pp. 295–314). New York, NY: Guilford Press.

Park, C. L., & Folkman, S. (1997). Meaning in the context of stress and coping. *Review of General Psychology, 1*, 115–144.

Parquart, M. (2002). Creating and maintaining purpose in life in old age: A meta-analysis. *Aging International, 27*, 90–114.

Peterson, C., Seligman, M. E. P., & Vaillant, G. E. (1994). Pessimistic explanatory style is risk factor for physical illness: A thirty-five-year longitudinal study. In A. Steptoe & J. Wardle (Eds.), *Psychosocial processes and health: A reader* (pp. 235–246). New York, NY: Cambridge University Press.

Pohlmann, K., Karin, P., Gruss, B., & Joraschky, P. (2006). Structural properties of personal meaning systems: A new approach to measuring meaning in life. *Journal of Positive Psychology, 1*, 109–117.

Reker, G. T. (1991, July). *Contextual and thematic analysis of sources of provisional meaning: A life-span perspective.* Paper presented at the Biennial Meeting of the International Society for the Study of Behavioral Development, Minneapolis, Minnesota.

Reker, G. T. (1997). Personal meaning, optimism, and choice: Existential predictors of depression in community and institutional elderly. *Gerontologist, 37*, 709–716.

Reker, G. T., & Chamberlain, K. (2000). Introduction. In G. T. Reker & K. Chamberlain (Eds.), *Exploring existential meaning: Optimizing human development across the life course* (pp. 1–4). Thousand Oaks, CA: Sage.

Reker, G. T., & Peacock, E. J. (1981). The Life Attitude Profile (LAP): A multidimensional instrument for assessing attitudes toward life. *Canadian Journal of Behavioral Sciences, 13*, 264–273.

Rensvold, R. B., & Cheung, G. W. (1998). Testing measurement invariance models for factorial invariance: A systematic approach. *Educational and Psychological Measurement, 58*, 1017–1034.

Rook, K. S. (1984). The negative side of social interaction: Impact on psychological well-being. *Journal of Personality and Social Psychology, 46*, 1097–1108.

Rook, K. S. (1987). Social support versus companionship: Effects of life stress, loneliness, and evaluations of others. *Journal of Personality and Social Psychology, 52*, 1132–1147.

Rook, K. S., & Pietromonaco, P. (1987). Close relationships: Ties that heal or ties that bind? In W. H. Jones & D. Perlman (Eds.), *Advances in personal relationships* (Vol. 1, pp. 1–35). London, England: Kingsley.

Schnell, T., & Becker, P. (2006). Personality and meaning in life. *Personality and Individual Differences, 41, 117–129.*

Settersten, R. A. (2002). Social sources of meaning in later life. In R. S. Weiss & S. A. Bass (Eds.), *Challenges of the third age: Meaning and purpose in later life* (pp. 55–79). New York, NY: Oxford University Press.

Smith, B. W., & Zautra, A. J. (2004). The role of purpose in life in recovery from knee surgery. *International Journal of Behavioral Medicine, 11*, 197–202.

Spilka, B., Hood, R. W., Hunsberger, B., & Gorsuch, R. (2003). *The psychology of religion.* New York, NY: Guilford Press.

Stark, R., & Finke, R. (2000). *Acts of faith: Explaining the human side of religion.* Berkeley: University of California Press.

Staudinger, U. M. (2001). Life reflection: A social-cognitive analysis of life review. *Review of General Psychology, 5*, 148–160.

Steger, M. F., Frazier, P., Oishi, S., & Kaler, M. (2006). The Meaning of Life Questionnaire: Assessing presence and search for meaning in life. *Journal of Counseling Psychology, 53*, 80–93.

Tedeschi, R. G., & Calhoun, L. G. (2004). Posttraumatic growth: Conceptual foundations and empirical evidence. *Psychological Inquiry, 15*, 1–18.

Tedeschi, R. G., Park, C. L., & Calhoun, L. G. (1998). *Posttraumatic growth: Positive changes in the aftermath of crisis.* Mahwah, NJ: Erlbaum.

Tornstam, L. (1997). Gerotranscendence: The contemplative dimensions of aging. *Journal of Aging Studies, 11*, 143–154.

U.S. Department of Health and Human Services. (2004). *Health, United States, 2004, Special Excerpt: Trend Tables on 65 and older population.* Washington, DC: Government Printing Office.

Wethington, E., & Kessler, R. C. (1986). Perceived support, received support, and adjustment to stressfull life events. *Journal of Health and Social Behavior, 27*, 78–89.

Wong, P. T. P. (1998). Implicit theories of meaningful life and development of the Personal Meaning Profile. In P. T. P. Wong & P. S. Frey (Eds.), *The human quest for meaning: A handbook of psychological research and clinical applications* (pp. 111–140). Mahwah, NJ: Erlbaum.

20

Personal Meaning in Life and Psychosocial Adaptation in the Later Years

GARY T. REKER and PAUL T. P. WONG

Trent University

The aim of this chapter is to explore the role of personal meaning in life in promoting and enhancing positive psychosocial adaptation in the later years. Current focus on meaning in life and psychosocial adaptation falls within the contemporary emphasis on positive psychology. Indeed, optimal psychosocial adaptation is commonly associated with and reflects many of the characteristics of successful aging.

Four specific objectives are addressed. First, following a definition of terms, Reker and Wong's (1988) conceptualization of global and situational meaning is described and presented in the context of a top-down, bottom-up model of personal meaning. Second, the findings from the Ontario Successful Aging Project on the contribution of global meaning to successful aging in older adults are presented. Third, available evidence on the contribution of global and situational meaning to positive psychosocial functioning and the underlying mechanism through which personal meaning promotes health in older adults is reviewed. Finally, an integrative model of global and situational meaning and its application in adapting to chronic health problems (e.g., stroke) and life-threatening illnesses (e.g., cancer) is proposed. It is concluded that a complete understanding of personal meaning and its role in promoting psychosocial adaptation in the later years can be achieved only when the joint and interactive influences of global meaning and situational meaning are taken into account.

Personal Meaning in Life

It is useful to conceptualize the construct of meaning in life as consisting of two different but interrelated aspects. The first, termed *global meaning*, refers to the existential belief that life has purpose and coherence whereby the individual attempts to understand how life events fit into a larger context. It addresses the *experience of meaning* and asks such questions as "What is worth living for?" and "What is the purpose in life?" Global meaning is the preferred term over such other labels as ultimate meaning, existential meaning, meaningfulness, purpose in life, or meaning-as-comprehensibility that have been used in the literature to describe this aspect of personal meaning in life. The second, termed *situational meaning*, refers to the attachment of personal significance to specific experiences in life whereby the individual tries to make sense of that experience. It involves the process of assigning or structuring meaning and addresses the *meaning of experience*, such as the "meaning of growing old." Situational meaning is the preferred term over such other labels as provisional meaning, meaning of the moment, definitional meaning, or meaning-as-significance. Situational meaning and global meaning are important constructs in fully understanding human experiences. They are interrelated insofar as experiences requiring the realization of situational meaning can often initiate and enhance the search for global meaning.

Although there is general agreement as to the importance of global meaning and situational meaning, the conceptualization of what constitutes each differs widely. For example, working within the stress and coping paradigm, Park and Folkman (1997) define global meaning as an abstract and generalized level of meaning that refers to people's basic goals and assumptions, beliefs, and expectations about the world. Situational meaning, in contrast, is tied to the processes of appraisal (i.e., appraised meaning) and reappraisal (i.e., meaning making) and is the outcome of an interaction between a person's global meaning and the circumstances of a person–environment transaction. Davis, Nolen-Hoeksema, and Larson (1998) differentiate between two construals of meaning or ways of understanding: sense making and benefit finding. The former is more closely tied to the concept of global meaning; the latter to situational meaning. Similarly, Janoff-Bulman and Frantz (1997) distinguish between meaning-as-comprehensibility (making sense of life events) and meaning-as-significance (the value or worth of life events).

Global Meaning

Working within an existential paradigm, we define global meaning as the cognizance of order, coherence, and purpose in one's existence; the pursuit and attainment of worthwhile goals; and the accompanying sense of fulfillment (Reker & Wong, 1988). Reker and Wong (1988) proposed a model of the structure of global meaning consisting of three interrelated components: cognitive, motivational, and affective. An expanded model of global meaning is depicted in Figure 20.1.

As can be seen in Figure 20.1, the cognitive component of beliefs, worldviews, and value schemas forms the cornerstone in the model that directs both the selection of goals and engenders feelings of worthiness. The motivational component of wants, needs, and goal strivings leads to satisfaction,

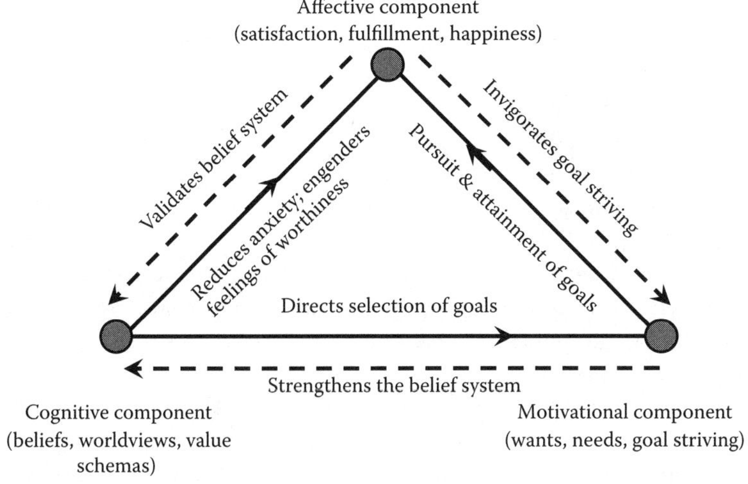

Figure 20.1 The three-component model of the structure of personal meaning. Solid arrows represent the direction of influence; dashed arrows represent feedback. (Adapted from Reker, G. T., and Wong, P. T. P., in *Emergent theories of aging*, 214–246, New York, NY, Springer, 1988.)

fulfillment, and happiness. In addition, there are feedback loops. Feelings of satisfaction, fulfillment, and happiness invigorate goal strivings and validate one's belief system. Successful goal attainment strengthens the belief system. Thus, a person high on global meaning has a clear life purpose, has a sense of direction, strives for goals consistent with life purpose, feels satisfied with past achievements, and is determined to make the future meaningful. A relatively large number of empirical studies have clearly demonstrated that global meaning in life is an important variable in the buffering of stress; in the enhancement of physical, psychological, and mental well-being; and in transcending negative life experiences (e.g., Fry, 2000, 2001; Newcomb & Harlow, 1986; Reker, 1994; Reker & Chamberlain, 2000; Reker, Peacock & Wong, 1987; Vickberg, Bovbjerg, DuHamel, Currie, & Redd, 2000; Zika & Chamberlain, 1992).

Situational Meaning

Situational or provisional meaning refers to attempts to understand the value and purpose of specific encounters and experiences in life that occur on a day-to-day basis. The ongoing quest to extract the "meaning of the moment" serves as a source for the attainment of a higher, ultimate, or global meaning. For Frankl (1963), meaning stems from three broad sources: (a) creative, or what one accomplishes from creative work; (b) experiential, or what one derives from beauty, truth, or love; and (c) attitudinal, or what one derives from reflections on such aspects of life as pain and suffering. Research has shown that individuals derive meaning from a variety of specific sources that vary according to cultural and ethnic background, sociodemographics, and developmental stage (DeVogler-Ebersole & Ebersole, 1985; Kaufman, 1987; O'Connor & Chamberlain, 1996; Prager, Savaya, & Bar-Tur, 2000; Reker, 1988, 1991, 1996; Wong & Fry, 1998; Yalom, 1980). Reker (1991) surveyed the available literature and generated a list of the most common sources of meaning. The list includes personal relationships, altruism, religious activities, creative activities, personal growth, maintenance of basic needs, financial security, leisure activities, personal achievement, leaving a legacy, enduring values and ideals, traditions and culture, social and political causes, humanistic concerns, hedonistic activities, material possessions, and relationship with nature. A 7-point rating scale, the Sources of Meaning Profile–Revised (SOMP-R), was developed to assess the degree of meaningfulness of each source (Reker, 1996). Many of the individual sources of meaning, as assessed by the SOMP-R, are associated with global meaning and with psychological and physical well-being (Reker, 1988, 1991, 1994).

Psychosocial Adaptation

Psychosocial adaptation is defined as the process of putting oneself in harmony with the changing circumstances of life so as to enhance one's sense of competence, identity, well-being, and long-term survivorship. Putting oneself in harmony means changing the self, changing the situation or the environment, or changing both. Psychosocial adaptation is achieved through the processes of assimilation (i.e., incorporating new information into existing structures) and accommodation (i.e., changing existing structures to accommodate new information), involving both the psychological domain (e.g., changes in perception, attitude, behavior, motivation) and the social domain (e.g., change in one's social environment). Traditional outcome indicators of effective psychosocial adaptation include, but are not limited to, the maintenance of good physical health, life satisfaction, good mental health, positive life and death attitudes, low levels of existential distress (e.g., fear of aging, fear of death, regrets in life), and a stable personality. The ability of individuals to find meaning in life is postulated to impact positively on adaptational processes and psychosocial outcomes.

Top-Down and Bottom-Up Model of Personal Meaning

Reker and Wong (1988) postulate that a full understanding of personal meaning requires both a top-down (holistic) and a bottom-up (elemental) view of life. It is not meaningful to talk about life as a whole as having meaning; life contains only meanings that are actualized through specific activities, quests, and goals. To achieve an enduring type of personal meaning, however, specific sources (i.e., situational meaning) need to be integrated into a larger and higher purpose (i.e., global meaning). Based on Frankl's (1990) conviction that the full meaning of life can be achieved only by transcending self-interests and on Rokeach's (1973) hierarchy of values in which certain values hold greater significance than others, Reker and Wong (1988) proposed a contextual model of personal meaning consisting of four levels: self-preoccupation with hedonistic pleasure and comfort, devotion of time and energy to the realization of personal potential, service to others and commitment to a larger societal or political cause, and the entertainment of values that transcend individuals and encompass cosmic meaning and ultimate purpose. The model is presented in Figure 20.2.

As shown in Figure 20.2, the situational and global components of personal meaning are integrated on the major dimension of comprehensiveness, ranging from least to most comprehensive, characterized by increasing abstractness and inclusiveness in understanding ideas, facts, or relationships. Whereas individuals *create* meaning through making choices, taking actions, and entering into relationships, they *discover* meaning through reflection on the givens of life, such as the existence of the universe or the existence of life. Each level is postulated to be qualitatively different in terms of the depth of meaning that is obtained, and each provides a horizon or backdrop against which meaning is created or discovered. Individuals who find meaning through self-preoccupation with hedonistic pleasure and comfort are at the shallow end, whereas those who find meaning through serving others and transcend the self are at the deep end. The implication of such a hierarchical structure is that individuals will be able to integrate the contradictions,

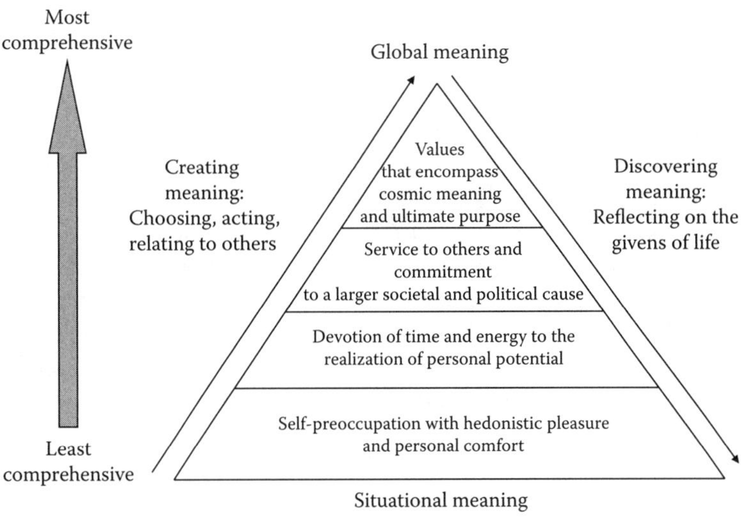

Figure 20.2 A contextual model of personal meaning in life.

conflicts, and absurdities of life by rising above them and viewing them in the context of a more comprehensive horizon.

The proposed contextual model of meaning has been subjected to empirical validation using quantitative (Reker, 1991) and qualitative (O'Connor & Chamberlain, 1996) approaches. Consistent with expectation, a principal-components factor analysis of the SOMP-R conducted by Reker (1991) resulted in the extraction of the four primary factors. The factors, the factor labels assigned, and the sources of meaning associated with each factor are as follows: *self-preoccupation* (maintenance of basic needs, financial security, hedonistic activities, material possessions); *individualism* (leisure activities, creative activities, personal achievement, personal growth); *collectivism* (social and political causes, traditions and culture, leaving a legacy, humanistic concerns) and; *self-transcendence* (personal relationships, religious beliefs and activities, service to others, enduring values and ideals, relationship with nature). Moreover, Reker (1991) demonstrated that individuals who experience meaning at deeper levels through collectivism and self-transcendence score higher on a measure of global meaning and are more fulfilled and satisfied with life compared to individuals who experience meaning through self-preoccupation and individualism. These findings provide strong support for Frankl's (1963) view that a deeper sense of meaning can be discovered only when an individual moves toward a self-transcendent state.

Global Meaning and Optimal Psychosocial Adaptation

In the past two decades, gerontological studies have investigated growth models of aging under the general heading of successful aging (e.g., Baltes & Baltes, 1990; Rowe & Kahn, 1997; Ryff, 1989; Schulz & Heckhausen, 1996). These models differ in the way successful aging is conceptualized, but there is still no generally agreed-upon definition nor is there agreement as to what constitutes success. The prevailing view is that successful aging requires consideration of multiple criteria and multiple adaptive patterns.

Researchers attempting to understand the factors involved in predicting successful aging have traditionally worked within the stress and coping paradigm, focusing on environmental factors, personal characteristics, lifestyle factors, social resources, and coping strategies in explaining variation in successful aging. Although much has been learned from this perspective, little emphasis has been given to the existential needs and concerns of older adults that touch on issues of human suffering, mortality, religiousness, spirituality, self-transcendence, and meaning in life. Reker, Peacock, and Wong (1987) have proposed that the existential construct of global meaning has value in facilitating optimal adaptation to life's changing circumstances that accompany the aging process. Indeed, global meaning has been shown to be related to a number of measures of psychological, physical, and mental well-being and is a major source for bolstering self-esteem, life satisfaction, and personal growth (Fry, 2000, 2001; Reker, 1994, 1997; Reker & Butler, 1990; Reker et al., 1987; Zika & Chamberlain, 1992).

In a stimulating theoretical article, Wong (1989) reviewed a number of theories and empirical findings that implicate the importance of personal meaning in promoting health and successful adaptation to aging. He proposed that the discovery or creation of meaning through inner and spiritual resources is a promising way of transcending personal losses and despair in old age. He introduced four meaning-enhancing strategies that are especially relevant to the elderly, namely, reminiscence, commitment, optimism, and religiosity. Wong (1989) concluded that

> at present, most of the societal resources have been directed to meeting the physical, social and economic needs of the elderly. While these efforts are essential, one must not overlook personal meaning as an important dimension of health and life satisfaction. Prolonging life without providing any meaning for existence is not the best answer to the challenge of aging. Greater research efforts are needed to provide a firm scientific basis for the application of personal meaning as a means of promoting successful aging. (p. 522)

Study 1: The Ontario Successful Aging Project

In the mid-1980s, Wong and Reker launched a longitudinal study on the profile and processes of successful aging in institutionalized and community-residing older adults that came to be known as the Ontario Successful Aging Project (OSAP). Only the findings relevant to meaning in life and successful aging are briefly summarized here. For more details on these findings, the reader is referred to Reker (2002).

The project involved an in-depth baseline screening procedure of successful aging, a comprehensive index of successful aging at 14-month follow-up, and a large number of traditional and existential predictor variables. In keeping with a multiple-criteria approach, successful aging was operationalized as the attainment of a relatively high level of physical well-being, psychological well-being, and adjustment. Participants were screened through an initial interview by a research assistant (using nine questions) and by a panel of three professionals (psychiatrist, geriatric nurse, and gerontological recreation worker) based on questions relevant to each professional's area of expertise. All interviewers completed three 11-point rating scales that assessed physical well-being, psychological well-being, and adjustment. The ratings were combined to form a reliable rating score. Participants were rank-ordered according to the total score and classified (using the median split) into either successful or unsuccessful agers. The classification was done separately for community-residing and institutionalized elderly. A total of 82 community-residing and 63 institutionalized elderly completed a large number of measures at the outset and at an average of 14 months later. At follow-up, a composite index of successful aging was generated using reliable and valid self-report measures of the presence of psychological well-being, physical well-being, and life satisfaction, as well as the absence of physical health problems, depression, and psychopathology.

To assess the role of global meaning in predicting successful aging, two sets of predictor variables were created. Traditional predictors included measures of social resources (meaningful social contacts), intellectual competence, and cognitive competence. Existential predictors included measures of purpose in life, religiousness, and death acceptance. Using hierarchical regression analysis and after controlling for demographic variables and baseline successful aging, it was found that social resources, purpose in life, and low religiousness predicted successful aging in community-residing older adults, whereas social resources and purpose in life predicted successful aging in institutionalized elderly. In both samples, purpose in life was found to be a potent predictor accounting for unique variance in successful aging beyond that accounted for by demographic, baseline successful aging and traditional predictor variables. The expectation that death acceptance, a positive interpretational construct, would make a significant contribution to the prediction of successful aging was not supported, although findings were in the predicted direction, particularly for the community-residing elderly.

Of particular interest is the way in which the construct of religiousness resulted in differential predictions for community-residing and institutionalized elderly individuals. For community-residing elderly individuals, religiousness made a significant but negative contribution to successful aging; for institutionalized elderly individuals, religiousness made a positive but nonsignificant contribution. The residence-differential predictive pattern is consistent with results reported by Fry (2000), who found that religiousness was a strong predictor of well-being in elderly individuals in institutional care but not for the community-residing older adults. Our finding that antireligious attitudes and practices predicted successful aging in community-residing elderly individuals is contrary to what is generally reported in the literature (e.g., see Wong & Fry, 1998). In the current study, both samples reported low but similar levels of religious involvement, so initial differences in the involvement aspect of religiousness appears not to be a factor. It may be that the community-residing elderly are still able to maintain a stable and varied repertoire of resources that allow them to acquire goals and compensate for losses without the benefit of religiousness. This notion raises the possibility that religiousness may have its primary impact on aging well when the individual is undergoing a crisis (loneliness, grief) and/or is severely under-resourced. Future studies are needed to examine the moderating effect of religiousness on successful aging for the in-crisis as well as the resource-rich and resource-poor elderly.

It is also possible that religious involvement through religious affiliation or religious behavior is not enough to contribute to successful aging. Several studies have shown that the strength of the faith, the belief, or the religious commitment is more critical in producing positive psychosocial outcomes than are religious affiliations or religious behaviors per se. A strong faith provides a strong sense of meaning and purpose, which in turn leads to feelings of well-being and psychosocial adjustment. The hypothesis that global meaning mediates or intervenes between religious involvement and well-being has received some empirical support (Kennedy & Kanthamani, 1995; Zika & Chamberlain, 1992).

Our findings underscore the importance of existential constructs, especially global meaning, in understanding why many older adults continue to age well in the face of difficult life situations. This is particularly so for the elderly living in institutions, who are more likely to suffer from depleted resources, declining functional status, poor health, and multiple losses and who, under these conditions, face the existential question "Why survive?" (Reker, 2002; Wong, 1989). According to Lukas (1992), purpose in life can give rise to an inner calm and composure and to the perception that life is unconditionally worth living.

Stress, Global Meaning, and Health Promotion

Global meaning has been identified as a powerful personal resource that is importantly related to a variety of health outcomes. The negative impact of stress on health outcomes is also well documented. In the context of stressful encounters, a related question is the nature of the mechanism through which global meaning promotes health. Global meaning may function as a stress moderator, a stress mediator, a generalized health-enhancer, or some combination of these. Moderation involves determining whether an observed relationship between two variables (e.g., life stress and physical health) is different at different levels of the moderator (e.g., global meaning). An effective moderator variable is said to function as a *buffer*. Mediation implies a causal hypothesis whereby an independent variable (e.g., life stress) causes a mediator (e.g., global meaning), which causes a dependent variable (e.g., physical health). An effective mediator variable is said to function as a *damper*.

Global Meaning as a Moderator of Stress

In a study of stressful life transitions involving housing relocation to a congregate living facility, Lutgendorf, Vitaliano, Tripp-Reimer, Harvey, and Lubaroff (1999) found that a sense of coherence (global meaning) moderated the relationship between relocation stress and natural killer-cell activity in healthy older adults. Specifically, in older adults anticipating relocation, those with low global meaning were found to have poorer immune function, whereas the immune function of movers with high global meaning was less compromised. As suggested by Lutgendorf et al. (1999), possible psychological mechanism underlying the health-protecting effect include (a) appraisal of relocation as a challenge as opposed to a stressor, (b) greater use of appropriate coping strategies to deal with moving-related difficulties, or (c) decreased physiological reactivity in response to a benign appraisal of moving.

In a study of global meaning as a moderator of everyday stress and well-being (Reker & Butler, 1990), 103 community-residing older adults, ranging in age from 60 to 90 years, completed measures of everyday stress, global meaning, perceived well-being, self-esteem, and physical health. It was found that global meaning functioned as a stress buffer for physical health. Older adults low on global meaning had increasing physical symptoms under high levels of everyday stress, whereas those high on global meaning were virtually unaffected by stress. In addition, global meaning enhanced levels of perceived psychological well-being and self-esteem (Reker & Butler, 1990). In a related study of physically healthy California elderly, results showed that global meaning moderated life event stress for perceived psychological well-being, but not for physical health (Reker, 1994). Finally, in Underhill's (1991) study of relatively healthy older adults, global meaning enhanced levels of psychological well-being and physical health at all levels of daily hassles and life event stress.

Recently, Krause (2007) investigated the stress-buffering function of meaning in life in the relationship between traumatic events at any point in one's lifetime and depressive affect and somatic symptoms. He found that more traumatic events are associated with more depressed affect and greater somatic symptom reporting for older adults who have a relatively weak sense of global meaning, whereas the effect of lifetime trauma on depressed affect was almost completely eliminated for those with a relatively strong sense of global meaning.

The health-protecting function of global meaning was also explored by Vickberg et al. (2000) in a sample of 61 women (mean age 59 years) who had survived breast cancer. Previous research has consistently demonstrated a positive relationship between intrusive thoughts about stressful experiences and psychological distress. The strength of the association has, however, varied across different studies. Vickberg et al. (2000) identified global meaning as a possible third variable that could moderate the relationship between intrusive thoughts and psychological distress. Intrusive thoughts were assessed with the Impact of Events Scale (IES; Horowitz, Wilner, & Alvarez, 1979), global meaning was assessed with the Personal Meaning Index of the LAP-R (Reker, 1992), and psychological distress was assessed with the Global Symptom Index of the Brief Symptom Inventory (BSI-GSI; Derogatis & Spence, 1982). Vickberg et al. (2000) found results consistent with a moderator hypothesis. Among women with lower global meaning, more frequent intrusive thoughts about cancer were associated with higher psychological distress, whereas no association was found among women with higher global meaning.

Global Meaning as a Mediator of Stress

Only a few studies have examined the role of global meaning as a mediator of stress. In one prospective study investigating a specific source of stress, the death of a family member, Davis et al. (1998) found that making sense of the event mediated the impact of antecedent factors (age at death, religious beliefs, preloss distress) on psychological adjustment at six months following the loss.

In a recent study of relatively healthy older adults, Reker (2008) assessed the mediating role of global meaning in the relation between stressful life events and subjective well-being, existential regret, and physical health. In this study, 146 older adults (55% female), ranging in age from 54 to 94 years, completed measures of stressful life events (stress rating, negative stress, general stress), life satisfaction, depression, existential regret (inner struggle, limited life, neglecting others, self-deprecation, undoing the past), and physical health. Using the latent construct approach and structural equation modeling, it was found that global meaning partially mediated the relationship between life stress and subjective well-being and existential regret. There was a mediation trend for physical health, but it did not reach statistical significance. Given that this study was not longitudinal, the direction of the causal influence is always open to question. To address this question, reverse causal mediation was also assessed. A causal interpretation of the mediating effects from life stress to global meaning to subjective and existential well-being was strengthened by the finding that reverse causal mediation (from subjective and existential well-being to global meaning to life stress) was not statistically significant.

Taken together, the research findings pertaining to stress, global meaning, and health promotion clearly demonstrate that global meaning functions as an effective buffer of life stress (health-protecting) and as a generalized enhancer of psychological well-being, physical well-being, and self-esteem (health-promoting). A high level of global meaning not only shields one from the negative impact of stress but also enhances one's level of wellness. Whether or not global meaning operated as a moderator of stress depended on the nature of the outcome variable and the general health of the older participants. For older adults with some physical health problems, global meaning buffered the effects of stress on physical health; for relatively healthy older adults, global meaning either buffered the effects of stress on psychological well-being or enhanced levels of well-being and self-esteem. In addition, the direct impact of life stress on measures of subjective and existential well-being was significantly mediated through global meaning. In sum, older adults high in global meaning perceive life events as less stressful. Finding meaning in a stressful situation, in turn, promotes positive psychosocial functioning.

Situational Meaning and Psychosocial Adaptation

As noted, unlike global meaning, which addresses the experience of meaning, situational meaning focuses on the meaning of experience. The bulk of prior research has been directed toward the study of global meaning and its role in positive psychosocial functioning. In recent years, there has been increasing research activity in the study of situational meaning per se as reflected in such themes as the meaning of love (e.g., Chapter 9, this volume) and the meaning of death (e.g., Chapter 10, this volume); as a developmental process across the life span (e.g., Bar-Tur, Savaya, & Prager, 2001; Prager, 1996; Prager et al., 2000; Reker & Chamberlain, 2000; Wong & Fry, 1998); in coping with traumatic life experiences (e.g., Chapters 22, 23, 24, and 25, this volume); and in the context of caregiving (e.g., Farran & Kuhn, 1998).

Within a developmental framework, cross-sectional studies of young, middle-aged, and older adults have shown that whereas an overall sense of global meaning remains high and relatively stable across the life span, the sources from which meaning is derived (i.e., situational meaning) show both stability and change, depending on one's developmental stage and points of transition between stages (Prager, 1996; Reker, 1991). Even within a specified age group of older adults, there are many different pathways through which to experience life as meaningful. A variety of sources have been shown to contribute to overall psychosocial adjustment (Reker, 1991). For example, Reker (1994) found that in one sample of older adults, having a relatively large network of meaningful sources (high breadth vs. low breadth) and experiencing meaning at deeper levels culminated in a heightened sense of meaning fulfillment and greater subjective well-being. Taken together, the findings suggest that individuals develop *personal meaning orientations* that individually and collectively contribute to positive psychosocial functioning.

Study 2: Personal Meaning Orientations and Psychosocial Adjustment

The purpose of Study 2 was to explore the personal meaning orientations of older adults and to assess the association of meaning orientations to measures of psychosocial adjustment. Relatively little is known about the content and the function of sources of meaning and the meaning system that older individuals create for themselves. Furthermore, the literature has not addressed the differential impact of meaning orientations on positive and negative indicators of psychosocial functioning.

Two main hypotheses were formulated. First, older adults will be characterized by personal meaning systems that reflect transcendent, collectivistic, individualistic, and self-preoccupied meaning orientations. Second, older adults who derive meaning from transcendent sources will show significantly better psychosocial adjustment and reduced existential distress compared to older adults who find meaning through self-serving values, interests, and activities. In this second study, 120 community-residing older adults (52% female) aged 52 to 93 years completed measures of sources of meaning, global meaning, and a number of psychosocial adjustment measures, including physical health, life satisfaction, death acceptance, depression, personality, existential regret, and attitude toward aging.

The first hypothesis was tested using K-means cluster analysis of cases on the SOMP-R. In the cluster analysis approach, the focus is on discovering groups, sets, or clusters of individuals in a multidimensional space defined by the domains of situational meaning. Individuals are thus characterized not as having high or low situational meaning but as expressing situational meaning in different ways. This conceptualization is consistent with a typological or taxonomic approach. A taxonomic approach not only provides useful summaries of the data but also allows for the exploration of changes in an individual's cluster placement at different points over an entire life span. In addition, cluster placement may be differentially related to a variety of psychosocial variables that could, in turn, identify possibilities for future interventions.

As hypothesized, cluster analysis performed on the SOMP-R scores revealed four distinct groups of individuals. The cluster profiles are presented in Figure 20.3. Cluster 1, labeled *self-transcendent meaning orientation*, consisted of 32 (27%) individuals oriented toward such transcendent sources of meaning as engaging in religious rituals and activities, preserving human values and ideals, leaving a legacy for the next generation, having an interest in humanistic concerns, and having a relationship with nature. Cluster 2 (*collectivistic meaning orientation*) comprised 24 (20%) individuals who found

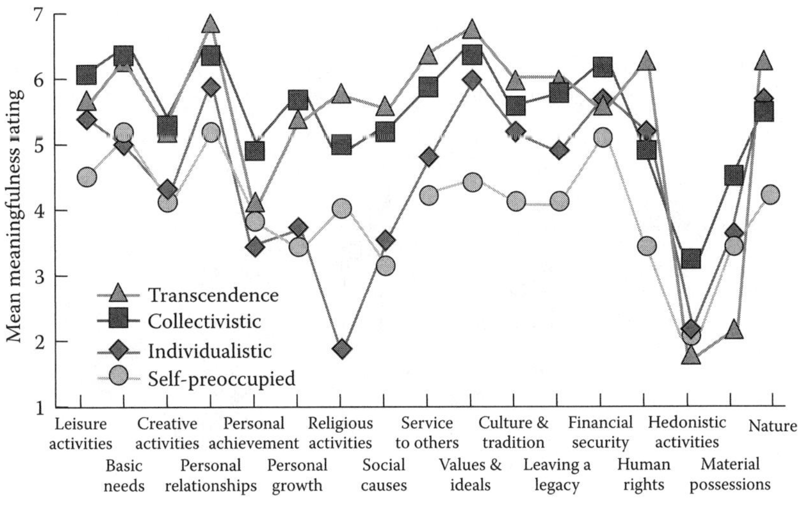

Figure 20.3 Plot of means of sources of meaning in life for each cluster.

meaning in personal relationships, service to others, and commitment toward larger societal and political causes. Cluster 3 (*individualistic meaning orientation*) consisted of 34 (28%) individuals who found meaning through devoting their time and energy to realizing such personal potential as taking part in creative activities, experiencing personal growth, and taking part in religious activities. Cluster 4 (*self-preoccupied meaning orientation*) identified 30 (25%) individuals who were primarily oriented toward finding meaning through pursuing self-serving interests without any real commitment to personal development, interpersonal relationships, or social causes. Although the individualistic orientation was found to be most salient in this sample of North American elderly individuals, there is little evidence that one meaning orientation predominates over another.

Are these pathways differentially related to psychosocial adjustment? The second hypothesis addressed this question. A 2 (Gender) × 4 (Meaning Orientation) between-subjects multivariate analysis of covariance (MANCOVA) was performed on a number of psychosocial variables. Age, education level, marital status, and financial satisfaction served as covariates. Significant multivariate main effects were found for meaning orientation and gender. The Gender × Meaning Orientation interaction was not statistically significant. Results of significant univariate effects for meaning orientation are presented in Figures 20.4 and 20.5.

Older adults with a transcendent meaning orientation have significantly greater purpose and coherence in life (global meaning), perceive to have more choice, fear death less, and continue to seek new challenges compared to older adults characterized by a self-preoccupied orientation. Transcendent older adults are also more extraverted, agreeable, and

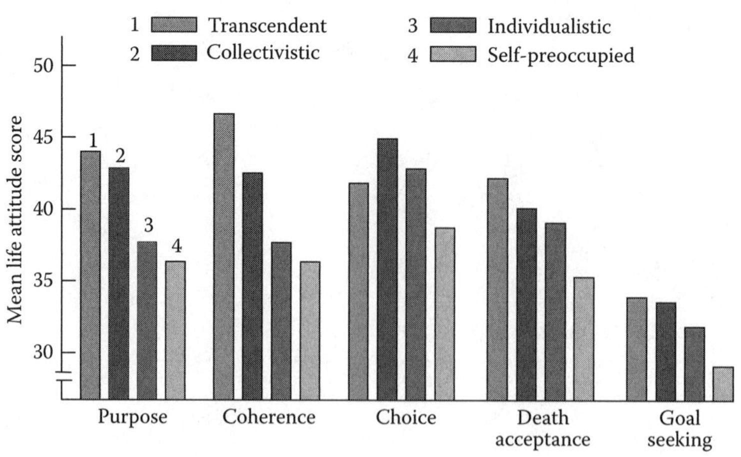

Figure 20.4 Life attitudes as a function of personal meaning orientations.

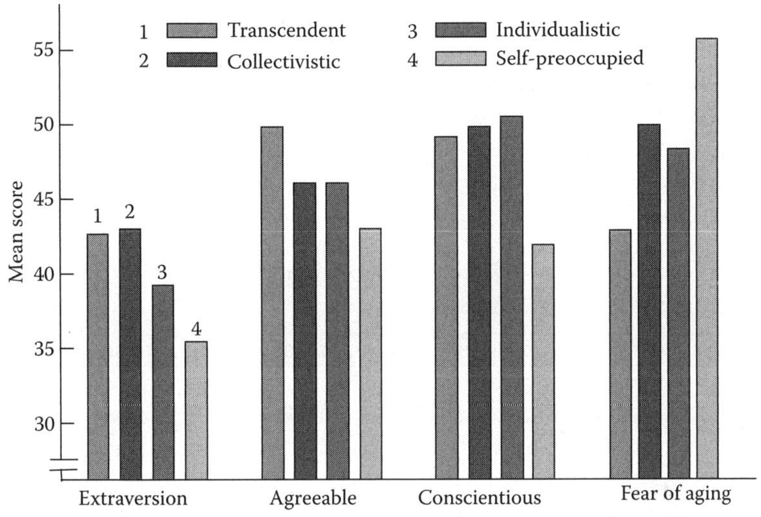

Figure 20.5 Personality traits and fear of aging as a function of meaning orientations.

conscientious and show less fear of aging compared to their self-preoccupied counterparts (see Figure 20.5). No significant differences were found for physical health, life satisfaction, depression, existential regrets, openness to experience, neuroticism, and existential vacuum. Thus, the second hypothesis was supported for some of but not all the psychosocial variables. Regarding gender differences, older males were found to be more extraverted, expressed greater purpose in life, and were lower on neuroticism compared to older females.

Our findings clearly demonstrate that there are a variety of different pathways through which older adults experience life as meaningful. Those older individuals with a transcendent meaning orientation show significantly better adjustment on a number of life attitudes and personality traits compared to those who find meaning through self-serving values, interests, and activities. Moreover, existential distress, as expressed through fear of aging and fear of death, was also significantly reduced in transcendent older adults. Consistent with Tornstam's (1977) concept of gerotranscendence, it appears that older men and women who see the "bigger picture" by discovering and creating meaning from transcendent sources hold positive life attitudes and exhibit prosocial personality characteristics that are conducive to optimal adaptation in the later years (see also Chapter 5, this volume). Schnell and Becker's (2006) recent study investigating the link between middle-aged adults' personality and meaning in life supports our conclusion. The researchers found that meaningfulness was predicted by extraversion–openness, conscientiousness, and disagreeableness; but most important, self-transcendence—as indexed by spirituality, generativity, attentiveness, nature, and religion—mediated between personality and meaningfulness. Indeed, Costa, Metter, and McCrae (1994) have noted that stable personality dispositions assist with shaping an individual's own life history, contribute to the coherence of the self-concept, and provide a dependable basis for adaptation to a changing world. They conclude, "For better or worse, we are what we are, and the recognition of that fact is a crucial step in successful aging" (p. 57).

Personal Meaning and Psychosocial Adaptation to Chronic and Life-Threatening Illnesses

Although personal meaning plays an important role in restoring, maintaining, and enhancing wellness in individuals across the life span, it plays an even greater role for those individuals who face such traumatic life events as brain injury, cardiovascular disease, or cancer. Most individuals assume that their lives are purposeful and coherent, but traumatic life events may challenge that assumption and trigger a renewed search for meaning (Park & Folkman, 1997; Reker & Wong, 1988). This process is diagrammed in Figure 20.6.

Individuals experience incongruence when the meaning they attach to the experience of a traumatic life event (i.e., situational meaning) does not match their beliefs, values, purpose, goals, and sense of coherence (global meaning). When that happens, the result is *shattered global meaning*: The life plan is disrupted, existential distress sets in, and adaptational difficulties emerge. Shattered global meaning prompts a search for meaning to achieve reintegration. There are two ways to achieve reintegration: Change global meaning, or change the meaning of the traumatic life event. Given the durability and stability of global meaning, the individual is more likely able to change the

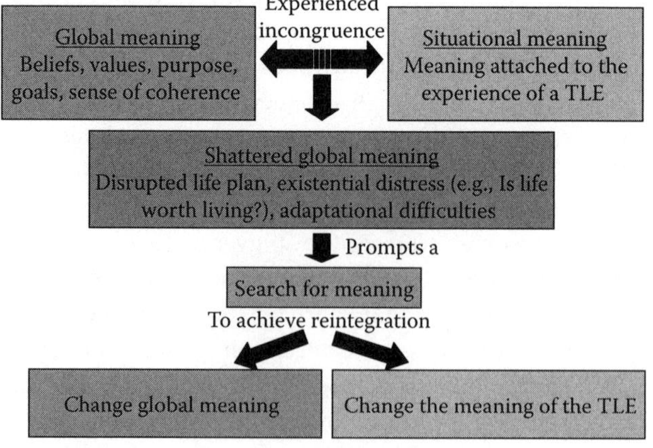

Figure 20.6 An integrated model of global and situational meaning in the context of traumatic life experiences (TLEs).

meaning attached to the traumatic experience than to change global meaning, although changes to both are possible outcomes.

By what processes does an individual change the meaning of a traumatic life event or change global meaning? Before addressing that question, it would be useful to find a way to assess the degree of incongruence between global meaning and situational meaning. One approach is to calculate a meaning congruence index, expressed as a ratio of global meaning scores over situational meaning scores. When global meaning scores are identical to situational meaning scores, the ratio is 1 and total congruence is indexed. As situational meaning scores decrease relative to global meaning scores, the ratio becomes increasingly larger, indexing greater incongruence. A measure of global meaning can be provided by the Purpose and Coherence subscales of the LAP-R (Reker, 1992). A sensitive measure of situational meaning would need to be developed for each traumatic life event.

Reker (2007) developed a situational meaning measure for individuals who suffered a stroke. Based on preliminary findings by Thompson (1991), an eight-item, 7-point Likert scale was constructed that addressed the following themes: appreciate life more following a stroke; have learned to slow down more; have a deeper appreciation for family, friends, and community; have become more compassionate; have grown personally; have become more spiritual; have not found any meaning; often ask myself, "Why me?" The maximum score on both the global meaning measure and the situational meaning measure is 56, the minimum is 8. A high score indicates greater global and situational meaning. When using both measures, the meaning congruence index can range from 1 (*congruence*) to 7 (*incongruence*). The cut-off score for incongruence would need to be established empirically.

It is now possible to determine the extent of shattered global meaning at any point in time and to chart progress in reestablishing personal meaning as a function of therapeutic interventions. Of particular interest are meaning-centered interventions designed to restore, maintain, or enhance a sense of meaning in life. For a comprehensive review of therapeutic approaches, including logotherapy, meaning-centered counseling, narrative therapy, and life review, see Reker, Birren, and Svensson (Chapter 18, this volume) and Wong (1998; Chapter 28, this volume).

Changing the Meaning of a Traumatic Life Event

The goal of changing the meaning of a traumatic life event is to effect posttraumatic growth in which the individual acknowledges the devastation of the traumatic event and begins to embrace a positive posttraumatic life that is subjectively valued (see Chapter 25, this volume). This goal is achieved through meaning-based coping strategies that include, but are not limited to, (a) finding purpose in the traumatic event, (b) engaging in positive reappraisal of the traumatic event, and (c) engaging in existential reattribution.

Finding purpose in the traumatic event may be achieved by realizing that the event revealed a previously unrecognized inner strength, or that the event heightened a renewed appreciation of life, or that the event improved relationships with significant others. Engagement in positive reappraisal could lead to feeling lucky that the experience was not worse, or to a judgement that one is better off compared to others, or to simply putting negative aspects aside. Existential reattribution would involve seeking answers to such key questions as "Why did the traumatic event happen to me?" "What caused the traumatic event?" "Who is responsible for the traumatic event?" and "What impact will the traumatic event have on me?"

Changing Global Meaning The goal of changing global meaning is to achieve a renewed sense of purpose and coherence in which the individual becomes more aware of the "bigger picture" through transformative and transcendence processes. This goal is achieved through global meaning-making processes that include, but are not limited to (a) rethinking one's values, (b) resetting new goals, and (c) revising one's belief system. Rethinking one's values might involve spending more time with family and friends, reevaluating ordinary events, or shifting from instrumental to terminal values (Rokeach, 1973). Resetting new goals might involve setting realistic goals that are more attainable, reordering priorities, or striving for higher level goals. Revising one's belief system might involve reevaluating spiritual and religious beliefs and practices, reconnecting with spiritual roots, or associating with individuals holding similar beliefs.

A renewed sense of purpose emerges when the individual begins to acknowledge that misfortunes in life are not unexpected, that goals are attainable despite negative life experiences, and that one can cope with life's vagaries through the positive attitudinal self-declaration "I will survive" (i.e., transformative processes). Renewed coherence may be achieved through greater spiritual or religious connectedness whereby the individual perceives that God puts obstacles in one's path but also gives one the strength to overcome them (i.e., transcendence processes).

Intervention Strategies

Meaning in life is a very personal, subjective, and private issue, particularly in the context of global–situational meaning incongruence. When it comes to intervention, one size does not fit all. In order to facilitate changes in meaning, a number of formalized individually tailored intervention strategies are needed. Four potential interventions are briefly described here: (a) cognitive reframing with a facilitator, (b) assessment of sources of meaning, (c) sharing of personal "stories" in a group environment, and (d) temporal reflections.

Cognitive reframing with a facilitator could assist with changing the meaning of the traumatic experience by focusing on and exploring answers to such "bigger" questions as "Why did this happen to me?" and "Why me?" The former seeks answers to the specific cause of the traumatic event; the latter reflects a general existential attribution. The simultaneous exploration of answers to both questions can lead to a deeper understanding, a fuller awareness, and a final acceptance of the traumatic event.

An assessment of the sources of meaning (e.g., personal relationships, creative activities, and traditions and culture) that are important to the individual facing a traumatic life event may provide a vehicle for promoting greater involvement in meaningful activities. Engagement in a variety of meaningful activities at deeper levels can facilitate both situational meaning and global meaning, reduce the experienced incongruence between them, and foster increased feelings of self-worth and well-being.

The sharing of personal "stories" in a group environment can facilitate personal understanding of the traumatic event and offer validation of the experience by others facing similar challenges. In the context of guided autobiography, Reker, Birren, and Svensson (2008) have shown that the sharing of life stories with others, known as the "developmental exchange," leads to greater actual self–ideal self congruence, greater actual self–social-image self congruence, a more positive evaluation of life at present, and a more positive evaluation of others. In other words, the sharing of life stories moves participants closer to their ideal selves. Participants also view others as more like themselves, but they do not necessarily view their actual and ideal selves differently (see also Chapter 18, this volume). By extension, it is proposed that sharing a traumatic life event with others has the potential to reduce the experienced incongruence between global meaning and situational meaning.

Finally, the encouragement of temporal reflections on the present, past, and future in the context of a traumatic life experience may be one way to stimulate self-awareness of the condition and promote a deeper understanding and acceptance of the traumatic event. For example, a present probe may ask, "What's it like living with a traumatic life event? Next follows a past probe that may ask, "What was life like before the traumatic event?" Finally there follows a future probe asking, "What will life be like in the future?" One outcome of having the individual reflect on these temporal questions may be to remove or reduce a sense of denial that often accompanies the experience of a traumatic event. The probes can set the stage for a more realistic self-assessment, one based more on actual and future actions than on emotional reactions that have come to be associated with the traumatic event.

Changed Personal Meaning, Recovery, and Adjustment An integrative model of global and situational meaning and its application to traumatic life events has been proposed, but is there any evidence that changed personal meaning leads to recovery and adjustment? Available evidence from qualitative and quantitative studies seems to suggest that the ability to find meaning in the traumatic event (situational meaning) contributes to positive psychological adjustment and improved quality of life. For example, in a study of stroke patients, Thompson (1991) reported that finding meaning in the stroke experience was associated with positive psychological adjustment not only in the patients but also in the caregivers. Individuals in both groups were less depressed and had higher levels of meaningfulness. Taylor (1983) reported that in a qualitative study of cancer patients, results showed that meaning gained from the cancer experience brought renewed self-confidence, gains in self-knowledge, a new attitude toward life, and a reestablished sense of control over one's body and over one's life generally. Skaggs and Barron (2006) found that in a case study of a 40-year-old coronary artery disease patient, after a second myocardial infarction the patient reevaluated priorities, spent more time with family and friends, and set realistic present goals that led to a greater appreciation for family, friends, and community, personal growth, and realistic goal setting in the future.

In the context of mental health, Ridgeway (2001) found that the narrative accounts of women who recovered from prolonged psychiatric disability contained descriptions of how they moved from feelings of alienation to achieving personal meaning and personal goals. The women reported that they found "a deep source of meaning through being actively involved in a process of giving back, in helping other people who experience psychiatric disabilities … to begin their own journeys of recovery" (Ridgeway, 2001, p. 339). Edmonds and Hooker (1992) and Gamino and Sewell (2004) found that finding meaning following the death of a loved one led to reduced feelings of grief and better bereavement adjustment. The work of Davis et al. (1998) on the sense-making and benefit-finding aspects of situational meaning revealed an interesting time-since-the-event psychological adjustment trajectory. Making sense of the death of a loved one predicted lowered psychological distress up to one year after the event, and finding benefit predicted lowered distress 13 and 18 months later.

The ability to maintain a sense of global meaning despite the traumatic event may also contribute to psychological adjustment after the event. In a well-designed quantitative study of psychological adjustment in survivors of bone marrow transplantation, Vickberg et al. (2001) found that after controlling for physical functioning, stressor severity, and gender, their study revealed that the ability to maintain one's belief about purpose and coherence in life was related to lower general psychological distress, lower bone marrow transplant–related psychological distress, and higher mental health quality of life as indexed by measures of emotional and social functioning. Similar findings on the role of global meaning in psychological adjustment (reduced anxiety) have been reported for individuals diagnosed with cancer (Mullen, Smith, & Hill, 1993) and infected with HIV (Linn, Lewis, Cain, & Kimbrough, 1993).

Taken together, the findings reveal that both situational meaning and global meaning play an important role in the recovery and adjustment processes of individuals who are challenged by traumatic life events.

Conclusion and Future Directions

The evidence reviewed in this chapter on the role of global and situational meaning in life and psychosocial adaptation in the later years clearly reveals the importance of personal meaning as a key factor in the buffering of stress; in the enhancement of physical, psychological, and mental well-being; and in the ability to transcend negative life experiences. Both the global aspects and the situational aspects of meaning in life enhance our conceptual understanding of the meaning construct, and both contribute uniquely and interactively to positive psychosocial outcomes. As such, personal meaning can be seen as a potentially significant component of psychological resilience. Existing conceptualizations and measures of resilience have focused on personality traits; the psychological dimensions of control, challenge, and commitment; and the use of a variety of adaptive coping strategies. To our knowledge, none have included the construct of personal meaning and other relevant existential variables. It is our view that our understanding of psychological resilience can be further enhanced by the addition of existential variables that include, but are not limited to, personal meaning in life, spirituality, existential regret, and death attitudes.

In response to this challenge and in the context of positive psychology, Woo (2008) recently proposed a strength-based conceptual model of resilience comprised of three primary domains: (a) psychological (control, challenge, commitment), (b) behavioral (active problem solving, positive emotional coping, social relations coping, tenacious coping, flexible coping), and (c) existential (personal meaning, spirituality). Measures of the components of the model are currently being tested in a large sample of older adults. Preliminary findings on the psychometric properties of the new scale are very promising. Future research should be directed toward the exploration of the expanded components of psychological resilience and their unique and combined contributions to psychosocial adaptation in the later years.

In practice, medical and rehabilitation professionals are beginning to embrace holistic models of health care that simultaneously address the physiological, psychological, social, existential, and spiritual needs of clients. For example, the Rehabilitation Research and Training Center on Community Integration for Persons with Traumatic Brain Injury in Houston, Texas, has specifically identified finding meaning in life and spirituality as potentially important factors in achieving community integration of clients with traumatic brain injury (State of the Science Conference, 2007). Future research needs to evaluate the effectiveness of meaning-centered interventions, beyond those provided by traditional approaches, in promoting recovery and adjustment.

References

Baltes, P. B., & Baltes, M. M. (1990). Psychological perspectives on successful aging: The model of selective optimization with compensation. In P. B. Baltes & M. M. Baltes (Eds.), *Successful aging: Perspectives from the behavioural sciences* (pp. 1–34). New York, NY: Cambridge University Press.

Bar-Tur, L., Savaya, R., & Prager, E. (2001). Sources of meaning in life for young and old Israeli Jews and Arabs. *Journal of Aging Studies, 15*, 253–269.

Costa, P. T., Metter, J. E., & McCrae, R. R. (1994). Personality stability and its contribution to successful aging. *Journal of Geriatric Psychiatry, 27*, 41–59.

Davis, C. G., Nolen-Hoeksema, S., & Larson, J. (1998). Making sense of loss and benefiting from the experience: Two construals of meaning. *Journal of Personality and Social Psychology, 75*, 561–574.

Derogatis, L. R., & Spence, P. (1982). *The Brief Symptom Inventory (BSI) Administration, Scoring and Procedures Manual–I.* Baltimore, MD: Copyrighted manuscript.

DeVogler–Ebersole, K., & Ebersole, P. (1985). Depth of meaning in life: Explicit rating criteria. *Psychological Reports, 56*, 303–310.

Edmonds, S., & Hooker, K. (1992). Perceived changes in life meaning following bereavement. *Omega: Journal of Death and Dying, 25*, 307–318.

Farran, C. J., & Kuhn, D. (1998). Finding meaning through caring for persons with Alzheimer's disease: Assessment and intervention. In P. T. P. Wong & P. S. Fry (Eds.), *The human quest for meaning: A handbook of psychological research and clinical applications* (pp. 335–358). Mahwah, NJ: Erlbaum.

Frankl, V. E. (1963). *Man's search for meaning.* New York, NY: Washington Square Press.

Frankl, V. E. (1990). Facing the transitoriness of human existence. *Generations, 15*, 7–10.

Fry, P. S. (2000). Religious involvement, spirituality, and personal meaning for life: Existential predictors of psychological wellbeing in community-residing and institutional care elders. *Aging and Mental Health, 4*, 375–387.

Fry, P. S. (2001). The unique contribution of key existential factors to the prediction of psychological well-being of older adults following spousal loss. *Gerontologist, 41*, 1–13.

Gamino, L. A., & Sewell, K. W. (2004). Meaning constructs as predictors of bereavement adjustment: A report from the Scott & White grief study. *Death Studies, 28*, 397–421.

Horowitz, M., Wilner, N., & Alvarez, W. (1979). Impact of Events Scale: A measure of subjective distress. *Psychosomatic Medicine, 41*, 209–218.

Janoff-Bulman, R., & Frantz, C. M. (1997). The impact of trauma on meaning: From meaningless world to meaningful life. In M. Power & C. R. Brewin (Eds.), *The transformation of meaning in psychological therapies* (pp. 91–106). New York, NY: Wiley.

Kaufman, S. R. (1987). *The ageless self: Sources of meaning in late life.* New York, NY: Meridian.

Kennedy, J. E., & Kanthamani, H. (1995). *Empirical support for a model of well-being, meaning in life, importance of religion, and transcendent experiences.* Unpublished manuscript.

Krause, N. (2007). Evaluating the stress-buffering function of meaning in life among older people. *Journal of Aging and Health, 19*, 792–812.

Linn, J. G., Lewis, F. M., Cain, V. A., & Kimbrough, G. A. (1993). HIV-illness, social support, sense of coherence, and psychological well-being in a sample of help seeking adults. *AIDS Education and Prevention, 5*, 254–262.

Lukas, E. (1992). Meaning and goals in the chronically ill. *International Forum for Logotherapy, 15*, 90–98.

Lutgendorf, S. K., Vitaliano, P. P., Tripp-Reimer, T., Harvey, J. H., & Lubaroff, D. M. (1999). Sense of coherence moderates the relationship between life stress and natural killer cell activity in healthy older adults. *Psychology and Aging, 14*, 552–563.

Mullen, P. M., Smith, R. M., & Hill, E. W. (1993). Sense of coherence as a mediator of stress for cancer patients and spouses. *Journal of Psychosocial Oncology, 11*, 23–46.

Newcomb, M. D., & Harlow, L. L. (1986). Life events and substance use among adolescents: Moderating effects of powerlessness and meaninglessness in life. *Journal of Personality and Social Psychology, 51*, 564–577.

O'Connor, K., & Chamberlain, K. (1996). Dimensions of life meaning: A qualitative investigation at midlife. *British Journal of Psychology, 87*, 461–477.

Park, C. L., & Folkman, S. (1997). Meaning in the context of stress and coping. *Review of General Psychology, 1*, 115–144.

Prager, E. (1996). Exploring personal meaning in an age-differentiated Australian sample: Another look at the Sources of Meaning Profile (SOMP). *Journal of Aging Studies, 10*, 117–136.

Prager, E., Savaya, R., & Bar-Tur, L. (2000). The development of a culturally sensitive measure of sources of life meaning. In G. T. Reker & K. Chamberlain (Eds.), *Exploring existential meaning: Optimizing human development across the life span* (pp. 123–136). Thousand Oaks, CA: Sage.

Reker, G. T. (1988). *Sources of personal meaning among young, middle-aged and older adults: A replication.* Paper presented at the Annual Meeting of the Gerontological Society of America, San Francisco, California.

Reker, G. T. (1991). *Contextual and thematic analyses of sources of provisional meaning: A life-span perspective.* Paper presented at the Biennial Meetings of the International Society of the Study of Behavioral Development, Minneapolis, Minnesota.

Reker, G. T. (1992). *Manual of the Life Attitude Profile–Revised (LAP-R).* Peterborough, ON, Canada: Student Psychologists Press.

Reker, G. T. (1994). Logotheory and logotherapy: Challenges, opportunities, and some empirical findings. *International Forum for Logotherapy, 17*, 47–55.

Reker, G. T. (1996). *Manual of the Sources of Meaning Profile–Revised (SOMP-R).* Peterborough, ON, Canada: Student Psychologists Press.

Reker, G. T. (1997). Personal meaning, optimism, and choice: Existential predictors of depression in community and institutional elderly. *Gerontologist, 37*, 709–716.

Reker, G. T. (2002). Prospective predictors of successful aging in community-residing and institutionalized Canadian elderly. *Ageing International, 27*, 42–64.

Reker, G. T. (2007, April). *The search for meaning in life following traumatic brain injury: Conceptual, measurement, and application issues.* Invited paper presented at the Community Integration of Persons with Traumatic Brain Injury State of the Science Conference, Arlington, Virginia.

Reker, G. T. (2008). *Global meaning as a mediator of stressful life events and subjective well-being, existential regret, and physical health in older adults.* Unpublished manuscript, Trent University, Peterborough, ON, Canada.

Reker, G. T., Birren, J. E., & Svensson, C. (2008). *Self-aspect reconstruction through guided autobiography: Exploring underlying processes.* Summary Report of Research Findings, University of Southern California.

Reker, G. T., & Butler, B. (1990, October). *Personal meaning, stress, and health in older adults.* Paper presented at the Canadian Association on Gerontology, *42*, 44–49.

Reker, G. T., & Chamberlain, K. (Eds.). (2000). *Exploring existential meaning: Optimizing human development across the life span*. Thousand Oaks, CA: Sage.
Reker, G. T., Peacock, E. J., & Wong, P. T. P. (1987). Meaning and purpose in life and well-being: A life-span perspective. *Journal of Gerontology, 42*, 44–49.
Reker, G. T., & Wong, P. T. P. (1988). Aging as an individual process: Toward a theory of personal meaning. In J. E. Birren & V. L. Bengtson (Eds.), *Emergent theories of aging* (pp. 214–246). New York, NY: Springer.
Ridgway, P. (2001). Restorying psychiatric disability: Learning from first person recovery narratives. *Psychiatric Rehabilitation Journal, 24*, 335–343.
Rokeach, M. (1973). *The nature of human values*. New York, NY: Free Press.
Rowe, J. W., & Kahn, R. L. (1997). Successful aging. *Gerontologist, 37*, 433–440.
Ryff, C. D. (1989). Beyond Ponce de Leon and life satisfaction: New directions in quest of successful aging. *International Journal of Behavioral Development, 12*, 35–55.
Schnell, T., & Becker, P. (2006). Personality and meaning in life. *Personality and Individual Differences, 41*, 117–129.
Schulz, R., & Heckhausen, J. (1996). A life span model of successful aging. *American Psychologist, 51*, 702–714.
Skaggs, B. G., & Barron, C. R. (2006). Searching for meaning in negative events: Concept analysis. *Journal of Advanced Nursing, 53*, 559–570.
State of the Science Conference. (April, 2007). *Community integration and TBI: What is the state of our science?* Arlington, Virginia.
Taylor, S. E. (1983). Adjustment to threatening events: A theory of cognitive adaptation. *American Psychologist, 38*, 1161–1173.
Thompson, S. C. (1991). The search for meaning following a stroke. *Basic and Applied Social Psychology, 12*, 81–96.
Tornstam, L. (1997). Gerotranscendence: The contemplative dimension of aging. *Journal of Aging Studies, 11*, 143–154.
Underhill, S. C. (1991). *Personal meaning and personal optimism: Interactive moderators of life event stress and daily hassles in older adults* (Honors thesis). Trent University, Peterborough, ON, Canada.
Vickberg, S. M. J., Bovbjerg, D. H., DuHamel, K. N., Currie, V., & Redd, W. H. (2000). Intrusive thoughts and psychological distress among breast cancer survivors: Global meaning as a possible protective factor. *Behavioral Medicine, 25*, 152–160.
Vickberg, S. M. J., Duhamel, K. N., Smith, M. Y., Manne, S. L., Winkel, G., Papadopoulus, E., & Redd, W. H. (2001). Global meaning and psychological adjustment among survivors of bone marrow transplant. *Psycho-Oncology, 10*, 29–39.
Wong, P. T. P. (1989). Personal meaning and successful aging. *Canadian Psychology, 30*, 516–525.
Wong, P. T. P., & Fry, P. S. (Eds.). (1998). *The human quest for meaning: A handbook of psychological research and clinical applications*. Mahwah, NJ: Erlbaum.
Woo, L. (2008). *Toward a strength-based model of resilience in later life* (Unpublished master's thesis). Trent University, Peterborough, ON, Canada.
Yalom, I. D. (1980). *Existential psychotherapy*. New York, NY: Basic Books.
Zika, S., & Chamberlain, K. (1992). On the relation between meaning in life and psychological well-being. *British Journal of Psychology, 83*, 133–145.

21
Meaning and Agency in the Context of Genetic Testing for Familial Cancer

LISA G. ASPINWALL, SAMANTHA L. LEAF, and SANCY A. LEACHMAN

University of Utah

I cannot change the fact that my test results came out positive for *p16*. My belief [is] that God made me this way so I will do the best with what I have been given and if I do my best to enjoy life and make the best of any situation I will be rewarded in the end.

—33-year-old woman with no history of melanoma reflecting on *CDKN2A/p16*+ results

My religious beliefs allow me to see the future from a positive perspective. I know that I control my destiny and how I react to life's challenges. I choose to be positive and do what is best for myself and my family.

—37-year-old woman with a melanoma history reflecting on *CDKN2A/p16*+ results

I believe God sends us medical knowledge to give us an opportunity to overcome physical and medical challenges. To ignore the chance to find out about my genetic status and seek medical advice and/or treatment would be almost an insult to God and the help he has tried to provide mankind.

—32-year-old woman reflecting on *CDKN2A/p16*– results

The concept of finding meaning in adversity has been central to the study of how people respond to such negative life events as victimization, natural disasters, bereavement, and life-threatening illnesses and accidents (Bulman & Wortman, 1977; Frankl, 1946/1959; Janoff-Bulman, 1989; Silver, Boon, & Stones, 1983; Taylor, 1983; Taylor, Kemeny, Reed, Bower, & Gruenewald, 2000; Tedeschi & Calhoun, 2004; see also Chapters 7, 20, 23, and 25, this volume). Negative life events pose multiple threats to one's sense of the world as meaningful and orderly (Janoff-Bulman, 1989; Janoff-Bulman & Frieze, 1983;

Silver et al., 1983; see also Chapter 22, this volume): They may challenge core beliefs about self-worth and personal invulnerability, personal control over good versus bad outcomes, the predictability and fairness of such outcomes, the benevolence of the impersonal world, and, depending on the event, the benevolence of other people. Accordingly, evidence from multiple sources suggests that the joint tasks of finding meaning and preserving or restoring mastery are central, frequently interrelated goals for people managing serious illness and other forms of adversity (Collins, Taylor, & Skokan, 1990; Emmons, Colby, & Kaiser, 1998; Folkman & Moskowitz, 2007; Janoff-Bulman, 1989; Park & Folkman, 1997; Rothbaum, Weisz, & Snyder, 1982; Taylor, 1983; Tedeschi & Calhoun, 2004; Thompson, 1981; Thompson, Sobolew-Shubin, Galbraith, Schwankovsky, & Cruzen, 1993; Wong & Fry, 1998; see also Chapters 2, 4, 8, 11, and 25, this volume). Further, finding meaning in one's own or a loved one's serious illness seems to be prospectively associated with better mental and physical health outcomes, including immune function and AIDS-related mortality (Bower, Kemeny, Taylor, & Fahey, 1998; Bower et al., 2005; for discussion, see Taylor et al., 2000, and Chapter 11, this volume).

Religion is a primary means through which many people make sense of the world (see Ozorak, Paloutzian, & Park, 2005; Park, 2007). Religious beliefs provide a framework for understanding one's condition on a daily basis (McIntosh, 1995) and for making sense of specific difficulties that arise during one's life (e.g., Spilka, Hood, Hunsberger, & Gorsuch, 2003). As such, religious and spiritual beliefs and practices are thought to serve as a central component of an individual's general orienting system, which helps one to understand, appraise, and derive meaning from stressful life events and, ultimately, to decide whether and how to act to try to alter them (Acklin, Brown, & Mauger, 1983; Jenkins & Pargament, 1988; Pargament et al., 1992; Park, 2007; Wong, 1998b; see also Chapter 8, this volume).

Our goal in this chapter is to examine multiple, potentially interrelated aspects of meaning making and mastery beliefs among people receiving genetic test results for familial cancer, in this case melanoma. As reflected in the perspectives of familial melanoma patients and their family members with which we opened this chapter, we seek to examine the specific ways in which religious and spiritual understandings of genetic test results and family cancer history may provide meaning to this experience and a framework for personal and familial action. We also seek to examine the relation of religious understandings to such concepts as perceived control and cancer fatalism that have been shown to be central to how people understand and manage serious health risks. In doing so, we hope to illustrate how an understanding of religious and spiritual beliefs may be integrated with a more typical focus on health cognitions and coping strategies to provide a more complete picture of how people understand and manage serious health risks.

We begin by describing (a) some of the unique challenges posed by a positive *CDKN2A/p16* genetic test result for familial melanoma, (b) recent research on genetic determinism that suggests that information highlighting the genetic basis of health risks may undermine perceptions of personal control, and (c) current approaches to understanding the role of religious and spiritual beliefs in coping with serious illness, the practice of health behaviors, and attitudes toward genetic testing. We then present some preliminary results of our ongoing prospective study of responses to *CDKN2A/p16* genetic testing that examines (d) high-risk participants' accounts of how their religious and spiritual beliefs influence their understanding and management of their genetic test results and (e) the relationship of these beliefs to religious coping, health cognitions, and adherence to recommended health behaviors. We conclude with observations about the importance of religious and spiritual beliefs in providing a framework for meaning and agency among people at high risk for illness and offer suggestions for future research and practical application.

Psychological and Behavioral Challenges of Positive *CDKN2A/p16* Genetic Test Results for Familial Melanoma

Genetic testing for familial cancer provides an interesting and important applied context in which to examine meaning making and mastery beliefs for several reasons. First, whether one has a particular genetic mutation that confers disease risk is clearly outside one's direct personal control, and there is nothing one can do at present to modify such mutations. Second, a pathogenic mutation in *CDKN2A/p16*, a tumor suppressor that regulates cell cycle and senescence, confers an extraordinarily elevated lifetime melanoma risk—approximately 76% in U.S. samples, compared to 1% in the general population (Bishop et al., 2002; Hansen, Wadge, Lowstuter, Boucher, & Leachman, 2004). Third, melanoma is an aggressive and often fatal cancer. If it is detected late, afflicted individuals face a five-year survival rate of only 15% (Balch et al., 2001; Barnhill, Fine, Roush, & Berwick, 1996). Fourth, unlike other cancer syndromes for which there is a known genetic basis, the elevated risk conferred by the *CDKN2A/p16* mutation interacts with UV exposure, making preventive behaviors (i.e., photoprotection) essential.

These facts have several implications for patient counseling. For most cancers for which predictive genetic testing is available, the main recommendation provided to patients who receive positive test results is to engage in accelerated screening to increase the likelihood of early detection and successful treatment. Familial melanoma patients, however, are additionally counseled to practice daily photoprotective behaviors to avoid UV exposure. These behaviors—avoiding peak exposure, wearing and frequently reapplying sunscreen, and wearing protective clothing—are often perceived as cumbersome and expensive. Baseline practice of these precautions is suboptimal, even among high-risk patients (Aspinwall, Leaf, Kohlmann, Dola, & Leachman,

2009; Bergenmar & Brandberg, 2001; Brandberg, Jonell, Broberg, Sjoden, & Rosdahl, 1996). Thus, familial melanoma provides an ideal context for examining patients' beliefs about personal agency and understanding of extremely elevated personal risk for life-threatening illness on the one hand and cancer fatalism and the corresponding failure to practice precautionary and screening behaviors on the other hand. Further, it is unknown how religious and spiritual understandings of the origin, nature, and meaning of genetic vulnerability to disease may influence individuals' attempts to manage it.

Of particular importance to questions of meaning and mastery, the experience of familial cancer patients is likely to be different in important ways from that of patients whose disease is sporadic in nature. Our participants were part of the original Utah pedigrees enrolled to discover the genetic basis for melanoma (Cannon-Albright et al., 1992; Kamb et al., 1994). To be eligible for this original study, participants had to have at least three first-degree family members with a confirmed diagnosis of one or more melanomas. Thus, most participants have seen family members struggle with the disease and its treatment, which can be disfiguring. Many have lost family members, often parents, to this disease, leaving little question as to its lethality. Further, the high rates of melanoma in these families may lead some participants to believe that their own illness is inevitable.

Finally, it is important to note that family members who test negative for the *CDKN2A/p16* mutation also face multiple challenges. Even though their own results were favorable for them and for their biological children with respect to their melanoma risk, these participants are still seeking to understand and manage their familial cancer history (Hamann et al., 2000; Hughes et al., 2002; van Oostrom et al., 2007; Wagner Costalas et al., 2003). Issues of survivor guilt and the need to provide support and encouragement to family members with positive test results may be paramount in this group. In addition, because of their family history, *CDKN2A/p16–* family members still carry a 1.7-fold elevation in lifetime melanoma risk compared to the general population and thus are counseled to follow the same recommendations regarding precautionary and risk behaviors as *CDKN2A/p16+* family members.

Beliefs About Genetic Determinism and the Management of Genetic Risk for Illness

To date, research on how people understand the genetic basis of illness strongly suggests that people view the high level of risk conferred by a positive genetic test result as immutable and that such views influence their attitudes toward genetic testing and the management of genetic risks. For example, Senior, Marteau, and Weinman (2000) presented participants with fictitious vignettes that described them as being at an increased risk for developing mild forms of arthritis or heart disease. In half the vignettes the nature of the risk was unspecified, whereas in the other half the risk was said to come from a dominant gene. Participants who were given genetic risk information attributed less causal importance to lifestyle and diet and greater importance to genes and perceived the disease to be less personally preventable than those who were not told the cause of their high risk. The researchers concluded that providing genetic risk information may engender a sense of fatalism in patients. Consistent with these findings, scenario studies suggest that people are more interested in hypothetical genetic tests for conditions over which they would have some control than for uncontrollable conditions (Shiloh, Ben-Sinai, & Keinan, 1999). The hypothesis that people may be more fatalistic when an illness is caused by genetic factors receives support from people dealing with actual illnesses. For example, among survivors of gynecological cancers, the belief that one's cancer was caused by genetics, endorsed by 54% of the sample, was associated with depression, anxiety, and worry about reoccurrence (Costanzo, Lutgendorf, Bradley, Rose, & Anderson, 2005).

Such perceptions regarding the inevitability and uncontrollability of genetically linked illness may derive in part from participants' knowledge of such illnesses as Huntington's disease, for which the risk of illness among those who carry a particular genetic mutation is 100%. As noted earlier, however, this one-to-one relationship between a positive genetic test result and illness is not the case for familial melanoma, where research evidence supports the idea that penetrance rates, the frequency with which a particular genetic mutation results in measurable disease, depend on UV exposure (Bishop et al., 2002). At present, little is known about how members of high-risk cancer families think about the inevitability of risks conferred by particular genetic mutations. Some encouraging recent research suggests that individuals may not always conclude that genetic risk is immutable. Specifically, Hicken and Tucker (2002) found that participants who were given genetic test results suggesting that they were at a 30–40% risk of developing a fictitious digestive disorder reported greater perceived risk and greater intentions to take precautionary measures to prevent the disease than participants told they were at population risk (10–12%) of developing the disease. This type of finding provides hope for attempts to increase the use of important precautionary behaviors among people with a genetic predisposition toward the development of disease; it is not clear, however, whether these more encouraging results were obtained because the risk estimates provided to participants were moderate or because particular features of the illness (a digestive disorder) may be seen by participants as more similar to preventable conditions than are such illnesses as cancer.

Because research on psychological and social aspects of actual (i.e., not hypothetical) genetic testing among high-risk family members has focused on its impact on psychological distress, recommended annual cancer screening, and family communication and dynamics (Botkin et al., 2003; Claes et al., 2003; Lerman, Croyle, Tercyak, & Hamann, 2002; Marteau & Croyle, 1998; Marteau & Lerman, 2001; Peterson et al., 2003; Smith, West, Croyle, & Botkin, 1999), relatively little is known about perceived control over important aspects of illness prevention among familial cancer patients receiving genetic test results and counseling. The small body of research that does exist suggests that high perceived control over the cause, development, or detection of an illness is associated with less use of emotion-focused coping after genetic testing, as well as higher levels of knowledge and greater satisfaction with counseling (Berkenstadt, Shiloh, Barkai, Katznelson, & Goldman, 1999; Shiloh et al., 1999; Shiloh, Berkenstadt, Meiran, Bat-Miriam-Katznelson, & Goldman, 1997). With respect to understanding the link between perceived control and the management of genetic risk, it is important to note that perceived control over disease development may not be relevant for genetically linked cancers for which there are no known precautionary behaviors that would be effective in reducing one's risk. Even less is known about how genetic test results and associated beliefs about personal control and risk immutability may be understood in the context of social, religious, and other cultural beliefs about the meaning, causation, and management of health and illness. Accordingly, one goal of the present research was to assess such beliefs and their implications for the understanding and management of genetic test results for familial cancer among high-risk patients.

Religiosity and Health: Understanding How Religious Beliefs Influence Coping With Illness, Health Behaviors, and Attitudes Toward Genetic Testing

The multiple challenges associated with receiving genetic test results and being a member of a melanoma-prone family make it a particularly interesting area for studying the role of religious beliefs in the understanding and management of this experience. Researchers have identified multiple pathways through which religious and spiritual beliefs may positively influence health outcomes, including emotional pathways (e.g., reducing stress and depression associated with a physical illness), social pathways (e.g., religious groups providing social support, which is associated with better health outcomes), behavioral pathways (e.g., religious mandates that may reduce the likelihood of engaging in such risk behaviors as smoking or drinking), and cognitive pathways (religious beliefs that may help people to understand and derive meaning from an illness or to change their appraisals of illness to make it less threatening; see, e.g., McIntosh, Silver, & Wortman, 1993; Park, 2007; and Chapter 23, this volume, for reviews; see also Gall & Cornblat, 2002, for a particularly detailed account of these processes among women with breast cancer; Pargament, 1997). For example, research suggests that people facing serious medical problems will often appraise the situation as being God's will (Bulman & Wortman, 1977; Pargament, Sullivan, Tyler, & Steele, 1982), an appraisal that has been shown to lead to higher self-esteem and better ratings of behavioral adjustment to illness among cancer patients receiving chemotherapy (Jenkins & Pargament, 1988). Similarly, among men diagnosed with prostate cancer in the past five years, believing that one's cancer was a result of God's will was positively associated with one's ability to manage the illness and with experiencing positive changes in health over the past year (Gall, 2004). Religious and spiritual beliefs may also be important in the management of illness by specifying how to care for the body, affirming the importance or sanctification of the body (Holt & McClure, 2006; Mahoney et al., 2005; Park, 2007), and by promising a rewarding afterlife in which one will be reunited with family members.

Consistent with these ideas, research on coping with chronic illness and other health threats has identified religious beliefs and behaviors, such as faith and prayer, as one of the most frequently cited coping mechanisms (see, e.g., Bulman & Wortman, 1977; Carver et al., 1993; Sherman, Simonton, Latif, Spohn, & Tricot, 2005). However, one substantial limitation of many studies that examine religious coping in the context of other coping efforts is that the assessment of religious coping in such broad-based coping assessments as the Ways of Coping Inventory (Folkman & Lazarus, 1980) and the COPE (Carver, Scheier, & Weintraub, 1989) is necessarily limited to only a few items (e.g., finding new faith, praying, seeking God's help, finding comfort in religion). Further, these coping items have assessed only a subset of the hypothesized pathways through which religious coping may be related to the management of adversity. As a result, it has been difficult to determine whether and why particular aspects of religious belief and religious coping strategies may be linked to positive or negative mental and physical health outcomes; it has also been difficult to differentiate among different kinds of religious coping. As we will describe, new measures have been developed to provide a more detailed and differentiated view of religious coping and the functions it may serve.

Measurement and Taxonomies of Religious Coping

As just noted, research on religious coping is moving toward a more differentiated view of particular coping strategies and their functions. Early research on the relationships among religious variables and health used global measures of religiosity, such as participants' self-rated degree of religiousness or measures of church attendance, which did not provide information regarding the specific aspects of religious faith or religious participation that are most beneficial to future health outcomes. In the last two decades, several frameworks have been developed to assess aspects of religious beliefs and behaviors that may be particularly important to coping and problem solving among people facing threats to physical health (Koenig, Pargament, & Nielsen, 1998). In particular, Pargament and his colleagues have developed a highly-detailed Religious Coping Inventory (the RCOPE; Pargament, Koenig, & Perez, 2000), which consists of 63 items divided into 21 subscales examining diverse aspects of religious coping. This typology groups religious coping strategies into five potential functions: *searching for meaning, achieving a sense of control, finding comfort and closeness to God, gaining intimacy with other people and closeness to God*, and *achieving life transformation*. In addition to articulating specific functions that religious coping may serve, this typology was designed to examine both positive and negative religious coping methods. According to Pargament, Smith, Koenig, and Perez (1998), *positive religious coping* methods are those associated with a sense of spiritual connectedness with others and with God, whereas *negative religious coping* methods suggest a less secure relationship with God, an ominous view of the world, and a struggle to find meaning and significance in one's life.

Although a comprehensive review of the different frameworks developed to categorize religious coping and problem solving is beyond the scope of this chapter, we would like to briefly describe a third framework that may prove to be highly relevant to how people understand and manage threats to health. Pargament and colleagues (Pargament, Kennell, Hathaway, & Grevengoed, 1988) introduced distinctions among self-directing, collaborative, and passive or deferring religious problem-solving styles. *Self-directing religious problem solving* involves the belief that it is an individual's sole responsibility to solve his or her own problems, without God's intervention. Recent research has further subdivided this category into self-direction because of an abandoning God (God has abandoned a person, leaving him or her to cope alone) and self-direction because of a supportive but nonintervening God (God has given a person the agency and the necessary resources to lead his or her own life; Phillips, Pargament, Lynn, & Crossley, 2004). In *collaborative religious problem solving*, the individual and God are viewed as active partners in the problem-solving process, sharing responsibility for solving the problem. In *passive or deferring religious problem solving*, the individual takes no direct problem-solving action but instead prays to a God who is seen as omnipotent and responsible for solving problems.

Religious Coping and Health Outcomes

Research suggests that these distinctions among different forms of religious coping are important in understanding individual efforts to manage threats to health and well-being. In general, such negative forms of religious coping as spiritual discontent and interpersonal religious conflict have generally been associated with such negative mental health outcomes as higher rates of depressive symptoms, distress, and poorer quality of life and mental health (Koenig, George, et al., 1998; Sherman et al., 2005; Tarakeshwar et al., 2006), whereas such positive forms of religious coping as seeking spiritual support and seeing one's situation as part of God's plan have positive cross-sectional relations with mental health outcomes, such as lower rates of depressive symptoms and higher self-esteem, life satisfaction, and quality of life among adults coping with cancer and coronary heart disease (Ai, Park, Huang, Rodgers, & Tice, 2007; Koenig, Pargament, & Nielsen, 1998; Pargament et al., 1998). Positive religious coping has also been shown to predict better pain management (McBride, Arthur, Brooks, & Pilkington, 1998) and higher self-rated health (Krause, 1998).

Positive religious coping methods are not, however, always associated with positive physical health outcomes. Among adults currently dealing with serious medical problems, positive and negative religious coping were both associated with a higher number of concurrent medical diagnoses, lower functional status, and lower cognitive status (Pargament et al., 1998). These results illustrate a potential confound in much of the research examining religious coping among seriously ill populations, namely that people experiencing medical crises or entering long-term care may turn to religion or spirituality to cope with their deteriorating health, leading to negative associations between religious coping and health status. That is, these associations may reflect religious coping that occurred as a result of poor health, rather than poor health outcomes that resulted from particular ways of religious coping.

The proposed distinctions among self-directing, collaborative, and passive or deferring religious coping have also proven to be successful in predicting mental and physical health outcomes. Collaborative coping has been associated with higher self-esteem, lower depression, lower psychological distress, and other positive outcomes in female breast cancer survivors (Gall, Miguez de Renart, & Boonstra, 2000) and in adults receiving chemotherapy for a variety of cancers (Nairn & Merluzzi, 2003). In nonpatient samples of undergraduates and churchgoers, self-directing religious problem solving was associated with greater personal control and self-esteem, whereas deferring religious problem solving was negatively related to personal control, self-esteem, and competence at active problem solving (Hathaway & Pargament, 1990; Pargament et al., 1998; Phillips et al., 2004).[1] Deferring coping has,

[1] Other researchers have combined the coping subscales differently on the basis of factor analysis and obtained different results. For example, in a study of cancer patients, Nairn and Merluzzi (2003) found that a deferring-collaborative religious coping factor was positively related to self-efficacy, psychosocial adjustment to illness, and several subscales of the Cancer Behavior Inventory (i.e., maintaining greater activity and independence, accepting cancer and maintaining a positive attitude, and confidence in seeking social support if needed). In contrast, the self-directing religious coping factor, which was viewed by the authors as more closely associated with an abandoning God than a supportive God, was negatively related to psychosocial adjustment and perceived availability of social support. According to the authors, this pattern of results was obtained because the deferring-collaborative factor reflects beliefs in the usefulness of God in the coping process, whereas the self-directing factor reflects a belief that God is uninvolved in the coping process. These differing views of the nature of self-directing, collaborative, and deferring coping styles suggest that additional research on the different ways in which people may view God as involved or uninvolved in their coping may prove useful.

however, been associated with higher levels of spiritual well-being (Wong-McDonald & Gorsuch, 2004).

To date, only a few studies have examined relationships among the RCOPE subscales and mental and physical health outcomes. A two-year longitudinal study of mental and physical health outcomes in a large sample of medically ill hospitalized elderly patients found that several negative religious coping subscales (e.g., reappraisal of God's power, spiritual discontent) and two positive religious coping subscales (i.e., religious forgiveness and religious conversion) were associated with declines in everyday physical functioning (Pargament, Koenig, Tarakeshwar, & Hahn, 2004). In contrast, higher levels of seeking support from clergy or church members were associated with improvements in cognitive status. Similarly, in a large sample of participants aged 55 or over who were admitted to general medical inpatient services at a local hospital, several negative religious coping strategies, including pleading for direct intercession and self-directing religious coping, were associated with poorer physical health, whereas positive religious coping strategies were generally unrelated to physical health (Koenig, Pargament, et al., 1998). As noted earlier, these mixed findings regarding the benefits of positive religious coping methods may represent the fact that dealing with medical conditions is a stressor that may lead to greater levels of religious coping in general, regardless of one's current health. In addition, researchers have suggested that negative religious coping may not necessarily be problematic because negative aspects of religious coping may be a precursor to growth (Pargament et al., 1998; Pargament et al., 2000).

Religious Coping and Health Behavior

Research examining the relationships among aspects of religiosity and the performance of health behaviors has yielded mixed results. Some large-scale studies suggest that measures of religiosity are positively related to the performance of such screening behaviors as mammography and breast self-exams (Benjamins, 2006; Benjamins, Trinitapoli, & Ellison, 2006), cholesterol screening (Benjamins, 2005), and blood pressure measurement (Felix Aaron, Levine, & Burstin, 2003). Other research has, however, found no influence of religion or, in some cases, a negative relation of religion to the performance of illness-detecting health behaviors (see, e.g., Fox, Pitkin, Paul, Carson, & Duan, 1998). In a study of 52 unaffected African American women from a large kindred with a *BRCA1* mutation, Kinney, Emery, Dudley, and Croyle (2002) found that women who believed that God controlled their health were less likely to adhere to clinical breast exam and mammography recommendations than were those who did not endorse this belief. According to the authors, these findings may reflect the fact that individuals who rely on God to reduce their risk of developing or dying from cancer may be less likely to rely on such early detection behaviors as mammography to do so. This finding suggests that external views of causation may undermine individuals' own active problem-solving efforts and may especially interfere with the practice of early detection measures (e.g., mammography).[2]

Religious Beliefs and Attitudes Toward Genetic Testing

Little is known about the relationships between religious beliefs and interest in, uptake of, and responses to genetic testing for disease susceptibility. Existing research suggests, however, that religious beliefs may be negatively related to interest in genetic testing. Multiple studies suggest that highly religious individuals are less likely than others to receive or intend to receive different types of prenatal and carrier genetic testing (e.g., fragile-X and Tay Sachs carrier tests; Sher, Romano-Zelekha, Green, & Shohat, 2003; but see Kastrinos, Stoffel, Balmana, & Syngal, 2007). Although more research in this area is needed, these findings suggest that other aspects of religious belief, such as attitudes toward abortion, may also play an important role in beliefs about genetic testing in the context of pregnancy.

Relatively little work has examined religious beliefs in the context of predictive genetic testing for cancer. Among women with a family and a personal history of breast or ovarian cancer who perceived themselves to be at low risk of developing cancer again, higher ratings of the strength of one's religious or spiritual faith predicted lower levels of uptake of *BRCA1/2* genetic testing for breast and ovarian cancer susceptibility (Schwartz et al., 2000). The authors hypothesized that this finding may be attributable to the fact that cancer patients often use religious or spiritual beliefs to find meaning in a cancer diagnosis and may feel that they do not need genetic testing to understand their cancer experiences. They further suggested that people high in religious faith may hold other beliefs, such as greater acceptance of a cancer diagnosis and greater attribution of health threats to external (e.g., environment) rather than internal factors (e.g. heredity), that may contribute to a less positive attitude toward genetic testing. It is important to note that this relationship was found only among women who perceived their risk of developing cancer again to be low, suggesting that spiritual beliefs were not detrimental to the genetic testing intentions of women who believed they might develop cancer again.

[2] A discussion of the complex relationships among religious belief, ethnicity, and health outcomes is beyond the scope of this chapter. It is important to note, however, that particular forms of religious coping have been shown to be associated with different outcomes in different ethnic groups (Bantha, Moskowitz, Acree, & Folkman, 2007; Tarakeshwar, Hansen, Kochman, & Sikkema, 2005), with, for example, different results for African Americans and Latinos than for Caucasians.

Method

The present study was designed to examine the role of religious and spiritual beliefs in the understanding and management of genetic test results in a high-risk sample. One-year following *CDKN2A/p16* genetic test reporting and counseling, 25 members of high-risk melanoma families completed an open-ended assessment of how their religious and spiritual beliefs influenced their understanding and management of their genetic test results, as well as the full version of the RCOPE. Responses to these two measures were then compared and related to concurrent measures of perceived control, cancer fatalism, and adherence to recommended health behaviors.

Participants

Demographics Participants were 25 adult members of high-risk melanoma families (48% men; average age = 46.3, *SD* = 14.3, range = 21–74), who received genetic testing and counseling for a *CDKN2A/p16* gene mutation and completed both a one-year follow-up assessment and a supplemental spirituality questionnaire.[3] (See Aspinwall, Leaf, Dola, Kohlmann, & Leachman, 2008, for details of participant recruitment and enrollment into the parent and follow-up studies.) All participants were Caucasian. The majority were married (84%) and reported education at the high school level or greater (96%). Median annual income was between $60,000 and $69,000.

Genetic Test Results and Melanoma History Forty-eight percent of respondents were *CDKN2A/p16*- mutation-positive. At baseline, 28% had a confirmed diagnosis of one or more melanomas.

Religious Affiliation and Central Beliefs of the Latter-day Saints Faith All participants reported an affiliation with the Church of Jesus Christ of Latter-day Saints (LDS). Headquartered in Salt Lake City, Utah, the Church is one of the fastest growing religions in the world, reporting 13 million members (Church of Jesus Christ of Latter-day Saints, 2006, 2007). A central aspect of the LDS

---

[3] Of the 53 participants from the parent study who enrolled in the follow-up study, 30 (56.6%) returned materials from the one-year assessment. Of these, 28 respondents provided complete or partially usable data for the main questionnaire and the structured inventory of religious coping strategies, and 25 respondents completed the open-ended portion of the spirituality questionnaire. Although the 25 participants whose data are presented here constitute only 47.2% of eligible participants at follow-up, it is important to note that these participants did not differ from the parent sample in age, sex, marital status, melanoma history, *CDKN2A/p16* mutation status, baseline health cognitions, or baseline health behaviors. A significant difference was found for household income such that participants who completed the one-year follow-up and spirituality questionnaire reported significantly greater median income ($60,000 to $69,999) than those who did not ($40,000 to $49, 999; see Leaf, Aspinwall, & Leachman, 2010, for additional details).

faith is personal agency, the belief that God has given each person the ability to choose and act for him- or herself (Book of Mormon, 2 Nephi, 2:27). This agency allows people to grow and progress on their path toward salvation. As we will describe, this belief in personal agency may be especially relevant for health concerns because Mormon people believe they carry responsibility for caring for their earthly bodies. Another important belief is that trials and adversity, such as illness, are a part of every person's life and can, with God's help, lead to spiritual growth (Book of Mormon, 2 Nephi, 2:11–24; Alma: 36:3). A third key aspect of the LDS faith is that obeying the laws and doctrines of the Church will lead to eternal life, where after earthly death one lives on with one's family and with God (Book of Mormon, Articles of Faith, 1:3; Doctrine & Covenants, 131: 1–4).

Measures

The data described in this chapter were taken from our one-year follow-up assessment, which included a supplementary spirituality questionnaire.

Patients' Open-Ended Accounts of How Religious and Spiritual Beliefs Influence Their Understanding and Management of Genetic Test Results and Familial Cancer History Participants were first provided with an introduction to our interest in understanding religious and spiritual beliefs, as well as other aspects of participants' worldview, that may be related to their understanding and management of their genetic test results. The introduction provided brief definitions of religious beliefs, spiritual beliefs, and worldview and ended with the following instructions: "If your beliefs and values have <u>not</u> influenced your experience in receiving genetic test results or thinking about your family's cancer history, it will be important for you to tell us that, as well." Participants were then asked three questions:

1. "Please describe how your personal religious and spiritual beliefs and values may influence how you *understand* your own genetic test result and/or a family member's test result. By *understand*, we mean how you think about your test result and/or family cancer history, what it means to you and your family, and why you think you have the particular result that you do."
2. "Please describe how your personal religious and spiritual beliefs and values may influence how you *manage* your genetic test result and/or a family member's test result. By *manage*, we mean anything you may have done in response to your genetic testing results and experience. This could include ways that you have adjusted emotionally, ways your spiritual beliefs have changed or adapted, ways you may have tried to reduce your melanoma risk, or practical, everyday changes you have made in your life."

3. "Have your personal religious and spiritual beliefs and values influenced *some other aspect of your experience* in receiving genetic counseling and test results, seeking and receiving medical care for skin changes or other medical needs, or being a member of a family with high rates of melanoma?"

Responses to these three questions were pooled, and a coding system was developed in collaboration with graduate and undergraduate volunteer LDS consultants who provided personal insight and scriptural and cultural references relevant to interpreting participants' responses. Responses were coded by two independent raters with 95% agreement. Disagreements were resolved in conference.

Religious Coping Inventory Following the open-ended questions, participants were asked to complete the full 63-item RCOPE with respect to whether or not they had used or attempted to use the described strategies to understand or manage their own or family members' genetic test results since receiving them. As described earlier, the RCOPE is designed to assess five major hypothesized functions of religious coping: seeking meaning, gaining control, seeking comfort, seeking intimacy, and transformation (Pargament et al., 2000). All items were scored on a 5-point scale ranging from *not at all* (1) to *very much* (5).

Perceived Control Participants were asked, "Overall, how much personal control do you feel you have over whether you develop a melanoma in the future?" (1 = *no control*, 5 = *a lot of control*).

Cancer Fatalism Participants also completed 13 items assessing cancer fatalism, of which 9 were adapted from existing inventories (Michielutte, Dignan, Sharp, Boxley, & Wells, 1996; Powe, 1995) and four were created by us. A factor analysis of these same items at baseline in the larger parent sample yielded four interpretable factors: (1) melanoma is always fatal (e.g., "I believe melanoma will kill you no matter how it is treated," $\alpha = .83$); (2) melanoma is meant to be (e.g., "I believe if someone is meant to get melanoma, they will get it no matter what they do," $\alpha = .85$); (3) once melanoma develops, it is too late to do anything about it ($\alpha = .76$); and (4) one cannot reduce one's risk of melanoma (e.g., "A person with a past history of a lot of sun exposure will not benefit from reducing sun exposure from now on because the damage has been done," $\alpha = .75$). All responses were made on 5-point scales ranging from *strongly disagree* (1) to *strongly agree* (5).

Sun-Protection Behaviors For each of the major photoprotective behaviors recommended by the American Academy of Dermatology (sunscreen use, wearing protective clothing, and avoiding peak UV exposure; American Academy of Dermatology, 2001; Lim et al., 2001), participants were asked to report the percentage of time they had practiced each precaution over the past six months, with responses ranging from "about 0% of the time" (1 = *never used*) to "about 100% of the time" (7 = *all the time*).

Sunburns and Tans Participants were asked to indicate the number of sunburns they had received in the past six months. Participants also indicated how much of this time they had been tan (1 = *none of the time*, 5 = *all the time*). For ease of presentation, these responses were converted to the percentage of time participants reported being tan. Responses to these summary items showed close correspondence to responses to a more detailed assessment of sunburns and tans on nine specific body sites.

Results

Religious Themes Identified by Participants

Of the 25 participants who completed the open-ended questions, 22 (88%) listed one or more ways in which their religious beliefs influenced their understanding and management of genetic test results.[4] The number of themes listed ranged from 0 to 8 (M = 3.48, SD = 2.47). Because themes did not differ as a function of *CDKN2A/p16* test results, we present combined results for carriers and noncarriers. It is important to note that these data represent the proportion of participants who spontaneously mentioned a specific theme in response to one of the questions, not the proportion who might express agreement with it on a closed-ended scale.

Belief in Personal Agency and Responsibility for Health The most frequently cited theme overall (listed by 60% of respondents), personal agency and responsibility for health included beliefs that God has given each of us the ability to choose and act for ourselves and a responsibility for taking good care of our earthly bodies. As one *CDKN2A/p16*– participant wrote, "Since I don't have the gene, it means God has put it in my hands. I can control whether or not I am at high risk or low risk for getting skin cancer based on my actions and choices regarding sun exposure." Similar responses were found among *CDKN2A/p16*+ participants; for example, a participant expressed, "I believe I am responsible for my part. Now, I know and I must be aggressive about checking my skin, covering up, applying sunscreen, etc."

[4] Four participants indicated that their religious beliefs had no effect on how they understood or managed their genetic test results; however, one of these participants indicated in a later section of the supplemental spirituality questionnaire that his genetic test results led him to contemplate the afterlife.

Belief in Cancer as God's Will or Plan for Individuals Endorsed by 56% of respondents, the next most frequently cited theme was the belief that a positive genetic test result and any subsequent cancer are parts of God's will and/or plan for each individual. Several participants indicated that they viewed cancer or a positive genetic test result as trials provided by God to help one become a better person. For example, one *CDKN2A/p16–* participant wrote, "We are all on this earth only temporarily. No matter what our test result may be, good or bad, it is all a part of our test here and part of God's plan for us," whereas another *CDKN2A/p16–* participant explained, "I guess genetic skin cancer just wasn't meant to be one of my life trials."

Belief That Religion Provides Emotional Benefits More than one third of participants (40%) listed one or more emotional benefits of religious beliefs and faith as important to how they manage their genetic test result. One *CDKN2A/p16+* participant wrote, "My religious beliefs allow me to see the future from a positive perspective"; and another wrote, "My religious beliefs make me happier and less [worried]." Similarly, one *CDKN2A/p16–* participant wrote, "If we have faith and trust in God—we can accept whatever comes our way."

Belief That God Provides Blessings and Guidance Of the 25 participants, 36% listed beliefs that God provides guidance, help, comfort, and love to those individuals facing problems and that God can bless and/or heal people through the actions of members of the Melchizedek Priesthood (the Church's term for the authority and responsibility to act in the name of Jesus Christ; Book of Mormon, Doctrine & Covenants, 107:101). For example, a *CDKN2A/p16–* participant stated, "I believe that God is a loving father of each one of us. I can go to Him in prayer for help, guidance, and comfort. I believe if we have faith and are obedient to his commandments that He will bless us as much as he can."

Belief That Science and Medicine Are Gifts From God The belief that medicine and science were given to humans by God to benefit humankind was listed by 24% of the sample. For example, one *CDKN2A/p16+* participant wrote, "We believe that through medical advancements (genetic testing, etc.) and treatments, that the Lord is helping us to solve our problem."

No Effect or Unsure of Effect A subset of respondents (16%) indicated that their religious beliefs had no effect on their understanding and management of genetic test results, that their beliefs would have an effect only if they were diagnosed with melanoma, or that they were currently unsure of the effect ("still trying to figure it all out").

Additional Themes Several additional themes were endorsed by smaller numbers of respondents. These include beliefs that the genetic mutation and melanoma are inherited aspects of one's family background just as is any other set of strengths and weaknesses, that LDS health and dress codes (e.g., modest clothing, no drinking or smoking) reduce cancer risk, that religion leads to stronger relationships with family and others, that an afterlife exists in which one will be reunited with one's eternal family, that religion makes one a better person, and that helping others is important.

Religious Coping Scale Results

Figure 21.1 presents the mean endorsement of each of the 21 subscales of the RCOPE by participants receiving positive and negative *CDKN2A/p16* genetic test results. The figure groups the strategies according to the original framework developed by Pargament and colleagues (2000) that delineates religious coping attempts in terms of their hypothesized function. As shown in Figure 21.1, only four strategies received endorsements at or above the midpoint of the scale: *collaborative religious coping* ("I worked together with God as partners," $M = 2.90$, $SD = 1.26$), *active religious surrender* ("I did my best and then turned the situation over to God," $M = 3.52$, $SD = 1.48$), *seeking spiritual support* ("I sought God's love and care," "I looked to God for strength, support, and guidance," $M = 3.69$, $SD = 1.53$), and *religious helping* ("I prayed for the well-being of others," "I tried to give spiritual strength to others," $M = 3.36$, $SD = 1.43$). It is of particular interest that there were no significant differences between *CDKN2A/p16+* and *CDKN2A/p16–* participants in the endorsement of these four strategies.

We next examined the endorsement of groups of religious coping strategies hypothesized to serve different functions.

Finding Meaning Consistent with the findings from the open-ended questions, *benevolent religious appraisal* ("I saw my situation as part of God's plan," "I tried to find a lesson from God in the event," $M = 2.40$, $SD = 1.44$) was most frequently endorsed among the religious coping strategies directed at finding meaning. Also consistent with the open-ended responses, there was little to no endorsement of coping strategies that involve feelings of being punished by God, reappraisal of God's powers, or believing the devil to be responsible for one's situation.

Gaining Control In support of the idea that preserving or restoring mastery is a central task of coping with adversity, all strategies in this group received at least some endorsement. As noted earlier, *collaborative religious coping* and *active religious surrender* were the most frequently endorsed, followed by *passive religious deferral* ($M = 1.83$, $SD = 0.92$) and *pleading for direct intercession* ($M = 1.69$, $SD = 0$ .94). It is of interest that although the *self-directing religious coping* scale received relatively low overall endorsement ($M = 1.65$, $SD = 0.70$), the single item "I tried to make sense of the situation on my own"

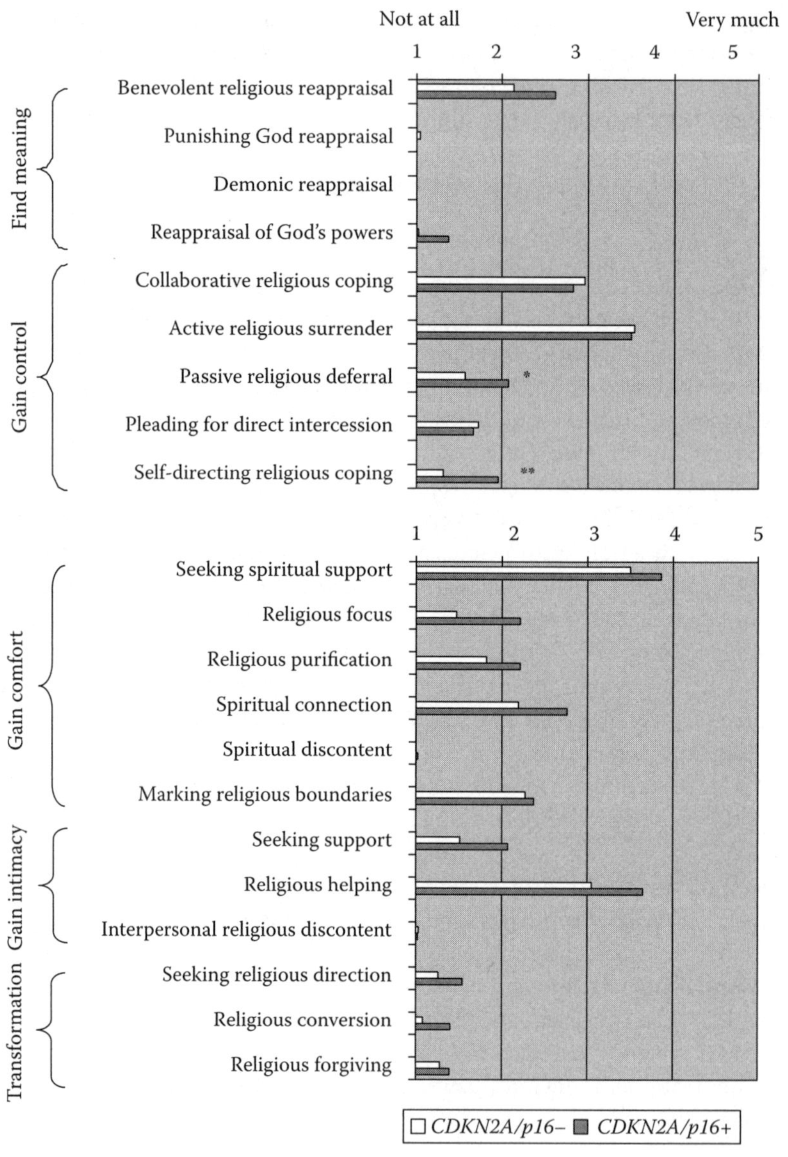

Figure 21.1 Mean endorsement of religious coping (RCOPE) strategies thought to serve each of five functions of religious coping by *CDKN2A/p16+* and *CDKN2A/p16–* participants. Asterisks are used to denote significant differences between carrier and noncarrier family members; $*p < .05$, $**p < .01$.

was more strongly endorsed than such items as "I tried to deal with my feelings without God's help," especially among participants receiving positive test results.

Strategies in this group were also the only ones to show significant differences between carriers and noncarriers. Specifically, as shown in Figure 21.1, participants who tested positive for the *CDKN2A/p16* mutation reported greater use of passive religious deferral than did those who tested negative (Ms = 2.07 vs. 1.55, respectively; F (1, 18) = 6.82, $p < .02$) and were also more likely to report self-directing religious coping (Ms = 1.95 vs. 1.31, respectively; F (1, 18) = 9.18, $p < .01$).

Seeking Comfort As noted earlier, *seeking spiritual support* was most strongly endorsed, followed by *seeking spiritual connection* ("I looked for a stronger connection with God," "I thought about how my life is part of a larger spiritual force," M = 2.50, SD = 1.36), *marking religious boundaries* ("I followed the teachings and practices of my religion," "I ignored advice that was inconsistent with my faith," M = 2.33, SD = 0.86), and to a lesser extent, *religious focus* ("I prayed to get my mind off my problems," M = 1.87, SD = 0.95) and *religious purification* ("I asked forgiveness for my sins," M = 2.04, SD = 1.21). *Spiritual discontent* ("I wondered whether God had abandoned me") received little to no endorsement.

Seeking Intimacy As noted earlier, consistent with the idea that a major aspect of familial cancer involves helping one's relatives manage positive genetic test results, *religious helping* was strongly endorsed in the sample. *Seeking support from clergy* received modest endorsement ("I looked for love and concern from the members of my church," M = 1.80, SD = 0.90), whereas *interpersonal religious discontent* ("I wondered whether my church had abandoned me") received little endorsement.

Seeking Transformation As shown in Figure 21.1, none of the three transformative religious coping strategies received even moderate levels of endorsement. Accordingly, these strategies were excluded from further analysis.

How Do the Religious Themes Identified by Patients Compare to the RCOPE Results?

We next examined the relationships between the most frequently endorsed religious themes identified by participants in the open-ended measures and the RCOPE subscales that received at least moderate endorsement in the sample. In interpreting this and subsequent findings, it is important to keep in mind that (a) the sample size is small and (b) the use of a dichotomous variable (e.g., endorsement vs. nonendorsement of religious themes) placed a ceiling on the magnitude of the association that could be obtained between the patient-identified themes and any other measure (Thorndike, 1978). As shown in Table 21.1, there are several points of convergence between religious themes identified as important by participants and reports of religious coping in the

Table 21.1 Correlations Between Frequently Endorsed Patient-Identified Religious Themes and Selected Religious Coping (RCOPE) Strategies

	Selected RCOPE Scales and Their Hypothesized Functions							
	Meaning	**Control**				**Comfort**		**Intimacy**
Patient-Identified Religious Themes	Benevolent Religious Reappraisal	Collaborative Religious Coping	Active Religious Surrender	Passive Religious Deferral	Self-Directing Religious Coping	Seeking Spiritual Support	Spiritual Connection	Religious Helping
Personal agency and responsibility for health	0	0.29	0.27	0.10	−0.03	0.32	0.27	0.31
Belief in God's will or plan	0.35	0.24	**0.54****	0.12	−0.31	**0.48***	0.15	**0.41***
Emotional benefits of religious faith	**0.54****	0.27	0.39^	0.28	−0.02	**0.42***	**0.44***	**0.61****
God provides blessings and assistance	**0.43***	0.04	**0.43***	0.13	−0.27	**0.48***	0.23	**0.54****
Science and medicine are gifts from God	0.18	−0.07	0.30	−0.07	−0.06	0.03	0.03	0.09
No effect	−0.20	−0.31	−0.27	−0.02	0.11	−0.34	−0.14	−0.35

Values in bold indicate significant correlations. *$p < .05$; **$p < .01$; ^$p < .10$.

year following receipt of genetic test results. There are also three religious themes that do not appear from these preliminary results to have counterparts in the RCOPE. We will briefly discuss each set of findings in turn.

Points of Convergence Between the Open-Ended Religious Themes and the RCOPE Subscales As shown in Table 21.1, there was noteworthy convergence between three of the patient-identified themes (belief in God's will or plan, emotional benefits of religious faith, and God provides blessings and assistance) and multiple RCOPE strategies. Specifically, endorsement of the emotional benefits of religious faith and the belief that God would provide assistance were both significantly associated with greater benevolent religious reappraisal of their own or a family member's genetic test results. In addition, the belief in God's will or plan, endorsement of the emotional benefits of faith, and the belief that God provides blessings and assistance were associated with greater reports of active religious surrender, seeking spiritual support, and religious helping (e.g., praying for others). Endorsement of the emotional benefits of religious faith was also a significant predictor of spiritual connection. Thus, there was a good correspondence between patient-identified themes in the context of genetic testing for familial cancer and at least one RCOPE scale for four out of five hypothesized functions of religious coping (seeking meaning, control, comfort, and intimacy).

Unique Elements of the Open-Ended Religious Themes As just noted, there were three religious themes identified by patients as important to their understanding and management of genetic test results that were not related to religious coping as assessed by the RCOPE: personal agency and responsibility for health, scientific and medical advances as gifts from God, and no effect. We will discuss each in turn.

First, although the RCOPE includes four subscales designed to address efforts to gain control through religious coping, none of the control-oriented scales were significantly related to beliefs in personal agency and responsibility for health described by 60% of our participants in the open-ended protocols. In particular, the lack of a relationship between patient-identified personal agency beliefs and collaborative or self-directing religious coping suggests that the personal agency reported by our participants was not conceptualized as coping in partnership with God or coping on one's own without God's help. Instead, participants' open-ended responses suggested that they viewed personal agency with respect to health and other matters as a God-given set of choices and responsibilities. Although this concept is similar to views that self-directing religious coping may have multiple forms (i.e., self-direction as a result of an abandoning God vs. self-direction as a result of a supportive but nonintervening God who has given the person agency and other necessary resources; Phillips et al., 2004), it does not appear that the self-directing religious coping subscale of the RCOPE, which contains items that assess efforts to make decisions without God's help, captures this form of self-direction.

The belief that science and medicine are gifts from God intended to benefit humans also emerged as a unique aspect mentioned by patients. As illustrated by the quotations from patients at the start of this chapter, this belief seems to have provided a strong framework for understanding and valuing genetic testing and medical treatments as a way to manage familial melanoma risk. As we have described elsewhere (Leaf et al., 2010), these beliefs also present a strong counterpoint to the idea that members of conservative religions will necessarily oppose scientific and medical advances or view the use of such advances as counter to God's will.

The third unique element to emerge from the open-ended religious themes that does not seem to have a clear counterpart in the RCOPE results is the presence of a subset of participants who indicated clearly that their religious or spiritual beliefs were unrelated to their understanding and management of the genetic test results or that they were still working on figuring out the relationship. It is not clear whether one could modify the administration of the RCOPE to allow participants a chance to clearly indicate that they did not use any form of religious coping to manage their situation. At present, it seems that such participants would simply indicate the lowest response option (e.g., *never* or *not at all*) for each scale, making it difficult to determine whether the person did not use religious means to cope, did not use the particular religious means presented in the inventory, or did not feel a need to cope.

Unique Elements of the RCOPE Finally, there were also some concepts captured by the RCOPE that did not emerge in the patient-identified themes. Most notably, we saw no evidence of collaborative religious coping or passive religious deferral in the open-ended responses, and none of the patient-identified themes were significantly associated with any of these RCOPE strategies.

Do Patient-Identified Religious Themes and Coping Strategies Predict Perceived Control and Cancer Fatalism?

We next examined whether the religious themes identified and coping strategies reported by patients were associated with greater or lesser perceived control and cancer fatalism. The only predictor of perceived control over the development of a new melanoma was personal agency and responsibility for health ($r = 0.36$, $p < .08$). Supplementary analyses revealed that this relationship was strongly moderated by melanoma history such that patients with a melanoma history who reported deriving a sense of personal agency and responsibility for their own health from their religious beliefs reported significantly higher perceived control ($M = 4.50$) than those who did not (M = 2.80, $t(5)$ = 3.98, $p < .02$), whereas this relationship was not significantly different among participants without a personal history of melanoma (personal agency, M = 4.00; no personal agency, M = 3.92, $t < 1$, *n.s.*).

Although levels of cancer fatalism were low overall, there were a few significant correlates of different aspects of cancer fatalism. Specifically, belief in cancer as God's will was a significant predictor of greater belief in the idea that melanoma is inevitably fatal ($r = 0.43$, $p < .03$). Among the RCOPE strategies, passive religious deferral predicted greater endorsement of the belief that if one has melanoma, it was meant to be ($r = 0.43$, $p < .04$). Finally, people who reported engaging in self-directing religious coping were less likely to believe that once melanoma had developed, it would be too late to do something about it ($r = -0.46$, $p < .03$).

Do Religious Themes and Coping Strategies Predict Adherence to Recommended Health Behaviors?

As shown in Table 21.2, all patient-identified themes and all but three RCOPE scales were significantly correlated with reports of at least one photoprotective or risk behavior in the past six months. With respect to the three photoprotective behaviors, it is important to note that they are functionally interrelated such that a person who employs one photoprotective behavior may not need to simultaneously employ another (e.g., someone who reports avoiding UV exposure between 10:00 a.m. and 4:00 p.m. does not need to simultaneously wear sunscreen or protective clothing, and vice versa). Thus, although there are no published guidelines for evaluating patterns of adherence across these multiple recommended health behaviors, the consistent practice of at least one measure may constitute adherence to medical recommendations (see Aspinwall et al., 2009, for discussion).

Performance of Sun-Protective Behaviors As shown in Table 21.2, participants who listed emotional benefits of religious beliefs or a belief that science and medicine were gifts from God reported greater UV avoidance in the past six months, as did those who reported engaging in benevolent religious appraisal, seeking spiritual connection, or religious helping as ways of coping with their own or a family member's genetic test results. On average, participants who endorsed one of the foregoing religious themes reported avoiding UV exposure 79.1% of the time, compared to 59.9% of the time for those who did not.[5] Similarly, several of the RCOPE strategies predicted more frequent reported sunscreen use. Specifically, benevolent religious appraisal, active religious surrender, and seeking spiritual connection predicted greater sunscreen use,

[5] See Leaf et al. (2010) for additional information about these analyses, including large sex differences in the reported practice of photoprotective behavior.

Table 21.2 Correlations of Frequently Endorsed Patient-Identified Religious Themes and Selected Religious Coping (RCOPE) Strategies With Reports of Sun-Protective and Risk Behaviors in the Past Six Months

Patient-Identified Religious Themes	**Sunscreen Use**	**Protective Clothing Use**	**Avoidance of UV Exposure**	**Number of Sunburns**	**Frequency of Tans**
Personal agency and responsibility for health	0.12	0.16	0.35	−0.31	**−0.70*****
Belief in God's will or plan	0.19	−0.07	0.22	−0.27	**−0.46***
Emotional benefits of religious faith	0.37	0.04	**0.44***	−0.30	**−0.49***
God provides blessings and assistance	0.28	−0.25	0.38^	−0.26	**−0.44***
Science and medicine are gifts from God	−0.09	0.18	**0.45***	−0.21	−0.29
No effect	−0.12	**−0.52****	**−0.45***	**0.62****	**0.64****
Selected RCOPE Strategies					
Benevolent religious appraisal	**0.44***	−0.22	**0.43***	−0.11	−0.22
Collaborative religious coping	0.17	0.12	0.37^	−0.15	−0.32
Active religious surrender	**0.43***	−0.15	0.39^	−0.09	−0.40^
Passive religious deferral	**0.44***	−0.03	0.16	0.02	−0.20
Self-directing religious coping	0.20	0.25	0.16	0.31	−0.02
Seeking spiritual support	0.21	−0.03	0.40^	−0.20	−0.40^
Spiritual connection	**0.44****	−0.06	**0.45***	−0.03	−0.30
Religious helping	0.31	0.07	**0.55****	−0.24	**−0.46***
Mean (*SD*)	45.4% (30.5)	70.0% (23.8)	65.9% (19.9)	1.12% (2.60)	16.7% (25.2)

Values in bold indicate significant correlations. $^*p < .05$; $^{**}p < .01$; $^{***}p <. 001$; $^\wedge p < .10$.

as did passive religious deferral, which typically shows an inverse relationship to the practice of health behaviors. A tertiary split based on religious coping scores was used to illustrate the magnitude of these differences. Participants reporting the most frequent use of the foregoing religious coping strategies reported using sunscreen twice as often as did participants reporting the least frequent use of these strategies (61.4% vs. 30.6%).

Finally, as shown in Table 21.2, the only religious theme or coping strategy to predict lower reported practice of photoprotective behaviors was the *no effect* response. Participants who reported that their religious and spiritual beliefs were unrelated to their understanding and management of genetic test results reported substantially less protective clothing use (42.5% vs. 75.2%) and less avoidance of UV exposure (45.6% vs.69.8%) than did other participants.

Performance of Risk Behaviors As shown in Table 21.2, all but one of the religious themes were reliable predictors of the reported practice of risk behaviors in the past six months. Specifically, personal agency and responsibility for health, belief in God's will and plan, endorsement of the emotional benefits of religious faith, and the belief that God provides blessings and assistance each predicted decreased frequency of being tan in the past six months, as did endorsement of religious helping as a coping strategy on the RCOPE. On average, participants who endorsed the foregoing religious themes reported being tan virtually none of the time in the past six months (3.9%), compared to 30.2% among participants who did not endorse one of these themes. Finally, consistent with the findings for decreased precautionary behaviors in this group, *no effect* participants reported substantially more sunburns (4.75 vs. 0.42) and a greater frequency of being tan (58.3% vs. 10.7%) in the past six months than did other respondents.

Discussion

The results of our study of some of the first participants to receive *CDKN2A/p16* genetic test results for familial melanoma suggest that religious and spiritual beliefs play a role in the understanding and management of genetic test results and familial cancer for most members of these high-risk families. Further, these beliefs seem to serve several specific functions for both carriers and noncarriers. In both patient-identified themes and responses to a structured inventory of religious coping strategies, we found evidence for the role of religious and spiritual beliefs in finding meaning, control, and comfort in managing one's own or family members' positive genetic test results and in providing support to others. These results suggest that religious beliefs provide a framework for both understanding and managing multiple behavioral and emotional challenges faced by cancer-prone families.

These results extend prior research on religiosity and health in a number of ways. First, most research on relationships among religiosity, religious coping, and mental and physical health outcomes has been conducted with participants who were either healthy (and therefore unlikely to be acutely concerned with any specific aspect of their health) or seriously ill. As noted earlier, researchers have long suspected that reports of positive and especially of negative forms of religious coping may be highly influenced by concurrent health status and associated psychological distress. Such confounds make it difficult to understand the relations between religious coping and mental and physical health outcomes. In contrast, our research, like earlier work by Kinney et al. (2002), assessed the ways in which participants who are not currently ill, but who are at extremely high risk for serious illness or its recurrence, use religious beliefs to understand, cope with, and manage a genetic test result that provides critically important information about their future health.

Second, we examined the relationship of patient-identified religious themes and religious coping strategies to health cognitions and medical adherence. We found a few cases in which specific religious themes and coping strategies were related to greater perceived control over the development of a future melanoma and to either increased or decreased cancer fatalism, such as whether melanoma is inevitably fatal and meant to be. Perhaps most important, we found that all the patient-identified religious themes and several of the religious coping strategies were associated with clinically meaningful differences in the reported practice of photoprotective and risk behaviors. In particular, all the patient-identified religious themes predicted greater reported avoidance of UV exposure, decreased frequency of being tan, or both. Similarly, several of the selected RCOPE strategies predicted greater reported use of sunscreen and UV avoidance, and religious helping predicted decreased tanning. These findings suggest that in addition to their role in providing important means of interpretive and/or vicarious control (see, e.g., Rothbaum et al., 1982; Thompson, 1981), religious and spiritual beliefs may foster actual behavioral control over one's melanoma risk, even among participants who receive positive test results. These results join a growing body of findings suggesting that such religious behaviors as church attendance are associated with such greater practice of health-promoting behaviors as physical activity and eating a healthy diet (Arredondo, Elder, Ayala, Campbell, & Baquero, 2005).

Beyond Health Cognitions: The Importance of Understanding the Meaning of Genetic Test Results to Participants

These results also suggest that there is much to be gained from studying the interplay of religious beliefs and health cognitions regarding particular illnesses. Specifically, studies of psychological and behavioral responses to genetic test results might profitably focus on the meaning of these results to participants. As we reviewed, earlier research has examined whether people see hypothetical genetic conditions as immutable risks and so may be less likely to adhere to recommended health behaviors but, understandably, researchers did not assess the meaning of such hypothetical results to participants and their families. In the present study, more than half of respondents indicated that they saw their own or a family member's genetic test results as God's will and as a personal trial selected by God to test and strengthen them, whereas 60% indicated that such results provided an important context in which to exercise God-given personal agency.

Understanding how religious and spiritual beliefs may influence the meaning that people ascribe to a positive genetic test result or family cancer history may help us understand other results from our earlier assessments in the parent sample of participants receiving *CDKN2A/p16* genetic test results and counseling, such as our findings that (a) reports of cancer worry, depression, and anxiety following genetic test reporting and counseling were generally low and (b) acceptance and religious coping were the most frequently endorsed ways of coping with genetic test results one month following genetic test reporting and counseling (Aspinwall, Taber, Leaf, Kohlmann, & Leachman, in press). Specifically, people who believe that a positive test result or cancer diagnosis is God's will and/or part of God's individual plan or trial for them have a coherent and meaningful framework with which to understand their genetic test results (Kinney et al., 2002; Pargament & Hahn, 1986). Further, several participants in the present study reported multiple emotional benefits of religious beliefs or faith, such as reducing worry, staying positive, and increasing acceptance, which could account for the low rates of psychological distress. Still others viewed genetic test results and other medical advances in the diagnosis and treatment of melanoma as gifts from God to help them manage their condition. In this context, then, a positive genetic test result (paired with counseling about how to manage one's risk) may be interpreted as a personally meaningful and less threatening outcome by people who are already acutely aware of their family's elevated cancer risk.

Understanding the Relationship Between Conceptions of Personal Agency and God's Will

This discussion of the meaning that patients may ascribe to a positive test result or cancer diagnosis brings us to our next major observation from this initial study: Beliefs about personal agency and responsibility seem to coexist with a strong endorsement of genetic test results and familial cancer as God's will. In contrast to studies that suggest that belief in God's will might undermine beliefs about personal agency and responsibility for health, patient-identified themes of personal agency and God's will frequently appeared together in the open-ended responses. This finding suggests that these concepts may be complementary, rather than competing: For people who see a positive genetic test result as a personal trial and test of faith, the key element seems to be how they will use their God-given agency to manage that test. Further, in the present study, belief in God's will or plan was associated with decreased reports of tanning frequency. These preliminary results present a challenge to the ideas that people with strong religious beliefs will necessarily hold an external or deferring view of their role in managing threats to health and well-being, or that seeing a medical diagnosis as part of God's will or plan will necessarily undermine personal agency with respect to its management.

The joint belief in personal agency and God's will found in our sample seems to be close to Pargament and colleagues' (2000) concept of active religious surrender (doing one's best and giving the rest up to God). Consistent with this idea, we found little endorsement of either the original form of self-directing religious coping, in which participants try to manage their situation on their own without God's help, or passive religious deferral. Although passive religious deferral was endorsed infrequently (though more so by participants receiving positive test results), asking God to take control of and solve one's problems was associated with greater cancer fatalism (e.g., believing that if one has melanoma, it was meant to be) and, surprisingly, greater reported sunscreen use. Although these findings await replication in a larger sample, they do suggest that passive religious deferral may not always be associated with decreased precautionary behavior. It will be important to continue to study the psychological and behavioral impact of genetic test results in diverse social and cultural contexts in which passive or deferring coping is more frequent (see, e.g., Kinney et al., 2002) and in which personal agency and responsibility for health are less frequently endorsed.

The Value of Multiple Methods of Examining Religious Themes and Coping Strategies

Our results also extend prior work by jointly assessing patient-identified religious themes by means of open-ended measures and religious coping strategies by means of structured inventory. The patient-identified themes showed some, but not complete, overlap with concepts assessed by the RCOPE. As noted earlier, good convergence between the two measures was noted for religious themes involving the belief in cancer as God's will or plan, the belief that God provides blessings and assistance, and the emotional benefits of religious faith. Of particular interest, our analysis yielded three religious themes that were not represented in the RCOPE inventory: personal agency and responsibility for health, belief in medical and scientific advances as gifts from God, and belief that one's religious and spiritual beliefs had no effect on one's understanding and management of genetic test results.

The first two unique findings may be results of the focus on a particular medical context, beliefs particular to members of the Church of Jesus Christ of Latter-Day saints, or both. It is also possible, however, that the identification of additional themes may be in part attributable to asking participants about such concepts as understanding and management, rather than coping. Specifically, participants may report coping only if they have some distress to manage and, as just described, reports of psychological distress and cancer worry following genetic test reporting and counseling were generally low. In contrast, questions about religious and spiritual understandings may have seemed relevant to a broader set of cognitions and behaviors, such as broader views of the role of personal agency in caring for one's health and responding to health threats and seeing medical advances as opportunities provided by God for humans to improve their situation.

The third unique finding—the identification of the *no effect* group—suggests that it is important for the study of religious coping to allow (and even to invite) participants to indicate that their religious beliefs are unrelated to their understanding and management of genetic test results or familial cancer history. Roughly one in six of our high-risk participants indicated that his or her religious beliefs had no effect on the understanding and management of genetic test results. We cannot tell from our results whether such responses reflect lower levels of religious belief or faith, whether these participants simply did not perceive a relationship between their religious faith and their management of genetic test results, or whether such participants had sought meaning in their religious beliefs but had not found it (see Chapter 23, this volume, for discussion). Given the strong pattern of lower preventive and higher risk behaviors found among these participants, however, it will be important for future research to understand how best to counsel and support such patients in reducing risk behaviors.

Limitations of the Present Study

Some limitations of the present study should be noted. First, the sample size of this initial study is small; thus, these results await replication with a larger sample. In future research, we have the opportunity to extend these findings by offering genetic test reporting and counseling to a sample of more than 300 first-degree relatives of members of the initial Utah pedigrees. The larger sample size will allow us to test whether there are particular constellations or clusters of religious themes and coping strategies associated with key health cognitions, adherence to recommended health behaviors, and psychological well-being, as well as whether particular religious themes and coping strategies have unique associations with these outcomes. We will also be better able to examine whether there are particular patterns associated with age, gender, personal melanoma history, and mutation status. Finally, we will be able to examine such relationships prospectively, rather than concurrently.

Second, because all participants reported an affiliation with the Church of Jesus Christ of Latter-day Saints, we are unable to generalize our findings to members of other faiths. It will be important to examine the prevalence and patterning of beliefs in personal agency and responsibility for health and beliefs in cancer or other illness as God's will among members of other faiths facing decisions about the uptake of genetic testing. It will also be important to examine religious coping and its relation to health cognitions and adherence among members of faiths who may believe that illness is a punishment from God or the work of the devil. As noted earlier, we found little to no evidence for these forms of religious coping in the present sample. Further, it will be important to examine the relationship of ethnicity and socioeconomic status to the concepts examined here.

Finally, it will be important to understand whether these findings may generalize to high-risk participants who receive genetic test results and counseling in other contexts (e.g., participants who are not part of research studies designed to find the genetic basis for their familial illness). Our participants had received extensive prior counseling regarding photoprotective and risk behaviors (although, as noted earlier, baseline practice of these behaviors was suboptimal). Further, our *CDKN2A/p16+* participants' elevated lifetime risk for melanoma was unlikely to have been surprising, given their familial and, in some cases, personal history of melanoma. It will be important to examine religious beliefs and coping in situations in which participants may have less information and fewer medical and social resources available to them.

Potential Applications to Genetic Counseling

It is our hope that this and other research designed to elucidate the social, cultural, and religious aspects of genetic testing for familial cancer will facilitate the development of culturally sensitive genetic counseling protocols. Personal religious and spiritual understandings of genetic test results and familial cancer history may prove to be important in helping people to manage the emotional and behavioral demands of accelerated screening and, where applicable, preventive behaviors. A greater understanding of this context may help promote ways of counseling people regarding familial cancer and other genetic risks that capitalize on religious beliefs that show a strong cross-sectional association with preventive health behaviors and address any specific beliefs or coping strategies that prove to be detrimental to the effective management of these risks (see also Chapters 1 and 22, this volume; Wong, 1998a).

Our results to date suggest that researchers and practitioners seeking to develop such protocols might profitably focus on understanding (a) people's beliefs about personal agency and responsibility for health, people's beliefs about whether illness is God's will, and the relationship between these two concepts and (b) particular religious beliefs regarding the nature and value of medicine, science, and technology in general. These latter beliefs may predict important attitudes concerning the use of emerging medical technology for the prediction, early detection, and treatment of cancer and other illnesses.

Further, such protocols need to continue to be sensitive to the familial context of cancer. For example, understanding particular religious and spiritual beliefs may prove to be important in counseling high-risk families about how to discuss their familial cancer risk and associated need for prevention and screening behaviors with their minor children and other minor family members (i.e., nieces and nephews). In the case of melanoma, such counseling may be especially important, given emerging evidence about the role that early childhood sunburns play in the development of melanoma (Bauer & Garbe, 2003; Noonan et al., 2001; Wachsmuth et al., 2001). Although *CDKN2A/p16* testing is not yet routinely offered to minor children, our participants have indicated strong interest in such testing (Taber, Aspinwall, Kohlmann, Dow, & Leachman, 2010). Finally, it will likely be important for counseling protocols for noncarriers to include information about how best to support family members who receive positive test results.

Conclusion

With the successful mapping of the human genome, progress in identifying genetic vulnerabilities to serious illness will be rapid. Researchers are currently working to untangle complex interplays of genetic vulnerability, individual behavior, and/or environmental exposure in the development of life-threatening and/or chronic diseases. As this work proceeds, it will become increasingly important to study how people understand and manage the part of their risk for such illnesses that can be controlled. The present results suggest that rather than approaching such risks with a sense of fatalism, people often derive from their religious and spiritual beliefs an understanding that they are responsible for taking care of their health and for seeking medical treatment when appropriate, even though their genetic risk is high. This work may provide a useful framework for understanding the multiple ways in which people may derive meaning and a sense of personal agency as they face cancer and other illnesses for which both genetic vulnerabilities and effective precautions are identified.

Acknowledgments

This work was supported by a Funding Incentive Seed Grant, Office of the Vice President for Research, University of Utah, awarded to Lisa G. Aspinwall and Sancy A. Leachman. Support was also received from the Huntsman Cancer Foundation (HCF), the Tom C. Mathews Jr. Familial Melanoma Research Clinic endowment, the Pedigree and Population Resource of Huntsman Cancer Institute, and a Templeton Positive Psychology Prize, awarded to Aspinwall by the John Templeton Foundation and the American Psychological Association. Samantha L. Leaf was supported in part by a Graduate Research Fellowship from the Graduate School, University of Utah. We acknowledge the use of the genetic counseling core facility supported by the Huntsman Cancer

Foundation. We especially appreciate the assistance of Brian Jones, Camila Rodrigues, and Trisha Weeks in sharing their understanding of cultural and religious beliefs relevant to the interpretation of participants' responses, and we gratefully acknowledge the willing and generous participation of all the family members in this study, without whom this project would not have been possible. We appreciate also the assistance of Amber Kostial, Michelle Welch, Emily Bullough, and Angela Newman.

References

Acklin, M. W., Brown, E. C., & Mauger, P. A. (1983). The role of religious values in coping with cancer. *Journal of Religion & Health, 22*(4), 322–333.

Ai, A. L., Park, C. L., Huang, B., Rodgers, W., & Tice, T. N. (2007). Psychosocial mediation of religious coping styles: A study of short-term psychological distress following cardiac surgery. *Personality and Social Psychology Bulletin, 33*(6), 867–882.

American Academy of Dermatology. (2001). Parents' guide to sun protection for children. Retrieved from http://www.newswireone.com/NW2005/C_AAD_CH/AAD3001456/assets/downloads/03sep_sun_protection.pdf

Arredondo, E. M., Elder, J. P., Ayala, G. X., Campbell, N. R., & Baquero, B. (2005). Is church attendance associated with Latinas' health practices and self-reported health? *American Journal of Health Behavior, 29*(6), 502–511.

Aspinwall, L. G., Leaf, S. L., Dola, E. R., Kohlmann, W., & Leachman, S. A. (2008). *CDKN2A/p16* genetic test reporting improves early detection intentions and practices in high-risk melanoma families. *Cancer Epidemiology, Biomarkers & Prevention, 17*, 1510–1519.

Aspinwall, L. G., Leaf, S. L., Kohlmann, W., Dola, E. R., & Leachman, S. A. (2009). Patterns of photoprotection following *CDKN2A/p16* genetic test reporting and counseling. *Journal of the American Academy of Dermatology, 60*, 745–757.

Aspinwall, L. G., Taber, J. M., Leaf, S. L., Kohlmann, W., & Leachman, S. A. (in press). Genetic testing for hereditary melanoma and pancreatic cancer: A longitudinal study of psychological outcome. *Psycho-Oncology*.

Balch, C. M., Buzaid, A. C., Soong, S. J., Atkins, M. B., Cascinelli, N., Coit, D. G., … Thompson, J. F. (2001, August). Final version of the American Joint Committee on Cancer staging system for cutaneous melanoma. *Journal of Clinical Oncology, 19*(16), 3635–3648.

Bantha, R., Moskowitz, J. T., Acree, M., & Folkman, S. (2007). Socioeconomic differences in the effects of prayer on physical symptoms and quality of life. *Journal of Health Psychology, 12*(2), 249–260.

Barnhill, R. L., Fine, J. A., Roush, G. C., & Berwick, M. (1996). Predicting five-year outcome for patients with cutaneous melanoma in a population-based study. *Cancer, 78*(3), 427–432.

Bauer, J., & Garbe, C. (2003). Acquired melanocytic nevi as risk factor for melanoma development: A comprehensive review of epidemiological data. *Pigment Cell Research, 16*(3), 297–306.

Benjamins, M. R. (2005). Social determinants of preventive service utilization: How religion influences the use of cholesterol screening in older adults. *Research on Aging, 27*(4), 475–497.

Benjamins, M. R. (2006). Religious influences on preventive health care use in a nationally representative sample of middle-age women. *Journal of Behavioral Medicine, 29*(1), 1–16.

Benjamins, M. R., Trinitapoli, J., & Ellison, C. G. (2006). Religious attendance, health maintenance beliefs, and mammography utilization: Findings from a nationwide survey of Presbyterian women. *Journal for the Scientific Study of Religion, 45*(4), 597–607.

Bergenmar, M., & Brandberg, Y. (2001). Sunbathing and sun-protection behaviors and attitudes of young Swedish adults with hereditary risk for malignant melanoma. *Cancer Nursing, 24*(5), 341–350.

Berkenstadt, M., Shiloh, S., Barkai, G., Katznelson, M. B., & Goldman, B. (1999). Perceived personal control (PPC): A new concept in measuring outcome of genetic counseling. *American Journal of Medical Genetics, 82*(1), 53–59.

Bishop, D. T., Demenais, F., Goldstein, A. M., Bergman, W., Bishop, J. N., Bressac-dePaillerets, B.,… Melanoma Genetics Consortium (2002). Geographical variation in the penetrance of CDKN2A mutations for melanoma. *Journal of the National Cancer Institute, 94*(12), 894–903.

Botkin, J. R., Smith, K. R., Croyle, R. T., Baty, B. J., Wylie, J. E., Dutson, D.,… Lyon, E. (2003). Genetic testing for a BRCA1 mutation: Prophylactic surgery and screening behavior in women 2 years post testing. *American Journal of Medical Genetics, 118A*, 201–209.

Bower, J. E., Kemeny, M. E., Taylor, S. E., & Fahey, J. L. (1998). Cognitive processing, discovery of meaning, CD4 decline, and AIDS-related mortality among bereaved HIV-seropositive men. *Journal of Consulting and Clinical Psychology, 66*(6), 979–986.

Bower, J. E., Meyerowitz, B. E., Desmond, K. A., Bernaards, C. A., Rowland, J. H., & Ganz, P. A. (2005). Perceptions of positive meaning and vulnerability following breast cancer: Predictors and outcomes among long-term breast cancer survivors. *Annals of Behavioral Medicine, 29*(3), 236–245.

Brandberg, Y., Jonell, R., Broberg, M., Sjoden, P.-O., & Rosdahl, I. (1996). Sun-related behaviour in individuals with dysplastic naevus syndrome. *Acta Derm Venereol (Stockholm)*, 76, 381–384.

Bulman, R. J., & Wortman, C. B. (1977). Attributions of blame and coping in the "real world": Severe accident victims react to their lot. *Journal of Personality and Social Psychology, 35*(5), 351–363.

Cannon-Albright, L. A., Goldgar, D. E., Meyer, L. J., Lewis, C. M., Anderson, D. E., Fountain, J. W.,… Skolnick, M. H. (1992, November 13). Assignment of a locus for familial melanoma, MLM, to chromosome 9p13–p22. *Science, 258*(5085), 1148–1152.

Carver, C. S., Pozo, C., Harris, S. D., Noriega, V., Scheier, M. F., Robinson, D. S.,… Clark, K.C. (1993). How coping mediates the effect of optimism on distress: A study of women with early stage breast cancer. *Journal of Personality and Social Psychology, 65*(2), 375–390.

Carver, C. S., Scheier, M. F., & Weintraub, J. K. (1989). Assessing coping strategies: A theoretically based approach. *Journal of Personality and Social Psychology, 56*(2), 267–283.

Church of Jesus Christ of Latter-day Saints. (2006). Church is the second-fastest growing religion in the United States. *Newsroom.* Retrieved from http://newsroom.lds.org/article/church-is-the-second-fastest-growing-religion-in-the-united-states

Church of Jesus Christ of Latter-day Saints. (2007). One million missionaries, thirteen million members. *Newsroom.* Retreived from http://newsroom.lds.org/article/one-million-missionaries-thirteen-million-members

Claes, E., Evers-Kiebooms, G., Boogaerts, A., Decruyenaere, M., Denayer, L., & Leguis, E. (2003). Communication with close and distant relatives in the context of genetic testing for hereditary breast and ovarian cancer in cancer patients. *American Journal of Medical Genetics, 116A*, 11–19.

Collins, R. L., Taylor, S. E., & Skokan, L. A. (1990). A better world or a shattered vision? Changes in life perspectives following victimization. *Social Cognition, 8*(3), 263–285.

Costanzo, E. S., Lutgendorf, S. K., Bradley, S. L., Rose, S. L., & Anderson, B. (2005). Cancer attributions, distress, and health practices among gynecologic cancer survivors. *Psychosomatic Medicine, 67*, 972–980.

Emmons, R. A., Colby, P. M., & Kaiser, H. A. (1998). When losses lead to gains: Personal goals and the recovery of meaning. In P. T. P. Wong & P. S. Fry (Eds.), *The human quest for meaning: A handbook of psychological research and clinical applications* (pp. 163–178). Mahwah, NJ: Erlbaum.

Felix Aaron, K., Levine, D., & Burstin, H. R. (2003). African American church participation and health care practices. *Journal of General Internal Medicine, 18*(11), 908–913.

Folkman, S., & Lazarus, R. S. (1980). An analysis of coping in a middle-aged community sample. *Journal of Health and Social Behavior, 21*(3), 219–239.

Folkman, S., & Moskowitz, J. T. (2007). Positive affect and meaning-focused coping during significant psychological stress. In M. Hewstone, H. A. W. Schut, J. B. F. DeWit, K. vanDenBos, & M. S. Stroebe (Eds.), *The scope of social psychology: Theory and applications* (pp. 193–208). New York, NY: Psychology Press.

Fox, S. A., Pitkin, K., Paul, C., Carson, S., & Duan, N. (1998). Breast cancer screening adherence: Does church attendance matter? *Health Education & Behavior, 25*(6), 742–758.

Frankl, V. E. (1959). *Man's search for meaning.* New York, NY: Pocket Books. (Originally published 1946)

Gall, T. L. (2004). Relationship with God and the quality of life of prostate cancer survivors. *Quality of Life Research, 13*, 1357–1368.

Gall, T. L., & Cornblat, M. W. (2002). Breast cancer survivors give voice: A qualitative analysis of spiritual factors in long-term adjustment. *Psycho-Oncology, 11*(6), 524–535.

Gall, T. L., Miguez de Renart, R. M., & Boonstra, B. (2000). Religious resources in long-term adjustment to breast cancer. *Journal of Psychosocial Oncology, 18*(2), 21–37.

Hamann, H. A., Croyle, R. T., Venne, V. L., Baty, B. J., Smith, K. R., & Botkin, J. R. (2000). Attitudes toward the genetic testing of children among adults in a Utah-based kindred tested for a BRCA1 mutation. *American Journal of Medical Genetics, 92*(1), 25–32.

Hansen, C. B., Wadge, L. M., Lowstuter, K., Boucher, K., & Leachman, S. A. (2004). Clinical germline genetic testing for melanoma. *Lancet Oncology, 5*(5), 314–319.

Hathaway, W. L., & Pargament, K. I. (1990). Intrinsic religiousness, religious coping, and psychosocial competence: A covariance structure analysis. *Journal for the Scientific Study of Religion, 29*(4), 423.

Hicken, B., & Tucker, D. (2002). Impact of genetic risk feedback: Perceived risk and motivation for health protective behaviours. *Psychology, Health & Medicine, 7*(1), 25–36.

Holt, C. L., & McClure, S. M. (2006). Perceptions of the religion–health connection among African American church members. *Qualitative Health Research, 16*(2), 268–281.

Hughes, C., Lerman, C., Schwartz, M., Peshkin, B. N., Wenzel, L., Narod, S., & Main, D. (2002). All in the family: Evaluation of the process and content of sisters' communication about BRCA1 and BRCA2 genetic test results. *American Journal of Medical Genetics, 107*(2), 143–150.

Janoff-Bulman, R. (1989). Assumptive worlds and the stress of traumatic events: Applications of the schema construct. *Social Cognition*, *7*(2), 113–136.

Janoff-Bulman, R., & Frieze, I. H. (1983). A theoretical perspective for understanding reactions to victimization. *Journal of Social Issues*, *39*(2), 1–17.

Jenkins, R. A., & Pargament, K. I. (1988). Cognitive appraisals in cancer patients. *Social Science & Medicine*, *26*(6), 625–633.

Kamb, A., Shattuck-Eidens, D., Eeles, R., Liu, Q., Gruis, N. A., Ding, W.,... Cannon-Albright, L. A. (1994). Analysis of the *p16* gene (CDKN2) as a candidate for the chromosome 9p melanoma susceptibility locus. *Nature Genetics*, *1*, 23–26.

Kastrinos, F., Stoffel, E. M., Balmana, J., & Syngal, S. (2007). Attitudes toward prenatal genetic testing in patients with familial adenomatous polyposis. *American Journal of Gastroenterology*, *102*(6), 1284–1290.

Kinney, A. Y., Emery, G., Dudley, W. N., & Croyle, R. T. (2002). Screening behaviors among African American women at high risk for breast cancer: Do beliefs about God matter? *Oncology Nursing Forum*, *29*(5), 835–843.

Koenig, H. G., George, L. K., Cohen, H. J., Hays, J. C., Larson, D. B., & Blazer, D. G. (1998). The relationship between religious activities and cigarette smoking in older adults. *Journals of Gerontology: Series A. Biological Sciences and Medical Sciences*, *53*(6), M426–M434.

Koenig, H. G., Pargament, K. I., & Nielsen, J. (1998). Religious coping and health status in medically ill hospitalized older adults. *Journal of Nervous and Mental Disease*, *186*(9), 513–521.

Krause, N. (1998). Neighborhood deterioration, religious coping, and changes in health during late life. *Gerontologist*, *38*(6), 653–664.

Leaf, S. L., Aspinwall, L. G., Dola, E., Kohlmann, W., & Leachman, S. A. (2010). *Psychological outcomes and patient reports of the costs and benefits of p16 genetic test reporting in a prospective study of familial melanoma patients.* Manuscript in preparation.

Leaf, S. L., Aspinwall, L. G., & Leachman, S. A. (2010). God and agency in the era of molecular medicine: Religious beliefs predict sun protection behaviors following melanoma genetic test reporting. *Archive for the Psychology of Religion, 32*, 87–112.

Lerman, C., Croyle, R. T., Tercyak, K. P., & Hamann, H. A. (2002). Genetic testing: Psychological aspects and implications. *Journal of Consulting and Clinical Psychology*, *70*, 784–797.

Lim, H. W., Naylor, M., Honigsmann, H., Gilchrest, B. A., Cooper, K., Morison, W.,... Scherschum, L. (2001). American Academy of Dermatology Consensus Conference on UVA protection of sunscreens: Summary and recommendations. Washington, DC, February 4, 2000. *Journal of the American Academy of Dermatology*, *44*(3), 505–508.

Mahoney, A., Carels, R. A., Pargament, K. I., Wachholtz, A., Edwards Leeper, L., Kaplar, M., & Frutchey, R. (2005). The sanctification of the body and behavioral health patterns of college students. *International Journal for the Psychology of Religion*, *15*(3), 221–238.

Marteau, T. M., & Croyle, R. T. (1998). Psychological responses to genetic testing. *British Medical Journal*, *316*, 693–696.

Marteau, T. M., & Lerman, C. (2001). Genetic risk and behavioural change. *British Medical Journal*, *322*, 1056–1059.

McBride, J. L., Arthur, G., Brooks, R., & Pilkington, L. (1998). The relationship between a patient's spirituality and health experiences. *Family Medicine*, *30*(2), 122–126.

McIntosh, D. N. (1995). Religion-as-schema, with implications for the relation between religion and coping. *International Journal for the Psychology of Religion, 5*(1), 1–16.

McIntosh, D. N., Silver, R. C., & Wortman, C. B. (1993). Religion's role in adjustment to a negative life event: Coping with the loss of a child. *Journal of Personality and Social Psychology, 65*(4), 812–821.

Michielutte, R., Dignan, M. B., Sharp, P. C., Boxley, J., & Wells, H. B. (1996). Skin cancer prevention and early detection practices in a sample of rural women. *Preventive Medicine, 25*(6), 673–683.

Nairn, R. C., & Merluzzi, T. V. (2003). The role of religious coping in adjustment to cancer. *Psycho-Oncology, 12*(5), 428–441.

Noonan, F. P., Recio, J. A., Takayama, H., Duray, P., Anver, M. R., Rush, W. L., … Merlino, G. (2001, September 20). Neonatal sunburn and melanoma in mice. *Nature, 413*(6853), 271–272.

Ozorak, E. W., Paloutzian, R. F., & Park, C. L. (2005). Cognitive approaches to religion. In R. F. Paloutzan & C. L. Park (Eds.), *Handbook of the psychology of religion and spirituality.* (pp. 216–234). New York, NY: Guilford Press.

Pargament, K. I. (1997). *The psychology of religion and coping: Theory, research, practice.* New York, NY: Guilford Press.

Pargament, K. I., & Hahn, J. (1986). God and the just world: Causal and coping attributions to God in health situations. *Journal for the Scientific Study of Religion, 25*(2), 193–207.

Pargament, K. I., Kennell, J., Hathaway, W., & Grevengoed, N. (1988). Religion and the problem-solving process: Three styles of coping. *Journal for the Scientific Study of Religion, 27*(1), 90–104.

Pargament, K. I., Koenig, H. G., & Perez, L. M. (2000). The many methods of religious coping: Development and initial validation of the RCOPE. *Journal of Clinical Psychology, 56*(4), 519–543.

Pargament, K. I., Koenig, H. G., Tarakeshwar, N., & Hahn, J. (2004). Religious coping methods as predictors of psychological, physical and spiritual outcomes among medically ill elderly patients: A two-year longitudinal study. *Journal of Health Psychology, 9*(6), 713–730.

Pargament, K. I., Olsen, H., Reilly, B., Falgout, K., Ensing, D. S., & Van Haitsma, K. (1992). God help me (II): The relationship of religious orientations to religious coping with negative life events. *Journal for the Scientific Study of Religion, 31*(4), 504.

Pargament, K. I., Smith, B. W., Koenig, H. G., & Perez, L. (1998). Patterns of positive and negative religious coping with major life stressors. *Journal for the Scientific Study of Religion, 37*(4), 710–724.

Pargament, K. I., Sullivan, M. S., Tyler, F. B., & Steele, R. E. (1982). Patterns of attribution of control and individual psychosocial competence. *Psychological Reports, 51*(3), 1243–1252.

Park, C. L. (2007). Religiousness/spirituality and health: A meaning systems perspective. *Journal of Behavioral Medicine, 30*(4), 319–328.

Park, C. L., & Folkman, S. (1997). Meaning in the context of stress and coping. *Review of General Psychology, 1*(2), 115–144.

Peterson, S. K., Watts, B. G., Koehly, L. M., Vernon, S. W., Baile, W. F., Kohlmann, W. K., & Gritz, E. R. (2003). How families communicate about HNPCC genetic testing: Findings from a qualitative study. *American Journal of Medical Genetics, 119C,* 78–86.

Phillips, R. E., III, Pargament, K. I., Lynn, Q. K., & Crossley, C. D. (2004). Self-directing religious coping: A deistic God, abandoning God, or no God at all? *Journal for the Scientific Study of Religion, 43*(3), 409–418.

Powe, B. D. J. A. (1995). Fatalism among African Americans: Philosophical perspectives. *Journal of Religion and Health, 34*(2), 119–125.

Rothbaum, F., Weisz, J. R., & Snyder, S. S. (1982). Changing the world and changing the self: A two-process model of perceived control. *Journal of Personality and Social Psychology, 42*(1), 5–37.

Schwartz, M. D., Hughes, C., Roth, J., Main, D., Peshkin, B. N., Isaacs, C., . . . Lerman, C. (2000). Spiritual faith and genetic testing decisions among high-risk breast cancer probands. *Cancer Epidemiology, Biomarkers & Prevention, 9*(4), 381–385.

Senior, V., Marteau, T. M., & Weinman, J. (2000). Impact of genetic testing on causal models of heart disease and arthritis: An analogue study. *Psychology & Health, 14*(6), 1077–1088.

Sher, C., Romano-Zelekha, O., Green, M. S., & Shohat, T. (2003). Factors affecting performance of prenatal genetic testing by Israeli Jewish women. *American Journal of Medical Genetics. Part A, 120*(3), 418–422.

Sherman, A. C., Simonton, S., Latif, U., Spohn, R., & Tricot, G. (2005). Religious struggle and religious comfort in response to illness: Health outcomes among stem cell transplant patients. *Journal of Behavioral Medicine, 28*(4), 359–367.

Shiloh, S., Ben-Sinai, R., & Keinan, G. (1999). Effects of controllability, predictability, and information-seeking style on interest in predictive genetic testing. *Personality and Social Psychology Bulletin, 25*(10), 1187–1195.

Shiloh, S., Berkenstadt, M., Meiran, N., Bat-Miriam-Katznelson, M., & Goldman, B. (1997). Mediating effects of perceived personal control in coping with a health threat: The case of genetic counseling. *Journal of Applied Social Psychology, 27*(13), 1146–1174.

Silver, R. L., Boon, C., & Stones, M. H. (1983). Searching for meaning in misfortune: Making sense of incest. *Journal of Social Issues, 39*(2), 81–101.

Smith, K. R., West, J. A., Croyle, R. T., & Botkin, J. R. (1999). Familial context of genetic testing for cancer susceptibility: Moderating effects of siblings' test results on psychological distress one to two weeks after BRCA1 mutation testing. *Cancer Epidemiology, Biomarkers & Prevention, 8*, 385–392.

Spilka, B., Hood, R. W., Hunsberger, B., & Gorsuch, R. (2003). *The psychology of religion: An empirical approach* (3rd ed.). New York, NY: Guilford Press.

Taber, J. M., Aspinwall, L. G., Kohlmann, W., Dow, R., & Leachman, S. A. (2010). Parental preferences for CDKN2A/p16 genetic testing of minors. *Genetics in Medicine, 12*, 823–838.

Tarakeshwar, N., Hansen, N., Kochman, A., & Sikkema, K. J. (2005). Gender, ethnicity and spiritual coping among bereaved HIV-positive individuals. *Mental Health, Religion & Culture, 8*(2), 109–125.

Tarakeshwar, N., Vanderwerker, L. C., Paulk, E., Pearce, M. J., Kasl, S. V., & Prigerson, H. G. (2006). Religious coping is associated with the quality of life of patients with advanced cancer. *Journal of Palliative Medicine, 9*(3), 646–657.

Taylor, S. E. (1983). Adjustment to threatening events: A theory of cognitive adaptation. *American Psychologist, 38*(11), 1161–1173.

Taylor, S. E., Kemeny, M. E., Reed, G. M., Bower, J. E., & Gruenewald, T. L. (2000). Psychological resources, positive illusions, and health. *American Psychologist, 55*(1), 99–109.

Tedeschi, R. G., & Calhoun, L. G. (2004). Posttraumatic growth: Conceptual foundations and empirical evidence. *Psychological Inquiry, 15*(1), 1–18.

Thompson, S. C. (1981). Will it hurt less if I can control it? A complex answer to a simple question. *Psychological Bulletin, 90*(1), 89–101.

Thompson, S. C., Sobolew-Shubin, A., Galbraith, M. E., Schwankovsky, L., & Cruzen, D. (1993). Maintaining perceptions of control: Finding perceived control in low-control circumstances. *Journal of Personality and Social Psychology, 64*(2), 293–304.

Thorndike, R. M. (1978). *Correlational procedures for research.* New York, NY: Gardner.

Van Oostrom, I., Meijers-Heijboer, H., Duivenvoorden, H. J., Brocker-Vriends, A. H. J. T., van Asperen, C. J., Sijmons, R. H.,… Tibben, A. (2007). A prospective study of the impact of genetic susceptibility testing for BRCA1/2 or HNPCC on family relationships. *Psycho-Oncology, 16*(4), 320–328.

Wachsmuth, R. C., Gaut, R. M., Barrett, J. H., Saunders, C. L., Randerson-Moor, J. A., Eldridge, A., … Newton Bishop, J. A. (2001, August). Heritability and gene–environment interactions for melanocytic nevus density examined in a U.K. adolescent twin study. *Journal of Investigative Dermatology, 117*(2), 348–352.

Wagner Costalas, J., Itzen, M., Malick, J., Babb, J. S., Bove, B., Godwin, A. K., & Daly, M. B. (2003). Communication of BRCA1 and BRCA2 results to at-risk relatives: A cancer risk assessment program's experience. *American Journal of Medical Genetics: Part C. Seminars in Medical Genetics, 119*(1), 11–18.

Wong, P. T. P. (1998a). Meaning-centered counseling. In P. T. P. Wong & P. S. Fry (Eds.), *The human quest for meaning: A handbook of psychological research and clinical applications* (pp. 395–435). Mahwah, NJ: Erlbaum.

Wong, P. T. P. (1998b). Spirituality, meaning, and successful aging. In P. T. P. Wong & P. S. Fry (Eds.), *The human quest for meaning: A handbook of psychological research and clinical applications* (pp. 359–394). Mahwah, NJ: Erlbaum.

Wong, P. T. P., & Fry, P. S. (Eds.). (1998). *The human quest for meaning: A handbook of psychological research and clinical applications.* Mahwah, NJ: Erlbaum.

Wong-McDonald, A., & Gorsuch, R. L. (2004). A multivariate theory of God concept, religious motivation, locus of control, coping, and spiritual well-being. *Journal of Psychology & Theology, 32*(4), 318–334.

III
Applications

22
Clinical Approaches to Discrepancies in Meaning
Conceptualization, Assessment, and Treatment

JEANNE M. SLATTERY
Clarion University

CRYSTAL L. PARK
University of Connecticut

> Although few conservative Presbyterian churches actually worship in the Puritan way, the Puritan theology of worship remains the standard orthodoxy among them. This discrepancy sometimes leads to guilty consciences.
>
> **—John Frame**

People are by nature meaning-making creatures: We have beliefs about how things are and expectations about how they should be (Baumeister, 1991), and we try to make sense of our world when reality differs from our expectations. As John Frame described, negative affect often follows experiences of major discrepancies between how the world is and how we think it should be (or how we should be). This chapter describes the ways in which such discrepancies may present in therapy and offers therapeutic approaches to resolving them.

Meaning Systems

To understand people, one must first recognize their unique perspectives and ways of understanding their world (Evans, 1993). In the course of a day, people use meaning as a heuristic to structure their lives and assign meanings to daily life events (Hogarth, 1981; Thompson, Armstrong, & Thomas, 1998). These meaning heuristics are both derived from and reflective of their understanding of the world (Park & Folkman, 1997). The meaning systems approach assumes that people's behaviors, problems, and attempted solutions are understandable once their individually constructed global and situational meanings and given context are understood (Park & Slattery, 2009; Slattery,

2004). This assumption applies equally to people at their best, to those who are actively delusional or psychotic, and to those who have violated basic societal laws and norms (e.g., Andrea Yates; cf. Slattery, 2004).

Global meaning refers to a broadly encompassing entity composed of beliefs, goals, and purpose, which exerts powerful influences on people's thoughts, actions, and feelings (Park & Folkman, 1997). Global beliefs are basic and often broad assumptions about the world, including whether it is benevolent, fair, or just (Koltko-Rivera, 2004). People also hold more personal beliefs, that is, whether they are lucky, good, safe, or vulnerable, have control, or can change a situation (e.g., Bandura, 1997; Janoff-Bulman, 1992; Koltko-Rivera, 2004; Thompson et al., 1998). These beliefs help people interpret and make sense of their lives and experiences. Beliefs can be explicit and conscious, or implicit and consciously denied yet still influence behavior (Briñol, Petty, & Wheeler, 2006). Global goals are high-level ideals, states, or objects toward which people work (Karoly, 1999). Most commonly reported global goals include relationships, intimacy, religion, and achievement (Emmons, 2005). Often, people set and meet a series of short-term, concrete goals that help them to meet their higher level goals (see Austin & Vancouver, 1996, for a review). Finally, most people experience a sense of meaning or purpose in life. This felt meaning or purpose has been referred to as the emotional aspect of global meaning (Klinger, 1977; Reker & Wong, 1988). Meaningfulness is thought to come from seeing one's actions as oriented or progressing toward a desired future state or goal (Baumeister, 1991; McGregor & Little, 1998).

According to the meaning system perspective, people continuously assign meanings to their daily lives, their own behaviors, and the situations that they encounter. Thus, *appraised meaning* refers to the specific understanding or significance that individuals assign to particular objects, relationships, situations, or events. People often enter therapy as a result of particularly challenging appraised meanings (e.g., derived from bereavement, relationship endings, or discord, violence, or trauma) that are inconsistent with their global meanings.

Discrepancies Among Aspects of Meaning

Discrepancies occur when individuals assign meanings to situations that violate their global beliefs (e.g., that the world is fair, but not getting a job despite being the best candidate), goals (e.g., failing to be accepted to graduate school, despite years of preparation), or purpose (e.g., having children leave home for college and therefore feeling one's life no longer has purpose). Discrepancies also arise when global beliefs or goals are in conflict with one another (e.g., wanting to fully express one's sexuality but being afraid of displeasing God; Exline, 2002). In addition, discrepancies can develop when events are appraised as differing from personal ideals (Alexander & Higgins,

1993; Avants, Margolin, & Singer, 1994; Higgins, 1987) or from developmental, cultural, or community norms and expectations (Lansford et al., 2005; Park & Slattery, 2009).

Events are often interpreted as being consistent with global beliefs regardless of the nature of the event (Festinger, 1957; Taylor & Brown, 1988, 1994). These global beliefs seem resistant to change, although some events—including both personal traumas (e.g., rape and assault) and more communal ones (e.g., terrorist attacks or natural disasters)—may be discrepant enough to disrupt global beliefs (Janoff-Bulman, 1992). Consistency among various aspects of individuals' appraised and global meanings creates a sense of contentment and harmony. On the other hand, discord among aspects of meaning increases negative affect and ruminations about the discrepant information, and decreases positive affect, psychological well-being, and life satisfaction (Briñol et al., 2006; Hardin, Weigold, Robitschek, & Nixon, 2007). Because of this distress, individuals are typically motivated to reduce such discrepancies. Presumably, ruminations and intrusive thoughts are attempts to do so (Briñol et al., 2006; Dalgleish & Power, 2004; Gray, Maguen, & Litz, 2007; Horowitz, 1986).

Although the motivation to reduce or resolve discrepancies can be a positive force, tolerating the negative emotions generated in the process of adaptively resolving discrepancies can be difficult (Greenberg & Pascual-Leone, 1997). Some people may create consistency in dysfunctional ways by, for example, concluding that one is bad or deserving of bad outcomes following a trauma, that is, that "bad things happen to bad people" (Foa, Ehlers, Clark, Tolin, & Orsillo, 1999). Helping clients identify strategies for resolving meaning-related discrepancies in more positive ways can be an important task for therapy.

People's behavior and experience are often discrepant from their reported values and goals (Baumeister, 1991; Emmons, 2005; Park, 2005). For example, they may want a teaching job but not engage in the behaviors that could help them get one. Mismatches between goals or motives and behaviors are "hidden stressors" and predictive of deficits in psychological well-being and physical health (Baumann, Kaschel, & Kuhl, 2005). When appraised meanings of events or situations do not fit with their global meaning, people typically attempt to change or distort their appraisals to incorporate them into their global meaning (assimilation; Joseph & Linley, 2005). A woman who believes that people are generally good may appraise being knocked to the ground by a passerby as an unfortunate accident, an interpretation consistent with her belief that accidents happen. If knocked to the ground and attacked, however, she might change her global meaning (accommodation) in order to make sense of her attack.

Research demonstrates that people naturally assimilate discrepant events without being consciously aware of doing so (Joseph & Linley, 2005). Arabs and Israelis viewing the same news report, for example, interpret it from within their distinct political and ethnic worldviews (Liebes & Riback, 1994). Homosexuals identify more discrimination than do members of a heterosexual population, although presumably seeing the same kinds of acts (Peyser, 1988). People with more optimistic worldviews before an assault were less likely to develop posttraumatic stress disorder (PTSD) than those who had been more pessimistic, presumably because they assimilated the attack into their experience in a way that allowed them to continue feeling safe (Ali, Dunmore, Clark, & Ehlers, 2002).

Unconscious avoidance of discrepant information appears to be a pervasive process. For example, a series of clever experiments had participants view a video, during which a gorilla walked across the screen or a woman crossed a basketball court with an open umbrella (reviewed in Most, Scholl, Clifford, & Simons, 2005). Only about 25% of people viewing these unusual stimuli saw them—even when prompted to do so. Most et al. (2005) concluded that although properties of the stimulus affect our ability to perceive and attend to it, our perception is largely an active process and that what is seen and remembered depends on our attentional set.

Overlooking or at least not focusing on everyday failings and weaknesses can be adaptive (Taylor & Brown, 1988). Although distorting experience, this strategy also organizes it and increases the ability to remember information consistent with global beliefs (Schachter, 1999). Overlooking discrepant events can, however, be maladaptive for people who are depressed or dysthymic and selectively attend to depression-relevant stimuli (Gotlib, Krasnoperova, Yue, & Joorman, 2004). Because of their negatively toned global meaning, such individuals consistently confirm their negative expectations by failing to register positive events. Helping them to recognize and incorporate positive events (e.g., good days, accomplishments) can be one important therapeutic task (Brown, Jeglic, Henriques, & Beck, 2006). Similarly, PTSD is maintained, in part, because people with this diagnosis adopt very negative beliefs about themselves and the world, then engage in trauma-avoiding behaviors that do not allow them to incorporate stimuli inconsistent with those negative beliefs. Their avoidance maintains their negative views of self and world (Foa, Huppert, & Cahill, 2006).

When the discrepancy between appraised and global meanings is too great, people are often forced to change their global meaning to *accommodate* new life events (Joseph & Linley, 2005; Park & Folkman, 1997). For example, William Maxwell, a writer and editor of the *New Yorker*, was 10 years old when his mother died during the 1918 flu epidemic.

> "I realized for the first time, and forever, that we were not safe. We were not beyond harm," he remembered eight decades later. "From that time on there was a sadness, which had not existed before, a deep down

> sadness that never quite went away.... Terrible things could happen—to anybody." (in Kreiser, 2006, p. 29)

People try to make meaning in response to life events, integrating appraised meanings into global meaning (Park & Folkman, 1997). People who are unable to incorporate new events into their global meaning experience more ruminations, intrusive thoughts, and depression (Gray et al., 2007). As Maxwell's life shows, these new global meanings can be persistent and long-lasting, defended and maintained even in the face of contradictory evidence.

Cultural and Social Clock Discrepancies

People adopt many aspects of their global meaning from external bodies, including culture, family, religions, and the media. Identifying these sources of global meaning is important, for doing so allows us to generate hypotheses about people's worldview through knowledge of the groups with which they identify (e.g., gender, race, ethnicity, social class, and sexual orientation). Understanding cultural groups also provides a source of hypotheses about sources of anxiety, depression, guilt, or other dysphoric emotions (Park & Slattery, 2009). For example, violations of cultural norms about marriage, childrearing, and being successful in a man's world may influence a 35-year-old unmarried Latina's anxiety levels. Hypotheses such as these should remain tentative until more data are available, however (Slattery, 2004; Tweed & Conway, 2006). People may focus on different aspects of a situation in drawing appraised meanings (e.g., Liebes & Riback, 1994; Peyser, 1988; Vohs, Baumeister, & Chin, 2007). That is, the Latina in the foregoing example could perceive being unmarried and childless in many ways, including as a failure to meet her cultural values of *familism* and *marianisma*, which she sees as both a relational and a moral failure. She could instead focus on her successful career as a source of meaning that supports and brings honor to her family.

Another well-studied source of discrepancies involves that between the "social clock" (e.g., being unmarried, without children, or without an established career) and actual behaviors and life situations; these discrepancies often have negative consequences for self-esteem and status (Helson, Mitchell, & Moane, 1984; Neugarten, 1979). These discrepancies influence goal pursuit or disengagement, the latter when achieving the prescribed goal appears impossible (Heckhausen, Wrosch, & Fleeson, 2001). People whose behavior is consistent with their social clock are generally happier and have more positive self-esteem and social status than do those whose behavior is discrepant from their social clock (Heckhausen et al., 2001).

Similarly, although people within a culture differ, knowledge of cultural norms can help identify culture-related discrepancies in meaning (Slattery, 2004; Tweed & Conway, 2006). For example, Lansford and colleagues' (Lansford et al., 2005) cross-cultural research on parental discipline suggests that children's reactions to abusive parental discipline depended in part on their parents' behavior, but also on cultural norms. Children who received culturally normative discipline—even if that discipline would be perceived as abusive from another culture's viewpoint—acted out less than did children in cultures for whom that discipline was perceived as nonnormative and abusive.

Most people subscribe to multiple clocks and expectations, which often have contradictory expectations (Helson et al., 1984; Slattery, 2004). These discrepancies can have negative consequences. For example, as a result of perceiving conflicting cultural expectations, bicultural women appear to be at greater risk of eating disorders than are monocultural people of color (reviewed by Harris & Kuba, 1997). That is, African American women and Latinas may experience pressures from their cultures to be heavy and curvy but perceive very different pressures (i.e., to be thin) when they enter predominantly Euro-American universities or workplaces.

Assessing Discrepancies in Meaning in the Course of Therapy

> Nothing that grieves us can be called little: by the eternal laws of proportion a child's loss of a doll and a king's loss of a crown are events of the same size.
>
> **—Mark Twain**

In observing people both within and across time and cultures, it is clear that nothing—not material goods, money, or success—inevitably causes happiness or depression (Beck, 1976). The meaning systems approach to therapy, like other cognitively based treatments, concludes that it is not events themselves that make one happy or unhappy but how one thinks about the events that does. Specifically, the way we think about an event can cause a negatively toned discrepancy, which makes us depressed, anxious, or afraid. Doing poorly in school does not cause psychological symptoms; negative discrepancies from global meaning do (e.g., "I should be doing well in school and am not. That's bad."). As a result, our thesis is that assessments should identify negatively toned discrepancies and that effective therapy helps clients develop strategies for adaptively resolving these discrepancies.

Discrepancies can be assessed in a variety of ways, although very little empirical effort has yet been put into development of standardized procedures. One approach is to compare client values on global meaning with population norms. For example, in the Trauma and Attachment Belief Scale (TABS), Pearlman (2003) focuses on aspects of worldview that are typically relevant to people who have been exposed to a trauma (Safety, Trust, Control, Intimacy, and Esteem). The TABS and such other measures as Janoff-Bulman's (1989) World Assumptions Scale and Foa and colleagues' (Foa et al., 1999) Posttraumatic Cognition Inventory assess beliefs associated with trauma. Individuals' scores are then compared to norms derived, purportedly, from nontraumatized samples. The extent of deviance from norms is interpreted as indicating the individuals' accommodation of their global beliefs as a result of trauma exposure. Although this assumption may be valid for some people in some situations, it is clear that there is great individual variation in how traumatic events are perceived and that these perceptions are influenced by other contextual variables, including past trauma history, childhood factors, and psychiatric history (Gray et al., 2007). In addition, global meaning is informed by many influences other than any given trauma exposure (e.g., Power & Brewin, 1997).

Our Approach

Discrepancies between current or ongoing appraised meanings and global meaning can be clinically important. Because of the range of possible discrepancies that may underlie a client's distress, systematically gathering and organizing information into a psychosocial history can identify potential hot spots that might otherwise be overlooked. Consequently, we advocate identifying discrepancies in a broad number of domains (e.g., health, family, work, spirituality) during an open-ended interview, then comparing these attitudes and experiences to personal, developmental, cultural, and other contextual norms (Park & Slattery, 2009; Slattery, 2004). Domains assessed should be tailored for the client's multiple cultures, presenting issues, and settings (Park & Slattery, 2009; see also Table 22.1). In particular, assessments should include the following specifics:

1. Spiritual and secular meanings ascribed to precipitating events, as well as to cognitive, affective, behavioral, and physical symptoms
2. Places where events are assimilated into global meaning, and the distortions required to do so
3. Violations of global meaning and attempts to accommodate to it
4. Discrepancies among aspects of appraised and global meanings
5. Discrepancies among life events, attitudes, beliefs, values, or behavior and the client's personal, cultural, spiritual, or developmental norms and expectations (Park & Slattery, 2009)

Clinicians need to have a thorough understanding of cultural and religious norms, developmental norms and benchmarks, and the values and functions of events in order to meet the assessment goals outlined in the foregoing list. Because most people are multicultural, that is, identifying with several cultural groups simultaneously (e.g., as a deaf, upper-middle-class, Italian American, college-attending male from New York City), discrepancy assessment processes require therapists to maintain a flexible cognitive style and a willingness to view a particular client from multiple perspectives (Slattery, 2004; Snibbe & Markus, 2005). In addition, developing hypotheses about discrepancies requires being aware of clients' theories about the world and prescriptions for behavior, both those that clients are able to verbalize and

Table 22.1 Questions to Guide Organization and Hypothesis Generation During the Case Conceptualization Process

The problem

Current problem or symptoms

What symptoms does the client report? How severe are they? How chronic? When did they begin? How much are they interfering with functioning? Are they specific to certain situations, or do they occur across situations? What are the client's beliefs about what is wrong? About the appropriate treatment for his or her symptoms? Does the client expect to get better?

Because clients often have difficulty reporting "bad" symptoms, be careful to assess major concerns, especially about suicide, rather than expecting clients to disclose them freely. Ask, "What else?"

Precipitating event and other recent events

Why is the client having problems now? Why is he or she entering treatment now?

What negative or positive events have occurred recently at home, work, and school and in important relationships? What ongoing stressors? Are reactions proportional or disproportional to the stressor?

Personal and family history of psychological disorders

Has the client or family experienced either similar symptoms or different ones at some time in the past? How were problems handled? What was helpful? Specifically assess whether suicide was considered as a way to cope with problems.

If either the client or family received formal treatment in the past, how might this affect current treatments? Were previous therapists respectful? hopeful? effective? empowering? Is current therapy an extension of previous work or, from the client's viewpoint, working on the same issues or totally new and unrelated ones?

Current context

Physical condition

How is the client's physical health? Can any medical conditions account for the symptoms reported? Have these been ruled out? What health-promoting (or -interfering) practices has the person been engaged in or is currently using?

Drug and alcohol use

Is the client taking any drugs (medicinal or recreational) that could cause symptoms? Is he or she taking any street drugs that could interact with medications prescribed to treat symptoms? Has the client been compliant with medications and treatment in the past?

Intellectual and cognitive functioning

What are the client's intellectual strengths and deficits? Could symptoms be caused by cognitive deficits?

Table 22.1 Questions to Guide Organization and Hypothesis Generation During the Case Conceptualization Process (continued)

Coping style

Is the client engaging in generally adaptive or maladaptive coping strategies? When is he or she most successful in coping with the problem? What works? Are coping strategies generally short-term or long-term solutions? How do these coping strategies fit with spiritual and religious goals?

Self-concept

What are the client's beliefs about him- or herself (e.g., "I'm helpless with regard to the winds of fate")? What beliefs about self or problems in the past are particularly helpful? Does he or she have a generally strong or weak sense of self-efficacy?

Sociocultural background

In what culture was the client raised? If the client is an immigrant, how long has he or she been in this country? Why did he or she come to this country? What are the client's connections to his or her homeland? What is his or her level of acculturation? What other group identifications (e.g., race, affectional orientation, gender, age, physical abilities) are most important?

How does the client's culture or group influence reactions to symptoms? How does cultural background influence symptoms? Could the behavior be "normal" in his or her culture but not in the therapist's (or vice versa)? Could differences in group identification influence the nature and quality of your relationship?

Spirituality and religion

What, if any, religious affiliation does the client report? Is religion important to the person? In what ways? How do spiritual and religious beliefs, values, goals, behaviors, and resources influence current functioning? Do they provide a supportive network? Are beliefs culture-typical or -atypical? How does the nature of the beliefs influence feelings of support and acceptance in the community?

Resources and barriers

Individual resources

What does the client do particularly well or feel good about? How can these attributes (e.g., persistence, loyalty, optimism, intelligence) be resources for treatment? How might they undermine it?

Relational style

What relationship style characterizes most of the client's relationships? Open? Trusting? Suspicious? Manipulative? What are the client's general views of others? What is the therapeutic relationship like? Can the client be honest about symptoms, actions, side effects, and concerns? Can he or she honestly disclose the level of compliance with recommendations? Does he or she feel comfortable correcting any misassumptions made in the course of treatment?

continued

Table 22.1 Questions to Guide Organization and Hypothesis Generation During the Case Conceptualization Process (continued)

Mentors and models
What real, historical, or metaphorical figures serve as pillars of support or spiritual guides? How have they handled similar problems? Note that some models may be primarily negative in tone. What are the positive aspects of these "negative" models?
Sense and source of meaning
What sense of meaning does the client have and from where? Is life meaningful? Chaotic? Unpredictable? What is his or her worldview? From where is meaning drawn? Does the person have a strong sense of purpose or mission in life? A strong sense of direction? How well does the client perceive his or her life to be progressing regarding ultimate sources of meaning and purpose?
Social resources (friends, family, and school or work)
How supportive are the client's family, friends, and work relationships? Are they sufficient in quantity and quality to meet the client's needs? Do they increase or decrease the client's stress levels? Do they empower or undermine him or her?
Community resources
What agencies, if any, are involved? How supportive are they? How well do they work together? Are they at loggerheads, undermining each other's recommendations, or do they generally share information in an open and collaborative manner?
Community contributions
How does the client contribute to the community? Does this feel useful and meaningful to the client? Are contributions acknowledged by important people in his or her support system? Are they related to and do they feed spiritual goals?
Obstacles and opportunities to change process
What things might serve as potential obstacles or aids to the change process? These can be financial, educational, social, intellectual, spiritual, and so on. What does the client believe will (or might) happen when change occurs (e.g., marriage will dissolve; family will work together more effectively; he or she will lose financial support, will be excommunicated from the Church)?

Source: Modified from Park, C. L., & Slattery, J. M., in *Spirituality and the therapeutic practice: A comprehensive resource from intake to termination*, American Psychological Association, Washington, DC, 2009.

those they cannot, considering the relevance of these to a particular situation (Tweed & Conway, 2006).

Coping responses vary; what is normative for one culture may not be for another. As Tweed and Conway (2006) note, however, cultural imperatives and coping strategies can be unhealthy (e.g., North Americans' reliance on catharsis). Identifying culturally normative beliefs, goals, and coping mechanisms during an assessment does not suggest accepting them as the best solution to a problem; doing so does acknowledge their influence on clients' behavior and patterns of symptoms.

An Example

Case Conceptualization Lucy is a 22-year-old Euro-American woman who recently graduated from a small private college.[1] In the months since graduating, she was experiencing free-floating anxiety and panic symptoms. Other stressors included choosing whether to attend the graduate school to which she was accepted or to look for a "real job." Her friends were leaving the area and getting started in their career, getting married, or both. She had been in a serious relationship of several years but became very panicked and irritable when attending a friend's wedding reception and picked an argument with her boyfriend. He broke off their relationship, escalating her anxiety and bringing her to treatment on the recommendation of her best friend. She reported being baffled by the anxiety she had been having.

Discussion of Case Conceptualization

As described in Table 22.2, each of these factors is stressful because it violates developmental, cultural, or familial norms and expectations. Lucy has a number of strengths (e.g., her intellectual functioning and successful admission to graduate school), yet the way she perceives these strengths also creates negative discrepancies and anxiety. Finally, she normalizes some "weaknesses" (e.g., her occasionally obsessive eating and exercise patterns), which do not appear to cause discrepancies.

A Model for Working With Meaning Discrepancies in Therapy

According to the model discussed here, distress arises when people's appraised meaning of an event challenges or violates their global beliefs, goals, and sense of purpose. Such discrepancies cause tension (Festinger, 1957). The tension of minor discrepancies can be stimulating or motivating (e.g., "I'd like to find just the right way of expressing this!"), albeit sometimes irritating. Major discrepancies between global and appraised meanings can, however, be overwhelming, anxiety provoking, or depressing, interfering with behavior (Dalgleish & Power, 2004; Higgins, Bond, Klein, & Strauman, 1986). After a trauma, people must somehow reconcile their previous beliefs with the discrepant aspects of trauma that many people experience (e.g., betrayal, shame, and problems with trust; Gray et al., 2007). In fact, posttraumatic symptoms may reflect vacillations between an awareness of a discrepancy and a desire to avoid it (Gray et al., 2007; Horowitz, 1986).

[1] All case material is disguised through the use of pseudonyms. Identifying material is changed and in some cases reflects composites of several people.

Table 22.2 Meaning-Based Case Conceptualization of Lucy, a 22-Year-Old Recent College Graduate

	Objective Description	Client's Global and Situational Meanings	Potential Discrepancies Among Meanings
The problem			
Presenting problem or symptoms	Client reports feeling considerable anxiety, as if a weight is lying on her chest. She feels indecisive, a feeling she has been trying to avoid.	Feels weak, indecisive, and overwhelmed.	Presents self as strong and competent. Feels uncomfortable, needy, and weak.
Precipitating event and other recent events	Client has recently graduated from college, has undetermined future, is underemployed, and is beginning to accumulate significant debt. Her boyfriend has recently questioned the seriousness of their relationship. Her closest friends are moving or getting married.	Afraid of being a "failure" in meeting developmental goals (e.g., marriage, getting a good job, having stable and mature lifestyle).	Friends are addressing major life goals, apparently successfully, and she feels less competent and capable than they, although she has historically been "the together one" in her group of friends.
Personal and family history of psychological problems	She has a history of avoidant responses to stressors, often attempting to stay busy, but also by exercising and controlling her weight. She reports that her mother has a history of mild depressive episodes.	Does not recognize herself as having a history of psychiatric problems.	Relative to her friends (at least two of whom have serious eating disorders), her weight and body image problems are relatively normal. She sees herself as "fine" with regard to diet and exercise issues.

Current context			
Physical health	Exercises and appears to be in good shape.	Values her health.	Her friends are less health oriented than she is; relative to a college population, her health habits are better than average.
Drug or alcohol use	Frequent binge drinking during college with two alcohol-related offenses, although client's drinking has been much more moderate since she graduated.	Does not identify this as a problem.	Sees her alcohol use as normative for her group, although her parents are very negative about any drug use.
Intellectual and cognitive functioning	Very bright (gifted program in grade school), but also unfocused. Does not like to read or engage in intellectual pursuits, but is very "street smart."	Simultaneously feels smart and competent and incompetent.	Believes she "should be" more successful and focused, especially because her parents and extended family are very successful professionally.
Coping style	Exercises, engages in "retail therapy," cleans, binges on sweets, talks to friends when stressed. Tends to not think about problems, reacting rather than being proactive.	"I'm doing fine."	Panic symptoms take her by surprise because she does not usually recognize and feel a problem.
Self-concept	Sees self as bright and competent, but also admits that she is insecure and "covers this well."	Generally positive, but context-dependent self-concept.	Compares self to friends, with whom she fares well, but comparisons to family create some insecurity.

continued

Table 22.2 Meaning-Based Case Conceptualization of Lucy, a 22-Year-Old Recent College Graduate (continued)

	Objective Description	**Client's Global and Situational Meanings**	**Potential Discrepancies Among Meanings**[a]
Sociocultural background	White, upper-middle class, professional background. Raised in small, rural community.	Sees self-in-community as competent and privileged, but also describes self as a "small-town nobody."	Now living in affluent urban area and sometimes feels "like a hick," although draws from and is proud of successes in nuclear and extended family.
Religious background	Catholic with nine years of Catholic school. Does not attend church.	Not described as important.	Not a source of support, but this does not seem problematic, given that her family and friends are not particularly religious.
Resources and barriers			
Individual resources	Very bright, hard-working, "street smart," with strong writing and people skills. Networks well.	Generally positive, but context-dependent self-concept.	In comparison with "adults" and urban professionals around her, feels insecure.
Relational style	Open, enthusiastic, and charming, although describes self as "shy" when out of her element.	Generally feels good about her social skills.	Currently feeling out of her element and wonders how she will do in comparison with peers.
Mentors and models	A favorite college professor actively mentored her, especially helping her see how she used her feminine wiles rather than her mind to accomplish goals.	Beginning to see herself as capable with more to offer than only charm.	Created a discrepancy in how she saw herself, a primary motivator for attending graduate school and choosing a challenging internship.

Sense and sources of meaning in life	Feels goal-less and without a sense of direction since graduating from college.	Feels lost and inadequate.	Has difficulty recognizing her loss of direction because her friends seem to feel the same way.
Social resources (family and friends)	Small, strong community of close friends both in high school and in college, although the central core changed every year or two with proximity. Friends have graduated and are in the process of moving throughout the country. Family is warm and supportive, and her relationship with her sister has become increasingly close.	Her support from friendships seems shaky, although her relationship with her family is becoming more important.	Wants more support than she is getting and is feeling insecure because of this loss.
Work and school	School performance is strong but variable, with a large number of As and Bs, but also Ds in "stupid" courses. Worked 20–40 hours per week throughout college, often in positions with significant responsibility and independence.	Questions her own intellectual skills, although sees herself as a hard worker. Sees herself as able to be successful in a small, local environment.	Her recent move to an affluent urban area may be influencing her sense of insecurity about academic and professional issues, especially as she is working in the service industry for a wealthy clientele.
Community resources	Has a good relationship with her doctor and her advisor.	Feels supported.	Relationships are normative or better.
Community contributions	Volunteers in some areas but has not found this work important.	Feels good about her contributions to the community.	Volunteers more than average and recognizes this.

[a] Includes personal meanings and those of culture, family, and friends.

Creating a more consistent and coherent set of meanings should lead to resolving or adjusting to a trauma or other challenge to global meaning (e.g., McIntosh, Silver, & Wortman, 1993; Resick & Schnicke, 1992). Changing either the appraised or global meaning can create a more consistent and coherent set of meanings (Klinger, 1998; Parkes, 1993). Therapy, then, is an opportunity for reducing discordance, developing a coherent and positive life narrative, and making sense of life and experience in a hopeful and useful way (Neimeyer & Stewart, 2000). In the course of pursuing these goals, issues of control, self-efficacy, intimacy, and meaning are often addressed.

Park and her colleagues (Park, Edmondson, & Mills, 2010) note, however, that it is not enough to simply reduce the discrepancy; instead, changes must occur in a more positive or benign direction. For example, a woman who is raped might shift her previously optimistic global meaning to a more pessimistic one, reducing the discrepancy. Concluding that bad things happen and that the world is bad is rarely satisfying, however; for the woman in the foregoing example, doing so is likely to interfere with her life, causing her to avoid objectively safe places in a way that exacerbates feelings of vulnerability, a sense of ineptness, and posttraumatic symptoms (Gray et al., 2007). Instead, she needs to create a narrative that helps her develop coherent and consistent global and appraised meanings that are understandable and consistent within her culture and context. Until she is able to create satisfying context-consistent resolutions between global and appraised meanings, she is likely to remain symptomatic (Gray et al., 2007).

Engagement in the Change Process

Not all clients enter treatment aware of a meaning-related discrepancy. Some clients are symptomatic but do not consciously experience a discrepancy; these are people Prochaska and Norcross (2001) would describe as being in precontemplation. Many of these clients get into treatment involuntarily, referred by family members, the legal system, or Child Protective Services. Others may observe a discrepancy but perceive that discrepancy as unimportant (e.g., not having family around, but also not seeing this as important; Higgins, 1999). In order to engage clients in the change process, however, we believe (a) there must be a discrepancy from or within global beliefs, goals, or sense of purpose; (b) clients must recognize the discrepancy and experience some degree of distress (anxiety or depression); (c) clients must attribute the problem to themselves; and (d) the anxiety or depression must be large enough to be motivating, but not so large as to be overwhelming.

Clients in precontemplation do not recognize discrepancies from their beliefs, goals, or sense of purpose; thus becoming aware of a discrepancy would be an initial treatment goal with this population (Prochaska & Norcross, 2001). For other clients, there might be awareness of discrepancies, but that awareness may not cause enough dysphoria to motivate engagement in treatment. Clients might also attribute the problem to someone or something else (e.g., a family member, employer, or "the system"), which interferes with their ability to change. Nonetheless, many clients recognize meaning-related discrepancies that cause some sort of dysphoric response and identify themselves as the problem (e.g., they want to be good parents but lose their temper with their children).

Finally, it is important to consider the size of the discrepancy experienced by a client. A large discrepancy may feel overwhelming and immobilizing, which can cause intense feelings of anxiety, depression, and hopelessness, interfering with treatment (Prochaska & Norcross, 2001). In this case, therapy must focus on decreasing the size of the discrepancy among meanings, perhaps through some sort of supportive intervention. Decreasing the discrepancy ultimately increases hopefulness and frees the person to change (Brown et al., 2006; Linehan, 1993). When the discrepancy is too small, however, as with many clients in precontemplation (Prochaska & Norcross, 2001), therapy must first increase the awareness of discrepancy and thereby increase the motivation to change.

Strategies for Treating Meaning-Related Discrepancies

Although most therapeutic approaches talk about neither meaning nor discrepancies, most do seem to help people draw new, more adaptive meanings. Strategies that change meaning include attempting to understand an event or one's reactions to it (e.g., why one was assaulted), and drawing new attributions about the event and its sequelae (e.g., that flashbacks mean that the client is not going crazy but attempting to understand the event). They also include changing goals to ones that are more consistent with new meanings (e.g., focusing on the importance of family following diagnosis with breast cancer), finding purpose in the face of apparent meaninglessness (e.g., joining Mothers Against Drunk Driving following the death of a child in an alcohol-related accident), and identifying perceived benefits deriving from the traumatic event (e.g., that losing one's job was best in the long run; Gray et al., 2007). Although some of these interventions can be primarily cognitive in focus, behavioral and affective interventions (e.g., problem solving, acquisition of social skills, affect regulation strategies, or exposure) also help people draw new meanings and close discrepancies.

The goal of discrepancy-reducing treatment is not to simply close discrepancies but to close them in a systematic and adaptive manner. When depressed and suicidal, people may feel hopeless and lost (Brown et al., 2006)—this, in a culture that suggests that one should have purpose and hope. Clinicians can begin challenging these global, stable, and persistent attributions, helping clients make more specific and changeable appraisals (Garratt, Ingram, Rand, & Sawalani, 2007). Although bad things happen, so do good things. Although clients have weaknesses, they also have strengths. When clients feel unable to cope with stressors (but believe that they should be able to), interventions may focus on helping the clients develop skills that will help them manage affect effectively and better cope with stressors (Baumann et al., 2005; Linehan, 1993). As Rogers (1992) suggested, this approach should be taken in a warm and accepting environment, which also helps clients challenge discrepancies (e.g., "I believe I am shameful and unacceptable, but my therapist treats me respectfully and believes that I am acceptable").

Gray and his colleagues (2007) suggest that clients often treat meanings drawn after a trauma as truisms rather than possibilities. Although these new meanings seem designed to protect clients, they often do so at an unacceptable cost. New meanings and behavioral strategies may not be wrong, however; just too extreme and overgeneralized (e.g., "All men are bad and are going to hurt me"). Healthier strategies for closing discrepancies in meanings may take a middle ground, noting the self-protective nature of the newer meaning but making it more moderate and adaptive (e.g., recognizing when one is less safe, but also identifying how one is able to stay safer).

Many discrepancy-based interventions encourage clients to challenge assumptions or reframe behavior (Mosak & Maniacci, 1989). Symptoms might be described as an attempt to resolve a problem. The adaptive nature of a behavior can be highlighted (e.g., yelling at one's teenager as an attempt to help her avoid mistakes), although clients might be encouraged to identify other mechanisms for meeting those goals. Reframes can also be used to help clients avoid dysfunctional behaviors by increasing a discrepancy and making it unacceptable (e.g., describing as "enabling" a parent who is serving as communication conduit between children and the other parent; Mosak & Maniacci, 1989). The effectiveness of this sort of reframe seems to come from both the discrepancy and clients' attributions about the discrepancy; that is, for example, if the family had seen enabling as a good thing, there would have been no reason to change. In a similar vein, one of the difficult aspects of working with substance-abusing clients is that their behavior is often normative and accepted within their substance-abusing subculture (Bennett, Reynolds, & Lehman, 2003). Change often includes helping such clients identify the behavior as problematic and staying away from people and places that interfere with their motivation to change (Prochaska & Norcross, 2001). Motivational interviewing, a technique often used with substance-abusing clients (Miller & Rollnick, 2002), is designed to elicit ambivalence and discrepancies, heightening motivation to change.

Problem–Intervention Match in Treatment Plans

The most effective way to close some meaning-based discrepancies depends in part on the nature of the discrepancy (Park, Folkman, & Bostrom, 2001). Some problems are best addressed through some sort of behavioral-change process. This decision might be made based on either cultural expectations about change (Slattery, 2004) or whether symptoms are easily addressed through behavioral strategies alone (Prochaska & Norcross, 2001). Other problems may best be addressed through developing adaptive coping mechanisms prior to more challenging interventions (Brown et al., 2006; Linehan, 1993). When the problem cannot be directly repaired or solved (e.g., in sexual assault, illness, or death), meaning-making efforts are often central to the change process (Mattlin, Wethington, & Kessler, 1990). Finally, in some instances, it may be adaptive to readjust goals (e.g., in accepting more realistic health and exercise goals when aging; Cheng, 2004). Hardin and her colleagues (2007) suggest that therapists should, in addition to seeking problem resolution, focus on growth or transformation because people with higher growth motives tend to experience less anxiety and more positive affect. This focus on growth may lead to more consistent reductions of discrepancies. Some of these meaning-focused discrepancy reduction strategies are seen in the following case example.

An Example

Treatment Lucy's distress appeared related to significant discrepancies between her current state of affairs and what she believed she should be doing as a new college graduate. Because she was simultaneously distressed by and not consciously aware of these discrepancies, we first explored social-clock issues (e.g., career, graduate school, and marriage). Simply naming these issues seemed to help her calm down, perhaps by labeling and organizing her experience, as well as by heightening her sense of control over her decisions. During this exploration, she concluded that she did not want to attend that particular graduate school but would apply to a wider range of schools in the following year. Given her plans to return to graduate school soon and her desire to travel, she decided that she valued her freedom more than a "real job" at this point. She began dating other men as she became more aware that she wanted a stable and supportive relationship. Each of these decisions closed a discrepancy.

The real therapeutic changes seemed to come as Lucy identified her values and goals and made decisions consistent with them. She decided to discuss her decisions and concerns with her parents, who were very accepting of her decisions—as long as her bills were being paid. The last was a concern that she shared also; this issue was resolved when she discussed her work hours with her employer and also as her work became busier, as the tourist season brought steadier hours and more predictable tips. As she made these decisions, her anxiety levels decreased and she reported less frequent and less severe panic symptoms.

We briefly discussed Lucy's health behaviors relative to her health goals. Although her exercise habits and diet were problematic, they were not acutely dangerous; nor were they issues on which she was interested in working in treatment at this point. Had these behaviors been more dangerous or more explicitly the focus of her own goals for therapy, we would have highlighted these issues, perhaps using negative reframes, to increase the discrepancies and her motivation to work on them.

Discussion of Treatment
Although a range of interventions from numerous theoretical backgrounds can be useful in treatment, they have several factors in common. First, they reduce discrepancies between real behavior and values, goals, beliefs, norms, or expectations. As seen with Lucy, they also reduce discrepancies among various values, goals, beliefs, norms, and expectations (e.g., wanting to be professionally successful while also wanting a period of freedom). Second, addressing discrepancies generally decreases the negative emotions associated with them (e.g., that putting off getting a "real job" does not mean Lucy is a failure). Third, highlighting and working with discrepancies can return a person's sense of control (e.g., putting off getting a job was Lucy's choice and one that she could change when she was ready). Fourth, not all discrepancies are perceived by clients as problematic (e.g., Lucy saw her eating and exercise habits as normal even though they were discrepant from national health guidelines). Finally, as alluded to in some of the previous points, addressing discrepancies changes people's sense of meaning (e.g., putting off career decisions is a choice and healthy, rather than a failure in accepting responsibility, as she had initially seen it).

In our previous writings and research, we have focused on discrepancies produced by trauma and other highly stressful events (e.g., Park, 2007; Park, Edmondson, Fenster, & Blank, 2008; Park et al., 2010). What is clear in this case example is that discrepancies also occur in relatively healthy people and in "normal" situations. Nonetheless, these "minor" discrepancies can also cause anxiety and, when addressed, lead to growth.

Conclusions

Discrepancy-changing therapy is a meaning-focused approach to therapy processes that is consistent with other therapeutic approaches in many ways. Its focus, however, is on clients' discrepancies in meanings and how these discrepancies produce symptoms. We argue that people's meanings do not, per se, cause symptoms; rather, symptoms arise when their appraised meanings differ from their beliefs, values, goals, expectations, and sense of purpose.

Because there are many different strategies for closing discrepancies, this approach focuses primarily on identifying the goals of treatment and clients' readiness for change. We have presented an assessment rubric for gathering a comprehensive psychosocial history (Park & Slattery, 2009; Slattery, 2004). This assessment process is not solely to gather information; more important, the process aims to identify probable discrepancies to address in the course of treatment.

Discrepancies among appraisals of reality and cultural, developmental, and familial norms or personal values and goals can cause psychiatric symptoms, including depression and anxiety (Higgins, 1987; Higgins et al., 1986). Discrepancies are also associated with motivation for change, although in an inverted-U fashion (Prochaska & Norcross, 2001): Large discrepancies tend to immobilize rather than energize change, and small perceived discrepancies tend to be insufficient to motivate the change process. Clinicians must consider the size and direction of the discrepancy to make sure that it is sufficiently motivating without being overwhelming.

Once discrepancies are identified and motivation for change is at a useful level, change strategies that address and close discrepancies can be introduced. Most psychological interventions described elsewhere can close meaning-based discrepancies. Rather than rejecting clients' new meanings, it may be more helpful to help them assess the accuracy of their new meanings, challenge inaccurate and unhelpful meanings, and incorporate the useful parts of new meanings into older ones (Gray et al., 2007).

References

Alexander, M. J., & Higgins, E. T. (1993). Emotional trade-offs of becoming a parent: How social roles influence self-discrepancy effects. *Journal of Personality and Social Psychology, 65*, 1259–1269.

Ali, T., Dunmore, E., Clark, D., & Ehlers, A. (2002). The role of negative beliefs in posttraumatic stress disorder: A comparison of assault victims and non victims. *Behavioural and Cognitive Psychotherapy, 30*, 249–257.

Austin, J. T., & Vancouver, J. B. (1996). Goal constructs in psychology: Structure, process, and content. *Psychological Bulletin, 120*, 338–375.

Avants, S. K., Margolin, A., & Singer, J. L. (1994). Self-reevaluation therapy: A cognitive intervention for the chemically dependent patient. *Psychology of Addictive Behaviors, 8*, 214–222.

Bandura, A. (1997). *Self-efficacy: The exercise of control.* New York, NY: Freeman.

Baumann, N., Kaschel, R., & Kuhl, J. (2005). Striving for unwanted goals: Stress-dependent discrepancies between explicit and implicit achievement motives reduce subjective well-being and increase psychosomatic symptoms. *Journal of Personality and Social Psychology, 89*, 781–199.

Baumeister, R. F. (1991). *Meanings of life.* New York, NY: Guilford Press.

Beck, A. T. (1976). *Cognitive therapy and the emotional disorders.* New York, NY: International Universities Press.

Bennett, J. B., Reynolds, G. S., & Lehman, W. E. K. (2003). Cautious optimism and recommendations: A call for more research from applied psychology. In J. B. Bennett & W. E. K. Lehman (Eds.), *Preventing workplace substance abuse: Beyond drug testing to wellness* (pp. 239–258). Washington, DC: American Psychological Association.

Briñol, P., Petty, R. E., & Wheeler, S. C. (2006). Discrepancies between explicit and implicit self-concepts: Consequences for information processing. *Journal of Personality and Social Psychology, 91*, 154–170.

Brown, G. K., Jeglic, E., Henriques, G. R., & Beck, A. T. (2006). Cognitive therapy, cognition, and suicidal behavior. In T. E, Ellis (Ed.), *Cognition and suicide: Theory, research, and therapy* (pp. 53–74). Washington, DC: American Psychological Association.

Cheng, S.-T. (2004). Age and subjective well-being revisited: A discrepancy perspective. *Psychology and Aging, 19*, 409–415.

Dalgleish, T., & Power, M. J. (2004). Emotion-specific and emotion-non-specific components of posttraumatic stress disorder (PTSD): Implications for a taxonomy of related psychopathology. *Behaviour Research and Therapy, 42*, 1069–1088.

Emmons, R. A. (2005). Emotion and religion. In R. F. Paloutzian & C. L. Park (Eds.), *Handbook of the psychology of religion and spirituality* (pp. 235–252). New York, NY: Guilford Press.

Evans, I. M. (1993). Constructional perspectives in clinical assessment. *Psychological Assessment, 5*, 264–272.
Exline, J. J. (2002). Stumbling blocks on the religious road: Fractured relationships, nagging vices, and the inner struggle to believe. *Psychological Inquiry, 13*, 182–189.
Festinger, L. (1957). *A theory of cognitive dissonance.* Stanford, CA: Stanford University Press.
Foa, E. B., Ehlers, A., Clark, D. M., Tolin, D. F., & Orsillo, S. M. (1999). The Posttraumatic Cognitions Inventory (PTCI): Development and validation. *Psychological Assessment, 11*, 303–314.
Foa, E. B., Huppert, J. D., & Cahill, S. P. (2006). Emotional processing theory: An update. In B. O. Rothbaum (Ed.), *The nature and treatment of pathological anxiety* (pp. 3–24). New York, NY: Guilford Press.
Garratt, G., Ingram, R. E., Rand, K. L., & Sawalani, G. (2007). Cognitive processes in cognitive therapy: Evaluation of the mechanisms of change in the treatment of depression. *Clinical Psychology: Science and Practice, 14*, 224–239.
Gotlib, I. H., Krasnoperova, E., Yue, D. N., & Joormann, J. (2004). Attentional biases for negative interpersonal stimuli in clinical depression. *Journal of Abnormal Psychology, 113*, 127–135.
Gray, M. J., Maguen, S., & Litz, B. T. (2007). Schema constructs and cognitive models of posttraumatic stress disorder. In L. P. Riso, P. L. du Toit, D. J. Stein, & J. E. Young, (Eds.), *Cognitive schemas and core beliefs in psychological problems: A scientist-practitioner guide* (pp. 59–92). Washington, DC: American Psychological Association.
Greenberg, L. S., & Pascual-Leone, J. (1997). Emotion in the creation of personal meaning. In M. J. Power & C. R. Brewin (Eds.), *The transformation of meaning in psychological therapies* (pp. 157–173). Hoboken, NJ: Wiley.
Hardin, E. E., Weigold, I. K., Robitschek, C., & Nixon, A. E. (2007). Self-discrepancy and distress: The role of personal growth initiative. *Journal of Counseling Psychology, 54*, 86–92.
Harris, D. J., & Kuba, S. A. (1997). Ethnocultural identity and eating disorders in women of color. *Professional Psychology: Research and Practice, 28*, 341–347.
Heckhausen, J., Wrosch, C., & Fleeson, W. (2001). Developmental regulation before and after a developmental deadline: The sample case of "biological clock" for childbearing. *Psychology and Aging, 16*, 400–413.
Helson, R., Mitchell, V., & Moane, G. (1984). Personality and patterns of adherence and nonadherence to the social clock. *Journal of Personality and Social Psychology, 46*, 1079–1096.
Higgins, E. T. (1987). Self-discrepancy: A theory relating self and affect. *Psychological Review, 94*, 319–340.
Higgins, E. T. (1999). Why do self-discrepancies have specific relations to emotions? The second-generation question of Tangney, Niedenthal, Covert, and Barlow (1998). *Journal of Personality and Social Psychology, 77*, 1313–1317.
Higgins, E. T., Bond, R. N., Klein, R., & Strauman, T. (1986). Self-discrepancies and emotional vulnerability: How magnitude, accessibility, and type of discrepancy influence affect. *Journal of Personality and Social Psychology, 51*, 5–15.
Hogarth, R. M. (1981). Beyond discrete biases: Functional and dysfunctional aspects of judgmental heuristics. *Psychological Bulletin, 90*, 197–217.
Horowitz, M. (1986). *Stress response syndromes* (2nd ed.). New York, NY: Jason Aronson.
Janoff-Bulman, R. (1989). Assumptive worlds and the stress of traumatic events: Applications of the schema construct. *Social Cognition: Social Cognition and Stress* [Special issue], *7*, 113–136.

Janoff-Bulman, R. (1992). *Shattered assumptions.* New York, NY: Free Press.
Joseph, S., & Linley, P.A. (2005). Positive adjustment to threatening events: An organismic valuing theory of growth through adversity. *Review of General Psychology, 9,* 262–280.
Karoly, P. (1999). A goal systems-self-regulatory perspective on personality, psychopathology, and change. *Review of General Psychology, 3,* 264–291.
Klinger, E. (1977). *Meaning and void.* Minneapolis: University of Minnesota Press.
Klinger, E. (1998). The search for meaning in evolutionary perspective and its clinical implications. In P. T. P. Wong & P. S. Fry (Eds.), *The human quest for meaning: A handbook of psychological research and clinical applications* (pp. 27–50). Mahwah, NJ: Erlbaum.
Koltko-Rivera, M. E. (2004). The psychology of worldviews. *Review of General Psychology, 8,* 3–58.
Kreiser, C. M. (2006, December). The enemy within. *American History, 41*(5), pp. 23–29.
Lansford, J. E., Chang, L., Dodge, K. A., Malone, P. S., Oburu, P., Palmérus, K.,… Quinn, N. (2005). Physical discipline and children's adjustment: Cultural normativeness as a moderator. *Child Development, 76,* 1234–1246.
Liebes, T., & Riback, R. (1994). In defense of negotiated readings: How moderates on each side of the conflict interpret Intifada news. *Journal of Communication, 44,* 108–124.
Linehan, M. M. (1993). *Cognitive-behavioral treatment of borderline personality disorder.* New York, NY: Guilford Press.
Mattlin, J. A., Wethington, E., & Kessler, R. (1990). Situational determinants of coping and coping effectiveness. *Journal of Health and Social Behavior, 31,* 103–122.
McGregor, I., & Little, B. R. (1998). Personal projects, happiness, and meaning: On doing well and being yourself. *Journal of Personality and Social Psychology, 74,* 494–512.
McIntosh, D. N., Silver, R. C., & Wortman, C. B. (1993). Religion's role in adjustment to a negative life event: Coping with the loss of a child. *Journal of Personality and Social Psychology, 65,* 812–821.
Miller, W. R., & Rollnick, S. (2002). *Motivational interviewing: Preparing people for change* (2nd ed.). New York, NY: Guilford Press.
Mosak, H. H., & Maniacci, M. (1989). The case of Roger. In D. Wedding & R. J. Corsini (Eds.), *Case studies in psychotherapy* (pp. 22–49). Itasca, IL: F. E. Peacock.
Most, S. B., Scholl, B. J., Clifford, E. R., & Simons, D. J. (2005). What you see is what you set: Sustained inattentional blindness and the capture of awareness. *Psychological Review, 112,* 217–242.
Neimeyer, R. A., & Stewart, A. E. (2000). Constructivist and narrative psychotherapies. In C. R. Snyder & R. E. Ingram (Eds.), *Handbook of psychotherapy* (pp. 337–357). New York, NY: Wiley.
Neugarten, B. L. (1979). Time, age, and the life cycle. *American Journal of Psychiatry, 136,* 887–894.
Park, C. L. (2005). Religion as a meaning-making framework in coping with life stress. *Journal of Social Issues, 61,* 707–730.
Park, C. L. (2007, August). Testing the meaning making model of coping with loss. In M. Steger (Chair), *Search for meaning—Emerging research spanning the juncture of social and clinical psychology.* Symposium conducted at the meeting of the American Psychological Association, San Francisco, California.
Park, C. L., Edmondson, D., Fenster, J. R., & Blank, T. O. (2008). Meaning making and psychological adjustment following cancer: The mediating roles of growth, life meaning, and restored just world beliefs. *Journal of Consulting and Clinical Psychology, 76,* 863–875.

Park, C. L., Edmondson, D., & Mills, M. A. (2010). Religious worldviews and stressful encounters: Reciprocal influence from a meaning making perspective. In T. W. Miller (Ed.), *Handbook of stressful transitions across the lifespan* (pp. 485–501). New York, NY: Springer.

Park, C. L., & Folkman, S. (1997). Meaning in the context of stress and coping. *General Review of Psychology, 1*, 115–144.

Park, C. L, Folkman, S., & Bostrom, A. (2001). Appraisals of controllability and coping in caregivers and HIV+ men: Testing the goodness-of-fit hypothesis. *Journal of Consulting and Clinical Psychology, 69*, 481–488.

Park, C. L., & Slattery, J. M. (2009). Including spirituality in case conceptualizations: A meaning systems approach. In J. Aten & M. Leach (Eds.), *Spirituality and the therapeutic practice: A comprehensive resource from intake to termination* (pp. 121–142). Washington, DC: American Psychological Association.

Parkes, C. M. (1993). Bereavement as a psychosocial transition: Processes of adaptation to change. In M. S. Stroebe, W. Stroebe, & R. Hansson (Eds.), *Handbook of bereavement* (pp. 91–101). Cambridge, England: Cambridge University Press.

Pearlman, L. A. (2003). *Trauma and Attachment Belief Scale.* Torrance, CA: Western Psychological Services.

Peyser, M. (1998, August 17). Battling backlash. *Newsweek*, 50–52.

Power, M. J., & Brewin, C. R. (1997). Foundation for the systematic study of meaning and therapeutic change. In M. Power & C. R. Brewin (Eds.), *The transformation of meaning in psychological therapies* (pp. 193–207). London, England: Wiley.

Prochaska, J. O., & Norcross, J. C. (2001). Stages of change. *Psychotherapy: Theory, Research, Practice, Training, 38*, 443–448.

Reker, G. T., & Wong, P. T. P. (1988). Aging as an individual process: Toward a theory of personal meaning. In J. E. Birren & V. L. Bengston (Eds.), *Emergent theories of aging* (pp. 214–246). New York, NY: Springer.

Resick, P. A., & Schnicke, M. K. (1992). Cognitive processing therapy for sexual assault victims. *Journal of Consulting and Clinical Psychology, 60*, 748–756.

Rogers, C. R. (1992). The necessary and sufficient conditions of therapeutic personality change. *Journal of Consulting and Clinical Psychology, 60*, 827–832.

Schachter, D. L. (1999). The seven sins of memory: Insights from psychology and cognitive neuroscience. *American Psychologist, 54*, 182–203.

Slattery, J. M. (2004). *Counseling diverse clients: Bringing context into therapy.* Belmont, CA: Brooks/Cole.

Snibbe, A. C., & Markus, H. R. (2005). You can't always get what you want: Educational attainment, agency, and choice. *Journal of Personality and Social Psychology, 88*, 703–720.

Taylor, S. E., & Brown, J. D. (1988). Illusion and well-being: A social psychological perspective on mental health. *Psychological Bulletin, 103*, 193–210.

Taylor, S. E., & Brown, J. D. (1994). Positive illusions and well-being revisited: Separating fact from fiction. *Psychological Bulletin, 116*, 21–27.

Thompson, S. C., Armstrong, W., & Thomas, C. (1998). Illusions of control, underestimations, and accuracy: A control heuristic explanation. *Psychological Bulletin, 123*, 143–161.

Tweed, R. G., & Conway, L. G. (2006). Coping strategies and culturally influenced beliefs about the world. In P. T. P. Wong & L. C. J. Wong. (Eds.), *Handbook of multicultural perspectives on stress and coping* (pp. 133–153). New York, NY: Springer.

Vohs, K. D., Baumeister, R. F., & Chin, J. (2007). Feeling duped: Emotional, motivational, and cognitive aspects of being exploited by others. *Review of General Psychology, 11*, 127–141.

23
Meaning and Meaning Making in Cancer Survivorship

CRYSTAL L. PARK

University of Connecticut

Meaning and meaning making are important for all humans, but they are particularly salient for individuals who experience life-threatening experiences (Moadel et al., 1999). Such highly stressful encounters often bring meaning to the fore (Lee, Cohen, Edgar, Laizner, & Gagnon, 2006). This chapter focuses on how meaning and meaning making determine, in part, the psychological adjustment of cancer survivors, people who have been forced by circumstance to face the possibilities of great suffering and a foreshortened future (Little & Sayers, 2004). Cancer survivors encounter many challenges as they leave primary treatment and return to lives altered by their experiences of cancer diagnosis and treatment. However, in addition to the commonly reported lingering fears and physical fragility (Bower et al., 2005; Demark-Wahnefried, Aziz, Rowland, & Pinto, 2005), survivorship also presents opportunities for individuals to transform their experiences and create a more meaningful life (Jim, Richardson, Golden-Kreutz, & Andersen, 2006). This chapter details the roles of meaning and meaning making in the psychological adjustment of individuals with cancer as they transition into longer-term survivorship. First, issues of cancer survivorship are discussed. Then, a model of the meaning-making process is presented, distinguishing between meaning making and meanings made. Within this framework, the literature relevant to meaning making in the context of cancer survivorship is reviewed. Clinical applications and directions for future research conclude the chapter.

Cancer Survivorship

Terminology and Statistics

In recent years, the term *survivor* has been actively promoted and widely used to refer to individuals who have experienced cancer. *Survivorship* is a term that has come to indicate the state or process of living after a diagnosis of cancer regardless of how long a person lives (National Cancer Institute [NCI], 2007). By this definition, an individual is considered to be a cancer survivor at the point of diagnosis and remains a survivor throughout treatment and through the balance of his or her life (NCI, 2007). Other sources, however, define survivorship as starting at the end of primary cancer treatment (e.g., Hewitt, Greenfield, & Stovall, *2005)*.

There are an estimated 12 million cancer survivors in the United States, representing approximately 4% of the population (NCI, 2009), and an estimated 25 million survivors worldwide (Stull, Snyder, & Demark-Wahnefried, 2007). Many of these survivors are in longer-term survivorship; approximately 14% of the 12 million estimated cancer survivors in the United States were diagnosed over 20 years ago (NCI, 2009).

Phases of Treatment: From Primary Treatment to Longer-Term Posttreatment Survivorship

Although the current definition of cancer survivorship includes anyone who has been diagnosed with cancer, individuals typically perceive themselves as patients during active treatment and may be reluctant to embrace the identity of survivor at that point. Once active treatment ends, the term *survivor* seems to be more readily adopted, although not universally (Bellizzi & Blank, 2007; Park, Zlateva, & Blank, 2009). The transition period from primary treatment to longer-term survivorship is a critical time, setting the course of psychological adjustment for years to come. While a patient remains in primary treatment, for that individual the cancer experience often becomes life's central focus, involving intensive and immediate coping with medical issues, decision making, and the many chaotic emotions that ensue, including fear, hope, pain, and grief (Ganz et al., 2004).

Transitioning from primary treatment, though a relief in many ways, is often highly stressful in its own right (Beisecker et al., 1997; Hewitt et al., 2005; Stanton et al., 2000; Tross & Holland, 1989) in part because of reduced frequency of visits with and access to medical providers, change in daily routines, adjustment to treatment-related side effects, and uneasiness about being on one's own (Ganz et al., 2004; Holland & Reznik, 2005; Lethborg, Kissane, Burns, & Snyder, 2000).

Issues of meaning appear to be particularly important during the transition to longer-term survivorship (Holland & Reznik, 2005). During primary treatment, when participants are dealing with the impact of the diagnosis and making treatment decisions, coping tends to be more problem focused, dealing with the immediate demands of the situation. Coping appears to become more reflective as survivors return to their everyday post–primary treatment lives (Stanton et al., 2000; S. E. Taylor, Lichtman, & Wood, 1984; Tomich & Helgeson, 2002).

Posttreatment Quality of Life

Many studies indicate that cancer survivors' quality of life does not differ much from that of their peers who did not have cancer (e.g., Tomich &

Helgeson, 2002). The relationship of survivorship status to quality of life depends, however, on the specific dimensions of well-being under consideration. Traditionally, studies of health-related quality of life have focused on mental health, physical functioning, and sometimes social functioning. For example, in breast cancer survivors, lingering health decrements, particularly pain and fatigue, have been documented (e.g., Broeckel et al., 2000; Jacobsen et al., 1999), although mental health appears to be, on average, about the same as that of those who have not had cancer (e.g., Ganz et al., 2004; Tomich & Helgeson, 2002).

Other aspects of postcancer quality of life have recently been recognized as important. For example, feelings of vulnerability and anxieties over recurrence appear to linger for many survivors even many years after treatment (Bower et al., 2005). On the other hand, some domains of quality of life, such as spirituality and life meaning, may be enhanced relative to those who did not experience cancer (Broeckel et al., 2000; Widows, Jacobsen, Booth-Jones, & Fields, 2005; Zebrack, Ganz, Bernaards, Petersen, & Abraham, 2006). Quality-of-life domains appear to be separate and somewhat independent in that survivors may simultaneously experience an enhanced sense of meaningfulness in life and a heightened sense of vulnerability and worry (Andrykowski et al., 2005; Bower et al., 2005). Further, these domains appear to result from different coping pathways (Carver, 2005).

The Role of Meaning in Cancer Survivors' Psychological Adjustment

The Meaning-Making Model

Many frameworks and theories regarding meaning and the making of meaning in stressful experiences have been put forward (e.g., Baumeister, 1991; Gillies & Neimeyer, 2006; Janoff-Bulman, 1992; Lepore, 2001; S. E. Taylor, 1983). Although differing in language and emphases, these theoretical frameworks converge on an underlying model of meaning and meaning making (Lepore, Silver, Wortman, & Wayment, 1996; Park, Edmondson, Fenster, & Blank, 2008). A foundational meaning-making model, based on these prior works, has been proposed and elaborated by Park and her colleagues (Park, in press; Park et al., 2008). According to this model, individuals possess global meaning systems comprising global beliefs, global goals, and a sense of meaning in life. These global meaning systems guide individuals' responses to situations of potential stress through situational meaning.

Global meaning consists of cognitive, motivational, and affective components, termed, respectively, global beliefs, global goals, and a sense of meaning or purpose (Park, in press; Reker & Wong, 1988). Global beliefs concerning fairness, justice, luck, control, predictability, coherence, benevolence, personal vulnerability, and identity comprise the core schemas through which people interpret their experiences of the world (Janoff-Bulman & Frantz, 1997;

Koltko-Rivera, 2004). Global goals are individuals' ideals, states, or objects toward which they work to be, obtain, accomplish, or maintain (Karoly, 1999; see Chapter 4, this volume). A subjective sense of meaning and purpose in life is thought to be derived through individuals' global beliefs and goals (Park, in press; see Chapter 8, this volume). Together, global beliefs and goals, and the resultant sense of life meaning, form individuals' meaning systems. Meaning systems comprise the lens through which individuals interpret, evaluate, and respond to their experiences.

Situational meaning involves the interaction of global meaning with specific encounters in which a particular situation is appraised vis-à-vis one's global beliefs or goals (Janoff-Bulman & Frantz, 1997). Confrontation with a severe stressor is thought to have the potential to violate or even shatter global meaning systems (i.e., individuals' global beliefs about the world and themselves and their overarching goals). Such violations or discrepancies are thought to initiate individuals' cognitive and emotional processing—meaning-making efforts—to rebuild their meaning systems. Meaning making involves individuals' efforts to understand and conceptualize a stressor in a way more consistent with their global meaning and to incorporate that understanding into their larger system of global meaning through assimilation and accommodation (Park & Folkman, 1997).

Following highly stressful events, individuals' meaning-making processes typically involve the individuals in reconsidering their beliefs and searching for some more favorable or consistent understanding of the event and its implications for their view of themselves and their lives. Meaning making may also entail revising goals (see Chapter 24, this volume) and questioning or revising one's sense of meaning in life (see Chapter 8, this volume). This rebuilding process is assumed to lead to better adjustment, particularly if adequate meaning is found or created (for reviews, see Collie & Long, 2005; Lee, Cohen, Edgar, Laizner, & Gagnon, 2004; Skaggs & Barron, 2006). Protracted attempts to assimilate or accommodate may, however, devolve into maladaptive rumination over time if satisfactory meanings cannot be constructed (Segerstrom, Stanton, Alden, & Shortridge, 2003).

Thus, the meaning-making model distinguishes between *attempts* to make meaning and the *successful creation* of meaning. A number of studies support the distinction between attempting to make meaning and having made meaning (Bower, Kemeny, Taylor, & Fahey, 1998; Davis, Nolen-Hoeksema, & Larson, 1998). The development of such "meanings made" or "products" of the meaning-making process, as well as the subsequent lessening of searching, is thought to differentiate between adaptive and maladaptive meaning making (Segerstrom et al., 2003). According to this perspective, meaning making is helpful primarily when there is some resolution achieved through the process. Studies have found ongoing efforts to make meaning to be associated with poorer adjustment (Silver, Boon, & Stones, 1983; Tait & Silver, 1989), whereas having found meaning is associated with better adjustment (Davis et al., 1998; Westling, Garcia, & Mann, 2007).

Meaning Making and Cancer

The foregoing theoretical model of meaning making is often applied to descriptions of cancer survivors adjusting to their experiences dealing with and recovering from cancer and transitioning into longer-term cancer survivorship (e.g., Brennan, 2001; Lepore, 2001; see Holland & Reznik, 2005); however, empirical evidence regarding the validity of this model has been scant. Only in recent years has a body of empirical studies become available to examine the accuracy of this model in reflecting cancer survivors' adjustment. The particular issues most commonly addressed in the literature and reviewed here concern (a) the extent to which survivors' appraised meaning of their cancer is related to their adjustment, (b) the extent to which survivors' meaning-making processes relate to their adjustment, (c) the meanings survivors make from cancer, and (d) relationships of survivors' made meaning with their adjustment.

Appraised Meaning and Adjustment Individuals appraise the meaning of their cancer along many dimensions; to date, researchers have mostly focused on primary appraisals (e.g., threat, loss, challenge), illness representation appraisals, and controllability appraisals.[1] Research on these various dimensions indicates that many of the meanings that survivors assign to their cancer experience are related to their subsequent psychological adjustment.

Primary appraisal, the extent to which situations are initially considered to be a threat, challenge, or loss, is generally linked to subsequent coping and adjustment (Aldwin, 2007; Roesch, Weiner, & Vaughn, 2002), and research conducted specifically with cancer survivors mostly supports this link. For example, a study of prostate cancer survivors found that individuals who appraised their cancer as a loss had higher levels of depression, whereas those who appraised their cancer as a threat had higher levels of anxiety (Bjorck, Hopp, & Jones, 1999). Similarly, a study of survivors of a variety of cancers found that threat appraisals were related to increased distress, although challenge appraisals were unrelated to distress (Silver-Aylaian & Cohen, 2001).

Following up on Lipowski's (1970) taxonomy of illness appraisals in a large sample of breast cancer survivors, Degner, Hack, O'Neil, and Kristjanson (2003) found that shortly after diagnosis most survivors appraised their cancer as a "challenge" (57.4%) or as having "value" (27.6%); few chose "enemy" (7.8%),

---

[1] Although attributions are also a part of initial appraised meanings of events, virtually no literature on immediate attributions for cancer is available. Most studies assess attributions long after the diagnosis, and thus attributions (or, more likely, reattributions) are considered here as a product of the meaning-making process.

"irreparable loss" (3.9%), "or "punishment" (.6%) in appraising their cancer. These appraisals were mostly unchanged three years later, and survivors who had initially appraised their cancer as a challenge or as having value reported less anxiety at follow up. Cross-sectionally, at follow-up, women who appraised the cancer negatively ("enemy," "loss," or "punishment") had higher levels of depression and anxiety and poorer quality of life than did women who appraised their cancer in more positive ways.

Studies assessing the influence of control appraisals have produced mixed results. For example, Silver-Aylaian and Cohen (2001), in the abovementioned study of survivors of various cancers, found that appraised uncontrollability of the cancer was related to increased distress, but appraised self-controllability of the cancer was unrelated to distress. A study of head and neck cancer survivors found little influence of control appraisals (Llewellyn, McGurk, & Weinman, 2007), but a study of ovarian cancer patients found a strong negative relationship between appraised control over the illness and psychological distress (Norton et al., 2005).

However, the meaning-making model proposes not only that appraised meaning is related to adjustment but, further, that the *discrepancy* between appraised and global meaning is the actual impetus for distress. That is, the more that individuals' assigned meanings of their cancer diagnosis are appraised as violating their beliefs and goals, the more resultant distress they will experience. Receiving a diagnosis of cancer can violate such important global beliefs as a belief in the fairness, benevolence, and controllability of the world as well as one's own sense of invulnerability and personal control (Holland & Reznik, 2005; Lepore, 2001). Beliefs in a loving God may also be violated (Gall, 2004). Further, having cancer almost invariably violates individuals' goals for their current lives and their plans for the future (Carver, 2005). It is likely that different types of cancer and the specifics of an individual's illness (e.g., prognosis) would greatly influence the situational meaning given and the extent of discrepancy with global meaning (e.g., McBride, Clipp, Peterson, Lipkus, & Demark-Wahnefried, 2000), although very little research has yet examined these issues.

This link between discrepancy of appraised and global meaning with adjustment in cancer survivorship has rarely been directly examined; that is, very few studies have specifically asked cancer survivors about violations to their global beliefs and goals. One cross-sectional study of gastrointestinal cancer patients found that higher levels of discrepancies in beliefs and goals were related to more anxiety and depression (Nordin, Wasteson, Hoffman, Glimelius, & Sjödén, 2001). A longitudinal study of survivors of various cancers found that the extent to which the cancer was appraised as violating their beliefs in a just world was negatively related to their psychological well-being across the year of the study, mediated through ruminative thinking about the cancer (Park et al., 2008). Further, the role of discrepancy as the driver of the meaning-making process is indirectly supported by the earlier cited studies demonstrating that higher levels of appraising the meaning of cancer as a loss are related to more distress (i.e., loss implies violation of a desired goal or state; Klinger, 1998). Nonetheless, research is needed that more directly addresses this central component of the meaning-making model.

Meaning-Making Processes and Adjustment Early (S. E. Taylor, 1983; S. E. Taylor et al., 1984) and subsequent (e.g., Moadel et al., 1999; Schroevers, Ranchor, & Sanderman, 2004; Tomich & Helgeson, 2002) studies have suggested that for survivors, efforts to make meaning of their cancer experience are a near-universal experience, although some researchers have argued that survivors often simply accept their cancer experience or, once it has ended, have little need to think or reflect on it (Blank & Bellizzi, 2006; Dirksen, 1995). It is not clear, however, how well assessments of meaning making in these studies correspond to the phenomenon of meaning making as defined in the meaning-making model. That is, according to this model, meaning making following cancer involves survivors' attempts to integrate their understanding (i.e., appraisal) of the cancer together with their global meaning to reduce the discrepancy between them (Horowitz, 2001; Park & Folkman, 1997). Such simple questions as "How often have you found yourself searching to make sense of your illness?" and "How often have you found yourself wondering why you got cancer or asking, 'Why me?'" (e.g., Roberts, Lepore, & Helgeson, 2005), though perhaps having some face validity, do not directly or comprehensively assess the process of attempting to reduce discrepancies between global meanings and appraisals of the cancer experience (Park, in press).

The model proposes that survivors' meaning-making processes involve such deliberate coping efforts as reappraising the event, reconsidering their global beliefs and goals, and searching for some understanding of the cancer and its implications for themselves and their lives (e.g., Lepore, 2001; Redd et al., 2001). In addition, meaning-making processes apparently often occur beneath the level of awareness or without conscious efforts (e.g., in the form of intrusive thoughts; Greenberg, 1995; Lepore, 2001). Researchers have posited that these meaning-making efforts are essential to adjustment by helping survivors either assimilate the cancer experience into their preexisting global meaning or helping them to change their global meaning to accommodate it (Lepore, 2001); indeed, it is difficult to imagine that survivors could get through a cancer experience without some reconsideration of their lives vis-à-vis cancer.

Many researchers have proposed, therefore, that meaning making is critical in successfully navigating these changes (Lepore, 2001; Moadel et al., 1999; S. E. Taylor, 1983; Zebrack et al., 2006). Yet research with cancer patients indicates that reports of searching for meaning and cognitive and emotional processing are typically related to poorer adjustment (e.g., Kernan & Lepore, 2009; Roberts et al., 2005; Tomich & Helgeson, 2002). A study of breast cancer survivors completing treatment found that positive reinterpretation, or attempting to see the cancer in a more positive light or find benefits in it, was unrelated to adjustment, whereas emotional processing, or attempting to understand the reasons underlying one's feelings, was actually associated with subsequently higher levels of distress (Stanton et al., 2000). Stanton et al. (2000) noted that posttreatment, emotional processing may actually reflect ruminative processes signaling a failure to make meaning.[2] A cross-sectional study of long-term breast cancer survivors found that searching for meaning was related to poorer adjustment (Tomich & Helgeson, 2002), and a recent study of prostate cancer survivors shortly after treatment found that meaning-making efforts were related to higher levels of distress both concurrently and three months later (Roberts et al., 2005). Similar findings were reported in a longitudinal study of recently diagnosed breast cancer survivors (Kernan & Lepore, 2009). Still other studies have failed to find any relationship between searching for meaning and adjustment following cancer (Cordova, Cunningham, Carlson, & Andrykowski, 2001; Gotay, 1985; S. E. Taylor et al., 1984), whereas a few have found that searching for meaning was positively related to well-being (Dirksen, 1995; Park et al., 2008).

The inconsistency between theory and findings on this central point, the adaptive nature of meaning making, is very important and deserves explication. The lack of strong support for the adaptive value of meaning making in these studies may be a result of methodological or conceptual issues. For example, the operational definitions employed in studies of meaning making and cancer are problematic. As noted, although asking survivors whether they have been searching for meaning may seem reasonable to assess, the extent to which it maps on to the proposed underlying assimilation–accommodation process is questionable; virtually no study has employed design and measurement strategies adequate to the task of capturing this process. In fact, much of the integration between global meaning and situational meaning may lie beneath individuals' awareness, precluding their ability to report on meaning (Lepore, 2001). Longitudinal assessments of appraised meanings and discrepancies between situational meaning and global meaning and change in them over time are necessary to adequately capture this assimilation–accommodation process.

Further, the meaning-making model proposes that meaning making per se is not necessarily adaptive and may, in fact, be indistinguishable from rumination, without attention to whether meaning has actually been made. The failure of most extant studies to distinguish between adaptive meaning making and

---

[2] Note, however, that this notion does not necessarily mean that meaning making is *causing* the distress, just that meaning making and stress are co-occurring. The meaning-making model posits that the failure to make meaning is creating the distress, a possibility not examined in that study.

maladaptive rumination may account for the lack of a more consistently demonstrated salubrious effect of meaning making (Park et al., 2008; Segerstrom et al., 2003). It may be that when survivors search for meaning, either through deliberate efforts or through more automatic processes, and achieve a reintegration of their cancer experience and their global meaning, they experience less distress and also engage in less subsequent meaning making. When meaning making efforts fail, however, the cancer experience may remain highly distressing. Survivors unable to assimilate their cancer experience into their belief system or accommodate their previously held beliefs to account for their experience may experience a loss of personal or spiritual meaning, existential isolation, and apathy (Holland & Reznik, 2005) and may persist in meaning-making efforts even years afterward (e.g., Tomich & Helgeson, 2002), accounting for the positive relationship between searching for meaning and distress.

To date, only two studies of cancer survivorship have assessed both the search for meaning and the finding of meaning and have tested their combined effects on adjustment. In a study of breast cancer survivors in the first 18 months postdiagnosis, Kernan and Lepore (2009) examined survivors' patterns of searching and finding meaning in their cancer. The researchers found that women who never searched and those who searched and found meaning did not differ on negative affect but that both groups were significantly higher on negative affect than were women who were searching for but had not found meaning over time. As well, a study of younger adult survivors of various cancers (Park et al., 2008), described earlier, assessed meaning making (as positive reappraisal) and meanings made (as growth, reduced discrepancies with global meaning). Results indicated that positive reappraisal led to increases in perceived growth and life meaning, which was related to reduced violations of belief in a just world. This process was related to better psychological adjustment (Park et al., 2008). Aside from these studies, this notion that meaning making may be helpful to the extent that it is related to actually making meaning, whereas searching for meaning without successfully finding it may simply signify a lack of resolution or satisfactory meaning, remains a tantalizing possibility awaiting future research. In the meantime, a number of studies have identified products of the meaning-making process and examined the extent to which these products are adaptive.

Meaning Made From the Cancer Experience Studies have examined a number of psychological phenomena that may be conceptualized as outcomes or products of the search for meaning in cancer survivors and the relationships between these meanings made and psychological adjustment. Among the most commonly studied meanings made are (a) perceptions of positive life changes or posttraumatic growth, (b) understanding regarding the cancer's occurrence (usually assessed as attributions), and (c) integration of cancer and survivorship into identity (Gillies & Neimeyer, 2006).

Growth Considerable research has demonstrated that many—even the majority—of cancer survivors report posttraumatic growth as a result of their experience with cancer (Stanton, Bower, & Low, 2006). These positive changes include improved relationships, increased self-confidence and coping skills, and higher levels of spirituality and appreciation for life (Tedeschi & Calhoun, Chapter 25, this volume; Tomich & Helgeson, 2004; see Stanton et al., 2006, for a review). Survivors' perceptions of positive changes appear to result from meaning-making coping processes based on reinterpreting the cancer experience in a more positive light (e.g., Bellizzi & Blank, 2006; Sears, Stanton, & Danoff-burg, 2003). Survivors' reports of growth following their cancer experience are sometimes (e.g., Carver & Antoni, 2004), but not always (e.g., Bellizzi, Miller, Arora, & Rowland, 2007; Cordova et al., 2001), related to better psychological adjustment.

Causal Understanding Several theorists have proposed that having an understanding of the cause of an event (i.e., an attribution for its occurrence) is an important type of made meaning (e.g., Davis et al., 1998; Janoff-Bulman & Frantz, 1997). Research with cancer survivors has indicated, however, that although most survivors have ideas or explanations regarding the cause of their cancer, possessing such explanations for their cancer is often associated with greater distress, not less (e.g., Costanzo, Lutgendorf, Bradley, Rose, & Anderson, 2005; Kulik & Kronfeld, 2005). It may be that the specific nature of the attribution determines its ability to aid successful establishment of meaning. A recent meta-analysis of people with a variety of illnesses found that attributions to controllable causes were associated with positive psychological adjustment, whereas attributions to stable and uncontrollable causes were associated with poorer psychological adjustment (Roesch & Weiner, 2001). Further, an understanding of the occurrence of cancer may involve understanding proximal (i.e., how) as well as distal (i.e., why) causes and selective incidence (i.e., why me as opposed to someone else; Park & Folkman, 1997; E. J. Taylor, 1995).

Specific to cancer, E. J. Taylor (1995) reviewed the literature on breast cancer survivors, concluding that better adjustment was related to attributions to such predictable and controllable causes as pollution and stress or such lifestyle factors as smoking. Feeling that one caused one's own cancer (self-blame) has, however, consistently been shown to be negatively related to adjustment. (e.g., Bennett, Compas, Beckjord, & Glinder, 2004; Friedman et al., 2007; Glinder & Compas, 1999; Malcarne, Compas, Epping-Jordan, & Howell, 1995).

The link between having made meaning by identifying causes of the cancer and adjustment is therefore more complicated than it might at first appear. This complexity is illustrated in a study of women with gynecological cancers (Costanzo et al., 2005), in which most attributions (e.g., genetics and heredity, stress, hormones, and environmental factors) were related to elevated levels of anxiety and depression. However, survivors who attributed their cancer to potentially controllable causes were more likely to be practicing healthy behaviors. Similarly, women citing health behaviors as important in preventing recurrence reported greater anxiety, but these women were also more likely to practice positive health behaviors. Further, health behavior attributions interacted with health practices in predicting distress. For example, among women who had not made positive dietary changes, rating lifestyle as important in preventing recurrence was associated with greater distress, whereas having made a positive change in diet was associated with less distress. Thus, it appears that behaviors consistent with attributions can be effective in reducing discrepancies in meaning and therefore related to better adjustment.

Most distal attributions also seem to be related to more distress. For example, in a sample of prostate cancer survivors, any causal attribution of the cancer to God, including to a loving or purposeful God, was related to poorer functioning, although attributions to an angry God were even more strongly related to distress (Gall, 2004). Attributions of the cancer to God's will in the abovementioned study of gynecological cancer survivors was related to worry about recurrence, but not to anxiety or depressive symptoms (Costanzo et al., 2005). However, attributions to luck or chance were unrelated to distress.

Integration of Cancer and Survivorship Into One's Life Narrative and Identity Another potentially important outcome of meaning-making processes involves the integration of the experience of cancer into survivors' ongoing life story and sense of self (see Sommer, Baumeister, & Stillman, Chapter 14, this volume). Surviving cancer has been described as a process of identity reconstruction through which survivors integrate the cancer experience into their self-concept, developing a sense of living through and beyond cancer (Brennan, 2001; Deimling, Kahana, & Schumacher, 1997; Foley et al., 2006; Zebrack, 2000). The extent to which having cancer becomes organically interwoven with other experiences in survivors' narratives may reflect their successful making of meaning, having come to terms with the cancer. Such narrative integration is widely viewed within the trauma literature as an important aspect of recovery (e.g., Monson et al., 2006). Little empirical research has, however, framed the cancer recovery process as narrative reconstruction or examined these processes.

A few studies have examined the extent to which cancer survivors embrace labels that refer to their cancer status and how that identification is related to well-being. An early study by Deimling and his colleagues (1997) examined cancer-related identities in a sample of older, long-term survivors of a variety of cancers. Asked whether they identified themselves as survivors (yes or no), 90% answered affirmatively. Other labels were endorsed less frequently: 60% identified as ex-patients, 30% as victims, and 20% as patients. Considering oneself a victim or a survivor was, however, unrelated to mastery, self-esteem, anxiety, depression, or hostility. It should be noted that this study was conducted prior to the mid-1990s, when the term *survivor* began to be actively promoted (NCI, 2007). A more recent longitudinal study of long-term survivors of colon, breast, or prostate cancer by the same group of researchers using the same measurement strategy found that 86% of the sample identified themselves as a "cancer survivor," 13% saw themselves as a "patient," and 13% identified themselves as a "victim" (Deimling, Bowman, & Wagner, 2007).

Several more recent studies have addressed postcancer self-identifications. When Bellizzi and Blank (2007) asked longer-term prostate cancer survivors which term best described them, over 50% chose "someone who has had cancer" and 25% chose "survivor," with smaller numbers choosing "patient" or "victim." Only identifying as a survivor was related to having more positive affect, and no label was related to levels of negative affect. Finally, Park and her colleagues (2009) asked younger adult cancer survivors about their postcancer identities and found that 83% endorsed survivor identity; 81%, the identity of "person who has had cancer"; 58%, "patient"; and 18%, "victim" (all at least "somewhat"). These four identities were minimally correlated with one another. Survivor and person who has had cancer identities correlated with involvement in most cancer-related activities, including wearing cancer-related items and talking about prevention. Survivor identity correlated with better psychological well-being and posttraumatic growth, and victim identity with poorer well-being; neither identifying as a patient nor as a person with cancer was related to well-being.

Meaning-Making Interventions With Cancer Survivors

With increasing recognition of the importance of meaning making in the lives of cancer survivors has come the development of a number of psychosocial interventions for individuals with cancer that are based on issues of meaning. Some of these interventions are existential in nature, focusing on broader issues of meaning in life (e.g., Kissane et al., 2003). Breitbart, Gibson, Poppito, and Berg (2004) have developed a palliative care therapy for people with cancer, aiming to identify and enhance sources of meaning and patients' sense of purpose as they approach death.

Other interventions have more explicitly targeted issues of meaning making. For example, Lee and her colleagues (2006) recently reported results of an intervention designed to promote survivors' exploration of existential issues and their cancer experiences through the use of meaning-making coping strategies. Cancer survivors received up to four sessions in which they explored their cognitive appraisals of and emotional responses to their cancer experience within the context of their previous experiences and future goals. After treatment, participants in the experimental group showed significantly higher levels of self-esteem, optimism, and self-efficacy than did members of the control group, when taking into account baseline scores on those variables, demonstrating the effectiveness of a therapy that explicitly promotes meaning making.

Chan, Ho, and Chan (2007) noted that although these meaning-based interventions are proliferating, "there is a sad lack of a corresponding body of controlled outcome studies, without which we cannot answer two central questions: 1. Can meaning-making interventions facilitate or catalyze the meaning construction process? 2. How much (if any) improvement of the psychosocial well-being of patients is attributable to the catalyzed meaning construction process?" (p. 844). Developing a body of controlled outcome studies evaluating meaning making interventions is an important challenge for interventionists.

Future Research Directions

Much remains to be learned about the meaning-making processes of cancer survivors. A review of the literature on meaning making does not appear to provide strong support for the meaning-making model in spite of its theoretical popularity. Further, the studies conducted to date do not appear to have adequately tested the model. As noted, an adequate test of this model will require a thorough assessment of the range of meaning-making efforts, both deliberate and automatic, and will need to assess whether there are any end products or adaptive changes resulting from efforts at meaning making. To date, no study of cancer survivors has fully assessed the components of the meaning-making process, and much remains to be learned about meaning and meaning making in cancer survivorship.

In order to fully understand the role of meaning in transitioning to longer-term survivorship, much more attention must be given to both conceptual and measurement issues. A better understanding of the ways by which survivors create meaning through their experiences with cancer holds great promise for better appreciating the ways in which individuals differ in their adjustment and the myriad influences on this process. This knowledge should help to identify individuals needing more assistance in adjusting to survivorship, including informing interventions for those who may need help returning to their "new normal" lives.

References

Aldwin, C. M. (2007). *Stress, coping, and development: An integrative approach* (2nd ed.). New York, NY: Guilford Press.

Andrykowski, M. A., Bishop, M. M., Hahn, E. A., Cella, D. F., Beaumont, J. L., Brady, M. J.,... Wingard, J. R. (2005). Long-term health-related quality of life, growth, and spiritual well-being after hematopoietic stem-cell transplantation. *Journal of Clinical Oncology*, *23*, 599–608.

Baumeister, R. F. (1991). *Meanings of life*. New York, NY: Guilford Press.

Beisecker, A. E., Cook, M. R. Ashworth, J., Hayes, J., Brecheisen, M., Helmig, L.,... Selenke, D. (1997). Side effects of adjuvant chemotherapy: Perceptions of node-negative breast cancer patients. *Psycho-Oncology*, *6*, 85–93.

Bellizzi, K. M., & Blank, T. O. (2006). Predicting posttraumatic growth in breast cancer survivors. *Health Psychology*, *25*, 47–56.

Bellizzi, K. M., & Blank, T. O. (2007). Cancer-related identity and positive affect in survivors of prostate cancer. *Journal of Cancer Survivorship, 1*, 44–48.

Bellizzi, K. M., Miller, M. F., Arora, N. K., & Rowland, J. H. (2007). Positive and negative life changes experienced by survivors of non-Hodgkin's lymphoma. *Annals of Behavioral Medicine, 34*, 188–199.

Bennett, K. K., Compas, B. E., Beckjord, E., & Glinder, J. G. (2004). Self-blame and distress among women with newly diagnosed breast cancer. *Journal of Behavioral Medicine, 28*, 313–323.

Bjorck, J. P., Hopp, D., & Jones, L. W. (1999). Prostate cancer and emotional functioning: Effects of mental adjustment, optimism, and appraisal. *Journal of Psychosocial Oncology, 17*, 71–85.

Blank, T. O., & Bellizzi, K. M. (2006). After prostate cancer: Predictors of well-being among long-term prostate cancer survivors. *Cancer, 106*, 2128–2135.

Bower, J. E., Kemeny, M. E., Taylor, S. E., & Fahey, J. L. (1998). Cognitive processing, discovery of meaning, CD4 decline, and AIDS-related mortality among bereaved HIV-seropositive men. *Journal of Consulting and Clinical Psychology, 66*, 979–986.

Bower, J .E., Meyerowitz, B. E., Desmond, K. A., Bernaards, C. A., Rowland, J. H., & Ganz, P. A. (2005). Perceptions of positive meaning and vulnerability following breast cancer: Predictors and outcomes among long-term breast cancer survivors. *Annals of Behavioral Medicine, 29*, 236–245.

Breitbart, W., Gibson, C., Poppito, S. R., & Berg, A. (2004). Psychotherapeutic interventions at the end of life: A focus on meaning and spirituality. *Canadian Journal of Psychiatry, 49*, 366–372.

Brennan, J. (2001). Adjustment to cancer-coping or personal transition? *Psycho-Oncology, 10*, 1–18.

Broeckel, J. A., Jacobsen, P. B., Lodovico, B., Horton, J., & Lyman, G. H. (2000). Quality of life after adjuvant chemotherapy for breast cancer. *Breast Cancer Research and Treatment, 62*, 141–150.

Carver, C. S. (2005). Enhancing adaptation during treatment and the role of individual differences. *Cancer, 104*, 2602–2607.

Carver, C. S., & Antoni, M. H. (2004). Finding benefit in breast cancer during the year after diagnosis predicts better adjustment 5 to 8 years after diagnosis. *Health Psychology, 23*, 595–598.

Chan, T. H.Y., Ho, R. T. H., & Chan, C. L. W. (2007). Developing an outcome measurement for meaning-making intervention with Chinese cancer patients. *Psycho-Oncology, 16*, 843–850.

Collie, K. K., & Long, B. C. (2005). Considering "meaning" in the context of breast cancer. *Journal of Health Psychology, 10*, 843–853.

Cordova, M. J., Cunningham, L. L. C., Carlson, C. R., & Andrykowski, M. A. (2001). Posttraumatic growth following breast cancer: A controlled comparison study. *Health Psychology, 20*, 176–185.

Costanzo, E. S., Lutgendorf, S. K., Bradley, S. L., Rose, S. L., & Anderson, B. (2005). Cancer attributions, distress, and health practices among gynecologic cancer survivors. *Psychosomatic Medicine, 67*, 972–980.

Davis, C. G., Nolen-Hoeksema, S., & Larson, J. (1998). Making sense of loss and benefiting from the experience: Two construals of meaning. *Journal of Personality and Social Psychology, 75*, 561–574.

Degner, L., Hack, T., O'Neil, J., & Kristjanson, L. J. (2003). A new approach to eliciting meaning in the context of breast cancer. *Cancer Nursing, 26*, 169–178.

Deimling, G. T., Bowman, K. F., & Wagner, L. J. (2007). Cancer survivorship and identity among long-term survivors. *Cancer Investigation, 25*, 758–765.

Deimling, G., Kahana, B., & Schumacher, J. (1997). Life threatening illness: The transition from victim to survivor. *Journal of Aging and Identity, 2*, 165–186.

Demark-Wahnefried, W., Aziz, N., Rowland, J., & Pinto, B. M. (2005). Riding the crest of the teachable moment: Promoting long-term health after the diagnosis of cancer. *Journal of Clinical Oncology, 23*, 5814–5830.

Dirksen, S. R. (1995). Search for meaning in long-term cancer survivors. *Journal of Advanced Nursing, 21*, 628–633.

Foley, K. L., Farmer, D. F., Petronis, V. M., Smith, R. G., McGraw, S., Smith, K.,... Avis, N. (2006). A qualitative exploration of the cancer experience among long-term survivors: Comparisons by cancer type, ethnicity, gender, and age. *Psycho-Oncology, 15*, 248–258.

Friedman, L. C., Romero, C., Elledge, R., Chang, J., Kalidas, M., Dulay, M. F.,... Osborne, C. K. (2007). Attribution of blame, self-forgiving attitude and psychological adjustment in women with breast cancer. *Journal of Behavioral Medicine, 30*, 351–357.

Gall, T. L. (2004). Relationship with God and the quality of life of prostate cancer survivors. *Quality of Life Research, 13*, 1357–1368.

Ganz, P. A., Kwan, L., Stanton, A. L., Krupnick, J. L., Rowland, J. H., Meyerowitz, B. E.,... Belin, T. R. (2004). Quality of life at the end of primary treatment of breast cancer: First results from the moving beyond cancer randomized trial. *Journal of the National Cancer Institute, 96*, 376–387.

Gillies, J., & Neimeyer, R. A. (2006). Loss, grief, and the search for significance: Toward a model of meaning reconstruction in bereavement. *Journal of Constructivist Psychology, 19*, 31–65.

Glinder, J. G., & Compas, B. E. (1999). Self-blame attributions in women with newly diagnosed breast cancer: A prospective study of psychological adjustment. *Health Psychology, 18*, 475–481.

Gotay, C. C. (1985). Why me? Attributions and adjustment by cancer patients and their mates at two stages in the disease process. *Social Science and Medicine, 20*, 825–831.

Greenberg, M. A. (1995). Cognitive processing of traumas: The role of intrusive thoughts and reappraisals. *Journal of Applied Social Psychology, 25*, 1262–1296.

Hewitt, M., Greenfield, S., & Stovall, E. (Eds.). (2005). *From cancer patient to cancer survivor: Lost in transition*. Washington, DC: Institute of Medicine.

Holland, J. C., & Reznik, I. (2005). Pathways for psychosocial care of cancer survivors. *Cancer, 704*, 2624–2637.

Horowitz, M. J. (2001). *Stress response syndromes: Personality styles and interventions* (4th ed.). Northvale, NJ: Aronson.

Jacobsen P. B., Hann, D. M., Azzarello, L. M., Horton, J., Balducci, L., & Lyman, G. H. (1999). Fatigue in women receiving adjuvant chemotherapy for breast cancer: Characteristics, course, and correlates. *Journal of Pain and Symptom Management, 18*, 233–242.

Janoff-Bulman, R. (1992). *Shattered assumptions: Towards a new psychology of trauma*. New York, NY: Free Press.

Janoff-Bulman, R., & Frantz, C. M. (1997). The impact of trauma on meaning: From meaningless world to meaningful life. In M. Power & C. Brewin (Eds.), *The transformation of meaning in psychological therapies: Integrating theory and practice*. Chichester, England: Wiley.

Jim, H. S., Richardson, S. A., Golden-Kreutz, D. M., & Andersen, B. L. (2006). Strategies used in coping with a cancer diagnosis predict meaning in life for survivors. *Health Psychology, 25*, 753–761.

Karoly, P. (1999). A goal systems-self-regulatory perspective on personality, psychopathology, and change. *Review of General Psychology*, *3*, 264–291.

Kernan, W. D., & Lepore, S. J. (2009). Searching for and making meaning after breast cancer: Prevalence, patterns, and negative affect. *Social Science & Medicine*, *68*, 1176–1182.

Kissane, D. W., Bloch, S., Smith, G. C., Miach, P., Clarke, D. M., Ikin, J. M.,… McKenzie, D. (2003). Cognitive-existential group psychotherapy for women with primary breast cancer: A randomised controlled trial. *Psycho-Oncology*, *12*, 532–546.

Klinger, E. (1998). The search for meaning in evolutionary perspective and its clinical implications. In P. T. P. Wong & P. S. Fry (Eds.), *The human quest for meaning: A handbook of psychological research and clinical applications* (pp. 27–50). Mahwah, NJ: Erlbaum.

Koltko-Rivera, M. E. (2004). The psychology of worldviews. *Review of General Psychology*, *8*, 1–58.

Kulik, L., & Kronfeld, M. (2005). Adjustment to breast cancer: The contribution of resources and causal attributions regarding the illness. *Social Work in Health Care*, *41*, 37–57.

Lee, V., Cohen, S. R., Edgar, L., Laizner, A. M., & Gagnon, A. J. (2004). Clarifying "meaning" in the context of cancer research: A systematic literature review. *Palliative & Supportive Care*, *2*, 291–303.

Lee, V., Cohen, S. R., Edgar, L., Laizner, A. M., & Gagnon, A. J. (2006). Meaning-making intervention during breast or colorectal cancer treatment improves self-esteem, optimism, and self-efficacy, *Social Science and Medicine*, *62*, 3133–3145.

Lepore, S. J. (2001). A social-cognitive processing model of emotional adjustment to cancer. In A. Baum & B. Anderson (Eds), *Psychosocial interventions for cancer* (pp. 99–118). Washington, DC: American Psychological Association.

Lepore, S. J., Silver, R. C., Wortman, C. B., & Wayment, H. A. (1996). Social constraints, intrusive thoughts, and depressive symptoms among bereaved mothers. *Journal of Personality and Social Psychology*, *70*, 271–282.

Lethborg, C. E., Kissane, D., Burns, W. I., & Snyder, R. (2000). "Cast adrift": The experience of completing treatment among women with early stage breast cancer. *Journal of Psychosocial Oncology*, *18*, 73–90.

Lipowski, Z. J. (1970). Physical illness, the individual and the coping process. *Psychiatric Medicine*, *1*, 91–102.

Little, M., & Sayers, E. (2004). The skull beneath the skin: Cancer survival and awareness of death. *Psycho-Oncology*, *13*, 190–198.

Llewellyn, C. D., McGurk, M., & Weinman, J. (2007). Illness and treatment beliefs in head and neck cancer: Is Leventhal's common sense model a useful framework for determining changes in outcomes over time? *Journal of Psychosomatic Research*, *63*, 17–26.

Malcarne, V. E., Compas, B. E., Epping-Jordan, J. E., & Howell, D. C. (1995). Cognitive factors in adjustment to cancer: Attributions of self-blame and perceptions of control. *Journal of Behavioral Medicine*, *18*, 401–417.

McBride, C. M., Clipp, E., Peterson, B. L., Lipkus, I. M. & Demark-Wahnefried, W. (2000). Psychological impact of diagnosis and risk reduction among cancer survivors. *Psycho-Oncology*, *9*, 418–427.

Moadel, A., Morgan, C., Fatone, A., Grennan, J., Carter, J., Laruffa, G.,… Dutcher, J. (1999). Seeking meaning and hope: Self-reported spiritual and existential needs among an ethnically-diverse cancer patient population. *Psycho-Oncology*, *8*, 378–285.

Monson, C. M., Schnurr, P. P., Resick, P. A., Friedman, M. J., Yinong, Y. X., & Stevens, S. P. (2006). Cognitive processing therapy for veterans with military-related post-traumatic stress disorder. *Journal of Consulting and Clinical Psychology, 74,* 898–907.

National Cancer Institute. (2007, October 12). Cancer survivorship research. Retrieved from http://dccps.nci.nih.gov/ocs/definitions.html

National Cancer Institute. (2009, December 11). Retrieved from http://dccps.nci.nih.gov/ocs

Nordin, K., Wasteson, E., Hoffman, K., Glimelius, B., & Sjödén, P. O. (2001). Discrepancies between attainment and importance of life values and anxiety and depression in gastrointestinal cancer patients and their spouses. *Psycho-Oncology, 10,* 479–489.

Norton, T. R., Manne, S. L., Rubin, S., Hernandez, E., Carlson, J., Bergman, C., & Rosenblum, N. (2005). Ovarian cancer patients' psychological distress: The role of physical impairment, perceived unsupportive family and friend behaviors, perceived control, and self-esteem. *Health Psychology, 24,* 143–152.

Park, C. L. (in press). Making sense of the meaning literature: An integrative review of meaning making and its effects on adjustment to stressful life events. *Psychological Bulletin.*

Park, C. L., Edmondson, D., Fenster, J. R., & Blank, T. O. (2008). Meaning making and psychological adjustment following cancer: The mediating roles of growth, life meaning, and restored just world beliefs. *Journal of Consulting and Clinical Psychology, 76,* 863–875.

Park, C. L., & Folkman, S. (1997). Meaning in the context of stress and coping. *General Review of Psychology, 1,* 115–144.

Park, C. L., Zlateva, I., & Blank, T. O. (2009). Self-identity after cancer: "survivor", "victim", "patient", and "person with cancer." *Journal of General Internal Medicine* [Special issue on survivorship], *24*(Suppl. 2), S430–S435.

Redd, W. H., DuHamel, K., Johnson-Vickberg, S. M., Ostroff, J. L., Smith, M. Y.,... Manne, S. L. (2001). Long-term adjustment in cancer survivors: Integration of classical-conditioning and cognitive processing models. In A. Baum & B. Anderson (Eds), *Psychosocial interventions for cancer* (pp. 77–98). Washington, DC: American Psychological Association.

Reker, G. T., & Wong, P. T. P. (1988). Aging as an individual process: Toward a theory of personal meaning. In J. E. Birren & V. L. Bengston (Eds.), *Emergent theories of aging* (pp. 214–246). New York, NY: Springer.

Roberts, K. J., Lepore, S. J., & Helgeson, V. S. (2005). Social-cognitive correlates of adjustment to prostate cancer. *Psycho-Oncology, 14,* 1–10.

Roesch, S. C., & Weiner, B. (2001). A meta-analytic review of coping with illness: Do causal attributions matter? *Journal of Psychosomatic Research, 50,* 205–219.

Roesch, S. C., Weiner, B., & Vaughn, A. A. (2002). Cognitive approaches to stress and coping. *Current Opinion in Psychiatry, 15,* 627–632.

Schroevers, M. J., Ranchor, A. V., & Sanderman, R. (2004). The role of age at the onset of cancer in relation to survivors' long-term adjustment: A controlled comparison over an eight-year period. *Psycho-Oncology, 13,* 740–752.

Sears, S. R., Stanton, A. L., & Danoff-Burg, S. (2003) The yellow brick road and the emerald city: Benefit finding, positive reappraisal coping and post-traumatic growth in women with early-stage breast cancer. *Health Psychology, 22,* 487–497.

Segerstrom, S. C., Stanton, A. L., Alden, L. E., & Shortridge, B. E. (2003). A multidimensional structure for repetitive thought: What's on your mind, and how, and how much? *Journal of Personality and Social Psychology, 85,* 909–921.

Silver, R. L., Boon, C., & Stones, M. H. (1983). Searching for meaning in misfortune: Making sense of incest. *Journal of Social Issues, 39*, 81–102.

Silver-Aylaian, M., & Cohen, L. H. (2001). Role of major lifetime stressors in patients' and spouses' reactions to cancer. *Journal of Traumatic Stress, 14*, 405–412.

Skaggs, B. G., &. Barron, C. R. (2006). Searching for meaning in negative events: Concept analysis. *Journal of Advanced Nursing, 53*, 559–570.

Stanton, A. L., Bower, J. E., & Low, C. A. (2006). Posttraumatic growth after cancer. In L. Calhoun & R. Tedeschi (Eds.), *Handbook of posttraumatic growth* (pp. 138–175). Mahwah, NJ: Erlbaum.

Stanton, A. L, Danoff-Burg, S., Cameron, C. L., Bishop, M., Collins, C. A., Kirk, S. B.,… Twillman, R. (2000). Emotionally expressive coping predicts psychological and physical adjustment to breast cancer. *Journal of Consulting and Clinical Psychology, 68*, 875–882.

Stull, V. B., Snyder, D. C., & Demark-Wahnefried, W. (2007) Lifestyle interventions in cancer survivors: Designing programs that meet the needs of this vulnerable and growing population. *Journal of Nutrition, 137*, 243S–248S.

Tait, R., & Silver, R. C. (1989). Coming to terms with major negative life events. In J. S. Uleman & J. A. Bargh (Eds.), *Unintended thought* (pp. 351–382). New York, NY: Guilford Press.

Taylor, E. J. (1995). Whys and wherefores: Adult patient perspectives of the meaning of cancer. *Seminars in Oncology Nursing, 11*, 32–40.

Taylor, S. E. (1983). Adjustment to threatening events: A theory of cognitive adaptation. *American Psychologist, 38*, 1161–1173.

Taylor, S. E., Lichtman, R. R., & Wood, J. V. (1984). Attributions, beliefs about control, and adjustment to breast cancer. *Journal of Personality and Social Psychology, 46*, 489–502.

Tomich, P. L., & Helgeson, V. S. (2002). Five years later: A cross-sectional comparison of breast cancer survivors with healthy women. *Psycho-Oncology, 11*, 154–169.

Tomich, P. L., & Helgeson, V. S. (2004). Is finding something good in the bad always good? Benefit finding among women with breast cancer. *Health Psychology, 23*, 16–23.

Tross, S., & Holland, J. C. (1989). Psychological sequelae in cancer survivors. In J. C. Holland & J. H. Rowland (Eds.), *Handbook of psychooncology: Psychological care for the patient with cancer* (pp. 101–116). New York, NY: Oxford University Press.

Westling, E., Garcia, K., & Mann, T. (2007). Discovery of meaning and adherence to medications in HIV-infected women. *Journal of Health Psychology, 12*, 627–635.

Widows, M. R., Jacobsen, P. B., Booth-Jones, M., & Fields, K. K. (2005). Predictors of posttraumatic growth following bone marrow transplantation for cancer. *Healthy Psychology, 24*, 266–273.

Zebrack, B. J. (2000). Cancer survivor identity and quality of life. *Cancer Practice, 8*, 238–242.

Zebrack, B. J., Ganz, P. A., Bernaards, C. A., Petersen, L., Abraham, L. (2006). Assessing the impact of cancer: development of a new instrument for long- term survivors. *Psycho-Oncology, 15*, 407–421.

24

When Meaning Is Threatened

The Importance of Goal Adjustment for Psychological and Physical Health

CARSTEN WROSCH

Concordia University

MICHAEL F. SCHEIER

Carnegie Mellon University

GREGORY E. MILLER

University of British Columbia

CHARLES S. CARVER

University of Miami

This chapter discusses how people can adapt when goals are unattainable and thereby maintain their psychological well-being and physical health. On the basis of self-regulation theories (Carver & Scheier, 1981, 1998), we argue that the pursuit of meaningful goals provides purpose for living and is an essential contributor to a person's subjective well-being and physical health. In circumstances when an important life goal has become unattainable, however, a person's sense of meaning can be threatened. The person may experience high levels of psychological distress and the associated negative consequences on physical health. In such situations, we argue that a person needs to engage in adaptive self-regulation processes that allow disengagement from the unattainable goal and reengagement in other meaningful goals and activities. Those people who are better able to disengage from unattainable goals and engage in other new goals should be more likely to maintain a sense of purpose in life, and thereby prevent distress and physical health problems, than people who have more difficulty with goal disengagement and goal reengagement.

Self-Regulation of Personal Goals

Theories of self-regulation suggest that personality processes involved in the pursuit of personal goals play an important role in individuals' quality of life (Carver & Scheier, 1981, 1998; Emmons, 1986; Heckhausen & Schulz, 1995; Heckhausen, Wrosch, & Schulz, 2010). From this perspective, goals are important because they are the building blocks that structure people's lives and imbue life with purpose, both in the short run and on a long-term basis (Heckhausen, 1999; Ryff, 1989). In a very real sense, goals provide the impetus for action, give life its direction, and help to define who the person is. Further, to create adaptive outcomes, it is important that people adopt goals that are attainable and highly valued. In support of this assumption, a large body of research deriving from expectancy-value models of motivation (see Atkinson, 1964; Feather, 1982; Vroom, 1964) has demonstrated that people prefer pursuing goals that are both attainable and valued. Moreover, people who pursue personally meaningful goals experience greater psychological well-being (e.g., emotional well-being, low depression, or low perceived stress) and physical health, as compared with people who are engaged in less valued goal pursuits (Scheier et al., 2006). Thus, valued goals are important. They contribute to adaptive behaviors, fostering subjective well-being and physical health.

How do goals promote action and contribute to a good quality of life? Self-regulation theories assume that these processes form feedback loops, with goals providing important reference values for the person's behaviors (Carver & Scheier, 1981, 1998). A feedback loop consists of four elements—an input function, a reference value, a comparator, and an output function (see Figure 24.1; cf. G. A. Miller, Galanter, & Pribram, 1960).

In such a feedback loop, the input represents a person's perception, which is compared to a reference value (i.e., a goal) by means of the comparator. The output reflects a person's (behavioral) response, which is tied to the result of the comparison process. In discrepancy-reducing or negative feedback loops,

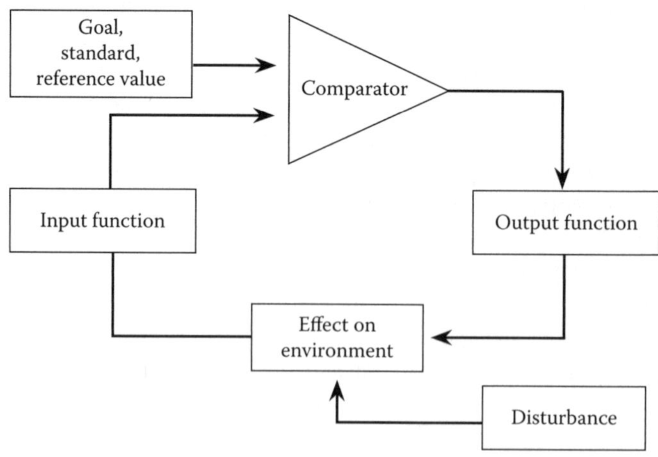

Figure 24.1 Schematic depiction of a feedback loop.

if the comparison does not detect a discrepancy between the input and the goal, the output does not change. If the comparison yields a discrepancy, however, the output changes, typically with the aim to reduce the perceived discrepancy. This process is targeted at approaching desired goals. We note that there are also discrepancy-enlarging or positive feedback loops. This happens when a person tries to increase a discrepancy between the input and a goal (typically if a person's goal is to avoid a negative outcome; see Elliot & Sheldon, 1997). In addition, feedback loops can be functionally organized in a hierarchical system (Powers, 1973), in which the output of a higher level feedback loop influences the reference value of a lower level feedback loop. However, positive loops and hierarchiality are not of primary importance for this chapter and are thus not discussed in more detail.

The preceding discussion makes clear that meaningful goals play an important role in adaptive self-regulation. However, a problem may occur when people experience difficulty attaining a goal they have set, such as not finishing a project on time, being unable to fix a problem, or not being able to find the time to go on a long-desired vacation. In such situations, when failure to make progress toward an important goal is encountered, people are likely to experience emotional distress. Thus, goal progress is functionally related to a person's emotional experiences (Carver & Scheier, 1990, 1998). This relationship is important because distress can compromise a person's physical health (Cohen, 1996). Stressful encounters trigger processes in the endocrine, immune, metabolic, and central nervous systems (e.g., cortisol disturbances of excessive inflammation) and thereby make people more vulnerable to the development of physical disease (Dickerson & Kemeny, 2004; Heim, Ehlert, & Hellhammer, 2000; Lupien et al., 1998; G. E. Miller, Chen, & Zhou, 2007; G. E. Miller & Wrosch, 2007; Willerson & Ridker, 2004).

Thus, people may need to adjust to the absence of goal progress to prevent the adverse downstream consequences for their psychological and physical health. Theories of self-regulation suggest that two categories of responses are involved in the management of failure in goal pursuits (Carver & Scheier, 1990, 1998; Kukla, 1972; Wright & Brehm, 1989). As depicted in Figure 24.2, the adaptive value of these two categories of responses should depend on a person's opportunities to attain the threatened goal in the future (see also Heckhausen & Schulz, 1995; Wrosch, Dunne, Scheier, & Schulz, 2006; Wrosch & Heckhausen, 1999).

One category of responses consists of continued engagement with one's goal and continued investing of effort. This response occurs if the person's expectations for goal attainment remain sufficiently positive. Continued effort can, in this case, promote positive outcomes if the opportunities for future goal attainment are favorable. In fact, in many situations people can overcome goal failure if they invest more effort, strengthen their psychological commitment toward, or find an alternative path to realizing the threatened

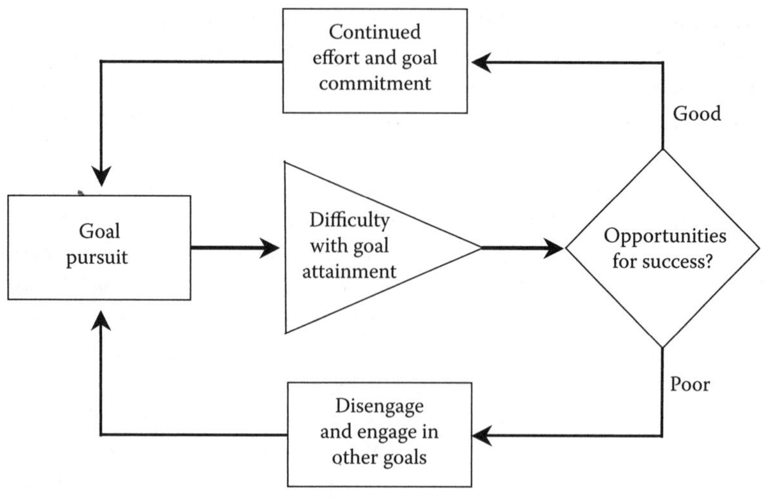

Figure 24.2 Adaptive self-regulation of difficulty with goal attainment.

goal (e.g., Bandura, 1997; Heckhausen, 1999). Thus, continued goal engagement should be adaptive as long as the goal is still within reach.

At times, however, it may not be possible to make further progress toward a desired goal because the opportunities for goal progress have become curtailed and the goal itself is unattainable. In such situations, a person may be more doubtful about future goal success and engage in a second category of self-regulation responses, aimed at goal disengagement and the pursuit of other meaningful goals (Carver & Scheier, 1990; Scheier & Carver, 2001; Wrosch, Scheier, Carver, & Schulz, 2003; Wrosch, Scheier, Miller, et al., 2003; Wrosch, Miller, Scheier, & Brun de Pontet, 2007). These processes of adaptive goal adjustment keep a person engaged in the pursuit of meaningful and attainable goals. They are the focus of this chapter.

Managing Unattainable Goals

Unfortunately, having a goal that can no longer be attained is a common experience in life. For example, research among college students has shown that young adults experience almost five unattainable and valued goals over a time span of five years (Wrosch, Scheier, Miller, Schulz, & Carver, 2003). Of importance, this finding was replicated in a more heterogeneous sample of young and older adults from different socioeconomic backgrounds (Bauer, 2004). Thus, people confront on average one valued but unattainable goal each year. This suggests that unattainable goals are a common and therefore important psychological phenomenon.

Goals may be unattainable for different reasons. For example, a person may select an unrealistic goal that is beyond the person's capacities and for that reason will never be attained (e.g., running a world record without having the necessary athletic skills). In addition, goals that were realistic and attainable at some point in a person's life may become unattainable over time. This may be caused by the occurrence of critical life events or age-related declines in the opportunities to attain a goal. An accident, unemployment, or growing older may render impossible the pursuit of a given goal—for example, staying in good health, buying a house, or having your own children. Finally, there are situations in which a person can no longer pursue a goal because the person needs to focus time and energy on the pursuit of more important and resource-intensive goals. For example, a person may no longer be able to pursue such valued leisure goals as seeing friends, going to the movies, or exercising because the person has to invest all available time and energy in the pursuit of such other goals as establishing a career or caring for a sick child that needs intensive care (Wrosch, Scheier, Carver, et al., 2003).

Regardless of why a goal becomes unattainable, having an unattainable goal may create a crisis for a person's sense of meaning because the desired outcome related to the person's overall sense of self or identity is no longer attainable. As discussed earlier, a person who cannot make progress toward a desired goal is likely to experience declines in subjective well-being (Carver & Scheier, 1990, 1998). In turn, the negative emotional consequences resulting from the experience of unattainable goals may influence a person's physical health (Wrosch, Miller, et al., 2007). Thus, having unattainable goals may not only compromise people's subjective well-being but also their physical health.

We have argued that people can avoid the negative psychological and physical consequences that result from the experience of unattainable goals if they engage in a form of adaptive self-regulation other than continued effort (Carver & Scheier, 1990; Wrosch, Miller, Scheier, & Brun de Pontet, 2007; Wrosch, Scheier, Miller, et al., 2003). More specifically, people can thrive in circumstances where valued goals have become unattainable if they are able to adjust their goals. This process should help maintain a sense of meaning in life and keeps a person engaged in the pursuit of valued activities. Thereby, it should further contribute to the person's psychological and physical health.

We have further suggested that goal adjustment involves two processes. First, a person needs to *disengage* from the unattainable goal. To disengage successfully, a person needs to withdraw effort and commitment from pursuing that goal (Wrosch, Scheier, Miller, et al., 2003). Goal disengagement should be adaptive because it prevents the person from experiencing the negative emotional consequences of repeated goal failure. In addition, successful goal disengagement should free resources that can be invested in the pursuit of other important goals (for beneficial effects of disengagement, see also Brandtstädter & Renner, 1990; Carver & Scheier, 1990, 1998; Heckhausen & Schulz, 1995; Klinger, 1975; Nesse, 2000).

The second process is that a person who confronts an unattainable goal needs to *reengage* goal-directed efforts elsewhere. To reengage successfully, a person needs to identify, commit to, and start to pursue alternative goals (Wrosch, Scheier, Miller, et al., 2003). Goal reengagement should help a person maintain a sense of purpose in life and buffer the negative emotions associated with the inability to make progress toward a desired goal.

In support of this argument, research has shown that people vary widely in their reactions to unattainable goals and that abandoning unattainable goals may help preserve a person's subjective well-being. Wrosch and Heckhausen (1999), for example, studied groups of younger and older persons who had recently experienced a separation from their spouses. It was assumed that the older persons in the study would face sharply reduced opportunities for establishing a new intimate relationship, thereby making disengagement from the general domain of partnership-related goals adaptive for older persons. The results showed that older persons in the study had disengaged from partnership goals more fully than had younger persons, as reflected in the number of partnership goals they reported. In addition, longitudinal data showed that deactivation of partnership goals predicted improvement of emotional well-being in older participants (Wrosch & Heckhausen, 1999).

Another prototypical example of such a situation in early midlife is the biological clock of childbearing. Heckhausen, Wrosch, and Fleeson (2001) studied women who had passed the deadline for having their own children. Among women whose biological clock had run out, those who failed to disengage from the goal of having their own children reported particularly high levels of depressive symptomatology.

In a similar vein, Tunali and Power (1993) examined how parents cope with the stress of having handicapped children. The researchers argued that when people are in such an inescapable situation, where their basic needs are threatened, they may "redefine what constitutes fulfillment of that need, and ... develop alternative means of achieving it" (Tunali & Power, 1993, p. 950). Consistent with this line of reasoning, Tunali and Power (1993) found that mothers of autistic children tended to downgrade the importance of career success in defining their life satisfaction and upgrade the importance of being a good parent in comparison to mothers who did not have an autistic child (cf. Carver & Scheier, 2000; Sprangers & Schwartz, 1999). Rated importance of being a successful parent was also strongly related to life satisfaction among the mothers of autistic children.

Related research by the Leventhals and their colleagues (Duke, Leventhal, Brownlee, & Leventhal, 2002) also documents the beneficial effects of goal reengagement. They studied a group of older adults, some of whom had to abandon physical activities because of health-related problems. Persons who replaced lost activities with new activities had higher positive affect one year after the onset of their illness than did those individuals who did not replace the activities.

There is also a body of research examining the roles played by goal disengagement and the pursuit of other new goals in the management of life regrets (for a review, see Wrosch et al., 2006). In this regard, it is important to bear in mind that it usually becomes more and more difficult to undo the negative consequences of regretted behaviors as people advance in age (e.g., having married the wrong person or having not become a lawyer; Wrosch, Bauer, & Scheier, 2005; Wrosch & Heckhausen, 2002). Intense regret has been shown to contribute to older adults' biological dysregulation and physical health problems (Wrosch, Bauer, Miller, & Lupien, 2007). Thus, to adaptively regulate the experience of regret, older adults need to disengage from trying to undo the consequences of their regretted behaviors and take up new goals.

In support of this argument, research has shown that older adults who failed to disengage from the effort to undo regretted behaviors and who had only a small number of goals to pursue in the future experienced particularly intense levels of regret and low levels of subjective well-being (e.g., depression or life satisfaction). In addition, the data were consistent with the idea that the adverse effects on compromised levels of subjective well-being mediated older adults' physical health problems (Wrosch et al., 2005). Finally, recent experimental research has demonstrated that engaging older adults in processes that support goal disengagement (e.g., making self-protective attributions and social comparisons; Bauer, Wrosch, & Jobin, 2008; Wrosch & Heckhausen, 2002), as well as the pursuit of other meaningful goals, can buffer an adverse effect of intense regret on the older adults' sleeping problems over time (Wrosch, Bauer, et al., 2007).

These studies document that abandoning unattainable goals and engaging in new goals can be adaptive and protect individuals from experiencing the negative effects of goal failure on their subjective well-being. It is important to note, however, that the work discussed thus far has focused on very specific goals (e.g., having a child, undoing the consequences of a regretted behavior, or building a new intimate relationship). It is also possible that there may be broader individual differences in goal regulation tendencies that affect the manner in which a person reacts and adjusts to unattainable goals. Stated differently, people may also vary more generally in their ability to adjust to unattainable goals, and individual differences in these capacities may determine how a person adjusts to the experience of an unattainable goal.

In this regard, we have argued that there may exist individual differences in people's general goal adjustment capacities. Some people might be better able than others to disengage from unattainable goals and reengage in alternative goals, regardless of the specific nature of the goals in question. Moreover, we have proposed that such individual differences can predict a person's quality of life (Wrosch, Scheier, Miller, et al., 2003; Wrosch, Miller, et al., 2007). People who are generally better able to abandon unattainable goals and to reengage in other meaningful activities should experience greater subjective well-being and better physical health than do people who have a more difficult time adjusting to their unattainable goals.

To start examining these propositions empirically, we developed a self-report instrument (Wrosch, Scheier, Miller, et al., 2003). This instrument contains 10 items that measure how people usually react if they can no longer pursue an important goal. Four items measure a person's tendency to disengage from unattainable goals (e.g., "it's easy for me to reduce my effort toward the goal") and six items measure the tendency to reengage in other new goals (e.g., "I start working on other new goals"). The items on these scales were written to reflect the components of goal disengagement and goal reengagement identified earlier—that is, withdrawal of effort and commitment with respect to goal disengagement; and the identification of, commitment to, and pursuit of alternative goals with respect to goal reengagement. Both scales are internally reliable and predict relevant outcome variables in a number of studies, which are discussed in more detail in the next section (Miller & Wrosch, 2007; Wrosch, Miller, et al., 2007; Wrosch, Scheier, Miller, et al., 2003). In addition, the effects of these self-regulation tendencies have been shown to be statistically independent of other coping constructs (e.g., assimilation and accommodation; Brandtstädter & Renner, 1990) and the personality traits of the five-factor model (Goldberg, 1992). This finding lends empirical support to the idea that individual differences in goal disengagement and goal reengagement tendencies are meaningful and independent predictors of a person's quality of life.

Goal Adjustment Capacities and Subjective Well-Being

A first set of empirical studies addressed the influence of general goal disengagement and goal reengagement capacities on indicators of subjective well-being. One study examined undergraduate students making the transition to college (Wrosch, Scheier, Miller, et al., 2003, Study 1). We reasoned that this transition may involve multiple potential losses, such as leaving friends and family behind at home, and an increased potential for failure experiences related to academic pursuits. Thus, students are likely to experience that some of their previously valued goals have become unattainable. In turn, students who are not able to adjust their goals may experience low levels of subjective well-being, whereas students who are better able to disengage and to engage in new goals may be protected from the potentially adverse emotional effects of this life transition.

In support of the hypotheses, this study showed that the capacity to withdraw effort and commitment from unattainable goals was related to lower levels of perceived stress and intrusive thoughts and to high levels of self-mastery. In addition, students who were able to reengage in alternative goals reported lower levels of perceived stress and intrusive thoughts as well as higher levels of purpose in life and self-mastery. Further, there was an interaction between goal disengagement and goal reengagement in predicting indicators of subjective well-being. Among students who reported difficulty disengaging from unattainable goals, those individuals with a higher capacity to reengage reported greater self-mastery and less perceived stress than did those less able to reengage. This pattern suggests that goal reengagement can buffer the negative effects of inability to disengage on subjective well-being.

Another study examined goal adjustment tendencies in a particularly stressful situation that could be expected to constrain important life goals (Wrosch, Scheier, Miller, et al., 2003, Study 3). Parents of children who had been diagnosed with cancer were compared with parents of physically healthy children. It was expected that the parents whose children had been diagnosed with cancer might have to redefine some of their goal priorities. In such a situation, goal disengagement and goal reengagement should be very important, given that the parents are forced to abandon certain goals they had adopted for themselves and their families in order to direct resources to this immediate challenge (e.g., giving up on work goals to spend more time with the sick children). In support of our assumptions, goal disengagement and goal reengagement tendencies were associated with fewer depressive symptoms, particularly among parents of children with cancer (Wrosch, Scheier, Miller, et al., 2003). In fact, among those parents of children with cancer who were better able to adjust to unattainable goals, depression scores were almost as low as the scores of parents of healthy children. These results are consistent with the idea that goal adjustment tendencies become particularly important in regulating well-being in the midst of stressors that are likely to interfere with previously established goal-directed activities.

In another study, Bauer (2004) examined the association between unattainable goals, goal adjustment tendencies, and positive and negative affect in a sample of adults. The participants were asked to report all the goals that were important to them and that became unattainable during the past five years. Unattainable goals exerted a cumulative effect on subjective well-being: As the number of unattainable goals increased, individuals reported lower levels of well-being. Moreover, adaptive goal disengagement predicted significantly lower levels of negative affect but were unrelated to individual differences in positive affect. Conversely, adaptive goal reengagement tendencies predicted high levels of positive affect but were not associated with negative affect. Finally, the study found a significant interaction effect between the capacity to disengage and the frequency of unattainable goals on negative affect. More specifically, having a high number of unattainable goals related to higher levels of negative affect, but only among those individuals who experienced difficulty disengaging from unattainable goals (Bauer, 2004).

Evidence for differential effects of goal disengagement and goal reengagement on a person's mood was also found in a recent longitudinal study of adolescent girls (Wrosch & Miller, 2009). In this study, participants who reported an increase in their goal disengagement capacities over the first year of study experienced a decline in their depressive mood over the subsequent six months. This effect was not obtained for participants' goal reengagement capacities, suggesting that goal disengagement contributes to relieving negative affect to a greater extent than does goal reengagement.

In another longitudinal study of older adults, we also examined the influence of goal adjustment capacities on subjective well-being over time. This study predicted changes in depressive symptomatology over a time span of two years (Dunne, Wrosch, & Miller, 2009). The findings showed that the depression scores among older adults significantly increased over time. However, this association was dependent on participants' goal disengagement capacities. Whereas older adults with poor goal disengagement capacities experienced a strong increase in depressive symptoms over time, depressive symptoms did not increase over time among older adults with adaptive levels of goal disengagement capacities. Goal reengagement capacities were statistically unrelated to changes in depressive symptoms.

We also collected cross-sectional data in a sample of older adults that directly address the associations between goal adjustment tendencies and purpose. As a measure of purpose, we administered the Life Engagement Test (LET; Scheier et al., 2006). In this study, adaptive levels of both goal disengagement and goal reengagement tendencies were associated with higher levels of purpose. In this regard, we note that the data also suggest that the association between goal reengagement and purpose was stronger than the association between goal disengagement and purpose, a finding that we had already observed in an earlier study using Ryff's (1989) measure of purpose in life (Wrosch, Scheier, Miller, et al., 2003, Study 1). Moreover, the pattern of findings was consistent with the idea that the beneficial effects of goal adjustment tendencies on low levels of depressive symptoms and perceived stress were mediated by purpose in life (Wrosch & Scheier, 2007). We find these findings very provocative because they suggest that being able to adjust to unattainable goals can help maintain a person's purpose in life and may thereby contribute to high levels of subjective well-being (Klinger, 1977).

Further evidence for this idea has been reported by Aviram (2009). In a study of older adults, she showed that baseline levels of goal reengagement tendencies (but not goal disengagement tendencies) predicted high levels of purpose in life two years later. In addition, the effect of goal reengagement tendencies on purpose mediated subsequent levels of physical health in that high levels of purpose were associated with a less pronounced increase of difficulties with instrumental activities of daily living over time.

Evidence that adaptive goal adjustment can provide purpose for living has also been reported in a cross-sectional study of 255 students from Scotland (O'Connor & Forgan, 2007). In that study, the authors related goal adjustment capacities to the frequency of suicidal thoughts. The findings showed that students who had difficulty finding and pursuing new goals when unattainable goals are encountered reported more suicidal thoughts than did students who had an easier time with goal reengagement. Goal disengagement tendencies were not related to the frequency of suicidal thoughts.

In a somewhat different approach, we examined whether goal adjustment capacities may lead to adaptive behaviors that can be expected to foster positive outcomes and well-being within the social setting of a family business. In this study, the business owners were approaching normative retirement age and were confronted with the task of transmitting their business to the next generation (typically their children). This does not seem to be an easy task: Research suggests that family businesses often fail in the transmission processes because the incumbents are hesitant to give up control and retire (e.g., Ward, 1987). Our research supports this argument by documenting that the incumbents' objective control over the business does not strongly decline when the successors gain more control over the business (Brun de Pontet, Wrosch, & Gagne, 2007). It is important to note, however, that not all family businesses fail in this process. We therefore reasoned that there may be individual differences in business owners' goal adjustment capacities that may facilitate the process of intergeneration business transmission.

Data from this longitudinal study of family business owners show that adaptive goal disengagement tendencies were associated with more favorable expectations about life after retirement (e.g., retirement as an opportunity to contribute in new ways to the community or to spend time with family and friends) and predicted an increase in retirement expectations over time (Brun de Pontet, Wrosch, & Gagne, 2008). In addition, adaptive goal disengagement was associated with concrete steps taken toward retirement and increased the steps taken toward retirement over time. Of interest is that the cross-sectional effects of goal disengagement were found only among struggling businesses. In this regard, research from the business arena has documented that entrepreneurs often have difficulty disengaging from business goals when they face a failing course of action, a phenomenon that has been described as entrapment (Brockner, 1992). The reported data suggest that in such circumstances, goal disengagement capacities may be become particularly important. They support behaviors that should contribute to the well-being and health of a business.

In sum, research on goal adjustment and indicators of subjective well-being has demonstrated in cross-sectional, quasi-experimental, and longitudinal studies that adaptive levels of goal adjustment tendencies can be associated with high levels of subjective well-being. In addition, the pursuit of new goals may buffer an adverse effect of difficulty with goal disengagement on a person's subjective well-being. Finally, the findings suggest a differential pattern, one in which goal disengagement tendencies often show a stronger effect on negative indicators of subjective well-being (e.g., low negative affect or low depression), whereas goal reengagement tendencies seem to be more closely related to positive indicators of subjective well-being (e.g., positive affect or purpose in life). This result may not be surprising, given that the main function of goal disengagement is to prevent the experience of emotional distress associated with a person's inability to make progress toward attaining important life goals. The primary function of goal reengagement, by contrast, is to provide purpose for living, which should be more likely to lead to increases in positive aspects of a persons' subjective well-being.

We note, however, that the studies discussed also suggest some deviations from this pattern of differential effects on positive and negative indicators of subjective well-being. These deviations may be a result of secondary functions of goal adjustment tendencies, in which goal disengagement may free resources that facilitate the pursuit of new purposeful goals, and thus goal reengagement may reduce the distress associated with not being able to make further progress toward an important but unattainable goal (for a more comprehensive discussion, see Wrosch, Miller, et al., 2007).

Goal Adjustment Capacities and Physical Health

We have also examined whether goal adjustment tendencies can influence indicators of physical health. As discussed earlier, we reasoned that such an association may emerge because the emotional distress from failed goal adjustment may trigger patterns of biological dysregulation in the immune or endocrine systems, for example, that increase a person's vulnerability to disease (for relations between distress, biological dysregulation, and physical health, see Dickerson & Kemeny, 2004; Heim et al., 2000; Kiecolt-Glaser, McGuire, Robles, & Glaser, 2002; McEwen, 1998; Miller, Chen, & Zhou, 2007; Segerstrom & Miller, 2004).

We started to examine this hypothesis in a heterogeneous and cross-sectional study of adults. We related participants' goal disengagement and goal reengagement tendencies to the number of reported physical health problems (e.g., eczema, migraine headaches, constipation; Wrosch, Miller, et al., 2007, Study 1). In support of our hypotheses, participants who were better able to let go of unattainable goals reported fewer health problems than did those who had more difficulty disengaging from unattainable goals. Goal reengagement, by contrast, did not relate to physical health problems.

The results from this study were also consistent with the assumption that subjective well-being can mediate the link between goal adjustment and physical health. Adaptive goal disengagement related to lower levels of depressive symptoms, and depressive symptoms predicted participants' physical health problems. It is important to note that when the effect of goal disengagement on physical health was controlled for depressive symptomatology, goal disengagement no longer significantly predicted participants' physical health problems.

The associations between goal adjustment tendencies and health-relevant biological variables were further examined in another sample of adults (Wrosch, Miller, et al., 2007, Study 2). This study included an assessment of participants' diurnal rhythms of cortisol secretion, a biological process that is widely thought to be a gateway through which distress increases vulnerability to clinical illness. Persons facing severe and long-term stressors often exhibit a flattened diurnal rhythm, characterized by low morning output and/or the failure to reduce secretion as the day progresses (e.g., Heim et al., 2000; Miller, Cohen, & Ritchey, 2002). There is also evidence that flattened diurnal cortisol rhythms are prognostic of adverse physical health outcomes (Heim et al., 2000; Matthews, Schwartz, Cohen, & Seeman, 2006; Sephton, Sapolsky, Kraemer, & Spiegel, 2000; Smyth et al., 1997). On the basis of these findings, we expected that participants who are better able to let go of unattainable goals and reengage in alternative goals would show a more normative (i.e., steeper) slope in diurnal cortisol secretion than would those who have more difficulties adjusting to unattainable goals.

The results showed that adaptive goal disengagement tendencies were associated with a steeper of slope of cortisol secretion over the day. As in the previously discussed study, goal reengagement did not relate to indicators of physical health. Of interest to us is that further analyses of the disengagement data found that differences in cortisol secretion as a function of goal disengagement occurred in the day and evening hours and not the morning hours (Wrosch, Miller, et al., 2007, Study 2). Our theoretical perspective holds that individual differences in goal adjustment tendencies should be particularly influential when people confront unattainable goals. Thus, it is not surprising that the influence of these tendencies is not large during the early morning hours, before people start their normal activities. As the day progresses, however, and people try to do what they set out to do, they may encounter situations in which goal attainment is difficult or impossible. Thus, unattainable goals are more likely to emerge later in the day, and differences in goal disengagement tendencies become important only then.

We have also examined the influence of goal adjustment tendencies on health-relevant variables in a sample of adolescent girls (Miller & Wrosch, 2007). Adolescents are a particularly interesting group in which to study goal adjustment. They are actively engaged in forming identities (Markus & Nurius, 1986), which often entails pursuing goals that later prove to be unrealizable. To evaluate the health impact of goal adjustment, we examined changes in C-reactive protein (CRP), a marker of systemic inflammation, over three measurement points spanning approximately one year of time. The immune system typically launches an inflammatory response when it detects an infection or injury, with the goal of eliminating pathogens and repairing tissue damage. The magnitude and duration of this process must, however, be carefully regulated because excessive inflammation may cause numerous medical conditions, among them long-term risk for diabetes or heart disease (Dandona, Aljada, Chaudhuri, Mohanty, & Garg, 2005; Willerson & Ridker, 2004). Given that psychological distress can contribute to excessive inflammation (Miller & Blackwell, 2006), we reasoned that goal adjustment capacities may be functionally associated with adaptive (i.e., lower) levels of C-reactive protein.

This study found that goal disengagement tendencies were associated with longitudinal trajectories of systemic inflammation (Miller & Wrosch, 2007). Among participants with poor disengagement capacities, levels of C-reactive protein increased twice as fast as it did for those with average disengagement capacities. In addition, levels of C-reactive protein even declined slightly among participants who had an easier time disengaging from unattainable goals (Miller & Wrosch, 2007). Similar to the previously discussed studies, goal reengagement tendencies were not related to trajectories of systemic inflammation. These findings are important because they show that goal disengagement tendencies predict changes over time in a clinically important biomarker. Because they were obtained prospectively in a sample of healthy young women, these data also bolster our confidence that goal adjustment is shaping health-related processes, rather than vice versa.

The hypothesis that goal adjustment can predict indicators of physical health was further tested in another longitudinal study, following a group of college students over the course of one semester (Wrosch, Miller, et al., 2007, Study 3). The study assessed goal adjustment tendencies at the beginning of the term and predicted self-reported physical health indicators (e.g., health symptoms, cold symptoms, sleep problems) at the end of the term. In addition, emotional well-being and life satisfaction were measured at the beginning and the end of the semester. Consistent with the previous studies, adaptive goal disengagement tendencies were associated with fewer health symptoms and better sleep efficiency at the end of the semester. There was no main effect of goal reengagement, although the findings did suggest evidence of a buffering effect of goal reengagement in that goal reengagement reduced the negative consequences of failure to disengage on participants' cold symptoms. Finally, the study provided further support for the mediating role of subjective well-being. Adaptive goal disengagement tendencies related to fewer increases in emotional distress across the course of the semester, and the effects of goal disengagement on changes in distress statistically explained the associations between goal disengagement and indicators of physical health.

Together, these studies demonstrate that individual differences in goal adjustment tendencies can be associated with physical health indicators. Failure in goal disengagement was shown to predict maladaptive levels of health-relevant biological processes (e.g., increased levels of cortisol secretion or systemic inflammations), which may increase a person's vulnerability to developing a clinical disease. In addition, difficulty with goal disengagement was associated with the occurrence of physical health problems (e.g., cold symptoms and physical health problems). Moreover, the findings suggest that the effects of failed goal disengagement on a person's physical health problems can be mediated by the experience of emotional distress.

Of importance, these studies did not show the same health effects for goal reengagement tendencies. That is, the main effect of goal reengagement was not related to health-relevant biological processes or physical health problems. We suggest that this may be a result of the previously discussed differential effect of goal adjustment tendencies on positive and negative indicators of subjective well-being. Presence of negative emotions may take a greater toll on a person's physical health than absence of positive emotions (for effects of positive and negative events and emotions on physical health, see Pressman & Cohen, 2005; Taylor, 1991). Thus, it is not surprising that goal disengagement tendencies can be a particularly strong predictor of physical health because the capacity to let go of unattainable goals seems to have a stronger effect on preventing the experience of emotional distress. We note, however, that the findings also showed that goal reengagement tendencies have the potential to buffer an adverse effect of failed goal disengagement on some physical health problems. This possibility implies that beneficial health effects of goal reengagement tendencies may be more complex and need to be further examined in future research (for a more comprehensive discussion, see Wrosch, Miller, et al., 2007).

Conclusions

We have argued that the pursuit of valued goals provides purpose for living and influences behavioral responses that lead to psychological well-being and good physical health. However, valued goals may also compromise a person's subjective well-being and physical health if the goals have become unattainable. In such situations, people need to engage in adaptive self-regulation to maintain their sense of meaning and avoid the negative consequences on their subjective well-being and physical health. In particular, processes aimed at goal disengagement and goal reengagement can prevent the adverse effects of unattainable goals on a person's quality of life.

In support of these arguments, research demonstrates that people who are better able to let go of unattainable goals tend to experience lower levels of emotional distress than do people who have more difficulty with goal disengagement. This process was further shown to mediate adaptive levels of biological functioning and physical health. Goal reengagement capacities were also shown to predict higher levels of subjective well-being. In general, goal reengagement seems not to be associated with physical health outcomes or important health indicators, although there is some minimal evidence that goal reengagement can buffer the health-damaging effects of the failure to disengage. The relationship between goal reengagement and physical health needs to be studied more fully in the future.

Acknowledgments

Preparation of this chapter was supported in part by grants and awards from the Canadian Institutes of Health Research, the Social Science and Humanities Research Council of Canada, and the Michael Smith Foundation for Health Research and by funds awarded to the Pittsburgh Mind-Body Center at the University of Pittsburgh and Carnegie Mellon University (NIH HL076852 and HL076858).

References

Atkinson, J. W. (1964). *An introduction to motivation*. Princeton, NJ: Van Nostrand.

Aviram, T. (2009). *Having goals or having purpose: Differential associations with age and quality of life in older adulthood* (Master's thesis). Concordia University, Montreal, QC, Canada.

Bandura, A. (1997). *Self-efficacy: The exercise of control*. New York, NY: Freeman.

Bauer, I. (2004). *Unattainable goals across adulthood and old age: Benefits of goal adjustment capacities on well-being* (Master's thesis). Concordia University, Montreal, QC, Canada.

Bauer, I., Wrosch, C., & Jobin, J. (2008). I'm better off than most other people: The role of social comparisons for coping with regret in young adulthood and old age. *Psychology and Aging, 23*, 800–811.

Brandtstädter, J., & Renner, G. (1990). Tenacious goal pursuit and flexible goal adjustment: Explication and age-related analysis of assimilative and accommodative strategies of coping. *Psychology and Aging, 5*, 58–67.

Brockner, J. (1992). The escalation of commitment to a failing course of action: Toward theoretical progress. *Academy of Management Review, 17*, 39–61.

Brun de Pontet, S., Wrosch, C., & Gagne, M. (2007). An exploration of the generational differences in levels of control held among family businesses approaching succession. *Family Business Review, 20*, 337–354.

Brun de Pontet, S., Wrosch, C., & Gagne, M. (2008). *Goal disengagement and retirement among family business owners approaching retirement age*. Unpublished manuscript, Concordia University, Montreal, QC, Canada.

Carver, C. S., & Scheier, M. F. (1981). *Attention and self-regulation: A control-theory approach to human behavior*. New York, NY: Springer Verlag.

Carver, C. S., & Scheier, M. F. (1990). Origins and functions of positive and negative affect: A control-process view. *Psychological Review, 97*, 19–35.

Carver, C. S., & Scheier, M. F. (1998). *On the self regulation of behavior*. New York, NY: Cambridge University Press.

Carver, C. S., & Scheier, M. F. (2000). Scaling back goals and recalibration of the affect system are aspects of normal adaptive self-regulation: Understanding "response shift" phenomena. *Social Science & Medicine, 50*, 1715–1722.

Cohen, S. (1996). Psychological stress, immunity, and upper respiratory infections. *Current Direction in Psychological Science, 5*, 86–89.

Dandona, P., Aljada, A., Chaudhuri, A., Mohanty, P., & Garg, R. (2005). Metabolic syndrome: A comprehensive perspective based on interactions between obesity, diabetes, and inflammation. *Circulation, 111*, 1448–1454.

Dickerson, S. S., & Kemeny, M. E. (2004). Acute stressors and cortisol responses: A theoretical integration and synthesis of laboratory research. *Psychological Bulletin, 130*, 355–391.

Duke, J., Leventhal, H., Brownlee, S., & Leventhal, E. A. (2002). Giving up and replacing activities in response to illness. *Journal of Gerontology: Psychological Sciences, 57B*, 367–376.

Dunne, E., Wrosch, C., & Miller, G. E. (2009). *Goal adjustment and depressive symptomatology: Reciprocal associations in the context of older adults' functional disability.* Manuscript submitted for publication.

Elliot, A. J., & Sheldon, K. M. (1997). Avoidance achievement motivation: A personal goal analysis. *Journal of Personality and Social Psychology, 73*, 171–185.

Emmons, R. A. (1986). Personal strivings: An approach to personality and subjective well-being. *Journal of Personality and Social Psychology, 51*, 1058–1068.

Feather, N. T. (Ed.). (1982). *Expectations and actions: Expectancy-value models in psychology*. Hillsdale, NJ: Erlbaum.

Goldberg, L. R. (1992). The development of markers for the Big-Five factor structure. *Psychological Assessment, 4*, 26–42.

Heckhausen, J. (1999). *Developmental regulation in adulthood.* New York, NY: Cambridge University Press.

Heckhausen, J., & Schulz, R. (1995). A life-span theory of control. *Psychological Review, 102*, 284–304.

Heckhausen, J., Wrosch, C., & Fleeson, W. (2001). Developmental regulation before and after passing a developmental deadline: The sample case of "biological clock" for child-bearing. *Psychology and Aging, 16*, 400–413.

Heckhausen, J., Wrosch, C., & Schulz, R. (2010). A motivational theory of lifespan development. *Psychological Review, 117*, 32–60.

Heim, C., Ehlert, U., & Hellhammer, D. (2000). The potential role of hypocortisolism in the pathophysiology of stress-related bodily disorders. *Psychoneuroendocrinology, 25*, 1–35.

Kiecolt-Glaser, J. K., McGuire, L., Robles, T., & Glaser, R. (2002). Emotions, morbidity, and mortality: New perspectives from psychoneuroimmunology. *Annual Review of Psychology*, 53, 83–107.

Klinger, E. (1975). Consequences of commitment to and disengagement from incentives. *Psychological Review, 82*, 1–25.

Klinger, E. (1977). *Meaning and void: Inner experience and the incentives in people's lives.* Minneapolis: University of Minnesota Press.

Kukla, A. (1972). Foundations of an attributional theory of performance. *Psychological Review, 79*, 454–470.

Lupien, S. J., de Leon, M., De Santi, S., Convit, A., Tarshish, C., Nair, N. P. V.,… Meaney, M. J. (1998). Cortisol levels during human aging predict hippocampal atrophy and memory deficits. *Nature Neuroscience, 1*, 69–73.

Markus, H., & Nurius, P. (1986). Possible selves. *American Psychologist, 41*, 954–969.

Matthews, K. M., Schwartz, J., Cohen, S., & Seeman, T. (2006). Diurnal cortisol decline is related to coronary calcification: CARDIA study. *Psychosomatic Medicine 68*, 657–661.

McEwen, B. S. (1998). Protective and damaging effects of stress mediators. *New England Journal of Medicine, 338*, 171–179.

Miller, G. A., Galanter, E., & Pribram, K. H. (1960). *Plans and the structure of behavior.* New York, NY: Holt, Rinehart, & Winston.

Miller, G. E., & Blackwell, E. (2006). Turn up the heat: Inflammation as a mechanism linking chronic stress, depression, and heart disease. *Current Directions in Psychological Science, 15*, 269–272.

Miller, G. E., Chen, E., & Zhou, E. S. (2007). If it goes up, must it come down? Chronic stress and the hypothalamic-pituitary-adrenocortical axis in humans. *Psychological Bulletin, 133*, 25–45.

Miller, G. E., Cohen, S., & Ritchey, A. K. (2002). Chronic psychological stress and the regulation of pro-inflammatory cytokines: A glucocorticoid resistance model. *Health Psychology, 21*, 531–541.

Miller, G. E., & Wrosch, C. (2007). You've gotta know when to fold 'em: Goal disengagement and systemic inflammation in adolescence. *Psychological Science, 18*, 773–777.

Nesse, R. M. (2000). Is depression an adaptation? *Archives of General Psychiatry, 57*, 14–20.

O'Connor, R. C., & Forgan, G. (2007). Suicidal thinking and perfectionism: The role of goal adjustment and behavioral inhibition/activation systems. *Journal of Rational-Emotive & Cognitive-Behavior Therapy* [Published online]. doi:10.1007/s10942-007-0057-2

Powers, W. T. (1973). *Behavior: The control of perception.* Chicago, IL: Aldine.

Pressman, S. D., & Cohen, S. (2005). Does positive affect influence health? *Psychological Bulletin, 131*, 925–971.

Ryff, C. D. (1989). Happiness is everything, or is it? Explorations on the meaning of psychological well-being. *Journal of Personality and Social Psychology*, 57, 1069–1081.

Scheier, M. F., & Carver, C. S. (2001). Adapting to cancer: The importance of hope and purpose. In A. Baum & B. L. Andersen (Eds.), *Psychosocial interventions for cancer* (pp. 15–36). Washington, DC: American Psychological Association.

Scheier, M. F., Wrosch, C., Baum, A., Cohen, S., Martire, L. M., Matthews, K. A.,... Zdaniuk, B. (2006). The Life Engagement Test: Assessing purpose in life. *Journal of Behavioral Medicine, 29*, 291–298.

Segerstrom, S. C., & Miller, G. E. (2004). Stress and the human immune system: A meta-analytic review of 30 years of inquiry. *Psychological Bulletin, 130*, 601–630.

Sephton, S. E., Sapolsky, R. M., Kraemer, H. C., & Spiegel, D. (2000). Diurnal cortisol rhythm as a predictor of breast cancer survival. *Journal of the National Cancer Institute, 92*, 994–1000.

Smyth, J. M., Ockenfels, M. C., Gorin, A. A., Catley, D., Porter, L. S., Kirschbaum, C.,... Stone, A. A. (1997). Individual differences in the diurnal cycle of cortisol. *Psychoneuroendocrinology, 22*, 89–105.

Sprangers, M. A. G., & Schwartz, C. E. (1999). Integrating response shift into health-related quality of life research: A theoretical model. *Social Science & Medicine, 48*, 1507–1515.

Taylor, S. E. (1991). Asymmetrical effects of positive and negative events: The mobilization–minimization hypothesis. *Psychological Bulletin, 110*, 67–85.

Tunali, B., & Power, T. G. (1993). Creating satisfaction: A psychological perspective on stress and coping in families of handicapped children. *Journal of Child Psychology and Psychiatry and Allied Disciplines, 34*, 945–957.

Vroom, V. H. (1964). *Work and motivation.* New York, NY: Wiley.

Ward, J. L. (1987). *Keeping the family business healthy*. San Francisco, CA: Jossey-Bass.

Willerson, J. T., & Ridker, P. M. (2004). Inflammation as a cardiovascular risk factor. *Circulation, 109*, 2–10.

Wright, R. A., & Brehm, J. W. (1989). Energization and goal attractiveness. In L. A. Pervin (Ed.), *Goal concepts in personality and social psychology* (pp. 169–210). Hillsdale, NJ: Erlbaum.

Wrosch, C., Bauer, I., Miller, G. E., & Lupien, S. (2007). Regret intensity, diurnal cortisol secretion, and physical health in older individuals: Evidence for directional effects and protective factors. *Psychology and Aging, 22*, 319–330.

Wrosch, C., Bauer, I., & Scheier, M. F. (2005). Regret and quality of life across the adult life span: The influence of disengagement and available future goals. *Psychology and Aging, 20*, 657–670.

Wrosch, C., Dunne, E., Scheier, M. F., & Schulz, R. (2006). Self-regulation of common age-related challenges: Benefits for older adults' psychological and physical health. *Journal of Behavioral Medicine, 29*, 299–306.

Wrosch, C., & Heckhausen, J. (1999). Control processes before and after passing a developmental deadline: Activation and deactivation of intimate relationship goals. *Journal of Personality and Social Psychology, 77*, 415–427.

Wrosch, C., & Heckhausen, J. (2002). Perceived control of life regrets: Good for young and bad for old adults. *Psychology and Aging, 17*, 340–350.

Wrosch, C., & Miller, G. E. (2009). Depressive symptoms can be useful: Self-regulatory and emotional benefits of dysphoric mood in adolescence. *Journal of Personality and Social Psychology, 96*, 1181–1190.

Wrosch, C., Miller, G. E., Scheier, M. F., & Brun de Pontet, S. (2007). Giving up on unattainable goals: Benefits for health? *Personality and Social Psychology Bulletin, 33*, 251–265.

Wrosch, C., & Scheier, M. F. (2007). *Goal disengagement, purpose in life, and distress among older adults*. Unpublished data, Concordia University.

Wrosch, C., Scheier, M. F., Carver, C. S., & Schulz, R. (2003). The importance of goal disengagement in adaptive self-regulation: When giving up is beneficial. *Self and Identity, 2*, 1–20.

Wrosch, C., Scheier, M. F., Miller, G. E., Schulz, R., & Carver, C. S. (2003). Adaptive self-regulation of unattainable goals: Goal disengagement, goal reengagement, and subjective well-being. *Personality and Social Psychology Bulletin, 29*, 1494–1508.

25
Pathways to Personal Transformation
Theoretical and Empirical Developments

RICHARD G. TEDESCHI and LAWRENCE G. CALHOUN

University of North Carolina at Charlotte

Personal transformations can be set in motion by intensely affective experiences that lead to revisions in the way individuals think of themselves, their worlds, the future, the universe and their place in it, human nature, good, and a variety of other matters. All of these diverse assumptions and beliefs are bound together in a narrative that can be revised at various times in life. Some experiences can challenge fundamental beliefs and the life narrative, and sometime those experiences can also produce major revisions of this narrative. What are the characteristics of these transformative experiences, and how do they change the sense of the meaning of one's life? We have focused much of our work on the power of intensely negative events to change the life narrative in ways that incorporate these events as turning points in life. Life narratives also change through other experiences, however, whether positive experiences, spiritual experiences, or something else. Those experiences that are designed to create changes (e.g., therapeutic encounters), those that contain some form of initiation (e.g., in military training, religious groups, youth gangs), or simple maturation may also produce positive change. In this chapter we will consider some of the similarities and differences among these kinds of transformations. We will focus on apparently positive transformations that yield more meaningful living, a sense of purpose, wisdom, or similarly described outcomes. But we recognize that experiences that lead to negative transformations (e.g., gang initiations) may have elements similar to those of the experiences that lead to positive transformations. In this chapter we will also add comments and suggestions regarding the current state and future of posttraumatic growth research.

Multiple Pathways to the Same Destination

Experiences that lead to positive transformation can have some degree of overlap. For example, military training might create a change in identity that is quite significant ("I am a soldier now") and be a first step toward a traumatizing combat experience. In an effort to cope, the soldier may receive some kind of healing response by becoming part of a religious group or entering psychotherapy. Positive experiences may be sought out and yet others are mixed with the negative experiences. A study of astronauts, for example, indicates that the experience of spaceflight produces positive outcomes similar to those reported by people who have endured negative experiences (Ihle, Ritsher, & Kanas, 2006). These astronauts took on personal challenges, discomfort, and danger in spaceflight, but it is unclear the degree to which they sought transformation or were even surprised by it. In contrast, people who enter psychotherapy and experience transformation may be open to change, even inviting it.

Transformative events seem to have in common an ability to challenge previously held views of one's life. Events can be defined as traumatic to the extent that these views are very strongly challenged or shaken and sometimes even shattered (Janoff-Bulman, 1992), and therapeutic changes are ushered in by challenging old ways of thinking and experiencing as well (the "corrective emotional experience"). Although cognitive therapies specifically focus on such changes in thinking, other forms of therapy also have this element to them. Spiritual or religious experiences can have an element of challenge, surprising people with a focus on sin or eternal love, salvation, or enlightenment. Military organizations can also emphasize some of the same focus on personal shortcomings and weaknesses, offering an opportunity to grow stronger, better, and be protected. Important interpersonal relationships (McMillen, 2004) and normative developmental processes (Aldwin & Levenson, 2004) may also serve as the impetus for personal growth. These different catalysts for growth are not mutually exclusive. People change in striking, transformative ways after trauma, but also after other kinds of experiences, and usually there are overlaps among these experiences. Still, we wonder if the changes wrought by trauma are similar to or different from personal growth that is a response to other life experiences.

The Struggle With Trauma as an Agent of Positive Change

Our work on posttraumatic growth has led us to continually revise our original model (Calhoun & Tedeschi, 2004, 2006; Tedeschi & Calhoun, 1995), and so currently (Calhoun, Cann, & Tedeschi, 2010) we argue for the interplay of several classes of variables as potentially central in the likelihood of posttraumatic growth developing after trauma. These variables include, among others, (a) cognitive processing, engagement, or rumination; (b) expression or disclosure of concerns surrounding traumatic events; (c) reactions of others to self-disclosures; (d) sociocultural context in which traumas occur and attempts to process, disclose, and resolve take place; (e) survivors' personal dispositions and the degree of resilience; and (6) degree to which events allow for the above processes to occur, or the degree to which events suppress them. We have also been examining the degree to which the domains of posttraumatic growth, as defined by the Posttraumatic Growth Inventory (PTGI; Taku, Cann, Calhoun, & Tedeschi, 2008; Tedeschi & Calhoun, 1996), occur cross-culturally and the possibility that these different domains of growth might also be associated with somewhat different processes. Finally, we have been interested in the degree to which posttraumatic growth is an ongoing process, what happens to people who report such growth after a long period of time, and how it may be associated with tendencies toward wisdom, satisfaction with life, and sense of purpose. Considering such positive aspects of living also suggests, however, that there are positive experiences that may be involved in producing such changes.

To What Degree Do People Attribute Growth to Highly Stressful Events as Opposed to Positive Experiences?

The PTGI (Tedeschi & Calhoun, 1996) and similar instruments (Joseph, Williams, & Yule, 1993; Park, Cohen, & Murch, 1996) that measure growth in the aftermath of challenging, negative events have been questioned as perhaps biasing respondents to exaggerate growth, since most of the inventories ask only about positive changes (Tomich & Helgeson, 2004; Park & Lechner, 2006). The kinds of experiences assessed by the PTGI may be found in people who are living through normative or positive experiences as well (Aldwin & Levenson, 2004). In attempts to address these different issues, researchers have created versions of the PTGI that add items that ask about negative changes in the aftermath of events (Baker, Kelly, Calhoun, Cann, & Tedeschi, 2008; Gottlieb, Still, & Newby-Clark, 2007). In one study (Gottlieb et al., 2007), young adults were asked about personal changes as measured by the PTGI and about "declines" that were mirror images of the PTGI items. In two studies reported by Baker et al. (2008), participants were asked to report both growth and "depreciation." For the Gottlieb et al. (2007) study, participants could attribute changes to negative events, positive events, or ongoing experiences that could not be classed as discrete events. In the Baker et al. studies, participants were asked to focus on the consequences of specific negative events. In both reports, positive changes were reported much more often than negative changes. Gottlieb et al. reported that growth was attributed to a variety of events and nonevents, whereas declines were attributed more uniformly to negative events.

Another recent study (Grubbs, 2006) asked participants to focus on either highly positive or highly negative life events to report growth on the PTGI. Both groups reported similar levels of growth. The positive-events group showed no relationship between growth and the amount of rumination about the event, but the negative events group did. The process by which positive events lead to reports of growth, then, may differ from the process for highly stressful, negative life events. This interpretation certainly makes intuitive sense because psychological distress may play a significant role in posttraumatic growth. Without distress to fuel attempts to change, what might be happening when persons confront positive events? Further, are there differences in processing and growth among events, positive or negative, that are attributed to one's own actions, those of others, or chance?

Are There Varying Routes to Posttraumatic Growth?

Our evolving model of posttraumatic growth (Calhoun et al., 2010) emphasizes cognitive-emotional processes that require people who have suffered trauma to navigate a difficult path to rebuilding a shattered assumptive world. This process has been described exquisitely by Janoff-Bulman (1992), who has proposed three posttraumatic growth processes: strength through suffering, existential reevaluation, and psychological preparedness (2006). The latter emphasizes the strength of the rebuilt assumptive world to withstand future shocks to the system, an inoculation of sorts that we have described with a metaphor of how communities rebuild stouter structures in the aftermath of earthquakes (Calhoun & Tedeschi, 1998). Work by Lykins, Segerstrom, Averill, Evans, and Kemeny (2007) suggests that processing that elicits posttraumatic growth may vary according to qualities of the goals individuals have. Their studies show that persons with intrinsic goals (e.g., building interpersonal relationships, improving the world), as opposed to extrinsic goals (e.g., making money, improving one's appearance), maintained their intrinsic goals when asked to reflect on their own deaths, whereas persons with extrinsic goals shifted toward more intrinsic goals after being exposed to a mortality-salience manipulation that was less emotionally challenging than the death reflection condition. Movement toward growth appears to be an interaction between tendencies toward more mature existential approaches to living and kinds of emotional-cognitive processing.

Another area of research that is relevant to cognitive processing that may produce the highest levels of personal growth includes the study of life transitions (Bauer & McAdams, 2004). A sample of people who had been through career or religious changes described their experiences, and the themes in their stories were classified. The classification reflected either intrinsic versus integrative themes (feeling better about one's life vs. thinking more complexly about one's life) and agentic versus communal themes (individual vs. collective aspects of personal growth). Persons who had the highest levels of ego development and well-being were in the minority, but they were characterized by life transition stories that emphasized integrative and intrinsic themes—what they had learned about important personal concerns as opposed to just learning anything or having a personally meaningful experience. In addition, the people with high levels of ego development also emphasized integrative and communal themes, that is, gaining new perspectives on personal relationships as opposed to just learning more or feeling better about themselves. A focus on learning about close relationships appeared to yield the best outcomes. Again, we may be seeing an interaction between individual characteristics and processing of experiences that lead to different levels of growth.

Personal characteristics may interact with posttraumatic growth (Norlander, von Schedvin, & Archer, 2005). A group of police officers and food product workers, men who were mostly in their 30s, were asked to report on the most negative event they had experienced in the past 10 years. Using a typology based on positive and negative affect, the researchers found that persons reporting both high positive and high negative affect also reported higher scores on the PTGI domains, except for spiritual growth, than did persons with low positive affect, or persons with high positive affect but low negative affect, who were intermediate scorers. Members of the latter group were labeled "self-actualizers" and appeared to be a resilient group that was able to recover well, without showing much growth. It appears that negative affect allows for the distress that we have cited as an impetus for growth (Tedeschi & Calhoun, 1995), whereas positive affect allows for some positive changes that contributes to posttraumatic growth. Indeed, measures of receptiveness to change and level of stress were both high for the high positive and negative affect group. According to our model, this is the fertile ground for growth.

Of interest are the studies by Bauer and McAdams (2004) and Lykins et al. (2007), which may or may not be studies of posttraumatic growth. Lykins et al. (2007) used an experimental manipulation where people were to imagine dying in a fire, and the transition stories recounted by the participants in the Bauer and McAdams (2004) study may not have been particularly traumatic. So we do not know the extent to which the results apply to people in real-life circumstances that are significantly distressing. The researchers suggest processes that may be operating among persons in the aftermath of trauma, but we cannot be sure. Their results may apply to growth processes that are operating in less stressful circumstances.

Constellations and Patterns of Posttraumatic Growth

Although inventories of growth tend to assess more than one dimension, the modal way of assessing stress-related growth has been to rely on the total score of the measure used. This formula has been, and continues to be, an important approach to employing quantitative summaries in order to conduct specific tests of hypotheses. Although available inventories appear to cover well the kinds of growth most typically reported by persons who have faced major life crises, it is not possible for one single, reasonably short inventory to cover all the possible positive changes experienced by all persons, given the wide array of tragedies and difficulties that human beings can encounter (McMillen, 2004; Park & Lechner, 2006).

An interesting additional area for investigation lies in examining the possible patterns and constellations of posttraumatic growth. One clear suggestion is the increased utilization of the factor scores, going beyond the simple reliance on total scores. As we can attest, it is often simpler and easier to use a single score of growth than to use multiple scores, and practical circumstances can place limitations on the feasibility of conducting statistical analyses with multiple scores rather than just one. But now seems to be the time to move to the next step of investigating subsets of posttraumatic growth, that is, to use multiple scores and not always rely on a single summary total score.

In a similar vein, it may be time to begin the search for constellations and patterns of growth that may tend to occur within populations facing similar challenges, attempting to identify stable patterns that tend to occur across problems and perhaps across populations and cultures. It does seem to be the case that the particular way in which the constellation of posttraumatic growth is manifested can be different for different persons. A report that gives insight into this pattern involves a study of family members who lost loved ones in a mine explosion (Davis, Wohl, & Verberg, 2007). The families participated in structured interviews eight years after their losses. Responses to open-ended questions selected a priori were coded by two of the experts conducting the investigation. Through the use of a particular statistical methodology, the researchers reduced the responses to three clusters of postloss experiences. One group was described as having been able to make sense of the loss, to report a benefit or gain (e.g., a change in public policy), to have experienced an increase in inner strength, to have "learned about themselves" (p. 704); but members of this group also tended to report the loss of something central to their lives. A second group reported that "nothing good had come" from the event; members of this group had not thought much about making sense or finding meaning in the loss, but they reported that "their philosophy of life had changed for the better" (p. 705). The third cluster of responses was characterized by having found no meaning in the loss, a philosophy of life changed for the worse, the loss of some assumptions related to the world as being just, and the view that "nothing good had come" (p. 705) from the loss. Although Davis et al. (2007) do not characterize their findings in this way, it seems that the first two clusters include elements of posttraumatic growth, but the third contains no evidence of any kind of growth. An interesting component of these findings is that only individuals whose responses were grouped in the third cluster reported a philosophy of life changed for the worse. Conversely, the proportion of reports of a positive change in philosophy of life was higher in the first two groups than in the third. Because the clusters were derived from questions selected in advance, it is not clear to what extent the responses, and consequently the clusters, represent what might have occurred naturally. Nonetheless, this study and its findings provide an intriguing suggestion for much additional investigation. For example, when growth is experienced in the aftermath of major loss, what are patterns, constellations, or clusters that best describe the experience?

Posttraumatic Growth and the Influence of the Immediate Sociocultural Context

One simple question about patterns of posttraumatic growth is the degree to which statistically based groupings of inventory items, originally developed with samples comprised primarily of North American young adults, are representative of the response patterns of persons in stable different samples, even across different national and cultural groups. Results from Australia (Morris, Shakespeare-Finch, Rieck, & Newbery, 2005) and a Spanish-speaking sample from the Americas (Weiss & Berger, 2006) suggest that the five factors originally reported for the PTGI tend to represent growth in those populations as well. However, results from a sample of young persons in Japan showed a four-factor solution in which Appreciation for Life and Spiritual Change merged into a single factor (Taku et al., 2007).

These various findings suggest two general possibilities for the experience in different cultural contexts. From the limited evidence so far, it does seem that there is some degree of commonality in the experience of posttraumatic growth across different national and cultural samples. But it is also clear that between large national and cultural groups, there may be differences in the ways in which growth from the struggle with crisis is experienced.

The behavior of individuals does not occur in a social vacuum. Yet it is quite interesting to witness the degree to which psychology, particularly the clinical and counseling areas, appears only recently to have discovered the important influence of culture, group membership, and other sociocultural variables. This inclusion of broader sociocultural variables in attempts to understand the experience of individuals is a welcome renaissance in the field. As with all other kinds of human experience, posttraumatic growth occurs in the context of macro, distal levels of social influences (Brofenbrenner, 1979), such as the common mass media of modern Western societies, and perhaps more important, in the context of such proximate, micro social influences as the family, neighborhood, local religious center, and the individual's other multiple primary reference groups. Another needed next step in the study of posttraumatic growth, as well as of the experience of the search for meaning in specific life crises, is to begin to systematically examine how these factors may be at play. We (e.g., Calhoun et al., 2010) and others (e.g., Wortman, 2004) have made some beginning suggestions regarding this possibility. The investigation of proximate sociocultural factors should include the interplay of the individual's desire and interest to disclose his or her experience with major stressors (especially growth themes), the process by which disclosure tends to occur, the form it takes, the responses of the proximate groups that have significant social influence over the individual, and the complex, mutual influence of these factors.

When We Study Posttraumatic Growth to What Degree Are We Studying Normative Development?

As is the case with many studies in psychology and related disciplines, in studies of posttraumatic growth the participants are often university students. Although evidence shows that these students are much like their adult counterparts in terms of experiences of traumatic events (Vrana & Lauterbach, 1994), these student populations may be unique in other ways that affect our findings. Arnett (2000) has suggested that in Western countries, the ages 18 to 25 mark a time of "emerging adulthood" that includes experiences and personal projects that are quite distinct from other times in life. Some of the aspects of emerging adulthood seem to be particularly salient for studies of trauma response and certainly for personal growth. Arnett states that at this time in life, "independent exploration of life's possibilities is greater for most people than it will be at any other period of the life course" (p. 469). What matters most to this age group is the development of character and self-sufficiency, especially accepting responsibility and making independent decisions. Explorations of identity and the changes in worldviews are also central to this time in life. Reexamining beliefs and values is important for both the college educated and those who are not. If Arnett's speculations are accurate, when we investigate growth in the aftermath of traumatic events in this college-age population, we may be assessing both posttraumatic changes and normal developmental processes. Perhaps these participants in our studies will be experiencing a baseline level of growth that is quite high. To what extent will they attribute their growth to trauma or other events, or to a developmental process they may be aware of? Still, the processes of change and growth may be similar across different age groups, but we should carefully look at what happens when traumatic events are experienced by persons who are relatively inexperienced in living, though most open to change, versus persons with more experience, but for whom change may be more threatening to established life investments in relationships, beliefs, and identity. This period of emerging adulthood may also be a time when people are developing coping strategies, given the need to develop self-responsibility and self-sufficiency. But the data indicate that there may be a decrease in negative coping strategies with little increase in positive ones (Aldwin, 2007). A close look at the details of how "emerging adults" handle particularly salient positive experiences and negative ones may help us understand the significant growth that is associated with this time of life. It is particularly telling that most of our military personnel are in this age group.

Fortunately, there are now many studies of posttraumatic growth in which the participants were not university or college students but adults older than traditional university age and dealing with a wide array of life challenges. Similar results and patterns of findings have been found in those studies as well (Val & Linley, 2006). So the concern about the confounding of posttraumatic changes with normal developmental changes seems to be assuaged, at least in part, by the broad pattern of findings with many different populations.

Individuals do indeed change as the result of development over the life span, and so the concern that normal development and posttraumatic growth may sometimes be difficult, if not impossible, to disentangle is a legitimate point of concern and research attention.

Growth by Every Other Name

Given that we coined the term *posttraumatic growth* (Tedeschi & Calhoun, 1996), we of course tend to prefer to use it to label the positive change experienced as the result of the struggle with major life challenges. A closely related expression, and one we believe also captures a similar phenomenon is *stress-related growth*. Even here, there may be differences in the pathways to growth if we take the terms literally. Trauma and stress are not the same. Experiences can be stressful without being traumatic, and stressful experiences may produce growth through somewhat different routes than trauma. The literature in this general area of investigation includes a wide variety of labels, with somewhat similar meanings, for example, *perceived benefits, construing benefits, positive by-products, thriving, positive reinterpretation, strength from adversity, discovery of meaning*, and *transformational coping*. Semantically, all these terms appear to be describing something similar. Maybe they are, and maybe they are not.

There is evidence to indicate that at least in some situations, measures designed to assess, for example, benefit finding and posttraumatic growth do not evidence the same relationships with other variables (Sears, Stanton, & Danoff-Burg, 2003). Compounding the potential errors of treating as similar the findings from studies that use different measures to assess similar sounding, but possibly different concepts is the reality that even when the same label, and presumably the same construct, is used, different researchers sometimes employ their own items to assess the phenomenon in question. So, what steps might be taken to help bring clarity and increased precision to the complicated matrix of different names for the same thing and different measures given the same label?

One step is to ensure that measures used to assess the phenomenon of interest in the domain of growth have very good reliability and at least some indication of validity. This step might, of course, mean that encouraging research in this area may be useful, to the extent that is quantitative, to rely on established measures of posttraumatic and stress-related growth and to discourage, for now, the use of items generated for use in individual studies but not used before. Relying on established measures and discouraging items generated for individual studies is an important step unless, of course, the items used can be shown to have good psychometric properties, which would include some evidence of validity as well.

Another step, to ensure that what is being measured is indeed the construct implied by the label, is to include more than one measure of the phenomenon of interest, and at least one of the measures should be one of the established and widely used instruments designed to assess growth. This suggestion also implies that the sole reliance on small sets of items, designed ad hoc for individual studies, without the inclusion of established inventories of growth is much less desirable or useful than it was in the early days of work in this area (Tedeschi, Calhoun, & Cann, 2007).

A third step, perhaps more in the aesthetic preference domain but relevant nevertheless, is to take into consideration the connotation of the label chosen to describe the positive changes associated with the struggle with trauma. Not surprisingly, researchers who tend to be skeptical about the reality of these experiences tend to select names that imply doubt or suspicion about the veracity of the experience, for example, *perceived benefits*, *construed benefits*, and the like (e.g., Frazier et al., 2009). Yet, researchers who tend to assume that such reports have some validity, or at least that the particular construction made by the survivor of the stressor should be respected, tend to prefer such terms as *posttraumatic growth*, *stress-related growth*, or *positive changes in outlook* (for more discussion about measurement and validity issues, see Aspinwall & Tedeschi, 2010; Park & Lechner, 2006; and Tedeschi & Calhoun, 2004). Scholars who are newly drawn to this area might do well to give consideration to which of these domains are more congruent with their own experiences, preferences, and biases and to select the label, construct, and measures that most clearly fit with their investigation's purpose.

So Is Posttraumatic Growth Different and United or Not?

At this point in time, our views about posttraumatic growth, as explained here, are based on studies concluded and published, as well as our own intuitive sense developed from talking in depth with many persons who describe this phenomenon in clinical settings. At the most fundamental level, or the core of personality, there is a tendency toward survival, enhancement, and growth, as Rogers (1961) described. But there is also a conservative tendency expressed in the struggle to defend one's preexisting constructs or views of the world—"hostility," as Kelly (1969) described, but what we label here as a tendency toward stability. It seems that unfettered movement toward change is not necessarily constructive. Certain purposes and understandings of life might be best maintained despite the challenges of unfortunate events. When these understandings and purposes approach wisdom, they tend more and more toward stability, no matter what the life circumstances might be. We will discuss further where wisdom fits in shortly.

All life events are being cognitively and emotionally processed with these competing motives influencing the interpretation of the events, as well as the broader context in which they are embedded, and the person experiencing them. Experienced events can be routine, or not, positive and desired, or not, planned or not. When events experienced are traumatic, events are unusual, negative, and unplanned. All this produces a great emotional challenge: sadness, fear, anger, and other negative affects. As a result, the relatively balanced system of growth versus stability is disrupted, but the competing motives toward growth and stability are still operating.

Personal characteristics, especially openness to experience and extraversion, will influence the degree to which growth is part of the posttrauma reports of trauma survivors. This is because the characteristics of openness and extraversion lead to tendencies toward certain coping patterns that are generally approach oriented rather than avoidant, in terms of cognitive processing and behavior patterns. It also appears that some degree of positive and negative affect is necessary in order to experience an event as truly distressing, whereas being able to have energy and relief from despair enables a person to continue to use approach coping strategies. Also to be considered are developmental aspects, that is, the degree to which a person is experiencing trauma at a time in life when change and insight are valued or not. These aspects also determine the degree to which a person approaches or avoids cognitive processing of the trauma and its aftermath and engages in behavior that tends to be prosocial. We have also posited early on (Tedeschi & Calhoun, 1995) that persons in the moderate range of psychological adjustment would show most growth compared to those who struggle with managing negative events and those who have already reached levels of insight, understanding, and prosocial behavior that withstand the onslaught of trauma (i.e., those who are wise).

So, fundamentally, posttraumatic growth is an extension of a system of basic motives, individual differences, and coping tendencies that are constantly in use. In this sense, posttraumatic growth is not a special case of how people live life. By definition, however, trauma is an extraordinary experience, and so there are clearly distinctive aspects of this experience as well that derive from the emotionality of it and the challenge to schemas or constructs. There are also varying domains of posttraumatic growth that may respond in distinctive ways. Spiritual change, for example, may not follow the same psychological pathway as developing new possibilities for one's life or discovering personal strength.

In recent years, social scientists have shown increasing interest in delineating core virtues (Dahlsgaard, Peterson, & Seligman, 2005), altruism (Staub, 2005), wisdom (Glück & Baltes, 2006; Linley, 2003; Schwartz & Sharpe, 2006; Webster, 2007), and related constructs (Ryan & Deci, 2001). We view posttraumatic growth as a process that can lead people to these places. Once people achieve these insights into living, develop their character, and behave according to these principles, a stability in personality is achieved. Further growth is incremental. On the road to wisdom and virtue, trauma can be a provocateur. We consistently hear from trauma survivors who have been provoked to growth by their experiences that they are quite aware that previous views of life seem shallow to them. So, in our growth toward meaningful, wise living, traumas can serve the purpose of the crystallization of discontent that Baumeister (1991) describes as provoking changes in meaning, or of the chaotic cognition noted by Finke and Bettle (1996), or of the cusp catastrophe that Carver (1998) applies to these situations. All these constructs are variations on the concepts of shattering of world assumptions from Janoff-Bulman's (1992) theory or our seismic metaphor for growth (Calhoun & Tedeschi, 1998). In all cases, theorists are saying that trauma is so disruptive to the way we feel, think, and live that those individuals who can learn, and still have a lot to learn, are provoked to greater meaning, wisdom, and virtue. Meanwhile, those individuals who have already learned, one way or another, say, "Yes, I am aware of all that, and life is meaningful nonetheless."

References

Aldwin, C. M. (2007). *Stress, coping and development* (2nd ed.). New York, NY: Guilford Press.

Aldwin, C. M., & Levenson, M. R. (2004). Posttraumatic growth: A developmental perspective. *Psychological Inquiry, 15*, 19–22.

Arnett, J. (2000). Emerging adulthood: A theory of development from the late teens through the twenties. *American Psychologist, 55*, 469–480.

Aspinwall, L. G., & Tedeschi, R. G. (2010). Of babies and bathwater: A reply to Coyne and Tennen's views on positive psychology and health. *Annals of Behavioral Medicine, 39*, 27–34.

Baker, J. M., Kelly, C., Calhoun, L. G., Cann, A., & Tedeschi, R. G. (2008). An examination of posttraumatic growth and posttraumatic depreciation: Two exploratory studies. *Journal of Loss and Trauma, 13*, 450–465.

Bauer, J. J., & McAdams, D. P. (2004). Personal growth in adults' stories of life transitions. *Journal of Personality, 72*, 573–602.

Baumeister, R. F. (1991). *Meanings of life*. New York, NY: Guilford Press.

Brofenbrenner, U. (1979). *The ecology of human development: Experiments by nature and design*. Cambridge, MA: Harvard University Press.

Calhoun, L.G., Cann, A., & Tedeschi, R. G. (2010). The posttraumatic growth model: Socio-cultural considerations. In T. Weiss & R. Berger, (Eds.), *Posttraumatic growth and culturally competent practice: Lessons learned from around the globe* (pp. 1–14). New York, NY: Wiley.

Calhoun, L. G., & Tedeschi, R. G. (1998). Posttraumatic growth: Future directions. In R. G. Tedeschi, C. L. Park, & L. G. Calhoun (Eds.), *Posttraumatic growth: Positive changes in the aftermath of crisis* (pp. 215–238). Mahwah, NJ: Erlbaum.

Calhoun, L. G., & Tedeschi, R. G. (2004). The foundations of posttraumatic growth: New considerations. *Psychological Inquiry, 15*, 93–102.

Calhoun, L. G., & Tedeschi, R. G. (2006). The foundations of posttraumatic growth: An expanded framework. In L. G. Calhoun & R. G. Tedeschi, (Eds.), *Handbook of posttraumatic growth* (pp. 1–23). Mahwah, NJ: Erlbaum.

Carver, C. S. (1998). Resilience and thriving: Issues, models, and linkages. *Journal of Social Issues, 54*, 245–266.
Dahlsgaard, K., Peterson, C., & Seligman, M. (2005). Shared virtue: The convergence of valued human strengths across culture and history. *Review of General Psychology, 9*(3), 203–213.
Davis, C. G., Wohl, M. J. A., & Verberg, N. (2007). Profiles of posttraumatic growth following an unjust loss. *Death Studies*, 31, 693–712.
Finke, R. A., & Bettle, J. (1996). *Chaotic cognition*. Mahwah, NJ: Erlbaum.
Frazier, P., Tennen, H., Gavian, M., Park, C., Tomich, P., & Tashiro, T. (2009). Does self-reported posttraumatic growth reflect genuine positive change? *Psychological Science, 20*, 912–919.
Glück, J., & Baltes, P. (2006). Using the concept of wisdom to enhance the expression of wisdom knowledge: Not the philosopher's dream but differential effects of developmental preparedness. *Psychology and Aging, 21*(4), 679–690.
Gottlieb, B. H., Still, E., & Newby-Clark, I. A. (2007). Types and precipitants of growth and decline in emerging adulthood. *Journal of Adolescent Research, 22*, 132–155.
Grubbs, A. (2006). Highly positive and highly negative life events: A comparison between their processes and outcomes (Unpublished master's thesis). University of North Carolina, Charlotte.
Ihle, E., Ritsher, J., & Kanas, N. (2006). Positive psychological outcomes of spaceflight: An empirical study. *Aviation, Space, and Environmental Medicine, 77*, 93–101.
Janoff-Bulman, R. (1992). *Shattered assumptions*. New York, NY: Free Press.
Janoff-Bulman, R. (2006). Schema-change perspectives on posttraumatic growth. In L. G. Calhoun & R. G. Tedeschi, (Eds.), *Handbook of posttraumatic growth: Research and practice* (pp. 47–67). Mahwah, NJ: Erlbaum.
Joseph, S., Williams, R., & Yule, W. (1993). Changes in outlook following disaster: Preliminary development of a measure to assess positive and negative responses. *Journal of Traumatic Stress, 6*, 271–279.
Kelly, G. (1969). *Clinical psychology and personality: The selected papers of George Kelly* (Brendan Maher, Ed.). New York, NY: Wiley.
Linley, P. A. (2003). Positive adaptation to trauma: Wisdom as both process and outcome. *Journal of Traumatic Stress, 16*, 601–610
Lykins, E., Segerstrom, S., Averill, A., Evans, D., & Kemeny, M. (2007). Goal shifts following reminders of mortality: Reconciling posttraumatic growth and terror management theory. *Personality and Social Psychology Bulletin, 33*(8), 1088–1099.
McMillen, J. C. (2004). Posttraumatic growth: What's it all about? *Psychological Inquiry, 15*, 48–52.
Morris, B. A., Shakespeare-Finch, J., Rieck, M., & Newbery, J. (2005). Multidimensional nature of posttraumatic growth in an Australian population. *Journal of Traumatic Stress, 18*, 575–585.
Norlander, T., von Schedvin, H., & Archer, T. (2005). Thriving as a function of affective personality: Relation to personality factors, coping strategies and stress. *Anxiety, Stress, and Coping, 18*, 105–116.
Park, C. L., Cohen, L., & Murch, R. (1996). Assessment and prediction of stress-related growth. *Journal of Personality, 64*, 645–658.
Park, C. L., & Lechner, S. (2006). Measurement issues in assessing growth following stressful life experiences. In L. G. Calhoun & R. G. Tedeschi (Eds.), *Handbook of posttraumatic growth: Research and practice* (pp. 47–67). Mahwah, NJ: Erlbaum.
Rogers, C. R. (1961). *On becoming a person*. Boston, MA: Houghton Mifflin.
Ryan, R., & Deci, E. (2001). On happiness and human potentials: A review of research on hedonic and eudaimonic well-being. *Annual Review of Psychology, 52*, 141–166.

Schwartz, B., & Sharpe, K. (2006). Practical wisdom: Aristotle meets positive psychology. *Journal of Happiness Studies, 7*(3), 377–395.

Sears, S. R., Stanton, A. L., & Danoff-Burg, S. (2003). The yellow brick road and the emerald city: Benefit-finding, positive reappraisal coping, and posttraumatic growth in women with early-stage breast cancer. *Health Psychology, 22*, 487–497.

Staub, E. (2005). *The roots of goodness: The fulfillment of basic human needs and the development of caring, helping and nonaggression, inclusive caring, moral courage, active bystandership, and altruism born of suffering*. Lincoln: University of Nebraska Press.

Taku, K., Calhoun, L. G., Tedeschi, R. G., Gil-Rivas, V., Kilmer, R. P., & Cann, A. (2007). Examining posttraumatic growth among Japanese university students. *Anxiety, Stress & Coping, 20*, 353–367.

Taku, K., Cann, A., Calhoun, L. G., & Tedeschi, R. G. (2008). The factor structure of the Posttraumatic Growth Inventory: A comparison of five models using confirmatory factor analysis. *Journal of Traumatic Stress, 21*, 158–164.

Tedeschi, R. G., & Calhoun, L. G. (1995). *Trauma and transformation*. Thousand Oaks, CA: Sage.

Tedeschi, R. G., & Calhoun, L. G. (1996). The posttraumatic growth inventory: Measuring the positive legacy of trauma. *Journal of Traumatic Stress, 9*, 455–471.

Tedeschi, R. G., & Calhoun, L. G. (2004). Posttraumatic growth: Conceptual foundations and empirical evidence. *Psychological Inquiry, 15*, 93–102.

Tedeschi, R., Calhoun, L., & Cann, A. (2007). Evaluating resource gain: Understanding and misunderstanding posttraumatic growth. *Applied Psychology: An International Review, 56*, 396–406.

Tomich, P. L., & Helgeson, V. S. (2004). Is finding something good in the bad always good? Benefit finding among women with breast cancer. *Health Psychology, 23*, 16–23.

Val, E. B., & Linley, P. A. (2006). Posttraumatic growth, positive changes, and negative changes in Madrid residents following the March 11, 2004, Madrid train bombings. *Journal of Loss and Trauma, 11*, 409–424.

Vrana, S., & Lauterbach, D. (1994). Prevalence of traumatic events and post-traumatic psychological symptoms in a nonclinical sample of college students. *Journal of Traumatic Stress, 7*, 289–302.

Webster, J. (2007). Measuring the character strength of wisdom. *International Journal of Aging & Human Development, 65*(2), 163–183.

Weiss, T., & Berger, R. (2006). Reliability and validity of a Spanish version of the Posttraumatic Growth Inventory. *Research on Social Work Practice, 16*, 191–199.

Wortman, C. B. (2004). Posttraumatic growth: Progress and problems. *Psychological Inquiry, 15*, 81–90.

26

The Human Heart or Recovering the Meaning of Life

A Theory Integrating Sexuality, Meaning of Life, and Sense of Coherence Applied in Holistic Therapy

SØREN VENTEGODT

Quality of Life Research Center

JOAV MERRICK

Ministry of Social Affairs and Social Services

A person who experiences life as depleted of meaning will most often have little energy, show little motivation for acting, lack libido and love, and have little interest in the outer world. Of interest to researchers is that this person can have what seems to be a perfectly normal health, both mentally and physically. The loss of meaning of life is a hidden killer; it is like a worm eating the apple from within. A total loss of meaning always signifies a major life crisis or even a life coming soon to its end, but most often meaning of life is only partially lost. This partial loss is really much more tricky than a total loss because people set up mental defenses that hinder them from noticing the loss. After a while, the lack of meaning of life will be materialized in poor quality of life, mental and somatic symptoms, including depression or pain, and reduced ability to function sexually, socially, and in work. When carefully examined in the holistic clinic, most patients evidence a problem with their meaning of life; so, in this area much work can be done, greatly benefiting the patients.

Current Practice

If a patient with compromised meaning of life goes to the physician, a careful examination will show the triad of poor health, low quality of life, and poor functioning ability in all or most of life's aspects. Because contemporary biomedical physicians are not trained to examine the state of a patient's existential core, they will fail to observe the patient's reduced degree of experienced meaning of life. Contemporary physicians will start to treat the patient, looking at one symptom at a time, and may prescribe pain killers, antidepressant drugs, Viagra, and the like.

This procedure most unfortunately hides the real reason for all the patient's problems, and so the patient now start to believe that he or she has medical problems, not existential ones. This situation is really very sad because most often the existential problems will remain unsolved for decades to come while the patient continues to try out all kinds of drugs on the market, none of which will solve his or her problems. The troublesome triad of health, quality-of-life, and ability problems will continue; perhaps the drugs will work a little, but they will never make up for the patient's general lack of motivation, libido, and personal energy.

If the physician and his or her patient understood better the cause of the poor state of being, the cure could in principle be simple: to recover the patient's basic meaning of life. Although a growing fraction of medical physicians are becoming aware of quality-of-life and existential issues these days, they can be of little help without proper theory and tools for helping. At most, their awareness often ends with an encouraging remark: "You should go and find some reason to be here. Look deep into your purpose of life!" Many young people follow this advice and go on vision quests with Native Americans; enter monasteries in Tibet, Japan, and Thailand; join men's development groups; take courses in meditation, Tantra, and yoga; perhaps experiment with mind-expanding drugs; and so forth. Reading books and talking honestly with friends, which might be the best solutions, is not that popular. The route to understanding life is often long and arduous, and if the medical physician were better prepared, many years of suffering could be avoided.

In existential therapy (Yalom, 1980, 2002) there are both theory and practical therapeutic tools for recovering the patient's mission in life (Ventegodt, 2003; Ventegodt, Andersen, & Merrick, 2003a, 2003b, 2003c; Vendegot & Merrick, 2003; Ventegodt, Flensborg-Madsen, Andersen, & Merrick, 2005; Ventegodt, Kroman, Andersen, & Merrick, 2004). But often this kind of therapy is both expensive and time consuming, and many times the patient is not much better even after numerous hours of hard work in therapy. If the physician convinces the patient that the cure is to be found in a long therapeutic process, the patient's sense of autonomy can be damaged, making the patient dependent on therapy in the same way he or she might become dependent on drugs or medicine.

The best way to help someone having little meaning of life is to give that person an exact understanding of the nature of the problem. When this can be done, the responsibility for the patient's life will be placed on the patient's shoulders. If the patient chooses to undergo therapy, which is only one route of many possible, the therapist is merely the patient's tool for recovering, and the patient is most likely to recover.

Contemporary Psychodynamic Models

In order to assist a patient in recovering his or her meaning of life, it is necessary for the physician to understand how the experience of meaning of life is related to the internal psychic and energetic structure of a human being, and how life meaning is lost and recovered.

Given that the structure of human existence is primarily an area for qualitative research, a theory of meaning of life is most likely to be a product of the researcher's conscious constructs. Nevertheless, much quantitative research has been conducted lately on the experience of quality of life, which is closely connected to the meaning of life (Ventegodt, 1995, 1996; Ventegodt, Flensborg-Madsen, Andersen, Nielsen, et al., 2005). The meaning of life is more difficult to measure and quantify than is quality of life because normal people do not have an existential philosophy of life that defines their possible experiences of positive meaning of life and thus their loss of this meaning. When you do not know what is possible for you to feel existentially, you can hardly rate your present experience on a relevant rating scale. Still, you can talk about it; and when doing so, you will carry the quality of your present being to the listener, who can experience you and your state of existence.

The interpretation of the human psyche and its structure has been a great research objective in the Western tradition since the work of Freud (Jones, 1961), Jung (1964), and Reich (1969), but before them these matters were explored for millenniums by the great thinkers of the Middle East, Asia, and ancient Europe.

Today many students and researchers work to modifiy these models for contemporary use. In Europe, for example, graduate students at the international campus of Interuniversity College in Graz, Austria, are eagerly engaged in remodeling the human psyche, working on an EU academic project on complementary medicine. Their model posits these key ideas (Torp, 2007):

- Human beings consist of body, mind, and spirit.
- Humans have three fundamental existential representations: the id, the ego, and the soul (higher self).
- The human psyche has a facility called "the human heart" integrating body, mind, and spirit though three global aspects of existence: sexuality, meaning of life, and sense of coherence.

Meaning of life is really a very subtle and hard-to-get-to quality of human consciousness. But when meaning of life finds its place between sexuality and one's sense of coherence, it may be approached through these two dimensions, which can much more easily be turned into exercises and practice. Sexuality is often a quality ascribed to the body, and sense of coherence is often a quality ascribed to the spiritual dimension of human beings; by seeing these qualities as being heart-qualities, love and sexuality are transformed to something more whole and holy. The most interesting thing about this model is that meaning of life, often seen as a psychic dimension of human beings, is placed between sexuality and spirituality and is most closely linked to these two other integrative, existential dimensions.

When the three global or ubiquitous aspects of the heart—sexuality, meaning of life, and sense of coherence—are understood as three layers of existence, meaning of life both bridges the other two and is being held by them. According to such a model, a strategy for rehabilitating the patient's meaning of life is to have the patient rehabilitate sexuality and the sense of coherence first.

Most unfortunately, there seem to be strong inner conflicts in every person that make such a rehabilitation project difficult. This difficulty is well demonstrated in Freud's famous model of the ego being in a difficult position between the demands of the id, the super-ego, and the outer world. Of course, Freud was not so interested in the spiritual dimensions as in sexuality carrying the life force of the person.

The need to revive both sexuality and the feeling of being an integrated part of the world—what sense of coherence is really about—will be challenging for the patient. Most modern Western patients are completely absorbed with mental activities, words, and administration, which leaves little space for spirituality and sexuality. Yet these are the very people who most often lack or lose their meaning of life; they are mentally engaged people with limited engagement in spiritual and erotic matters. You could say that the mind is for survival; but just surviving without a deeper meaning of being here will, in the end, be felt futile. Thus, many people, among them the well educated, will in the middle of their lives enter a deep existential crises, asking the famous existential questions "Who am I?" and "Why am I here?"

Helping the Patient to Accept Sexuality

To acknowledge, accept, and integrate all major aspects of life is what existential therapy is all about. Accepting and understanding ourselves has been the challenge for human beings since the birth of human kind.

Sigmund Freud did a marvelous job helping the West to accept sexuality. Since the 1960s, spiritual matters have been vividly explored by the young people of Western cultures, often using illegal mind-expanding drugs, shamanistic rituals, and the like. The time seems ripe for combining these two trends in a new trend for human development. In doing so in the Research Clinic for Holistic Medicine in Copenhagen, we have been able to rehabilitate dozens of patients, who had almost completely lost their meaning of life.

Since 1997, the therapists at the Clinic for Holistic Medicine in Copenhagen have been using a combination of models from Freud and Jung (Jones, 1961; Jung, 1964), Frankl (1985), Grof (1980), and Antonovsky (1985, 1987) to help patients integrate sexuality, mind, and spirituality and in this way recover a meaningful existence. Many of these patients were given up on by the established medical service system, with 40% not helped by psychiatric treatment (Ventegodt et al., 2006). Recent documentation research has shown that using this general strategy, we were able to help more that 50% of the patients coming with physical, mental, existential, or sexual problems (Ventegodt et al., 2006; Ventegodt et al., 2007a, 2007b. 2007c, 2007d, 2007e). Our understanding of what is happening in this therapy is called "existential healing," or salutogenesis, after Aaron Antonovsky (1923–1994) from the Ben Gurion University of the Negev, who chose this name for existential healing.

Although only one aspect among many, the issue of sexual ethics has received more attention in medicine than has any other ethical issue. In many fields of traditional medicine, the ethical rule regarding sexuality is quite simple: Do not engage in a sexual relationship with the patient. In holistic health care, this simple rule is more relevant than ever. Because sexuality is often much more subtle and much more present in such holistic therapies as psychotherapy and in bodywork than in other therapies, however, the issue of sexual ethics needs more clarification.

The first researcher to struggle with the problem of how to deal with sexuality in the holistic clinical setting was Sigmund Freud (1856–1939), who in his famous "Transference Love" gave clever advice to his fellow psychoanalysts (Freud, 1915/1985):

> It is, therefore, just as disastrous for the analysis if the patient's craving for love is gratified as if it is suppressed. The course the analyst must pursue is neither of these; it is one for which there is no model in real life. He must take care not to steer away from the transference-love, or to repulse it or to make it distasteful to the patient; but he must just as resolutely withhold any response to it [i.e. avoid acting out]. He must keep firm hold of the transference-love, but treat it as something unreal, as a situation which has to be gone through in the treatment and traced back to its unconscious origins and which must assist in bringing all that is most deeply hidden in the patent's erotic life into her consciousness and therefore under her control. The more plainly the analyst lets it be seen that he is proof against every temptation, the more readily will he be able to extract from the situation its analytical content. The patient, whose sexual repression is of course not yet removed but merely pushed into the background, will then feel safe enough to allow all her preconditions for loving, all the phantasies of her state of being in love, to come to light; and from these she will herself open the way to the infantile roots of her love. (p. 168)

Freud became famous for realizing the importance for the patient's health of healing her sexuality. He also realized that while the analyst was working on releasing the patient's sexuality from suppression, the female patient frequently felt in love with her male therapist. Further, he also noticed that this transferred love could reach extreme intensity. Most disturbing, Freud also noticed the impact of the transference love on the therapist, because it often gave a strong sexual countertransference as an involuntary response.

Transference love was a serious problem to psychoanalysis in its early days. Freud had two main concerns here: How could the therapy continue in spite of the seemingly locked situation where therapy turned into a love affair? And how could the therapist help himself to avoid getting sexually involved with his patient? Freud ingeniously realized that the mutual sexual attraction was unavoidable in the psychodynamic therapy; he also realized that it was a most useful artifact if the therapist had a sound response to the sexual interest of his female patient. Freud's solution was that the therapist's reaction should be neither so cold that her sexuality was rerepressed nor so hot that it came to acting out on the sexual desire.

On one hand, the therapist should give his full acceptance to every aspect of his patient's sexuality and also actively encourage the patient to go deeper into it; on the other, the therapist should completely resist the temptation of a sexually interested woman completely in his power—and this resistance should be accomplished in a loving, accepting, and caring way, actually letting the patient know that the therapist was also tempted but managed to firmly resist the temptation. Since 1912, this well-tempered response has been the solution to this severe therapeutic headache. Nonethless, the ethical and cultural aspects of this response are still debated and not settled universally.

Holistic health practitioners are often dealing with patients who remain chronically ill without improvement using standard treatment, including psychiatric and sexological treatment. Today's intensive holistic therapy with such patients often includes bodywork, and here every kind of sexual reactions is found, from the patient undergoing catharsis from remembering early sexual abuse—and sometimes even projecting the abuser on the therapist to avoid the emotional pain of the traumas—to the patient rediscovering her own sexuality in the therapy by sometimes having "unprovoked" orgasms, which happens suddenly, uncontrolled, and without any warning, often resulting from only a light touch on the patient's nonerogenous zones of the arms or back. The enhanced difficulties of sexual transference, when working directly on the body, makes the discovery of Freud's solution more actual than ever, and every student of holistic therapy must be trained to have a firm, proper, and constructive therapeutic response to the patient's transference of love.

It is important to remember that what happens in therapy must always be with the patient's full consent. When there is consent, the therapy can contain even the most radical elements, such as direct touching the genitals, or agreed-on elements of symbolic failure or abuse, or other "rough" and provocative therapeutic elements meant to facilitate the patient's reexperience of traumatic life events in order to enter the state of existential healing (salutogenesis) through the use of the famous principle of similarity. In principle, there are no limits to what can function as a tool for healing in holistic therapy; the excellent therapist continues the treatment as long as there is progress by continuing to invent original new steps of therapeutic intervention.

From the time of Hippocrates, it has been of crucial importance that the patient never be harmed, and this notion is even more important for the holistic practitioner today. It is also necessary that the holistic therapist always respects the laws of the country where he or she practices. National laws may set severe limits for what can be done in the holistic clinic, even with the written and oral consent of the patient. Thus in the best interest of patients, the holistic practitioner must continually be engaged in awakening the public's awareness of needed changes to the country's laws.

Research dispensations can temporarily free the holistic practitioner of some of the limitations of the national laws, and the holistic practitioner is encouraged to do the research needed to develop the clinical practice of holistic medicine and to document its effects in a scientific way.

Helping the Patient to Accept Spirituality

A most interesting and puzzling aspect of human life is that we are more than the sum of our parts. Our wholeness carries meaning and talent, and this is the area of the un-seen and abstract or what most people have chosen to call the spiritual side of human beings. Unfortunately, this labeling has caused alienation from traditional religions, with many people now replacing orthodox understanding of human existence with self-experienced understanding.

In our human wholeness, it seems that we all carry a major, social talent as well as several minor talents to support this. The major talent is seldom understood and appreciated either by the individual or by the individual's surroundings, and this lack calls for intensive human development. The core talent of human wholeness is really one's gift to the world. And finding that core talent, realizing that it is there, deeply within our human nature, is often one of the biggest experiences in a person's life. Indeed, finding that core talent is akin to realizing who you are meant to be.

The fact that such a rediscovery of self often happens in existential therapy has led us suggest a general theory of the spiritual meaning of life, or the life mission (Ventegodt, 2003; Ventegodt et al., 2003a, 2003b, 2003c; Ventegodt & Merrick, 2003):

1. *Life mission*: Let us assume that at the moment of conception all the joy, energy, and wisdom that our lives are capable of supporting is expressed in a "decision" as to the purpose of our lives. This first decision is quite abstract and all-encompassing and holds the intentions of the entire life for that individual. It may be called the

personal mission or the life mission. This mission is the meaning of life for that individual. It is always constructive and sides with life itself.

2. *Life pain*: The greatest and most fundamental pain in our lives derives from the frustrations encountered when we try to achieve our personal mission, be they frustrated attempts to satisfy basic needs or the failure to obtain desired psychological states.
3. *Denial and loss of meaning of life*: When the pain becomes intolerable, we can deny our life mission by making a counterdecision, which is then lodged in the body and the mind, partially or entirely canceling the life mission.
4. *Repair*: One or several new life intentions, more specific than the original life mission, may now be chosen relative to what is possible henceforth. The new life intention replaces the original life mission and enables the person to move forward again. The new mission can, in turn, be modified, when the individual encounters new pains experienced as unbearable (e.g., Mission 1 says, "I am good," but Denial 1 says, "I am not good enough," and then Mission 2 says, "I will become good," which implies I am not good, and so on).
5. *Repression and loss of responsibility*: The new life intention, which corresponds to a new perspective on life at a lower level of responsibility, is based on an effective repression of both the old life mission and the counterdecision that antagonizes and denies it. Such a repression causes the person to split in a conscious and one or more unconscious or subconscious ways. The end result is that we deny and repress parts of ourselves. Our new life intention must always be consistent with what is left undenied.
6. *Loss of physical health*: Human consciousness is coupled to the wholeness of the organism through the information systems that bind all the cells of the body into a unity. Disturbances in consciousness may thus disturb the organism's information systems, resulting in the cells being less perfectly informed of what they are to do where.

   Disruptions in the necessary flow of information to the cells of the organism and tissues hamper the ability of the cells to function properly. Loss of cellular functionality may eventually result in disease and suffering.
7. *Loss of quality of life and mental health*: In psychological and spiritual terms, people who deny their personal mission gradually lose their fundamental sense that life has meaning, direction, and coherence. They may find that their joy of life, energy to do important things, and intuitive wisdom are slowly petering out. The quality of their lives is diminished, and their mental health impaired.

8. *Loss of functionality*: When we decide against our life mission, we invalidate our very existence. This invalidation shows up as reduced self-worth and self-confidence. Thus, counterdecisions compromise not only our health and quality of life but also our basic powers to function physically, psychologically, socially, sexually, mentally, and physically.

Applying the Life Mission Theory

Spiegel, Bloom, Kraemer, and Gottheil (1989) asked women with metastatic breast cancer to talk to each other in group sessions about their illness. As described in the article, the women made an effort to improve the quality of their lives. Survival in this group improved radically relative to that of women in a control group. The explanation is, in our opinion, simply that when people confront and deal with their destructive cognitions or attitudes to life, counterdecisions recorded in their bodies and minds cause repressed pain to resurface in consciousness, where it can be dealt with; consequently, the fragmentation of the person slowly ceases. We heal and we become whole. Because fragmentation is one of the causes of the disease, resulting in decreased quality of life and ability to function, the internal repair will enable the person to become more healthy, happy, and functional. The inner qualities of joy, energy, and wisdom reexpress themselves. Other things being equal, there will be prophylactic effects on new outbreaks of disease, accidents, and loss of functionality.

Ornish et al. (1990) induced patients with coronary arteries severely constricted from atherosclerosis to adopt lifestyle changes and deal with the quality of their lives. These changes had beneficial effects on the arterial constrictions of these patients as compared with a control group.

The life mission theory may explain this improvement by reference to the systematic efforts exerted by the patients to modify their behaviors and the attitudes that go along with them. This means that people work to relinquish destructive attitudes to life that deny the life mission. As this denial recedes, the person more or less returns to his or her natural state of health, quality of life, and ability to function.

The theory predicts that when, for example, a person is helped along by her family physician who, through a clinical interviw or consultation, conducts a conversation about her quality of life, she can reestablish her life mission. The person can then recognize it as the proper purpose in her life. She can rearrange her life accordingly and achieve her true sense of humanity; she becomes a human being in full agreement with herself and life. This person can draw on her resources and potentials to the fullest degree. In her natural state as a human being, she is maximally valuable to herself and to the world around her. A consciousness-oriented (holistic) medicine based on this theory will help people become valuable not only to themselves but also to each other.

Conclusions: Four Steps From Death to Life and Meaning

Our strategy at the Research Clinic for Holistic Medicine in Copenhagen has been to take the patients through four steps, or *doors*, from a state of being "almost dead" into at state of feeling fully alive and real.

- Step 1: Going from being as if dead to being physically alive: awakening sexuality
- Step 2: Going from awareness of the body to awareness of the mind (psyche): working on emotions and feelings, including sexual feelings
- Step 3: Going from mind to spirit: rehabilitating the ability to love and the spiritual talents; stepping into character and starting to be of real value to others
- Step 4: Shifting from body, mind, and spirit to coming from the heart: using all talents—physical, mental, and spiritual—to contribute to one's beloved ones (especially to the partner in a one-to-one relationship) and to the world (most often through succeeding at work)

In our experience, most people who are willing to walk this route of personal development can easily and efficiently be helped to success in their one-to-one relationship and love life together with a functioning work life. When these two important sides of human life are conquered, people find their meaning of life is normally restored.

In Step 1, the patient is helped to reexperience him- or herself as bodily alive. Owing all kinds of feelings and emotions, having their offspring in the body, is necessary to start feeling life. Sexuality is often a strict taboo hidden by enormous amounts of shame, which can be released and treated in the clinic. Almost 100 years ago Sigmund Freud taught us all how this should be done.

The next step is conquering the psyche, that is, waking up and realizing our human nature as an attentive and knowing entity. Putting feelings to words seems to be necessary to conquer the mind. Freud did this by talking sexuality quite explicitly with his patients, and this is really a clever opening to the consciousness. When the patient has recovered consciousness, the issue of existential depths, love, and spiritual talents can be addressed. The realization of the purpose of life, or the life mission, seems to be the most important event in existential therapy; after meaning of life comes rehabilitation, which follows as soon as the patient learns how to use his or her talent in private life and in working life.

The most troublesome aspect of modern life still seems to be sexuality, so let us remember and appreciate the work done by Sigmund Freud and let us work bravely with the patients, who trust us for help and support. When it comes to the hard problems of rehabilitating meaning of life, our support and caring understanding is more needed than ever.

References

Antonovsky, A. (1985). *Health, stress and coping.* London, England: Jossey-Bass.

Antonovsky, A. (1987). *Unravelling the mystery of health: How people manage stress and stay well.* San Francisco, CA: Jossey-Bass.

Frankl, V. (1985). *Man's search for meaning.* New York, NY: Pocket Books.

Freud, S. (1958). Further recommendations on the technique of psychoanalysis: Observations on transference love. In *Collected works* (Vol. 12, pp. 147–171). London, England: Hogarth. (Originally published 1915)

Grof, S. (1980). *LSD psychotherapy: Exploring the frontiers of the hidden mind.* Alameda, CA: Hunter House.

Jones, E. (1961). *The life and works of Sigmund Freud.* (L. Trilling & S. Marcus, Eds.). New York, NY: Basic Books.

Jung, C. G. (1964). *Man and his symbols.* New York, NY: Anchor Press.

Ornish, D., Brown, S. E., Scherwitz, L. W., Billings, J. H., Armstrong, W. R., Ports, T.A.,... Gould, K. L. (1990). Can lifestyle changes reverse coronary heart disease? The Lifestyle Heart Trial. *Lancet, 336*(8708), 129–133.

Reich, W. (1969). *Die Function des Orgasmus.* Köln, Germany: Kiepenheuer Witsch.

Spiegel, D., Bloom, J. R., Kraemer, H. C., & Gottheil, E. (1989). Effect of psychosocial treatment on survival of patients with metastatic breast cancer. *Lancet, 2*(8668), 888–891.

Torp, M. (2007). Personal communication.

Ventegodt, S. (1995). *Livskvalitet I Danmark [Quality of life in Denmark: Results from a population survey].* Copenhagen, Denmark: Forskningscentrets Forlag.

Ventegodt, S. (1996). *Livskvalitet hos 4500 31–33 årige [The quality of life of 4,500 31–33 year-olds: Result from a study of the prospective pediatric cohort of persons born at the University Hospital in Copenhagen].* Copenhagen, Denmark: Forskningscentrets Forlag.

Ventegodt, S. (2003). The life mission theory: A theory for a consciousness-based medicine. *International Journal of Adolescent Medicine and Health, 15*(1), 89–91.

Ventegodt, S., Andersen, N. J., & Merrick, J. (2003a). The life mission theory II: The structure of the life purpose and the ego. *ScientificWorldJournal, 3*, 1277–1285.

Ventegodt, S., Andersen, N. J., & Merrick, J. (2003b). The life mission theory III: Theory of talent. *ScientificWorldJournal, 3*, 1286–1293.

Ventegodt, S., Andersen, N. J., & Merrick, J. (2003c). The life mission theory V: A theory of the anti-self and explaining the evil side of man. *ScientificWorldJournal, 3*, 1302–1313.

Ventegodt, S., Flensborg-Madsen, T., Andersen, N. J., & Merrick, J. (2005). The life mission theory VII: Theory of existential (Antonovsky) coherence: A theory of quality of life, health and ability for use in holistic medicine. *ScientificWorldJournal, 5*, 377–389.

Ventegodt, S., Flensborg-Madsen, T., Andersen, N. J., Nielsen, M., Mohammed, M., & Merrick, J. (2005). Global quality of life (QOL), health and ability are primarily determined by our consciousness: Research findings from Denmark, 1991-2004. *Social Indicator Research, 71*, 87–122.

Ventegodt, S., Kroman, M., Andersen, N. J., & Merrick, J. (2004). The life mission theory VI: A theory for the human character. *ScientificWorldJournal, 4*, 859–880.

Ventegodt, S., & Merrick, J. (2003). The life mission theory IV: A theory of child development. *ScientificWorldJournal, 3*, 1294–1301.

Ventegodt, S., Thegler, S., Andreasen, T., Struve, F., Enevoldsen, L., Bassaine, L.,... Merrick, J. (2006). Clinical holistic medicine: Psychodynamic short-time therapy complemented with bodywork: A clinical follow-up study of 109 patients. *ScientificWorldJournal, 6*, 2220–2238.

Ventegodt, S., Thegler, S., Andreasen, T., Struve, F., Enevoldsen, L., Bassaine, L.,... Merrick, J. (2007a). Self-reported low self-esteem. Intervention and follow-up in a clinical setting. *ScientificWorldJournal, 7*, 299–305.

Ventegodt, S., Thegler, S., Andreasen, T., Struve, F., Enevoldsen, L., Bassaine, L.,... Merrick, J. (2007b). Clinical holistic medicine (mindful, short-term psychodynamic psychotherapy complemented with bodywork) in the treatment of experienced mental illness. *ScientificWorld Journal, 7*, 306–309.

Ventegodt, S., Thegler, S., Andreasen, T., Struve, F., Enevoldsen, L., Bassaine, L.,... Merrick, J. (2007c). Clinical holistic medicine (Mindful, short-term psychodynamic psychotherapy complemented with bodywork) in the treatment of experienced physical illness and chronic pain. *ScientificWorld Journal, 7*, 310–316.

Ventegodt, S., Thegler, S., Andreasen, T., Struve, F., Enevoldsen, L., Bassaine, L.,... Merrick, J. (2007d). Clinical holistic medicine (mindful, short-term psychodynamic psychotherapy complemented with bodywork) improves quality of life, health, and ability by induction of Antonovsky-salutogenesis. *ScientificWorldJournal, 7*, 317–323.

Ventegodt, S., Thegler, S., Andreasen, T., Struve, F., Enevoldsen, L., Bassaine, L.,... Merrick, J. (2007e). Clinical holistic medicine (mindful, short-term psychodynamic psychotherapy complemented with bodywork) in the treatment of experienced impaired sexual functioning. *ScientificWorldJournal, 7*, 324–329.

Yalom, I. D. (1980). *Existential psychotherapy*. New York, NY: Basic Books.

Yalom, I. D. (2002). *The gift of therapy*. New York, NY: Harper Collins.

27
A Meaning-Centered Approach to Building Youth Resilience

PAUL T. P. WONG
Trent University

LILIAN C. J. WONG
Meaning-Centered Counselling Institute

Resilience has emerged as a major area of research in psychology (Hart & Sasso, 2011), especially in applied positive psychology (Seligman, 2011). In fantasyland, life would be experienced as a perpetual state of bliss, free from stress and strife; living in such a paradise, where every need is met and every desire fulfilled, would make resilience superfluous. But in reality, life for most people is full of hardship and problems; people need resilience in order to manage stress and maintain an acceptable level of well-being. For vulnerable populations, those living in poverty or war-torn zones or suffering from chronic conditions, for example, resilience takes on even greater importance. Although agreeing with Bonanno (2004) that most people are resilient, we also believe that children and youth can benefit a great deal from resilience training on how to grow and flourish in spite of adversities.

Research on resilience has evolved over the years. In the early days of resilience research, the focus was on "the invulnerable child," who did better than expected despite adversities and disadvantages (Garmezy, 1974, 1985; Werner, 1984); developmental psychologists were interested in individual differences and the protective factors that contributed to the development of the invulnerable child.

Subsequent research shifted the focus to person–situation interactions and emphasized contextual variables and the process of adaptation. Rutter (1993) even dismissed the concept of invulnerability as both misleading and unrealistic. He warned that resilience should not be assumed to be a "magic bullet" that enables individuals to resist all the stresses in life. He emphasized that "resilience may reside in the social context as much as within the individual" (p. 626). His concept of the "steeling" effect highlights the essence of resilience—the more experience you have in overcoming adversities, the more resilient you will become.

It is of interest to note that research on resilience has come full circle. Recently, on the basis of research on coping with loss and trauma, Bonanno (2004) concluded that some individuals are simply more resilient than others, a notion hearkening back to earlier research on invulnerability. The current consensus is that resilience is a matter of individual differences and adaptive processes, as well as context factors. Similar to Maddi (Chapter 3, this volume; see also Kobasa, Maddi, & Kahn, 1982), we recognize that some people are indeed more resilient or hardy by virtue of their genetic makeup, temperament, intelligence, or personal history; but context and training are also important.

In this chapter, we first develop a taxonomy of resilience and articulate the holistic, multidimensional nature of the resilience construct. We then briefly review the various theoretical perspectives and intervention programs. Finally, we describe our meaning-centered approach, which is based on the interactions between the three modules of the positive triad: (a) the PURE principles of meaningful living, (b) the ABCDE strategies of resilience, and (c) the five elements of tragic optimism.

Definitions of Resilience

Resilience was first conceptualized as a personal characteristic of at-risk children who appeared to do better than expected; these children were considered invulnerable (Garmezy, 1974; Pines, 1975; Werner, 1984). Resilient children were characterized by Garmezy (1974) as having high expectations, internal locus of control, self-esteem, self-efficacy, and autonomy in spite of disadvantages. Rutter (1987) defines resiliency as "the positive pole of individual differences in people's responses to stress and adversity" (p. 316). Garmezy (1991a) defines resiliency as "the capacity for recovery and maintained adaptive behavior that may follow initial retreat or incapacity upon initiating a stressful event" (p. 459). Benard (1991) concludes that resilient children also need meaning in life, goals, and interpersonal problem-solving skills.

Over the years, the definition of resilience has been revised and refined, focusing on the adaptive process and person–context interactions (Luthar, 2003; Luthar & Zelazo, 2003; Masten, 2001; Rutter, 1993). Masten and Reed (2002) define resilience as "a class of phenomena characterized by patterns of positive adaptation in the context of significant adversity or risk" (p. 75). Vanderbilt-Adriance and Shaw (2008) discuss the evolution of resilience and stress the importance of taking into account different types of adversities.

According to Ungar (2006, 2008), resilience needs to incorporate ecological and cultural factors. Thus, resilience is understood as the capacity of individuals to navigate difficult situations through accessing health-enhancing psychological, social, cultural, and physical resources. In sum, the term *resilience* may be operationally defined as a positive outcome in the context of risk or adversity, known to be associated with negative outcomes (Luthar,

Cicchetti, & Becker, 2000) as a result of effective utilization of available personal and ecological resources (Ungar, Brown, et al., 2008; Wong, 1993).

What Constitutes a Risk Factor?

Resilience is manifested when two conditions are met: (a) the presence of some risk or adversity, and (b) the presence of resistance or positive outcome in spite of risk. However, for each individual, the presence of such risk factors depends on the presence of protective resources and the appraisal of threat or danger. According to this transactional view, individuals possessing a great deal of internal and external resources may see risks not as risks but as opportunities for personal growth (Bonanno, 2004; Lazarus & Folkman, 1984; Wong, 1993). By the same token, those individuals with severe deficiency in internal and external resources may feel easily threatened and traumatized; they may become depressed and suicidal, for example, simply because of rejection by a boyfriend or girlfriend. In any event, resilience becomes necessary only when there is a perceived risk to one's psychological integrity or physical safety.

What Constitutes a Positive Outcome?

We need to be careful in how we conceptualize and measure the positive outcomes of resilience. Individuals who cope with grief by immersing themselves in work may appear resilient because of high levels of functioning, but they may be "dead" on the inside. Other people may cope with loss by seeking all kinds of distractions and cheap thrills and appear unscathed by grief, but they may feel empty and lost.

What is considered positive also depends on culture. Ungar (2004) points out that in some cultural contexts, resilience may take the form of aggression. In order to survive, it may be necessary for disadvantaged individuals, such as the urban poor and high school dropouts, to show a pattern of aggression and the absence of emotional engagement (Eggerman & Panter-Brick, 2010; Obradovic, Bush, Stamperdahl, Adler, & Boyce, 2010). However, although gang violence may temporarily protect marginalized individuals from falling prey to helplessness, whether such aggression constitutes good adaptation in the long run for the individual as well as society is debatable.

Generally, there are two kinds of criteria for good adaptation. *External* adaptation focuses on meeting the social, educational, and occupational expectations of society or culture, whereas *internal* adaptation focuses on achieving positive psychological well-being as determined by culture. These two criteria complement each other. Most cultures favor one criterion over the other. The internal orientation seems more adaptive because it focuses on psychological processes rather than situational factors. The transformative potential of meaning making and meaning reconstruction is an example of good internal adaptation.

The Bonanno Controversy: Recovery Versus Resilience

Bonanno (2004) differentiates between recovery and resilience. Recovery refers to individuals who often experience a period of "subthreshold symptom levels" before regaining normal levels of healthy functioning (p. 21). Resilience refers to an individual's "ability to maintain relatively stable, healthy levels of psychological and physical functioning" (p. 20). Given the large literature on resilience as recovery, we wonder whether there is any strong empirical evidence or compelling theoretical advantage to maintain a distinction between recovery and resilience. We argue that when we take into account the subjectively perceived severity of the trauma, the differences between recovery and resilience become blurred. For instance, individuals who perceive the tragic loss of their only child as devastating but eventually bounce back may actually exhibit greater resilience than those who remain relatively unaffected by the long anticipated loss of an ill and aging parent.

We propose that there are at least three prototypical patterns of resilience, which may occur in different contexts for different individuals. All three are manifestations of resilience; the differences can be attributed to different person–context interactions rather than individual differences in their resilience strength.

1. *Recovery*: bouncing back and returning to normal functioning
2. *Invulnerability:* remaining relatively unscathed by the adversity or trauma
3. *Posttraumatic growth:* bouncing back and becoming stronger

Bonanno acknowledges the multiple pathways to resilience, among them hardiness (Kobasa et al., 1982), self-enhancement (Greenwald, 1980; Taylor & Brown, 1988), and positive emotion (Fredrickson, Tugade, Waugh, & Larkin, 2003). Presumably, individuals are resilient because of a combination of their genetic makeup and prior experiences in those multiple pathways. We believe that meaning and purpose should also be included as a pathway to resilience (Wong & Fry, 1998).

Research on Resilience

Risk and Protective Factors in Youth Resilience

According to Masten and Reed (2002), protective factors include cognitive abilities, problem solving, faith and a sense of meaning in life, positive outlook on life, close relationships with caring adults, and connections to supportive and rule-abiding people. According to Bender, Thompson, McManus, and Lantry (2007), protective factors encompass intelligence, relationships, healthy beliefs, self-reliance, and self-efficacy.

Ungar, Brown, et al. (2008) studied the pathways to resilience among Canadian youth. They found that the youths' capacity to cope under stress depends on different degrees of access to seven mental health-enhancing experiences: (a) access to material resources, (b) access to supportive relationships, (c) development of a desirable personal identity, (d) experiences of power and control, (e) adherence to cultural traditions, (f) experiences of social justice, and (g) experiences of a sense of cohesion with others.

Hass and Graydon (2009) studied the sources of resiliency among successful foster youth. They identified such protective factors as a sense of competence, future goals, social support, and involvement in community services. The implication for improving foster youth services includes nourishing supportive relationships and empowering youth to help others.

A sense of personal agency involves the freedom and ability to make choices. Bender et al. (2007) emphasize that "as choice is essential to motivate change, youth who believe they have even modest personal control over their destinies will persist in mastering tasks and become more committed to making positive life changes" (p. 2).

Research on Meaning and Purpose in Youth Resilience

Bronk (2005) differentiated the characteristics in purposeful youth and non-purposeful youth. Results suggested that purposeful youth as a group shared a number of defining characteristics: They were relatively open, enthusiastic about their interests, and committed to core values. They also devised a number of creative strategies to overcome challenges, actively sought and created communities of like-minded peers, and established intense, long-term relationships with mentors. With a sense of purpose, they developed a strong sense of moral identity and resiliency. These are assets that prior empirical research has shown to play an important role in positive youth development.

Mariano (2007) studied the relationship between categories of purpose and character strengths (including vitality, self-control, optimism, agency, and pathways) in emerging adulthood. According to Mariano, there exists a critical period in youth for cultivating a commitment to positive purposes. In his review of past literature, he points out that a sense of purposelessness is related to destructive behaviors in youth, whereas a sense of purpose is positively correlated with the moral development and psychosocial health of youth. Across genders, participants considered family as most important, followed by career, academic achievement, the arts, social causes, religious faith or spirituality, and politics. The results also show that a sense of agency and hope is related to the presence of purpose in most areas of life.

Damon (2008) investigated young people's lack of career motivation. His study shows that only about one fifth of youth today are highly engaged with a clear sense of what they want to do with their lives. The other four fifths may dabble in various pursuits without any commitment, or they may entertain unrealistic dreams without understanding what is needed to achieve their life goals. Youths who are highly engaged and who respond resiliently to difficult circumstances have four key characteristics: (a) a sense of future purpose, (b) autonomy, (c) social competence, and (d) problem-solving skills.

Fry (1998) makes the case that the search for meaning starts during adolescence and, most importantly, contributes to identity development. Based on her research with adolescents (Fry, 1996), she found evidence of intrinsic motivation for self-knowledge, personal meaning, self-esteem, and the desire to improve the human condition. The development of meaning and wisdom depends, however, on a number of factors, among them the presence of mentors, tutors, and nurturing adults, who provide personal valuations and support for dealing with ontological anxiety. She also considers the need for hardiness training in early developmental years to facilitate adolescents' search for meaning and personal growth.

Cross-Cultural Factors in Youth Resilience

Because meaning is largely shaped by culture, this chapter also stresses the role of culture in youth resilience. Culture prescribes the values and expectations of what really matters and what constitutes positive functioning. Furthermore, culture assigns different values to various protective factors. For example, the Chinese people consider a close-knit family unit as the sole protective agent for their children's well-being. Most people are resilient because each cultural system has built-in mechanisms to protect children from being harmed; however, not all culturally prescribed protective mechanisms equally contribute to resilience. Thus, resilience is a cultural expression.

Many studies have explored the influences of culture on youth resilience (Ungar, 2005; Ungar et al., 2007). As indicated previously, resilience is multidimensional, and in order to fully understand the process of resilience, research needs to include the cultural dimension. Some cultures focus more on building character, whereas others focus on making children happy. In traditional Chinese culture, for example, the virtues of responsibility, discipline, and perseverance are deeply ingrained in children, thereby increasing the children's capacity for resilience (Wong, 2009a). Western cultures, in contrast, make little demand from youth and may thus unwittingly deprive young people of the opportunity to develop character strengths and hardiness. Therefore, resilience needs to be understood within the cultural context (Ungar, 2005).

Ungar, Liebenberg, et al. (2008) should be commended for their major international study of youth resilience, which involved 35 researchers from 11 countries in developing a child and youth resilience measure (CYRM) suitable for resilience research in different cultures. They were fully aware of the problems of cross-cultural research, among them construct equivalence, factorial invariance, and domain specificity. Their scale emphasizes four factors: individual, relational, community, and culture. Clearly, their measurement is based on an ecological model of resilience. It is worth noting that the domain of individual characteristics does not include any items related to meaning and purpose, which have been shown to be important in youth resilience (Damon, 2008; Fry, 1998).

Cross-cultural differences were also apparent in Mariano's (2007) study, such that participants with a Hispanic or Latino ethnic background found religious faith or spirituality significantly more important than other ethnic groups. Thus, which purpose is most important depends on culture. Similarly, Kiang and Fuligni (2010) found that Asian American adolescents reported higher search for meaning than their Latin and European counterparts. Pan, Wong, Chan, and Joubert (2008) examined the meaning of life as a protective factor of positive affect in acculturation with samples of Chinese university students in Australia and Hong Kong. Their analyses revealed that meaning of life strongly predicted positive affect in acculturation. They also found that meaning of life mediated the relationship between acculturative stress and positive affect in both samples.

In view of the foregoing, we favor an ecological and contextual perspective of youth resilience. We need to take into account the individual, family, school, church, and culture in order to understand what contributes to resilience. Secure attachment, a sense of meaning and purpose, and a supportive environment are all important factors in fostering youth resilience.

Theoretical Perspectives

Luthar, Doernberger, and Zigler (1993) provide an extensive discussion on how the definition of resilience has changed over the years and how, by nature, resilience is multidimensional. We propose that the first step toward a comprehensive theory of resilience is to develop a taxonomy of the various dimensions of resilience.

Taxonomy of Resilience

Cognitive Resilience How we interpret events that happen to us determines how we cope. There is a large literature on the importance of attribution (Wong & Weiner, 1981), appraisal (Lazarus & Folkman, 1984; Peacock & Wong, 1990), and attribution retraining (Hilt, 2003–2004; Seligman, 1990) in reacting to negative events. Evidence shows that academic persistence depends on the reasons or values attributed to education (Wong, 1998a). Resilience programs based on cognitive-behavioral therapy (CBT) capitalize on cognitive resilience.

Transactional Resilience Transactional resilience refers to how we negotiate changing circumstances and daily stressors in a way that allows us to survive and flourish. According to the transactional model (Lazarus & Folkman, 1984) and the resource-congruence model (Wong, 1993, 1995; Wong, Reker, & Peacock, 2006), resilience depends on having sufficient resources and effective coping strategies. We have demonstrated that the cultivation of internal and external resources and the use of situational and culturally appropriate coping strategies result in effective coping (Peacock & Wong, 1990; Wong, 1993; Wong, Reker, & Peacock, 2006).

Behavioral Resilience Behavioral resilience refers to the habit of persistence and endurance in the face of failure and obstacles. It is a habit acquired, as is any other habit, through a history of reinforcement and practice. In a series of experiments, Wong (1979, 1995) has demonstrated that animals can be trained through intermittent reinforcement, especially a progressively demanding schedule of reinforcement, to develop very high levels of persistence, which generalizes to other difficult situations. A similar kind of progressively more rigorous and demanding training regimen is also used to develop endurance and toughness in elite athletes.

Motivational Resilience Motivational resilience refers to whether you have a clear sense of purpose, and whether you are fully committed in pursuing a life goal. Individuals are more likely to give up unless they are convinced that their pursuit or calling is something worth dying for. Therefore, the will to live is importantly dependent on the will to meaning (Frankl, 1946/1985; Chapter 28, this volume).

Existential or Spiritual Resilience Motivational resilience becomes existential or spiritual resilience when one considers the ultimate meaning and purpose of human existence. Existential resilience becomes spiritual resilience when the person resorts to religious or spiritual perspectives to answer life's big questions. Existential or spiritual resilience is also related to the quest for meaning and purpose (Wong, 1998c). A number of studies have shown that adults and children both tend to believe that the natural world was created by someone or something for a purpose (Azar, 2010). Such beliefs provide a sense of stability and coherence during times of uncertainty and change.

Relational Resilience There are three types of relational resilience. The most basic type is based on secure attachment during early childhood development (Bowby, 1988; Siegel, 2001). Relational resilience also comes from bonding or close relationships between adults (Chapter 9, this volume). Finally, self-transcendence and altruism contribute to resilience through meaning and tragic optimism (Frankl, 1946/1985; Wong, 1998b, 2009b).

Emotional Resilience "A resilient child is an emotionally healthy child, equipped to successfully confront challenges and bounce back from setbacks" (Brooks & Goldstein, 2002, p. 5). There are three types of emotional resilience. First is one's ability, based on secure attachment, to tolerate rejection and negative emotions. Second is one's ability to maintain some level of self-confidence, hopefulness, and emotional stability through mental toughness or hardiness. Third, emotional resilience also comes from one's ability to confront and overcome existential anxieties through existential or spiritual experience.

Dimensions of Resilience

The foregoing discussion has shown that the seven dimensions of resilience are all related to the pivotal construct of meaning. In cognitive resilience, meaning is involved in cognitive reframing as well as retraining in attribution or explanatory styles. Transactional resilience involves appraisal and adopting appropriate coping strategies, including existential coping. Behavioral resilience involves forming the habit of persistence and endurance in goal striving. Motivational resilience involves commitment to a major life goal or a higher purpose. Relational resilience means that one draws strength and support from others. Emotional resilience implies that one is able to hold on to an anchor or find a refuge even when one feels overwhelmed and devastated. Resilience training is needed for every age group, but the approach needs to take into account developmental differences in resilience. A comprehensive meaning-centered resilience training program takes into account all seven dimensions of resilience because meaning seeking plays a role in all seven types of resilience.

Developmental Stages

The relative importance of various dimensions of resilience may vary according to developmental stages. For example, relational resilience and emotional resilience based on secure attachment are most important in early childhood. Behavioral resilience is more important for school-aged children than for older adults, who have already developed habitual patterns of behavior and thought. Cognitive resilience is more important in adults than in children because of adults' developed capacity for understanding and reasoning. During adolescence, the individual's developmental needs are primarily (a) autonomy, (b) relatedness, and (c) competence (Ryan & Powelson, 1991), as well as identity development (Erikson, 1963). Therefore, motivational resilience and existential or spiritual resilience are essential for adolescents in view of their need for self-identity, challenge (Damon, 2008), and self-determination (Ryan & Powelson, 1991; Chapter 4, this volume).

Humanistic-Existential Models

The humanistic-existential theory states that people have an innate desire for self-actualization (Maslow, 1965) and an innate tendency to overcome obstacles and setbacks in order to realize one's potentials. In a similar vein, Viktor Frankl (1946/1985) emphasized that all people have the will to meaning. In other words, individuals will strive to overcome obstacles in order to fulfill their meaning in life. Humanistic-existential models also focus on understanding human behavior within a larger context of existential issues (Robbins & Friedman, 2011; Wong & Tomer, 2011).

Contextual Models

Contextual models emphasize the social, political, and cultural factors in resilience (Jessor, 1993; Takanishi, 1993; Ungar, 2005). Most studies on resilience have such identified contextual factors as family, school, community, agency, and church as protective factors (e.g., Harvey & Delfabbro, 2004; Masten & Reed, 2002; Ungar, Brown, et al., 2008). Communities play a large role in fostering resilience. Benard (1991) identifies three characteristics of community support: (a) availability of social organizations that provide an array of resources to residents, (b) consistent expression of social norms so that community members understand what constitutes desirable behavior, and (c) opportunities for children and youth to participate in the life of the community as valued members. The clearest sign of a cohesive and supportive community is the presence of social organizations that provide healthy human development (Garmezy, 1991b). Luthar and Goldstein (2004) observe that individual resilience cannot be sustained over time when children are under continued and severe stress from the external environment; their suggested solution includes a reduction of community violence and fostering supportive relationships with significant adults.

Family also plays a crucial role. Brooks and Goldstein (2002) recognize the importance of teaching and modeling empathy, in addition to creating opportunities for children and youth to act responsibly and compassionately. Any family that emphasizes the value of assigned chores, caring for brothers or sisters, and the contribution of part-time work in supporting the family, helps to foster resilience (Werner & Smith, 1982).

In a related book, Brooks and Goldstein (2004) describe how adults can develop a "resilient mindset." They emphasize the importance of taking responsibility for one's actions and their impact on others. A resilient mindset also involves setting realistic goals and overcoming obstacles and adversities. Parental demonstration of a resilient mindset will impact their children because children learn responsibility and resilience vicariously from their parents.

Religious institutions are also protective factors. Williams and Lindsey (2010) reviewed the roles of spiritual practices in at-risk adolescents. They confirmed that the following three major spiritual themes were related to bolstering resilience: (a) having a personal relationship with God or a higher power, (b) finding meaning and purpose in life, and (c) embracing personally meaningful spiritual practices. The church's social life influences youth from poor communities more than doctrine does. Johnson (2002) also found that church attendance improves physical, social, and emotional health of students.

Individual Differences Models

The individual differences models focus on the roles of personal characteristics, personality traits, and competencies (Beardslee, 1989; Salovey & Sluyter, 1997). Resilience may also be conceptualized in terms of individual differences in character strengths. Certain character strengths, among them persistence, endurance, resourcefulness, courage, faith, and hope, are particularly important for resilience (Wong, 1995). As operationalized in Snyder's hope theory (1997), hope has been shown to be a key psychological strength in the face of adverse life events. Hope can be measured as either a trait or a state (Curry & Snyder, 2000).

Maddi's (Chapter 3, this volume) hardiness theory emphasizes the attitudes of commitment, control, and challenge, as well as meaning making through decisions. Commitment is the decision to do what is right and remain engaged with life. Individuals exercise control by taking the initiative of doing what is right within one's power as opposed to becoming passive and helpless. Challenge refers to the existential courage to confront adversities as an opportunity for personal growth.

Park and Peterson (2006) studied the Values in Action Inventory for Youth (VIA-Youth), which is a self-report questionnaire that measures 24 character strengths. Their factorial study of several samples of adolescents revealed four interpretable factors: temperance strengths (e.g., prudence, self-regulation, authenticity, perseverance), intellectual strengths (e.g., love of learning, curiosity, open-mindedness), theological strengths (e.g., hope, religiousness, love, zest, gratitude), and interpersonal strengths (e.g., kindness, modesty, bravery, teamwork).

Everly (2008) suggested seven lessons to develop character strengths in children: (a) developing strong relationships, (b) learning to make difficult decisions, (c) taking responsibility, (d) staying healthy, (e) thinking positively, (f) having a faith, and (g) possessing integrity. To this list, Brooks and Goldstein (2002) would add empathy, optimism, respect, unconditional love, listening skills, and the patience to practice these values.

Another individual difference has to do with the capacity for happiness and positive emotions, which also play an important role in meaningful living and resilience (Csikszentmihalyi & Csikszentmihalyi, 2006). There are clear individual differences in the happiness set point (Lykken, 1999). However, more recent research has shown that the pursuit of life goals can alter the happiness set point (Headey, 2008).

Narrative Models

The narrative approach makes use of the human capacity for narratives and storytelling to bring about personal transformation. The website http://www.selfauthoring.com contains a wealth of information on the power and benefits of narratives dealing with negative emotions and stimulating personal growth. Hauser, Allen, and Golden's (2008) project illustrates how resilient troubled teens made pivotal changes in their lives through telling their stories.

Cognitive-Behavioral Models

The cognitive-behavioral approach focuses on cognitive resilience. Examples of cognitive-behavioral models include cognitive-behavior therapy (CBT), rational-emotive behavior therapy (REBT), and problem-solving therapy (PST). According to Neenan (2009), having a stoic attitude toward adversity is at the heart of resilience. Neenan suggests that it is the cognitive meanings we attach to events, and not the events themselves, that determine our reactions to them. People can find constructive ways of dealing with their difficulties by using the techniques from CBT, as well as learning from the wisdom of those who have prevailed over adversity.

Holistic Models

Because resilience is multidimensional, it takes a village to produce a resilient youth. Tull (2007), for example, summarizes a number of factors that promote resilience; these include the ability to cope effectively with stress, being connected with family and friends, spirituality, and finding positive meaning. Werner (1995) distinguished three contexts for protective factors: (a) personal attributes, (b) the family, and (c) the community. Wexler, DiFluvio, and Burke (2009) find that meaning making and group identity can contribute to resilience in combating systemic discrimination and structurally based unfairness. This approach is particularly useful for marginalized groups. This notion is consistent with the meaning-centered approach, which recognizes that meaning making is based on personal as well as social construction. Community involvement also contributes to resilience. Price-Mitchell (2010) emphasizes the importance of engagement in civil responsibilities in promoting intrinsic motivation for self-efficacy, self-reflection, overcoming challenges, and moral development.

Reichert, Stoudt, and Kuriloff's (2006) study suggests that gang violence may be normative and actually adaptive in some communities. In order to reduce violence, it may be necessary to move beyond the individuals and take political actions to create safer communities. The researcher emphasize a need for structural change of societies and communities to reduce poverty, injustice, and discrimination.

The Meaning-Centered Approach to Resilience

The meaning-centered approach (Wong, 2010, 2011b; see also Chapter 1, this volume) represents a holistic and integrative theory for understanding resilience. This approach is based on managing the interactions between the three modules of the positive triad through the dual-systems model of approach

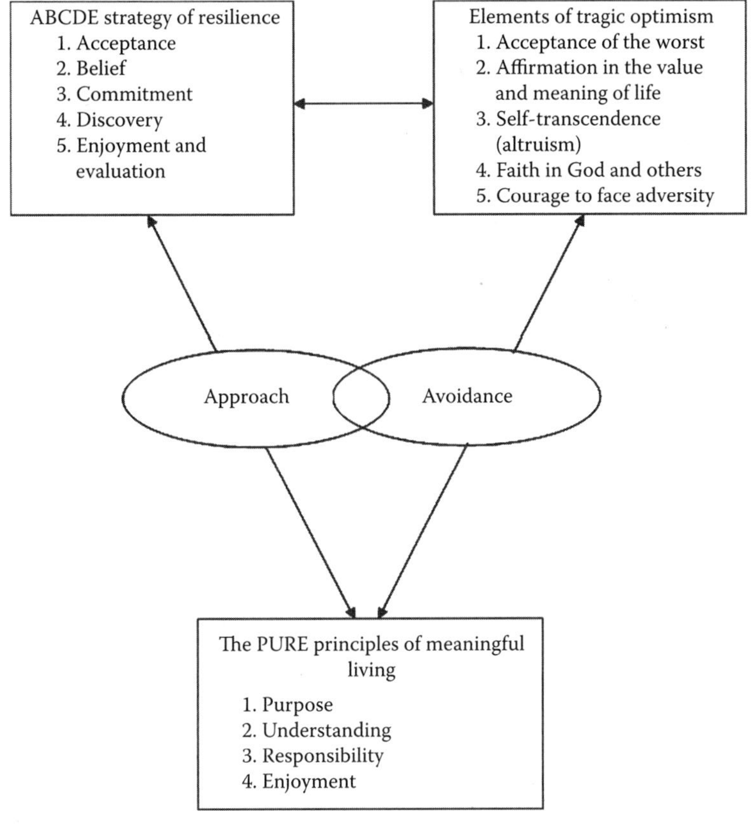

Figure 27.1 The meaning-centered positive triad of survival and flourishing as mediated by the dual-system of approach and avoidance.

and avoidance, as depicted in Figure 27.1. The three modules represent three meaning-centered positive intervention strategies. This positive triad provides a comprehensive way to enhance resilience in a variety of adverse situations, including the terror of death and tragic losses (Tomer, Grafton, & Wong, 2008; Wong, 2009b).

The PURE Principles

The first module of the positive triad consists of the PURE principles as shown in Table 27.1. PURE stands for purpose, understanding, responsible action, and enjoyment or evaluation. Elsewhere, we have elaborated on PURE (Chapter 28, this volume). Here, we explain why these four principles of meaningful living form the foundation of resilience.

The Imperative of Purpose Having the right purpose is perhaps the most important key to resilience and flourishing. One may volunteer for a good cause and

Table 27.1 The PURE Principles of Flourishing

	Source of Meaning
Purpose (motivation): • Direction, calling, passion, priority, value, choice • Purpose depends on understanding, wisdom, knowledge, and sound judgment	Positive emotions Achievement Relationship Self-acceptance Self-transcendence (altruism) Religion and spirituality Fairness and justice
Understanding (cognition): • Awareness, knowing, insight, belief, attitude • Understanding depends on having the right mindset, philosophy of life, and value systems	Meaning mindset Mindful awareness A sense of coherence Philosophy and religion Narratives, myths, and symbols Belief systems Self-identity and self-concept Realistic positive thinking about life
Responsibility (behavior): • Moral habit, ethical behavior, accountability, civic virtue • Responsibility depends on purpose and understanding	Doing the right thing Engaged in civic virtues Engaged in fulfilling potential Caring and compassion for others Living as a good person Leaving a good legacy Solving problems and coping with stress
Enjoyment (affect): • Feeling good about one's actions and life • Enjoyment depends on all the above	Happiness Eudaimonia, well-being Life satisfaction Fulfillment Harmony

engage in happiness-inducing and strength-enhancing exercises, but without a strong sense of life purpose, one is likely to lose one's way and see one's life derailed by making a wrong turn. In some cases, having the wrong life purpose is worse than having no purpose at all. Adolph Hitler, for example, had an evil purpose, as did Osama Bin Laden: Both devoted their lives to the evil purpose of destroying innocent people, and the world has suffered greatly because of them. To the extent that purpose is related to core values and beliefs, it is not morally neutral. Purpose can be right or wrong, good or bad. A good and right purpose will be constructive, realistic, achievable, consistent with one's gifts and strengths, and, more important, congruent with the best values for the person and society. Self-transcendence is one of the defining characteristics of a good purpose.

> Importantly, Erikson proposed that young people need to identify with values that have transcendence, that is, that supersede family and self and have historical continuity, commanding respect from others who have lived and who will live after them (Yates & Youniss, 1996). This sense of transcendence is important for young people because it provides them with a compelling purpose. (Wexler et al., 2009, p. 567)

Self-transcendence is part of the sources of meaning that make life worth living (Wong, 1998b). The eight sources of meaning identified by Wong map onto the pathways to flourishing and happiness (Seligman, 2011; see also Ecclesiastes, NIV; Myers, 1993). Therefore, only meaning-oriented life purposes are likely to enhance resilience and flourishing.

One's life purpose depends importantly on one's overall life orientation or the mindset with which one looks at life and makes significant choices. Elsewhere, Wong (2011d; see also Chapter 1, this volume) has made the distinction between a meaning mindset and a happiness mindset. For those individuals with a happiness mindset, the primary objective in life is to pursue whatever gives them optimal happiness, which may be money, power, fame, or pleasures. Thus, the happiness mindset may also be referred to as the success mindset. In contrast, for those individuals with a meaning mindset, the ultimate concern is to devote their lives to pursue something meaningful and virtuous for the common good. Thus, the meaning mindset can also be referred to as virtue mindset. The happiness mindset asks, "What can I get from life? How can I be happier?" whereas the meaning mindset asks, "What does life demand of me? How can I do more to make life better for others?" Research is underway to determine whether a meaning mindset, as compared to a happiness mindset, would lead to more eudaimonistic well-being, resilience, character strengths, and moral virtues.

Understanding Understanding is closely related to purpose and plays a vital role in meaningful living. It is doubtful whether one can live a meaning-filled life without a clear sense of the self and of one's place in the world. If you do not know who you are and what you are meant to be, how can you discover the right purpose and meaning in life? Similarly, one needs to have a pretty good understanding of reality, of the challenges and opportunities available in order to set life goals. Having a philosophical understanding of what really matters also contributes to the formation of life purpose. Finally, to understand the demands of each situation as well as one's own proper role in that situation is important for deciding on responsible actions.

Understanding is also related to a sense of coherence. Without a sense of coherence, life is incomprehensible, unpredictable, and unsettling. Without a sense of order and understanding of how the world works, we would have difficulty cultivating hardiness (Maddi, 1998). Without a clear sense of self-identity, we would not know what to do with our lives. The pursuit of self-understanding and self-knowledge is important for self-control (Baumeister, Heatherton, & Tice, 1994). Attribution and appraisal help us understand the nature of situational stress (Lazarus & Folkman, 1984; Peacock & Wong, 1990; Weiner, 1985; Wong & Weiner, 1981). Understanding also includes emotional intelligence (Salovey, Mayer, & Caruso, 2002). At a deeper level, enlightenment about life and death, as well as one's place in the larger scheme of things, is needed to discover the meaning of life (Wong & Tomer, 2011).

For young people with limited life experience, guidance and mentoring are needed to enhance the understanding of themselves, other people, and their responsibilities in the world. A big part of understanding has been referred to as social-emotional intelligence (Salovey et al., 2002), which will contribute to relational resilience.

There is also a sociocultural dimension to understanding. According to constructivist psychology (Raskin, Bridges, & Neimeyer, 2010), meaning making is involved in understanding self and the world, in navigating everyday life. Meanings are subjectively constructed based on one's personal history and idiographic way of experiencing the world, but the ways that we understand our world and ourselves are also shaped by culture, language, and ongoing relationships. Thus, curiosity, meaning seeking, myth making, and storytelling all contribute to our understanding of ourselves and the world we live in.

We are more likely to quest for meaning and understanding when our assumptive worlds are disrupted (Janoff-Bulman, 1992). Crisis serves as an opportunity for people to rework their understanding of their own lives and the cultural dynamics of their world (Becker, 1997). According to the meaning maintenance model (Heine, Proulx, & Vohs, 2006), when one's meaning systems are threatened by a variety of adverse events, one will seek alternative mental representations to regain a sense of meaning. Wong and Weiner (1981) demonstrated that when outcomes are unexpected or negative, people engage in both causal and existential attributions (Wong, 1991). Thus, our capacity for understanding is constantly challenged and stretched. We probe, explore, and search. We use imaginations, metaphors, myths, and analogues. We even learn how to see and hear beyond our senses in order to get a sense of our calling and destiny.

Damon (2008) emphasizes the need for self-assessment: "A sense of calling requires (1) a realistic awareness of one's own abilities; (2) an interest in how those abilities can serve some aspect of the world's needs; and (3) a feeling of enjoyment in using one's abilities in this way" (p. 46). Barber's (2008a, 2008b) research with youth in war-torn Bosnia and Gaza demonstrated the psychological importance of establishing a sense of personal identity and understanding the nature of the conflict in order to make sense of one's personal experiences of war. "He concludes that if young people can locate themselves in a historical context, identify with a collective purpose and play an active role to further that purpose, they will be better able to withstand hardship" (Wexler et al., 2009, p. 567).

Understanding also requires practical wisdom. Aristotle (trans. 2004) emphasized the importance of practical wisdom as well as rationality. In Sternberg's (2001) words, practical wisdom is "not simply about maximizing one's own or someone else's self-interest, but about balancing various self-interests (intrapersonal) with the interests of others (interpersonal) and of other aspects of the context in which one lives (extrapersonal), such as one's city or country or environment or even God" (p. 231). All the signature strengths without practical wisdom may lead to irresponsible decisions with disastrous consequences. That is why to Aristotle, practical wisdom and rationality are always needed in living the good life.

Responsibility Responsibility is concerned with doing what is right. With freedom comes responsibility. Because self-determination is one of the keys to happiness and the good life, the ability to make good decisions is paramount. Good decisions not only lead to successful or satisfying results for the individual but also meet ethical requirements and contribute to the well-being of others (e.g., Snyder & Feldman, 2000). According to Gallup's *Strengthfinders*, "People strong in the Responsibility theme take psychological ownership of what they say they will do. They are committed to stable values such as honesty and loyalty" (as cited in Snyder & Lopez, 2007, p. 56). To act responsibly, one must be accountable to self and others. A meaningful and optimal life, according to Csikszentmihalyi (1990; Csikszentmihalyi & Csikszentmihalyi, 1992, 2006), involves two processes, namely *differentiation* and *integration*. The former reflects a strong sense of personal responsibility for developing and using our unique talents, and the latter requires the wisdom to be responsible for others, given that we are all enmeshed in a network of relationships.

Enjoyment and Evaluation Typically, there are three sources of enjoyment of happiness: (a) hedonic happiness that comes from pleasant experiences, (b) eudaimonic happiness that comes from doing what is good and realizing one's potential, and (c) chaironic happiness that comes as a gift from grace, often unrelated to our own virtue and accomplishments. One is more likely to experience chaironic happiness when one is spiritually attuned. The pursuit of all eight sources of meaning will yield all three kinds of happiness. Even when we do all the right things, however, from time to time we may still experience periods of darkness. From our meaning-centered perspective, these difficult moments in life call for soul searching and reflection, which often results in adopting the ABCDE strategy, introduced next in this chapter.

Feeling good is the inevitable outcome from doing good in light of one's highest purpose and best understanding. One can feel satisfied with the decision and action even when one fails to achieve the desired result. When the situation worsens and when dissatisfaction sets in, self-regulation demands that one reevaluates one's purpose, understanding, and actions in order to make midcourse corrections. The evaluative component is necessary to ensure that one gets unstuck and moves forward. Here, discontent serves a positive function when it compels the unhappy person to make positive changes.

> The annals of the world's great religions are full of stories about men and women who maintain their dedication and mental balance despite severe persecution and hardships.... [Indeed,] far from feeling sorry for themselves, they felt gratitude, and even joy, for the hardships that had tested their faith. Their ordeals, they were convinced, had brought them closer to God. (Damon, 2008, p. 45)

The ABCDE Strategy of Resilience

The ABCDE model, which stands for acceptance, belief, commitment, discovery, and evaluation, is primarily an intervention strategy dealing with stress and adversity, as summarized in Table 27.2. Wong has elaborated on the therapeutic functions of ABCDE elsewhere (Wong, 2011b; see also Chapter 28, this volume). Whereas PURE provides the principles of meaningful living, ABCDE provides the principles of overcoming existential givens, misfortunes, and sufferings. Here, we simply highlight elements related to resilience.

Acceptance Acceptance plays a vital role in meaning-centered resilience training. It not only contributes to the source of meaning but also is a key element of the ABCDE strategy and tragic optimism. The reason acceptance is involved in all three modules of the positive triad is that practical wisdom is needed to accept what cannot be changed. Acceptance involves recognizing one's limitations as a person as well as one's finitude and fragility as a human being. Just as wisdom is needed for living an authentic life, a worthwhile life comes from the wisdom of self-acceptance.

Acceptance moves us beyond the immature defense mechanisms of denials and repression, and enables us to face the new reality to which we must adapt. A positive attitude toward life begins with accepting our limitations and external constraints (Wong, 1998b). The mindfulness approach emphasizes acceptance. Kabat-Zinn (1990) teaches his patients "to taste their own wholeness as they are, right now … to accept ourselves right now, as we are, symptoms or no symptoms, pain or no pain, fear or no fear" (pp. 279–280).

Belief It is difficult to conceive how we can maintain hope and confidence in the face of bleak prospects without some belief, be it religious faith, trust in others, or self-affirmation. Whereas CBT emphasizes the importance of challenging dysfunctional beliefs, meaning-centered counseling and therapy (MCCT) emphasizes the importance of positive belief that gives people hope

Table 27.2 The ABCDE Model of Resilience

	Description
Acceptance: Accepting what cannot be changed	Accepting reality, limitations, loss, trauma, existential givens
Belief: Affirming one's ideals and core values	Recognizing the intrinsic value and meaning of life Receiving support and help from others Turning to a personal God or higher power Growing and striving for positive transformation Believing in an eventual triumph of good over evil Recognizing the worthiness and authenticity of one's mission Recognizing and using one's competencies and abilities
Commitment: Moving forward and carrying out one's responsibility with determination	Doing what needs to be done regardless of feelings or circumstances Striving to fulfill one's responsibility no matter what Enduring hardship and pain for your cause Problem solving and effective coping Avoiding errors and temptations Practicing the PURE principle Pursuing realistic goals Reauthoring one's life story
Discovery: Learning something new about the self and life	Digging deeper, exploring farther, and searching higher Discovering one's hidden courage and strength Discovering the power of faith and spiritual resources Grasping the complexities of life and people
Enjoyment or evaluation: Savoring positive outcomes or reassessing one's progress	Feeling relief that the worst is over Savoring the moments of success Reflecting and reviewing one's life Receiving feedback from others Conducting assessments and making adjustments

and sustains goal striving. Positive belief also provides the motivation to change. The belief that life can be meaningful and significant inevitably leads to efforts to discover one's purpose and passion. For young people, it is particularly important that they believe that their future can be better and that life is worth living in spite of the present difficulties.

Commitment MCCT emphasizes human agency and the potency of action. "Agency is the motivational component that ensures a person will be able to begin and sustain the effort necessary to follow a particular pathway. Agency is characterized by internal speech, such as 'I am not going to be stopped'" (Valle, Huebner, & Suldo, 2006, p. 395). Commitment to persistent hard work is necessary to bring about change. There will always be setbacks and obstacles; therefore, persistence and resourcefulness are indispensable in achieving worthy goals. Real change begins when one takes the first concrete step in a new direction. We need to do whatever it takes to get out of a rut to create a better future. We all need to do what is demanded of us by a sense of responsibility or moral obligations. Just do it is the message, even when we do not feel like doing it. Both Morita therapy (Ishiyama, 1990) and acceptance-commitment therapy (Biglan, Hayes, & Pistorello, 2008) stress the importance of action over feelings in order to overcome depression and improve daily functioning. Commitment to goal setting and goal striving is important for academic achievement (Morisano, Hirsh, Peterson, Shore, & Pihl, 2010). Commitment also refers to the quest for meaning and significance, which makes one feel that life is worth living.

Discovery Viktor Frankl (1946/1985) has consistently emphasized that meaning is discovered more than created, and for good reason. Discovery of meaning involves soul searching, awakening, or enlightenment about how one ought to live. It also means discovering hidden talents in oneself, significance in mundane activities, and more important, one's sense of calling and mission. People are often unaware of how courageous and resilient they are until they are challenged to rise to the occasion. Young people do not usually discover what matters and what life demands of them until they are committed to the quest for meaning and personal growth.

Evaluation or Enjoyment Evaluation or enjoyment is an important component of self-regulation. If nothing seems to work and one remains miserable, then some adjustment is necessary. When the previous four steps work well and result in a satisfactory solution, then the ABCDE strategy will yield to PURE principles until one encounters another obstacle or crisis.

Tragic Optimism

Tragic optimism is a specialized module used to cope with extreme adversities and catastrophic events. It draws strengths from PURE and ABCDE to restore hope in the most hopeless situations. The five components of tragic optimism are acceptance, belief, courage, religious faith, and self-transcendence. Tragic optimism is the only kind of hope that can survive all the storms of life (Frankl, 1946/1985; Wong, 2009b; Wong & McDonald, 2002), for it is grounded in reality and rooted in faith. Horrible things happen to good people, and tragedy may strike without any notice. In such trying times, resilience begins with the courage to accept the horrors that have descended on us. Belief in the intrinsic worth and meaning of life prevents people from sinking into depression or committing suicide. Having faith in God or belief that rescue is forthcoming keeps hope alive. Self-transcendence connects suffering individuals with other victims in the solidarity of helping others and working together to overcome devastating traumas.

The Dual-Systems Model

The dual-systems model, as described by Wong (Chapter 1, this volume), is responsible for managing the interactions between the three modules. More specifically, it manages the coordination and interactions between the approach and avoidance systems. It is based on self-determination theory (Chapters 4 and 24, this volume), which emphasizes the process and the skills necessary for achieving desirable goals and overcoming obstacles. The mediating role of the dual-systems model is shown in Figure 27.1.

The dual-systems model also incorporates principles of effective coping and stress management, which are essential for well-being and resilience (Lazarus & Folkman, 1984; Wong & Wong, 2006). Preventive and transformative types of coping (as measured by Wong, Reker, & Peacock, 2006) are particularly important in planning for a desirable future and achieving the good life. The dual-systems model mediates between the interactions of PURE, ABCDE, and tragic optimism to ensure that the positive triad works in a balanced and efficient manner to enhance resilience and flourishing.

Ways of Building Resilience

Since the early days of research on the invulnerable child, many youth resilience programs have been developed as part of the positive youth movement (Catalano, Berglund, Ryan, Lonczak, & Hawkins, 1998; Lopez & McKnight, 2002); these interventions may have outpaced scientific research (Doll & Lyon, 1998).

There are different approaches to building resilience. The positive youth movement contributes to youth resilience primarily through extracurricular activities. According to America's Promise Alliance (2010), there are five promises of the positive youth movement: caring adults, safe places, a healthy start and healthy development, an effective education, and opportunities to help others through service. Some of the organizations that provide activities that contribute to positive youth development include Big Brothers and Big Sisters, Boy's Club, YMCA, and YWCA. According to Jamieson (2005), although positive youth programs come in different shapes and sizes, one can identify factors for youth programs that work: First, the more time committed to youths generally result in better outcomes. Second, the younger the participants, the more likely they are to develop competence. Third, the more structured the programs, the more likely these programs will produce consistent results.

Some programs are highly structured and are incorporated in the regular school curriculum. One example is the Penn Resiliency Program (PRP; Gillham & Reivich, 2004). The PRP consists of 12 scripted sessions in the classroom focusing on awareness of thought patterns and modifying explanatory styles of events. The program helps students think realistically and flexibly and is based on CBT.

Currently, there are numerous other programs based on the cognitive-behavioral approach to building resilience in children and youth. For example, the "FRIENDS for Life" program developed by Barrett (2004a, 2004b) has been used to reduce anxieties and reinforce desirable behavior in order to increase resilience (Barrett & Turner, 2001; Rose, Miller, & Martinez, 2009).

Reivich and Shatte's (2002) program is also based on CBT and emphasizes seven cognitive skills to finding one's inner strength and overcoming life's obstacles: (a) learning the ABCs of CBT, (b) avoiding thinking traps, (c) detecting icebergs, (d) challenging beliefs, (e) putting things in perspective, (f) calming and focusing, and (g) real-time resilience.

A Meaning-Centered Approach to Building Resilience

Given the multidimensional nature of resilience, only a holistic and integrative meaning-centered approach can deliver a comprehensive resilience program. A comprehensive resilience program for youth will incorporate all seven dimensions of resilience.

1. Relational and emotional resilience results from such protective factors as secure attachment and intimacy with a parent, caregiver, or caring adult.
2. Behavioral resilience comes from discipline and training, including forming good habits of focusing, persistence, endurance, and task completion.
3. Cognitive competence is also important: Learning how to think positively and resist negative thoughts builds cognitive resilience.
4. Youth need to realize that there is something bigger out there, bigger than one's self-interests. They can also learn to be attuned to spiritual transcendental realities, which give birth to feelings of awe and wonder. They need to develop the kind of faith that will work for them in times of tragedy. Spiritual-existential resilience entails the capacity for faith and prayer.
5. Transactional resilience comes from learning coping and problem-solving skills. It involves learning how to develop and access ecological resources and how to use culturally and situationally appropriate coping responses.

A comprehensive meaning-centered resilience program will cover the following themes: (a) purposes and life goals; (b) understanding the self and one's place in the world; (c) freedom and responsibility; (d) the right and wrong pathways to happiness; (e) the courage to accept internal and external constraints; (f) faith and belief in a better future; (g) commitment to growth;

(h) discovery of hidden dimensions of the self and new frontiers of life; (i) the power of self-transcendence, empathy, compassion, and altruism; and (j) Positive thinking, attribution and meaning-management.

Given that space will not permit a detailed description of all meaning-enhancing positive interventions (see Wong & Wong, in press), here we will highlight just a few exercises.

Interventions to Enhance Purposefulness

A purpose-driven life is more likely to endure adversities and setbacks. Thus, the meaning-centered approach focuses on discovering what really matters in life, reinforcing the will to meaning, and identifying concrete and realistic goals consistent with one's life purpose (Frankl, 1946/1985; Wong, 1998b, 2010). Damon (2008) shows that the key ingredient in guiding young people to meaningful choices is the development of a clear sense of purpose that transcends self-interest. Having a sense of purpose gives youth a strong sense of moral identity and resiliency (Bronk, 2005). Here are a few interventions that contribute to the discovery and enhancement of purpose.

1. Discover what makes your life worth living: Complete the Personal Meaning Profile (PMP; Wong, 1998b) to learn which sources of meaning are important to you.
2. Discover what matters most to you: Complete the Life Orientation Profile (LOP; Wong, 2011a) to learn whether your core values and ultimate concerns are primarily oriented toward pleasure, success, meaning, or virtue.
3. Describe in concrete, specific terms a mission statement for your life, career, or education. Ask a series of *why* questions until you are truly satisfied with your mission statement.
4. Conduct a dream analysis by asking yourself "What was my dream as a child?" and "What is my recurrent dream in life?" Write about these dreams, and reflect on their meaning and importance to you.
5. Consider a magic question: If you were granted one wish, what would that be? Why?
6. If you could carry only one thing with you to a faraway place for an extended period of time, what would it be and why?

Interventions to Enhance Self-Understanding

1. Mirror test (Part 1): Look at yourself in the mirror and ask yourself "Do I like what I see?" "What do I like about myself?" "What don't I like about myself?" "Is there a dark secret in me that needs to be dealt with?" "What changes do I need to make in order to make my life more meaningful and fulfilling?"
2. Mirror test (Part 2): Ask yourself "What do other people see in me?" "What do other people say about me?" "What are the most common

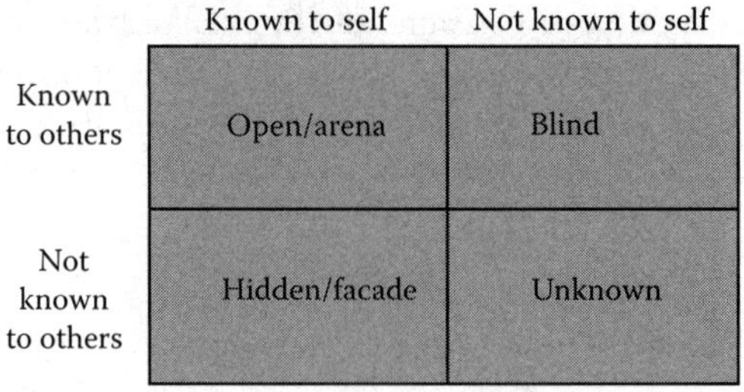

	Known to self	Not known to self
Known to others	Open/arena	Blind
Not known to others	Hidden/facade	Unknown

Figure 27.2 The Johari window.

compliments I receive?" "What are the most common criticisms I receive?" (If you are a believer, you can also ask yourself, "What does God see in me?")

3. The Johari window (see Figure 27.2; Luft & Ingham, 1955): This exercise is intended to help you discover what you know and don't know about yourself and what others know and don't know about yourself.
4. Journaling and self-authoring: Write something about your past, present, and future (see http://www.selfauthoring.com). Write about your emotional everyday life experiences (Pennebaker, 1997).
5. Identify and articulate the positive meanings for your education or career choice.
6. Reflect on meaningful moments (Wong, 2011c). A meaningful moment is defined as a moment marked by certain qualities that enrich life and provide insights to living.

Positive Exercises

1. Self-assessment: At the end of each day or week, identify the things you did that gave you a sense of satisfaction; also identify the things you failed to do or things you did that made you feel dissatisfied. Describe your negative feelings and plan actions to reduce or eliminate areas of dissatisfaction.
2. Positivity exercise (Part 1): Identify the most troublesome and negative areas in your life. Discover three positive benefits that can come from each of these negative areas. Explore ways to transform negative aspects of your life into positive assets for the future.
3. Positivity exercise (Part 2): Identify your most intrusive negative thoughts. Reframe these thoughts so they will no longer trouble you. The next step is to transform these thoughts into positive ideas for personal growth.
4. Silence exercise: Unplug yourself from everything. Switch off your iPhone, iPod, TV, radio, telephone, and so on. Get away from people and noise. Find a quiet spot and stay in complete solitude for one

hour. Meditate, pray, or simply savor the present moment without judgment or analysis. Afterward, describe what you experienced.

Acceptance Exercises

1. Ask a trusted friend to tell you honestly what is right and what is wrong with you. Throughout the exercise, do not defend yourself. Learn to listen quietly and carefully. After a time of reflection, write down your feelings and thoughts and describe how you have come to accept the parts of the criticisms that are true or partially true.
2. Discover and accept your limitations and find a way to get the job done despite your deficiencies.

Commitment Exercises

1. Contracting: Make a contract with yourself and/or with a trusted friend or counselor to make yourself accountable to a commitment you have made. The contract should include a realistic goal and a concrete plan of action.
2. Success story: Describe at least one incident in your life in which you had to endure and overcome a serious adversity or setback. Indicate what you learned from that experience.
3. Endurance test: Commit to a regime of gradually increasing your endurance in some activity or exercise without harming yourself. Focus on improving your ability to persist and concentrate on that task despite discomfort.
4. Team work: Commit yourself to becoming a valued member of a group. It can be a special interest club, community service group, or meet-up group (see http://www.meetup.com). Stay with that group until you feel as if you belong to the group as a significant, valued, and contributing member.
5. Good deeds: Do good deeds every week. Some good deeds may inconvenience you or call for self-sacrifice while benefiting others.
6. Challenge yourself: Do something challenging each week. Choose to do something outside your comfort zone or perform a task that is fairly difficult but still achievable.

Conclusions

We have shown that resilience is the capacity to grow and flourish in spite of setbacks and adversity. We have made the case that in order for children and youth to be resilient, we need a holistic and integrative approach that takes into account social, ecological, and cultural factors. We have shown that the meaning-centered positive triad incorporates all the dimensions of resilience. The PURE module provides the main sources of motivational, relational, and emotional resilience. Meaning and purpose give individuals direction, life goals, and the energy needed to succeed in life. Relationships and community resources provide the social support one needs. The positive emotions that ensue from meaningful pursuits are like icing on the cake, making life more pleasant and engaging.

The ABCDE module provides cognitive and behavioral resilience. Positive and realistic thinking enables one to make sound decisions and judgments. Acquiring the habit of persistence and flexibility enables one to persevere with courage, fortitude, and resourcefulness. Success in overcoming difficulties further increases one's cognitive resilience; one learns to attach positive meanings and attributions to adversity, perceiving them as challenges and opportunities, rather than threats, to becoming better and stronger.

Tragic optimism provides the existential or spiritual resilience one needs in catastrophic or hopeless situations. When one's assumptive world is shattered and when death seems inescapable, "will to meaning," according to Frankl (1946/1985), gives one the will to live. Life has meaning to its last breath. Suffering becomes bearable and death loses its sting when one has found something worth dying for. Tragic optimism offers a ray of hope even when all realistic hopes for survival and recovery have perished. In such desperate situations, tragic optimism often involves belief in miracles and an ultimate rescuer. Also, however, tragic optimism emphasizes the importance of self-transcendence, compassion, and solidarity in trying times. The burden becomes lighter and the pain becomes more bearable when people come together to help each other to survive yet another day.

The dual-systems model provides transactional resilience through managing the interactions between the approach and avoidance systems in order to minimize failure and maximize success. This meaning-centered self-regulation system capitalizes on people's capacities for meaning seeking, meaning making and meaning reconstruction in order to achieve important life goals.

In the final analysis, resilience has to be fueled by hope, faith, and love. Resilience demands all the courage one can muster, all the wisdom one can master, and all the support one can rally in order to become what one was meant to be and make worthy contributions to humanity. The holistic meaning-centered approach is designed to produce positive, mentally healthy youth by building character strengths, developing moral fortitude, fostering compassion for others, and cultivating supportive social ecologies.

Greitens (2011) provides a living example of meaning-centered resilience that combines true grit with compassion. He wrote in his autobiography:

> I've learned from nuns who fed the destitute in Mother Teresa's homes for the dying in India, aid workers who healed orphaned children in Rwanda, and Navy SEALs who fought in Afghanistan. As warriors, as humanitarians, they've taught me that without courage, compassion falters, and without compassion, courage has no direction. They've shown

> me that it is within our power, indeed the world requires of us—every one of us—to be both good and strong. (p. ix)

To Greitens, "The person who has nothing for which he is willing to fight, nothing which is more important than his own personal safety, is a miserable creature" (Back cover). This statement captures the essence of the meaning-centered positive triad for resilience and flourishing.

References

America's Promise Alliance (2010, December). *Positive youth development.* Retrieved from http://www.ncsl.org/IssuesResearch/HumanServices/WhatisPositiveYouthDevelopment/tabid/16375/Default.aspx

Aristotle. (2004). *Nichomachean ethics.* (F. H. Peters, Trans.) New York, NY: Barnes and Noble.

Azar, B. (2010, December). A reason to believe. *Monitor on Psychology, 41*(11), 52–56.

Barber, B. K. (2008a). Contrasting portraits of war: youths' varied experiences with political violence in Bosnia and Palestine. *International Journal of Behavioral Development, 32*(4), 298–309.

Barber, B. K. (2008b). Making sense and no sense of war: Issues of identity and meaning in adolescents' experience with political conflict. In B. K. Barber (Ed.), *Adolescents and war: How youth deal with political violence.* New York, NY: Oxford University.

Barrett, P. (2004a). *FRIENDS for life: Group leaders' manual for children.* Bowen Hills, Queensland, Australia: Australian Pearson Merrill Prentice Hall.

Barrett, P. (2004b). *FRIENDS for life: Workbook for children* (4th ed.). Bowen Hills, Queensland, Australia: Australian Academic Press.

Barret, P. M., & Turner, C. M. (2001). Prevention of anxiety symptoms in primary school children: Preliminary results from a universal school-based trial. *British Journal of Clinical Psychology, 40,* 399–410.

Baumeister, R. F., Heatherton, T. F., & Tice, D. M. (1994). *Losing control: How and why people fail at self-regulation.* San Diego, CA: Academic Press.

Beardslee, W. R. (1989). The role of self-understanding in resilient individuals: The development of a perspective. *American Journal of Orthopsychiatry, 59,* 266–278.

Becker, G. (1997). *Disrupted lives: How people create meaning in a chaotic world.* Los Angeles: University of California Press.

Benard, B. (1991). *Fostering resiliency in kids: Protective factors in the family, school and community.* Portland, OR: Northwest Regional Educational Laboratory.

Bender, K., Thompson, S. J., McManus, H., & Lantry, J. (2007, February). Capacity for survival: Exploring strengths of homeless street youth. *Child Youth Care Forum, 36*(1), 25–42. doi:10.1007/s10566-006-9029-4

Biglan, A., Hayes, S. C., & Pistorello, J. (2008, September). Acceptance and commitment: Implications for prevention science. *Prevention Science, 9*(3), 139–152. doi:10.1007/s11121-008-0099-4

Bonanno, G. A. (2004). Loss, trauma, and human resilience: Have we underestimated the human capacity to thrive after extremely aversive events? *American Psychologist, 59*(1), 20–28. doi:10.1037/0003-066X.59.1.20

Bowby, J. (1988). *A secure base: Parent-child attachment and healthy human development.* New York, NY: Basic Books.

Bronk, K. C. (2005). Portraits of purpose: A study examining the ways a sense of purpose contributes to positive youth development. *Dissertation Abstracts International.* (AAT 3187267)

Brooks, R., & Goldstein, S. (2002). *Raising resilient children: Fostering strength, hope, and optimism in your child.* New York, NY: McGraw-Hill.

Brooks, R., & Goldstein, S. (2004). *The power of resilience: Achieving balance, confidence, and personal strength in your life.* New York, NY: McGraw-Hill.

Catalano, R. F., Berglund, M. L., Ryan, J. A. M., Lonczak, H. S., & Hawkins, J. D. (1998). *Positive youth development in the United States: Research findings on evaluations of positive youth development programs.* Retrieved from http://aspe.hhs.gov/hsp/PositiveYouthDev99/

Csikszentmihalyi, M. (1990). *Flow: The psychology of optimal experience.* New York, NY: Harper & Row.

Csikszentmihalyi, M., & Csikszentmihalyi, I. S. (Eds.). (1992). *Optimal experience: Psychological studies of flow in consciousness.* New York, NY: Cambridge University Press.

Csikszentmihalyi, M., & Csikzentmihalyi, I. S. (Eds.). (2006). *A life worth living: Contributions to positive psychology.* New York, NY: Oxford University Press.

Curry, L., & Snyder, C. R. (2000). Hope takes the field: Mind matters in athletic performances. In C. R. Snyder (Ed.), *Handbook of hope: Theory, measures, and applications* (pp. 243–259). San Diego, CA: Academic Press.

Damon, W. (2008). *The path to purpose: Helping our children find their calling in life.* New York, NY: Free Press.

Doll, B., & Lyon, M. A. (1998). Risk and resilience: Implications for the delivery of educational and mental health services in schools. *School Psychology Review, 27*(3), 348–363.

Eggerman, M., & Panter-Brick, C. (2010). Suffering, hope, and entrapment: Resilience and cultural values in Afghanistan. *Social Science & Medicine, 71*, 71–83.

Erikson, E. H. (1963). *Childhood and society.* New York, NY: Norton.

Everly, G. S., Jr. (2008). *The resilient child: Seven essential lessons for your child's happiness and success.* New York, NY: DiaMedica.

Frankl, V. E. (1985). *Man's search for meaning* (Rev. and updated). New York, NY: Washington Square Press/Pocket Books. (Originally published 1946)

Fredrickson, B. L., Tugade, M. M., Waugh, C. E., & Larkin, G. R. (2003). What good are positive emotions in crisis? A prospective study of resilience and emotion following the terrorist attacks on the United States on September 11th, 2001. *Journal of Personality and Social Psychology, 84*, 365–376.

Fry, P. S. (1996). *Reflective and subversive dialogues with adolescents.* Research in progress, Trinity Western University, Langley, BC, Canada.

Fry, P. S. (1998). The development of personal meaning and wisdom in adolescence: A reexamination of moderating and consolidating factors and influences. In P. T. P. Wong & P. S. Fry (Eds.), *The human quest for meaning* (pp. 91–110). Mahwah, NJ: Erlbaum.

Garmezy, N. (1974, August). *The study of children at risk: New perspectives for developmental psychopathology.* Paper presented at the annual meeting of the American Psychological Association, New Orleans, Louisiana.

Garmezy, N. (1985). Stress-resistant children: The search for protective factors. In J. E. Stevenson (Ed.), *Recent research in developmental psychopathology: Journal of Child Psychology and Psychiatry Book Supplement 4* (pp. 213–233). Oxford, England: Pergamon Press.

Garmezy, N. (1991a). Resilience in children's adaptation to negative life events and stressed environments. *Pediatric Annals, 20*, 459–466.

Garmezy, N. (1991b). Resiliency and vulnerability to adverse developmental outcomes associated with poverty. *American Behavioral Scientist, 34*(4), 416–430.

Gillham, J. E., & Reivich, K. J. (2004). Cultivating optimism in childhood and adolescence. *Annals of the American Academy of Political and Social Science, 591*, 146–153.
Greenwald, A. G. (1980). The totalitarian ego: Fabrication and revision of personal history. *American Psychologist, 35*, 603–618.
Greitens, E. (2011). *The heart and the fist.* Boston, NY: Houghton Mifflin Harcourt.
Hart, K. E., & Sasso, T. (2011). Mapping the contours of contemporary positive psychology. *Canadian Psychology, 52*(2), 82–92.
Harvey, J., & Delfabbro, P. H. (2004). Resilience in disadvantaged youth: A critical overview. *Australian Psychologist, 39*, 3–13.
Hass, M., & Graydon, K. (2009). Sources of resiliency among successful foster youth. *Child and Youth Services Review, 31*, 457–463.
Hauser, S. T., Allen, J. P., & Golden, E. (2008). *Out of the woods: Tales of resilient teens.* Boston, MA: Harvard University Press.
Headey, B. (2008). Life goals matter to happiness: A revision of set-point theory. *Social Indicators Research, 86*(2), 213–231.
Heine, S. J., Proulx, T., & Vohs, K. D. (2006). The meaning maintenance model: On the coherence of social motivations. *Personality and Social Psychology Review, 10*(2), 88–110.
Hilt, L. M. (2003–2004). Attribution retraining for therapeutic change: Theory, practice, and future directions. *Imagination, Cognition and Personality, 23*(4), 289–307.
Ishiyama, F. I. (1990). Meaningful life therapy: Use of Morita therapy principles in treating patients with cancer and intractable diseases. *International Bulletin on Morita Therapy, 3*(2), 77–84.
Jamieson, K. H. (Ed.). (2005). *Treating and preventing adolescent mental health disorders: What we know and what we don't know.* New York, NY: Oxford University Press.
Janoff-Bulman, R. (1992). *Shattered assumptions: Towards a new psychology of trauma.* New York, NY: Free Press.
Jessor, R. (1993). Successful adolescent development among youth in high-risk settings. *American Psychologist, 48*, 117–126.
Johnson, A. A. (2002, May). Want better grades? Go to church. *Christianity Today, 46*(6). Retrieved from http://www.christianitytoday.com/ct/2002/may21/8.60.html
Kabat-Zinn, J. (1990). *Full catastrophe living.* New York, NY: Delacorte Press.
Kiang, L., & Fuligni, A. J. (2010). Meaning in life as a mediator of ethnic identity and adjustment among adolescents from Latin, Asian, and European American backgrounds. *Journal of Youth and Adolescence, 39*, 1253–1264. doi:10.1007/s10964-009-9475-z
Kobasa, S. C., Maddi, S. R., & Kahn, S. (1982). Hardiness and health: A prospective study. *Journal of Personality and Social Psychology, 42*, 168–177.
Lazarus, R. S., & Folkman, S. (1984). *Stress, appraisal, and coping.* New York, NY: Springer.
Lopez, S. J., & McKnight, C. (2002). Moving in a positive direction: Toward increasing the utility of positive youth development efforts. *Prevention and Treatment, 5*, http://journals.apa.org/prevention/volume5/pre0050019c.html
Luft, J., & Ingham, H. (1955). The Johari window, a graphic model of interpersonal awareness. *Proceedings of the western training laboratory in group development.* Los Angeles, CA: UCLA.
Luthar, S. S. (Ed.). (2003). *Resilience and vulnerability: Adaptation in the context of childhood adversities.* New York, NY: Cambridge University Press.
Luthar, S. S., & Goldstein, A. (2004). Children's exposure to community violence: Implications for understanding risk and resilience. *Journal of Clinical Child and Adolescent Psychology, 33*(3), 499–505.

Luthar, S. S., Cicchetti, D., & Becker, B. (2000). The construct of resilience: A critical evaluation and guidelines for future work. *Child Development*, *71*(3), 543–562.

Luthar, S. S., Doernberger, C. H., & Zigler, E. (1993). Resilience is not a unidimensional construct: Insights from a prospective study of inner-city adolescents. *Development and Psychopathology*, *5*(4), 703–717.

Luthar, S. S., & Zelazo, L. B. (2003). Research on resilience: An integrative review. In S. S. Luthar (Ed.), *Resilience and vulnerability: Adaptation in the context of childhood adversities* (pp. 510–549). New York, NY: Cambridge University Press.

Lykken, D. (1999). *Happiness: What studies on twins show us about nature, nurture, and the happiness set-point.* New York, NY: Golden Books.

Maddi, S. R. (1998). Creating meaning through making decisions. In P. T. P Wong & P. S. Fry (Eds.), *The human quest for meaning: A handbook of psychological research and clinical applications* (pp. 3–26). Mahwah, NJ: Erlbaum.

Mariano, J. M. (2007). The relationship of purpose to character strengths in emerging adulthood. *Dissertation Abstracts International.* (AAT 324590)

Maslow, A. H. (1965). *Eupsychian management: A journal.* New York, NY: Irwin.

Masten, A. S. (2001). Ordinary magic: Resilience processes in development. *American Psychologist*, *56*(3), 227–238.

Masten, A. S., & Reed, M. G. J. (2002). Resilience in development. In C. R. Snyder & S. J. Lopez (Eds.), *The handbook of positive psychology* (pp. 74–88). New York, NY: Oxford University Press.

Morisano, D., Hirsh, J. B., Peterson, J. B., Shore, B., & Pihl, R. O. (2010). Personal goal setting, reflection, and elaboration improves academic performance in university students. *Journal of Applied Psychology*, *95*, 255–264.

Myers, D. G. (1993). *The pursuit of happiness: Discovering the pathway to fulfillment, well-being, and enduring personal joy.* New York, NY: Avon Books.

Neenan, M. (2009). *Developing resilience: A cognitive-behavioural approach.* New York, NY: Routledge.

Obradović, J., Bush, N. R., Stamperdahl, J., Adler, N. E., & Boyce, W. T. (2010). Biological sensitivity to context: The interactive effects of stress reactivity and family adversity on socioemotional behavior and school readiness. *Child Development*, *81*(1), 270–289.

Pan, J. Y., Wong, D. F. K., Chan, C. L. W., & Joubert, L. (2008). Meaning of life as a protective factor of positive affect in acculturation: A resilience framework and a cross-cultural comparison. *International Journal of Intercultural Relations*, *32*, 505–514.

Park, N., & Peterson, C. (2006). Moral competence and character strengths among adolescents: The development and validation of the values in action inventory of strengths for youth. *Journal of Adolescence*, *29*, 891–909.

Peacock, E. J., & Wong, P. T. P. (1990). The Stress Appraisal Measure (SAM): A multidimensional approach to cognitive appraisal. *Stress Medicine*, 6, 227–236.

Pennebaker, J. W. (1997). Writing about emotional experiences as a therapeutic process. *Psychological Science*, *8*, 162–166.

Pines, M. (1975, December). In praise of "invulnerables." *APA Monitor*, 7.

Price-Mitchell, M. (2010). *Civic learning at the edge: Transformative stories of highly engaged youth* (Unpublished doctoral dissertation). Fielding Graduate University, Santa Barbara, California.

Raskin, J. D., Bridges, S. K., & Neimeyer, R. A. (2010). *Studies in meaning 4: Constructivist perspectives on theory, practice, and social justice.* New York, NY: Pace University Press.

Reichert, M. C., Stoudt, B., & Kuriloff, P. (2006). Don't love no fight: Healing and identity among urban youth. *Urban Review*. doi:10.1007/s11256-006-0033-7

Reivich, K., & Shatte, A. (2002). *The resilience factor: 7 essential skills for overcoming life's inevitable obstacles*. New York, NY: Broadway Books.

Robbins, B. D., & Friedman, H. (2011). Resiliency as a virtue: Contributions from humanistic and positive psychology. In K. M. Gow & M. J. Celinski (Eds.), *Continuity versus creative response to challenge: The primacy of resilience and resourcefulness in life and therapy*. Hauppauge, NY: Nova Science.

Rose, H., Miller, L., & Martinez, Y. (2009, August). "Friends for life": The results of a resilience-building, anxiety-prevention program in a Canadian elementary school. *Professional School Counseling, 12*(6), 400–407.

Rutter, M. (1987). Psychosocial resilience and protective mechanisms. *American Journal of Orthopsychiatry, 57*, 316–331.

Rutter, M. (1993). Resilience: Some conceptual considerations. *Journal of Adolescent Health, 14*, 626–631.

Ryan, R. M., & Powelson, C. L. (1991). Autonomy and relatedness as fundamental to motivation and education. *Journal of Experimental Education, 60*(1), 49–66.

Salovey, P., Mayer, J. D., & Caruso, D. (2002). The positive psychology of emotional intelligence. In C. R. Snyder & S. J. Lopez (Eds.), *The handbook of positive psychology* (pp. 159–171). New York, NY: Oxford University Press.

Salovey, P., & Sluyter, D. J. (1997). Emotional development and emotional intelligence: Educational implications. New York, NY: Basic Books.

Self authoring. (2010). Retrieved from http://www.selfauthoring.com

Seligman, M. E. (1990). *Learned optimism*. New York, NY: Knopf.

Seligman, M. E. (2011). *Flourish*. New York, NY: Free Press.

Siegel, D. J. (2001). *The developing mind: How relationships and the brain interact to shape who we are*. New York, NY: Guildford Press.

Snyder, C. R. (1997). Unique invulnerability: A classroom demonstration in estimating personal mortality. *Teaching of Psychology, 24*, 197–199.

Snyder, C. R., & Feldman, D. (2000). Hope for the many: An empowering social agenda. In C. R. Snyder (Ed.), *Handbook of hope: Theory, measures, and applications* (pp. 389–412). San Diego, CA: Academic Press.

Snyder, C. R., & Lopez, S. J. (2007). *Positive psychology: The scientific and practical explorations of human strengths*. Thousand Oaks, CA: Sage.

Sternberg, R. J. (2001). Why schools should teach for wisdom: The balance theory of wisdom in educational settings. *Educational Psychology, 36*, 227–245.

Takanishi, R. (1993). The opportunities of adolescence: Research, interventions, and policy. *American Psychologist, 48*, 85–87.

Taylor, S. E., & Brown, J. D. (1988). Illusion and well-being: A social psychological perspective on mental health. *Psychological Bulletin, 103*, 193–210.

Tomer, A., Grafton, E., & Wong, P. T. P. (Eds.). (2008). *Death attitudes: Existential & spiritual issues*. Mahwah, NJ: Lawrence Erlbaum Associates.

Tull, M. (2007). *Recovering from and overcoming trauma: Preventing the development of PTSD*. Retrieved from http://ptsd.about.com/od/causesanddevelopment/a/resiliency.htm

Ungar, M. (2004). *Nurturing hidden resilience in troubled youth*. Toronto, QC: University of Toronto Press.

Ungar, M. (2005). *Handbook for working with children and youth: Pathways to resilience across cultures and contexts*. Thousand Oaks, CA: Sage.

Ungar, M. (2006). *Strengths-based counseling for at-risk youth*. Thousand Oaks, CA: Corwin Press.

Ungar, M. (2008). Resilience across cultures. *British Journal of Social Work, 38*(2), 218–235.

Ungar, M., Brown, M., Liebenberg, L., Cheung, M., & Levine, K. (2008). Distinguishing differences in pathways to resilience among Canadian youth. *Canadian Journal of Community Mental Health*, *27*(1), 1–13.

Ungar, M., Brown, M., Liebenberg, L., Othman, R., Kwong, W. M., Armstrong, M. & Gilgun, J. (2007). Unique pathways to resilience across cultures. *Adolescence*, *42*(166), 287–310.

Ungar, M., Liebenberg, L., Boothroyd, R., Kwong, W. M., Lee, T. Y., Leblanc, J., . . . Makhnach, A. (2008). The study of youth resilience across cultures: Lessons from a pilot study of measurement development. *Research in Human Development*, *5*(3), 166–180.

Valle, M. F., Huebner, E. S., & Suldo, S. M. (2006). An analysis of hope as a psychological strength. *Journal of School Psychology*, *44*, 393–406.

Vanderbilt-Adriance, E., & Shaw, D. S. (2008, June). Conceptualizing and re-evaluating resilience across levels of risk, time, and domains of competence. *Clinical Child and Family Psychology Review*, *11*(1–2), 30–58. doi:10.1007/s10567-008-0031-2

Weiner, B. (1985). An attributional theory of achievement motivation and emotion. *Psychological Review*, *92*, 548–573.

Werner, E. E. (1984). Resilient children. *Young Children*, *40*(1), 68–72.

Werner, E. E. (1995). Resilience in development. *Current Directions in Psychological Science*, *4*, 81–85.

Werner, E., & Smith, R. (1982). *Vulnerable but invincible: A longitudinal study of resilient children and youth.* New York, NY: Adams, Bannister, & Cox.

Wexler, L. M., DiFluvio, G., & Burke, T. K. (2009). Resilience and marginalized youth: Making a case for personal and collective meaning-making as part of resilience research in public health. *Social Science & Medicine*, *69*, 565–570. doi:10.1016/j.socscimed.2009.06.022

Williams, N. R., & Lindsey, E. W. (2010). Finding their way home: Utilizing spiritual practices to bolster resiliency in youth at risk. *New Scholarship in the Human Services*, *9*(1), 1–16.

Wong, P. T. P. (1979). Frustration, exploration, and learning. *Canadian Psychological Review*, *20*, 133.

Wong, P. T. P. (1991). Existential vs. causal attributions. In S. Zelen (Ed.), *Extensions and new models of attribution theory* (pp. 84–125). New York, NY: Springer-Verlag.

Wong, P. T. P. (1993). Effective management of life stress: The resource-congruence model. *Stress Medicine*, *9*, 51–60.

Wong, P. T. P. (1995). A stage model of coping with frustrative stress. In R. Wong (Ed.), *Biological perspectives on motivated activities* (pp. 339–378). Norwood, NJ: Ablex.

Wong, P. T. P. (1998a). Academic values and achievement motivation. In P. T. P. Wong & P. S. Fry (Eds.), *The human quest for meaning: A handbook of psychological research and clinical applications* (pp. 261–292). Mahwah, NJ: Erlbaum.

Wong, P. T. P. (1998b). Implicit theories of meaningful life and the development of the Personal Meaning Profile (PMP). In P. T. P. Wong & P. S. Fry (Eds.), *The human quest for meaning: A handbook of psychological research and clinical applications* (pp. 111–140). Mahwah, NJ: Erlbaum.

Wong, P. T. P. (1998c). Spirituality, meaning, and successful aging. In P. T. P Wong & P. S. Fry (Eds.), *The human quest for meaning: A handbook of psychological research and clinical applications* (pp. 359–394). Mahwah, NJ: Erlbaum.

Wong, P. T. P. (2009a). Chinese positive psychology. In S. Lopez (Ed.), *Encyclopedia of positive psychology* (Vol. 1, pp. 148–156). Oxford, England: Wiley Blackwell.

Wong, P. T. P. (2009b). Viktor Frankl: Prophet of hope for the 21st century. In A. Batthyany & J. Levinson (Eds.), *Anthology of Viktor Frankl's logotherapy.* Phoenix, AZ: Zeig, Tucker & Theisen.

Wong, P. T. P. (2010). Meaning therapy: An integrative and positive existential psychotherapy. *Journal of Contemporary Psychotherapy, 40*(2), 85–93.

Wong, P. T. P. (2011a). The life orientation profile. Retrieved from http://inpm.org/wp-content/uploads/2011/06/Meaningful-Living-Project-Survey-1-LOP.pdf

Wong, P. T. P. (2011b). Meaning-centered counseling and therapy: An integrative and comprehensive approach to motivational counseling and addiction treatment. In W. M. Cox & E. Klinger (Eds.), *Handbook of motivational counseling: Goal-based approaches to assessment and intervention with addiction and other problems* (pp. 461–487). Chichester, England: Wiley.

Wong, P. T. P. (2011c). The meaningful living project. Retrieved from http://www.meaning.ca/archives/archive/art-meanignful-living-project-p-wong.html

Wong, P. T. P. (2011d). Positive psychology 2.0: Towards a balanced interactive model of the good life. *Canadian Psychology, 52*(2), 69–81.

Wong, P. T. P., & Fry, P. S. (Eds.). (1998). *The human quest for meaning: A handbook of psychological research and clinical applications*. Mahwah, NJ: Erlbaum.

Wong, P. T. P., & McDonald, M. (2002). Tragic optimism and personal meaning in counselling victims of abuse. *Pastoral Sciences, 20*(2), 231–249.

Wong, P. T. P., Reker, G. T., & Peacock, E. (2006). The resource-congruence model of coping and the development of the Coping Schema Inventory. In P. T. P. Wong & L. C. J. Wong (Eds.), *Handbook of multicultural perspectives on stress and coping* (pp. 223–283). New York, NY: Springer.

Wong, P. T. P., & Tomer, A. (2011). Beyond terror and denial: The positive psychology of death acceptance. *Death Studies, 35*(2), 99–106.

Wong, P. T. P., & Weiner, B. (1981). When people ask "why" questions and the heuristic of attributional search. *Journal of Personality and Social Psychology, 40*, 650–663.

Wong, P. T. P., & Wong, L. C. J. (2006). *The handbook of multicultural perspectives on stress and coping*. New York, NY: Springer.

Wong, P. T. P., & Wong, L. C. J. (in press). *A manual of meaning-centered positive interventions*. Abbotsford, BC: INPM Press.

28
From Logotherapy to Meaning-Centered Counseling and Therapy

PAUL T. P. WONG

Trent University

The quest for meaning represents not only a primary intrinsic motivation for life expansion but also a powerful capacity for personal transformation. Cognitive and existential therapies both emphasize that we are what we think; more precisely, we are how we make sense of ourselves and our place in the world. Having a healthy sense of self-identity and of one's mission in life is essential for well-being. Meaning is also a pivotal concept in understanding the complexity and predicaments of life as well as in developing faith and spirituality. It is no wonder that meaning is an essential component to all major schools of psychotherapy.

More than any other therapy, Viktor Frankl's logotherapy (1946/1985a, 1986) capitalizes on the characteristic of human beings as meaning-seeking and meaning-making creatures. Frankl died in 1997, but his enduring influence has continued to increase (Wong, 1998a, 2009). His autobiographical book *Man's Search for Meaning* still speaks to new generations of readers, and his impact on psychology and psychotherapy has been well documented (Batthyany & Guttmann, 2006; Batthyany & Levinson, 2009). Joseph Fabry and Elizabeth Lukas, two leading figures in logotherapy, contributed to the first edition of the *Human Quest for Meaning*; they were unable to revise their chapters because they passed away. Their contributions to logotherapy are included in this chapter, however. Here, I present the basic tenets and principles of logotherapy and then describe how logotherapy evolves into meaning-centered counseling and therapy (MCCT).

A Brief Overview of Logotherapy

Logotherapy simply means therapy through meaning. Frankl considered logotherapy a spiritually oriented approach toward psychotherapy. "A psychotherapy which not only recognizes man's spirit, but actually starts from it may be termed logotherapy. In this connection, logos is intended to signify 'the spiritual' and beyond that 'the meaning'" (Frankl, 1986, xvii). Of interest to note it has become common practice in academic psychology to define spirituality in terms of meaning and purpose (Wong, 1998d; Wong, Wong, McDonald, & Klaassen, 2007).

The term *existential analysis* implies a form of depth psychotherapy influenced by Sigmund Freud's psychoanalysis. Frankl, however, focused on clients' cries for meaning and purpose, both of which may lie latent at a subconscious level. For Frankl, existential analysis is the therapeutic process of making clients aware of their spirituality and capacity for meaning. "Inasmuch as logotherapy makes him aware of the hidden logos of his existence, it is an analytical process" (Frankl, 1985a, p. 125). In Frankl's writing, existential analysis and logotherapy are used interchangeably.

The Spiritual Dimension of Human Existence

One of the propositions of logotherapy is that the human spirit is our healthy core. The human spirit may be conceptualized as our basic yearnings and capacity for meaning and spirituality. The human spirit may be blocked by biological or psychological sickness, but it remains intact; the spirit does not get sick, even when the psychobiological organism is injured. The main objective of existential analysis is to remove the blockages and free the human spirit to fulfill its tasks.

According to Fabry (1994), the noetic dimension or the human spirit is the "medicine chest" of logotherapy, containing such various inner resources as love, the will to meaning, purpose in life, hope, dignity, creativity, conscience, and the capacity for choice. Existential analysis focuses on activating the noetic dimension through a variety of therapeutic means, among them the appealing technique, modification of attitude, Socratic dialogue, paradoxical intention, and dereflection.

Paradoxical intention is a very useful therapeutic technique. Simply put, it encourages the client to confront his or her worst nightmare. In fact, the client is encouraged to imagine a worst-case scenario that is so ridiculous and so impossible that the only logical response is to laugh at it. This technique is based on the human capacity of self-distancing or self-detachment. It is similar to the externalization technique used in narrative therapy, which asks the client to detach him- or herself from the problem and observe the problem as something external to the self. By distancing oneself from the problem, one gains some clarity and perspective so that the problem no longer defines or consumes the individual.

The second-most commonly used logotherapy technique is called dereflection. With dereflection, the client is asked to shift his or her focus from a seemingly intractable problem to something bigger and positive. This technique is based on the human capacity for self-transcendence. In other words, the client is asked to rise above or transcend the problem.

When existential analysis is effective, clients become more open and more accepting of themselves and also more tolerant of the complexities and dark aspects of human existence. They begin to feel free to engage the world and pursue their dreams in a responsible and courageous manner; as a result, clients become able to lead an authentic and meaningful life.

Basic Tenets of Logotherapy

The three fundamental tenets of logotherapy are (1) freedom of will, (2) will to meaning, and (3) meaning of life (Frankl, 1967/1985b). These three tenets are interconnected: People have the intrinsic motivation for meaning; they are free to choose and live a meaningful life because meaning can be found in all circumstances. Logotherapy is built on these three basic propositions.

Freedom of Will Without the capacity for freedom of will, people would not be able to choose how to respond to a given situation and decide on their own preferred life path. Freedom of will enables people to be responsible, moral agents. There is no escape from making choices, and people are accountable for the consequences of their decisions and actions. Frankl (1946/1985a) emphasized that freedom without responsibility would lead to chaos and nihilism. Therefore, freedom is always limited by responsibility. Fabry (1998) wrote, "This individual responsibility is a personal response to ultimate meaning and to the meanings of the moment as they are interpreted by the unique individual" (p. 298). We are responsible to ourselves, to other people, to societal values, and to the suprahuman dimension.

> In this suprahuman dimension dwells the order which I have defined as ultimate meaning. One could also call it "suprameaning"—an order whose laws we can violate only at our peril, regardless of whether we see the order in religious or secular terms: as God, Life, Nature, or the Ecosystem. (Fabry, 1994, p. 150)

According to Fabry (1994), "The switch from a vertical to a horizontal value system has caused confusion and meaninglessness because many people reject the traditional guidelines and have had no experience in finding their own" (p. 206). Fabry suggested that the demands of the suprahuman dimension may correct the widespread belief that individuals are free to do whatever they want to achieve success and happiness.

Will to Meaning The will to meaning refers to the primary motivation of seeking meaning and living a meaningful life. Human beings are not pushed by drives, instincts, and past histories of reinforcement but drawn forward by the need to fulfill future meanings. The ultimate purpose in life is not to gain pleasure or power but to find meaning and value in life. Will to meaning is essential for survival and health. The will to live is best understood as the will to meaning. A strong will to meaning enables people to endure unimaginable sufferings and to persist in pursuing their ideals (Frankl, 1969/1988).

Frankl considered Freud's pleasure principle and Adler's will to power as derivatives of the will to meaning. Accordingly,

> pleasure is a byproduct or side effect of the fulfillment of our strivings, but is destroyed and spoiled to the extent to which it is made a goal or target.... The will to pleasure mistakes the effect of the end, the will to power mistakes the means to an end for the end itself. (Frankl, 1967/1985b, p. 6)

Meaning of Life The third tenet, meaning of life, affirms that meaning can be found even in the most miserable and tragic circumstances. Life has meaning not only in specific situations but also in one's existence as a whole. The ultimate meaning of one's life, in Frankl's belief, is found in the spiritual dimension of human beings. Fabry (1998) wrote:

> People's lives will be meaningful to the extent their human spirit is able to tune in on the "Ultimate Meaning" (Frankl, 1985, p. 141) in the suprahuman dimension of the Spirit (with a capital S). Frankl translated the word *logos* both with "spirit" and "meaning." The biblical passage "In the beginning was *logos*, and *logos* was with God, and *logos* was God," to Frankl meant: In the beginning was Meaning, it is the center of the universe and calls out to people to discover it. It is the ultimate demand of life. (pp. 297–298)

Although Frankl (1946/1985a) believed in ultimate meaning and purpose, he chose to focus on specific meanings for concrete situations in psychotherapy: "What matters, therefore, is not the meaning of life in general, but rather the specific meaning of a person's life at a given moment" (p. 171). Every meaning is unique to each person, and each person has to discover the meaning of each particular situation for him- or herself. The therapist can only challenge and guide the client to potential areas of meaning.

Frankl (1946/1985a) emphasized the discovery rather than the creation of personal meaning: "The true meaning of life is to be discovered in the world rather than within man or his own psyche" (p. 133). The underlying assumption is that meaning can be detected only through one's reflection on life experiences, in addition to active engagement in the world and with people. Furthermore, one cannot create meaning without any reference to horizontal and vertical values. Personal meaning needs are based in universal and time-proven values. In the spiritual realm, meaning and values are closely related.

One cannot understand the meaning of life apart from the meaning of suffering because suffering is an inevitable aspect of human existence. To discover meaning in suffering is essential to meaningful living. Frankl's own life epitomized Nietzche's dictum: "He who has a *why* to live for can bear almost any *how*" (as cited in Frankl, 1946/1985a, p. 97). When individuals are stripped of everything that makes life worth living or when they are in the throes of battling with pain and despair, meaning makes suffering more bearable and provides reasons for living:

> It is precisely when facing such fate, when being confronted with a hopeless situation, that man is given a last opportunity to fulfill a meaning—to realize even the highest value, to fulfill even the deepest meaning—the meaning of suffering. (Frankl, 1967/1985b, p. 15)

The Calls of Meaning Fabry (1998) pointed out the calls of meaning as a fourth tenet implicit in the foregoing three: "Life challenges individuals with demands to which they have to respond if they are to live a fulfilled life" (p. 297). Thus, one's primary concern is to discover and surrender to the call of meaning. The significance of this meaning orientation needs to be fully grasped in order for individuals to live a truly fulfilling life because doing so entails the development of a meaning mindset as a frame of reference for looking at each event and life as a whole. We can never fully understand ultimate meaning because it is a matter of continued pursuit and incremental understanding, but having a sense of one's calling, no matter how vague, is an important guiding light in decision making and discovering the meaning of the moment.

Lukas (1998) further elaborated on the concept of the call of meaning: To live is to fulfill the call of meaning. Thus, the ultimate purpose of life is meaning rather than happiness and success. This meaning mindset makes all the difference how one lives and makes decisions. The key to living a truly meaningful life is to "build a bridge between the meaning of life as the guiding ray of providence that is invisible but perceptible and the personal life goals that are visible in acts of will and in wishes" (p. 311). The process of achieving congruence includes three elements: First, awareness of one's special purpose or mission in life. Setting life goals to fulfill this special mission depends on self-knowledge, that is, awareness of one's interests, talents, and limitations. It also depends on a guiding ray from a variety of such external sources as cultural values, societal norms, and religions. This guiding light "seeks to grant passage to the highest realization of a unique, irrevocable personal existence" (p. 309). Second, all people are given the necessary gifts, talents, and opportunities to fulfill their special mission. However, one needs to develop these innate strengths and gifts. Third, individuals must follow their conscience, their sense of responsibility, and their best light to set life goals and make decisions congruent with their calling. Logotherapy takes into account the clients' personal strengths, value systems, and understanding of ultimate meaning.

Frankl (1967/1985b) emphasized that we do not prescribe meaning for clients but educate them regarding the nature and pathways to meaning:

> While no logotherapist *prescribes* a meaning he may well *describe* it. This means describing what is going on in a man when he experiences

> something as meaningful, without applying to such experiences any preconceived pattern of interpretation. In short, our task is to resort to a phenomenological investigation of the immediate data of actual life experience. (pp. 28–29)

The Pathways to Meaning Frankl (1946/1985a) suggested three ways of finding meaning: (a) giving or contributing something to the world through our work, (b) experiencing something or encountering someone, and (c) choosing a courageous attitude toward unavoidable suffering. This deceptively simple formulation actually contains a great deal of wisdom and has clinical implications. The creative pathway to meaning emphasizes the human being as a responsible, creative, and free agent capable of self-regulation, self-determination, and goal striving. It also implies that the meaningful life is an achieving life, that is, that each person has the opportunities to develop his or her potentials and achieve something significant.

The experiential pathway is even richer in its implications. If the creative pathway focuses on giving gifts through the work you do, the experiential pathway focuses on receiving gifts from life. It means savoring every moment of the day and appreciating the gifts of relationships and gifts from nature. Our lives are enriched when we are mindful of whatever happens to us and around us. It means that we are open to all that life has to offer with sensitivity and gratitude, even when life hurts.

The attitudinal pathway is especially important in situations of unavoidable suffering. Frankl (1969/1988) claimed: "This is why life never ceases to hold meaning, for even a person who is deprived of both creative and experiential values is still challenged by a meaning to fulfill, that is, by the meaning inherent in the right, in an upright way of suffering" (p. 70). Indeed, attitudinal values are probably the most important to human survival and flourishing in times of adversity and tragedy. The attitudinal pathway encourages the defiant human spirit to go deeper, higher, and broader—digging deeper into one's inner resources, reaching higher for hope and inspiration, and reaching out to connect with other suffering people. This attitude is also based on the belief that an individual life cannot be destroyed if it is devoted to something bigger, higher, and more long-lasting than itself. Having the right attitude toward suffering and life indicates that one has reflected on one's life experiences and learned to make sense of the difficulties, predicaments, and paradoxes of life. Logotherapy recognizes that every crisis is an opportunity for personal transformation and developing a mature worldview. Clients are helped to revise their assumptions and attitudes so that they can adapt better to their life circumstances.

Existential Frustration

Existential frustration is a universal human experience because the quest for existential meaning can be blocked by external circumstances as well as internal hindrances. When the will to meaning is frustrated, existential vacuum may result, enveloping the individual with a general sense of meaninglessness or emptiness, as evidenced by a state of boredom. Such existential vacuum is a widespread phenomenon as a result of industrialization, the loss of traditional values, and the dehumanization of individuals in the modern world. Many people feel that life has no purpose, no challenge, and no obligation; they try to fill their existential vacuum with material goods or superficial things, but their misguided efforts lead only to frustration and despair (Frankl, 1946/1985a).

According to Frankl (1986), feelings of meaninglessness underlie "the mass neurotic triad of today, i.e., depression-addiction-aggression" (p. 298). A meaning-oriented therapist would explore the linkage between these psychological problems and the underlying existential vacuum.

Suffering and the Tragic Triad

About suffering, Frankl (1946/1985a) says: "If there is a meaning in life at all, then there must be a meaning in suffering. Suffering is an ineradicable part of life, even as fate and death" (p. 88).

Suffering is not a necessary condition for meaning, but suffering tends to trigger the quest for meaning. Paradoxically, our ability to embrace and transform suffering is essential for authentic happiness. Frankl (1967/1985b) observed that *homo sapiens* are concerned with success, whereas the *homo patiens* (the suffering human being) is more concerned about meaning. Through his own experience and observations of prisoners and clients, Frankl (1946/1985a, 1986) also observed that people are willing to endure any suffering if they are convinced that this suffering has meaning. Suffering without meaning, however, leads to the tragic triad.

Logotherapists do not ask for a reason for suffering but guide their clients toward the realization of concrete meanings and choosing the right attitudes. Many logotherapists appeal to their clients to take a heroic stand toward suffering by suggesting that unavoidable suffering gives them the opportunity to bear witness to dignity and the human potential.

The search for meaning is very likely to be occasioned by three negative facets of human existence: pain, guilt, and death. Pain refers to human suffering, guilt to the awareness of our fallibility, and death to our awareness of the transitory nature of life (Frankl, 1946/1985a, 1967/1985b). These negative experiences make us more aware of our needs for meaning and spiritual aspiration. Neuroses are more likely to originate from our attempt to obscure the reality of pain, guilt, and death as existential facts (Frankl, 1946/1985a, 1967/1985b).

Logotherapy provides an answer to the tragic triad through attitudinal values because worldviews and life orientation may have far more influence on how we live our lives than our cognitions and behaviors in specific situations.

This is usually accomplished through constructively confronting negative views and directly appealing to the defiant power of the human spirit.

Assessment of Logotherapy

The importance of spirituality in healing has gained widespread acceptance in today's therapeutic community, but Frankl was the first one to make spirituality the cornerstone of logotherapy. Frankl can also be credited as the father of existential positive psychology and positive psychotherapy (Wong, 2009) because rather than focusing on what is wrong with us, he focused on what is right with us and what is good about life, and he took this stand despite the horrors he personally endured. He emphasized our capacity to respond to the meaning potentials of aversive situations; through our affirmative and optimistic responses to events, he believed, we can transcend negative forces and live meaningful lives whatever our circumstances may be.

Because of its general holistic orientation, logotherapy can be applied to a wide variety of disciplines, ranging from medicine, counseling, and pastoral care to education and management. It can also be employed in all areas of our lives so that we can fulfill our potentials. There are, nonetheless, three limitations: First, logotherapy is often referred to by logotherapists as the Franklian philosophy. As an existential philosophy, logotherapy is difficult to subject to empirical tests or link to relevant psychology research. Frankl's antireductionism is also responsible for the lack of empirical research on logotherapy.

Second, Frankl intended logotherapy as an adjunct to whatever therapy one practices. Although logotherapy offers several logotherapeutic techniques to psychological problems related to the existential vacuum, it was not designed to provide a comprehensive and coherent framework of counseling or psychotherapy incorporating a wide range of skills and tools.

Third, many Frankl loyalists are opposed to any extension of logotherapy. Some even have a "guild" mentality, trying to ban others from making any reference to logotherapy without having taken a set of courses offered by them. They are more Catholic than the pope in their rigid and dogmatic approach to logotherapy. Their entrenched legalistic attitude has, however, actually done more harm than good in terms of advancing Frankl's ideas around the globe. In fact, Frankl always intended logotherapy to be used for the betterment of humanity, rather than being a clinical specialty for the career benefits of a few psychotherapists.

In the true spirit of Viktor Frankl, Joseph Fabry was progressive and forward looking (Wong, 1999a). Largely responsible for introducing logotherapy to North America, he was the founder of the Viktor Frankl Institute of Logotherapy and founding editor of the *International Forum of Logotherapy*. It was through his unfailing support and encouragement that I was able to develop MCCT (Wong, 1999a, 1999b).

Meaning-Centered Counseling and Therapy

Over the past decade, through MCCT I have elaborated and extended Frankl's classic logotherapy by introducing new constructs and skills that are consistent with the basic tenets of logotherapy (Wong, 1997, 1998a, 1999b). I have already alluded to the fact that some of the concepts and skills of logotherapy are related to the best practices of other approaches of psychotherapy. Although rooted in logotherapy, MCCT has evolved into an integrative therapy informed by advances in psychological research and new insights.

For MCCT, the key organizing construct is meaning, which is central to understanding culture and society (Bruner, 1990; Wong & Wong, 2006), physical and mental health (Wong & Fry, 1998), spirituality and religion (Wong, 1998c), and death and dying (Wong, 2008). Various constructs in cognitive and social psychology, among them cognitive reframing, existential and spiritual coping, attribution, stress appraisal, and life review, are also incorporated in MCCT (Wong, 1998c).

Consistent with all existentially oriented therapies, MCCT is primarily concerned with the meaning and quality of human existence. It emphasizes the importance of understanding what it means to be fully alive and how to live vitally in spite of suffering and the finiteness of life. It helps people acquire existential insight and psychological skills to transform and transcend unavoidable predicaments and pursue worthy life goals. Consistent with most faith traditions and the tenets of logotherapy, MCCT believes that the terminal value of self-centered pursuits of personal happiness and success often lead to disillusion and misery, whereas the ultimate concern of actualizing one's mission leads to authentic happiness and fulfillment.

May (1940) was explicit in his writings on meaning and purpose. He affirmed that life has meaning: "The creative person can affirm life in its three dimensions—affirm himself, affirm his fellow-men and affirm his destiny. To him life has meaning" (p. 19). Personal meaning comes not only from the continuous process of fulfilling potentials but also from religious beliefs: "The essence of religion is the belief that something matters—the *presupposition that life has meaning*" (pp. 19–20).

This unconditional affirmation of meaning—both provisional meaning and ultimate meaning—constitutes the bedrock foundation for MCCT. The following defining characteristics of MCCT more clearly indicate how it has evolved from logotherapy.

Defining Characteristics of Meaning-Centered Counseling and Therapy

MCCT Is Integrative and Holistic What would be your focus when a client walks into your office? Your diagnosis and treatment are likely to be shaped by your theoretical orientation. Given the complexity of psychological problems today, however, no one school of psychotherapy is sufficient by itself. The micro and macro forces that contribute to individual predicaments are beyond the scope of any single theoretical lens. An openness to integrate different ideas and a willingness to explore new alchemies of therapy may provide new clinical insight. Thus, a flexible integrative approach to psychotherapy may be more efficacious (Brooks-Harris, 2008; Norcross & Goldfried, 2005).

MCCT is one emerging integrative model that is open, flexible, and comprehensive. It assimilates cognitive-behavioral, narrative, cross-cultural, and positive therapies (Wong, 1998c, 2005, 2007, 2008) with its logotherapy and humanistic-existential roots.

Because the meaning construct itself is holistic, MCCT is *inherently* rather than *technically* integrative. Hoffman (2009) explains:

> The instillation of meaning is a primary component of all existential approaches to psychotherapy. The deepest forms of meaning can be experienced on the various realms of biological, behavioral, cognitive, emotional, and interpersonal; in other words, it is a holistic meaning. The attainment of meaning is one of the most central aspects of human existence and necessary to address in existential therapy. (p. 45)

Most important, MCCT is holistic by virtue of its focus on meaning and conceptualizing humans as biopsychosocial spiritual beings. Thus, a meaning-oriented therapist approaches the client not as a compartmentalized patient with some dysfunction or disease but as a troubled person seeking healing and wholeness in a broken world. Therefore, we propose that the best way to achieve a fuller understanding of the presenting problem is to place all clinical knowledge and findings within a meaning-centered integrative and holistic framework that recognizes the client as a complete human being in a specific historical and cultural context. By the same token, the best way to motivate positive change is to explore the many different modalities and avenues that resonate with the client.

MCCT Is Existential or Spiritual Viktor Frankl's logotherapy, which literally means therapy through meaning, may be translated as meaning-oriented or meaning-centered therapy. It incorporates spirituality, emphasizes the need to relate and respond to the ultimate meaning of life, and makes clients confront the logos within them. It focuses on our human responsibility to live meaningfully and purposefully in every situation on a daily basis in order to become what we are meant to be.

According to Frankl, three factors characterize human existence: spirituality, freedom, and responsibility. The spiritual dimension is the very core of our humanness, the essence of humanity. The defiant power of the human spirit refers to the human capacity to tap into the spiritual dimension in order to transcend the detrimental effects of stressful situations, illness, or the influence of the past.

As mentioned earlier, the human spirit is the most important resource in psychotherapy. It may be conceptualized as the inner resources of Wong's resource-congruence model of coping (Wong, 1993; Wong, Reker, & Peacock, 2006). Research has clearly demonstrated the vital role of these inner resources in achieving resilience (Wong & Fry, 1998; Wong & Wong, 2006). Both logotherapy and MCCT attempt to awaken people's awareness of the importance of spirituality, freedom, and responsibility in recovery and personal growth.

Based on his observations of inmates in concentration camps and patients in hospitals, Frankl (2000) concluded that the will to meaning and self-transcendence are essential for survival:

> Under the same conditions, those who were oriented toward the future, toward a meaning that waited to be fulfilled—these persons were more likely to survive. Nardini and Lifton, two American military psychiatrists, found the same to be the case in the prisoner-of-war camps in Japan and Korea. (p. 97)

MCCT recognizes that what defines human beings is that they are meaning-seeking and meaning-making creatures living in cultures based on shared meanings (Bruner, 1990). MCCT also recognizes that when a void engulfs human existence, all behaviors, in one way or another, are aimed at filling this vacuum (Baumeister, 1991; Klinger, 1977).

Van Deurzen and Adams (2011) summed up the notion of humans as meaning-making beings thus: "In the sense that life is about meaning creating, the spiritual dimension is the central axis of existential therapy" (p. 20). Spirituality entails meaning creation and myth making. Spiritual beliefs are important because when basic faith in God, transcendence, or some universal principle of value is absent, people feel less secure and less able to rise above existential crises that are beyond their control. Spiritual beliefs are also important for one's sense of well-being because they provide worldviews that make sense of life and provide values by which to live.

MCCT Is Relational Another crucial element of MCCT is the centrality of relationships for healing, meaning, and well-being (Wong, 1998b, 1998c), This basic tenet is based on the need to belong, which is a fundamental human motivation (Adler, 1964; Baumeister & Leary, 1995) and imperative to the therapeutic relationship as the key to effective therapy (Duncan, Miller, Wampold, & Hubble, 2009; Norcross, 2002). The phenomenal growth of social media (e.g. Facebook, Twitter) attests to the deep-seated human needs for social connection. In MCCT, the relationship goes beyond mere therapeutic alliance; it is more like an authentic encounter that reaches the deepest level of common humanity between two individuals. Therapeutic change necessarily involves some form of exchange of life, resulting in reciprocal change in both parties in the counseling setting. Each counseling session constitutes a genuine existential encounter. In this here-and-now encounter, information and energy flow back and forth between two human beings; thus, the messenger is more important than the message, and the therapist more important than the therapy. In fact, the therapist is the most important instrument in the entire therapeutic process. In addition to addressing interpersonal issues experienced by clients (Weissman, Markowitz, & Klerman, 2000) and capitalizing on the here-and-now interactions as the basis for diagnosis and therapy (Yalom, 1980), MCCT seeks to enhance clients' positive meanings through relationships. MCCT emphasizes the need for personal growth as an essential part of professional development. An MCCT practitioner needs to be a secure, centered person who possesses the personal qualities of genuineness, empathy, and unconditional positive regard, as emphasized by Carl Rogers.

These three qualities are incorporated in the practice of the five components of mindful presence: openness, compassion, empathy, acceptance, and nonjudgment. Such an oceanic mindful awareness of the here and now can have a powerful impact on the client. Mindful presence means that the therapist is psychologically and spiritually present and that he or she is relationally and emotionally attuned to the client.

The relationship is not only necessary for building rapport, trust, and therapeutic alliance but also curative in its own right. If one's sense of displacement, estrangement, and alienation are contributing factors to one's problems, then a renewed sense of connectivity and belonging is an antidote to these attachment deficits. Mindful presence provides a model for new ways of relating and demonstrates the importance of the self-regulation skill of mindful awareness.

MCCT Is Positive Because of its affirmation of life and the defiant human spirit to survive and flourish no matter what, MCCT is intrinsically positive. This approach emphasizes that there is always something worth living for. More important, it maintains that individuals have almost unlimited capacity to construct complex meaning systems that protect them from inevitable negative life experiences and also empower them to make life worth living during very difficult times. What makes MCCT a potent form of positive therapy is its stance that there are no hopeless cases for positive change. Healing and recovery can be a long and daunting uphill battle, but the struggle can make us better and stronger. MCCT provides both the motivation and the road map for positive transformation.

The concept of tragic optimism in logotherapy (Frankl, 1946/1985a; Wong, 2007) provides an answer to human suffering and death through attitudinal values:

> I speak of a tragic optimism, that is, an optimism in the face of tragedy and in view of the human potential which at its best always allows for:

> (1) turning suffering into a human achievement and accomplishment; (2) deriving from guilt the opportunity to change oneself for the better; and (3) deriving from life's transitoriness an incentive to take responsible action. (Frankl, 1946/1985a, p. 162)

Frankl maintains that meaning and hope can be found regardless of the circumstances up to the last breath. Born out of desperation and nurtured by adversity, tragic optimism is the kind of hope that can weather the worst storms and disasters. Wong (2009) has identified the following key ingredients of tragic optimism: acceptance, affirmation, courage, faith, and self-transcendence. These qualities are incorporated in the practices of both logotherapy and MCCT. The intervention strategies described later address all five components of tragic optimism. Tragic optimism can be very helpful in working with individuals suffering from drug addiction, chronic pain, disabilities, and terminal illnesses.

Seligman, Steen, Park, and Peterson (2005) demonstrated that exercises designed explicitly to increase positive emotion, engagement, and meaning are more efficacious in treating depression than is cognitive-behavioral therapy (CBT) without positive psychology (PP) exercises. MCCT goes beyond CBT and PP exercises by (a) addressing existential and spiritual issues involved in depression and other psychological disorders, (b) emphasizing the importance and the skills of transforming and transcending life crises and personal tragedies, and (c) equipping clients with the tools to succeed in their quest for a better and more fulfilling life. MCCT represents a meaning-oriented positive psychotherapy, which taps into people's innate capacities for self-reflection, meaning construction, responsible action, and personal growth.

For a meaning therapist, the client's ability to discover the calls of meaning and make sense of the complexities and paradoxes of life is just as important as enhancing the client's strengths and positive affect. In MCCT, positive psychotherapy is not a set of exercises adjunct to the traditional CBT. Instead, the positive orientation of restoring hope and meaning, as well as the cultivating of strengths and resilience, permeates the entire process of psychotherapy, from intake to end. In sum, MCCT represents the second wave of positive psychology, which recognizes both the downsides of positives and the upsides of negatives (Wong, in press; Yu, 2009). Here are some of the positive assumptions of MCCT:

- Meaning and hope can be found in the most helpless and hopeless situations.
- Humans are capable of self-transcendence.
- Humans always have the freedom and responsibility to choose their own destiny.

- Individuals are capable of growth regardless of internal and external limitations.
- Meaning is essential to healing, happiness, and well-being.
- Practice of compassion and altruism is essential to meaningful living.
- All negatives can be transformed into positives.
- All existential crises are opportunities for personal transformation.

MCCT Is Multicultural For several reasons, MCCT is inherently multicultural in its orientation and practice:

1. Because meaning is both individually and socially constructed, one's meaning systems are inevitably shaped by one's historical and sociocultural background.
2. Culture has a profound and pervasive influence on people's behaviors and attitudes. We cannot understand clients' behaviors and attitudes apart from their meaning systems and cultural backgrounds (Arthur & Pedersen, 2008).
3. Empathy demands cultural sensitivity in working with clients from different racial, ethnic, and cultural backgrounds. Pedersen, Crethar, and Carlson (2008) stress the need for inclusive cultural empathy as an antidote to cultural biases.
4. We cannot fully understand the meaning of behaviors unless it is viewed at all levels of the ecological context. An ecological approach enables us to understand the existential-phenomenological experiences of individuals in their interactions with the different contexts of their life circumstances.
5. In a multicultural society, personal meaning systems necessarily evolve through the long struggle of navigating the cross-currents of different cultures. Therefore, sensitivity, understanding, and knowledge of such struggles are essential to MCCT.
6. MCCT employs macrocounseling skills because behavior is always situated in an ecological context, which includes macrosystems, including culture, race, gender, history, and the human condition.

Wong (2008) emphasizes the following qualities that facilitate cross-cultural interactions: openness to new experiences, willingness to accept and tolerate differences, inclusive cultural empathy, respect for other cultures, and the humility to acknowledge one's own cultural blind spots and implicit racial biases.

Many of the main features suggested by the multicultural counseling theory (Sue & Sue, 2003) are implicit in MCCT. For example, MCCT also seeks to understand and motivate clients at different levels, including personal circumstances, the cultural context, and the universal existential givens. Meaning-centered therapists help clients define life goals that are consistent with their life experiences, cultural values, and the universal needs for meaning and relationship.

Given MCCT's concern with the client's social context and place in society, the MCCT approach shares many of the same objectives as multicultural counseling theory as listed by Nelson-Jones (2002). These counseling goals include providing support, encouraging reconciliation, facilitating acculturation, addressing issues of marginalization and discrimination, managing intergenerational conflict, helping clients manage cross-cultural relationships, and attaining a higher level of personal and societal development.

Thus, on a personal and societal level, the cultural orientation of MCCT contributes to the positive motivation for change by appealing to clients' culture-specific values and addressing societal problems resulting from cultural barriers and discrimination.

MCCT Is Narrative Meaning consists of more than isolated concepts and actions. Meaning is best understood and communicated in stories because of the "storied nature of human conduct" (Sarbin, 1986). Human beings lead storied lives; they also construct and communicate their activities and experiences as stories filled with meaning. Only narratives do full justice to the lived experience of individuals and their sociocultural contexts. We all need a story to live by—a story that crystallizes our core values, spiritual beliefs, and ethical principles.

In some way, all therapists depend on narratives from their clients for the purpose of diagnosis and treatment. Meaning-centered narrative therapy goes further and deeper in its emphasis on the power of reconstructing past meanings and reauthoring one's life story as a means of bringing about positive change. MCCT makes use of both local narratives and metanarratives to provide the guiding ray of meaning. Harnessing the motivation to pursue and live out one's preferred life can be a powerful impetus for change.

MCCT Is Psychoeducational MCCT favors a psychoeducational approach for two reasons. First, it is helpful to explain to clients the change process and the tools and strategies used to facilitate such change. The importance of meaning and relationship in achieving positive change must be explained quite clearly. So much depends on the clients' level of understanding. At a minimum, clients need to understand that their meaning-centered therapists are concerned with two basic practices: (a) how to make relationships work not only in the counseling room but also in real life situations and (b) how to decide and pursue what really matters in making life better in spite of inevitable setbacks.

Second, therapy is essentially a learning process, for it involves learning new ways of looking at life and new ways of living. The MCCT approach provides important guidelines and tools for living a life filled with meaning, purpose, and responsibility. Once clients master these tools and strategies, they can employ them effectively in real-life situations even long after termination of therapy.

The Conceptual Framework

Based on the foregoing basic assumptions and tenets, the conceptual framework of MCCT is expressed in two complementary theoretical models: the dual-systems model and the meaning-management theory (MMT).

Whereas dual-systems model is primarily concerned with the interactions between the approach and avoidance systems, MMT is concerned with the underlying psychological processes involved in self-regulation and focuses on meaning-related cognitive processes in (a) such automatic adaptive mechanisms in daily functioning as stress appraisal (Peacock & Wong, 1990) and attribution (Wong & Weiner, 1981) and (b) such executive decision-making processes as goal setting and making choices. A meaning-centered counselor would keep in mind how the interventions contribute to the underlying processes of meaning seeking, meaning making, and meaning reconstruction.

The Dual-Systems Model

The dual-systems model is explained in greater detail in Chapter 1 of this volume. Here I simply want to mention the importance of the dual-systems model in integrating approach and avoidance systems to optimize positive transformation of the individual as well as organizations. Given that negative events and suffering are an inevitable part of human existence, MCCT specializes in transforming problems and negative forces into positive potentials for clients. The ABCDE strategy is a good example of the use of meaning seeking, meaning reconstruction, and existential coping (Wong, Reker, & Peacock, 2006). These are examples of useful tools for effectively coping with negative life events. Tragic optimism (Frankl, 1985a; Wong, 2009) is yet another example of a meaning-based intervention that restores and reconstructs hope from the ashes of disaster and trauma. Budd and Budd (2010), for example, investigated how twelve wrongfully convicted and imprisoned men held onto hope. The research and interviews by Budd and Budd, revealed in their book *Tested*, showed that the secrets that enabled the twelve men to sustain their hope and maintain their sanity despite the gross injustice of wrongful conviction and the harsh environment of the prison system were, not surprisingly, components of tragic optimism. These components included accepting the horrible ordeal they had to endure, affirming that there is ultimate justice and having faith that in the end justice will prevail, transcending the negative circumstances, and finally having the courage to live through the terrible injustice. Likewise components of tragic optimism can be found in the case of the miners who were trapped for more than three days underground in Pennsylvania; again, what enabled them to keep their spirits up was faith in their eventual rescue and the mutual support and relationships with fellow miners (Goodell, 2002). In both cases, hope was not based on agency and resourcefulness as conceptualized by Snyder (2002) nor on the dispositional optimism of expecting good things to happen, as conceptualized by Scheier and Carver (1985); instead, hope was based more on acceptance, affirmation, and faith as emphasized by Frankl (1946/1985a). In short, the dual-systems model capitalizes on the potential of meaning and spirituality in transcending and transforming unimaginable, noxious life circumstances. Therefore MCCT, like logotherapy, is uniquely suited for extreme human conditions.

The Meaning-Management Theory

In MMT, the centrality of meaning seeking and meaning making in human adaptation is paramount. Meaning encompasses (a) the human quest for meaning and purpose, (b) the human capacity to discover and create meanings out of raw and perplexing life experiences, and (c) the capacity to reconstruct meaning through transforming one's worldviews and reauthoring one's life story. Whereas the dual-systems model provides a practical guide to clinical intervention, MMT provides a theoretical framework of such underlying meaning-related processes as meaning seeking, meaning making, and meaning reconstruction.

The quest for meaning is a biological imperative (Klinger, 1998; Sommer & Baumeister, 1998). Survival depends on (a) our capacity to predict and control our environment through learning the significance of events happening to us and (b) purposeful behavior to meet the basic needs for existence. This biological impulse can, however, be distorted and blocked by traumatic life experiences and oppressive circumstances.

Meaning is also imperative for self-expansion. Higher-order meanings, among them actualizing one's potentials, living an authentic life, improving the well-being of disadvantaged people, or doing God's will, are born from ideas and imaginations. The most powerful incentives are not money, power, or possessions but ideas that can make a difference in the world. Frankl (1946/1985a) considers the will to meaning as the primary motivation that makes us humane.

Traditional existential therapy focuses on reducing existential anxieties, especially death anxiety, whereas MCCT focuses on what makes life worth living. In the former case, we pursue meaning in life in order to reduce death anxiety; in the latter case, we pursue meaning in life for its own sake, even when such pursuit increases the likelihood of untimely death.

Meaning is also important in our search for understanding and coherence in the face of uncertainty, chaos, and absurdity. Our views about people and the world are essentially our generalized and crystallized experiences and understandings about human existence. Our own self-concept and identity are based on (a) our interpretation of how others treat us and (b) our own evaluation of what really matters in life and what we are meant to be.

The meaning we attribute to an event is more important than the event itself. The story we live by is more important than the actual chronology of our life history. The ideals we pursue are more important than our past achievements. The culture we create is more important than the physical environment we inhabit. In sum, it is the inner life full of meanings that determines the quality of life.

A meaning-centered therapist would pay attention to both the basic meaning-related processes and the client's meaning systems. An MCCT practitioner would at all times keep in mind this fundamental meaning question: "How does this intervention facilitate or enhance the client's capacity for meaning seeking, meaning making, and meaning reconstruction?"

After all, it is meaning that gives life clarity, direction, and passion. It is meaning that endows life with a sense of significance and fulfillment. It is meaning that helps us navigate through troubled waters. Meaning manifests itself in thoughts, emotions, and actions. Meaning management is about managing and regulating one's life successfully through meaning.

Therefore, to understand clients is to understand how they construe the world and their own existence, as well as how they make use and manage their world of meaning in making crucial decisions. Most clients see the world and people almost entirely in negative terms. They focus on the negative aspect of the environment; they construct a negative worldview, and they are unduly preoccupied by fear of failure in pursuing any life goals. Therefore, their lifestyle is dominated by the defensive avoidance tendency.

Meaning management supplements the dual-systems model by (a) focusing on meaning-related processes in approach and avoidance tendencies and (b) examining the construction and reconstruction of one's general meaning systems apart from specific goals or problems. Metasystems are shaped by both culture and one's life history, and they include worldviews, philosophies of life, values, and belief systems.

According to MMT, net positive meanings, after accepting and transforming negative realities, offer clients the best protection against tough times and the best chance for success in realizing their life goals. Thus, a meaning-centered therapist is in a good position to guide and motivate clients to make positive changes.

Intervention Strategies

The PURE Strategy of Life Expansion

Meaning is defined in terms of four interrelated components: purpose, understanding, responsible action, and evaluation (PURE). This PURE model is capable of incorporating most of meaning research (Wong, 2010a).

The PURE model can also be referred to as the four treasures of MCCT because they represent the best practices for building a healthier and happier future.

1. Purpose is the motivational component, including goals, directions, incentive objects, values, aspirations, and objectives. It is concerned with such questions as these: What does life demand of me? What should I do with my life? What really matters in life? What is the point of working so hard?
2. Understanding is the cognitive component, encompassing a sense of coherence, making sense of situations, understanding one's own identity and other people's, and effective communication. It is concerned with such questions as these: What's happened? Why isn't it working? What does this mean? What am I doing here? Who am I? Why did he do that? What does he want?
3. Responsible action is the behavioral component, including appropriate actions and reactions, doing what is morally right, finding the right solutions, and making amends. It is concerned with such questions as these: What is my responsibility in this situation? What is the right thing to do? What options do I have? What choices should I make?
4. Evaluation is the affective component, including assessing degree of satisfaction or dissatisfaction with the situation or life as a whole. It is concerned with such questions as these: Have I achieved what I set out to do? Am I happy with how I have lived my life? If this is love, why am I still unhappy?

Each of these components includes a set of intervention skills. Some of the commonly used skills include goal setting, decision making, reality checking, fast-forwarding to consequences of choices, engaging in Socratic questioning, using Wong's Personal Meaning Profile (1998b), and challenging irrational or unrealistic thoughts.

These four components of meaning work together and form an upward-spiral feedback loop. With each successful completion, one's positivity moves up one notch. When one encounters a serious setback, however, one will switch to the avoidance system for help.

The ABCDE Strategy

The ABCDE intervention strategy is the main tool of MCCT in dealing with negative life experiences. Completely different from the ABCDE sequence involved in the rational-emotive therapy process (Ellis 1962, 1987), this ABCDE is similar to acceptance-commitment therapy in its emphasis on action rather than thinking.

Simply put, in MCCT, *A* stands for acceptance, *B* for belief and affirmation, *C* for commitment to specific goals and actions, *D* for discovering the meaning and significance of the self and situations, and *E* for evaluation of outcomes and enjoying the positive results. These components generate the corresponding principles:

1. *Accept* and confront reality: *the reality principle*
2. *Believe* that life is worth living: *the faith principle*
3. *Commit* to goals and actions: *the action principle*
4. *Discover* the meaning and significance of the self and situations: *the Aha! principle*
5. *Evaluate* the foregoing: *the self-regulation principle*

The Power of Acceptance Central to both logotherapy and MCCT is the important role of acceptance. Recovery begins with accepting the fact that something is seriously wrong and that help is needed. Regardless of whether the problem is addiction or physical illness, over the long haul, denial kills whereas acceptance heals. The serenity prayer attributed to Reinhold Niebuhr has been embraced by so many people, especially among those suffering from addiction, because it recognizes the power of acceptance in facing adversities and healing one's brokenness: "God, grant me the serenity to accept the things I cannot change, the courage to change the things I can, and the wisdom to know the difference."

All clinicians have faced the problem of resistance and denial. A seasoned therapist will employ a variety of skills to reduce or bypass clients' unconscious defense mechanisms and intentional denial and avoidance. Motivational counseling is primarily concerned with overcoming such resistance and awakening clients' yearnings for positive change and happiness.

We need to be clear that acceptance does not mean giving up hope or change. Nor does it mean passively accepting reality as fate. It does mean that we need to honestly recognize the constraints of reality and the fact that we cannot turn back the clock. It also means that we try to make changes in areas where we have some control and surrender our control to God or fate in areas beyond our control. It is also important to recognize the different levels of acceptance: (a) cognitive acceptance simply acknowledges that something has happened as a matter of fact; (b) emotional acceptance involves a willingness to confront and reexperience negative emotions; (c) realistic acceptance recognizes honestly and unflinchingly the full impact of the event on one's life; (d) integrative acceptance incorporates the negative life event with the rest of one's life; (e) existential acceptance allows one to endure and live with what cannot be changed; (f) transcendental acceptance rises above an unsolvable problem; and (g) transformative acceptance entails the process of meaning reconstruction that transforms the negative event into something positive.

Different skills are involved in achieving each of the seven levels of acceptance. For example, exercises can be prescribed to practicing letting go behaviorally, cognitively, and emotionally and experiencing each moment as it comes without judgment through mindful meditation. However, it is beyond the scope of this chapter to describe these different skills.

Here are some of the interventions and exercises that facilitate acceptance. Any combinations of these skills can pave the way for healing and personal transformation.

- Describe the negative experience in greater detail.
- Retell the event from different perspectives.
- Reflect on the meaning of what has happened.
- Identify the patterns of maladaptive responses.
- Confront the client with facts and discrepancies.
- Learn to identify and challenge dysfunctional thinking.
- Learn to keep negative thoughts and feelings in the background while pursuing one's ideals.
- Identify what can be changed and what cannot.
- Accept one's own limitations and weaknesses as well as others'.
- Practice paradoxical intention.
- Practice externalization.
- Practice confession and forgiveness.
- Learn to let go cognitively, behaviorally, and emotionally.
- Accept life in its totality.
- Accept each moment as it comes without judgment through mindful meditation.
- Accept harsh realities with equanimity through existential and spiritual understanding.
- Learn to endure unavoidable difficulties with patience through narrative meanings.
- Learn to transcend and transform suffering through narrative, existential, and spiritual means.
- Learn precious lessons from losses and sufferings.
- Make sense of the transitory nature of life and the boundaries of the human condition.

The Power of Belief and Affirmation Another important component is belief, which is related to faith and positive expectations. Clients need to believe that some progress is attainable if they are committed to the regimen of change. They need to be patient and keep faith even when progress is slow. Acceptance without affirmation often leads to despair and depression (Klinger, 1977). Transcendental and transformative acceptances are predicated on belief in something positive. To some extent, the efficacy of any treatment depends on belief as attested by the placebo effect. Belief, whether it is religious faith or humanistic affirmation, gives people hope. Belief provides the motivation for change. If one believes that one can get better and that life is worth living, then one is more likely to be committed to taking the steps to change. In therapeutic conversations, the therapist needs to reinforce the belief that there is some goodness in life that is worth fighting for and that it is never too late to start over again regardless of how many past failures.

- Use encouragement and validation to reinforce positive beliefs.
- Practice daily affirmation and affirm the intrinsic value of life.
- Affirm that positive meaning can be found in any situation.
- Believe that one is not alone in troubled times.
- Explore various possibilities and opportunities.
- Employ metanarratives to inspire clients.
- Bring out the client's strengths and positive aspects of life.
- Explore possible benefits from misfortunes and mistakes.
- Reinforce belief in the possibility of positive change and a better future.
- Support and reinforce religious beliefs in divine intervention.
- Support the belief that there is some goodness in life that is worth fighting for.
- Support the belief that one can achieve one's life goal at least partially if one persists.
- Believe that one can become what one is meant to be.
- Learn to appreciate life in its worst and its best.
- Recognize that breathing is the basis for hope.

The Power of Action The MCCT model emphasizes human agency and the potency of action. Hard work is necessary to bring about change. There will always be setbacks and obstacles, but there is no substitute for persistence and hard work. Choice without commitment means that one remains stuck. Promise without following through is empty. Remorse is simply sentimentality without an actual change of direction. Real change is possible only when one takes the first concrete step in a new direction. As the Chinese proverb says, a journey of a thousand miles begins with one step. It is at this point of action that we branch out to the approach system of PURE, which will help transform negativity. There is some truth in the practice of "fake it until we make it." We need to act as if it is true even when we do not really feel it or believe it. We need to do what we ought to do as demanded by a sense of responsibility or moral obligation, even if we do not feel like doing it. Both Morita therapy and acceptance-commitment therapy stress the importance of action over feelings in order to overcome depression and improve daily functioning.

In equipping clients with self-regulation skills, therapists have the responsibility to clarify and demonstrate the assignment and drive home the significance of practicing it. For example, the therapist can explain that setting specific, concrete, and realistic goals is more likely to lead to successful implementation than setting ambitious but vague goals. The therapist can also demonstrate the usefulness of a daily and weekly checklist of goals in terms of increasing the likelihood of success and reinforcement. To practice one lesson consistently is more beneficial to the client than learning many lessons without practicing any. Commitment to action is one of the keys to getting started on the long hard road of recovery and transformation. Therapists need to use the principles of modeling, reinforcement, and meaning. If clients perceive a prescribed exercise as meaningful and attainable, they are more likely to practice it. Here a few helpful exercises:

- Contract to perform specific behavioral tasks.
- Develop and implement plans of action.
- Set concrete, specific, and realistic goals.
- Take small steps toward one's goals.
- Monitor one's progress on a daily basis.
- Keep making adjustments and improvements.
- Practice meaning-seeking and meaning-making skills.
- Never give up trying.
- Practice new ways of relating and managing one's emotions, new coping skills, and new habits.
- Practice the routine of transforming negative emotions into positive motivations.
- Practice the routine of letting go.

The Power of Discovery Recovery is akin to a sense of awakening, which is necessary for a successful existential quest (Wong & Gingras, 2010). For good reason, Frankl (1946/1985a) emphasized that meaning is discovered more than created. Whatever belief we may hold and whatever action we may take, discovery of meaning ultimately requires an Aha! response, a spark of insight to achieve optimal results. There is, so to speak, the turning on of a light bulb inside our heads. Out of the darkness of confusion and despair, suddenly therapy makes good sense, and there is indeed light at the end of the tunnel only if one keeps moving in the right direction.

Clinicians need to pay special attention to moments of awakening. Many skills can be used to help clients see life in a new way. Mindful meditation is useful in discovering the richness of present moments, whereas life review is useful in making sense of the past. Alert clients to the many possibilities of discoveries, as identified here:

- Discover the forgotten positive aspects of one's life.
- Discover the hidden strengths of oneself.
- Discover the significance of mundane matters.

- Discover joy in every step and every breath.
- Discover newness in old routines.
- Discover sacred moments in secular engagements.
- Learn to hear, see, and think deeply.
- Practice looking toward the sky beyond the horizon.
- Walk toward the sun and leave behind the shadow.
- Learn to pause and reflect.
- Discover creativity in drudgery.
- Discover the unique beauty of each season.
- Discover the bright and dark sides of life.

Evaluating and Enjoying the Outcomes Evaluation represents the affective component of self-regulation. If nothing seems to work and one remains miserable, then some adjustment is necessary.

Joy is inevitable if one successfully follows the aforementioned four strategic steps, which are dynamically interrelated. Positive feelings and outcomes reinforce positive practices. Here are a few examples of positive feelings that follow successful practice of the ABCDE strategy:

- Enjoy the liberty and relief that come from acceptance.
- Enjoy the feeling of freedom and the power of letting go.
- Enjoy the hope and consolation that come from belief in a better future.
- Enjoy a more positive outlook on life.
- Enjoy the healing and transformation that come from commitment.
- Enjoy the surprises and blessings of discovery.
- Enjoy a new understanding of the self.

The Double-Vision Strategy

The double-vision strategy is two-pronged approach that aims at addressing both the presenting problems and the "big picture" issues, among them the meaning of life and the injustice of society. Double vision is an important macro skill for several reasons:

1. If we focus on the trees, we may lose sight of the forest. We can gain deeper insight into our clients' predicaments by looking at the bigger picture.
2. If we can help restore our clients' passion and purpose for living, this will reinforce their motivation for change.
3. By looking beyond the pressing, immediate concerns, MCCT seeks to awaken clients' sense of responsibility to something larger than themselves.

MCCT is concerned with individuals' presenting problems and the larger context in which these problems are situated. It is helpful for clients to be aware that there are larger forces that limit their freedom of choice.

Macrocounseling skills help clients to view their predicaments in the larger scheme of things, thereby broadening and deepening their understanding of the meaning of their problems and their potential for positive change.

Conclusion

Fabry (1995) summarized Frankl's view in the following way:

> Self-actualization, a popular goal in affluent societies, is fulfilling only when it is oriented toward meaning, not pleasure, power, and riches. Logotherapy maintains that meaning comes from self-transcendence (to reach out beyond oneself and do things for the sake of others), not from self-actualization. (p. 9)

Similarly, Bettelheim (1991) believed that the most difficult achievement and the greatest satisfaction is to find meaning in life. In order to find meaning, people must transcend the narrow confines of self-centered existence and make a significant contribution to society.

Meaning-centered counseling adopts the basic tenets of logotherapy and it may be considered an extension of logotherapy. There are differences in its details and emphases, however. For example, Frankl (1969/1988) defined the will to meaning as the "basic striving of man to find and fulfill meaning and purpose" (p. 35). From the perspective of meaning-centered counseling, the will to meaning consists of two psychological processes: the motivation to seek the core meaning of a given life situation and the motivation to seek purpose and significance for one's life goals.

The main difference between logotherapy and meaning-centered counseling is that the former takes a philosophical and spiritual approach, whereas the latter favors a cognitive or psychological approach. For example, Frankl (1946/1985a, 1967/1985b) considered meanings and values as belonging to the noological dimension, separate from the psychological dimension; but Patterson (1986) argued that "it should not be necessary to consider meanings and values as constituting an independent aspect of the individual; they should be included as part of his or her psychological aspect" (p. 453). The present position is that all existential issues, including meanings and values, can be subjected to psychological analysis. For example, existential attribution is concerned with questions of meaning, purpose, and value (Wong, 1991).

In sum, MCCT equips clinicians with the fundamental principles and skills to (a) help clients develop a healthy understanding of their true identity and place in the world; (b) motivate and empower clients in their struggle for survival and fulfillment regardless of their life circumstances; (c) tap into people's capacity for meaning construction in order to help clients make sense of their predicaments and restore their purpose, faith, and hope; (d) provide necessary tools for clients to overcome personal difficulties and anxieties and fulfill their life's mission; and (e) establish a genuine healing relationship with clients and enhance their capacity to trust and relate with others.

The MCCT model incorporates not only empirically tested counseling practices but also relevant research findings from social-personality psychology and positive psychology. Furthermore, MMT, one of the conceptual frameworks for MCCT, is consistent with the research evidence, and its implications can be empirically tested.

In today's economic environment, when most people cannot afford long-term psychotherapy, MCCT offers short-term therapy (Wong, 2010b), which can be completed in 8 to 12 sessions, depending on the severity of the case. This short duration is made possible because of MCCT's psychoeducational emphasis, which equips clients to practice meaning-based adaptive tools on a daily basis. Furthermore, MCCT skills can readily be employed by coaches, both executive and life coaches. Different from most psychotherapies, MCCT takes a two-pronged approach: On the one hand, MCCT seeks to repair what is broken and reduce clients' debilitating symptoms by employing the most appropriate interventions; on the other hand, MCCT focuses on helping clients discover and cultivate meaning, resilience, and positive emotions in clients as well as empower them to fulfill their potentials and life dreams. In short, what makes MCCT appealing is its ability to deal with a variety of psychological problems while addressing the core existential issues of how to survive and flourish in spite of the limiting and destructive forces from within and without.

References

Adler, A. (1964). *Social interest: A challenge to mankind.* New York, NY: Capricorn Books.

Arthur, N., & Pedersen, P. (2008). *Case incidents in counseling for international transitions.* Alexandria, VA: American Counseling Association.

Batthyany, A., & Guttman, D. (2006). *Empirical research in logotherapy and meaning-oriented psychotherapy.* Phoenix, AZ: Zeig, Tucker & Theisen.

Batthyany, A., & Levinson, J. (Eds.). (2009). *Anthology of Viktor Frankl's logotherapy.* Phoenix, AZ: Zeig, Tucker & Theisen.

Baumeister, R. F. (1991). *Meanings of life.* New York, NY: Guilford Press.

Baumeister, R. F., & Leary, M. R. (1995). The need to belong: Desire for interpersonal attachments as a fundamental human motivation. *Psychological Bulletin, 117,* 497–529.

Bettelheim, B. (1991). *The uses of enchantment.* London, England: Thames & Hudson.

Brooks-Harris, J. E. (2008). *Multitheoretical psychotherapy: Key strategies for integration practice.* Boston, MA: Houghton-Mifflin.

Bruner, J. S. (1990). *Acts of meaning.* Cambridge, MA: Harvard University Press.

Budd, P., & Budd, D. (2010). *Tested: How twelve wrongfully imprisoned men held onto hope.* Dallas, TX: Brown Books.

Duncan, B. L., Miller, S. D., Wampold, B. E., & Hubble, M. A. (Eds.). (2009). *The heart and soul of change: Delivering what works in therapy* (2nd ed.). Washington, DC: American Psychological Association.

Ellis, A. (1962). *Reason and emotion in psychotherapy.* Oxford, England: Lyle Stuart.

Ellis, A. (1987). *The practice of rational-emotive therapy.* New York, NY: Springer.

Fabry, J. (1994). *The pursuit of meaning (Rev. ed.).* Abilene, TX: Institute of Logotherapy Press.

Fabry, J. (1995). Prescription for survival. *International Forum for Logotherapy, 18,* 7–12.

Fabry, J. (1998). *The cause of meaning.* In P. T. P. Wong & P. S. Fry (Eds.), *The human quest for meaning: A handbook of psychological research and clinical applications* (pp. 295–305). Mahwah, NJ: Erlbaum.

Frankl, V. E. (1985a). *Man's search for meaning.* New York, NY: Washington Square Press. (Originally published 1946)

Frankl, V. E. (1985b). *Psychotherapy and existentialism: Selected papers on logotherapy.* New York, NY: Washington Square Press. (Originally published 1967)

Frankl, V. E. (1986). *The doctor and the soul: From psychotherapy to logotherapy* (Rev. and expanded). New York, NY: Vintage Books.

Frankl, V. E. (1988). *The will to meaning: Foundations and applications of logotherapy.* New York, NY: World. (Originally published 1969)

Frankl, V. E. (2000). *Recollections: An autobiography.* New York, NY: Basic Books.

Goodell, J. (2002). *Our story: 77 hours that tested our friendship and our faith.* New York, NY: Hyperion.

Hoffman, L. (2009). Introduction to existential psychology in a cross-cultural context: An East–West dialogue. In L. Hoffman, M. Yang, F. J. Kaklauskas, & A. Chan (Eds.), *Existential psychology East–West* (pp. 1–67). Colorado Springs, CO: University of the Rockies Press.

Klinger, E. (1977). *Meaning and void: Inner experiences and the incentives in people's lives.* Minneapolis: University of Minnesota Press.

Klinger, E. (1998). The search for meaning in evolutionary perspective and its clinical implications. In P. T. P. Wong & P. S. Fry (Eds.), *The human quest for meaning: A handbook of psychological research and clinical applications* (pp. 27–50). Mahwah, NJ: Erlbaum.

Lukas, E. (1998). The meaning of life and the goals in life for chronically ill people. In P. T. P. Wong & P. S. Fry (Eds.), *The human quest for meaning: A handbook of psychological research and clinical applications* (pp. 307–316). Mahwah, NJ: Erlbaum.

May, R. (1940). *The springs of creative living: A study of human nature and God.* New York, NY: Abingdon-Cokesbury.

Nelson-Jones, R. (2002). Diverse goals for multicultural counseling and therapy. *Counseling Psychology Quarterly, 15,* 133–143.

Norcross, J. C. (Ed.). (2002). *Psychotherapy relationships that work: Therapist contributions and responsiveness to patients.* New York, NY: Oxford University Press.

Norcross, J. C., & Goldfried, M. R. (2005). *Handbook of psychotherapy integration.* New York, NY: Oxford University Press.

Patterson, C. H. (1986). *Theories of counseling and psychotherapy* (2nd ed.). New York, NY: HarperCollins.

Peacock, E. J., & Wong, P. T. P. (1990). The Stress Appraisal Measure (SAM): A multidimensional approach to cognitive appraisal. *Stress Medicine, 6,* 227–236.

Pedersen, P., Crethar, H., & Carlson, J. (2008). *Inclusive cultural empathy.* Washingon, DC: American Psychological Association.

Sarbin, T. R. (1986). *Narrative psychology: The storied nature of human conduct.* Westport, CT: Praeger.

Scheier, M. F., & Carver, C. S. (1985). Optimism, coping, and health: Assessment and implications of generalized outcome expectancies. *Health Psychology, 4,* 219–247.

Seligman, M. E. P., Steen, T., Park, N., & Peterson, C. (2005). Positive psychology progress: Empirical validation of interventions. *American Psychologist, 60,* 410–425.

Snyder, C. R. (2002). Hope theory: Rainbows in the mind. *Psychological Inquiry, 13,* 249–275.

Sommer, K. L., & Baumeister, R. F. (1998). The construction of meaning from life events: Empirical studies of personal narratives. In P. T. P. Wong & P. S. Fry (Eds.), *The human quest for meaning: A handbook of psychological research and clinical applications* (pp.143–162). Mahwah, NJ: Erlbaum.

Sue, D. W., & Sue D. (2003). *Counseling the culturally diverse: Theory and practice* (4th ed.). New York, NY: Wiley.

Van Deurzen, E., & Adams, M. (2011). *Skills in existential counseling & psychotherapy.* London, England: Sage.

Weissman, M. M., Markowitz, J. C., & Klerman, G. L. (2000). *Comprehensive guide to interpersonal psychotherapy.* New York, NY: Basic Books.

Wong, P. T. P. (1991). Existential vs. causal attributions. In S. Zelen (Ed.), *Extensions and new models of attribution theory* (pp. 84 –125). New York, NY: Springer-Verlag.

Wong, P. T. P. (1993). Effective management of life stress: The resource-congruence model. *Stress Medicine, 9,* 51–60.

Wong, P. T. P. (1997). Meaning-centered counseling: A cognitive-behavioural approach to logotherapy. *International Forum for Logotherapy, 20,* 85–94.

Wong, P. T. P. (1998a). The endurance of logotherapy. *International Forum for Logotherapy, 21*(1), 47.

Wong, P. T. P. (1998b). Implicit theories of meaningful life and the development of the Personal Meaning Profile (PMP). In P. T. P. Wong & P. S. Fry (Eds.), *The human quest for meaning: A handbook of psychological research and clinical applications* (pp. 111–140). Mahwah, NJ: Erlbaum.

Wong, P. T. P. (1998c). Meaning-centered counseling. In P. T. P Wong & P. S. Fry (Eds.), *The human quest for meaning: A handbook of psychological research and clinical applications* (pp. 395–435). Mahwah, NJ: Erlbaum.

Wong, P. T. P. (1998d). Spirituality, meaning, and successful aging. In P. T. P Wong & P. Fry (Eds.), *The human quest for meaning: A handbook of psychological research and clinical applications* (pp. 359–394). Mahwah, NJ: Erlbaum.

Wong, P. T. P. (1999a). Joe Fabry—A visionary storyteller. Available online at http://www.meaning.twu.ca/joefabry.htm

Wong, P. T. P. (1999b). Towards an integrative model of meaning-centered counseling and therapy. *International Forum for Logotherapy, 22,* 47–55.

Wong, P. T. P. (2005). Creating a positive participatory climate: A meaning-centered counseling perspective. Sandor Schuman (Ed.), *The IAF facilitation handbook.* San Francisco, CA: Jossey-Bass.

Wong, P. T. P. (2007). Transformation of grief through meaning: Meaning-centered counseling for bereavement. In A. Tomer, E. Grafton, & P. T. P. Wong (Eds.), *Death attitudes: Existential & spiritual issues* (pp. 375–396). Mahwah, NJ: Erlbaum.

Wong, P. T. P. (2008). Narrative practice and meaning-centered positive psychotherapy. [Review of the book *Maps of narrative practice*]. *PsycCRITIQUE, 53.*

Wong, P. T. P. (2009). Viktor Frankl: Prophet of hope for the 21st century. In A. Batthyany & J. Levinson (Eds.), *Anthology of Viktor Frankl's logotherapy.* Phoenix, AZ: Zeig, Tucker & Theisen.

Wong, P. T. P. (2010a). Meaning-therapy: An integrative, positive approach. *Journal of Contemporary Psychotherapy, 40*(2), 85–99.

Wong, P. T. P. (2010b, August). *Short term meaning therapy.* Given at the 6th Biennial International Meaning Conference in Vancouver, BC, Canada.

Wong, P. T. P. (in press). Positive psychology 2.0: Towards a balanced interactive model of the good life. *Canadian Psychology.*

Wong, P. T. P., & Fry, P. S. (Eds.). (1998). *The human quest for meaning: A handbook of psychological research and clinical applications.* Mahwah, NJ: Erlbaum.

Wong, P. T. P., & Gingras, D. (2010). Finding meaning and happiness while dying of cancer: Lessons on existential positive psychology. [Review of the film *Ikiru*]. *PsycCRITIQUES, 55.*

Wong, P. T. P., Reker, G. T. & Peacock, E. (2006). The resource-congruence model of coping and the development of the Coping Schemas Inventory. In P. T. P. Wong & L. C. J. Wong (Eds.), *Handbook of multicultural perspectives on stress and coping* (pp. 223–284). New York, NY: Springer.

Wong, P. T. P., & Weiner, B. (1981). When people ask "why" questions and the heuristic of attributional search. *Journal of Personality and Social Psychology, 40*, 650–663.

Wong, P. T. P., & Wong, L. C. J. (2006). *The handbook of multicultural perspectives on stress and coping.* New York, NY: Springer.

Wong, P. T. P., Wong, L. C. J., McDonald, M. J., & Klaassen, D. W. (Eds.). (2007). The positive psychology of meaning and spirituality. Abbotsford, BC: INPM Press.

Yalom, I. D. (1980). *Existential psychotherapy.* New York, NY: Basic Books.

Yu, M. (2009). *The power of negative thinking* (Chu, L. Z., Trans.). Taipei, Taiwan: ASA Publishing.

Author Index

A

C

D

H

L

M

N

O

Q

R

U

V

X

Y

Z

Subject Index

A

B

D

E

F

I

N

S

T